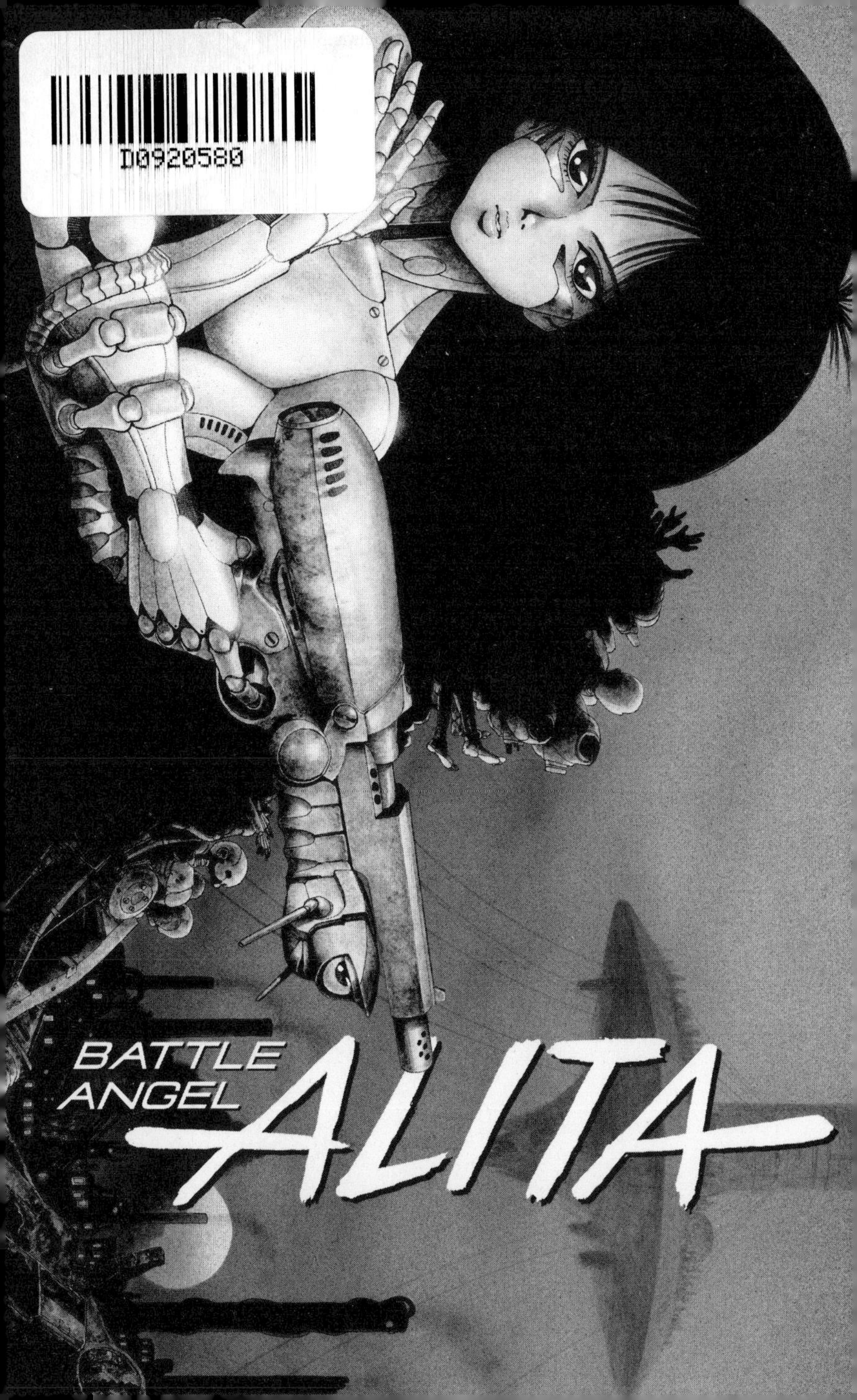
BATTLE
ANGEL
ALITA

RUE DES TEMPÊTES
2km
FACTORY
CONTENTS

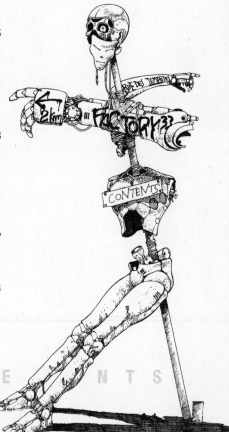

C O N T E N T S

FIGHT_001 Rusty Angel

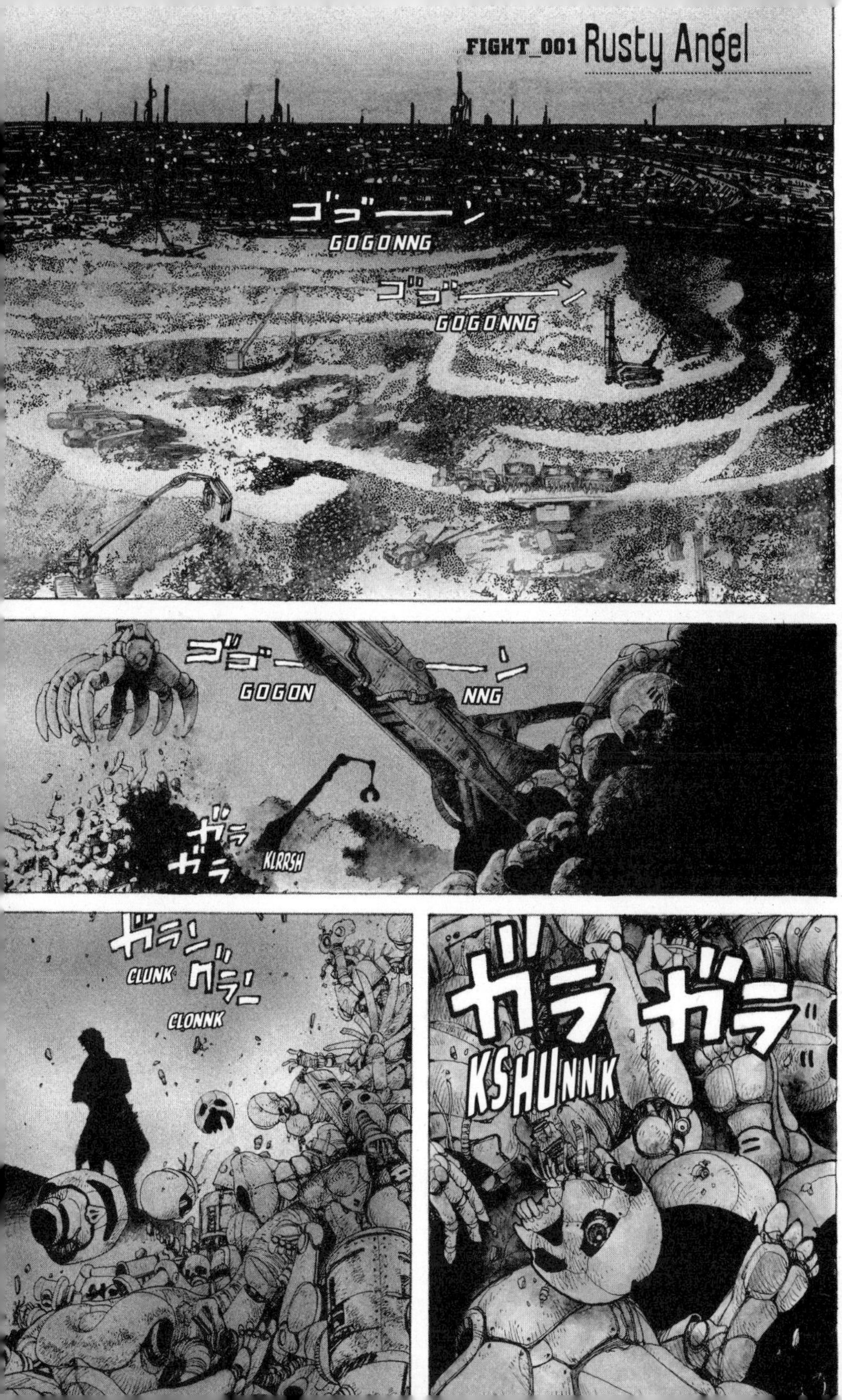

ゴゴーーン
GOGONNG
ゴゴーーーン
GOGONNG
ゴゴーーーン
GOGON
NNG
ガラ
ガラ
KLRRSH
ガラ ガラ
KSHUNNK
ガラン
CLUNK
グラン
CLONNK

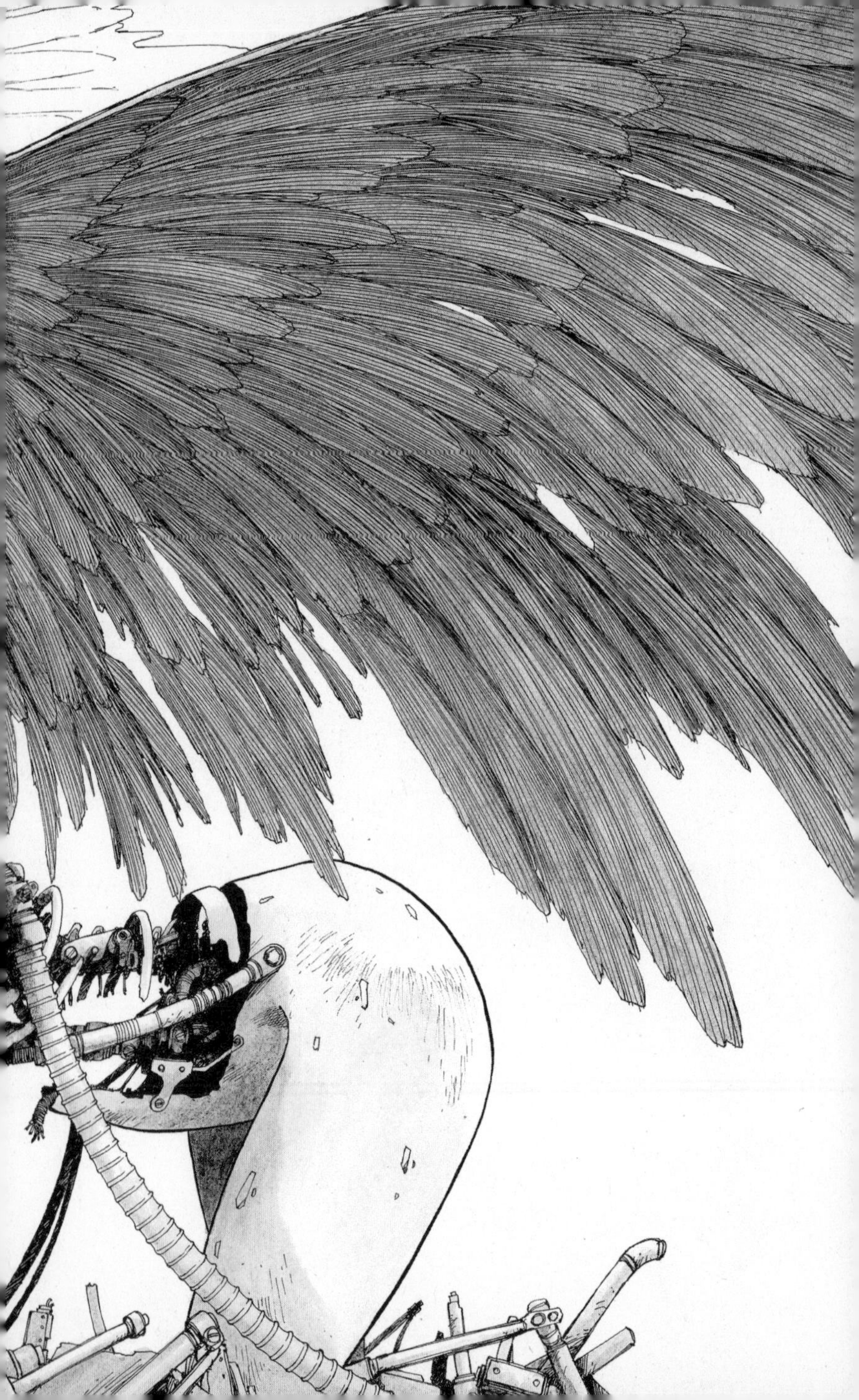

FIGHT_001 Rusty Angel

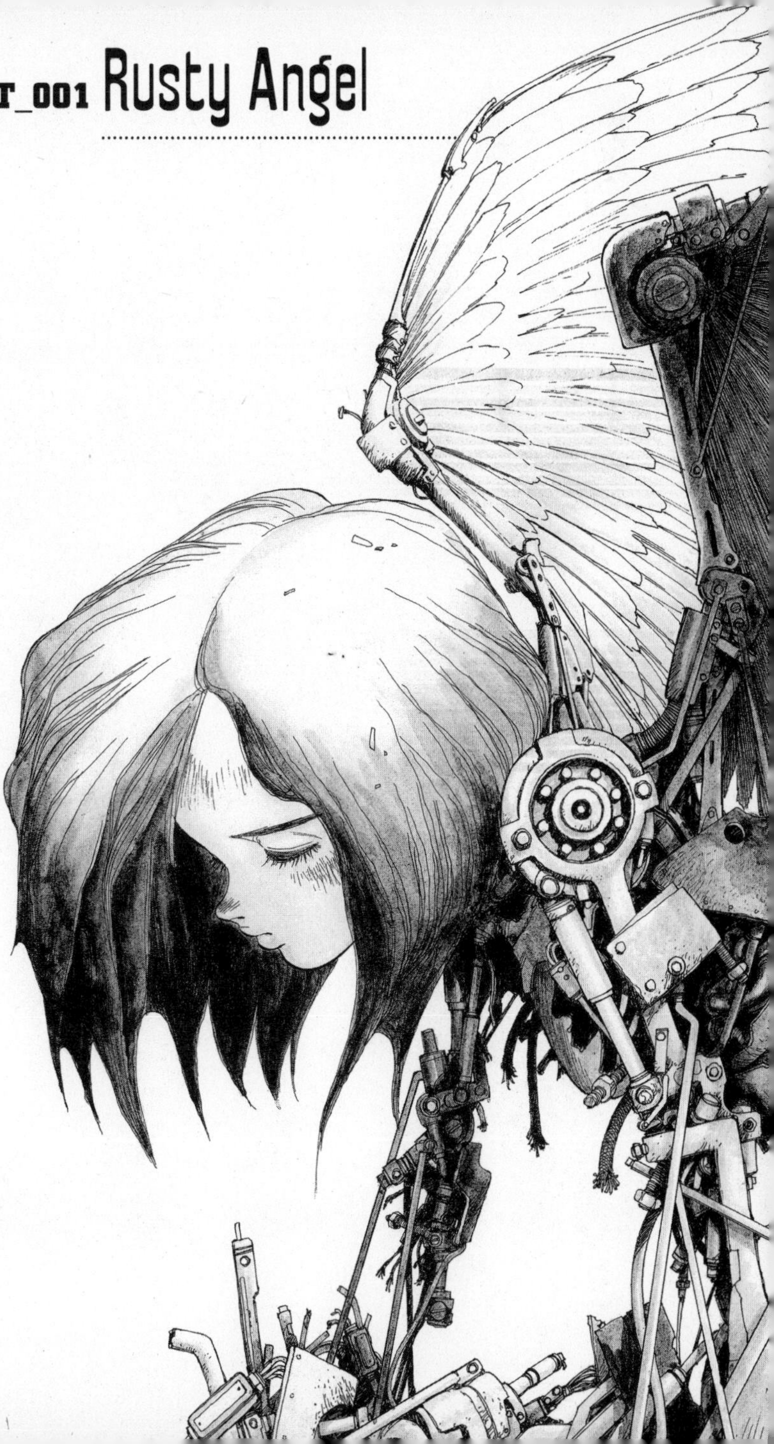

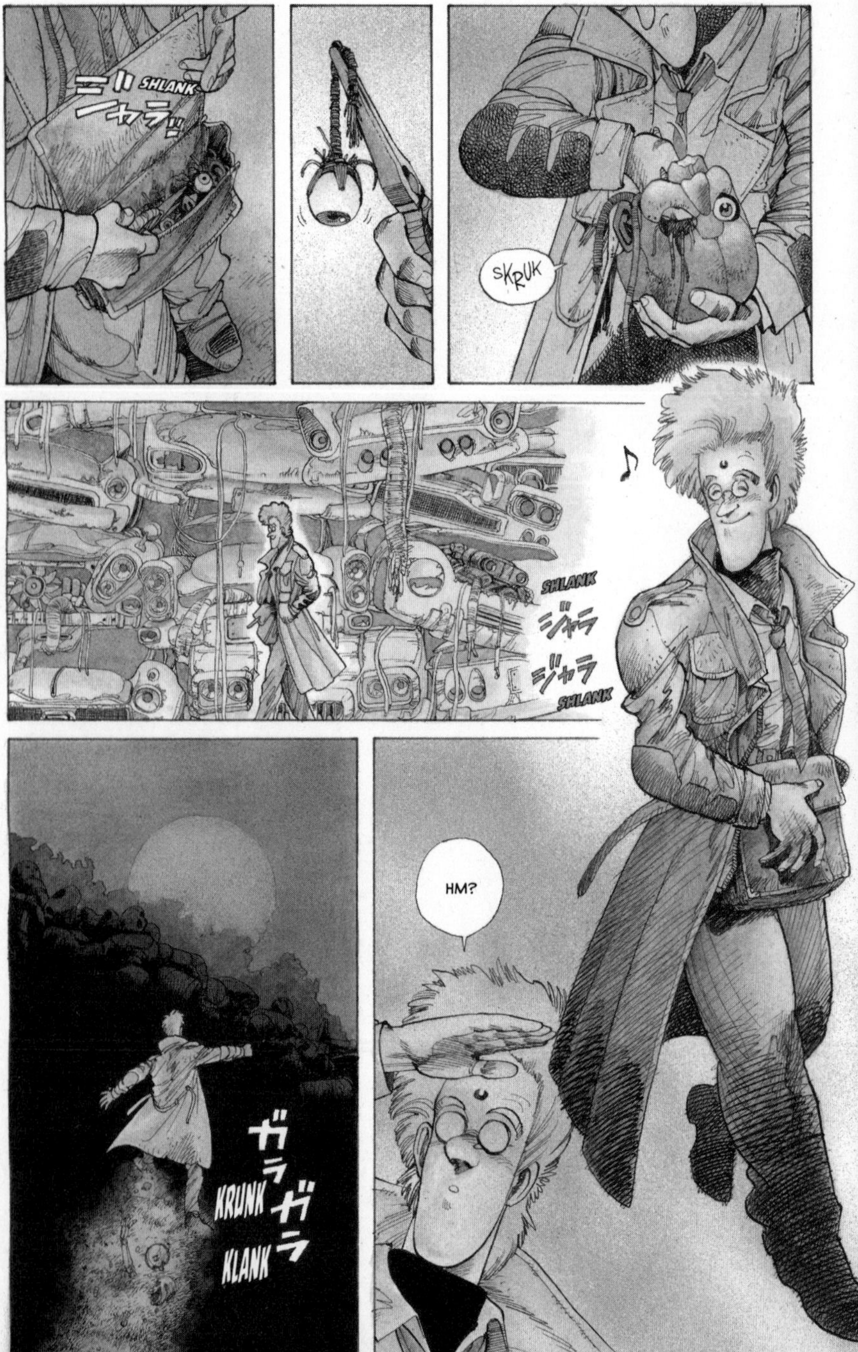
SKRUK
SHLANK
ジャラ!!
♪
SHLANK
ジャラ
ジャラ
SHLANK
HM?
ガラガラ
KRUNK
KLANK

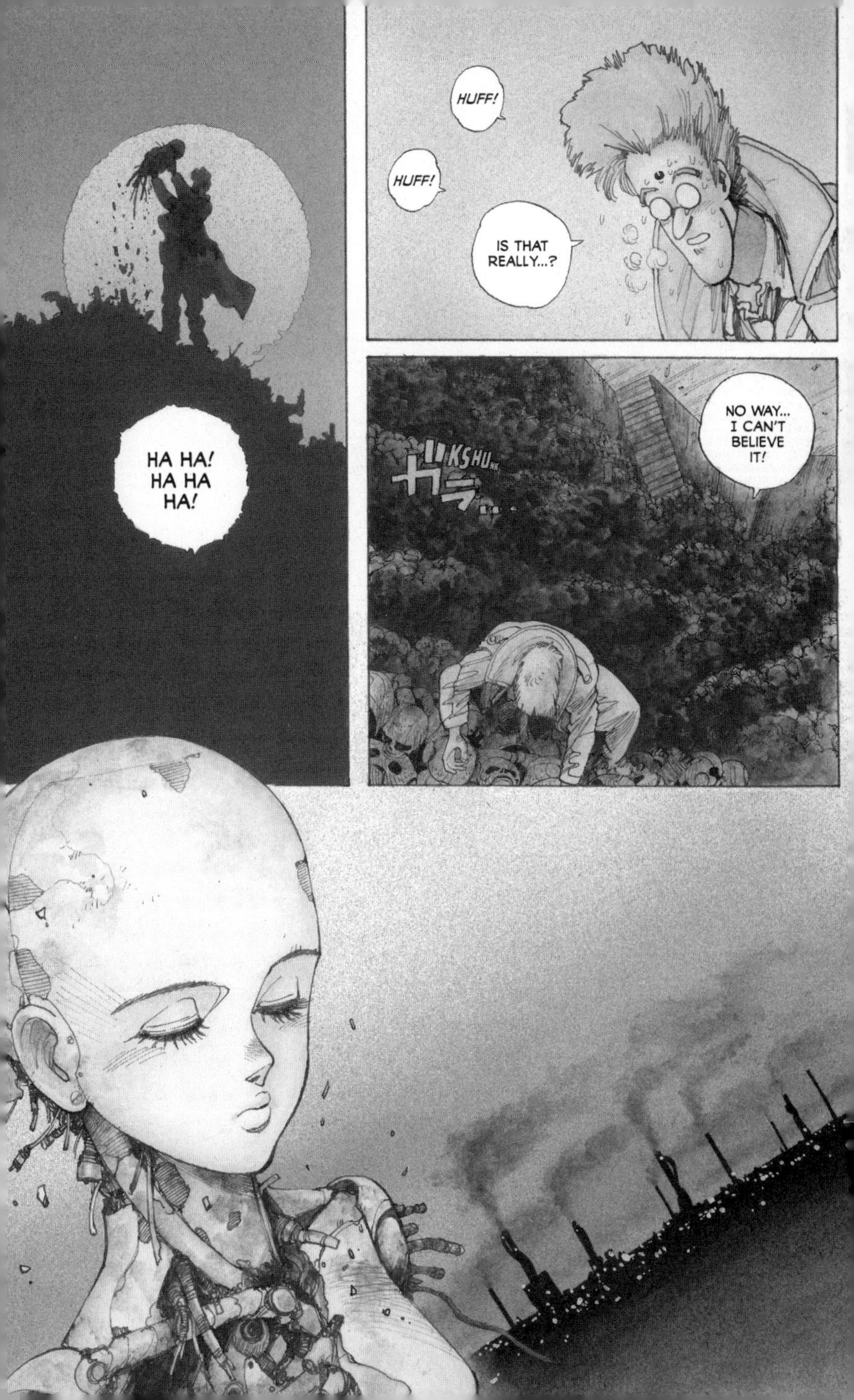
HUFF!
HUFF!
IS THAT REALLY...?
ガラ..
KSHUNK
NO WAY... I CAN'T BELIEVE IT!
HA HA! HA HA HA!

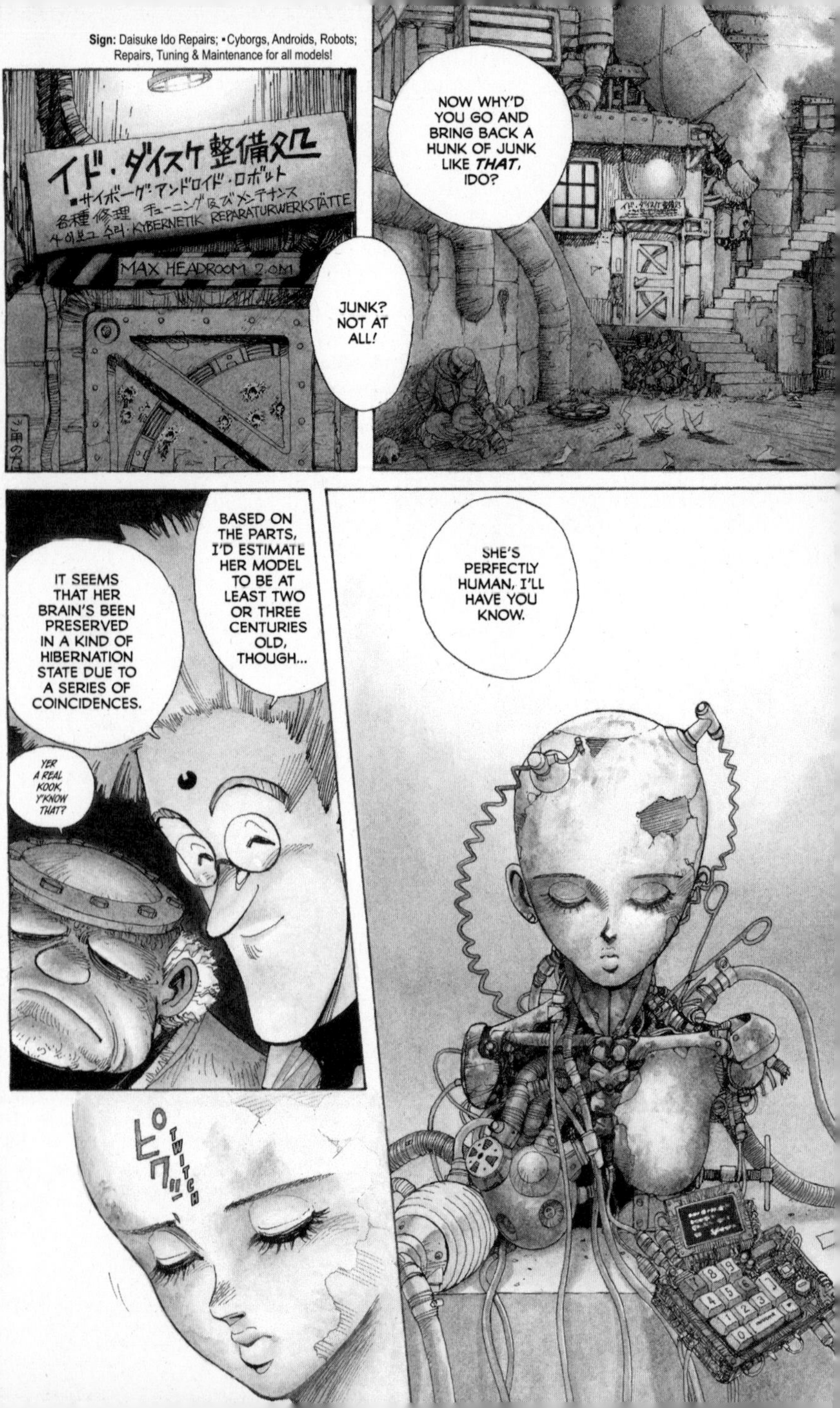
NOW WHY'D YOU GO AND BRING BACK A HUNK OF JUNK LIKE *THAT*, IDO?
JUNK? NOT AT ALL!
Sign: Daisuke Ido Repairs; ▪Cyborgs, Androids, Robots; Repairs, Tuning & Maintenance for all models!
イド・ダイスケ整備処
■サイボーグ・アンドロイド・ロボット
各種修理 チューニング及びメンテナンス
사이보그 수리・KYBERNETIK REPARATURWERKSTÄTTE
MAX HEADROOM 2.0M
SHE'S PERFECTLY HUMAN, I'LL HAVE YOU KNOW.
BASED ON THE PARTS, I'D ESTIMATE HER MODEL TO BE AT LEAST TWO OR THREE CENTURIES OLD, THOUGH...
IT SEEMS THAT HER BRAIN'S BEEN PRESERVED IN A KIND OF HIBERNATION STATE DUE TO A SERIES OF COINCIDENCES.
YER A REAL KOOK, Y'KNOW THAT?
ピクッ
TWITCH

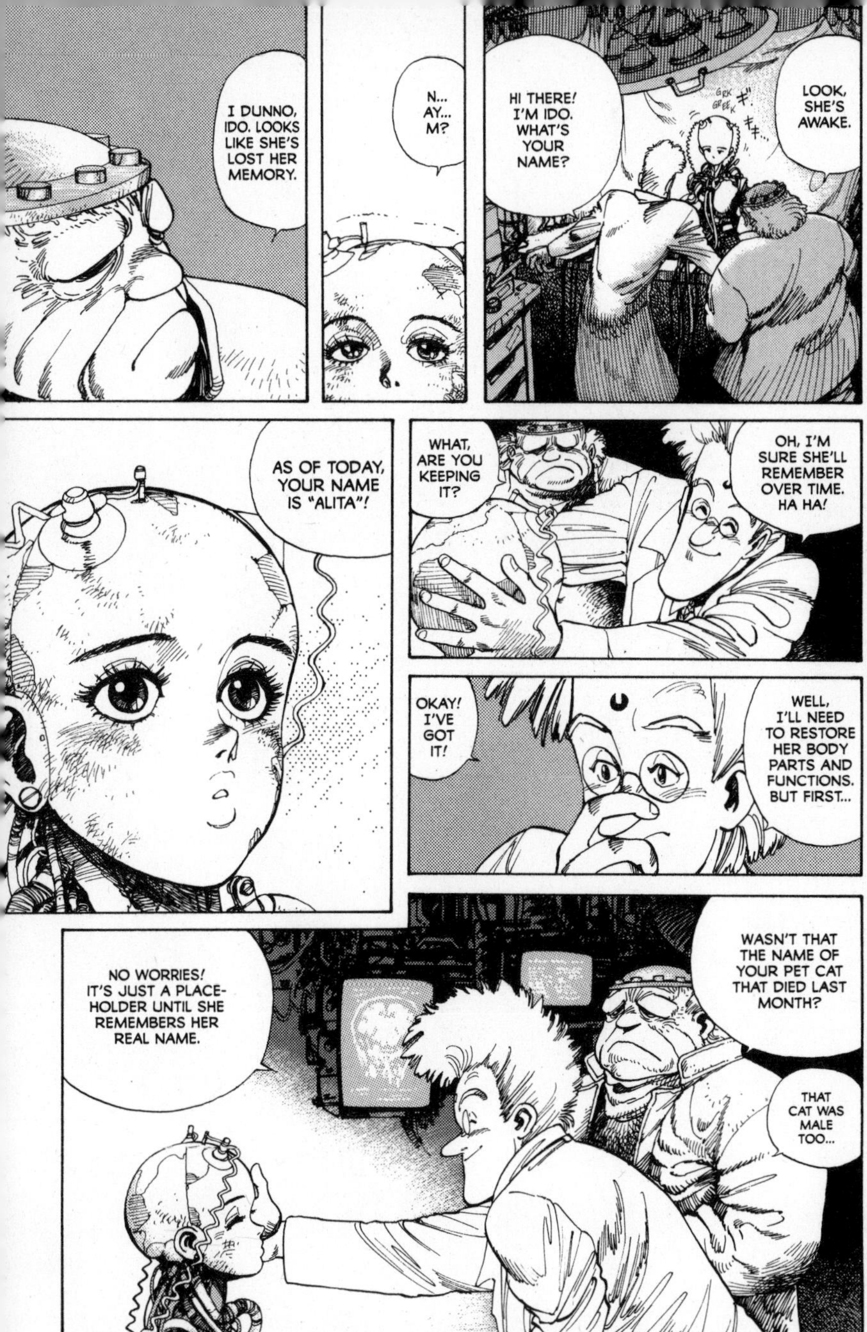
LOOK, SHE'S AWAKE.
GRK GREEK
HI THERE! I'M IDO. WHAT'S YOUR NAME?
N... AY... M?
I DUNNO, IDO. LOOKS LIKE SHE'S LOST HER MEMORY.
OH, I'M SURE SHE'LL REMEMBER OVER TIME. HA HA!
WHAT, ARE YOU KEEPING IT?
WELL, I'LL NEED TO RESTORE HER BODY PARTS AND FUNCTIONS. BUT FIRST...
OKAY! I'VE GOT IT!
AS OF TODAY, YOUR NAME IS "ALITA"!
WASN'T THAT THE NAME OF YOUR PET CAT THAT DIED LAST MONTH?
NO WORRIES! IT'S JUST A PLACE-HOLDER UNTIL SHE REMEMBERS HER REAL NAME.
THAT CAT WAS MALE TOO...

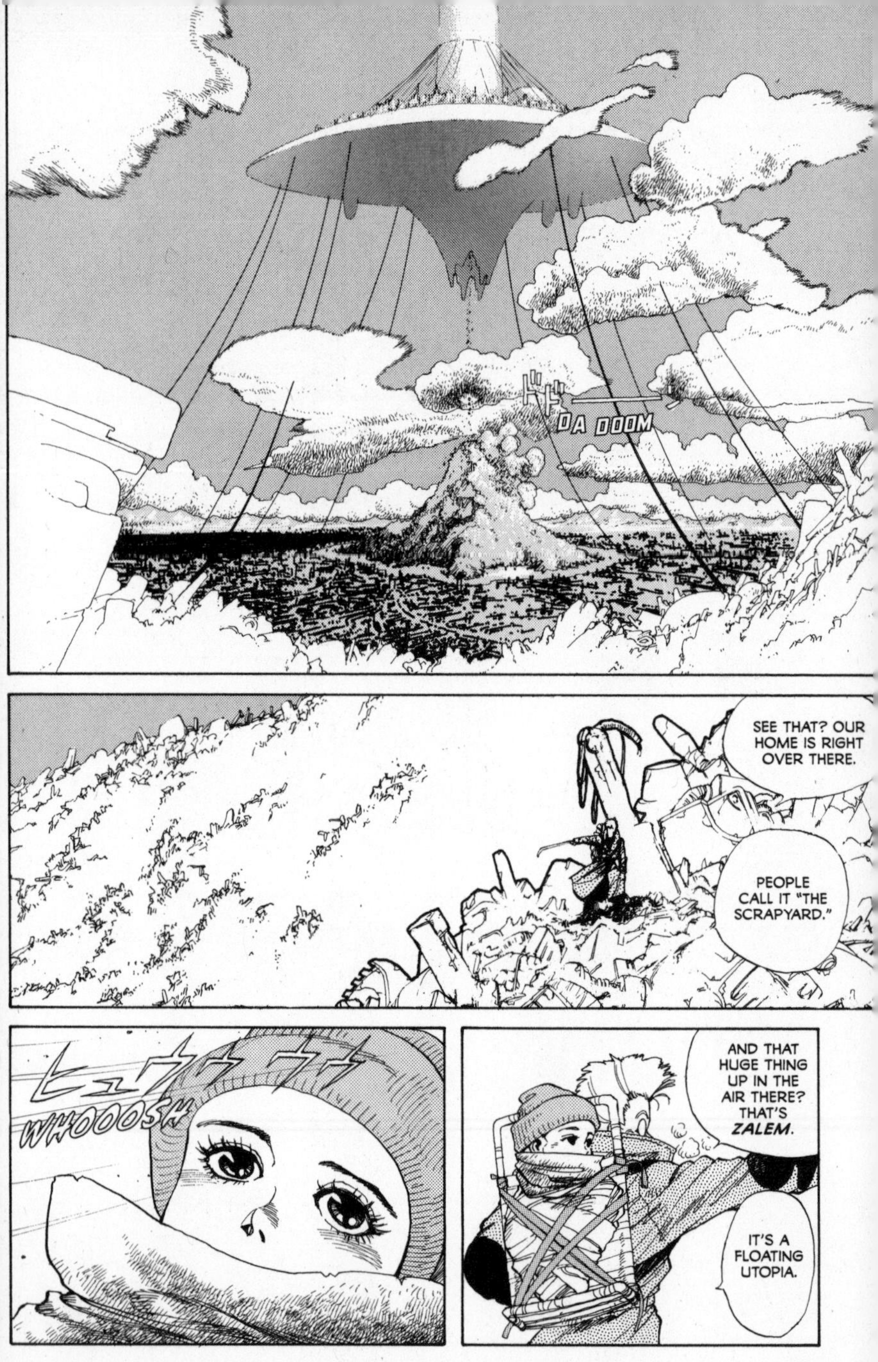
DA DOOM
SEE THAT? OUR HOME IS RIGHT OVER THERE.
PEOPLE CALL IT "THE SCRAPYARD."
AND THAT HUGE THING UP IN THE AIR THERE? THAT'S *ZALEM*.
IT'S A FLOATING UTOPIA.
WHOOOSH

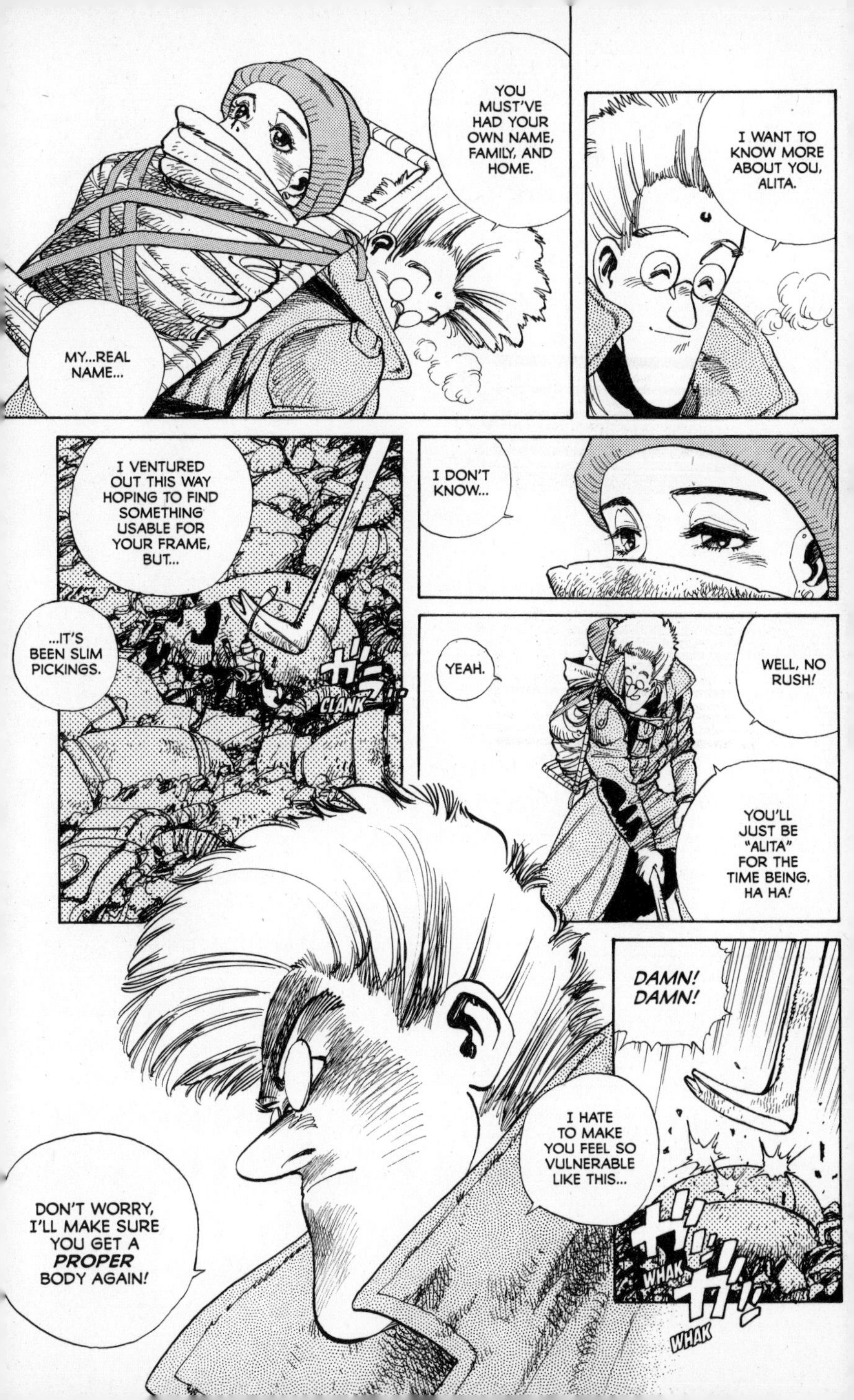

I WANT TO KNOW MORE ABOUT YOU, ALITA.
YOU MUST'VE HAD YOUR OWN NAME, FAMILY, AND HOME.
MY...REAL NAME...
I DON'T KNOW...
WELL, NO RUSH!
YOU'LL JUST BE "ALITA" FOR THE TIME BEING. HA HA!
YEAH.
I VENTURED OUT THIS WAY HOPING TO FIND SOMETHING USABLE FOR YOUR FRAME, BUT...
...IT'S BEEN SLIM PICKINGS.
CLANK
DAMN! DAMN!
WHAK
WHAK
I HATE TO MAKE YOU FEEL SO VULNERABLE LIKE THIS...
DON'T WORRY, I'LL MAKE SURE YOU GET A ***PROPER*** BODY AGAIN!

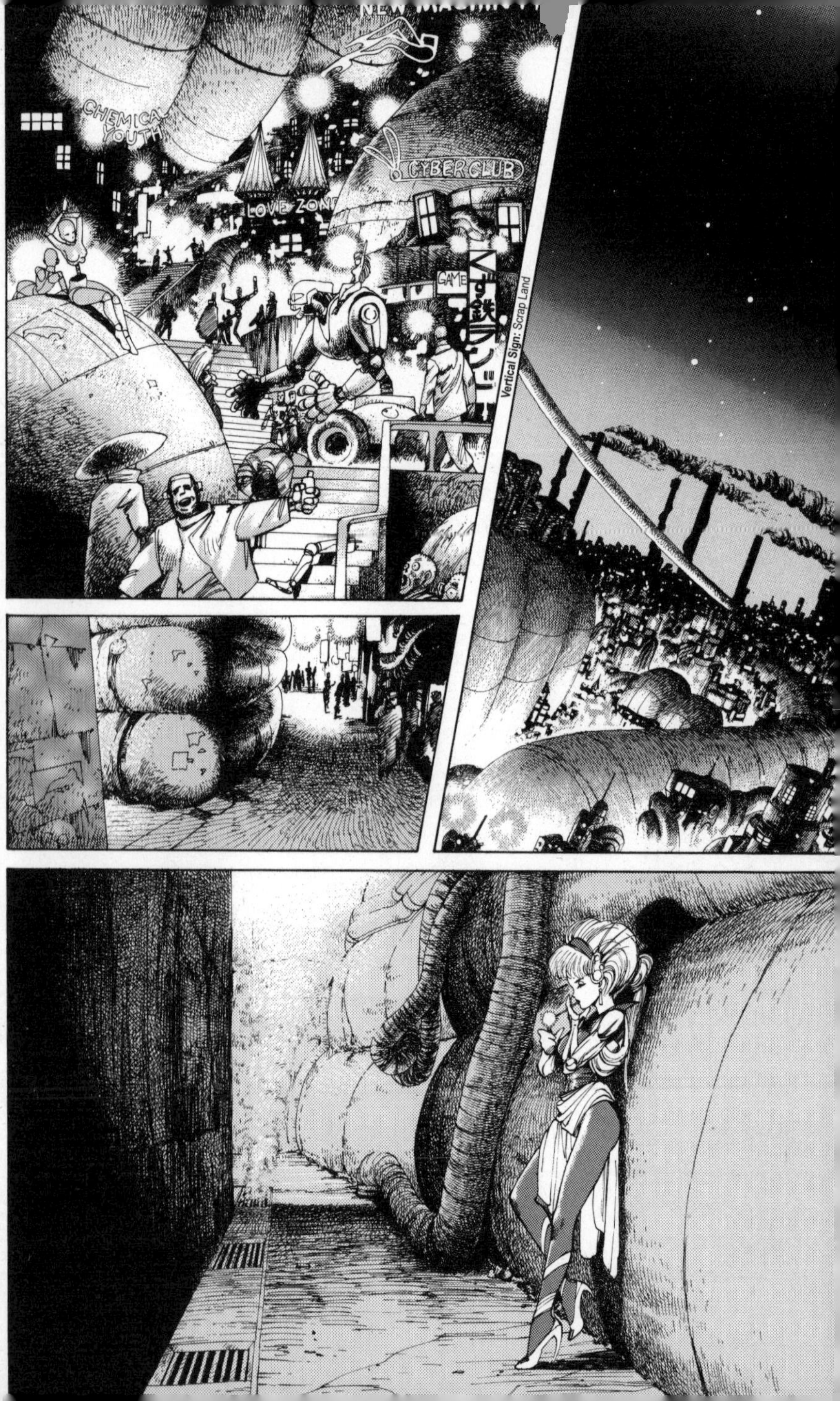
CHEMICAL YOUTH
CYBER CLUB
LOVE ZONE
GAME
Vertical Sign: Scrap Land

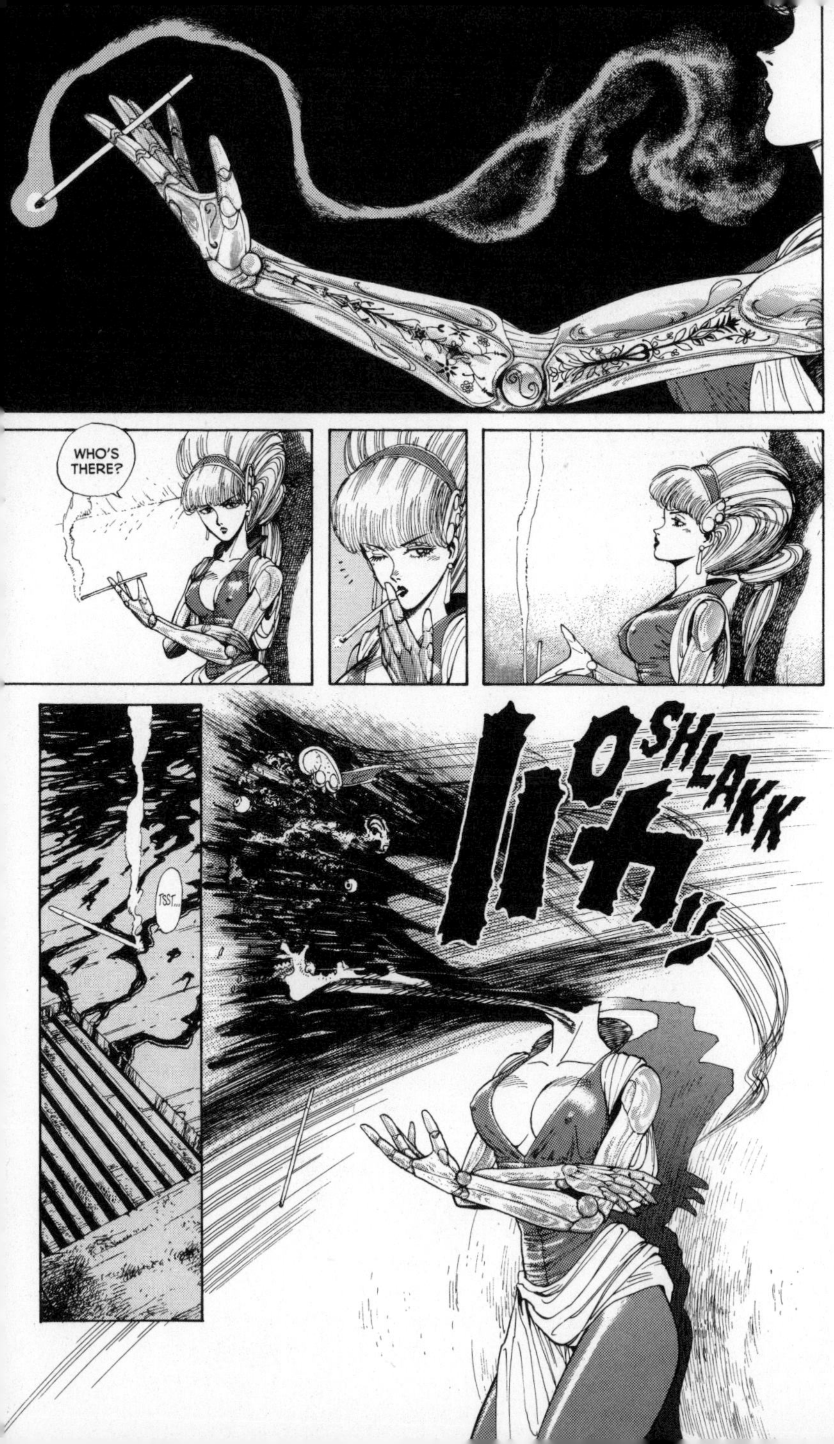
WHO'S THERE?
SHLAKK
TSST...

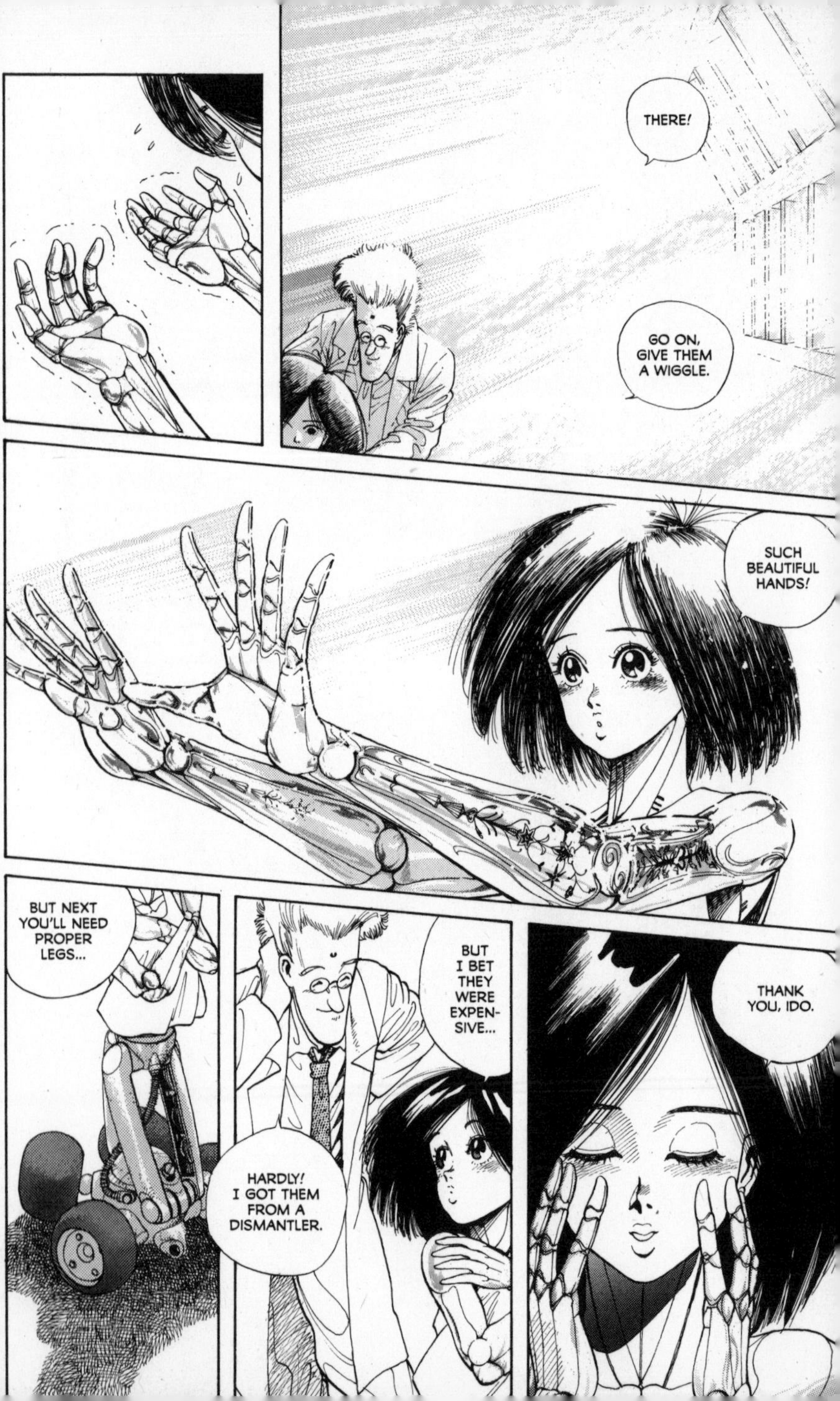
THERE!
GO ON, GIVE THEM A WIGGLE.
SUCH BEAUTIFUL HANDS!
THANK YOU, IDO.
BUT I BET THEY WERE EXPEN-SIVE...
HARDLY! I GOT THEM FROM A DISMANTLER.
BUT NEXT YOU'LL NEED PROPER LEGS...

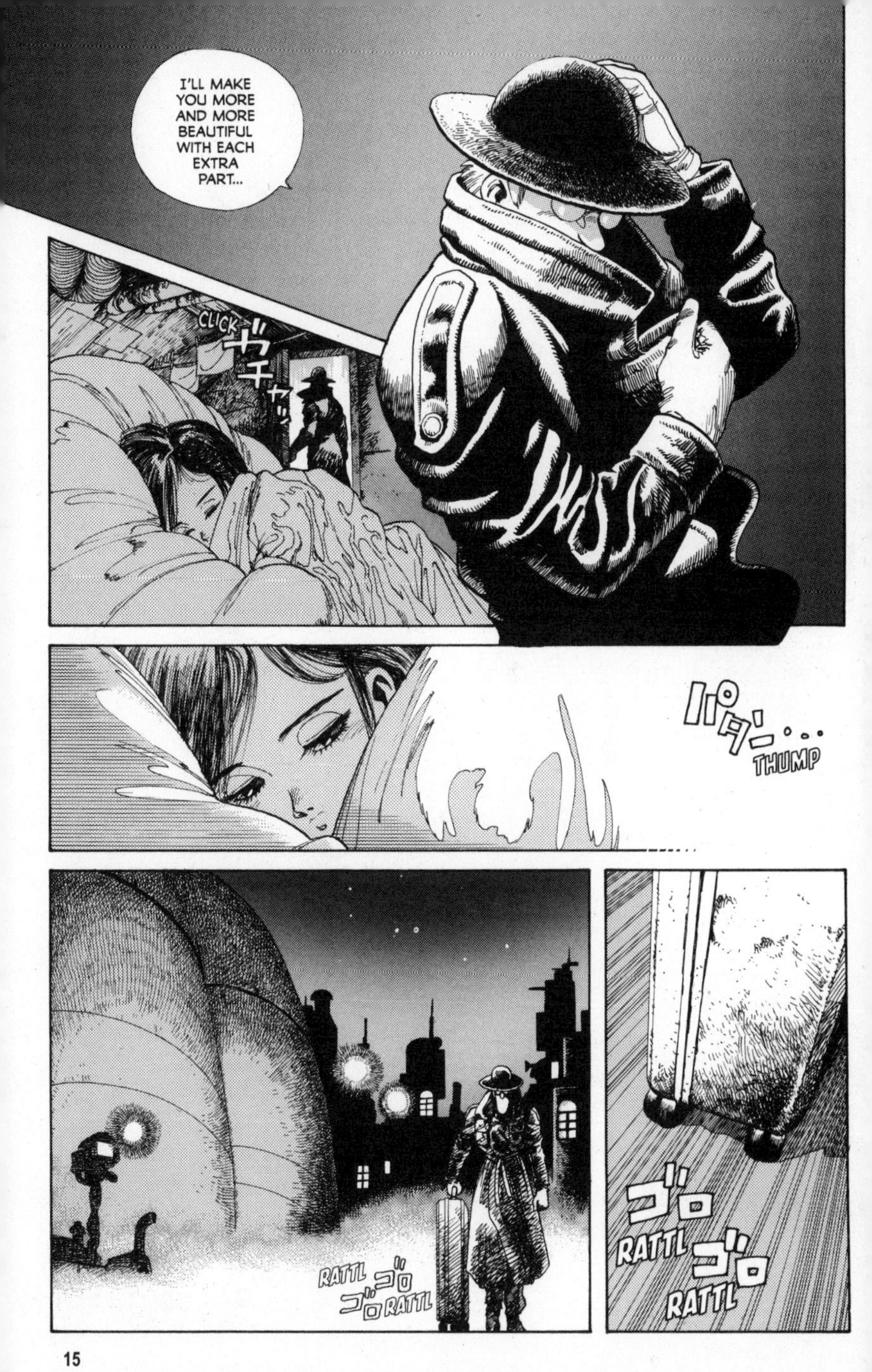
I'LL MAKE YOU MORE AND MORE BEAUTIFUL WITH EACH EXTRA PART...
ガチャッ
CLICK
パタ―。。。
THUMP
ゴロ
RATTL
ゴロ
RATTL
ゴロ
RATTL
ゴロ
RATTL

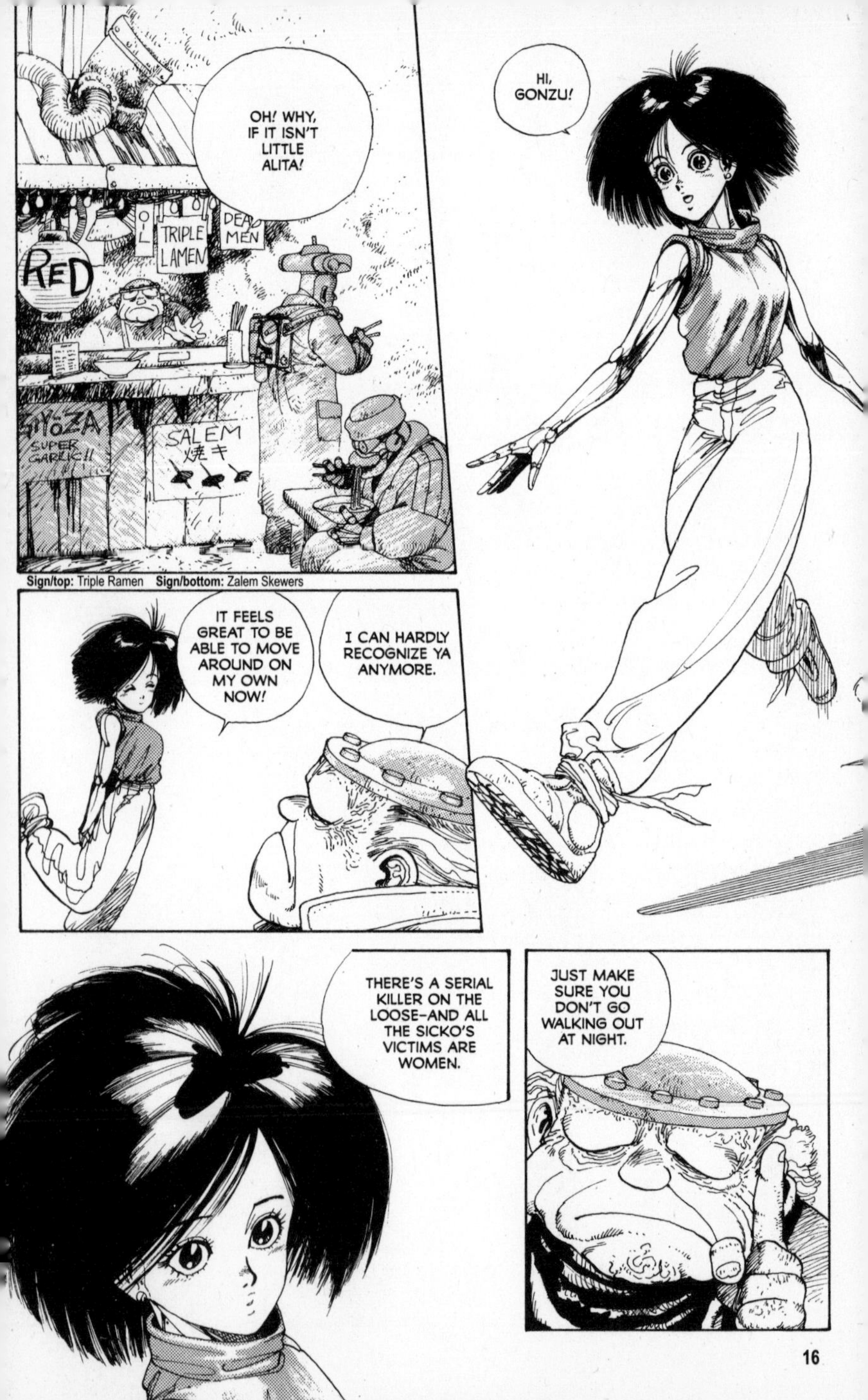
HI, GONZU!
OH! WHY, IF IT ISN'T LITTLE ALITA!
RED
OIL
TRIPLE LAMEN
DEAD MEN
GIYOZA
SUPER GARLIC!!
SALEM 焼キ
I CAN HARDLY RECOGNIZE YA ANYMORE.
IT FEELS GREAT TO BE ABLE TO MOVE AROUND ON MY OWN NOW!
JUST MAKE SURE YOU DON'T GO WALKING OUT AT NIGHT.
THERE'S A SERIAL KILLER ON THE LOOSE–AND ALL THE SICKO'S VICTIMS ARE WOMEN.

Sign/top: Triple Ramen **Sign/bottom:** Zalem Skewers

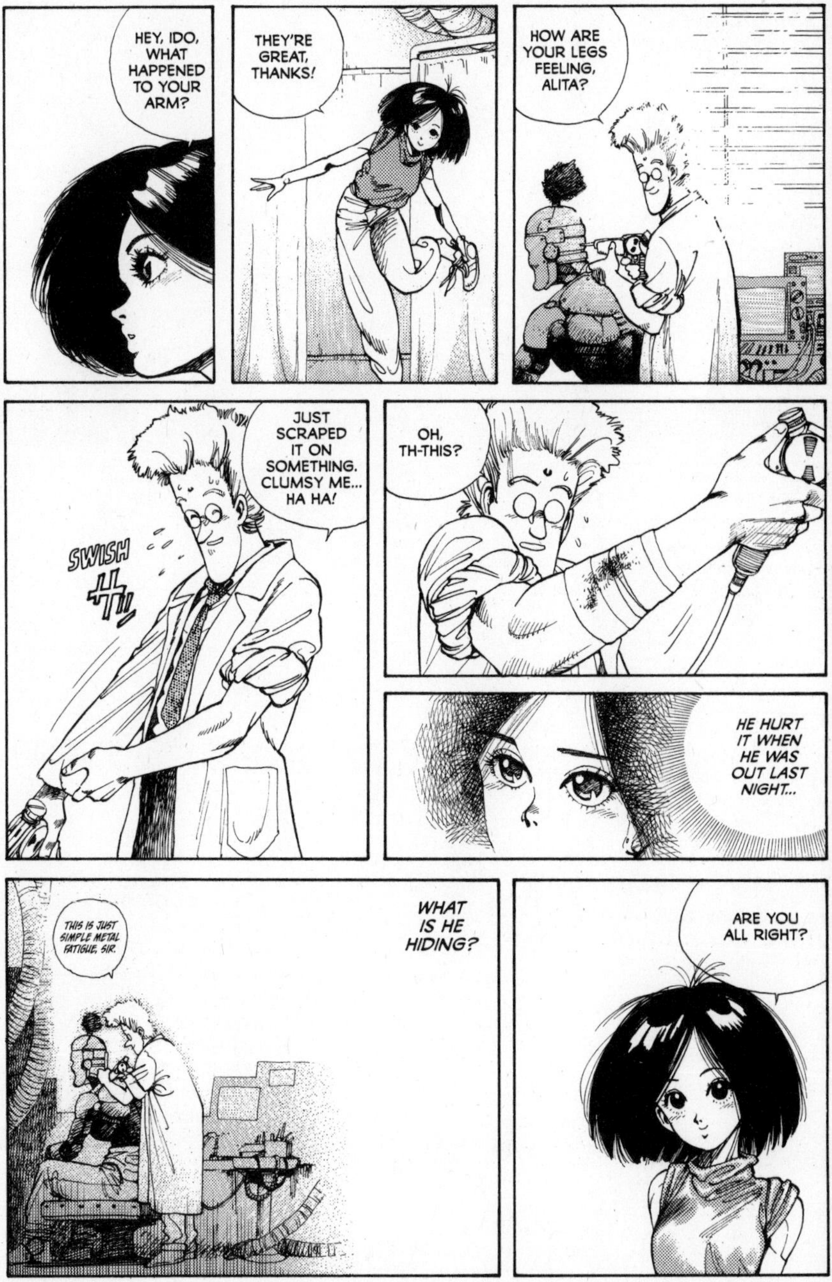
HOW ARE YOUR LEGS FEELING, ALITA?
THEY'RE GREAT, THANKS!
HEY, IDO, WHAT HAPPENED TO YOUR ARM?
OH, TH-THIS?
HE HURT IT WHEN HE WAS OUT LAST NIGHT...
JUST SCRAPED IT ON SOMETHING. CLUMSY ME... HA HA!
SWISH
ARE YOU ALL RIGHT?
WHAT IS HE HIDING?
THIS IS JUST SIMPLE METAL FATIGUE, SIR.

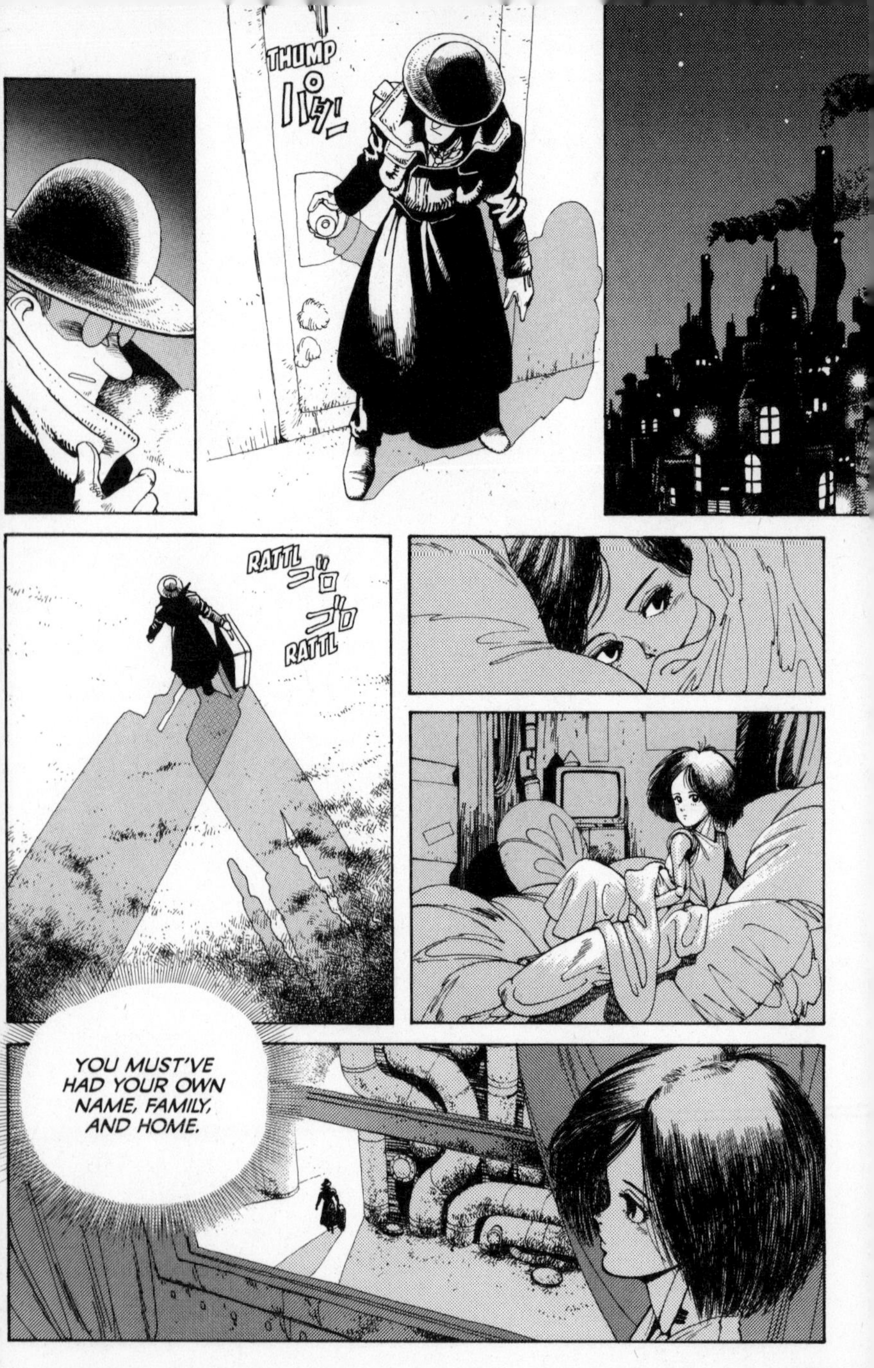
THUMP
パタン
RATTL
ゴロ
ゴロ
RATTL
YOU MUST'VE HAD YOUR OWN NAME, FAMILY, AND HOME.

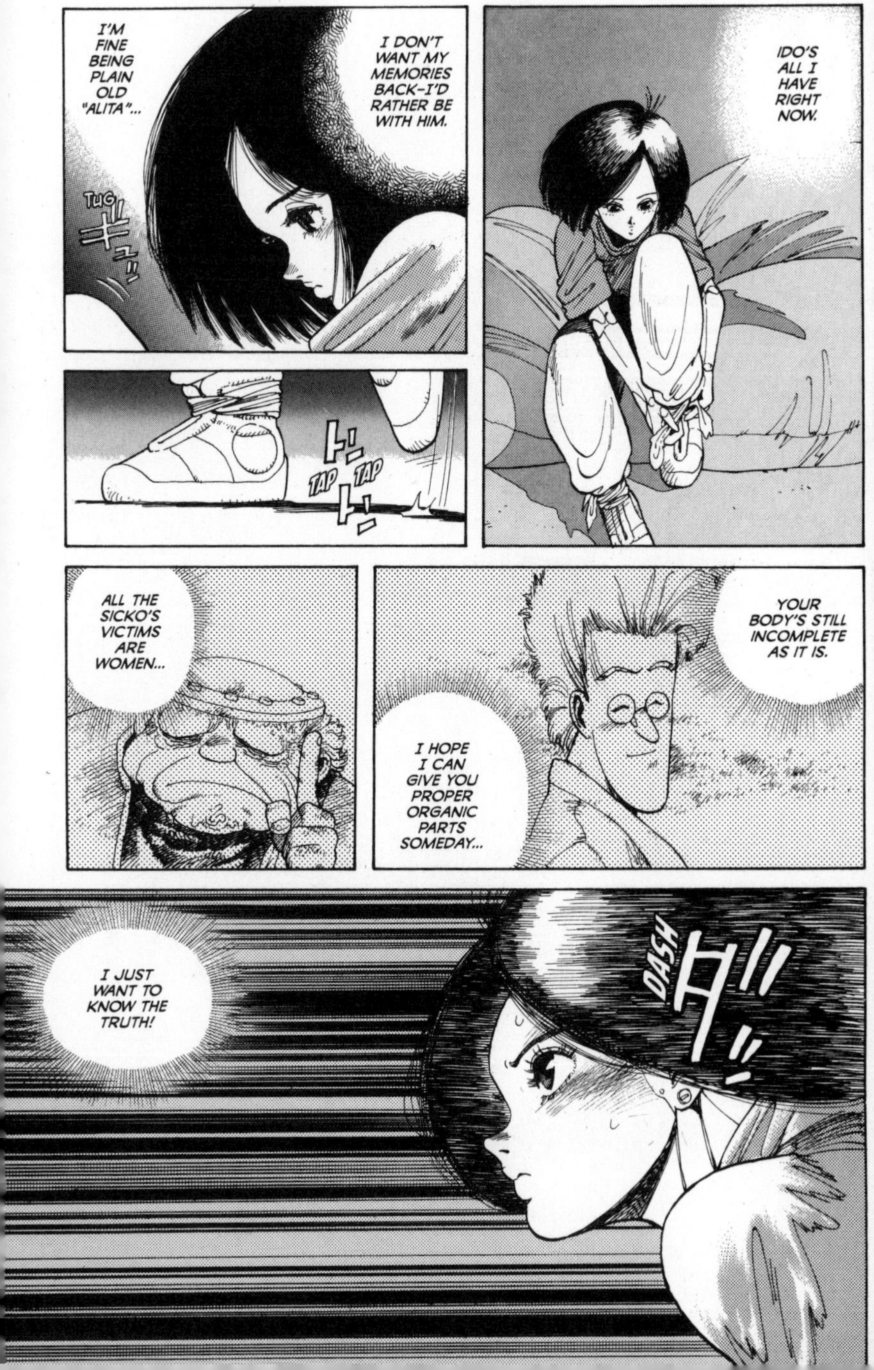
IDO'S ALL I HAVE RIGHT NOW.
I DON'T WANT MY MEMORIES BACK–I'D RATHER BE WITH HIM.
I'M FINE BEING PLAIN OLD "ALITA"...
TUG
TAP TAP
YOUR BODY'S STILL INCOMPLETE AS IT IS.
I HOPE I CAN GIVE YOU PROPER ORGANIC PARTS SOMEDAY...
ALL THE SICKO'S VICTIMS ARE WOMEN...
DASH
I JUST WANT TO KNOW THE TRUTH!

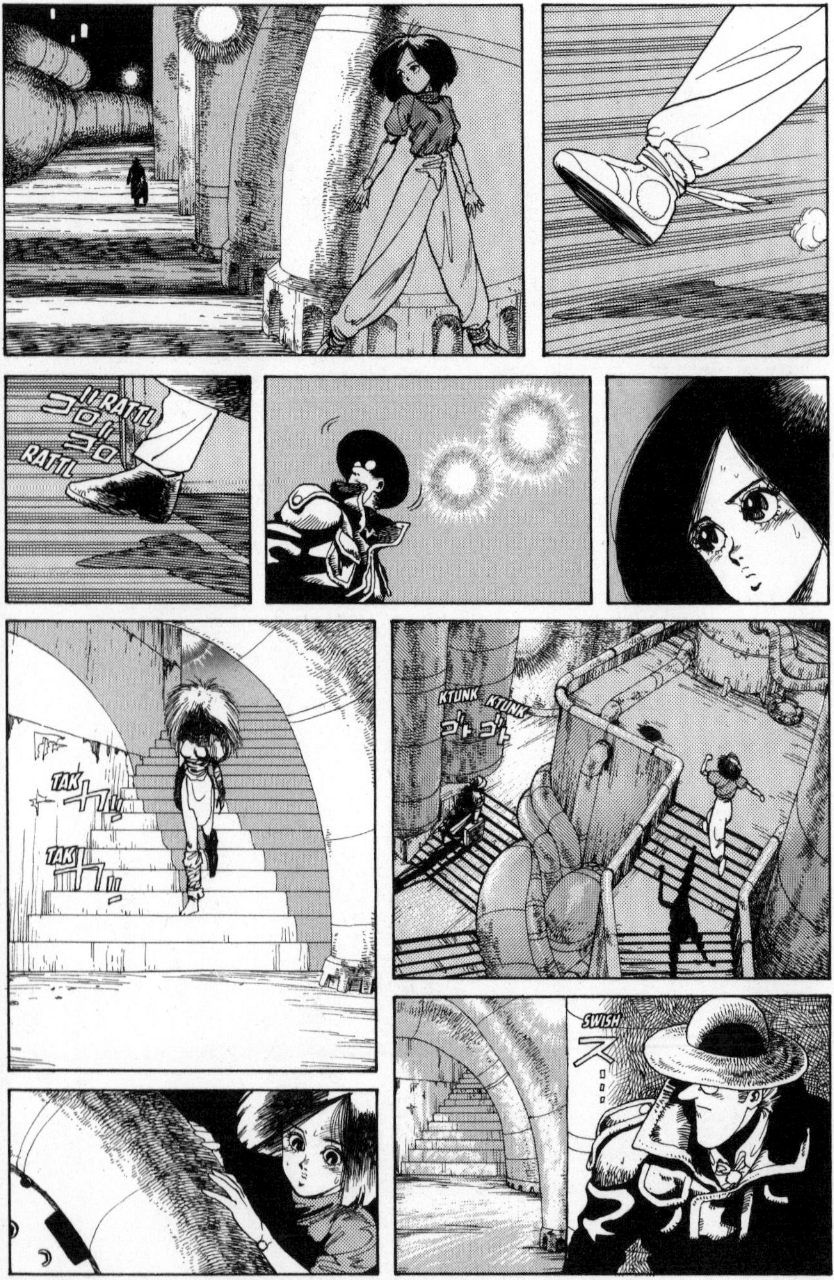
RATTL
ゴロ
ゴロ
RATTL
KTUNK KTUNK
ゴトゴト
TAK
カッ
TAK
カッ
SWISH
ス

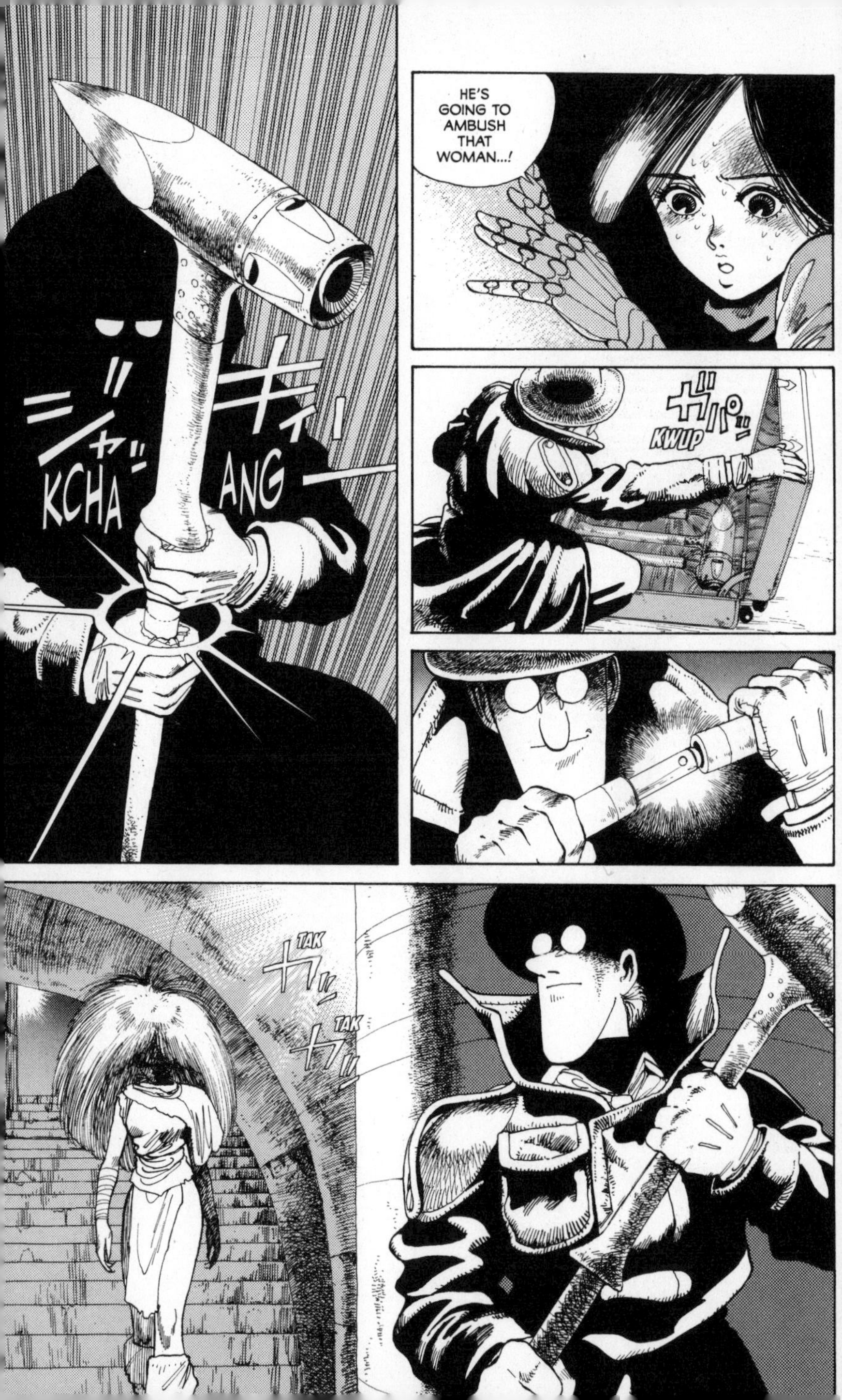
HE'S GOING TO AMBUSH THAT WOMAN...!
KWUP
KCHA
ANG
TAK
TAK

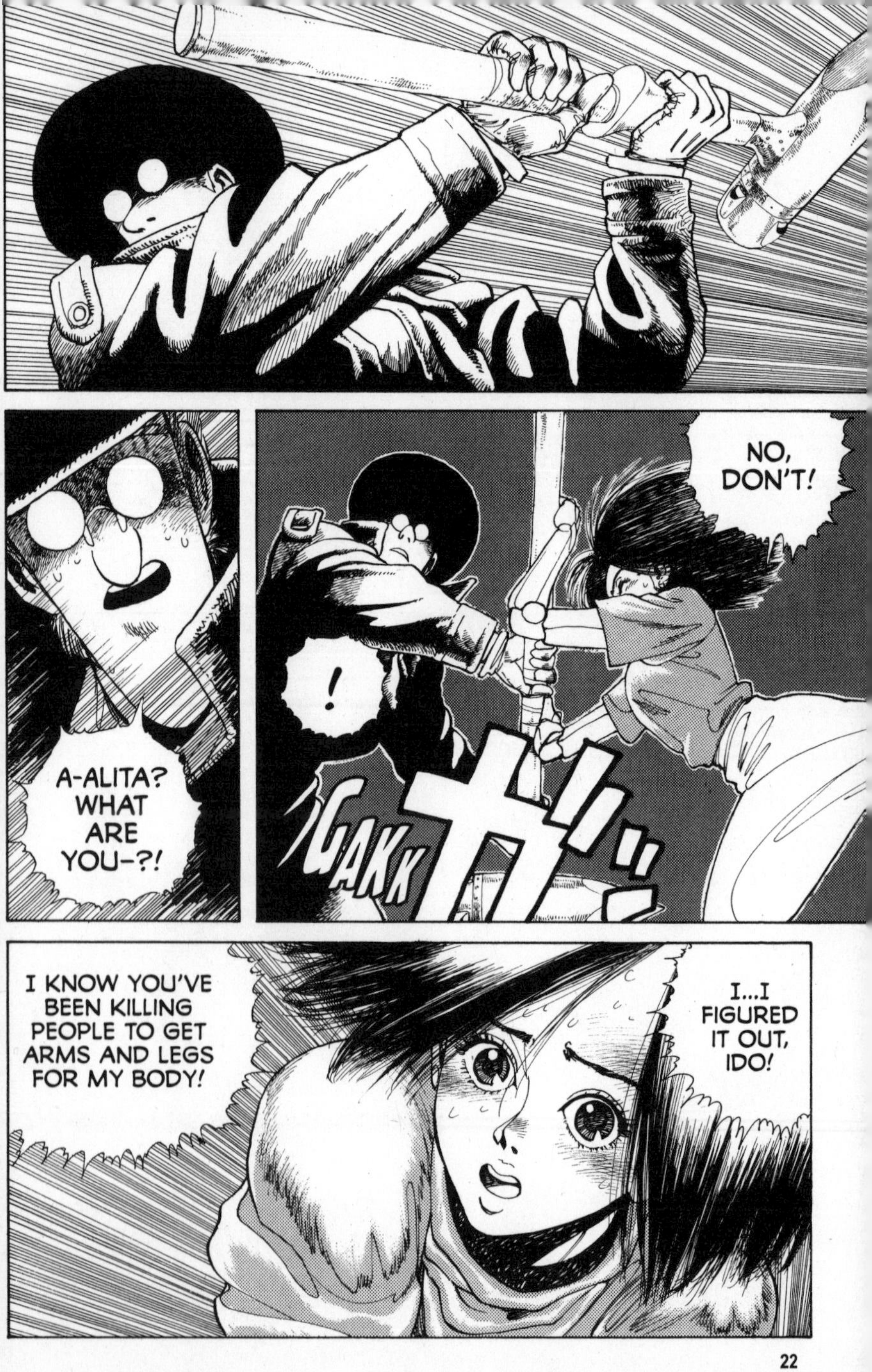
NO, DON'T!
!
GAKK
A-ALITA? WHAT ARE YOU-?!
I...I FIGURED IT OUT, IDO!
I KNOW YOU'VE BEEN KILLING PEOPLE TO GET ARMS AND LEGS FOR MY BODY!

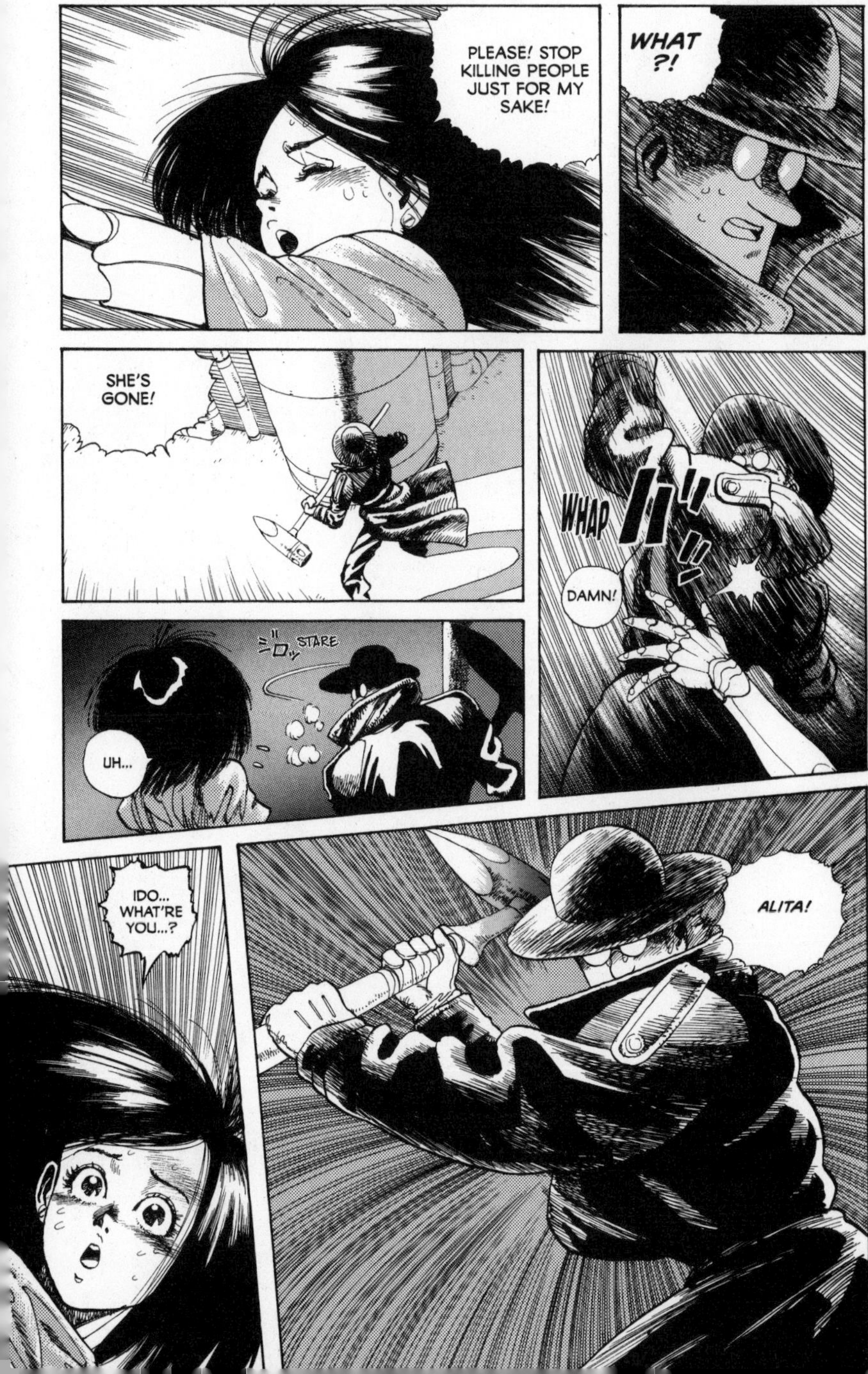
WHAT ?!
PLEASE! STOP KILLING PEOPLE JUST FOR MY SAKE!
WHAP
DAMN!
SHE'S GONE!
ジロッ STARE
UH...
ALITA!
IDO... WHAT'RE YOU...?

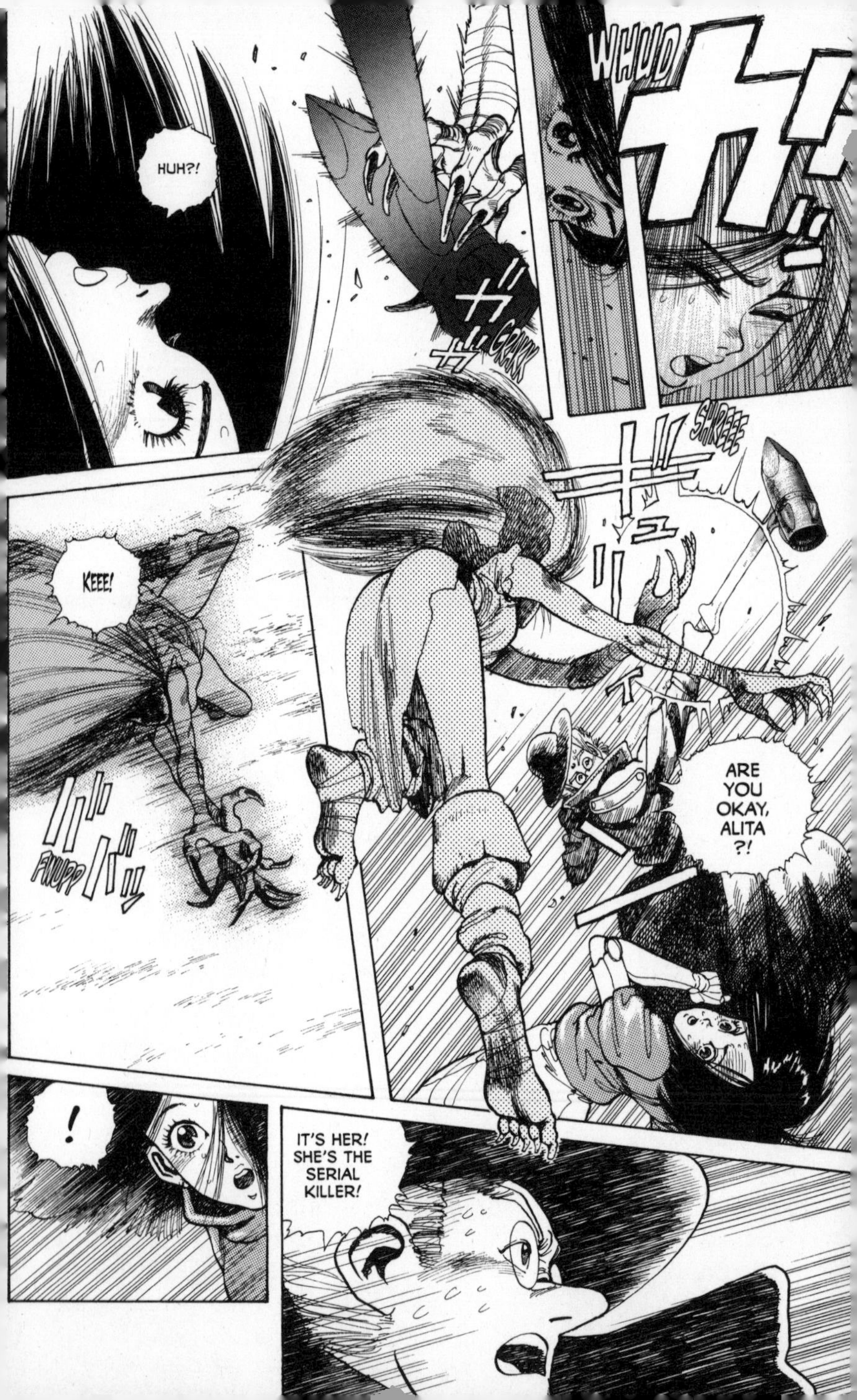
WHUD
GRAKK
HUH?!
SHREEE
ARE YOU OKAY, ALITA?!
KEEE!
FWUPP
IT'S HER! SHE'S THE SERIAL KILLER!
!

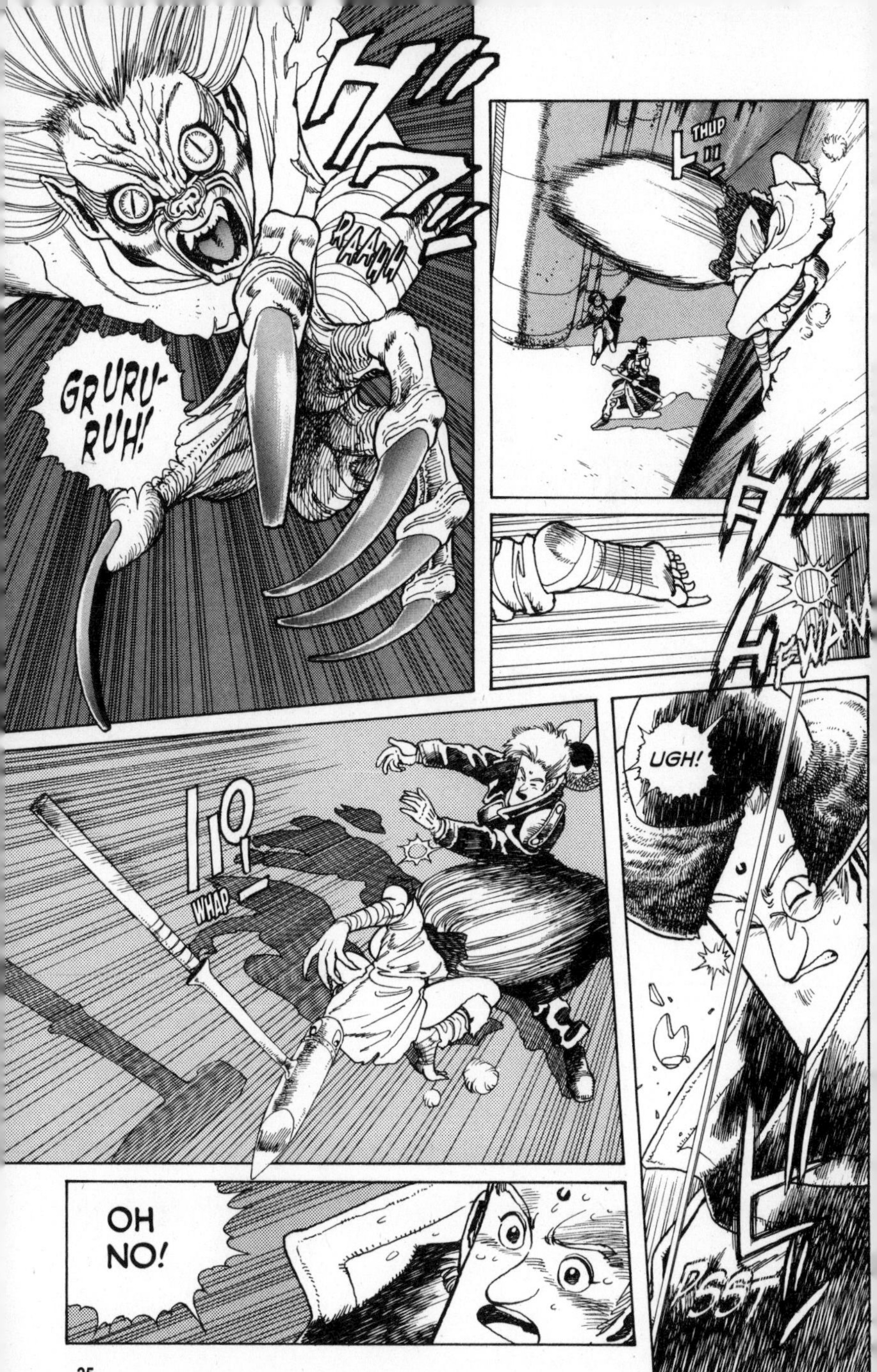
THUP
FWAM
GRURU-RUH!
RAAH!
UGH!
PSST
WHAP
OH NO!

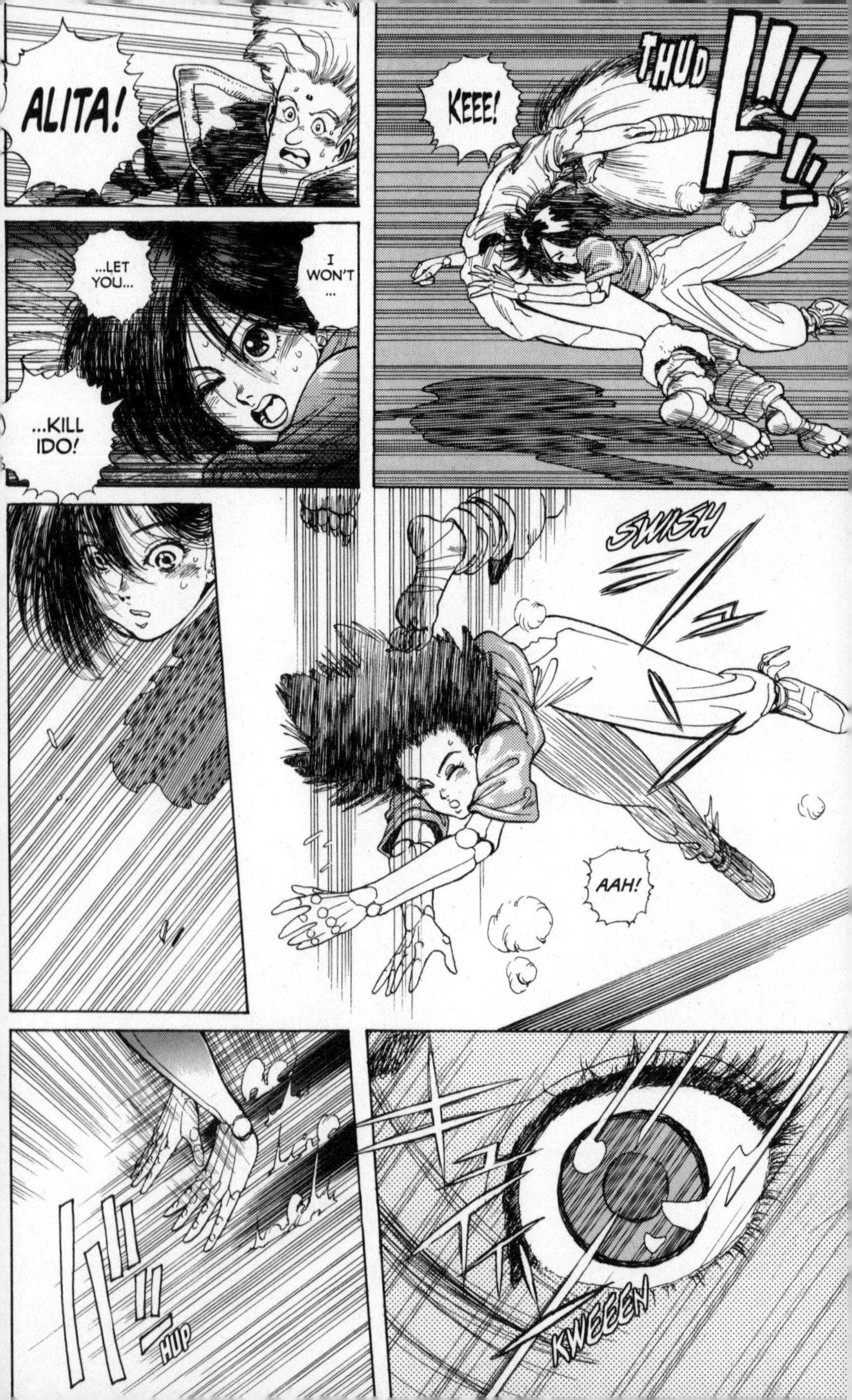
THUD
KEEE!
ALITA!
I WON'T ...
...LET YOU...
...KILL IDO!
SWISH
AAH!
KWEEEN
HUP

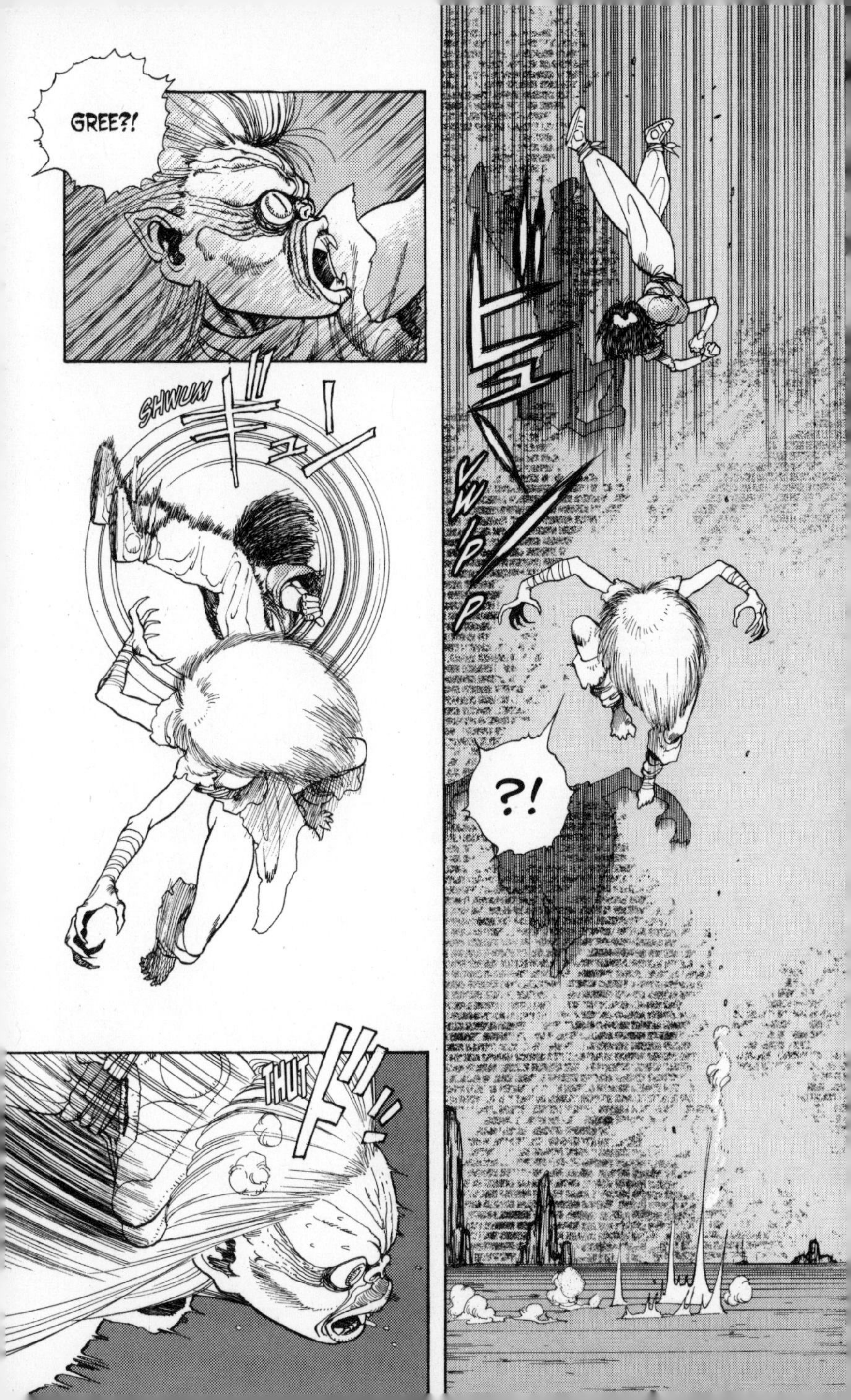
VWIPP
?!
GREE?!
SHWUM
THUT

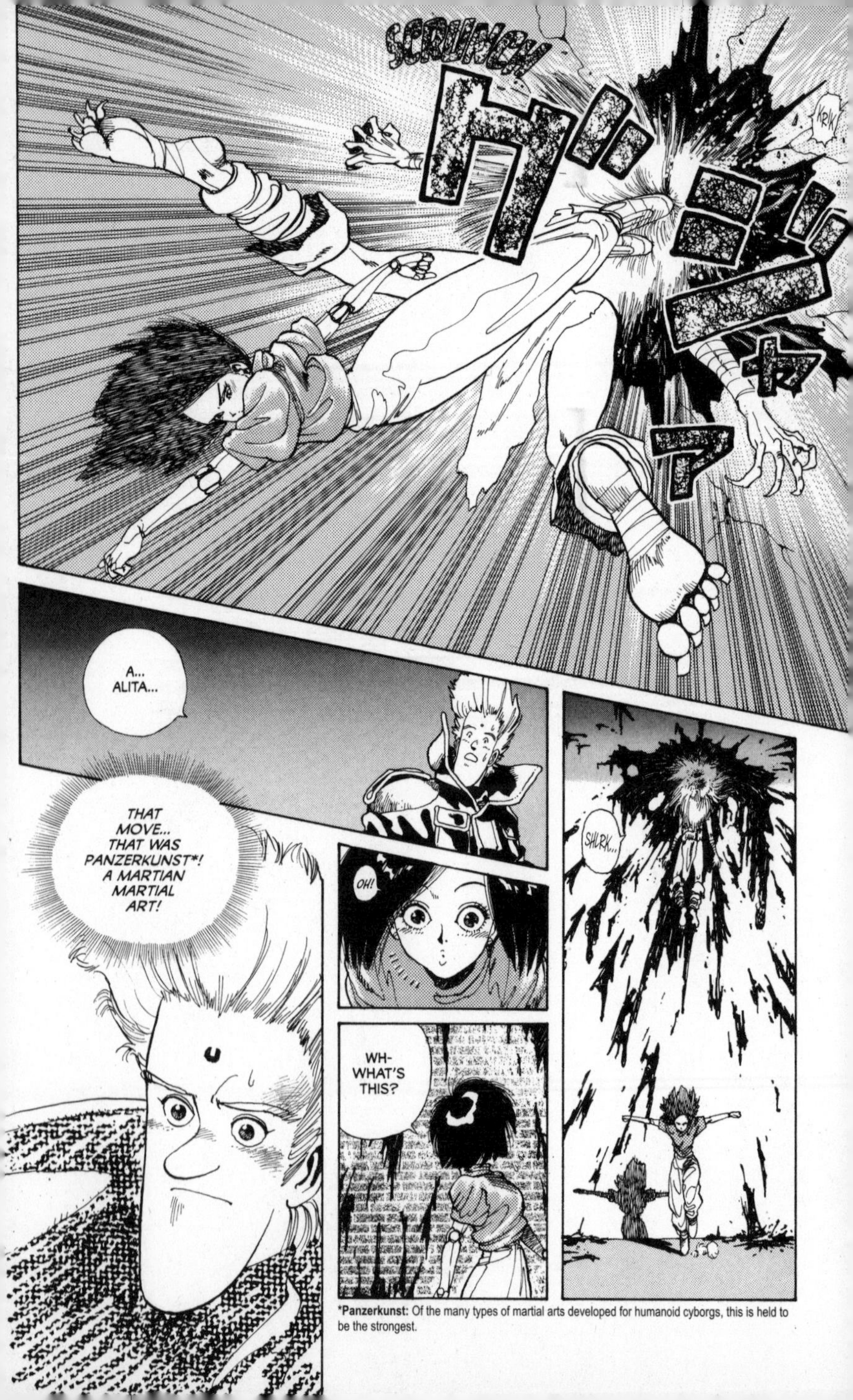
SCRUNCH
KRIK
SHLRK...
A... ALITA...
OH!
WH- WHAT'S THIS?
THAT MOVE... THAT WAS PANZERKUNST*! A MARTIAN MARTIAL ART!

***Panzerkunst:** Of the many types of martial arts developed for humanoid cyborgs, this is held to be the strongest.

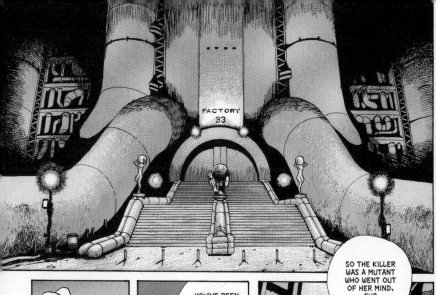

FACTORY 33
SO THE KILLER WAS A MUTANT WHO WENT OUT OF HER MIND, EH?
TAP
BEEP
TAP
GIVEN HER LOOKS, I GUESS I CAN SEE WHY SHE HAD SUCH A VENDETTA AGAINST PRETTY WOMEN.
TAK
TAP
YOU'VE BEEN ON THE WAR-PATH HUNTING DOWN ALL THESE WANTED TARGETS LATELY, IDO.
KSHH
WELL, HERE'S YOUR BOUNTY PAYOUT: 100,000 CHIPS.
WHAT, NOT GONNA BUY ANY FEMALE PARTS THIS TIME?

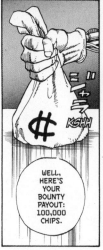

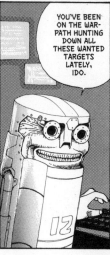

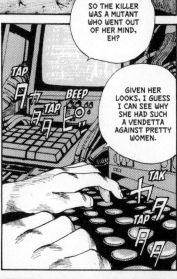

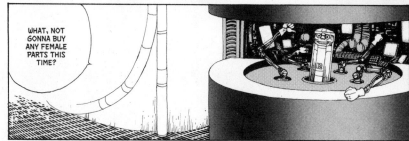

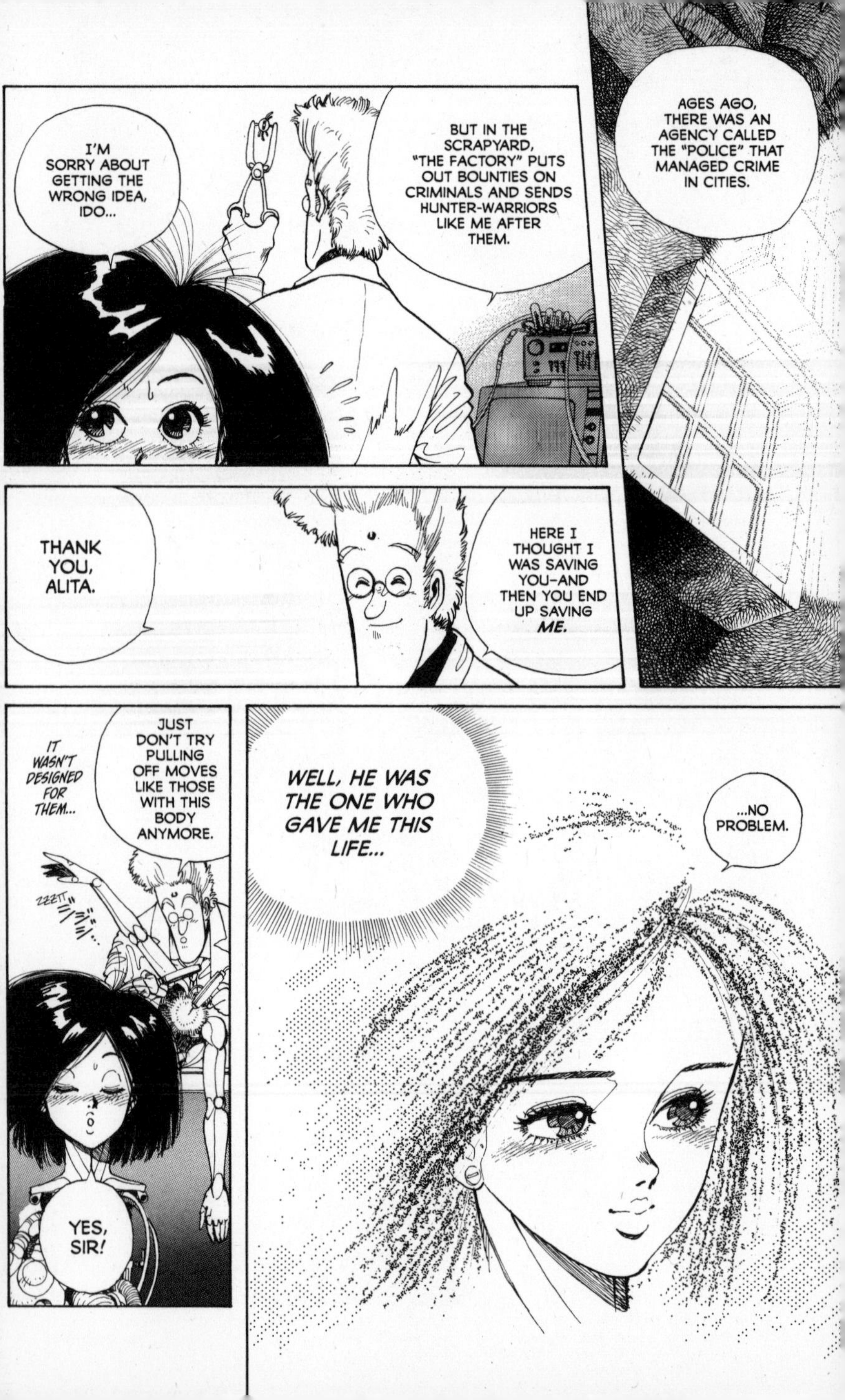
AGES AGO, THERE WAS AN AGENCY CALLED THE "POLICE" THAT MANAGED CRIME IN CITIES.
BUT IN THE SCRAPYARD, "THE FACTORY" PUTS OUT BOUNTIES ON CRIMINALS AND SENDS HUNTER-WARRIORS LIKE ME AFTER THEM.
I'M SORRY ABOUT GETTING THE WRONG IDEA, IDO...
HERE I THOUGHT I WAS SAVING YOU–AND THEN YOU END UP SAVING *ME.*
THANK YOU, ALITA.
...NO PROBLEM.
WELL, HE WAS THE ONE WHO GAVE ME THIS LIFE...
JUST DON'T TRY PULLING OFF MOVES LIKE THOSE WITH THIS BODY ANYMORE.
IT WASN'T DESIGNED FOR THEM...
ZZZTT
YES, SIR!

FIGHT_002 Fighting Instincts

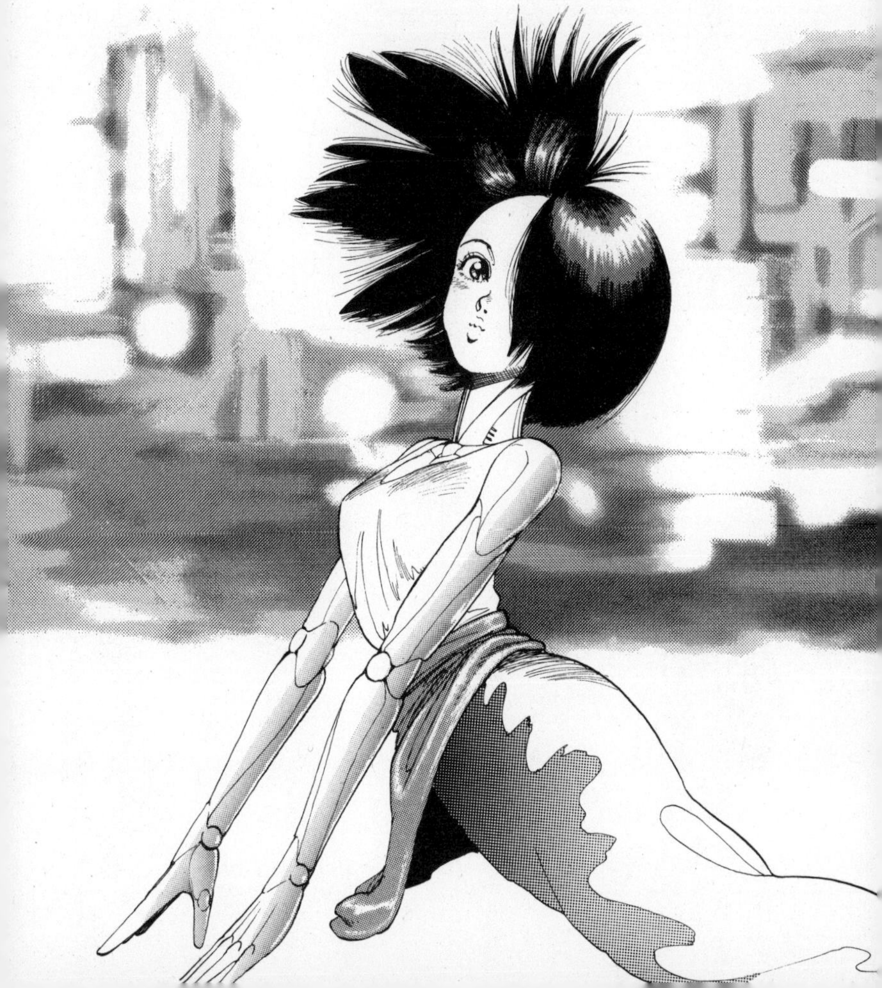

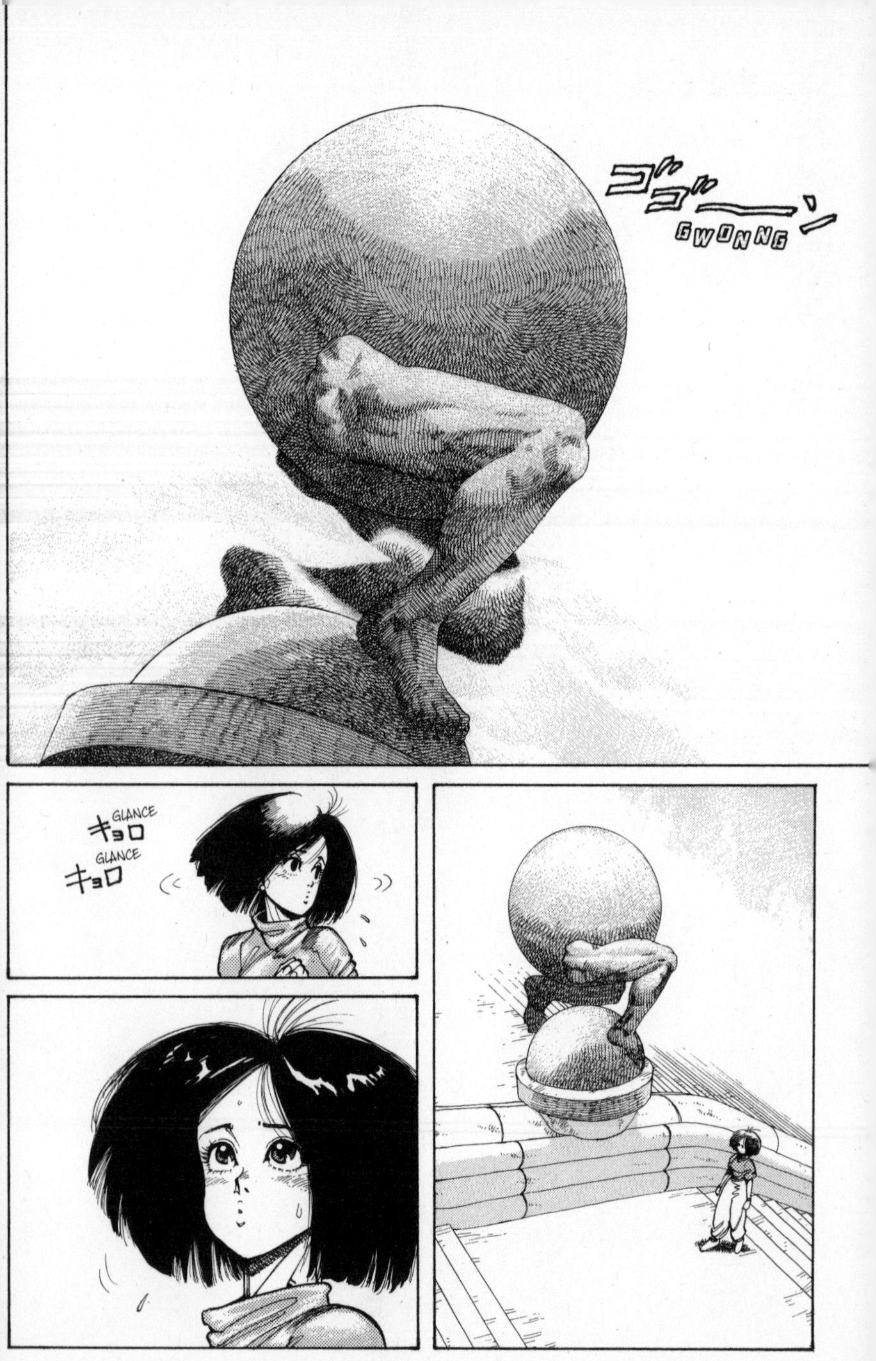
ゴゴーーン
GWONNG
キョロ
GLANCE
キョロ
GLANCE

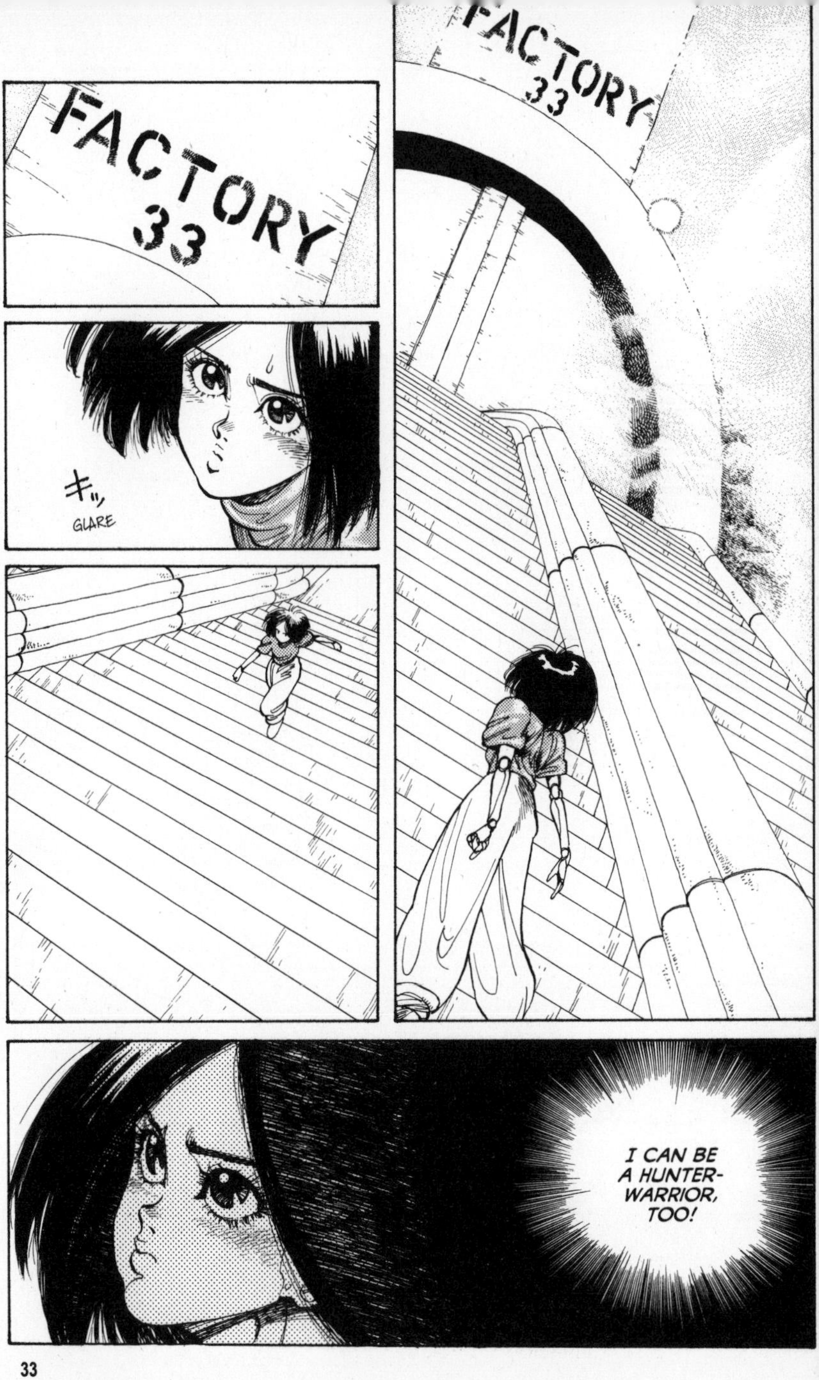
FACTORY 33
FACTORY 33
キッ
GLARE
I CAN BE A HUNTER-WARRIOR, TOO!

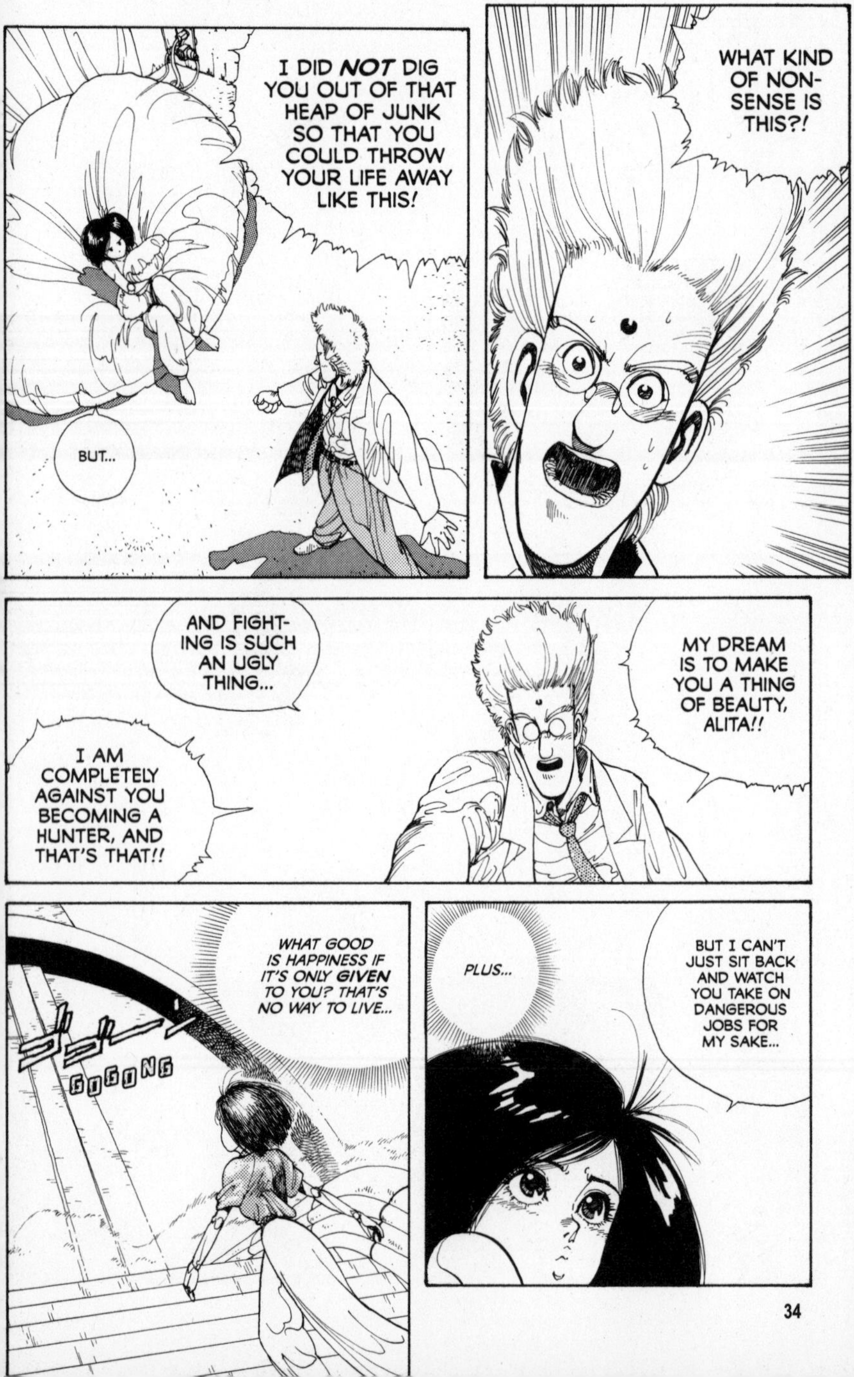
WHAT KIND OF NON-SENSE IS THIS?!
I DID NOT DIG YOU OUT OF THAT HEAP OF JUNK SO THAT YOU COULD THROW YOUR LIFE AWAY LIKE THIS!
BUT...
MY DREAM IS TO MAKE YOU A THING OF BEAUTY, ALITA!!
AND FIGHT-ING IS SUCH AN UGLY THING...
I AM COMPLETELY AGAINST YOU BECOMING A HUNTER, AND THAT'S THAT!!
BUT I CAN'T JUST SIT BACK AND WATCH YOU TAKE ON DANGEROUS JOBS FOR MY SAKE...
PLUS...
WHAT GOOD IS HAPPINESS IF IT'S ONLY GIVEN TO YOU? THAT'S NO WAY TO LIVE...
GOGONG

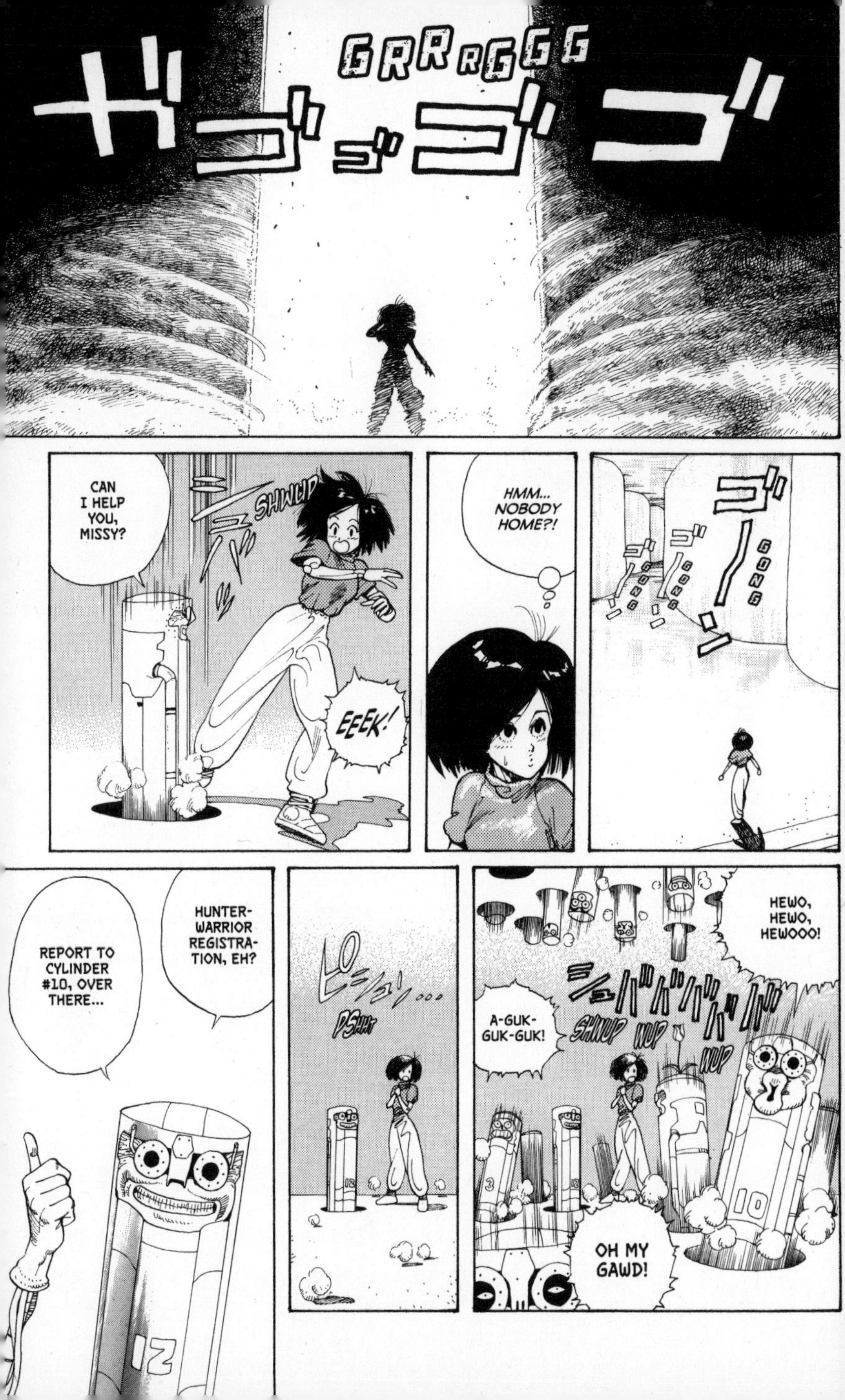
GRRRGGG
GONG
GONG
GONG
HMM... NOBODY HOME?!
CAN I HELP YOU, MISSY?
SHWUP
EEEK!
HEWO, HEWO, HEWOOO!
A-GUK-GUK-GUK!
SHWUP
WUP
WUP
OH MY GAWD!
DSHHT
HUNTER-WARRIOR REGISTRATION, EH?
REPORT TO CYLINDER #10, OVER THERE...

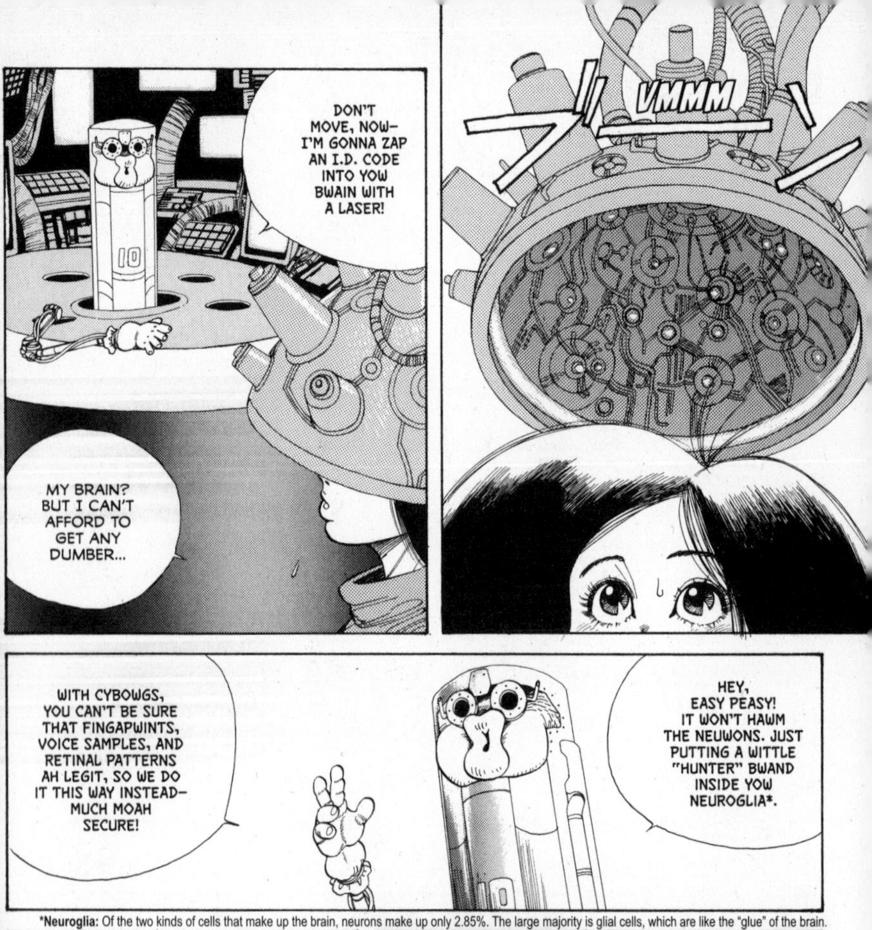
VMMM
DON'T MOVE, NOW– I'M GONNA ZAP AN I.D. CODE INTO YOW BWAIN WITH A LASER!
MY BRAIN? BUT I CAN'T AFFORD TO GET ANY DUMBER...
HEY, EASY PEASY! IT WON'T HAWM THE NEUWONS. JUST PUTTING A WITTLE "HUNTER" BWAND INSIDE YOW NEUROGLIA*.
WITH CYBOWGS, YOU CAN'T BE SURE THAT FINGAPWINTS, VOICE SAMPLES, AND RETINAL PATTERNS AH LEGIT, SO WE DO IT THIS WAY INSTEAD– MUCH MOAH SECURE!

***Neuroglia:** Of the two kinds of cells that make up the brain, neurons make up only 2.85%. The large majority is glial cells, which are like the "glue" of the brain.

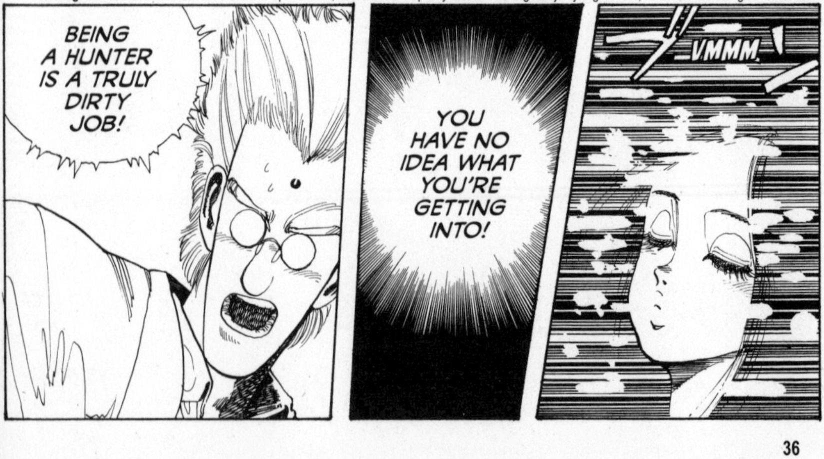
VMMM
YOU HAVE NO IDEA WHAT YOU'RE GETTING INTO!
BEING A HUNTER IS A TRULY DIRTY JOB!

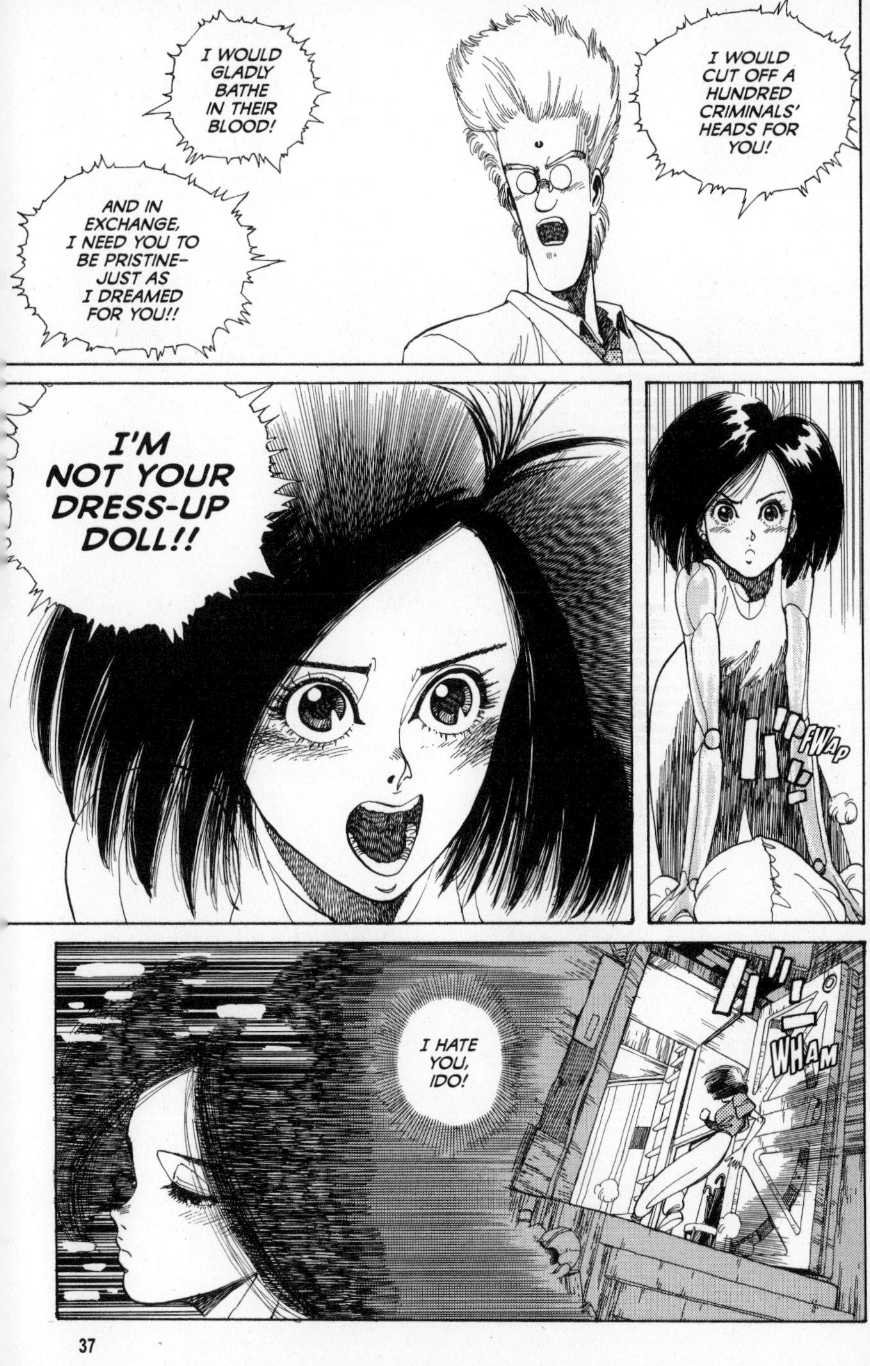
I WOULD CUT OFF A HUNDRED CRIMINALS' HEADS FOR YOU!
I WOULD GLADLY BATHE IN THEIR BLOOD!
AND IN EXCHANGE, I NEED YOU TO BE PRISTINE- JUST AS I DREAMED FOR YOU!!
FWAP
I'M NOT YOUR DRESS-UP DOLL!!
WHAM
I HATE YOU, IDO!

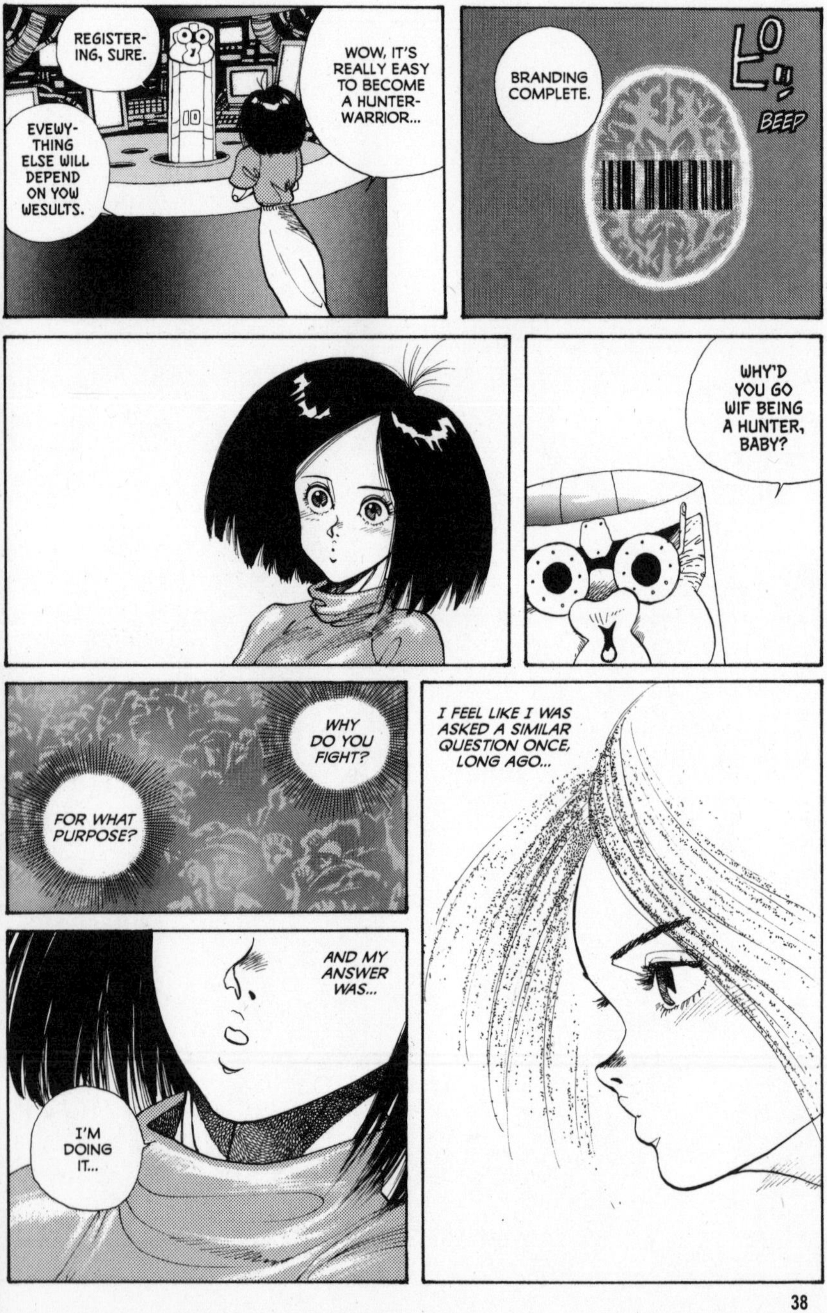

BRANDING COMPLETE.
ピッ
BEEP
WOW, IT'S REALLY EASY TO BECOME A HUNTER-WARRIOR...
REGISTERING, SURE.
EVEWYTHING ELSE WILL DEPEND ON YOW WESULTS.
WHY'D YOU GO WIF BEING A HUNTER, BABY?
I FEEL LIKE I WAS ASKED A SIMILAR QUESTION ONCE, LONG AGO...
WHY DO YOU FIGHT?
FOR WHAT PURPOSE?
AND MY ANSWER WAS...
I'M DOING IT...

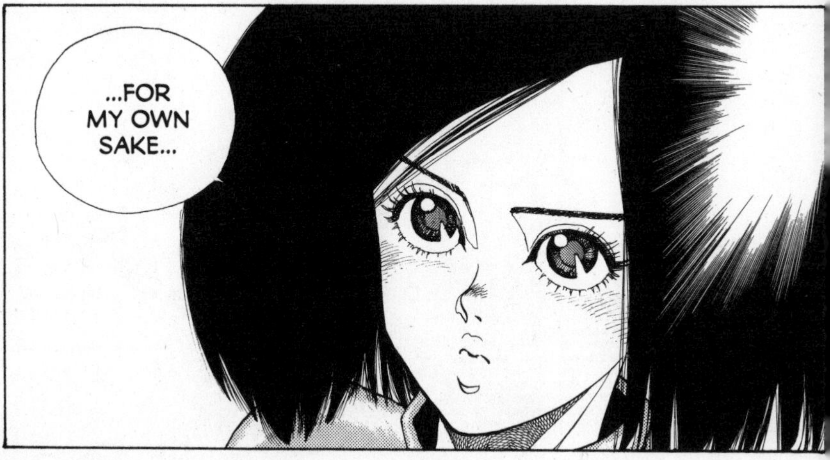
...FOR MY OWN SAKE...

Signs/L-to-R: Cyber, Udon, Meat Buns, Inari Sushi

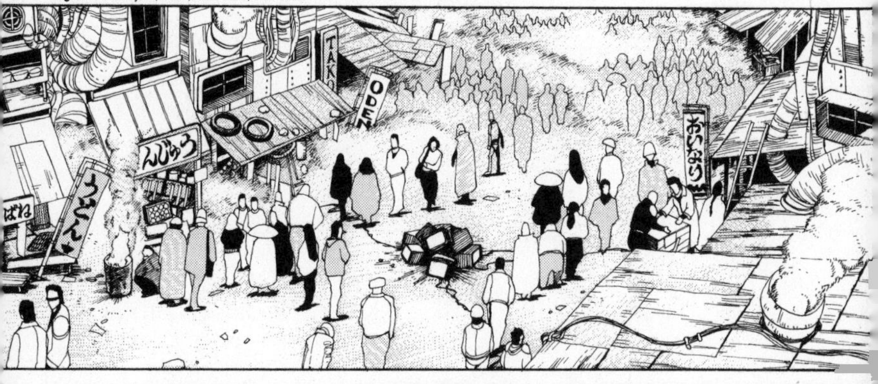
TAKO
ODEN

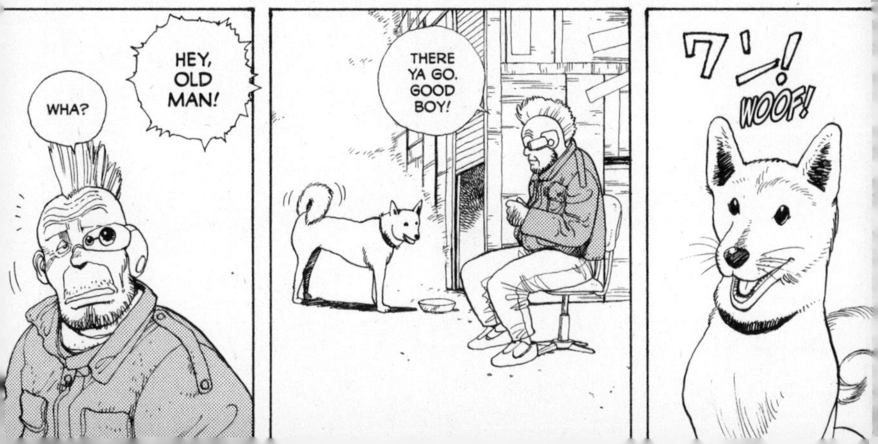
ワンー!
WOOF!
THERE YA GO. GOOD BOY!
HEY, OLD MAN!
WHA?

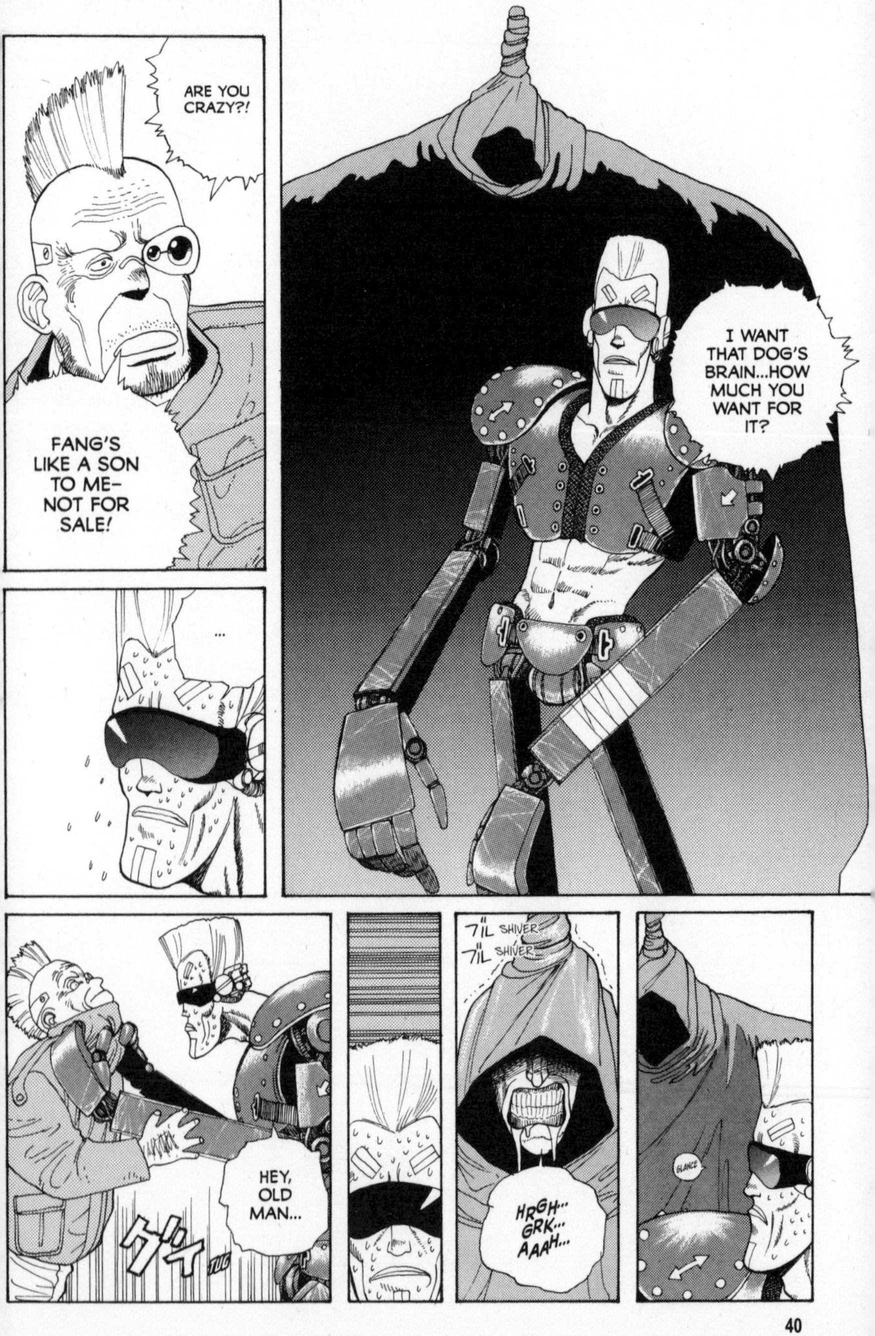
I WANT THAT DOG'S BRAIN...HOW MUCH YOU WANT FOR IT?
ARE YOU CRAZY?!
FANG'S LIKE A SON TO ME— NOT FOR SALE!
...
GLANCE
ブル SHIVER
ブル SHIVER
HRGH... GRK... AAAH...
HEY, OLD MAN...
グイ TUG

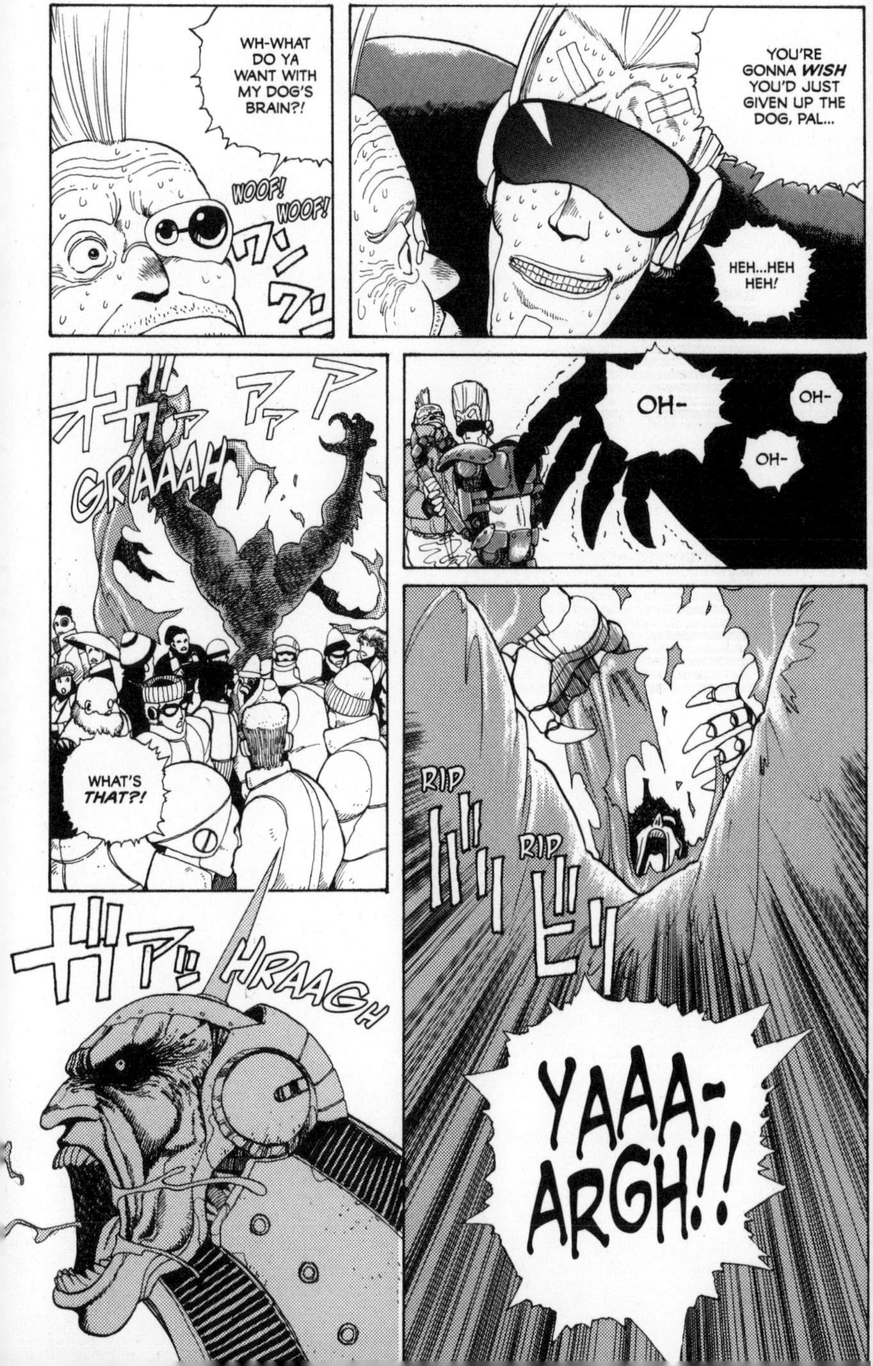
YOU'RE GONNA *WISH* YOU'D JUST GIVEN UP THE DOG, PAL...
HEH...HEH HEH!
WH-WHAT DO YA WANT WITH MY DOG'S BRAIN?!
WOOF!
WOOF!
OH-
OH-
OH-
RIP
RIP
YAAA-ARGH!!
GRAAAH
WHAT'S *THAT?!*
HRAAGH

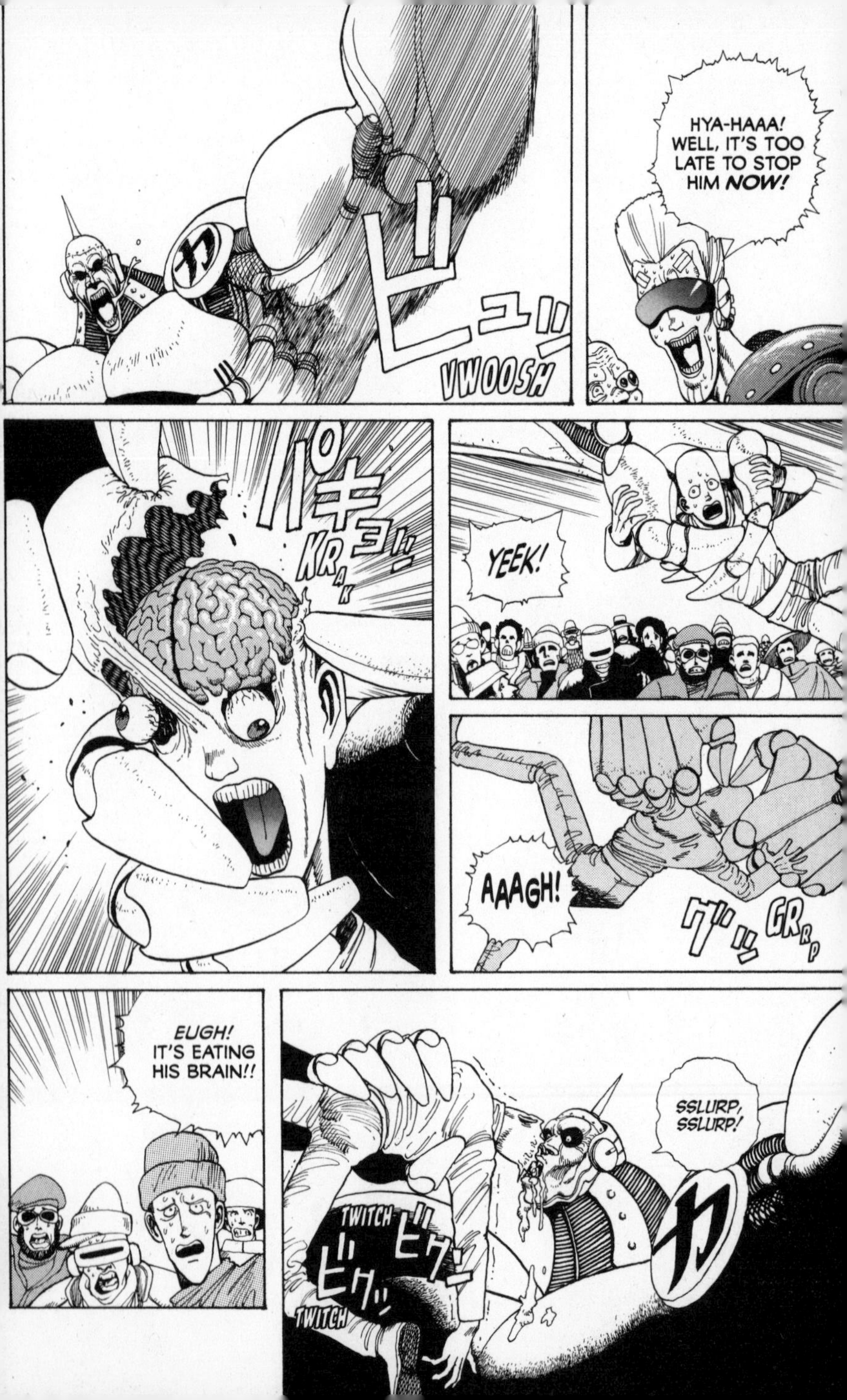
HYA-HAAA! WELL, IT'S TOO LATE TO STOP HIM *NOW!*
VWOOSH
YEEK!
AAAGH!
GRRP
KRAK
SSLURP, SSLURP!
TWITCH
TWITCH
EUGH! IT'S EATING HIS BRAIN!!

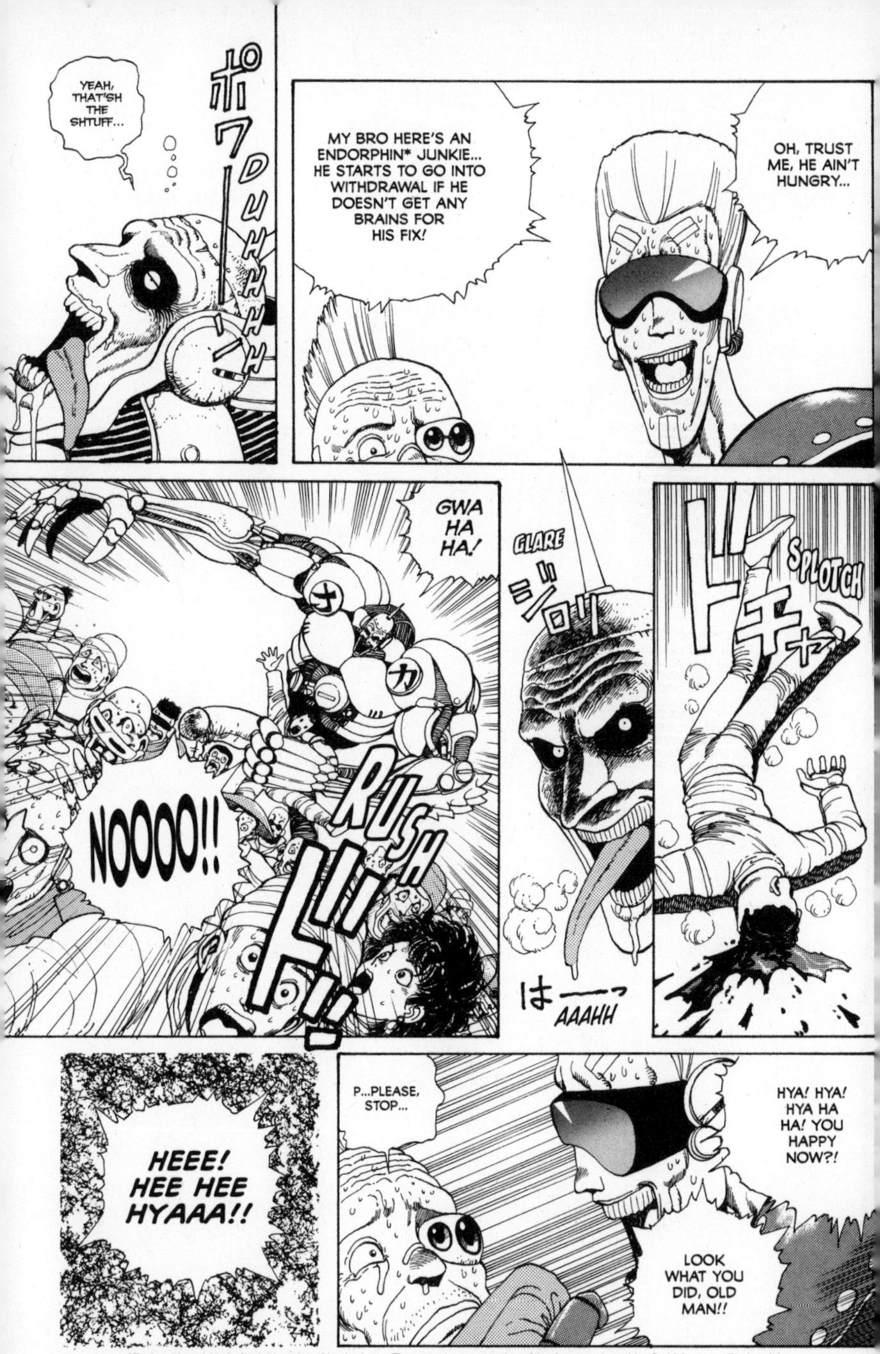
OH, TRUST ME, HE AIN'T HUNGRY...
MY BRO HERE'S AN ENDORPHIN* JUNKIE... HE STARTS TO GO INTO WITHDRAWAL IF HE DOESN'T GET ANY BRAINS FOR HIS FIX!
ポワ
DUHHHHHH
YEAH, THAT'SH THE SHTUFF...
SPLOTCH
GLARE
ジロリ
はーっ
AAAHH
GWA HA HA!
RUSH
NOOOO!!
HYA! HYA! HYA HA HA! YOU HAPPY NOW?!
P...PLEASE, STOP...
LOOK WHAT YOU DID, OLD MAN!!
HEEE! HEE HEE HYAAA!!

*Endorphins: A kind of opioid produced by the brain. The name is a contraction of "endogenous morphine," which means "body-originated morphine." Beta endorphins actually have 6.5 times the painkilling effect of morphine.

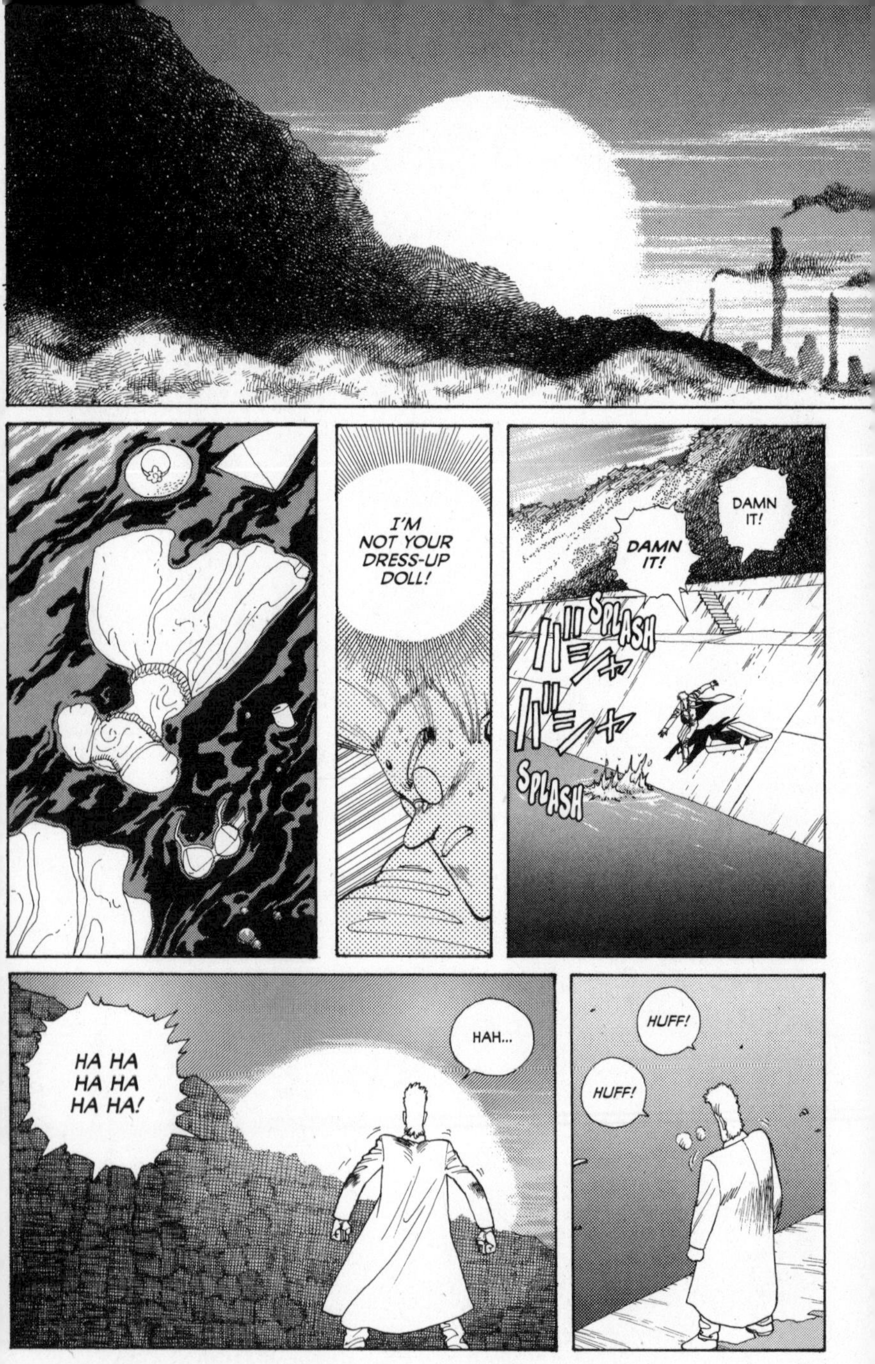
DAMN IT!
DAMN IT!
SPLASH
SPLASH
I'M NOT YOUR DRESS-UP DOLL!
HUFF!
HUFF!
HAH...
HA HA HA HA HA HA!

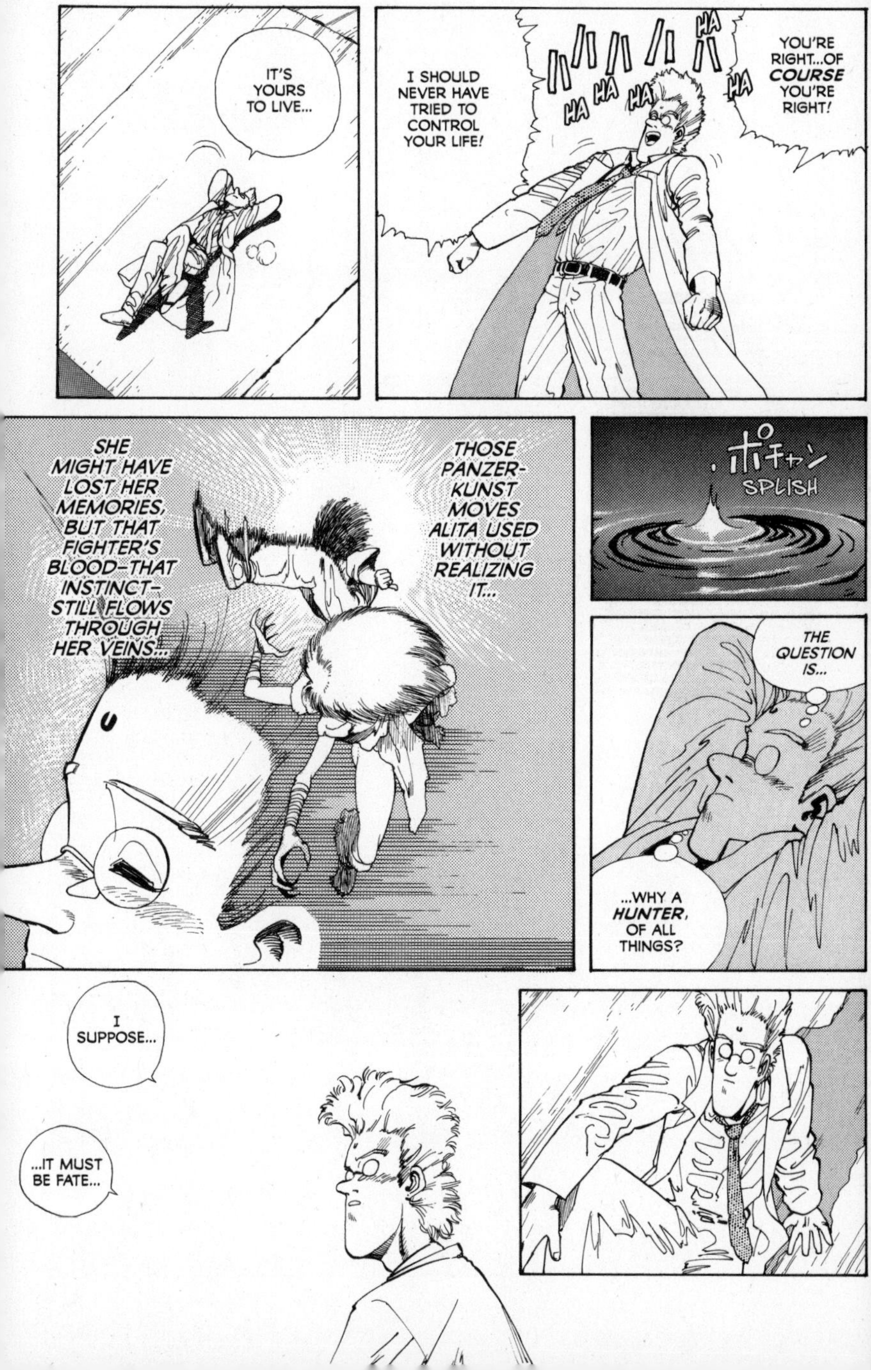
YOU'RE RIGHT...OF *COURSE* YOU'RE RIGHT!
ハハハハハハ
HA HA HA HA HA HA
I SHOULD NEVER HAVE TRIED TO CONTROL YOUR LIFE!
IT'S YOURS TO LIVE...
ポチャン
SPLISH
THE QUESTION IS...
...WHY A *HUNTER*, OF ALL THINGS?
THOSE PANZER-KUNST MOVES ALITA USED WITHOUT REALIZING IT...
SHE MIGHT HAVE LOST HER MEMORIES, BUT THAT FIGHTER'S BLOOD—THAT INSTINCT—STILL FLOWS THROUGH HER VEINS...
I SUPPOSE...
...IT MUST BE FATE...

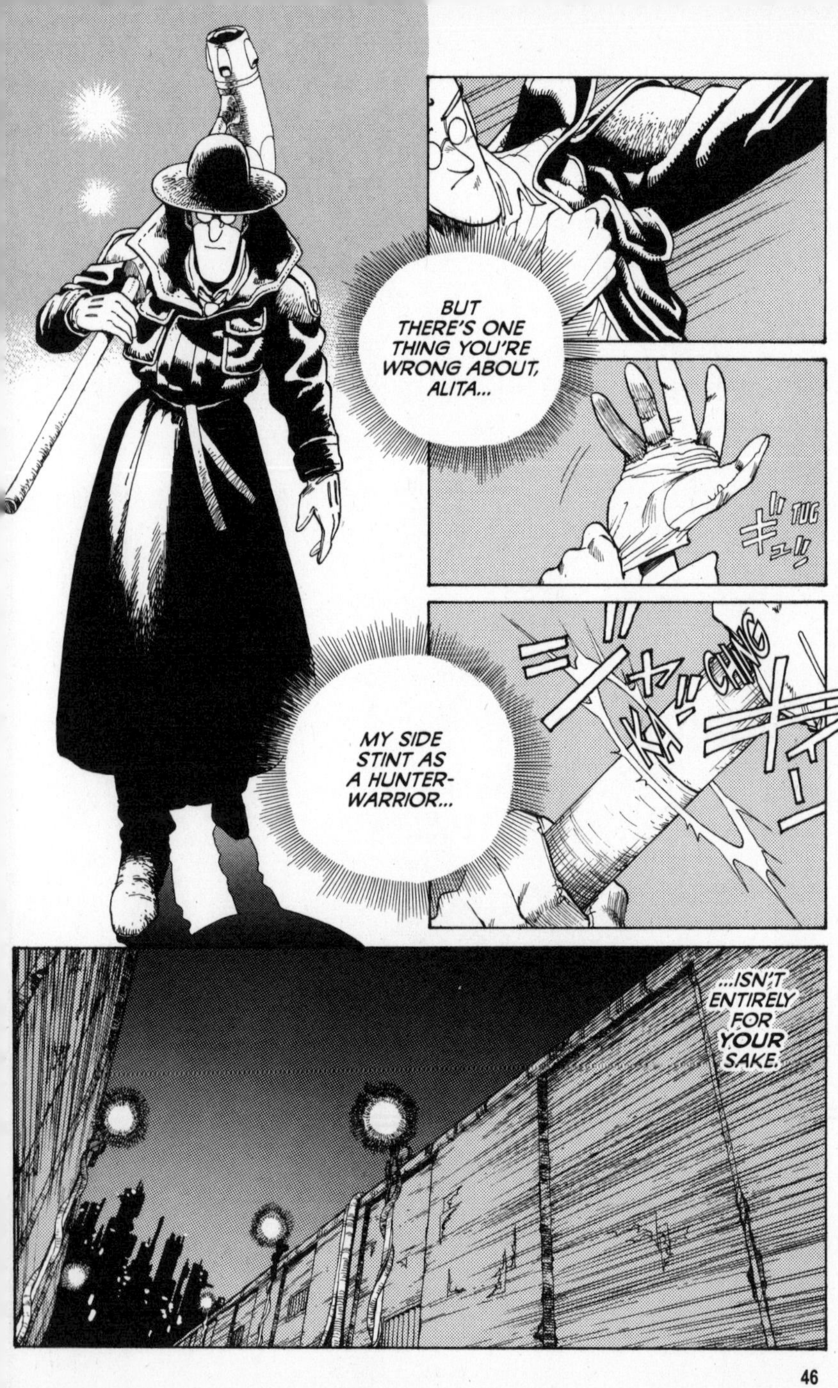
TUG
KA-CHING
BUT THERE'S ONE THING YOU'RE WRONG ABOUT, ALITA...
MY SIDE STINT AS A HUNTER-WARRIOR...
...ISN'T ENTIRELY FOR YOUR SAKE.

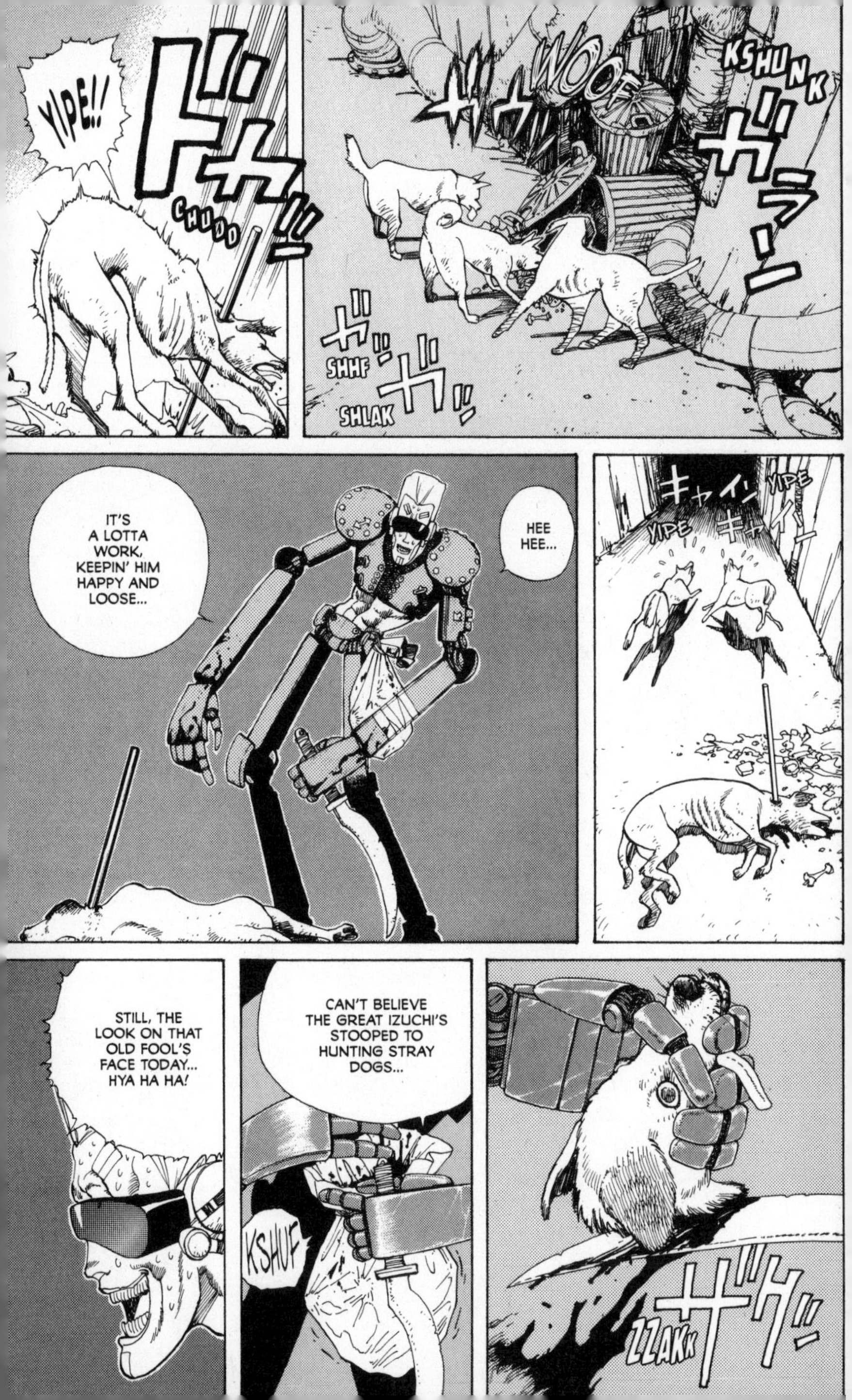
WOOF
KSHUNK
SHHF
SHLAK
YIPE!!
CHUDD
YIPE
YIPE
HEE HEE...
IT'S A LOTTA WORK, KEEPIN' HIM HAPPY AND LOOSE...
ZZAKK
CAN'T BELIEVE THE GREAT IZUCHI'S STOOPED TO HUNTING STRAY DOGS...
KSHUF
STILL, THE LOOK ON THAT OLD FOOL'S FACE TODAY... HYA HA HA!

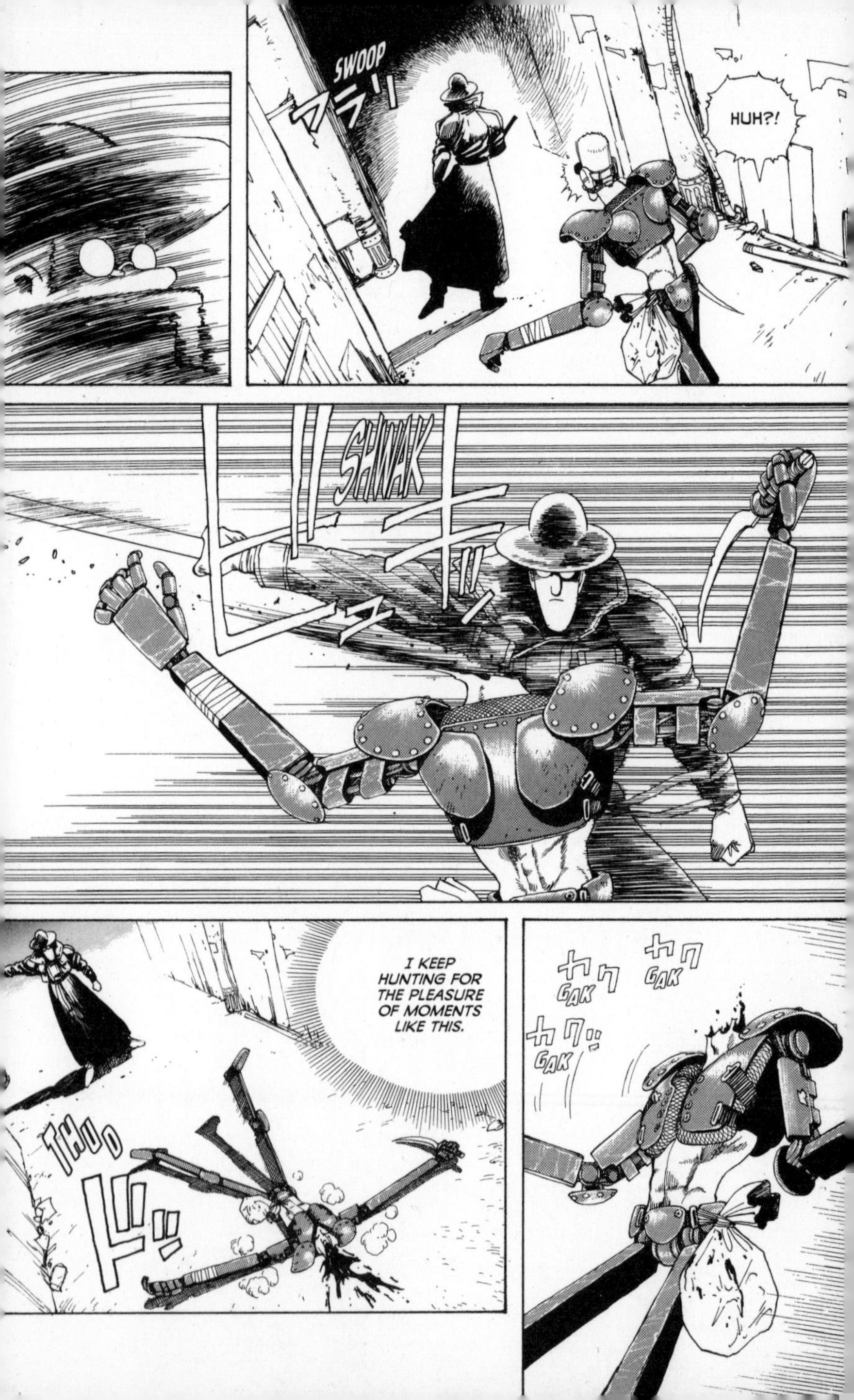
SWOOP
HUH?!
SHWAK
GAK
GAK
GAK
I KEEP HUNTING FOR THE PLEASURE OF MOMENTS LIKE THIS.
THUD

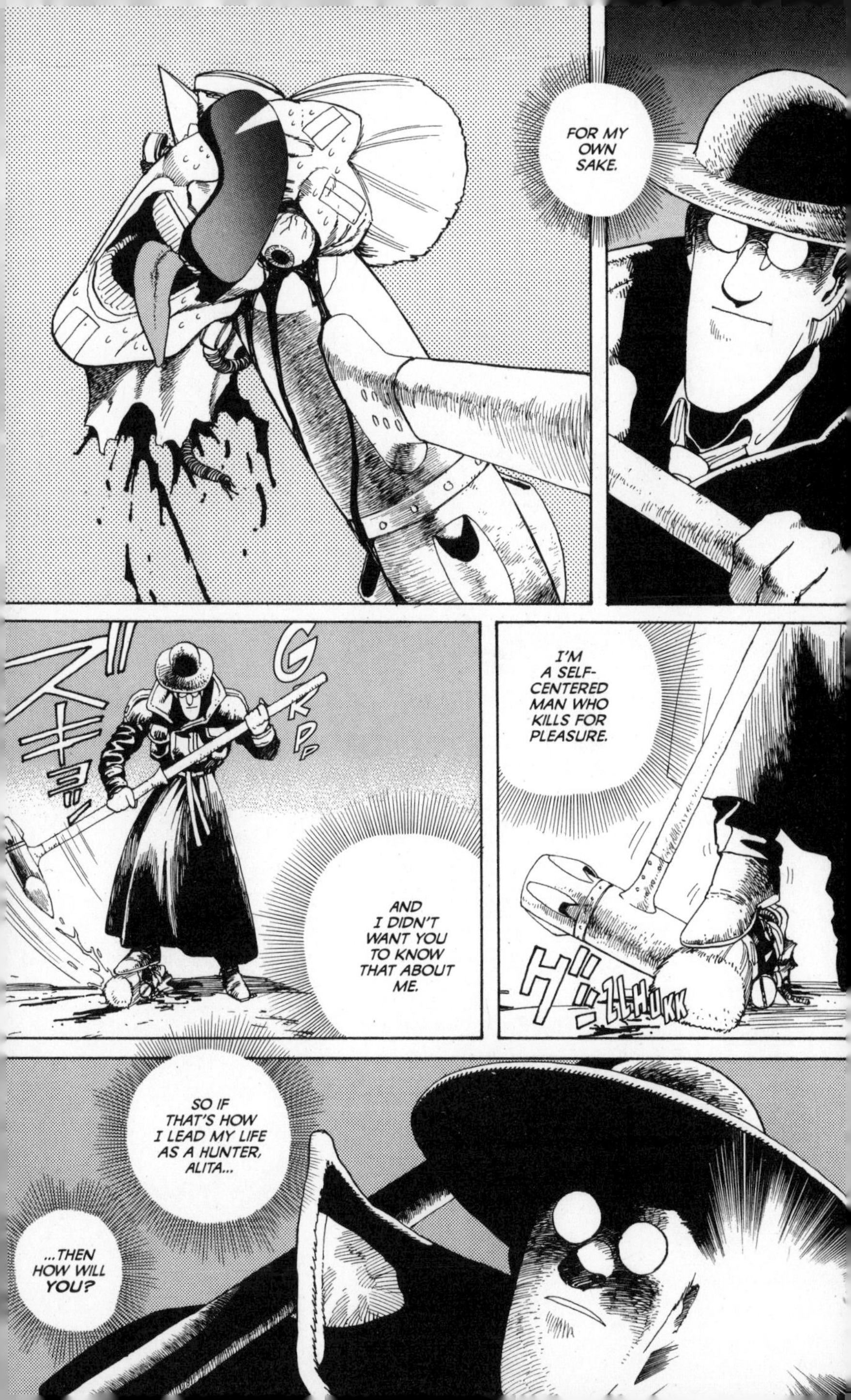
FOR MY OWN SAKE.
I'M A SELF-CENTERED MAN WHO KILLS FOR PLEASURE.
ZLHUKK
AND I DIDN'T WANT YOU TO KNOW THAT ABOUT ME.
GKPP
SO IF THAT'S HOW I LEAD MY LIFE AS A HUNTER, ALITA...
...THEN HOW WILL YOU?

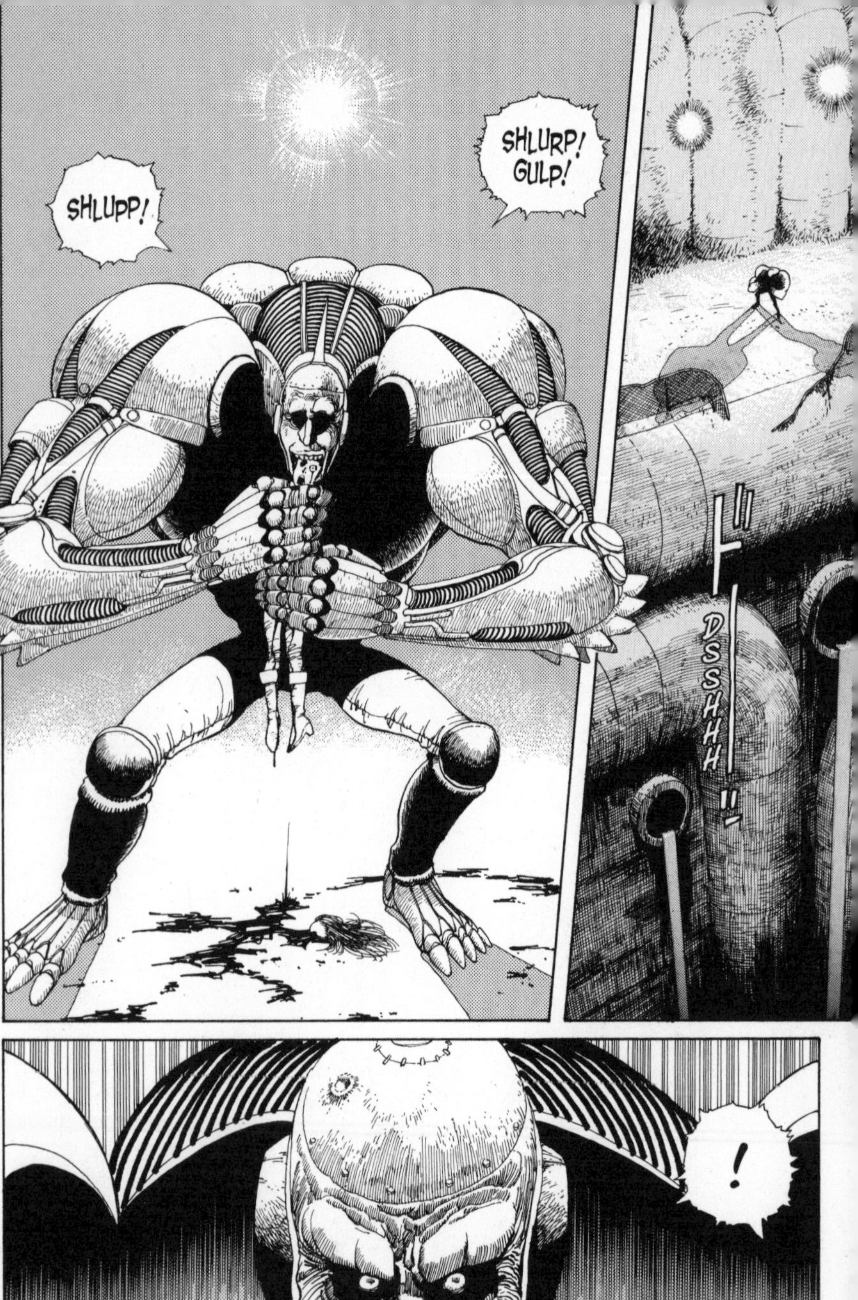
DSSHHH!!
SHLURP! GULP!
SHLUPP!
!

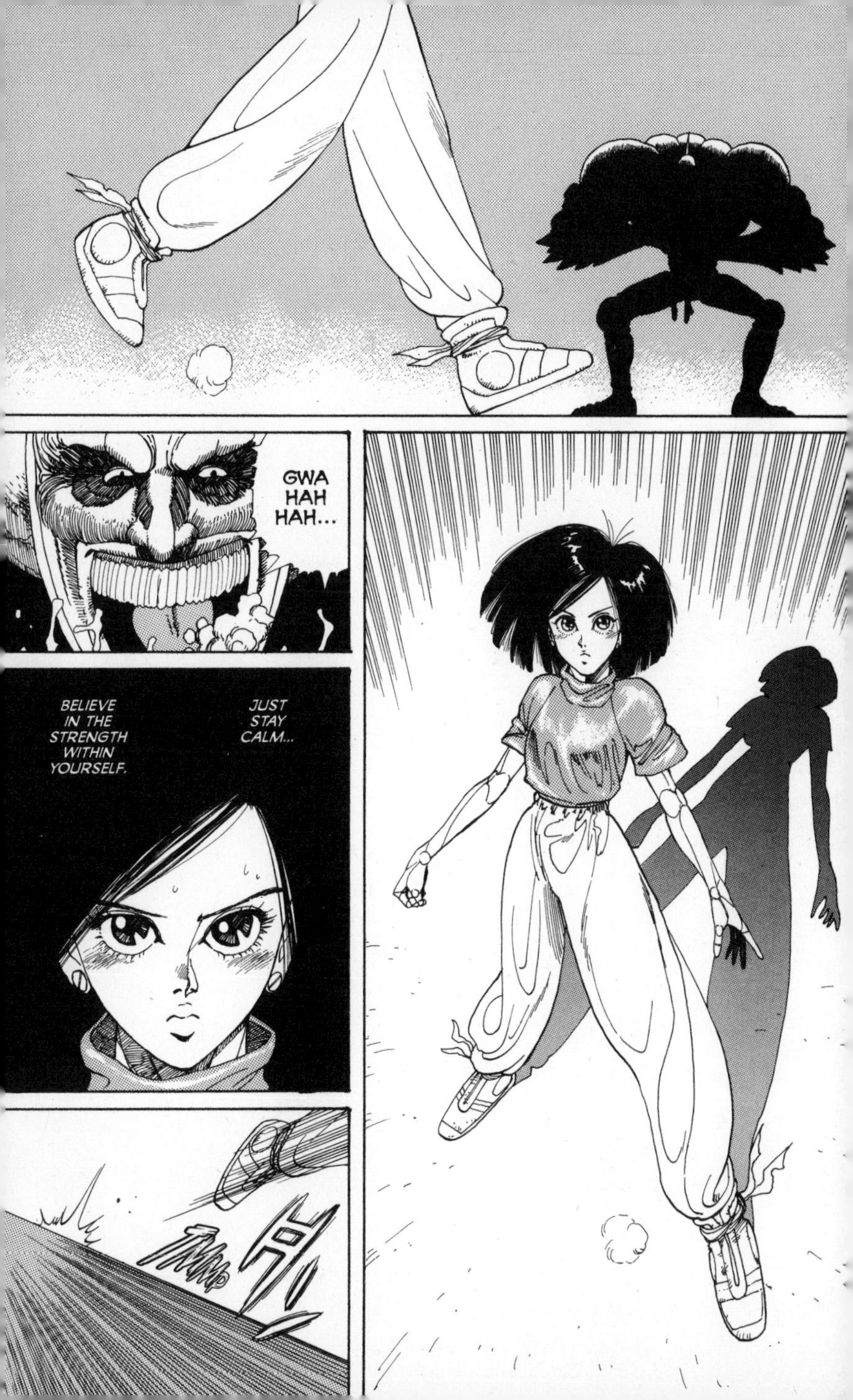
GWA HAH HAH...
JUST STAY CALM...
BELIEVE IN THE STRENGTH WITHIN YOURSELF.

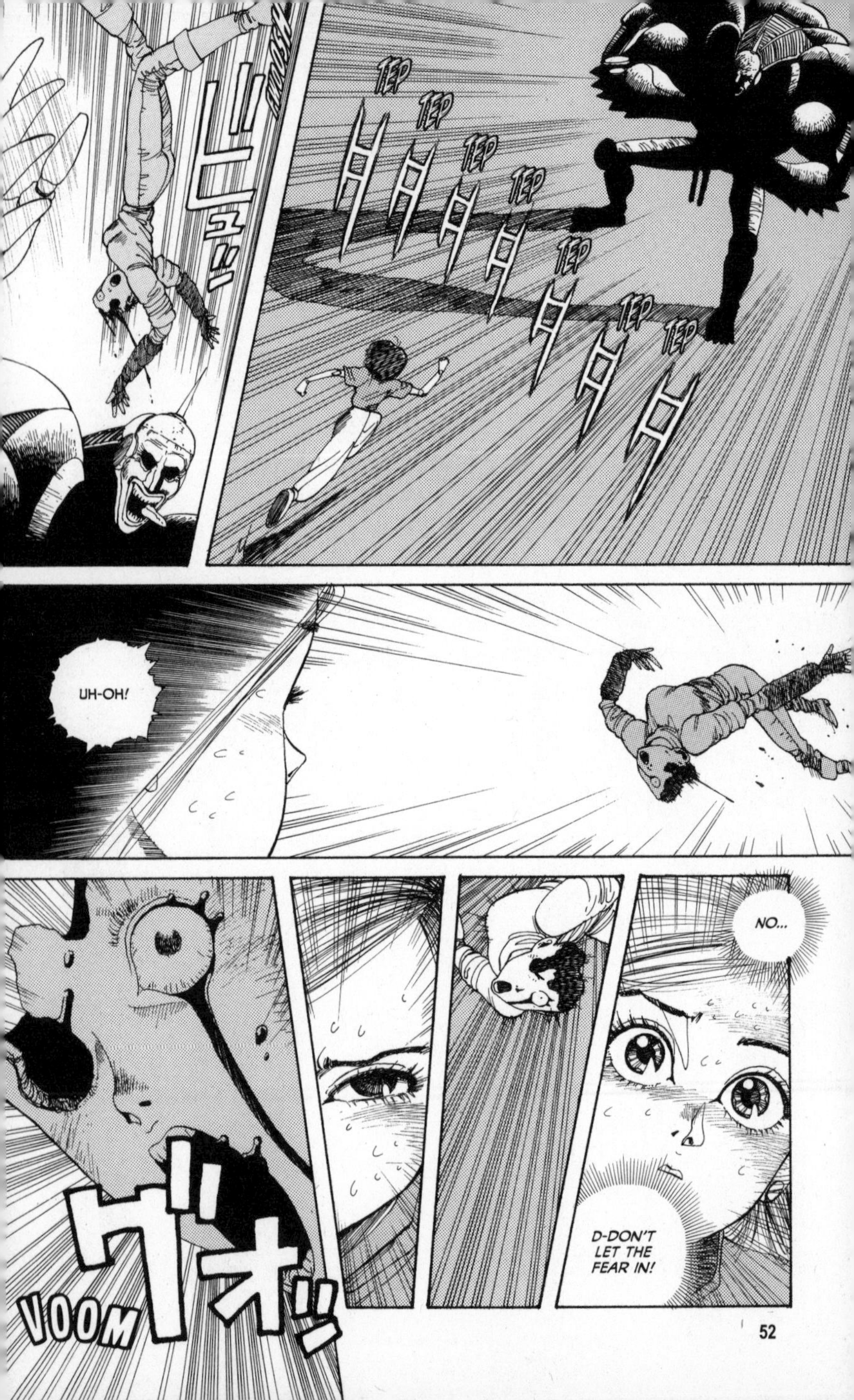
TEP
TEP
TEP
TEP
TEP
TEP
TEP
WHOOSH
UH-OH!
NO...
D-DON'T LET THE FEAR IN!
VOOM

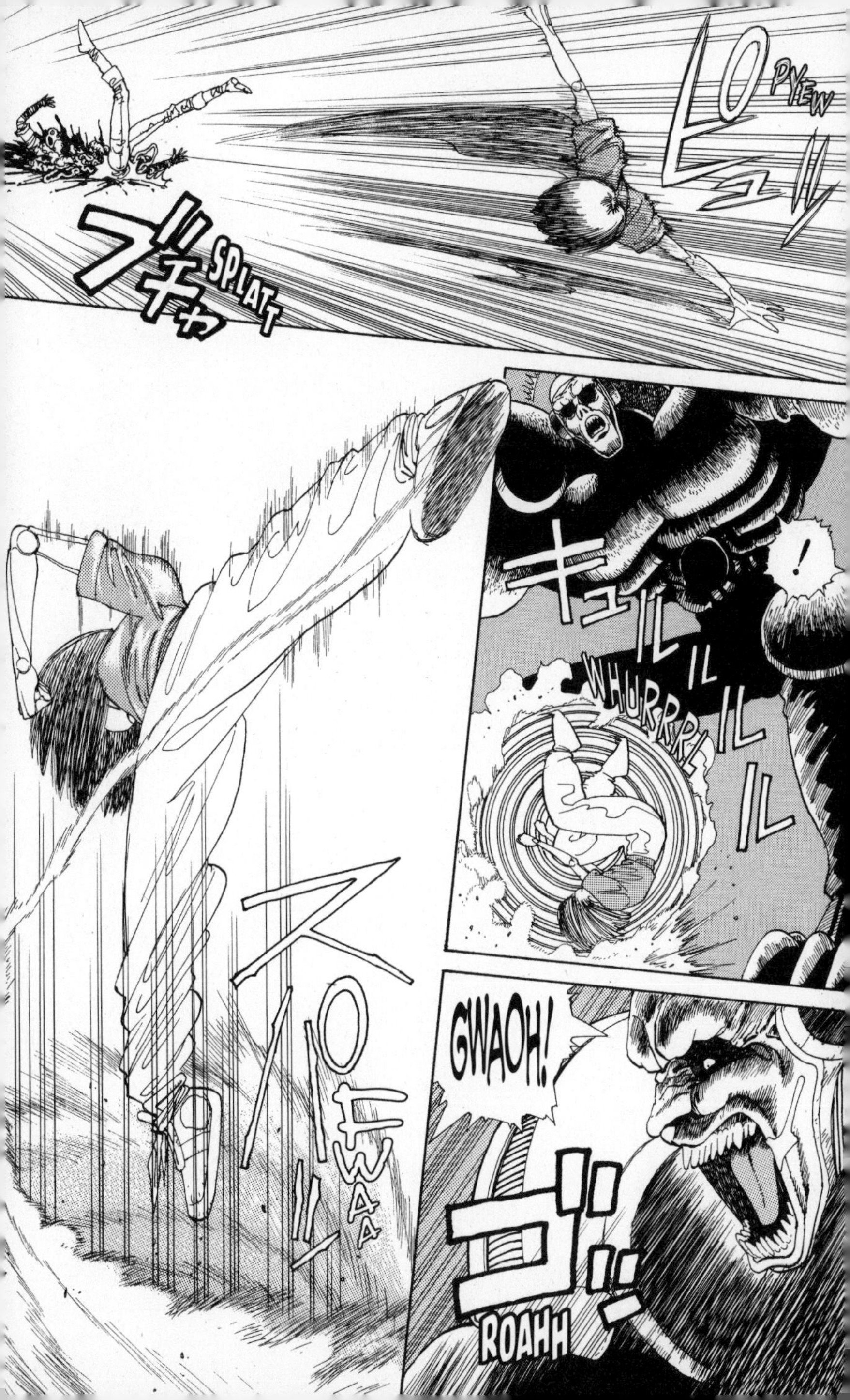
ヒュルッ
PYEW
ブギャ
SPLATT
キュルルルルル
WHURRRL
!
GWAOH!
ゴゴ
ROAHH
FWAA

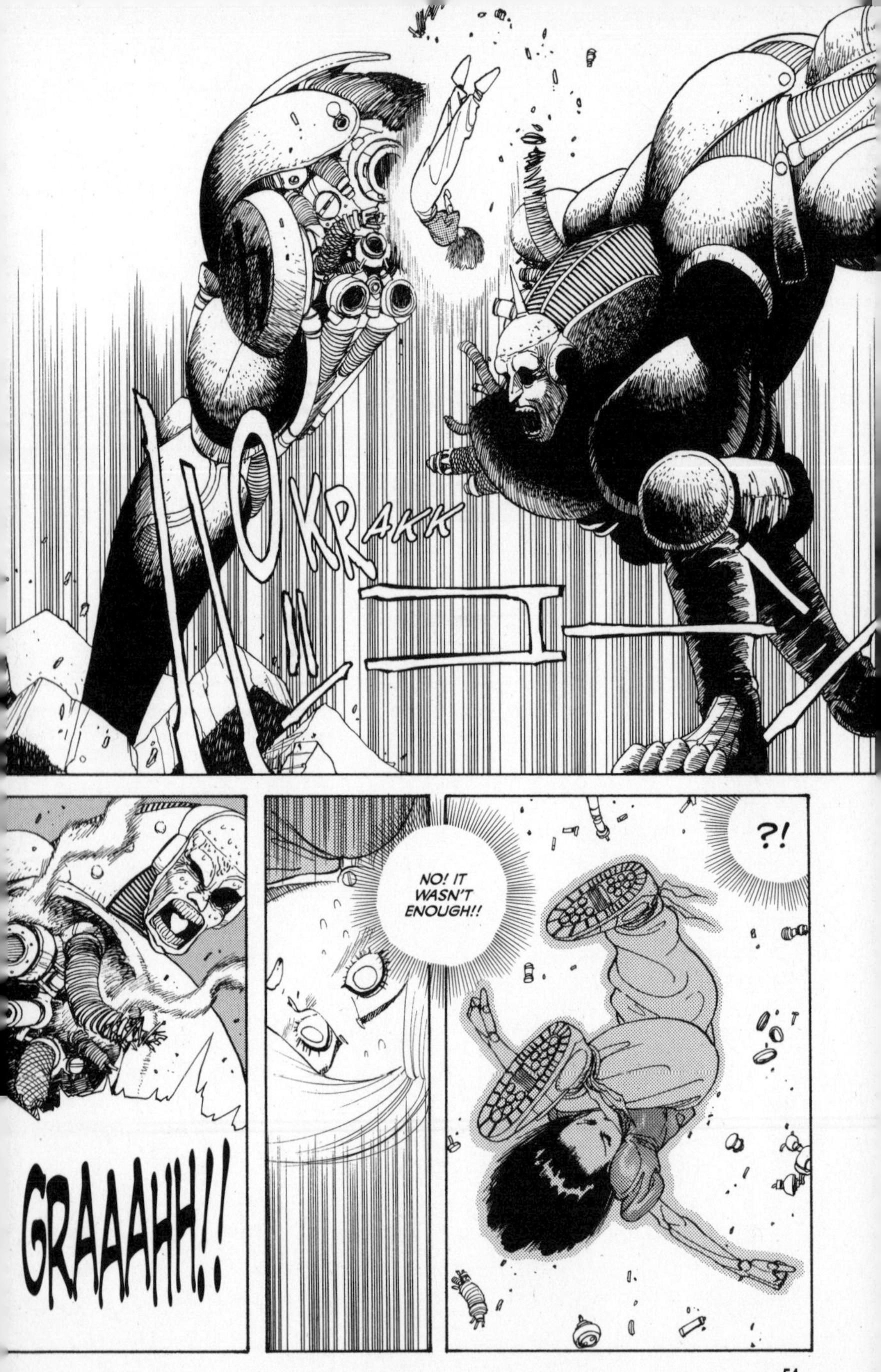
KRAKK
?!
NO! IT WASN'T ENOUGH!!
GRAAHH!!

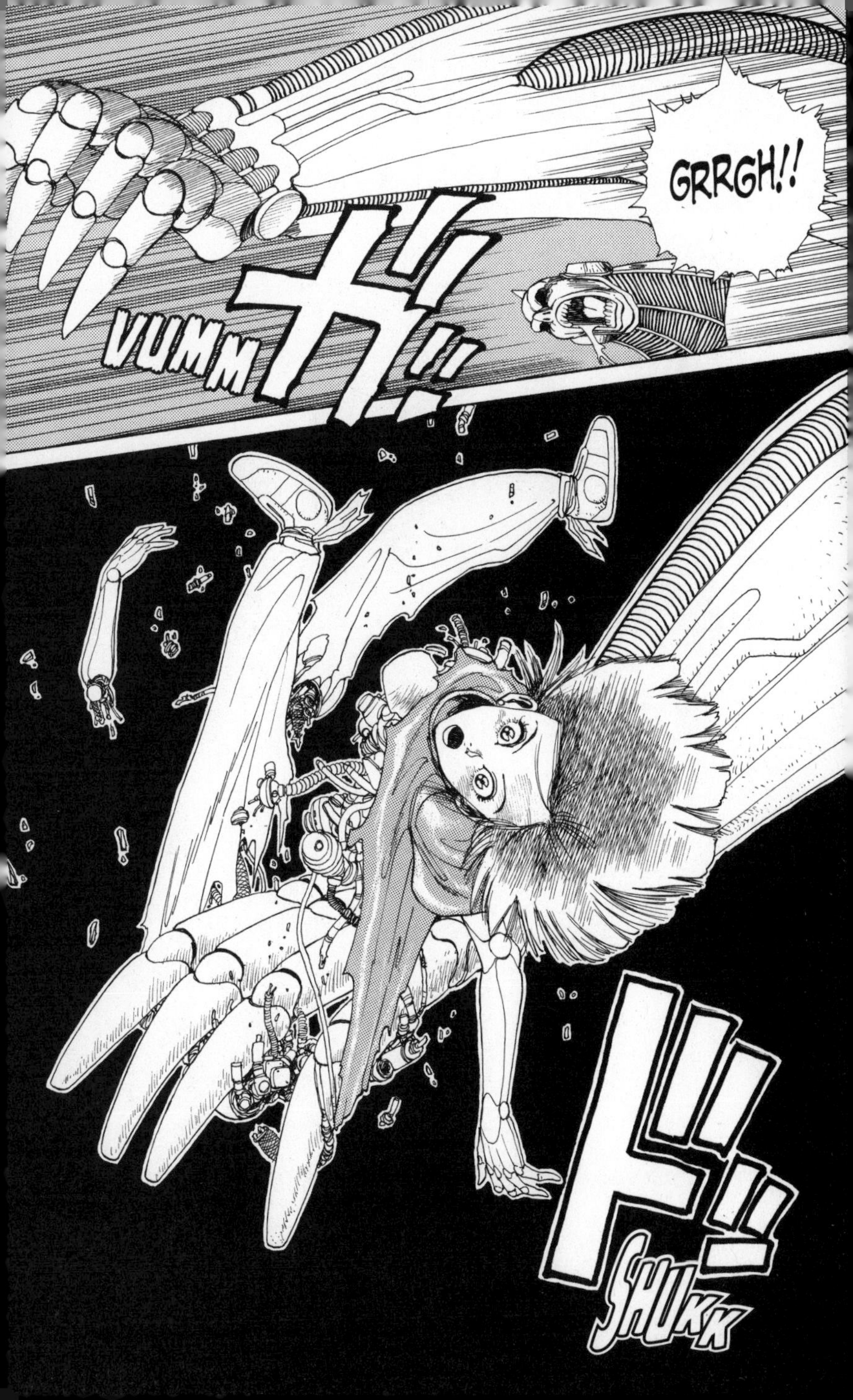
GRRGH!!
VUMM
SHUKK

FIGHT_003 What Has Value

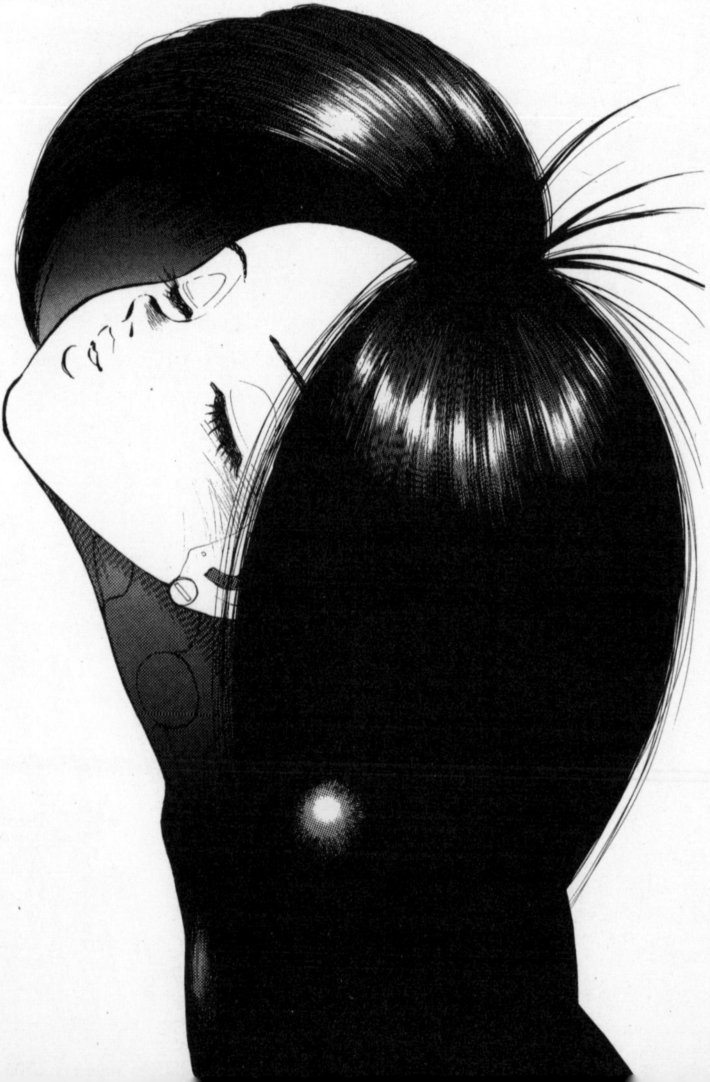

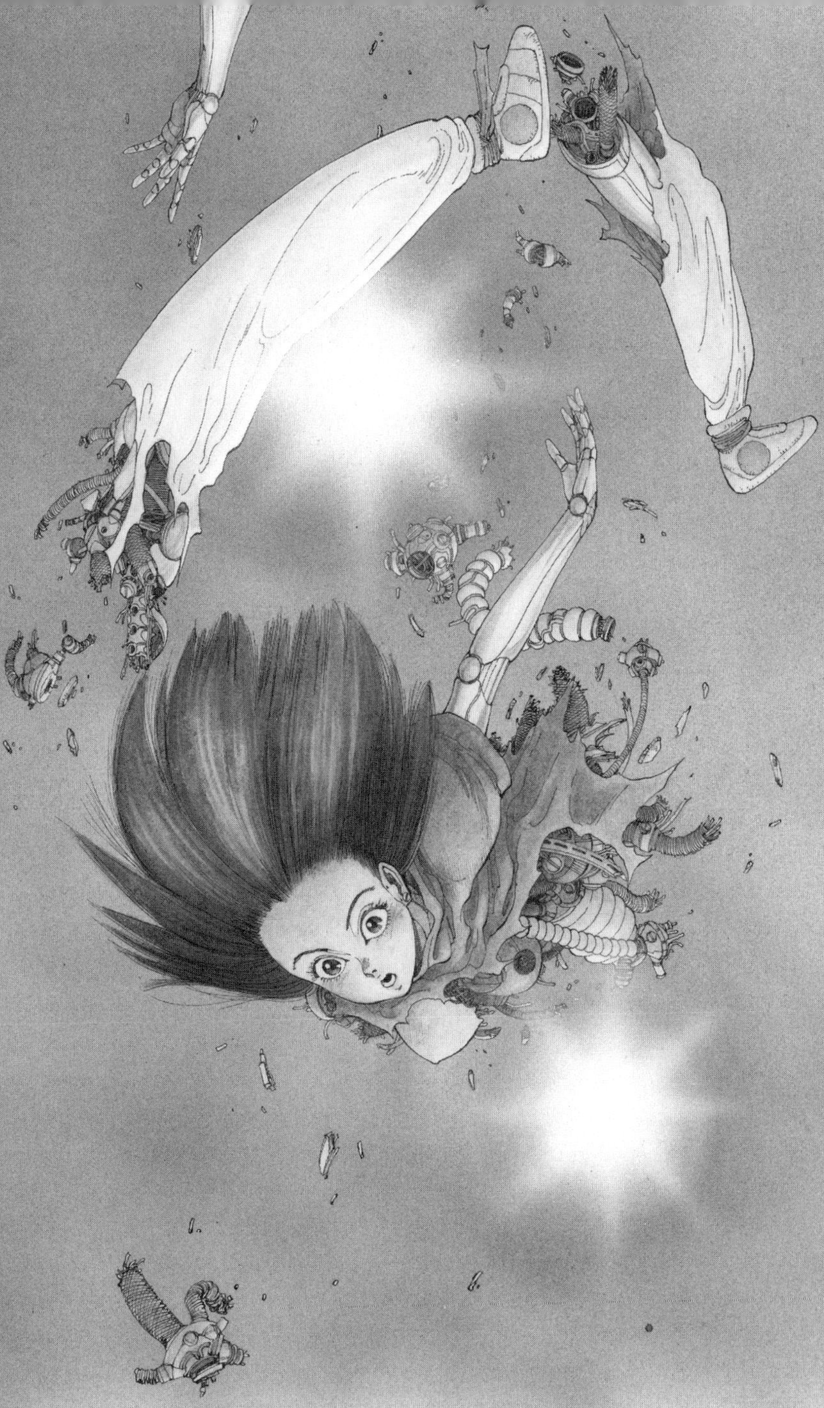

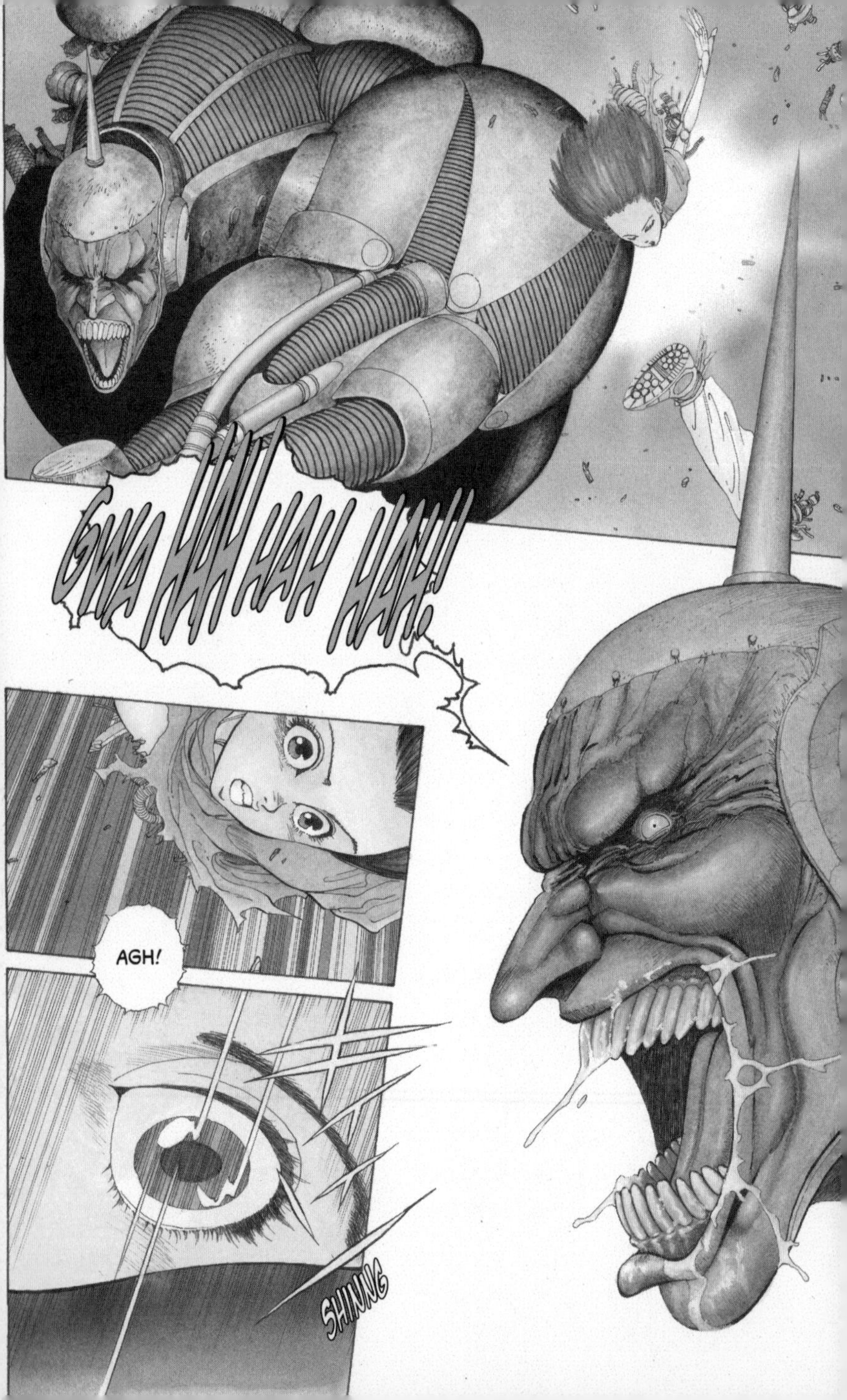
GWA HAH HAH HAH!!
AGH!
SHINNG

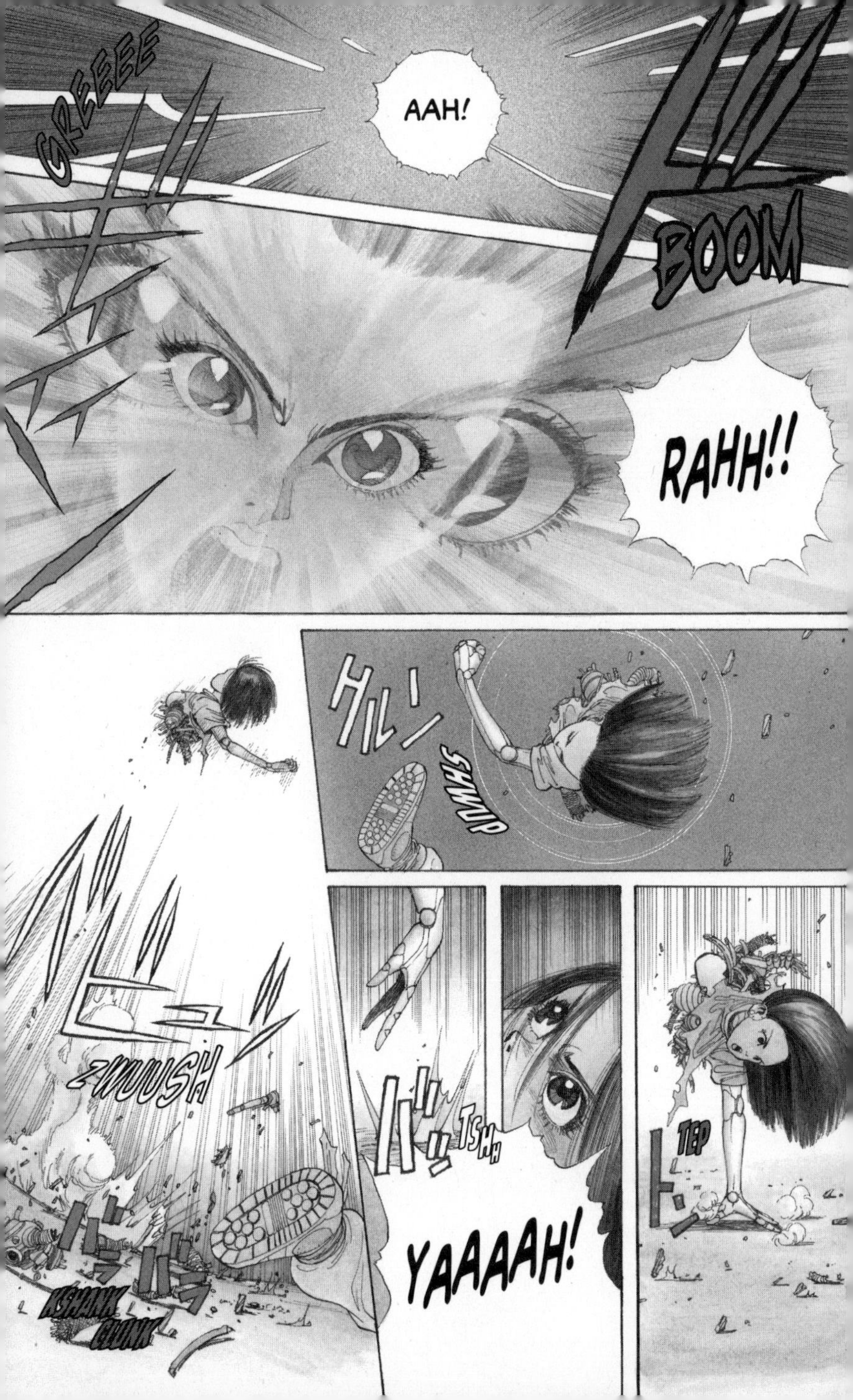
BOOM
AAH!
RAHH!!
GREEEE
SHWUP
TEP
YAAAAH!
TSHH
ZWUUSH
KSHANK
CLUNK

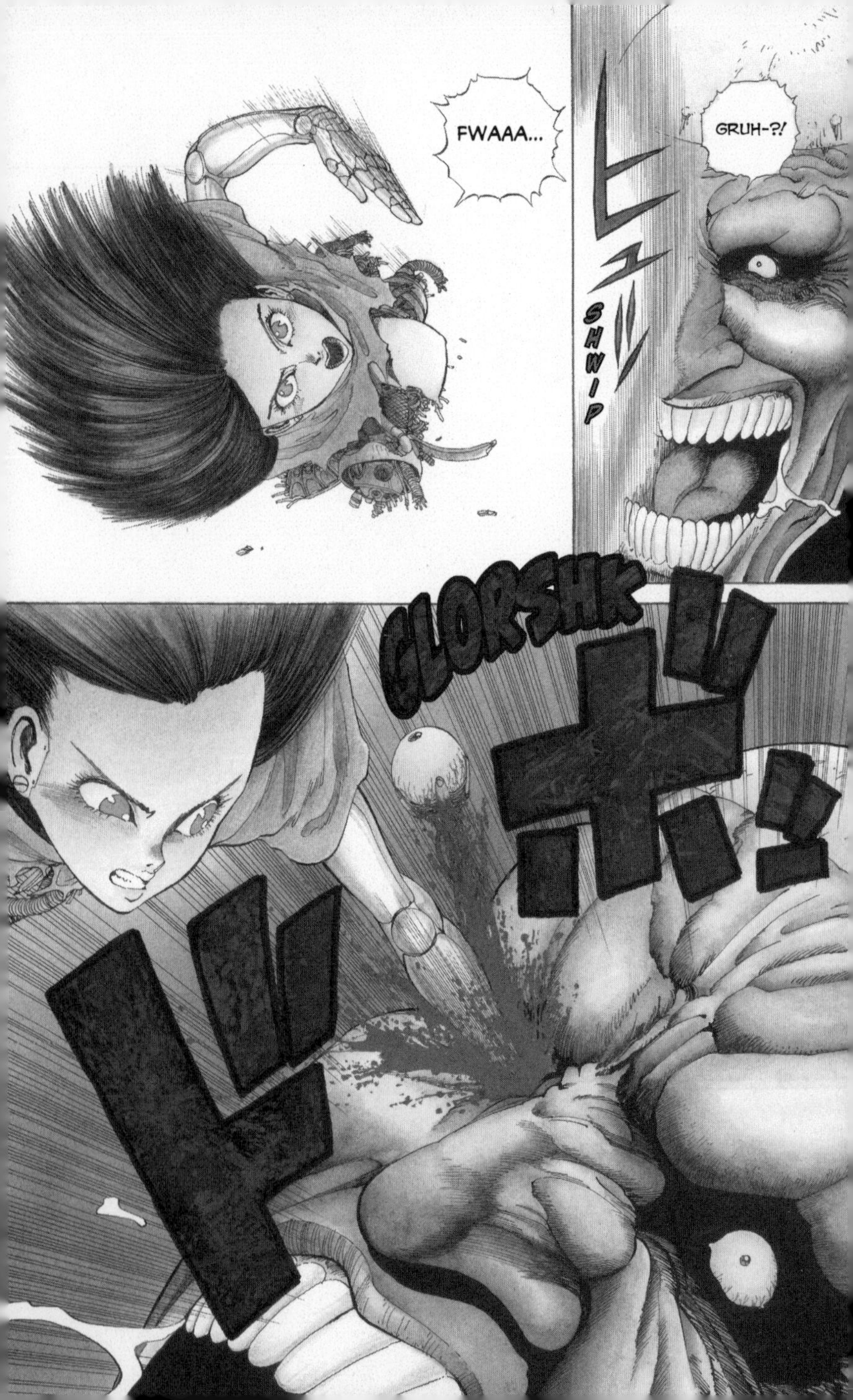
GRUH-?!
SHWIP
FWAAA...
GLORSHK

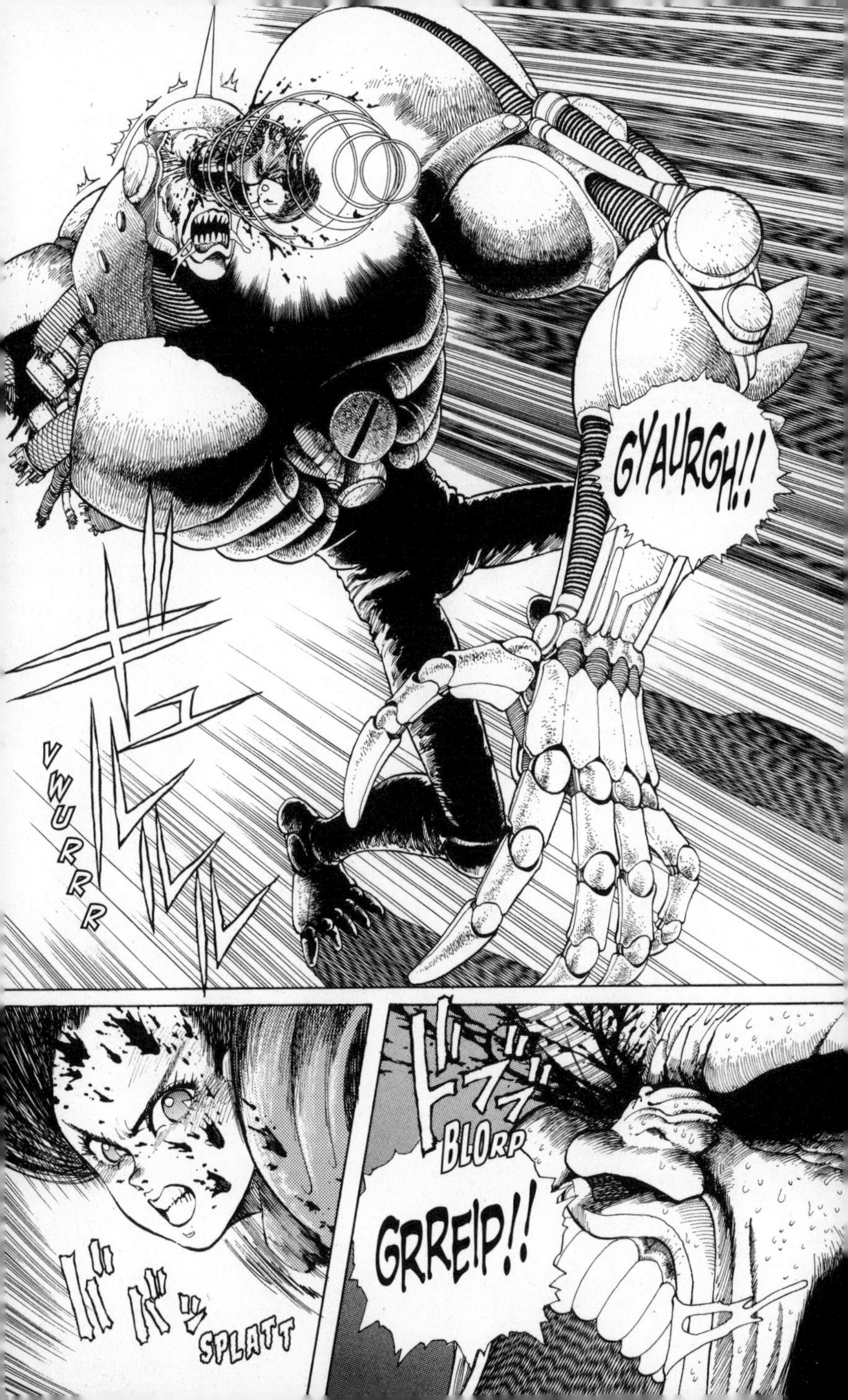
GYAURGH!!
VWURRR
BLORP
GRREIP!!
SPLATT

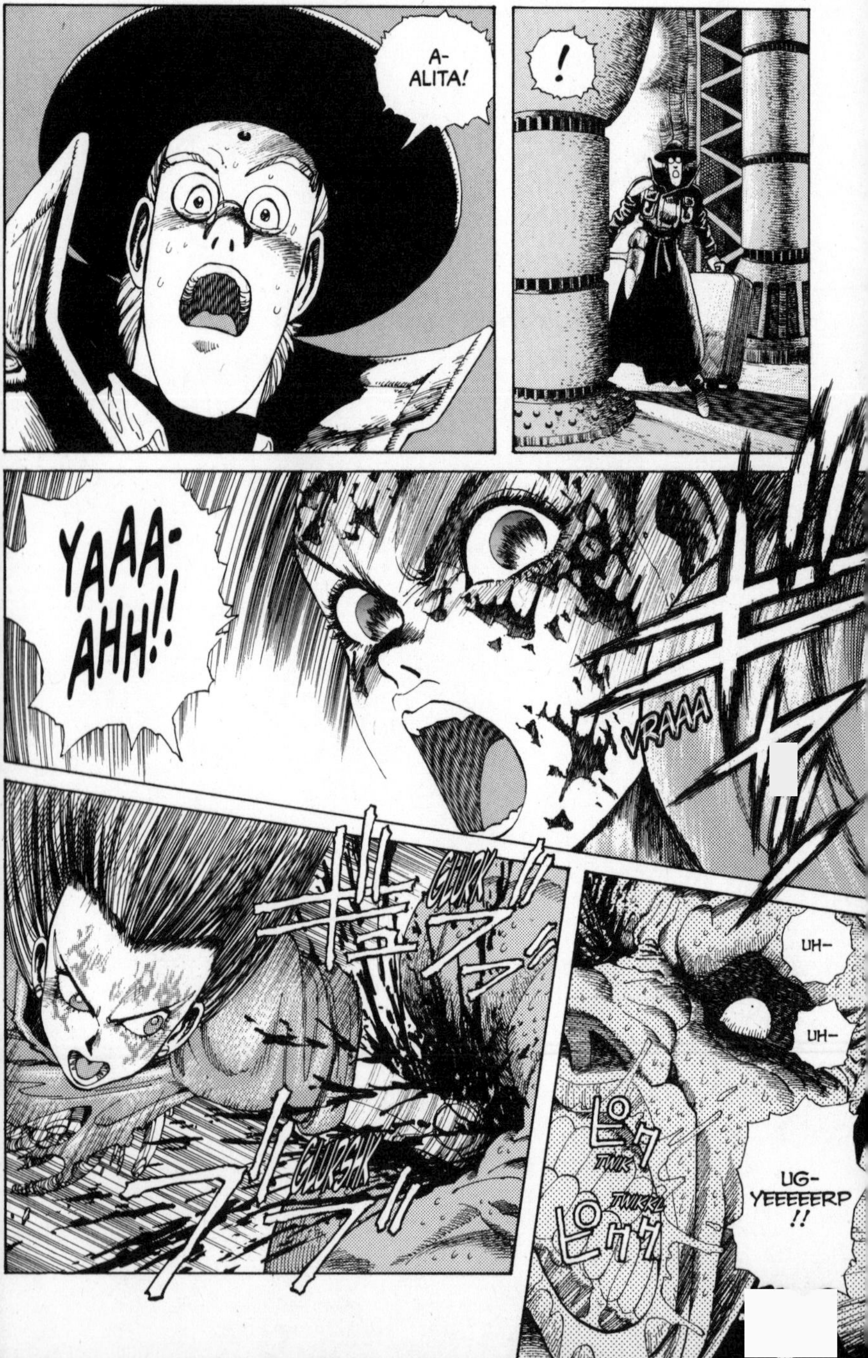
!
A- ALITA!
YAAA-AHH!!
VRAAA
UH-
UH-
UG-YEEEEERP!!
TWIK
TWIKRL
GLURK
GLURSHK

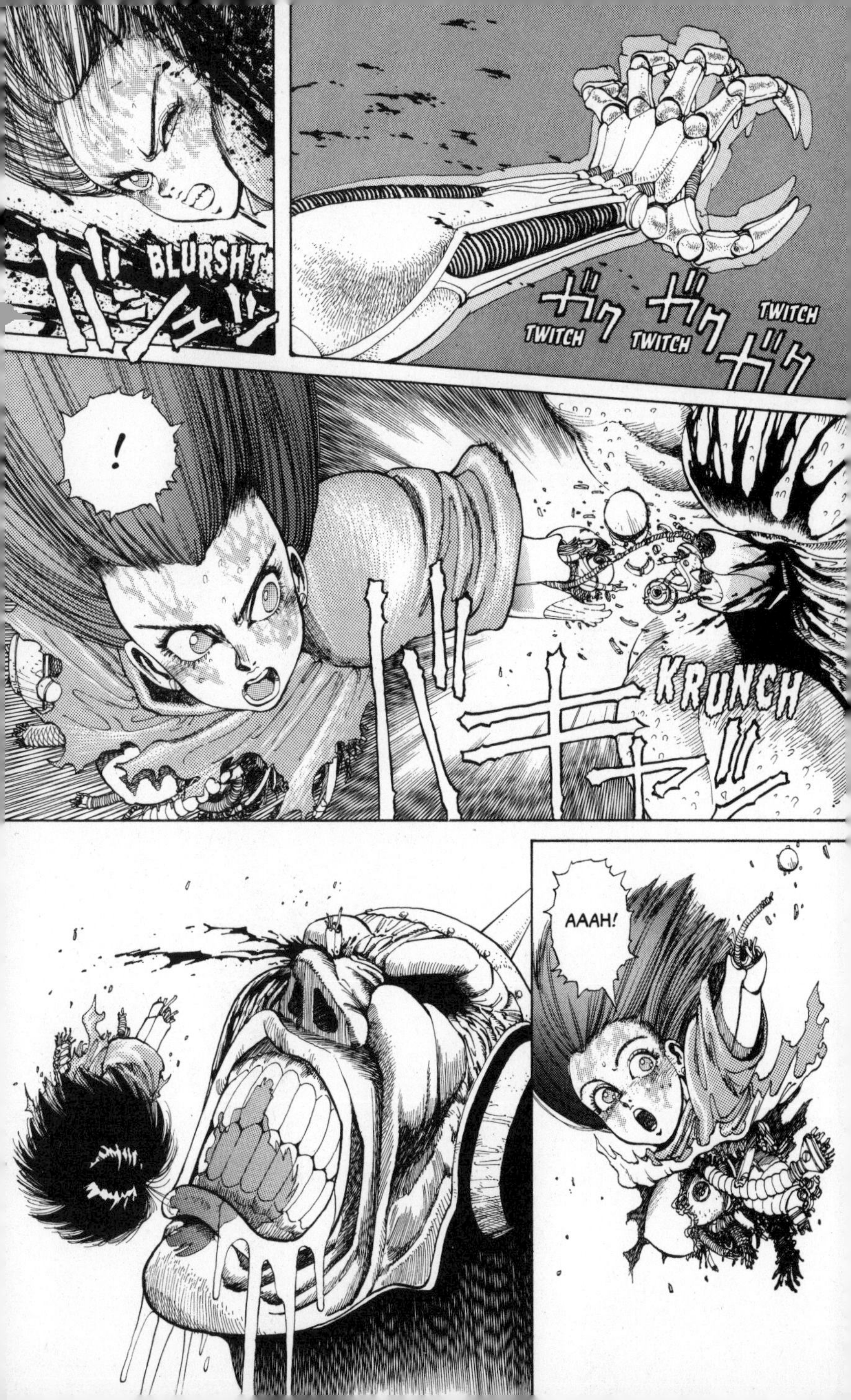
TWITCH
TWITCH
TWITCH
BLURSHT
KRUNCH
!
AAAH!

SNAGG!!

fLASH!!

GRRGH...

MRRH!

GUH-GUH...

GUH!

GUH-
GUH-
GUH-
GUH...

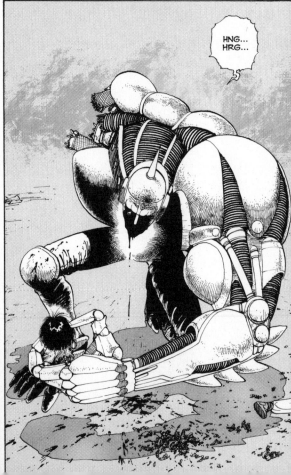

HNG...
HRG...

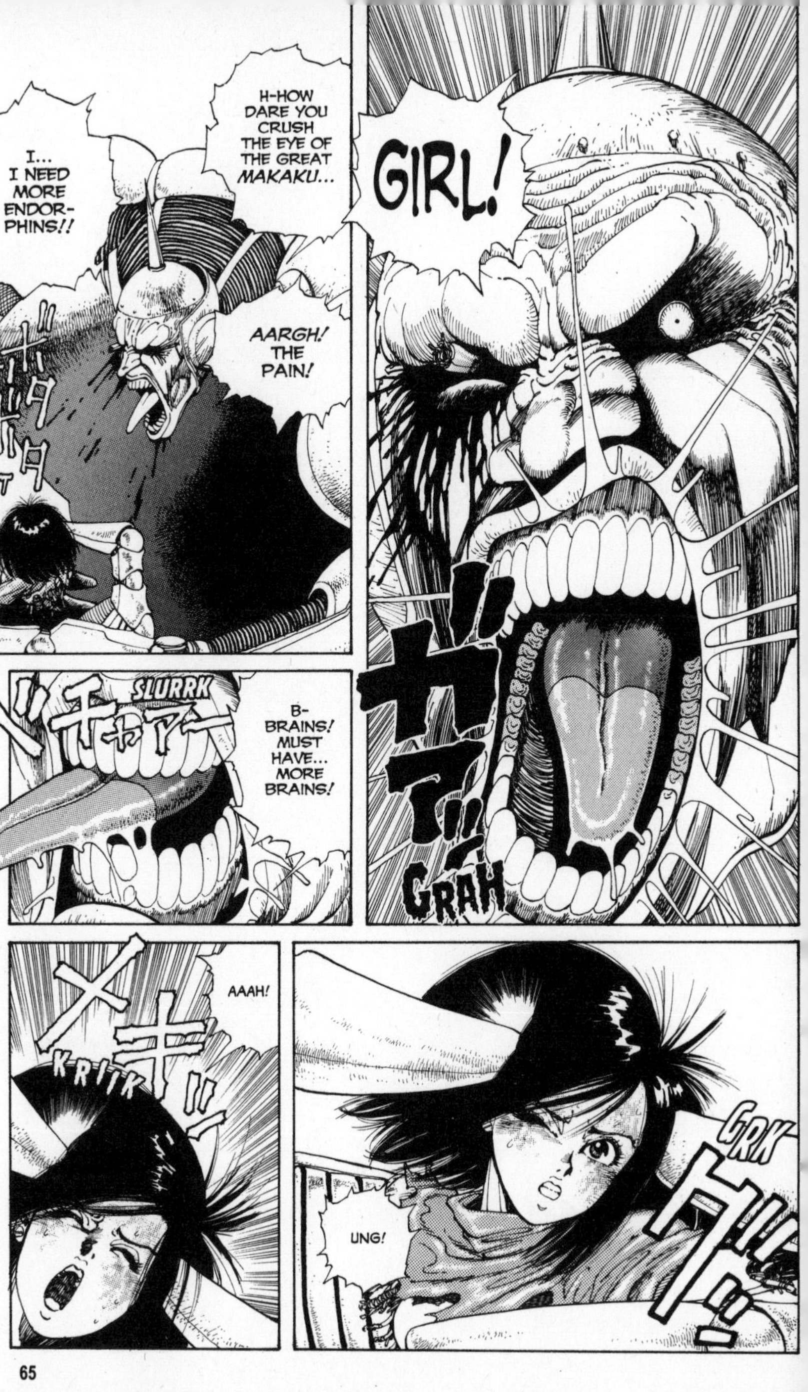
GIRL!
GRAH
H-HOW DARE YOU CRUSH THE EYE OF THE GREAT MAKAKU...
I... I NEED MORE ENDOR-PHINS!!
AARGH! THE PAIN!
BLOTT
BLOTT
SLURRK
B-BRAINS! MUST HAVE... MORE BRAINS!
GRK
UNG!
AAAH!
KRIIK

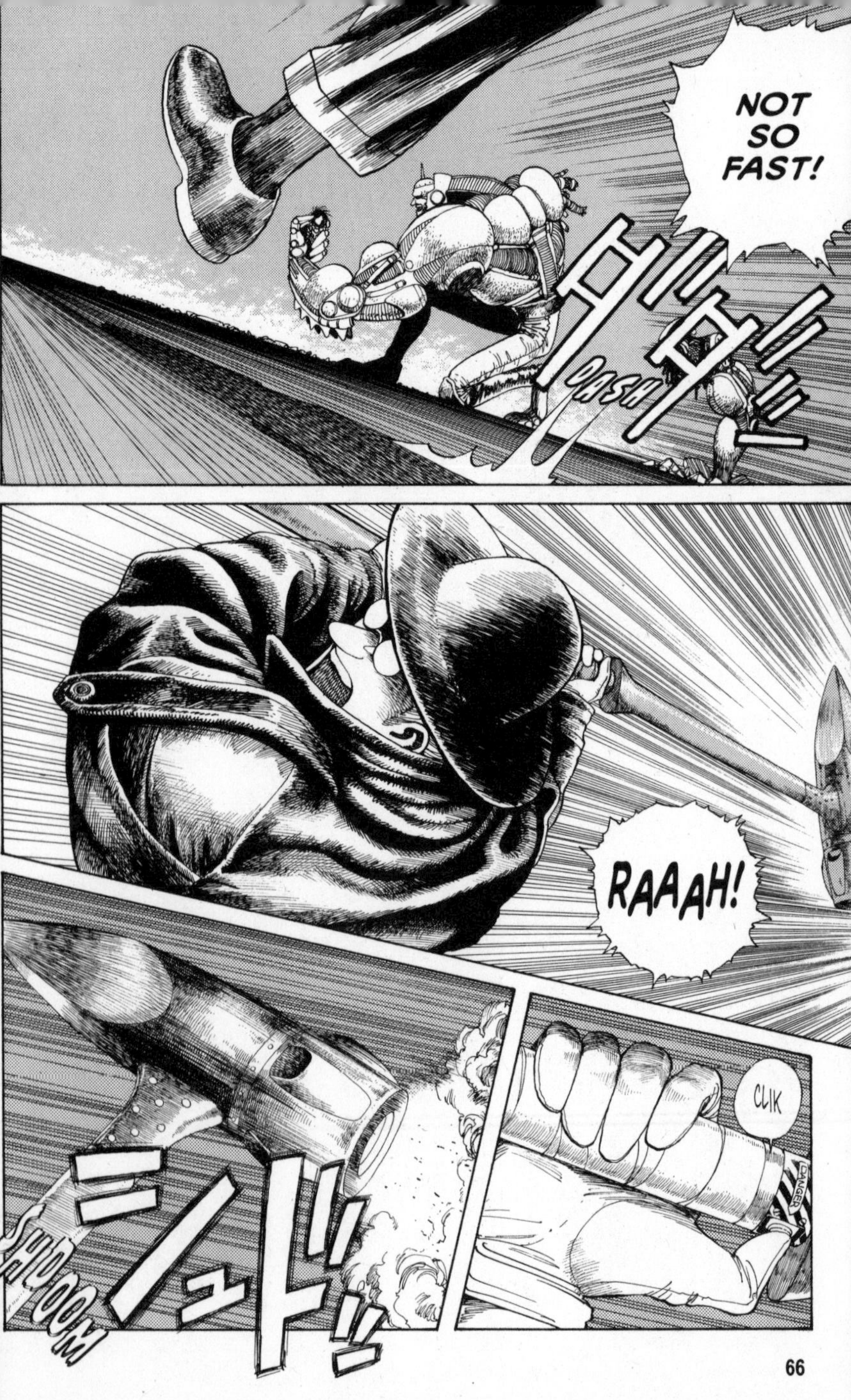
NOT SO FAST!
DASH
RAAAH!
CLIK
DANGER
SHOOOM

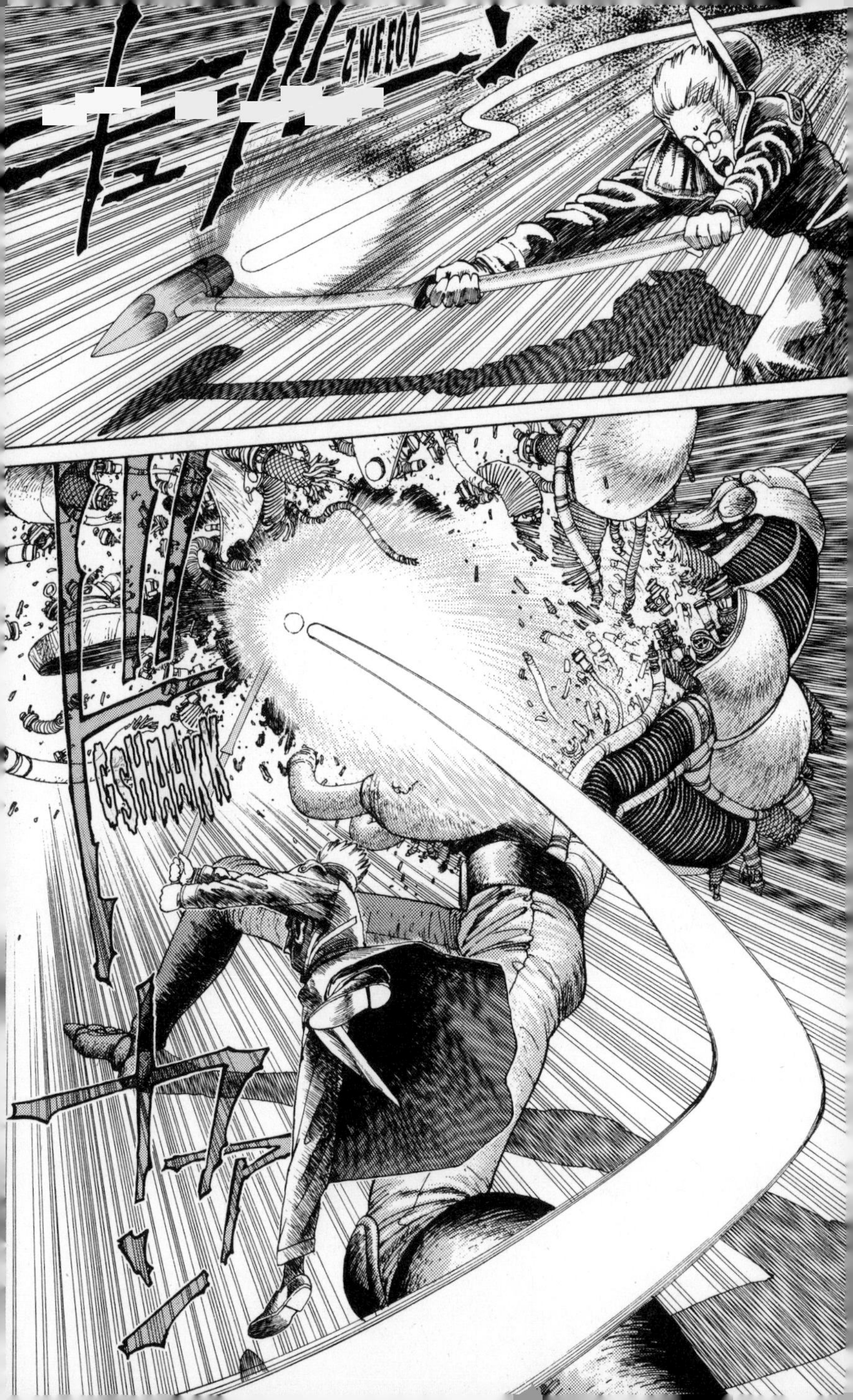
ZWEFOO
GSHAAKK

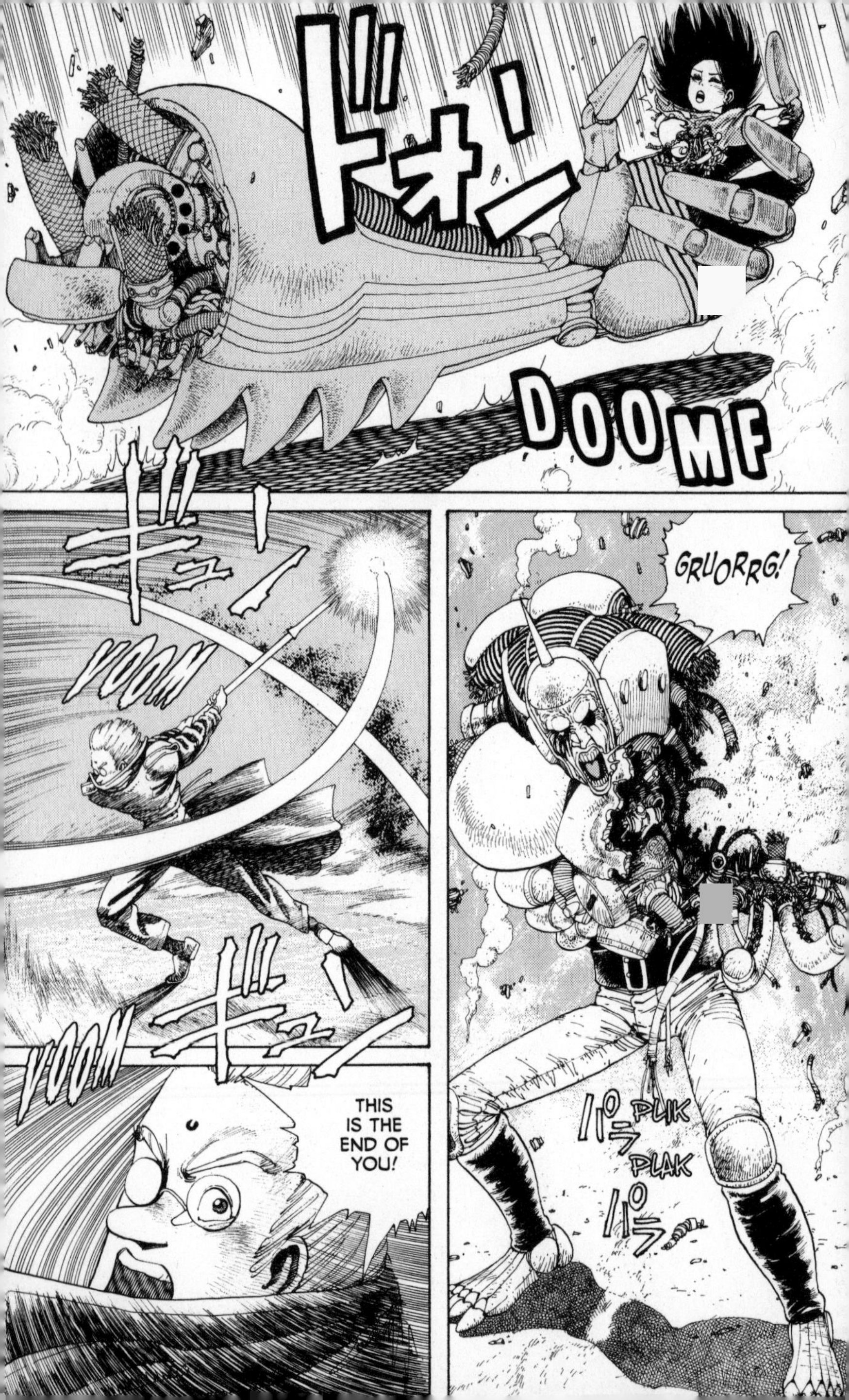
ドオーン
DOOMF
GRUORRG!
パラ PLIK
PLAK パラ
ギューン
VOOM
ギューン
VOOM
THIS IS THE END OF YOU!

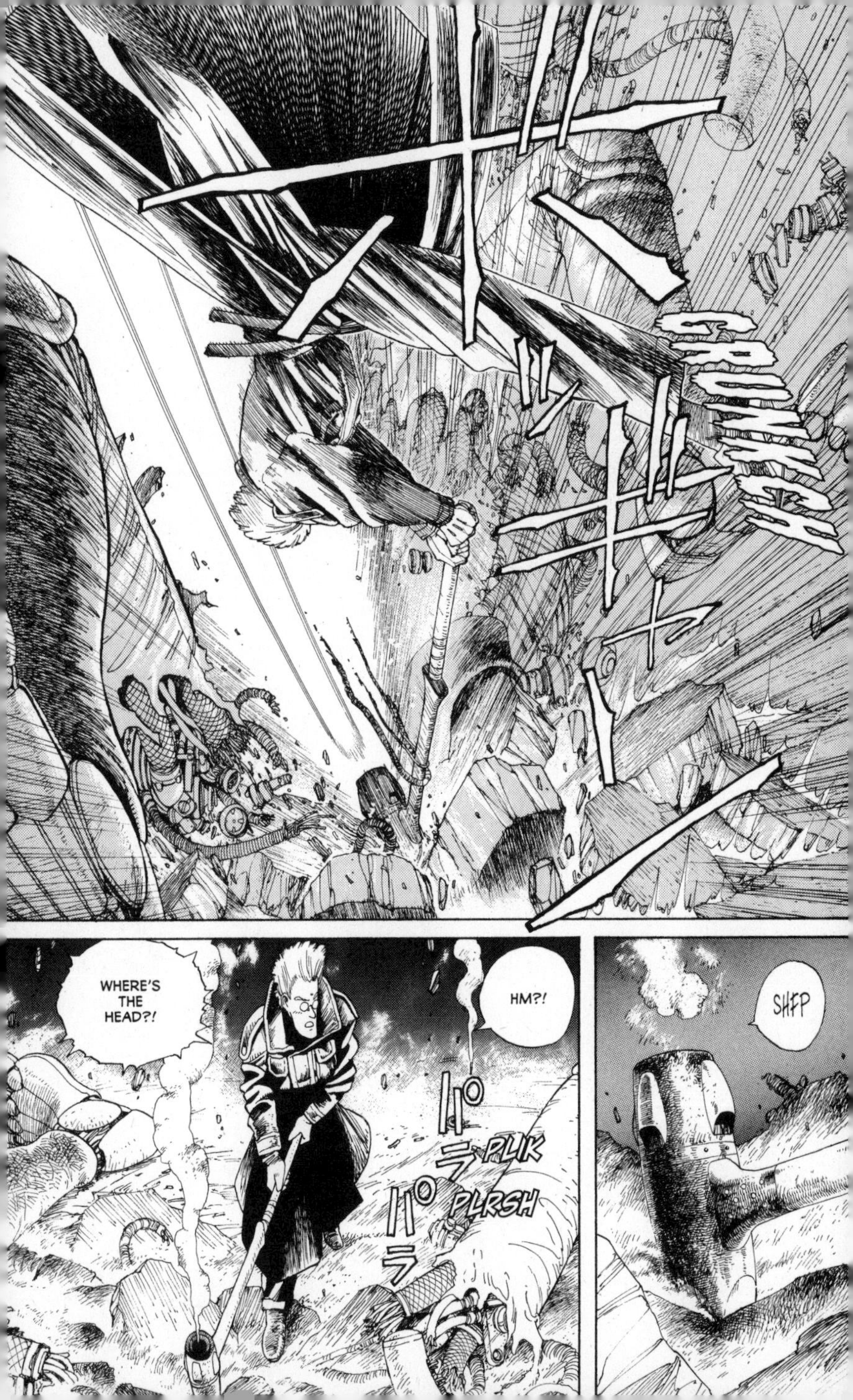
CRUNCH
SHFP
HM?!
WHERE'S THE HEAD?!
パラ
PLIK
パラ
PLRSH

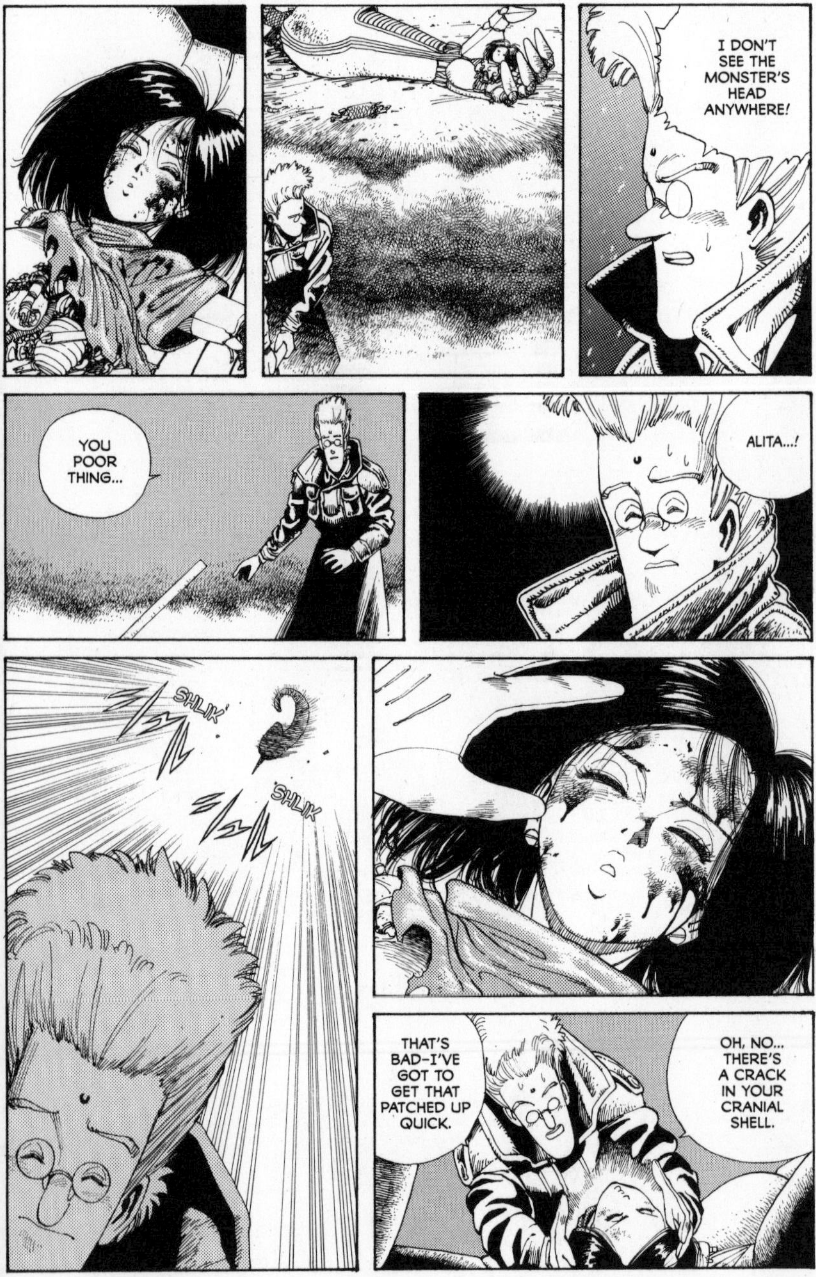
I DON'T SEE THE MONSTER'S HEAD ANYWHERE!
ALITA...!
YOU POOR THING...
OH, NO... THERE'S A CRACK IN YOUR CRANIAL SHELL.
THAT'S BAD–I'VE GOT TO GET THAT PATCHED UP QUICK.
SHLIK'
SHLIK

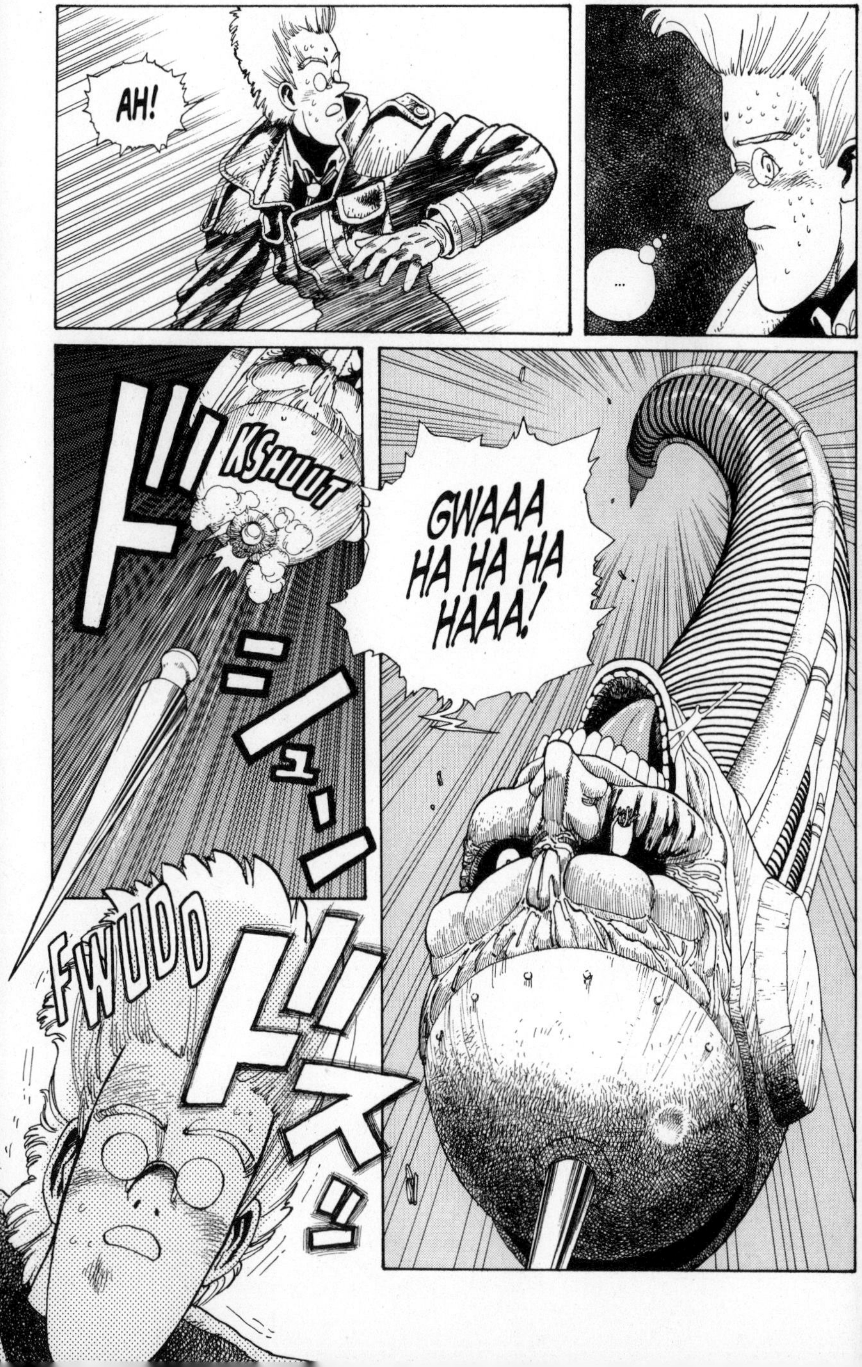
...
AH!
GWAAA HA HA HA HAAA!
KSHUUT
FWUDD

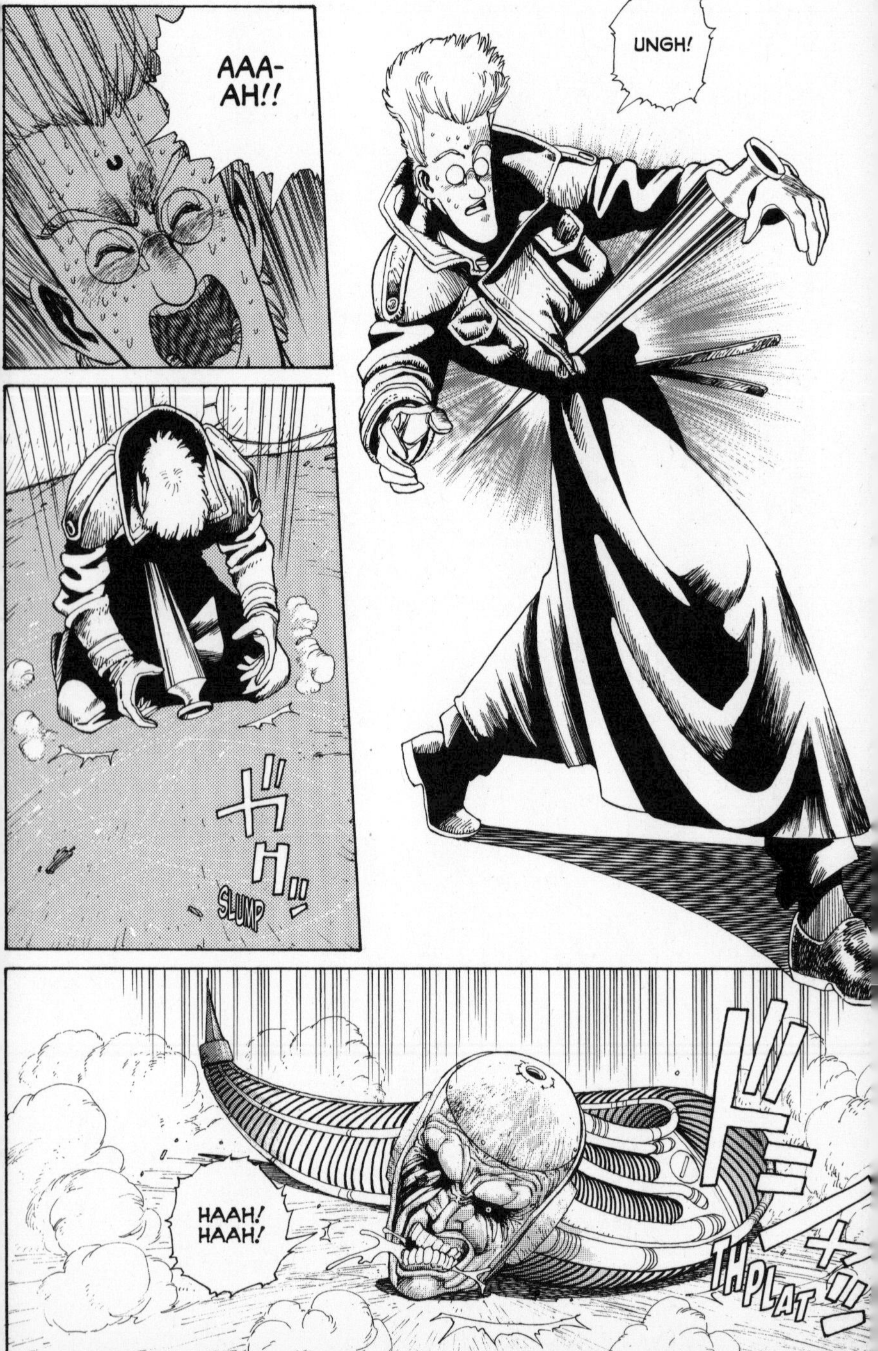
UNGH!
AAA-AH!!
SLUMP
THPLAT
HAAH! HAAH!

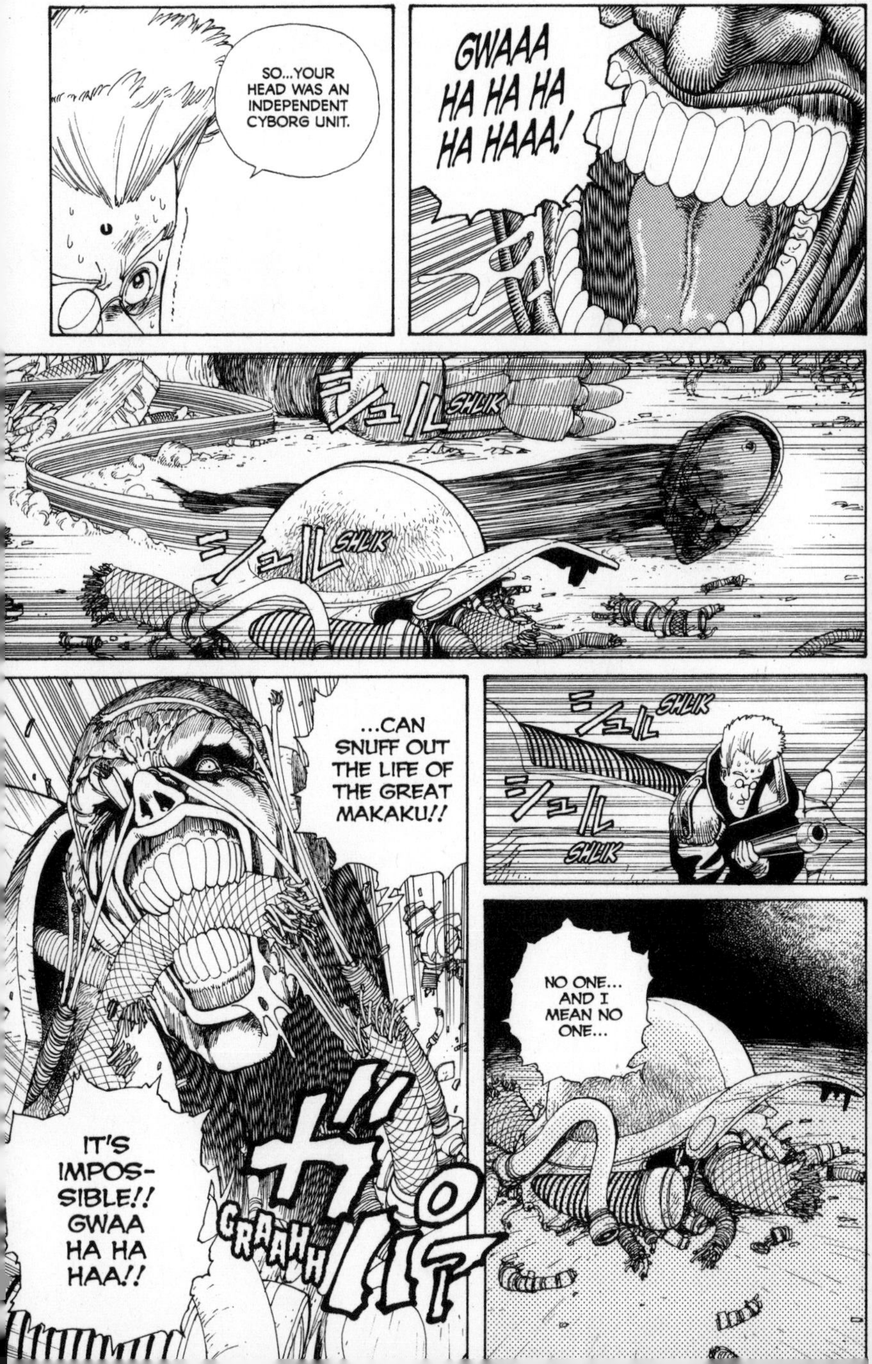
GWAAA HA HA HA HA HAAA!
SO...YOUR HEAD WAS AN INDEPENDENT CYBORG UNIT.
SHLIK
SHLIK
SHLIK
SHLIK
NO ONE... AND I MEAN NO ONE...
...CAN SNUFF OUT THE LIFE OF THE GREAT MAKAKU!!
IT'S IMPOS-SIBLE!! GWAA HA HA HAA!!
GRAAHH

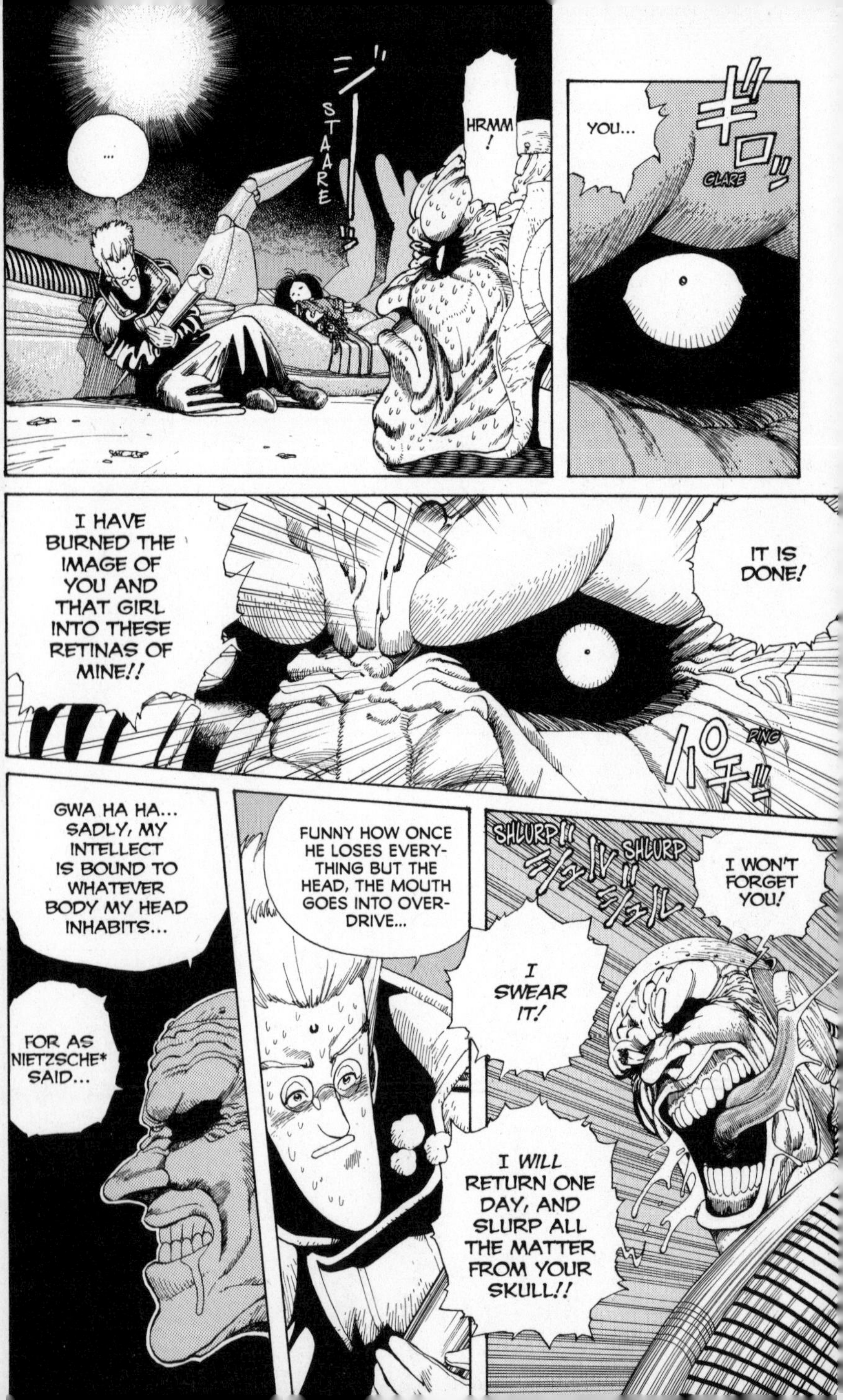
YOU...
ギロッ!!
GLARE
HRMM!
ジー!!
STAARE
...
IT IS DONE!
パチ!!
PING
I HAVE BURNED THE IMAGE OF YOU AND THAT GIRL INTO THESE RETINAS OF MINE!!
ジュル!!
SHLURP!!
ジュル
SHLURP
I WON'T FORGET YOU!
I SWEAR IT!
I WILL RETURN ONE DAY, AND SLURP ALL THE MATTER FROM YOUR SKULL!!
FUNNY HOW ONCE HE LOSES EVERY-THING BUT THE HEAD, THE MOUTH GOES INTO OVER-DRIVE...
GWA HA HA... SADLY, MY INTELLECT IS BOUND TO WHATEVER BODY MY HEAD INHABITS...
FOR AS NIETZSCHE* SAID...

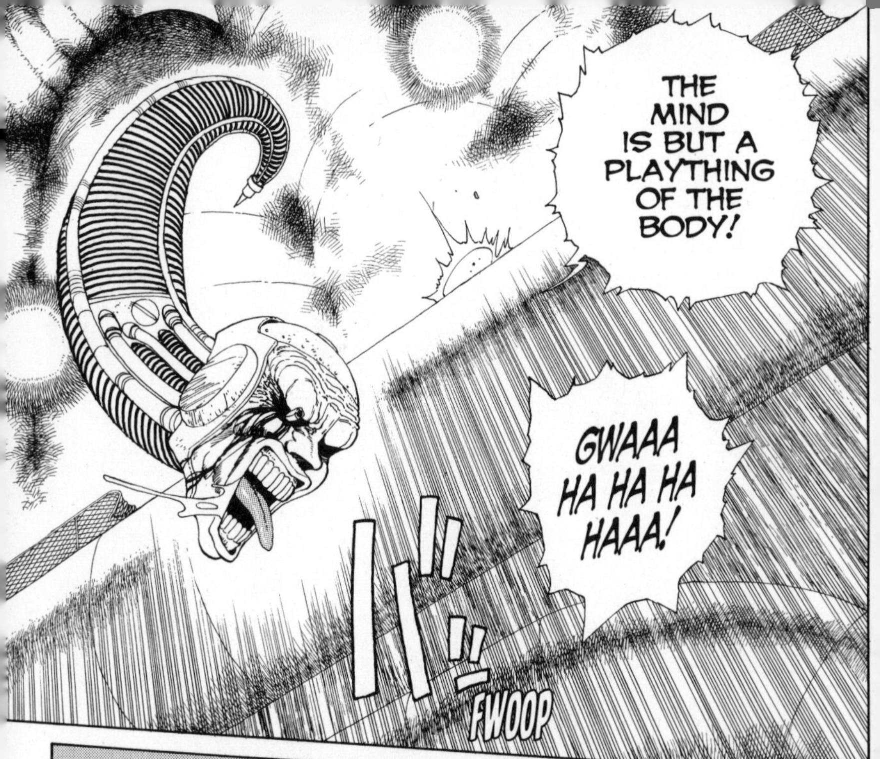
THE MIND IS BUT A PLAYTHING OF THE BODY!
GWAAA HA HA HA HAAA!
FWOOP

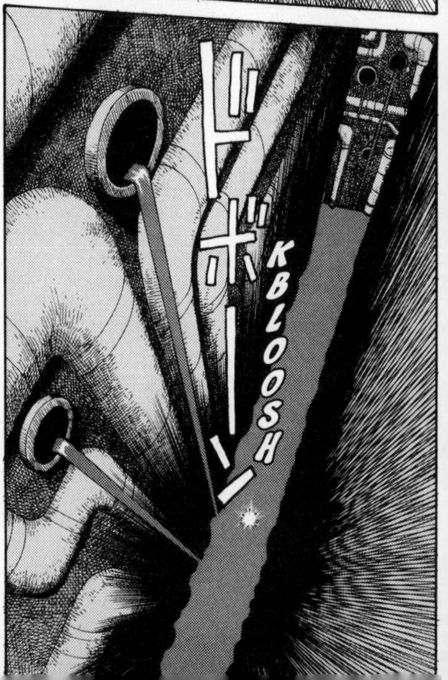
KBLOOSH

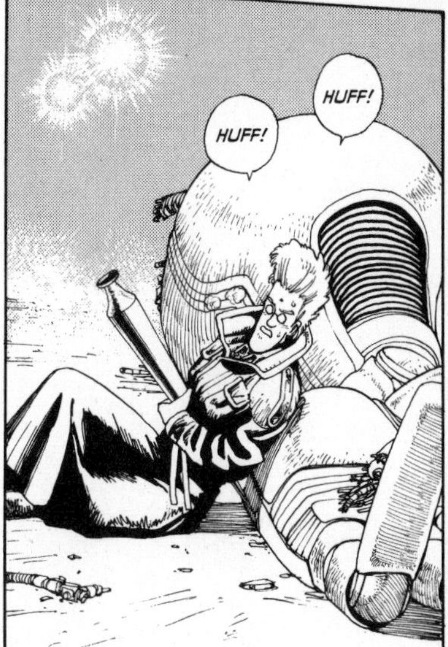
HUFF!
HUFF!

***Friedrich Wilhelm Nietzsche:** German philosopher (1844-1900). Author of *Thus Spoke Zarathustra*.

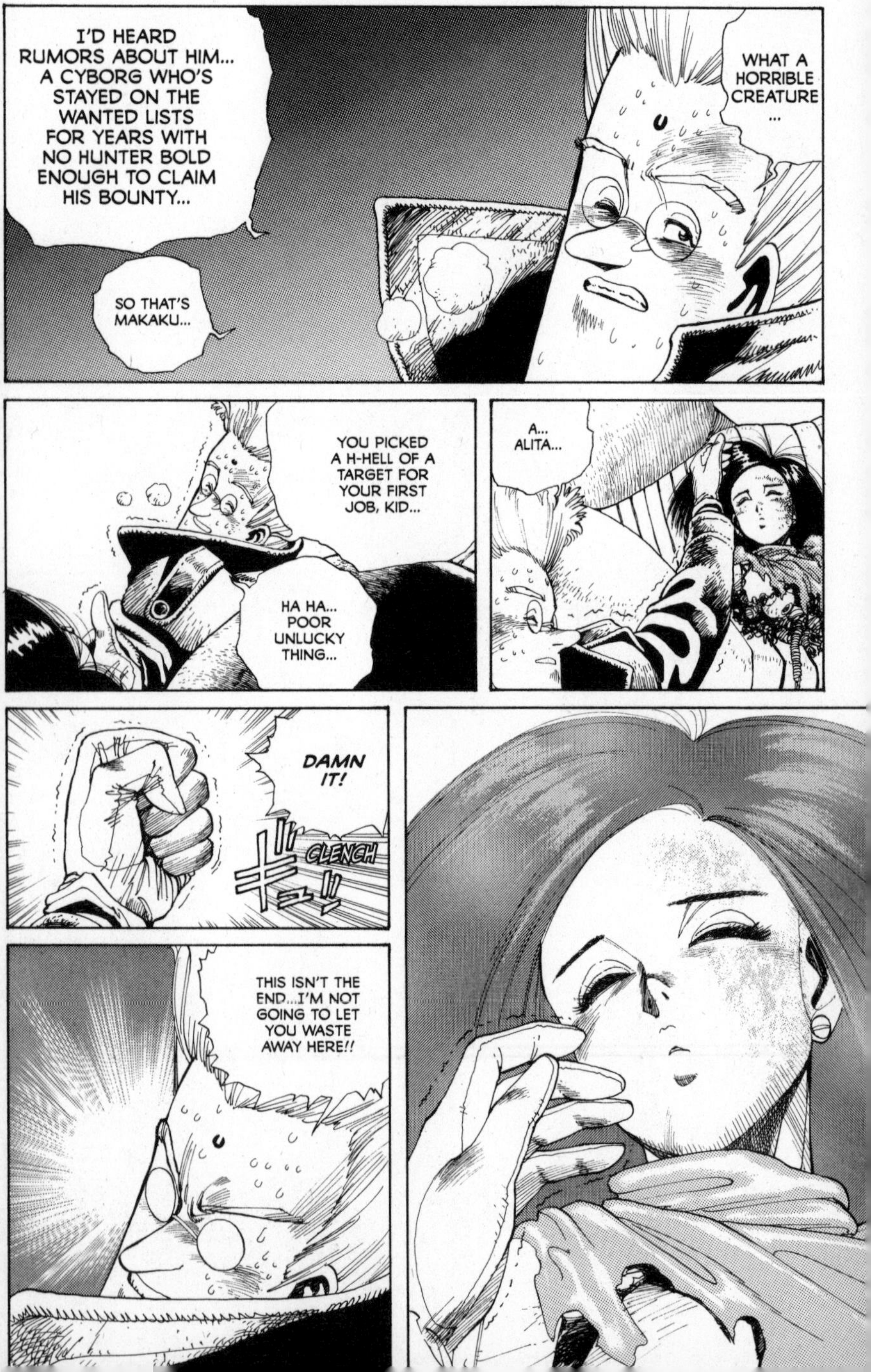
WHAT A HORRIBLE CREATURE ...
I'D HEARD RUMORS ABOUT HIM... A CYBORG WHO'S STAYED ON THE WANTED LISTS FOR YEARS WITH NO HUNTER BOLD ENOUGH TO CLAIM HIS BOUNTY...
SO THAT'S MAKAKU...
A... ALITA...
YOU PICKED A H-HELL OF A TARGET FOR YOUR FIRST JOB, KID...
HA HA... POOR UNLUCKY THING...
DAMN IT!
CLENCH
THIS ISN'T THE END...I'M NOT GOING TO LET YOU WASTE AWAY HERE!!

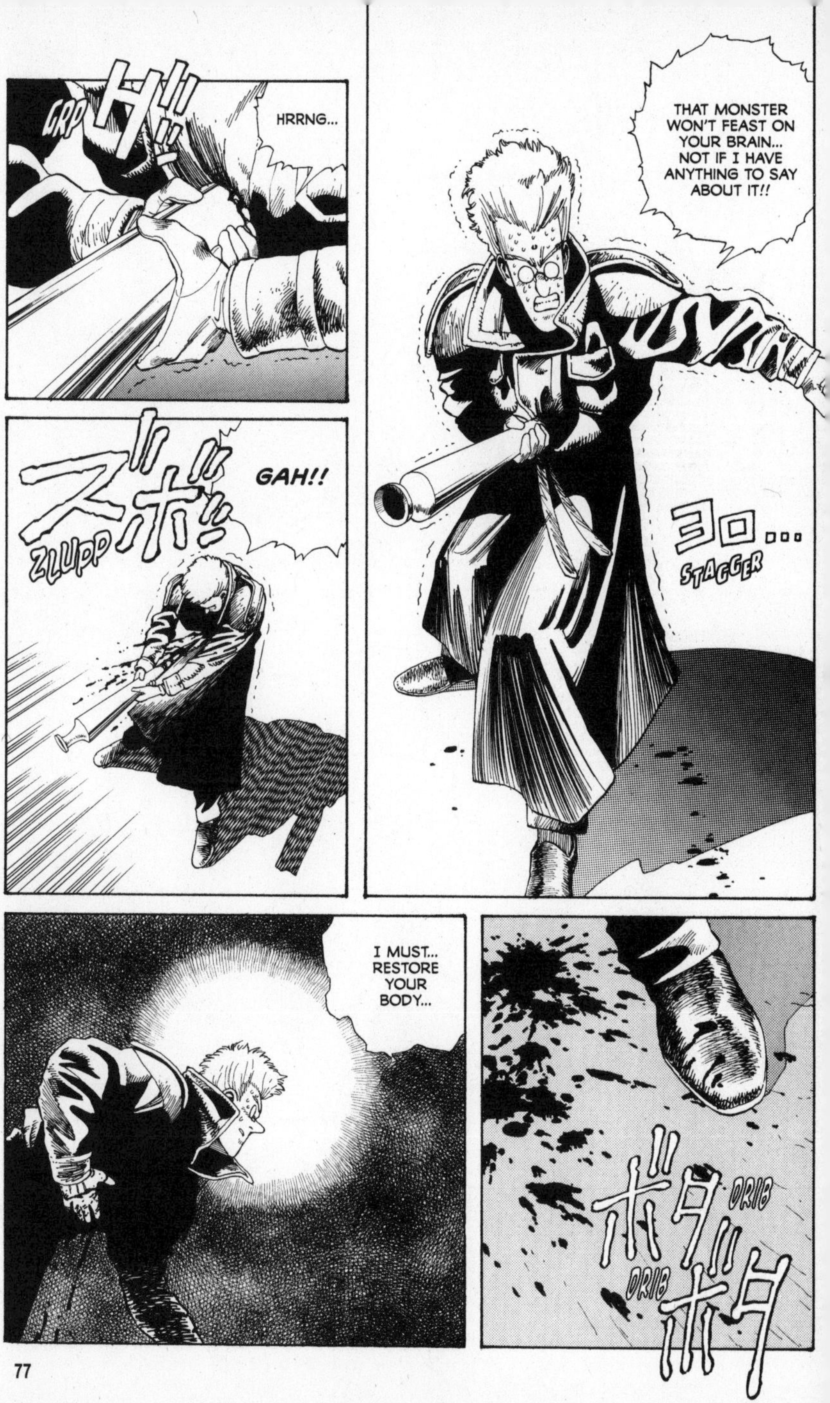
THAT MONSTER WON'T FEAST ON YOUR BRAIN... NOT IF I HAVE ANYTHING TO SAY ABOUT IT!!
ヨロ...
STAGGER
GRP
HRRNG...
ズボッ!!
ZLUPP
GAH!!
ポタポタ
DRIB DRIB
I MUST... RESTORE YOUR BODY...

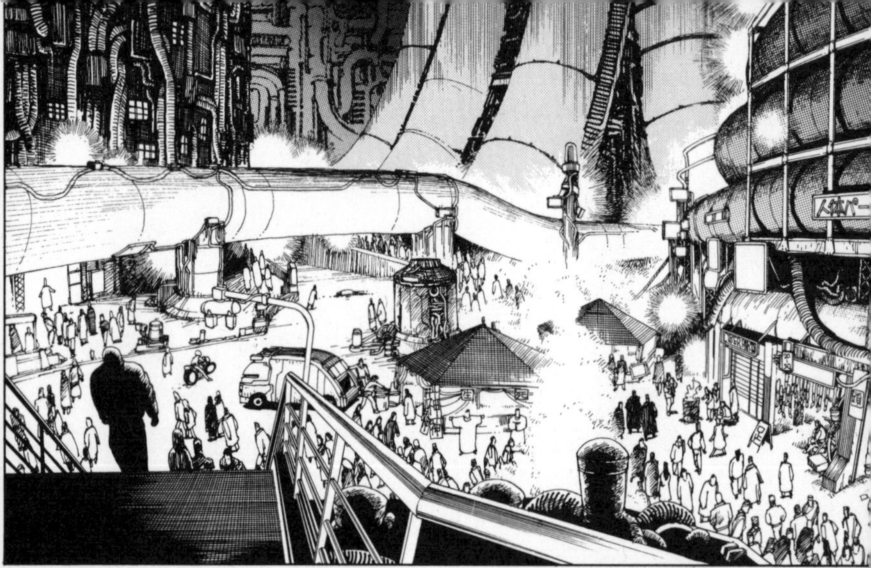
人体パー

Sign: Body Parts

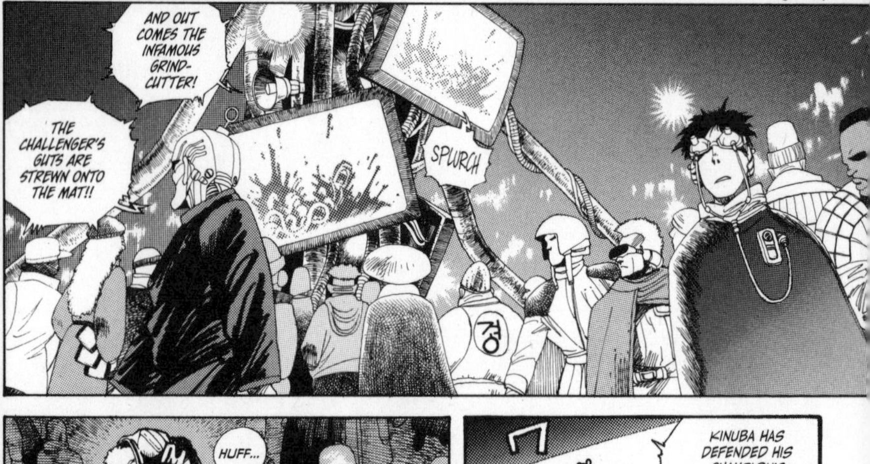
AND OUT COMES THE INFAMOUS GRIND-CUTTER!
SPLURCH
THE CHALLENGER'S GUTS ARE STREWN ONTO THE MAT!!
정

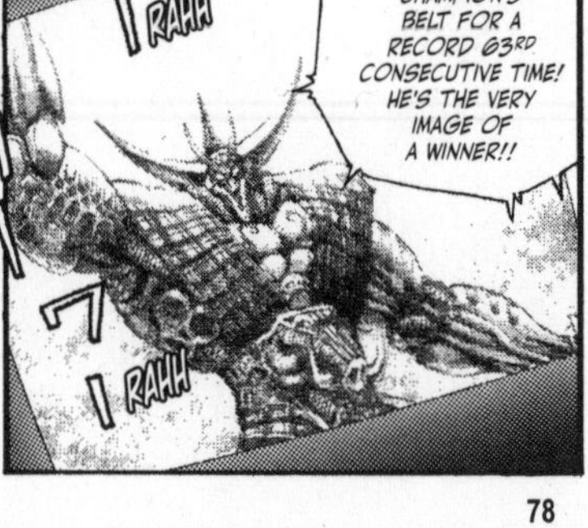
RAHH
KINUBA HAS DEFENDED HIS CHAMPION'S BELT FOR A RECORD 63RD CONSECUTIVE TIME! HE'S THE VERY IMAGE OF A WINNER!!
RAHH

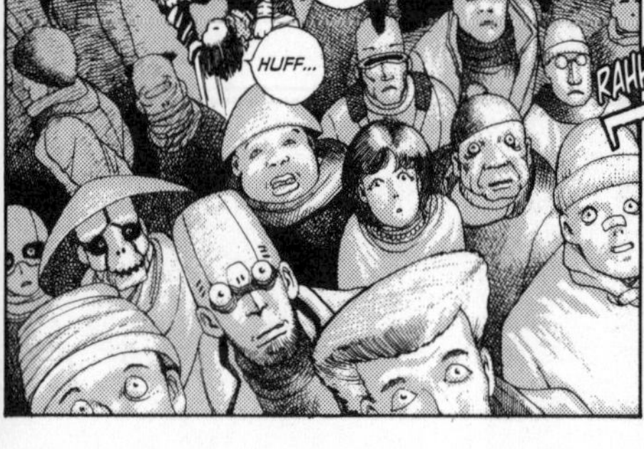
RAHH
HUFF...
HUFF...

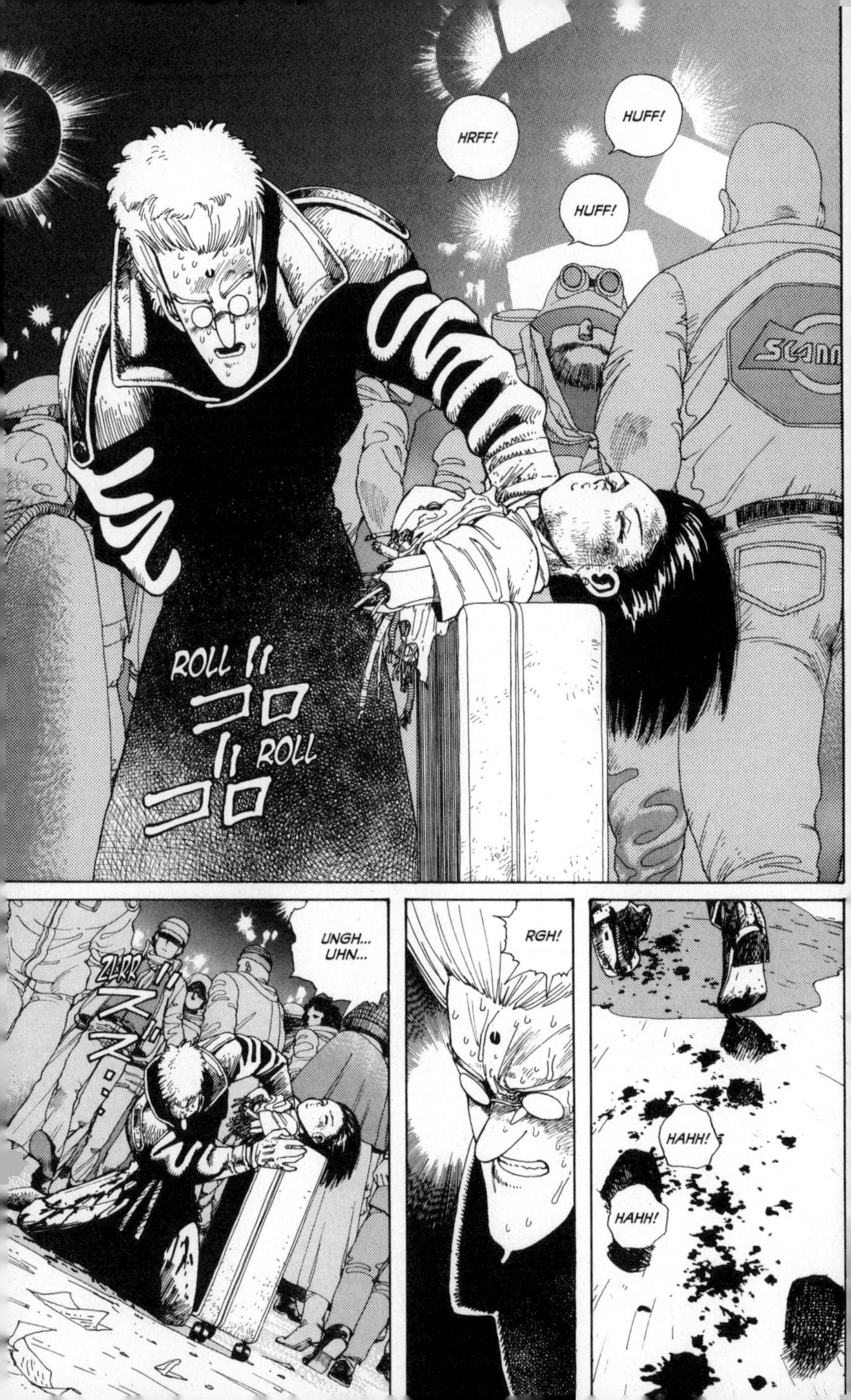
HUFF!
HRFF!
HUFF!
ROLL
コロ
ROLL
コロ
HAHH!
HAHH!
RGH!
UNGH... UHN...
ZLRR

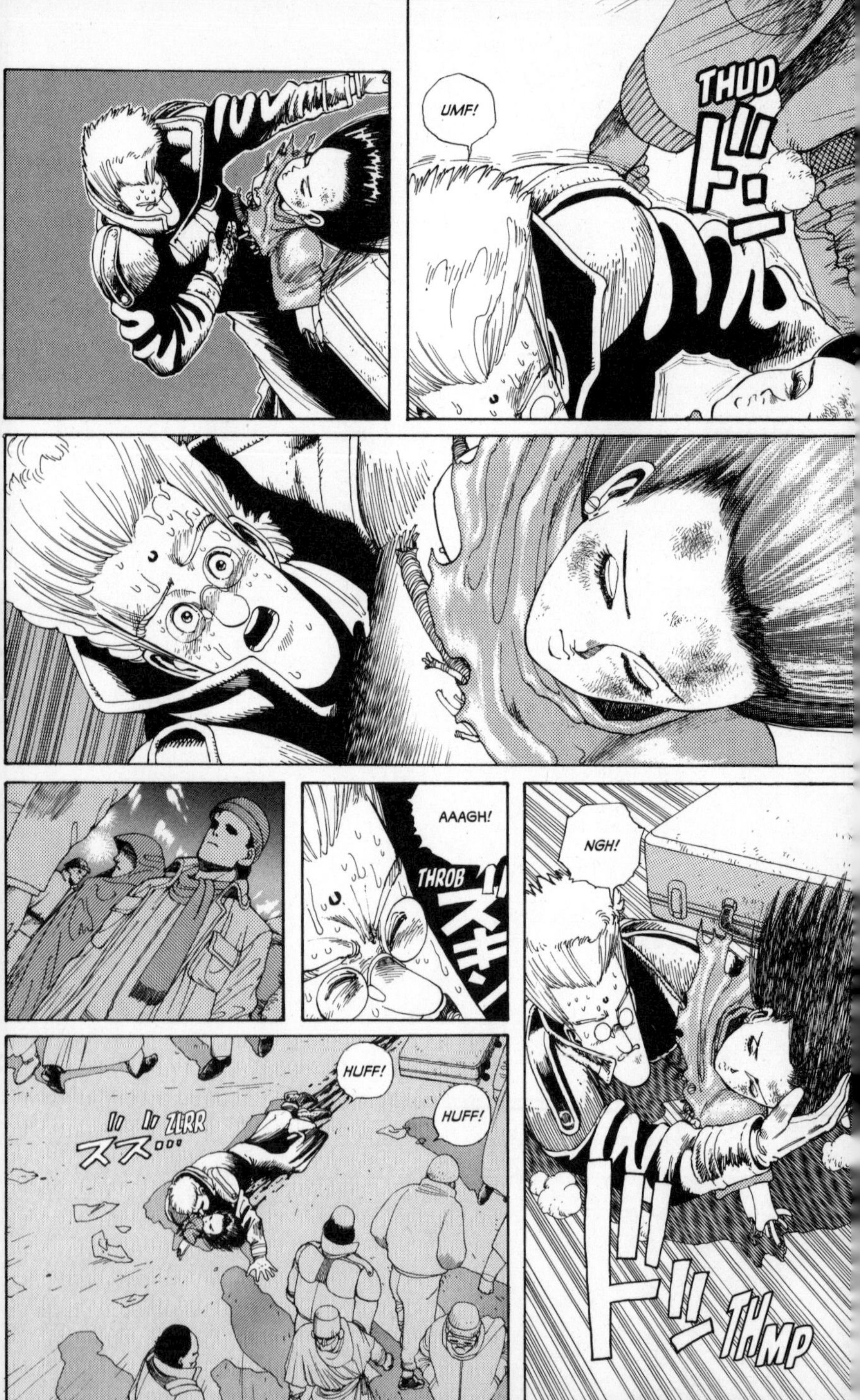
UMF!
THUD
NGH!
THMP
AAAGH!
THROB
HUFF!
HUFF!
ZLRR

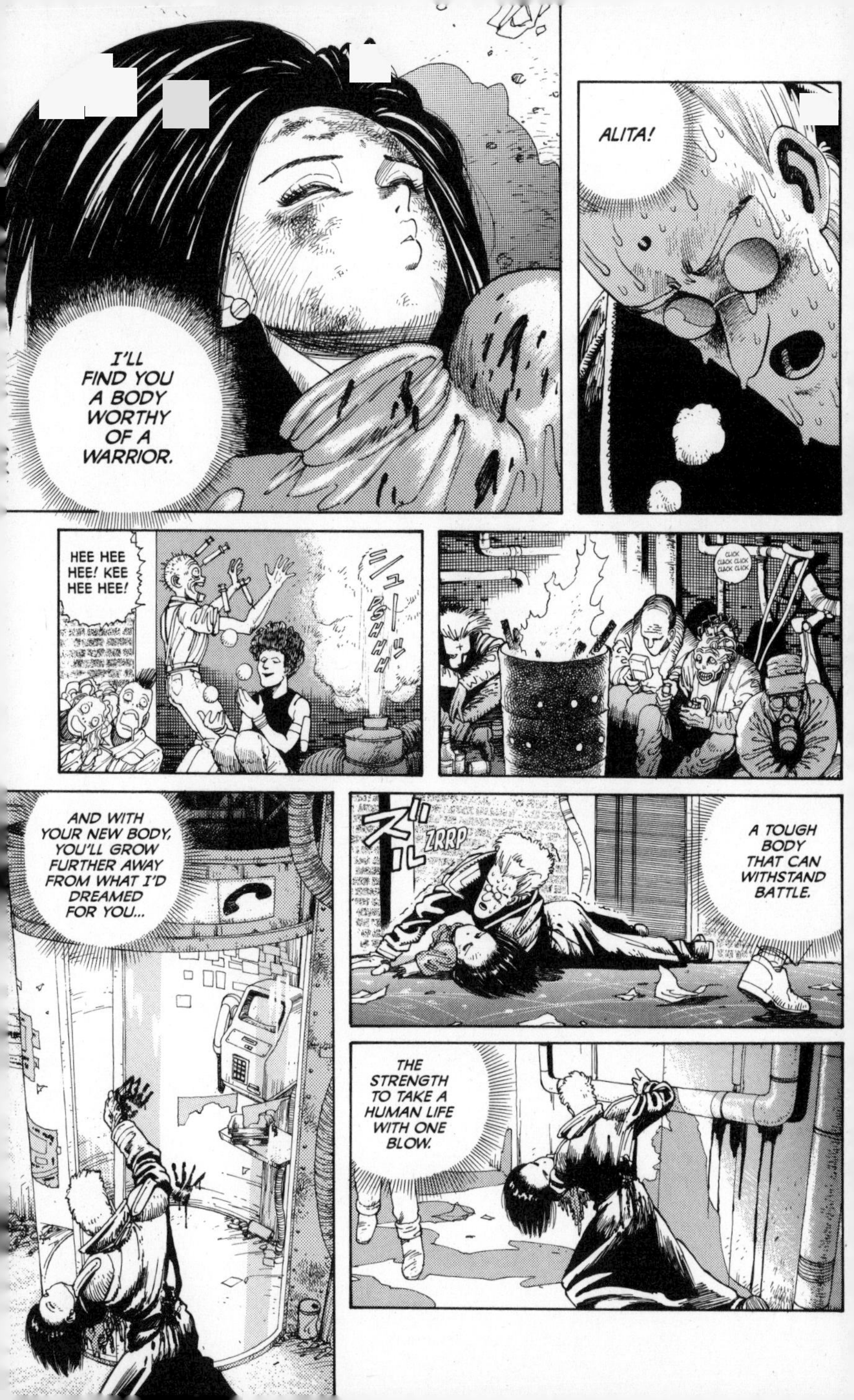
ALITA!
I'LL FIND YOU A BODY WORTHY OF A WARRIOR.
CLICK CLACK CLICK CLACK CLICK
HEE HEE HEE! KEE HEE HEE!
PSHHHH
A TOUGH BODY THAT CAN WITHSTAND BATTLE.
ZRRP
THE STRENGTH TO TAKE A HUMAN LIFE WITH ONE BLOW.
AND WITH YOUR NEW BODY, YOU'LL GROW FURTHER AWAY FROM WHAT I'D DREAMED FOR YOU...

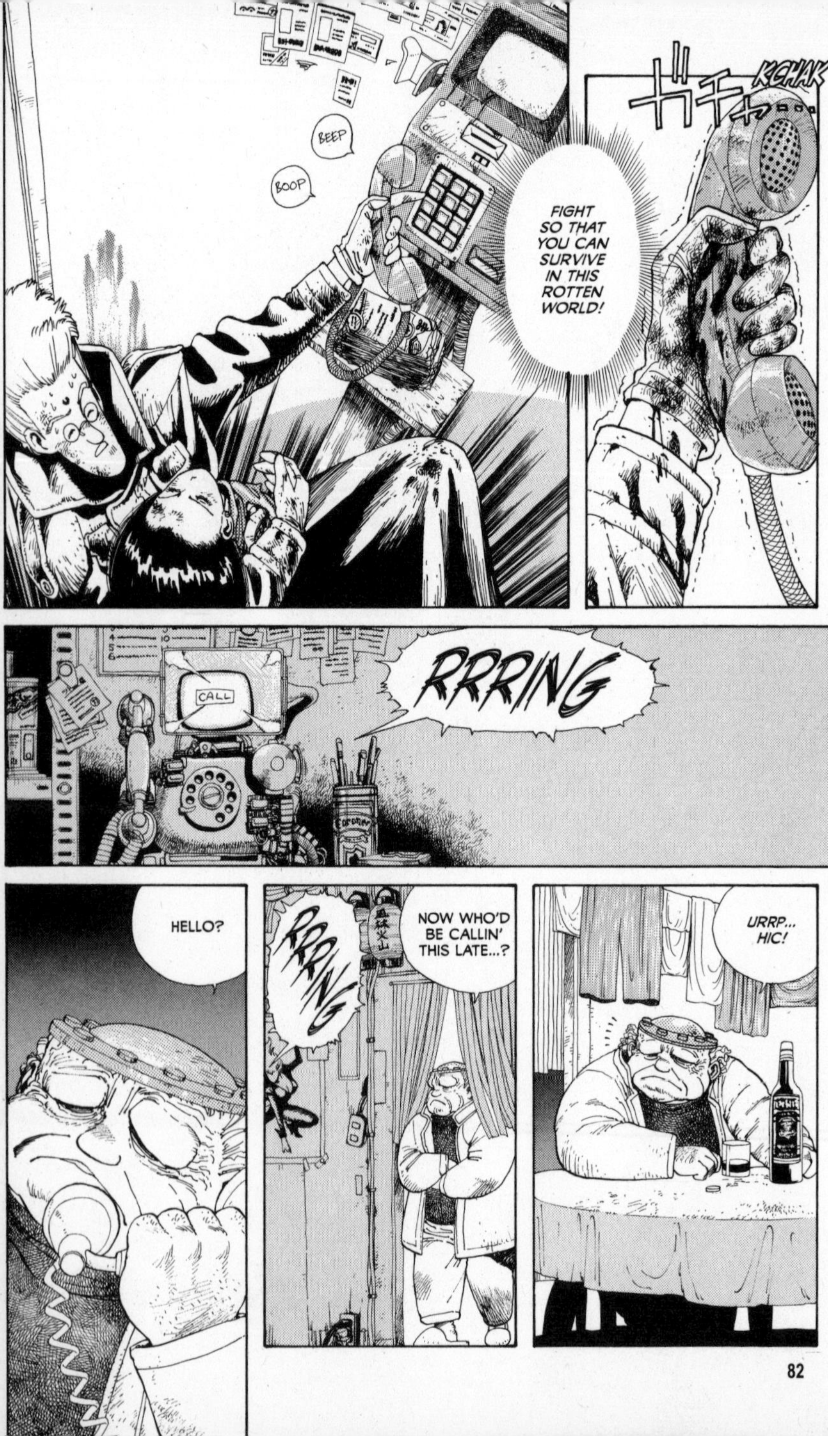
KCHAK
FIGHT SO THAT YOU CAN SURVIVE IN THIS ROTTEN WORLD!
BEEP
BOOP
RRRING
URRP... HIC!
NOW WHO'D BE CALLIN' THIS LATE...?
RRRING
HELLO?

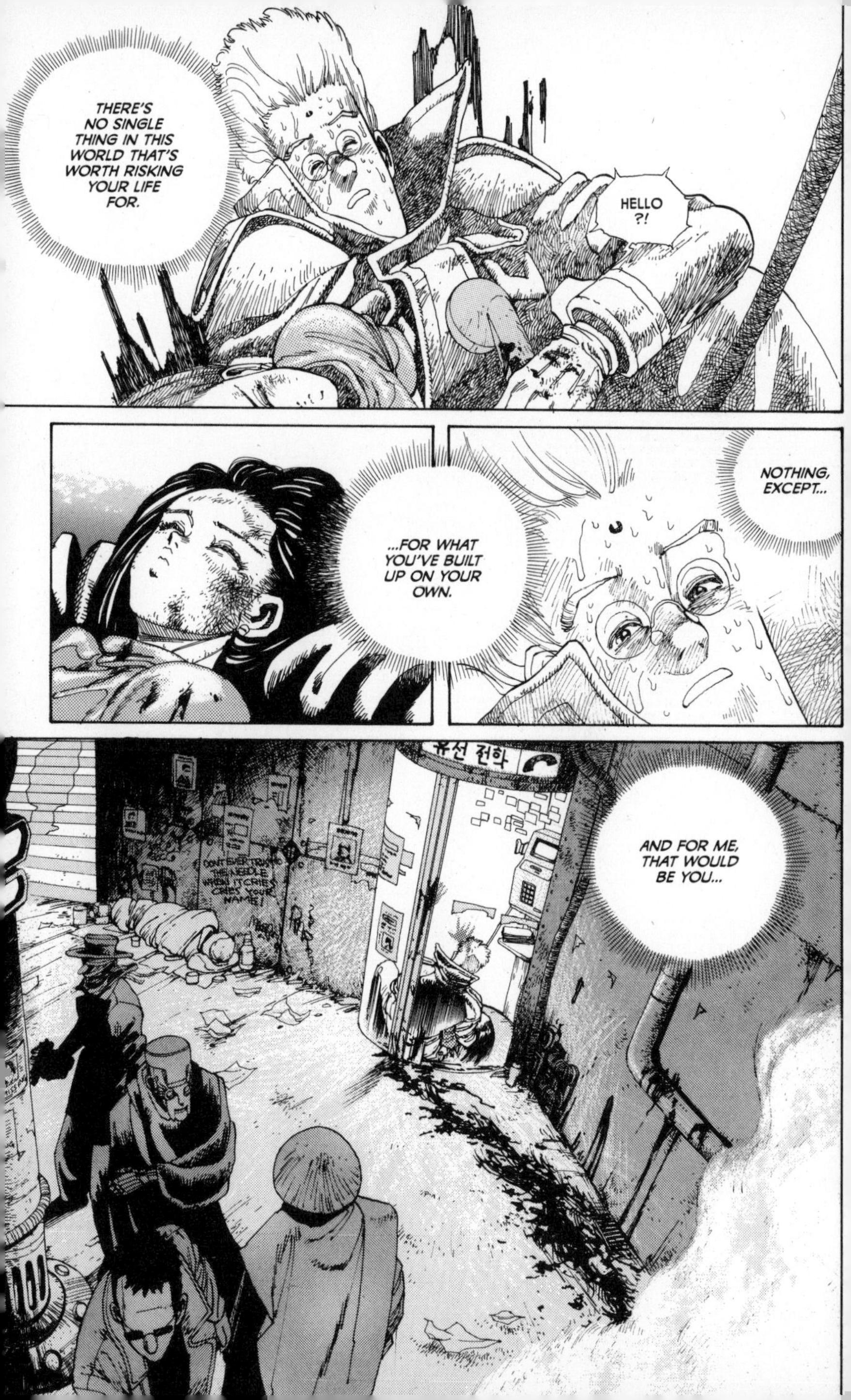
HELLO ?!
THERE'S NO SINGLE THING IN THIS WORLD THAT'S WORTH RISKING YOUR LIFE FOR.
NOTHING, EXCEPT...
...FOR WHAT YOU'VE BUILT UP ON YOUR OWN.
유선 전화
AND FOR ME, THAT WOULD BE YOU...

FIGHT_004 Resurgents

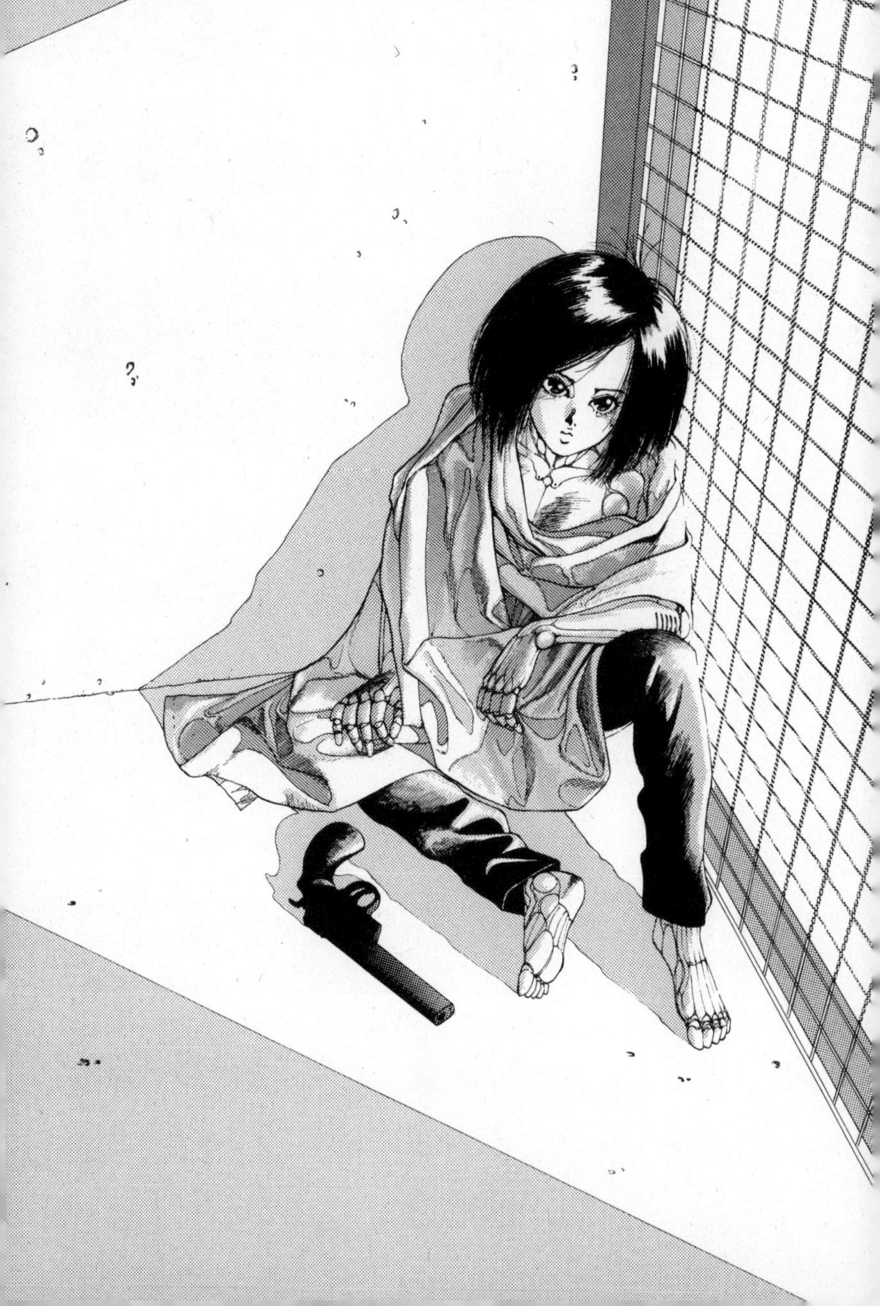

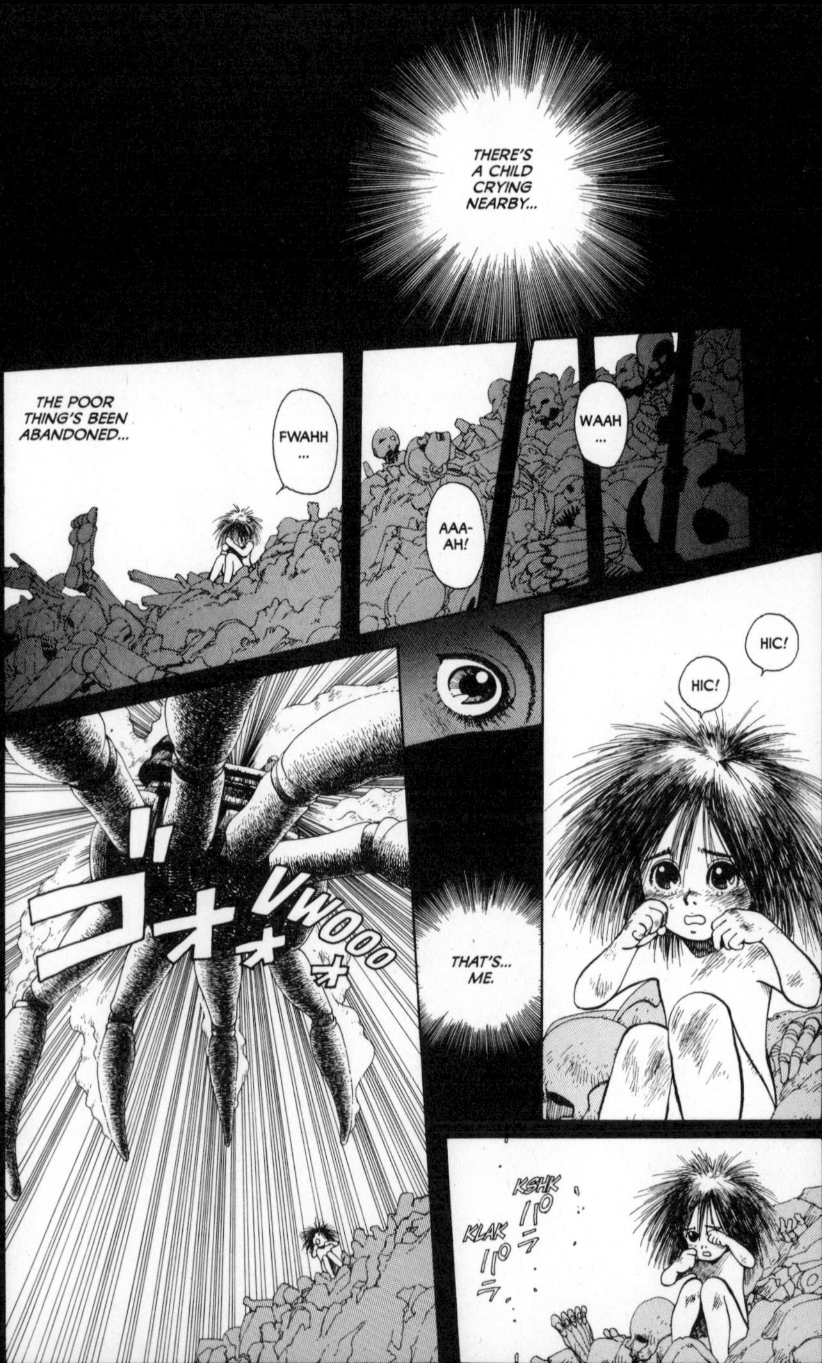
THERE'S A CHILD CRYING NEARBY...
WAAH ...
AAA-AH!
FWAHH ...
THE POOR THING'S BEEN ABANDONED...
HIC!
HIC!
THAT'S... ME.
VWOOOO
KSHK
KLAK

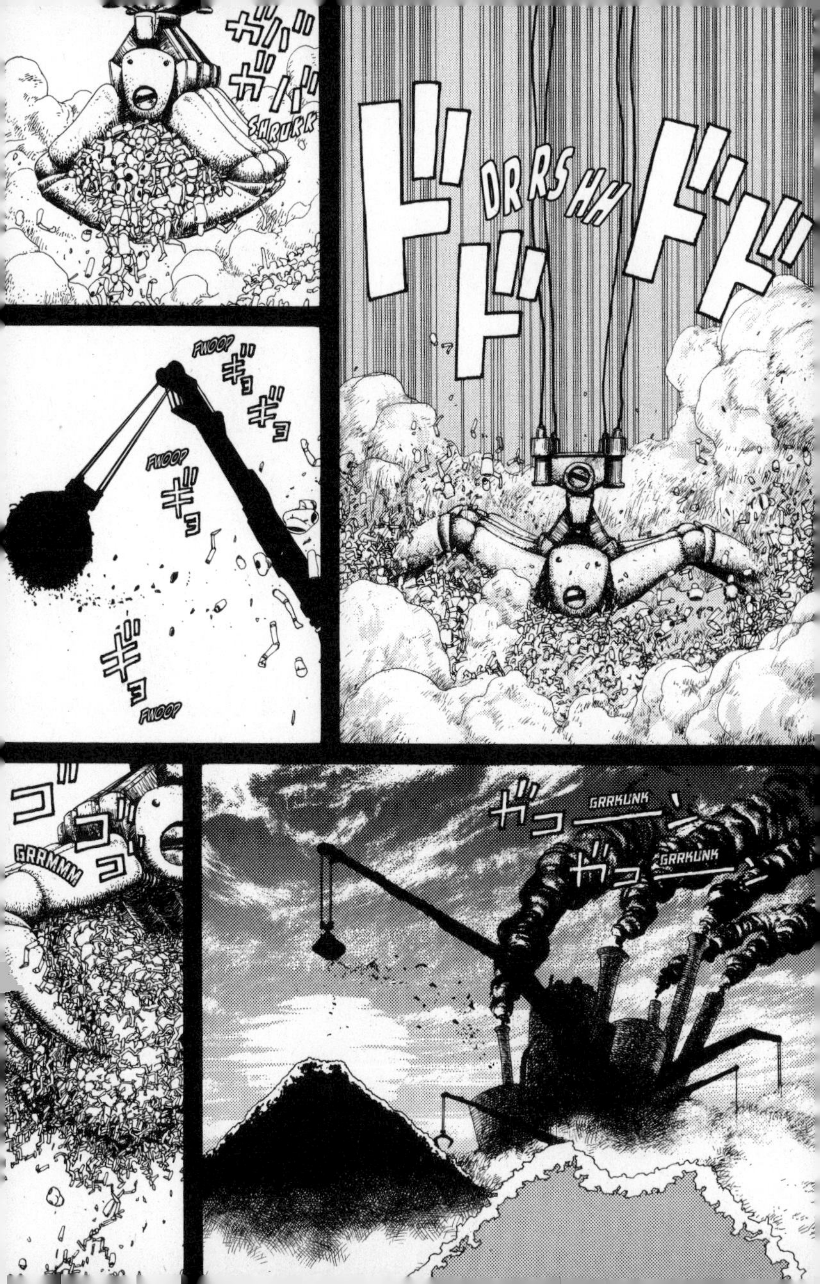

ドド
DRRSHH
ドドド
ガバガバ
SHRUKK
FWOOP
ギョギョ
FWOOP
ギョ
ギョ
FWOOP
ガコー
GRRKUNK
ガコー
GRRKUNK
ゴゴゴ
GRRMMM

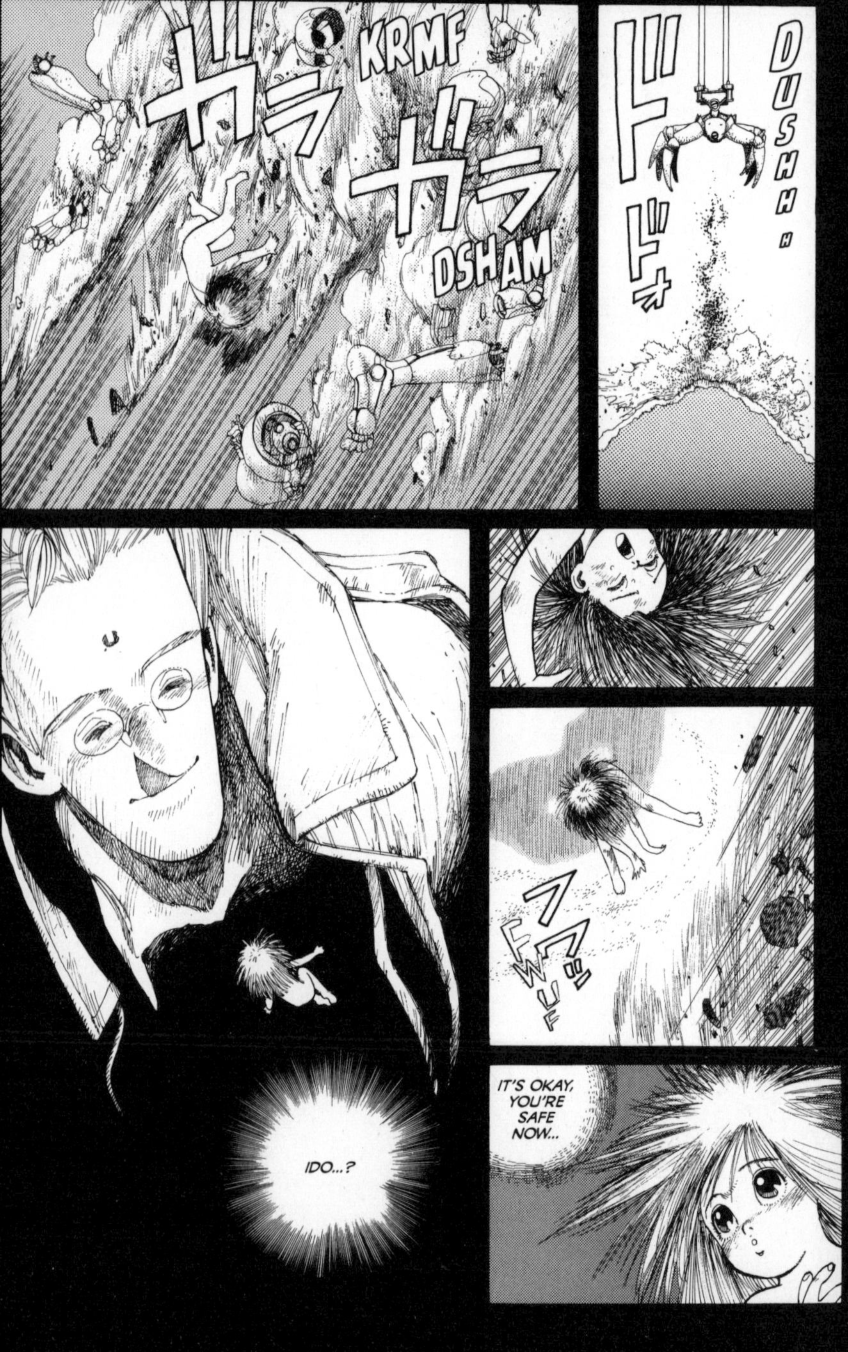
ドド
DUSHHH
ドォ
カラ
ガラ
KRMF
DSHAM
フワ
FWUF
IDO...?
IT'S OKAY, YOU'RE SAFE NOW...

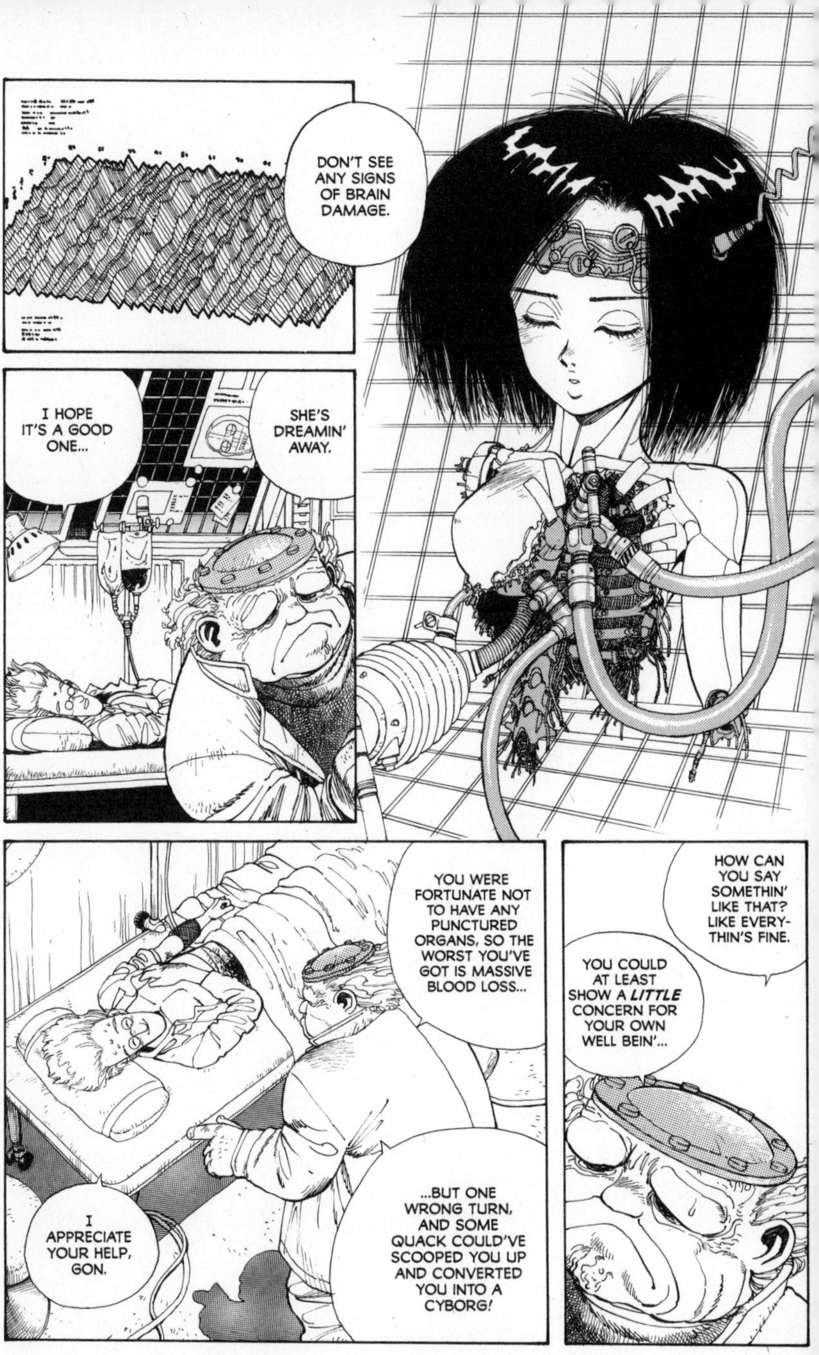
DON'T SEE ANY SIGNS OF BRAIN DAMAGE.
SHE'S DREAMIN' AWAY.
I HOPE IT'S A GOOD ONE...
HOW CAN YOU SAY SOMETHIN' LIKE THAT? LIKE EVERY-THIN'S FINE.
YOU COULD AT LEAST SHOW A *LITTLE* CONCERN FOR YOUR OWN WELL BEIN'...
YOU WERE FORTUNATE NOT TO HAVE ANY PUNCTURED ORGANS, SO THE WORST YOU'VE GOT IS MASSIVE BLOOD LOSS...
...BUT ONE WRONG TURN, AND SOME QUACK COULD'VE SCOOPED YOU UP AND CONVERTED YOU INTO A CYBORG!
I APPRECIATE YOUR HELP, GON.

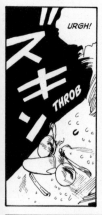

BEIN' A CYBORG'S NOT ALL BAD, BUT THE COST OF THAT BODY WILL PUT YOU INTO DEBT FOR LIFE. IT'S A MISERABLE FATE.
THOUGH IT DOES RAISE A DIFFICULT QUESTION: WHICH IS BETTER, TO BE ABANDONED TO YOUR DEATH, OR TO SURVIVE AND SUFFER DEBT SLAVERY? HA HA HA!
URGH!
ズキン
THROB
MAKAKU... THAT MONSTER'S GOING TO COME BACK FOR ALITA, NO DOUBT ABOUT IT...
I'VE GOT TO BE READY TO FIGHT BACK. GOT TO FIX ALITA'S BODY FOR HER...
ALL THAT WORK YOU PUT INTO BUILDING HER UP, AND LOOK AT HER NOW, POOR THING. HOW'RE YOU SUPPOSED TO FIX UP THIS BODY OF HERS?
I'VE... ALREADY MADE UP MY MIND...
HELP ME, GON.
HELP YOU?

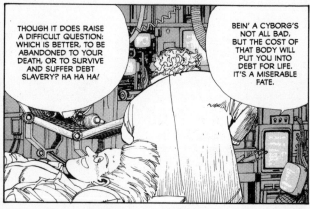

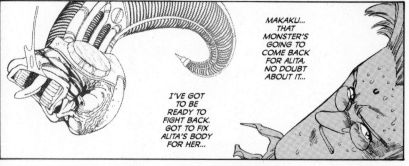

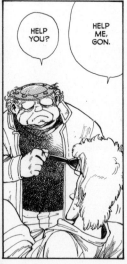

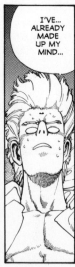

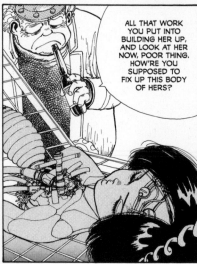

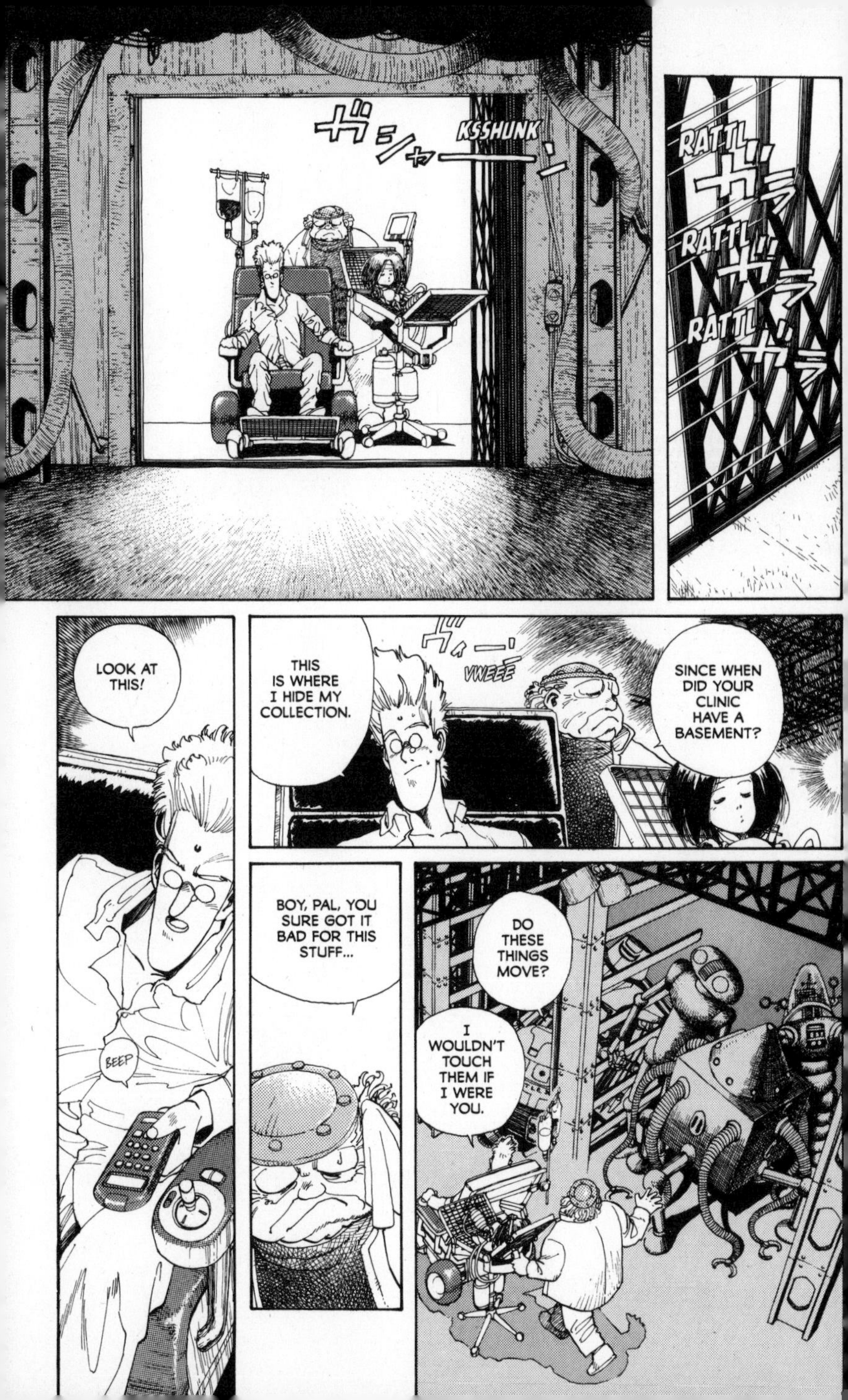
RATTL
ガラ
RATTL
ガラ
RATTL
ガラ
ガシャーン
KSSHUNK
ヴィーン
VWEEE
SINCE WHEN DID YOUR CLINIC HAVE A BASEMENT?
THIS IS WHERE I HIDE MY COLLECTION.
DO THESE THINGS MOVE?
I WOULDN'T TOUCH THEM IF I WERE YOU.
BOY, PAL, YOU SURE GOT IT BAD FOR THIS STUFF...
LOOK AT THIS!
BEEP

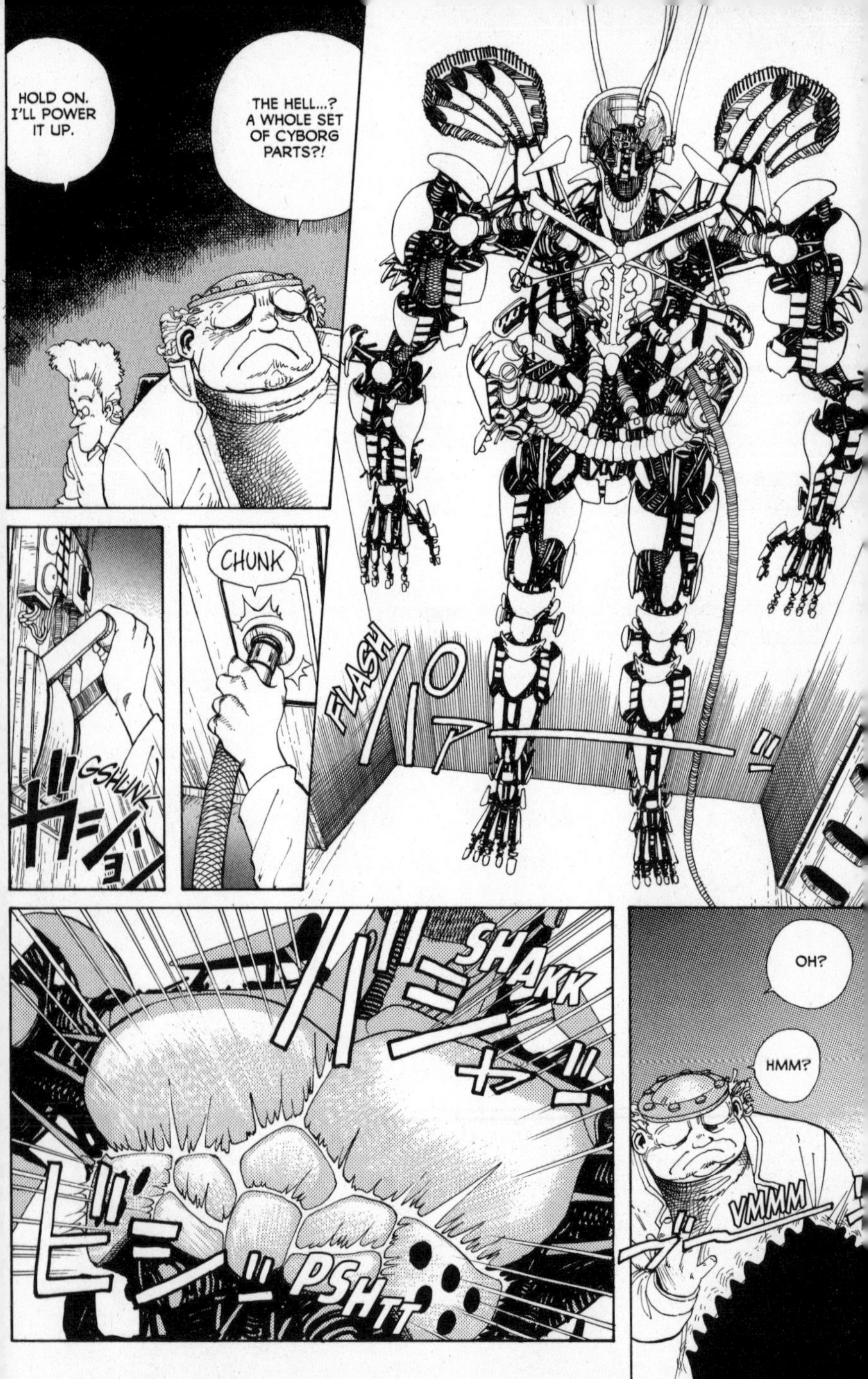
FLASH
THE HELL...? A WHOLE SET OF CYBORG PARTS?!
HOLD ON. I'LL POWER IT UP.
CHUNK
GSHUNK
OH?
HMM?
VMMM
SHAKK
PSHTT

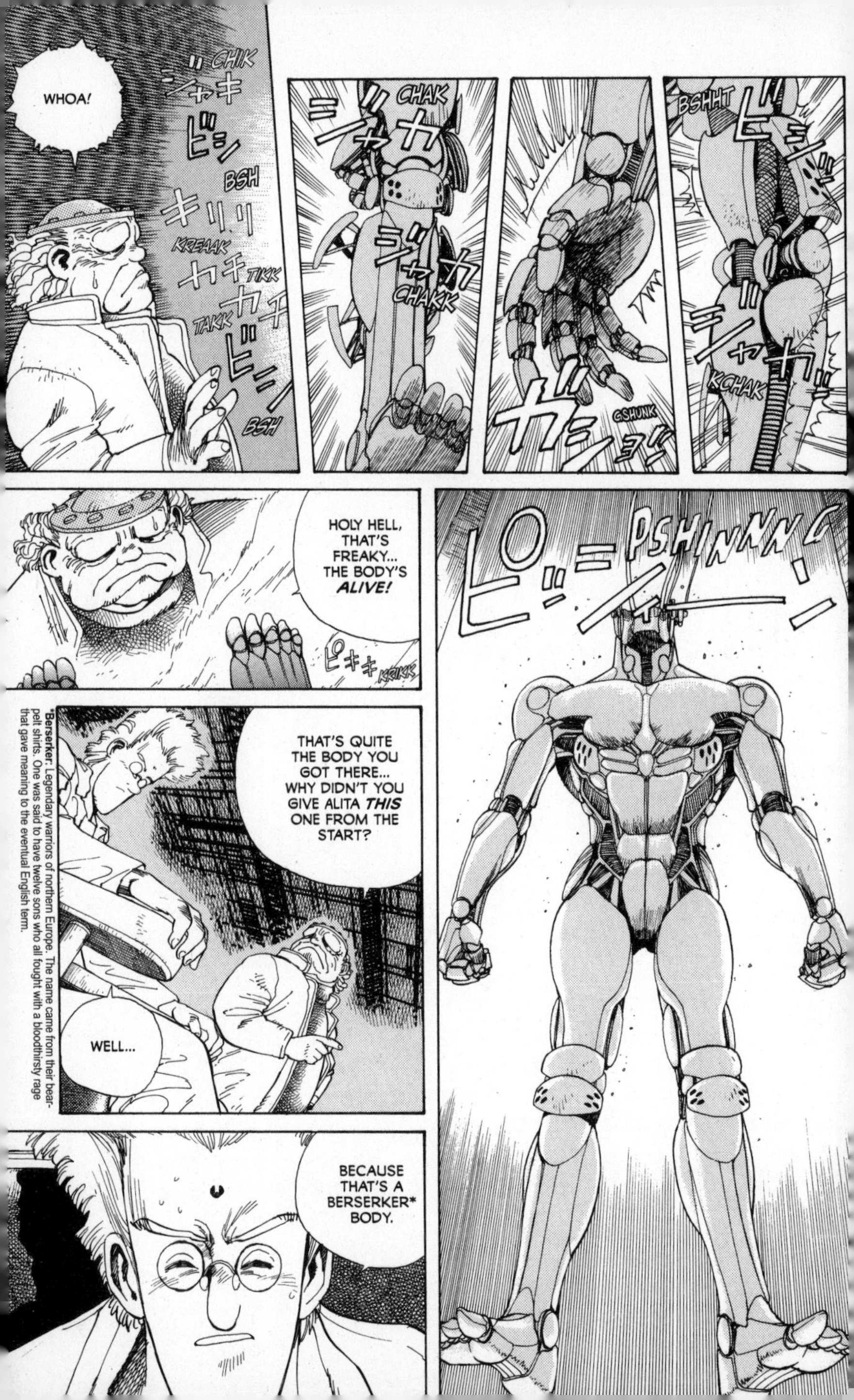
BSHHT
KCHAK
GSHUNK
CHAK
CHAKK
WHOA!
CHIK
BSH
KREAAK
TIKK
TAKK
BSH
PSHINNNG
HOLY HELL, THAT'S FREAKY... THE BODY'S *ALIVE!*
KRIKK
THAT'S QUITE THE BODY YOU GOT THERE... WHY DIDN'T YOU GIVE ALITA *THIS* ONE FROM THE START?
WELL...
BECAUSE THAT'S A BERSERKER* BODY.

***Berserker:** Legendary warriors of northern Europe. The name came from their bear-pelt shirts. One was said to have twelve sons who all fought with a bloodthirsty rage that gave meaning to the eventual English term.

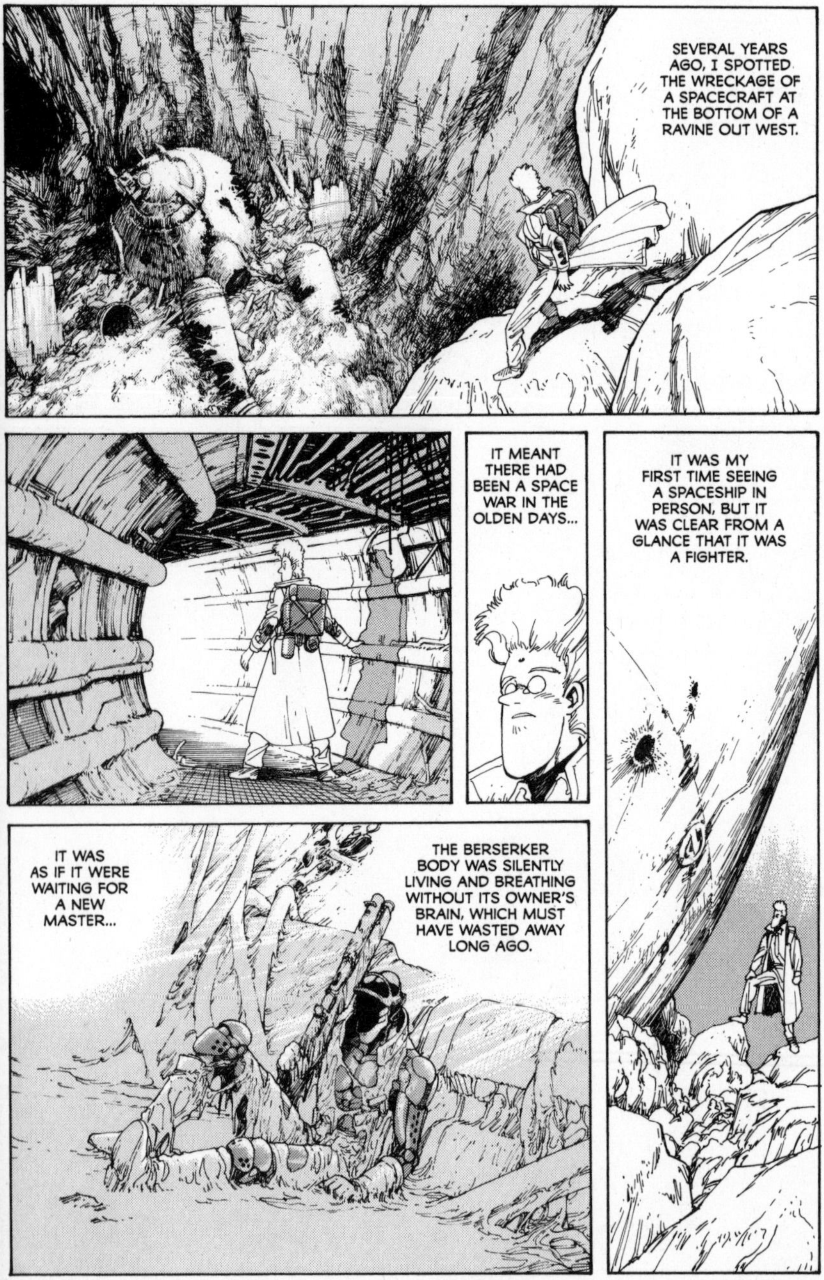
SEVERAL YEARS AGO, I SPOTTED THE WRECKAGE OF A SPACECRAFT AT THE BOTTOM OF A RAVINE OUT WEST.
IT WAS MY FIRST TIME SEEING A SPACESHIP IN PERSON, BUT IT WAS CLEAR FROM A GLANCE THAT IT WAS A FIGHTER.
IT MEANT THERE HAD BEEN A SPACE WAR IN THE OLDEN DAYS...
THE BERSERKER BODY WAS SILENTLY LIVING AND BREATHING WITHOUT ITS OWNER'S BRAIN, WHICH MUST HAVE WASTED AWAY LONG AGO.
IT WAS AS IF IT WERE WAITING FOR A NEW MASTER...

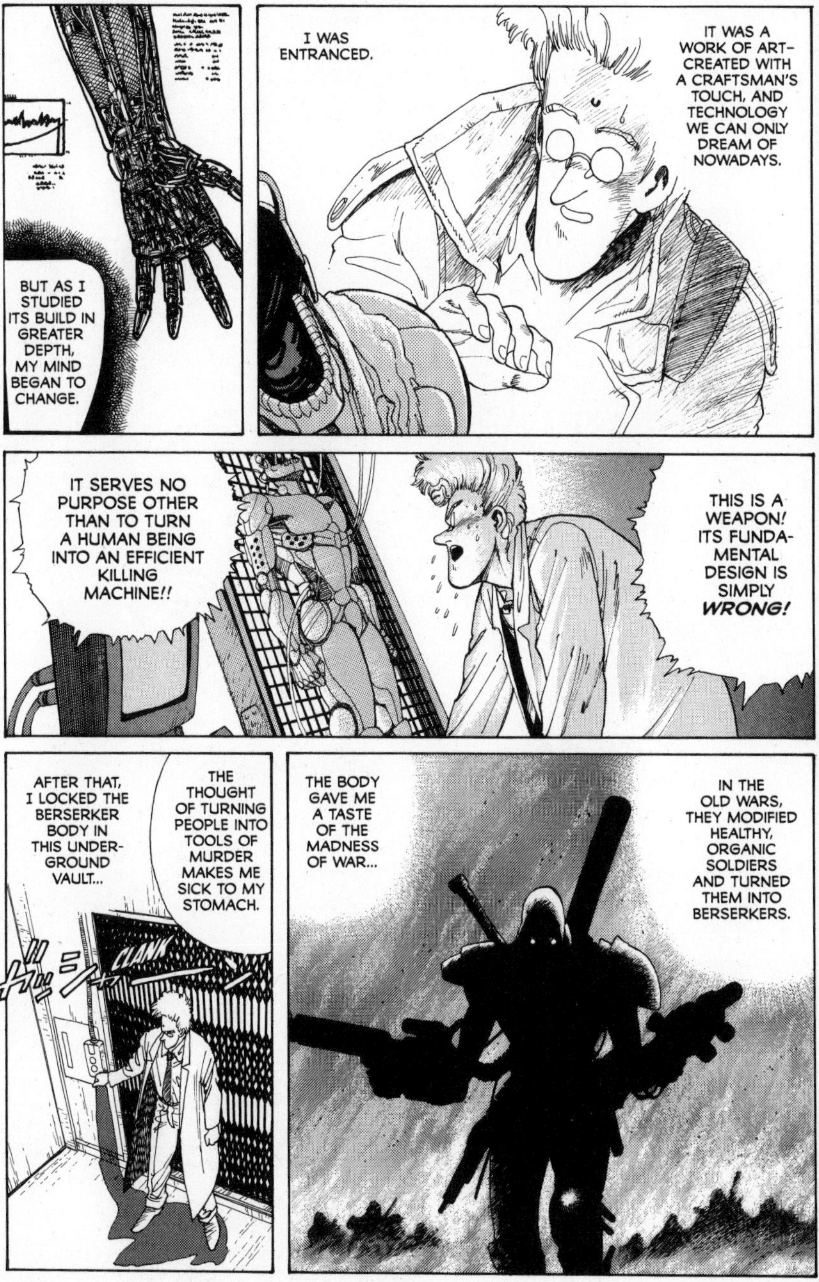
IT WAS A WORK OF ART—CREATED WITH A CRAFTSMAN'S TOUCH, AND TECHNOLOGY WE CAN ONLY DREAM OF NOWADAYS.
I WAS ENTRANCED.
BUT AS I STUDIED ITS BUILD IN GREATER DEPTH, MY MIND BEGAN TO CHANGE.
THIS IS A WEAPON! ITS FUNDA-MENTAL DESIGN IS SIMPLY *WRONG!*
IT SERVES NO PURPOSE OTHER THAN TO TURN A HUMAN BEING INTO AN EFFICIENT KILLING MACHINE!!
IN THE OLD WARS, THEY MODIFIED HEALTHY, ORGANIC SOLDIERS AND TURNED THEM INTO BERSERKERS.
THE BODY GAVE ME A TASTE OF THE MADNESS OF WAR...
THE THOUGHT OF TURNING PEOPLE INTO TOOLS OF MURDER MAKES ME SICK TO MY STOMACH.
AFTER THAT, I LOCKED THE BERSERKER BODY IN THIS UNDER-GROUND VAULT...
CLANK

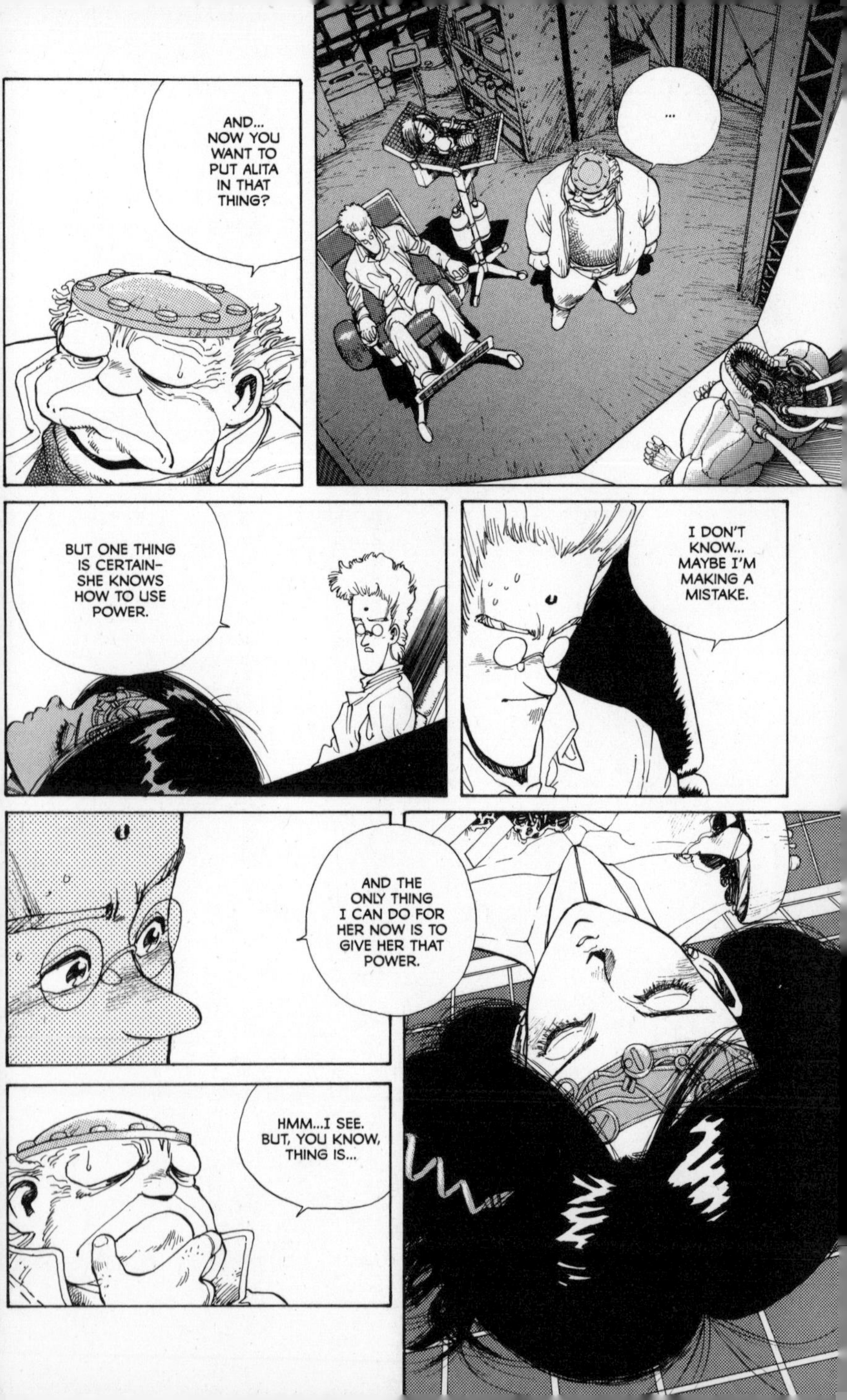
...
AND... NOW YOU WANT TO PUT ALITA IN THAT THING?
I DON'T KNOW... MAYBE I'M MAKING A MISTAKE.
BUT ONE THING IS CERTAIN– SHE KNOWS HOW TO USE POWER.
AND THE ONLY THING I CAN DO FOR HER NOW IS TO GIVE HER THAT POWER.
HMM...I SEE. BUT, YOU KNOW, THING IS...

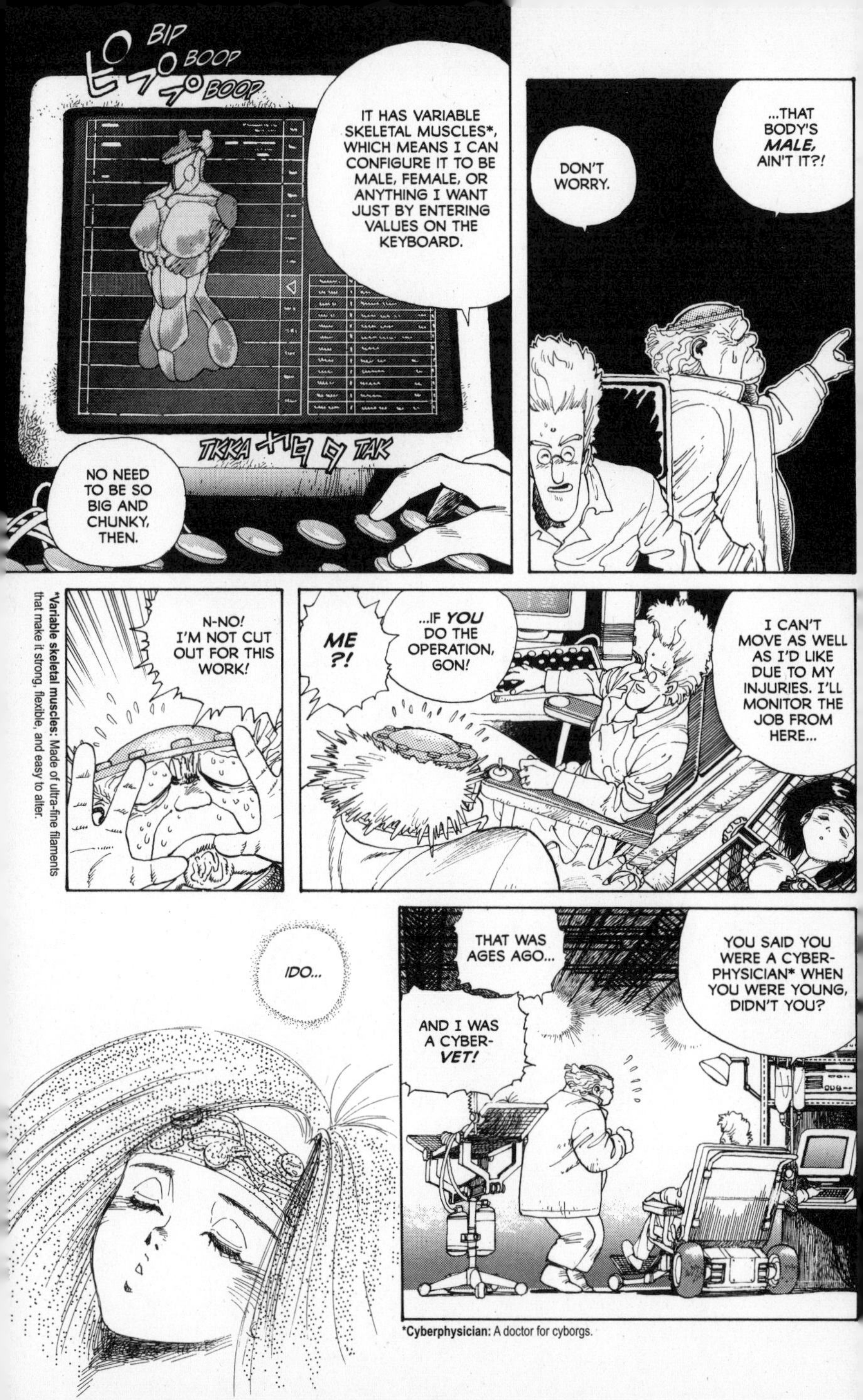
...THAT BODY'S *MALE,* AIN'T IT?!
DON'T WORRY.
BIP BOOP BOOP
IT HAS VARIABLE SKELETAL MUSCLES*, WHICH MEANS I CAN CONFIGURE IT TO BE MALE, FEMALE, OR ANYTHING I WANT JUST BY ENTERING VALUES ON THE KEYBOARD.
TKKA TAK
NO NEED TO BE SO BIG AND CHUNKY, THEN.
I CAN'T MOVE AS WELL AS I'D LIKE DUE TO MY INJURIES. I'LL MONITOR THE JOB FROM HERE...
...IF *YOU* DO THE OPERATION, GON!
ME ?!
N-NO! I'M NOT CUT OUT FOR THIS WORK!
YOU SAID YOU WERE A CYBER-PHYSICIAN* WHEN YOU WERE YOUNG, DIDN'T YOU?
THAT WAS AGES AGO...
AND I WAS A CYBER-*VET!*
IDO...

***Variable skeletal muscles:** Made of ultra-fine filaments that make it strong, flexible, and easy to alter.

***Cyberphysician:** A doctor for cyborgs.

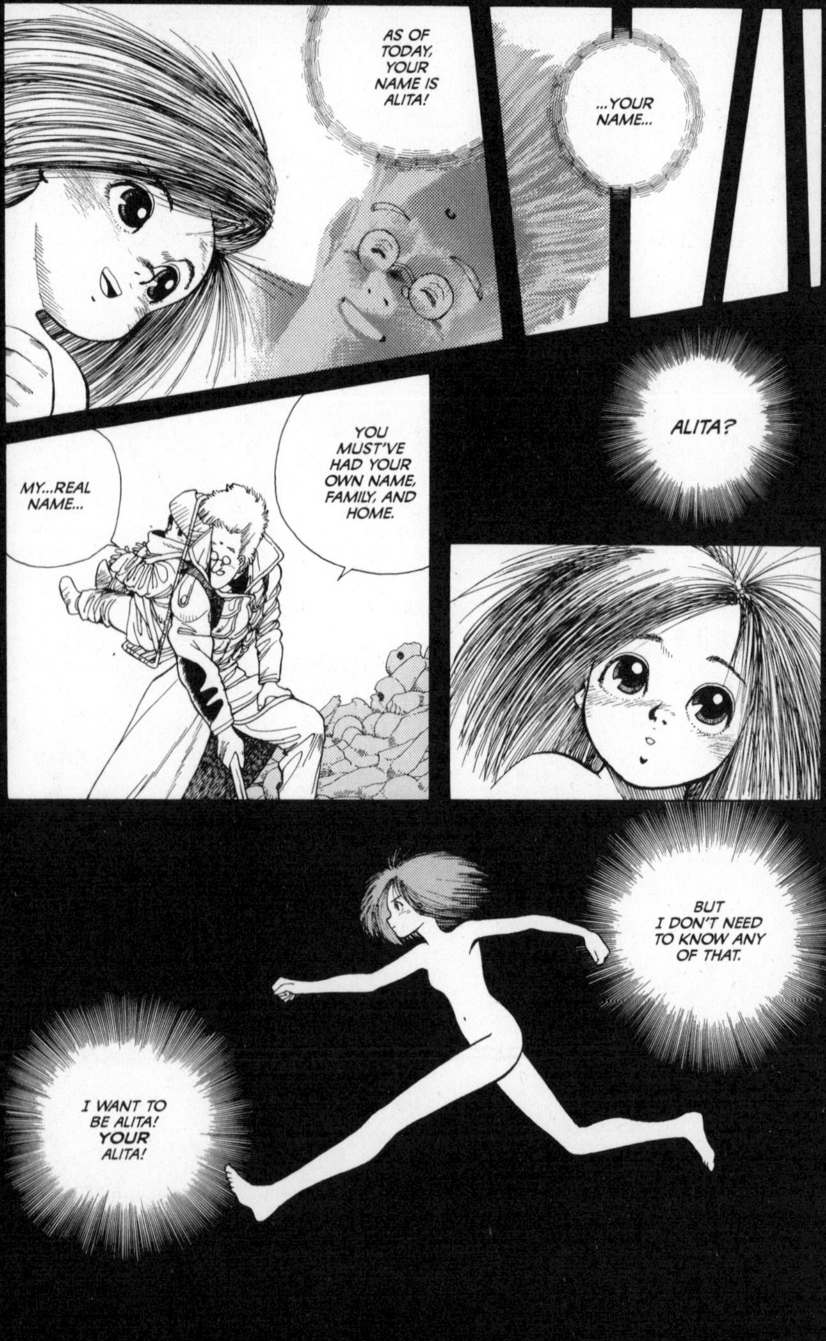
...YOUR NAME...
AS OF TODAY, YOUR NAME IS ALITA!
ALITA?
YOU MUST'VE HAD YOUR OWN NAME, FAMILY, AND HOME.
MY...REAL NAME...
BUT I DON'T NEED TO KNOW ANY OF THAT.
I WANT TO BE ALITA! **YOUR** ALITA!

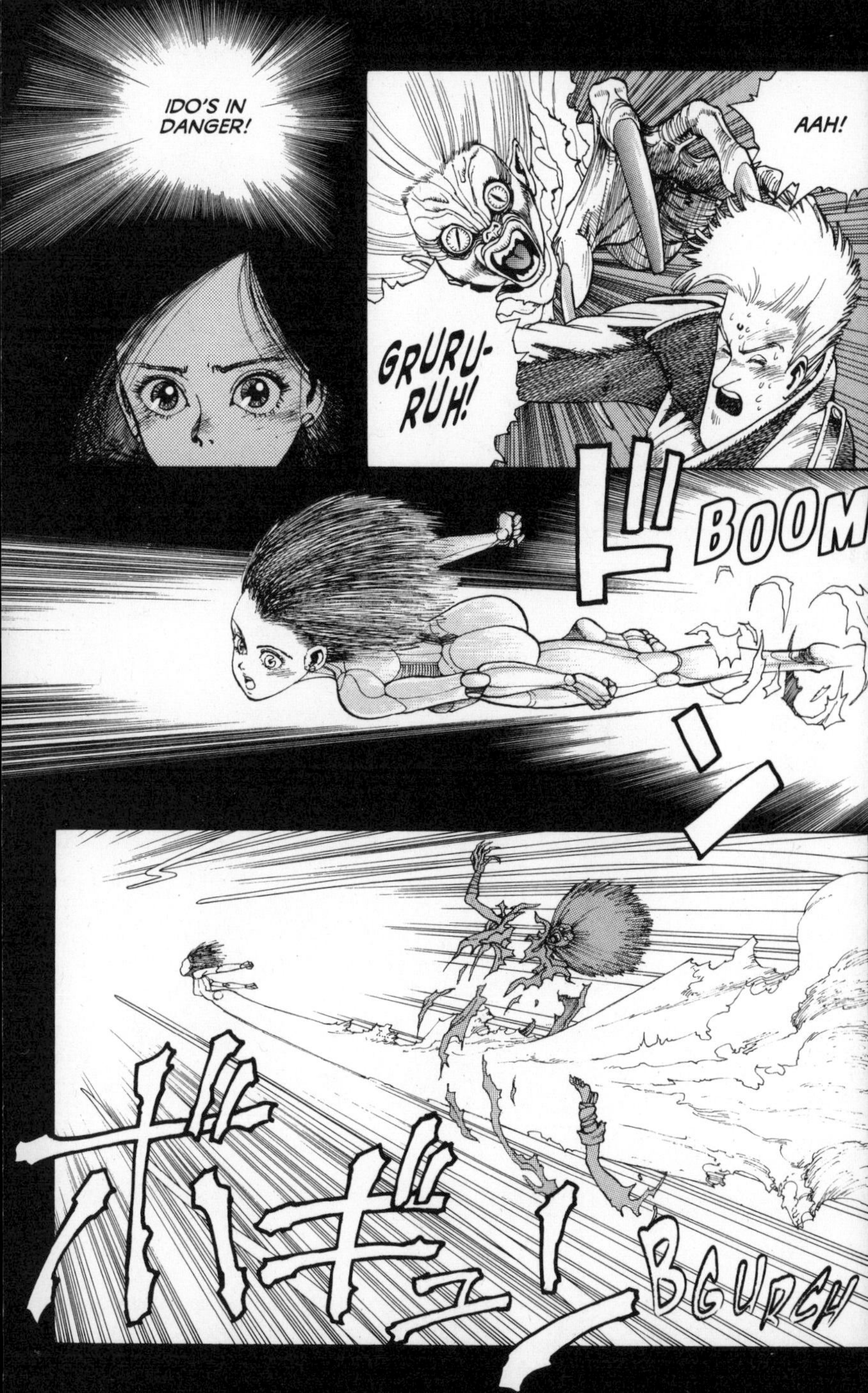
AAH!
GRURU-RUH!
IDO'S IN DANGER!
BOOM
BGURCH

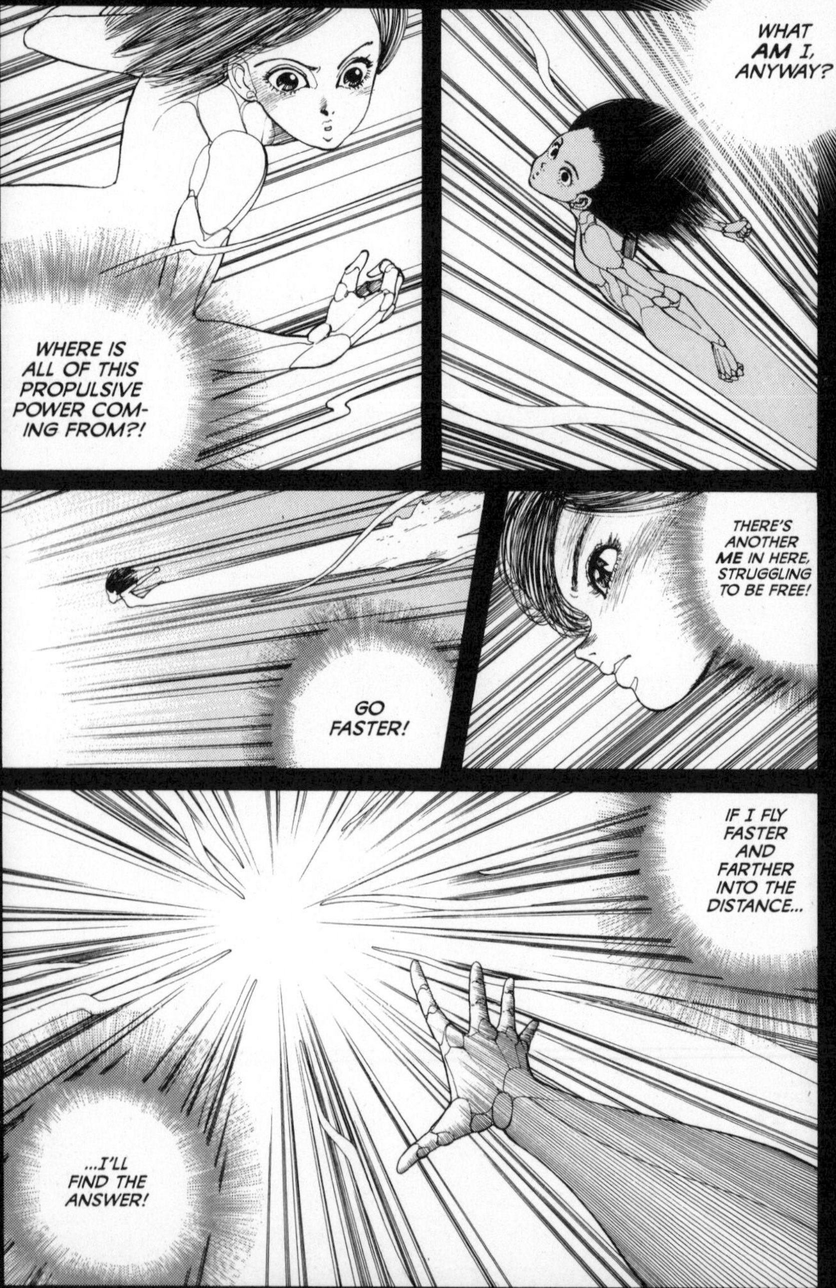
WHAT AM I, ANYWAY?
WHERE IS ALL OF THIS PROPULSIVE POWER COM-ING FROM?!
THERE'S ANOTHER ME IN HERE, STRUGGLING TO BE FREE!
GO FASTER!
IF I FLY FASTER AND FARTHER INTO THE DISTANCE...
...I'LL FIND THE ANSWER!

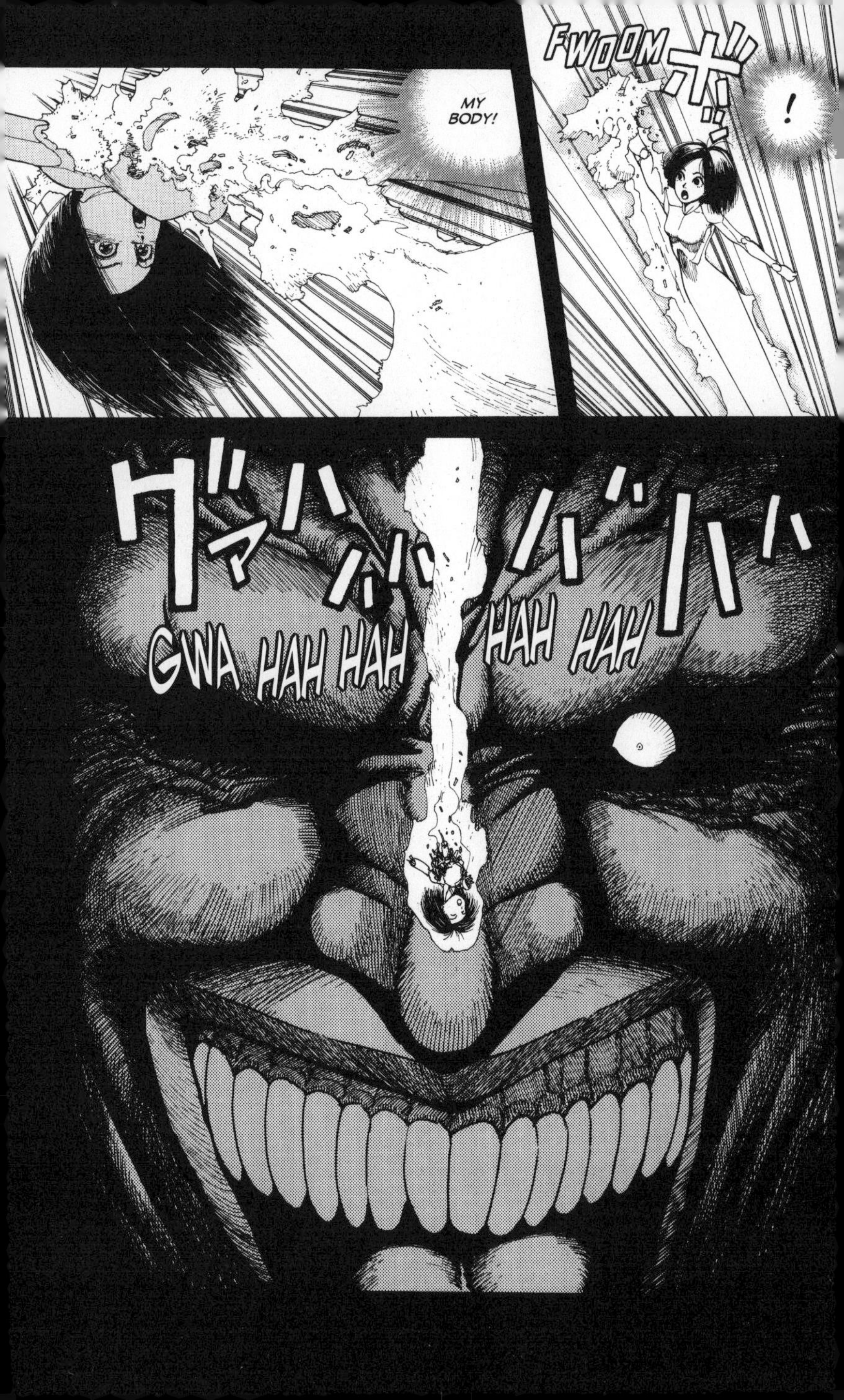
FWOOM
!
MY BODY!
GWA HAH HAH HAH HAH

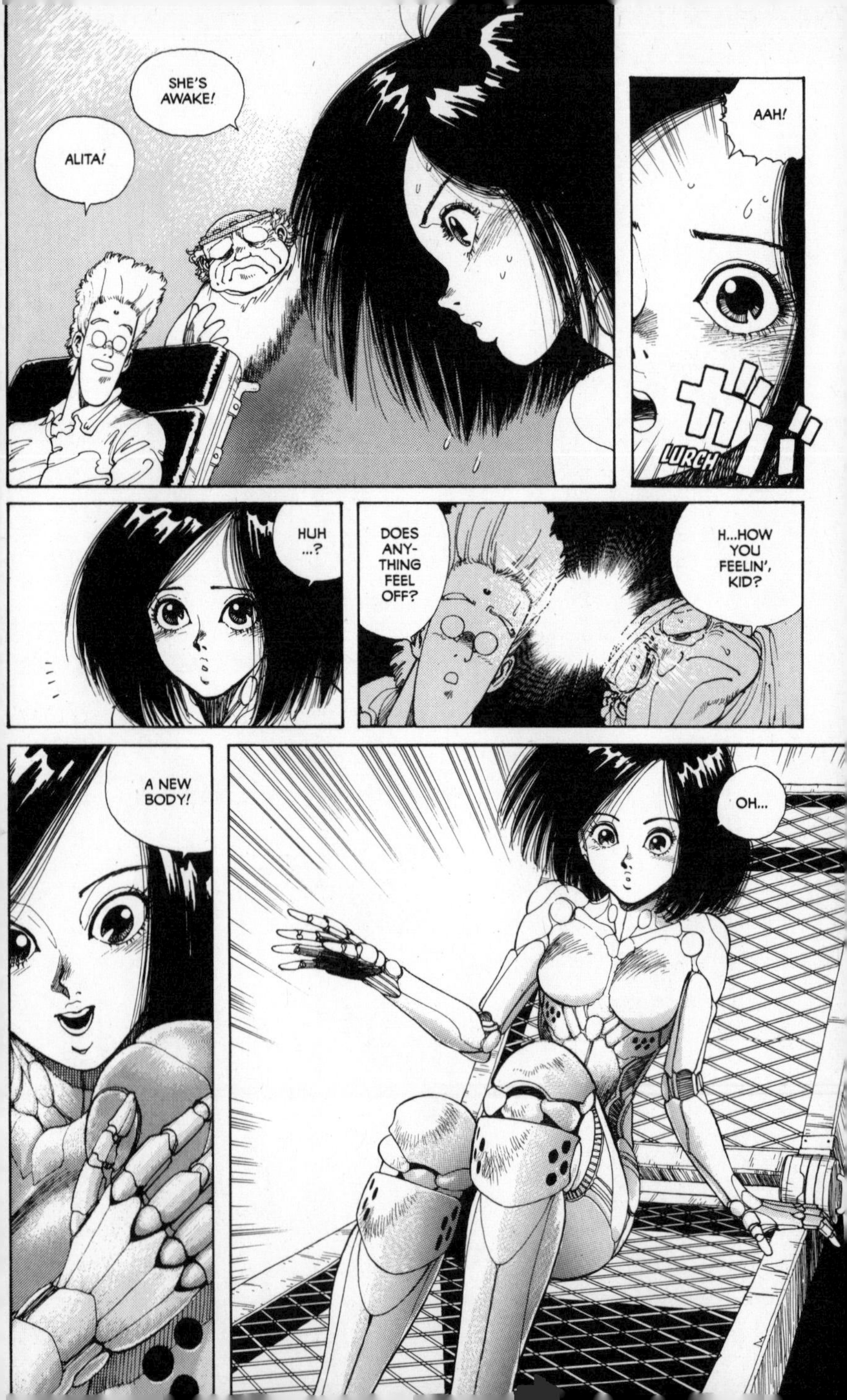
AAH!
ガバ
LURCH
SHE'S AWAKE!
ALITA!
H...HOW YOU FEELIN', KID?
DOES ANY-THING FEEL OFF?
HUH ...?
OH...
A NEW BODY!

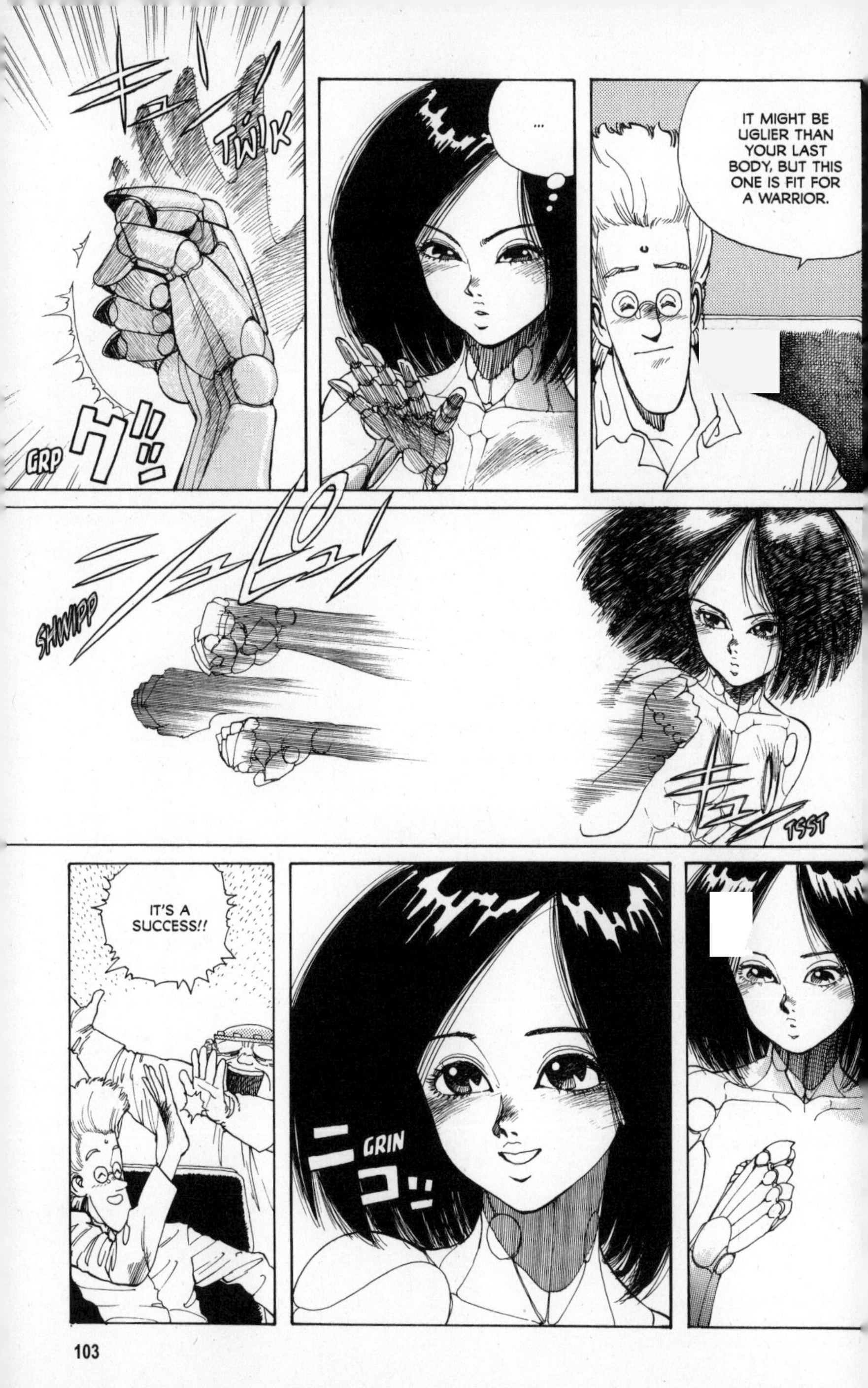

IT MIGHT BE UGLIER THAN YOUR LAST BODY, BUT THIS ONE IS FIT FOR A WARRIOR.
...
TWIK
GRP
TSST
SHWIPP
GRIN
IT'S A SUCCESS!!

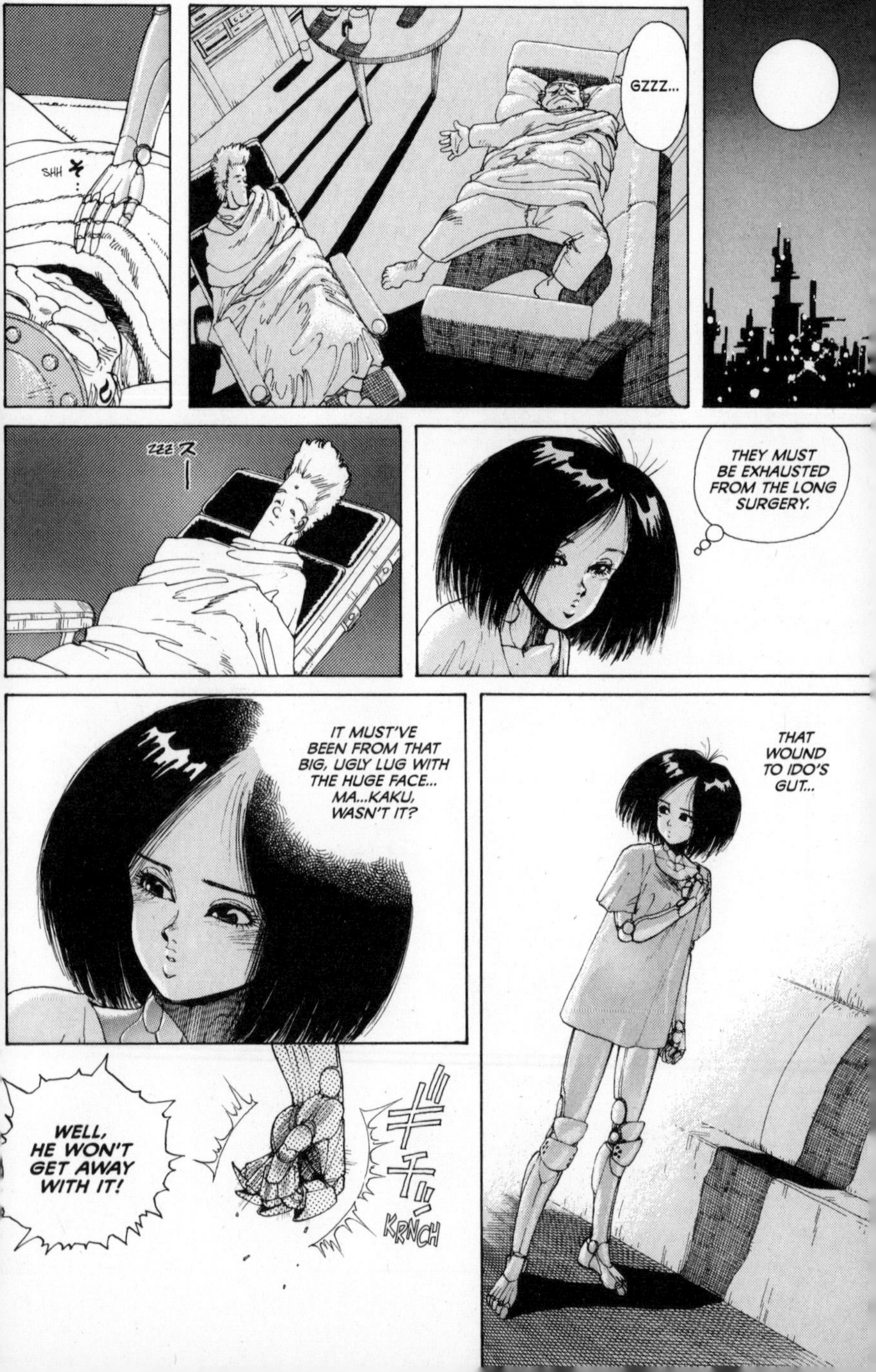
GZZZ...
SHH
THEY MUST BE EXHAUSTED FROM THE LONG SURGERY.
ZZZ スー
THAT WOUND TO IDO'S GUT...
IT MUST'VE BEEN FROM THAT BIG, UGLY LUG WITH THE HUGE FACE... MA...KAKU, WASN'T IT?
WELL, HE WON'T GET AWAY WITH IT!
KRNCH

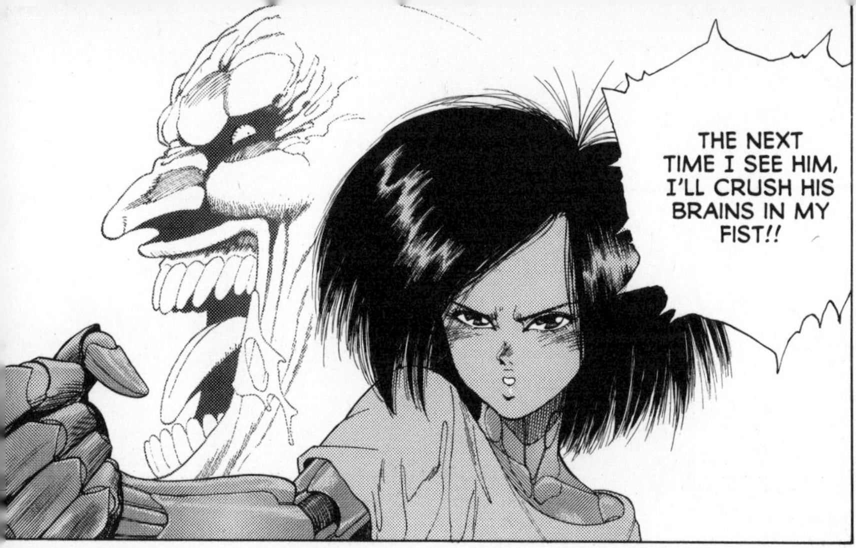
THE NEXT TIME I SEE HIM, I'LL CRUSH HIS BRAINS IN MY FIST!!

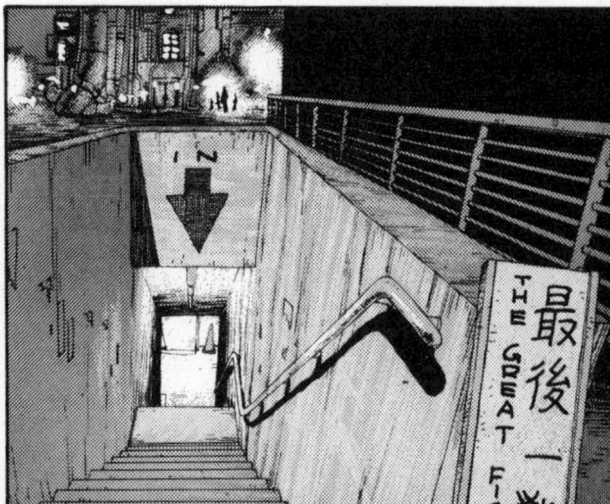
IN
最後一戦
THE GREAT FIGHT

Sign: Final Battle: The Great Fight

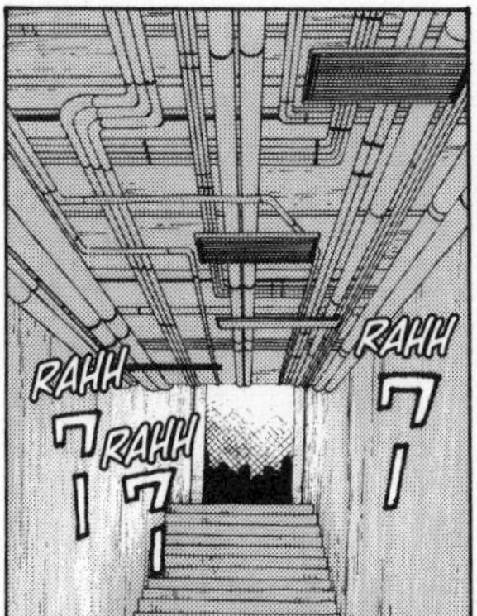
ワー
RAHH
ワー
RAHH
ワー
RAHH

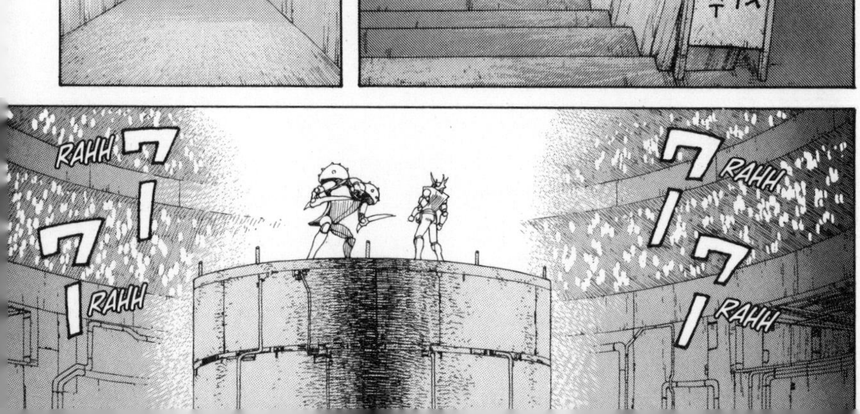
ワー
RAHH
ワー
RAHH
ワー
RAHH
ワー
RAHH

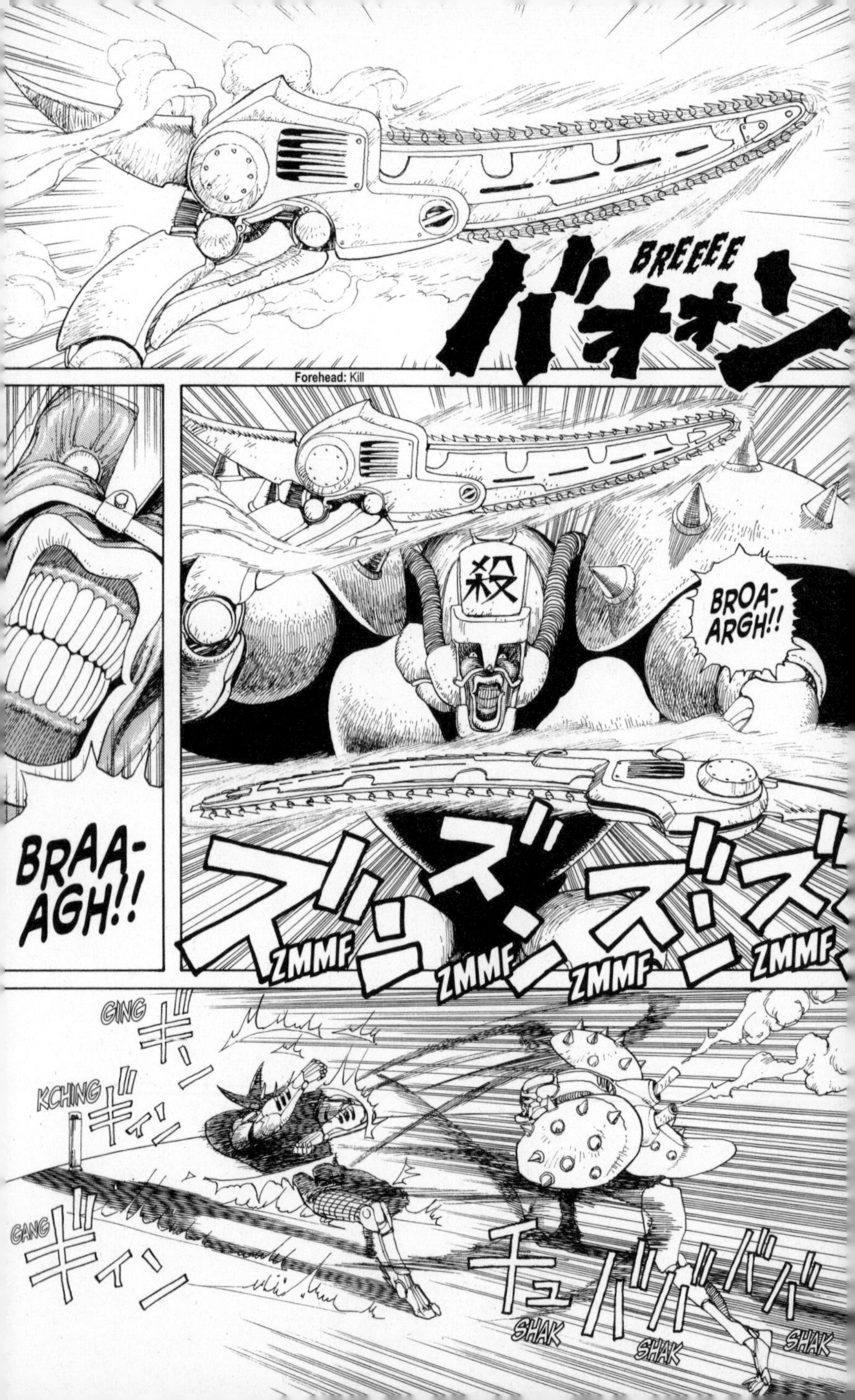
BREEEE
Forehead: Kill
BROA-ARGH!!
ZMMF
ZMMF
ZMMF
ZMMF
BRAA-AGH!!
GING
KCHING
GANG
SHAK
SHAK
SHAK

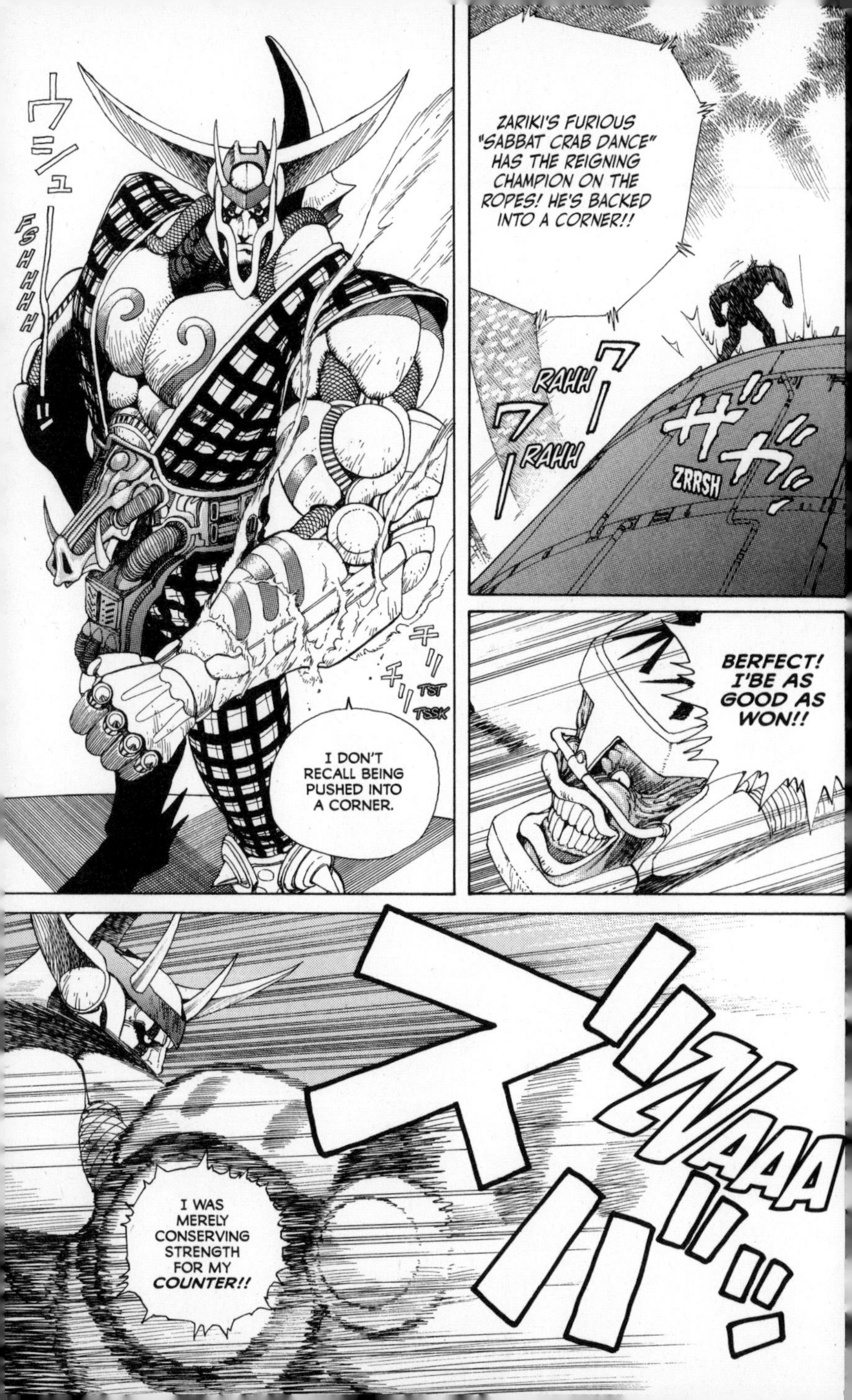

ZARIKI'S FURIOUS "SABBAT CRAB DANCE" HAS THE REIGNING CHAMPION ON THE ROPES! HE'S BACKED INTO A CORNER!!
ワー RAHH
ワー RAHH
ザザ ZRRSH
BERFECT! I'BE AS GOOD AS WON!!
ウシュー FSHHHHH
チリ TST
チリ TSSK
I DON'T RECALL BEING PUSHED INTO A CORNER.
I WAS MERELY CONSERVING STRENGTH FOR MY COUNTER!!
VAAA!!

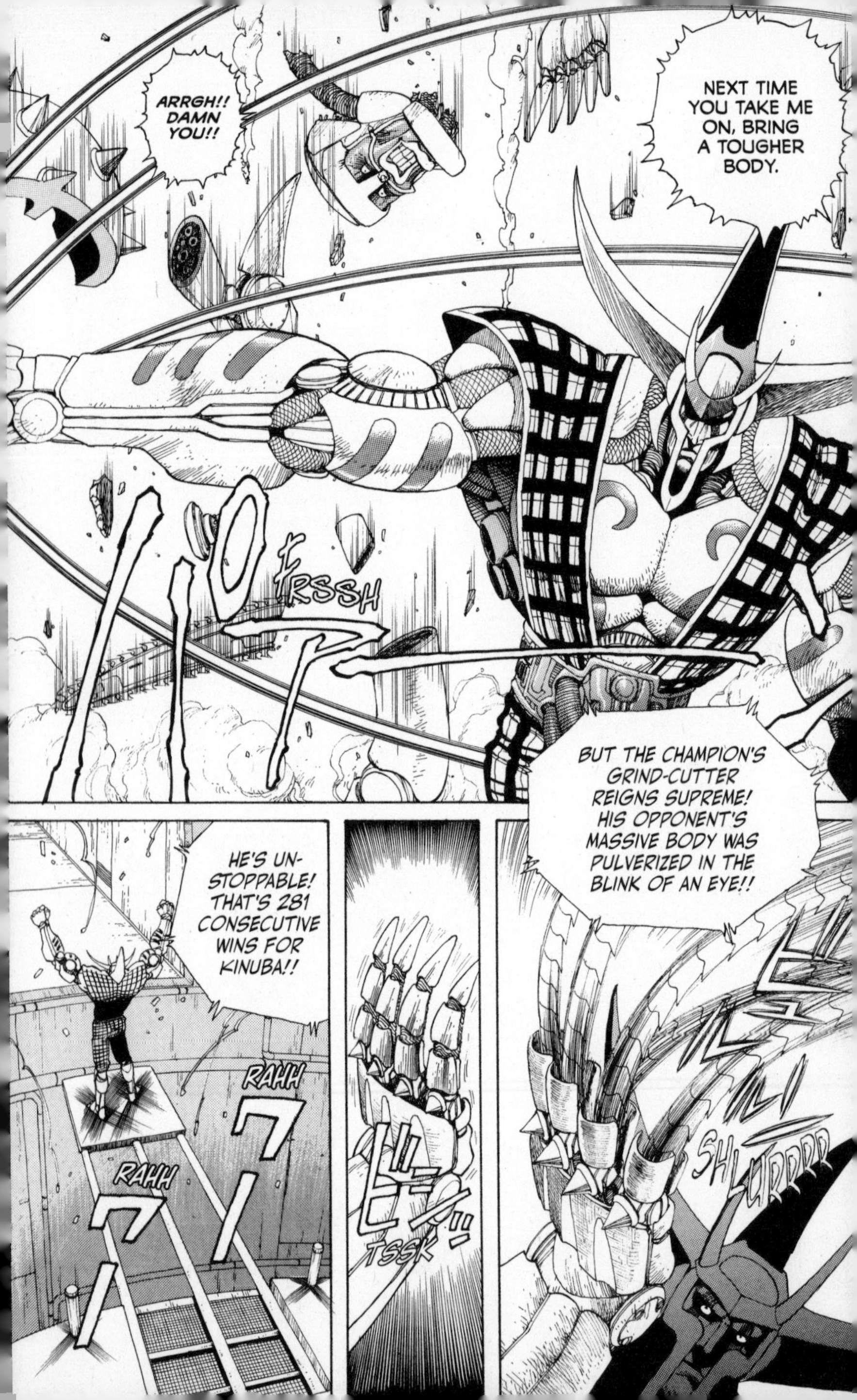
NEXT TIME YOU TAKE ME ON, BRING A TOUGHER BODY.
ARRGH!! DAMN YOU!!
FRSSH
BUT THE CHAMPION'S GRIND-CUTTER REIGNS SUPREME! HIS OPPONENT'S MASSIVE BODY WAS PULVERIZED IN THE BLINK OF AN EYE!!
SHLUDDDD
TSSK
HE'S UN-STOPPABLE! THAT'S 281 CONSECUTIVE WINS FOR KINUBA!!
RAHH
RAHH

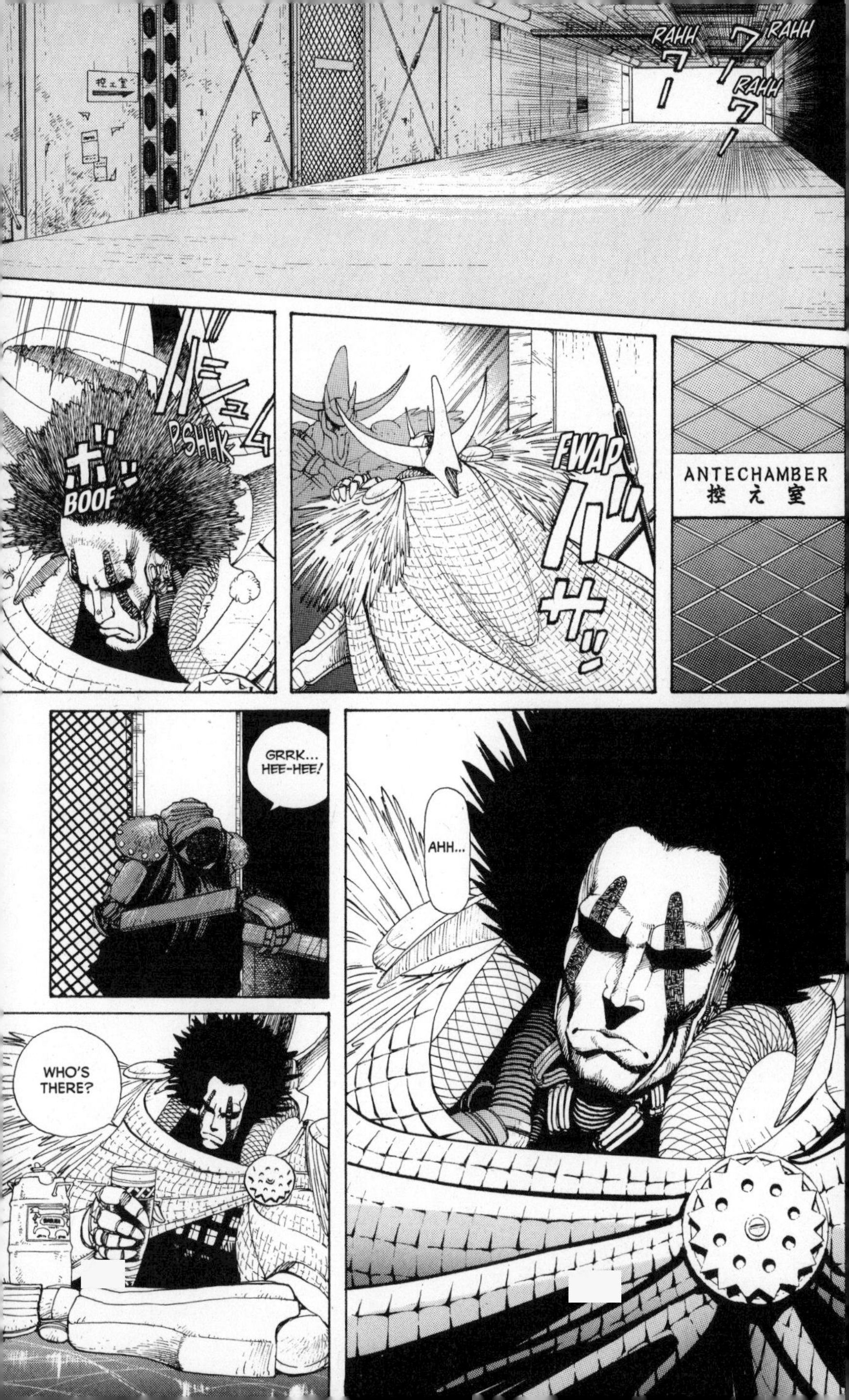
RAHH
RAHH
RAHH
ANTECHAMBER
控え室
FWAP
PSHHK
BOOF
AHH...
GRRK... HEE-HEE!
WHO'S THERE?

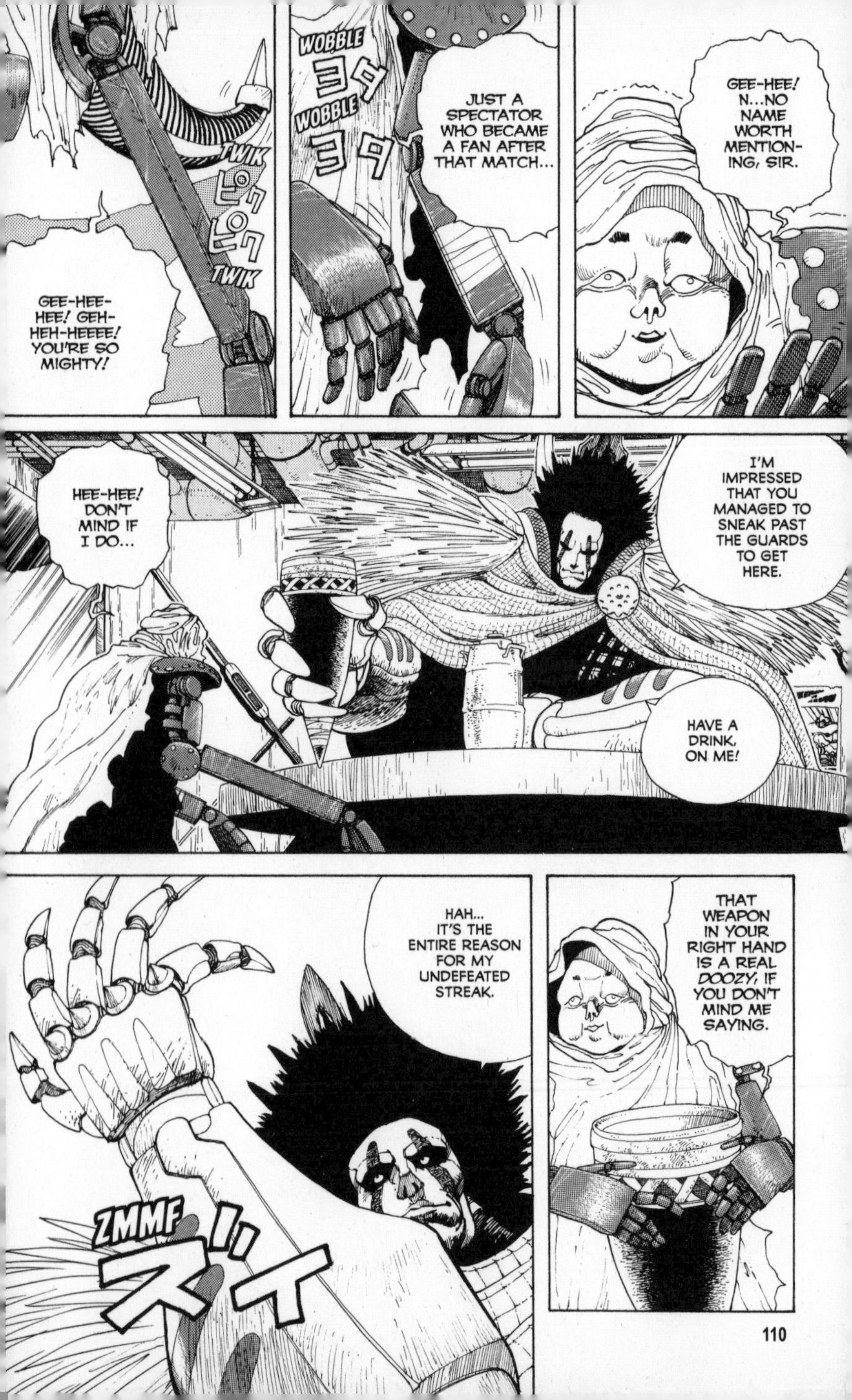
GEE-HEE! N...NO NAME WORTH MENTIONING, SIR.
JUST A SPECTATOR WHO BECAME A FAN AFTER THAT MATCH...
WOBBLE
ヨタ
WOBBLE
ヨタ
TWIK
ピク
ピク
TWIK
GEE-HEE-HEE! GEH-HEH-HEEEE! YOU'RE SO MIGHTY!
I'M IMPRESSED THAT YOU MANAGED TO SNEAK PAST THE GUARDS TO GET HERE.
HAVE A DRINK, ON ME!
HEE-HEE! DON'T MIND IF I DO...
THAT WEAPON IN YOUR RIGHT HAND IS A REAL *DOOZY,* IF YOU DON'T MIND ME SAYING.
HAH... IT'S THE ENTIRE REASON FOR MY UNDEFEATED STREAK.
ZMMF
ズイ

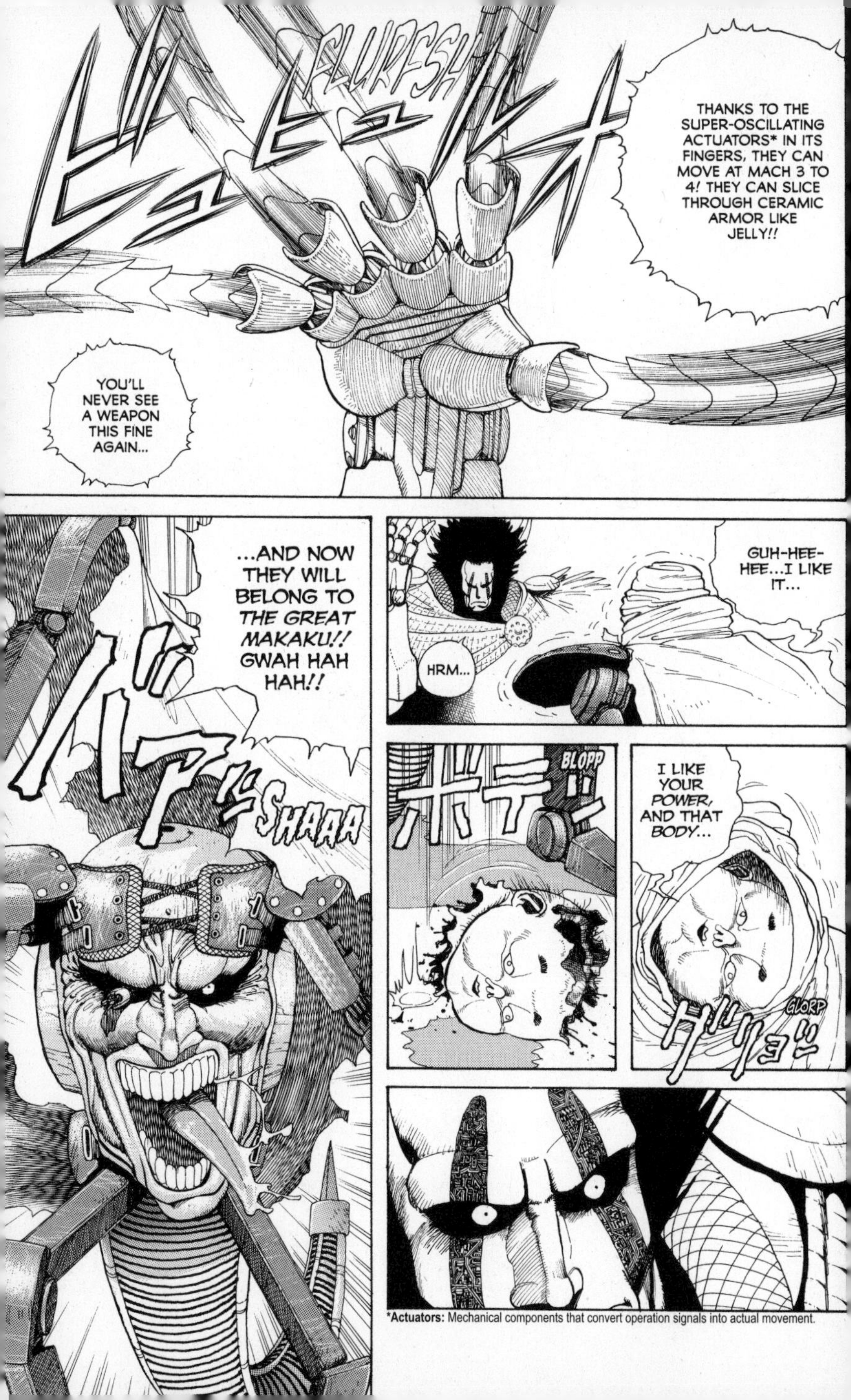
FLURFSH
THANKS TO THE SUPER-OSCILLATING ACTUATORS* IN ITS FINGERS, THEY CAN MOVE AT MACH 3 TO 4! THEY CAN SLICE THROUGH CERAMIC ARMOR LIKE JELLY!!
YOU'LL NEVER SEE A WEAPON THIS FINE AGAIN...
GUH-HEE-HEE...I LIKE IT...
HRM...
I LIKE YOUR POWER, AND THAT BODY...
GLORP
BLOPP
...AND NOW THEY WILL BELONG TO THE GREAT MAKAKU!! GWAH HAH HAH!!
SHAAA

*Actuators: Mechanical components that convert operation signals into actual movement.

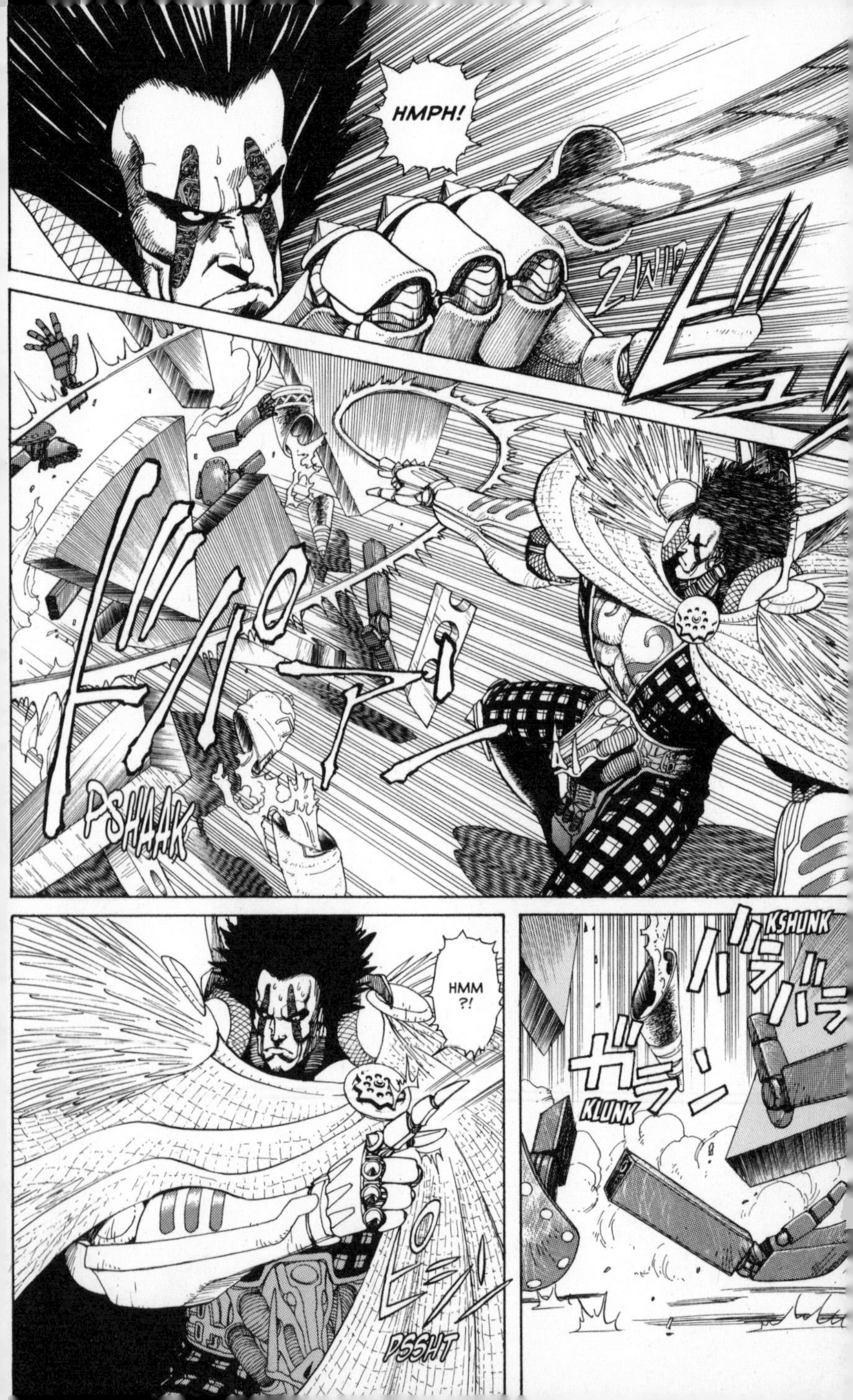
HMPH!
ZWIP
PSHAAK
KSHUNK
KLUNK
HMM ?!
PSSHT

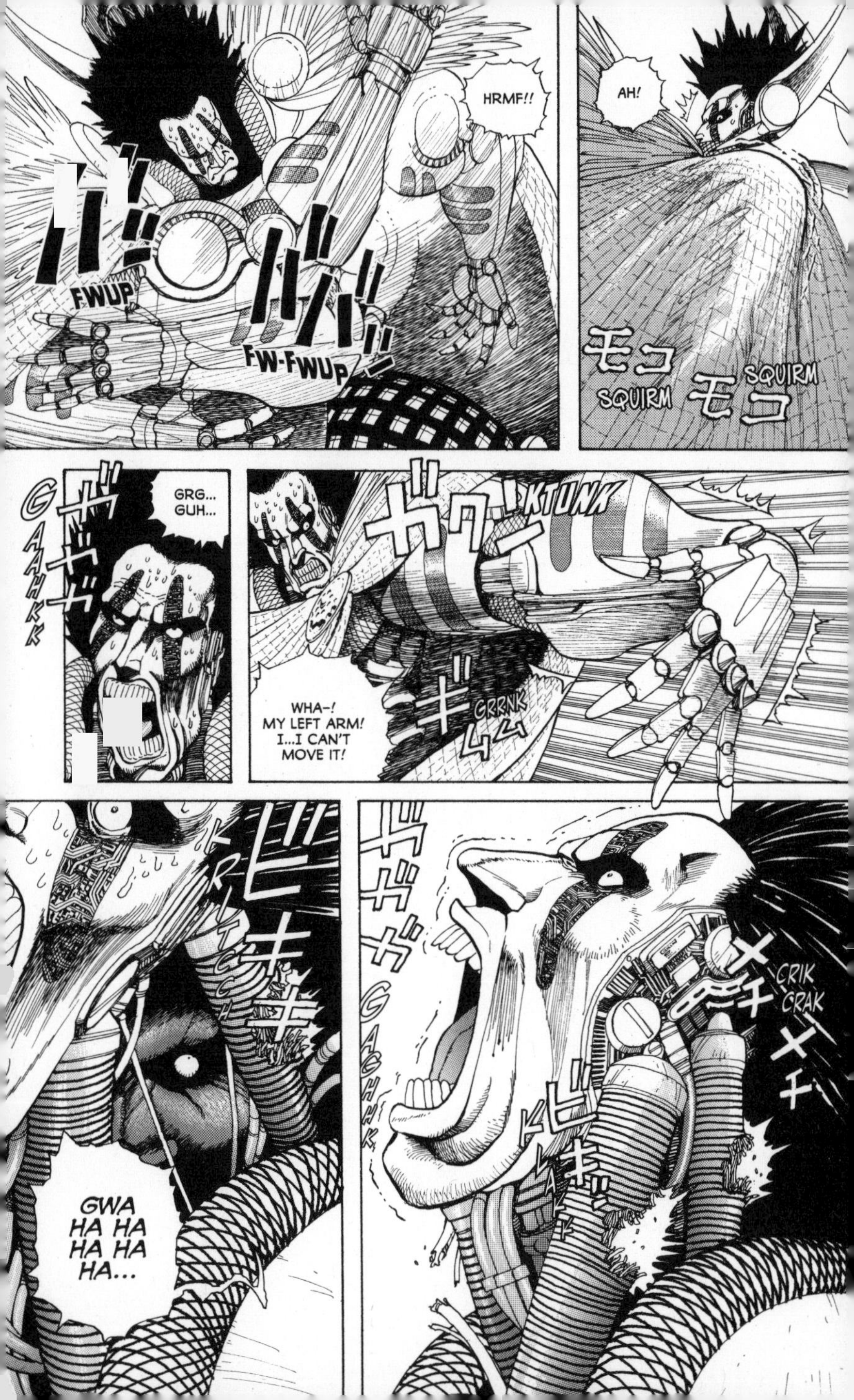
AH!
モコ
SQUIRM
モコ
SQUIRM
HRMF!!
FWUP
FW-FWUP
KTONK
WHA-! MY LEFT ARM! I...I CAN'T MOVE IT!
CRRNK
GRG... GUH...
GAAAHKK
CRIK CRAK
GACHHK
KRITCCH
GWA HA HA HA HA HA...

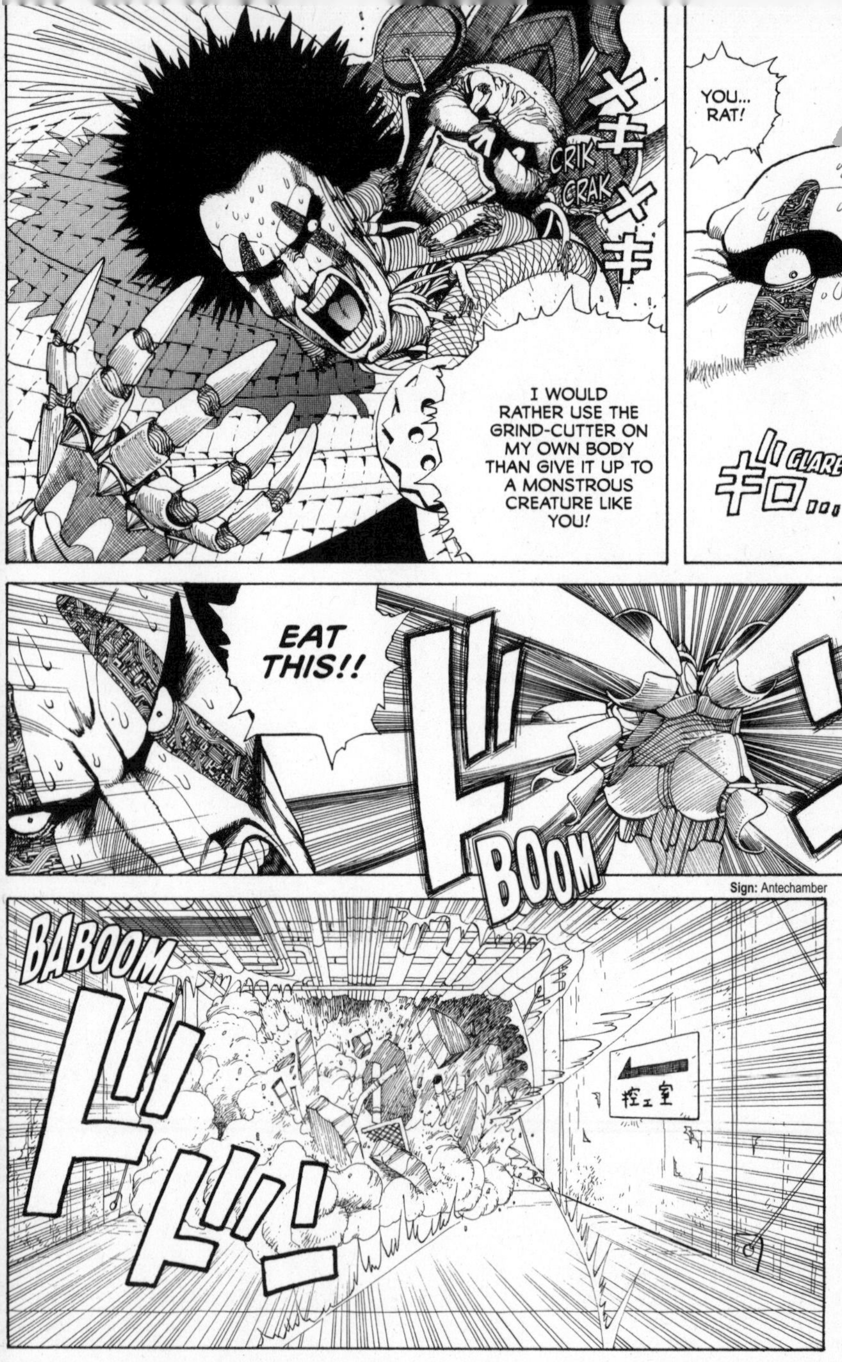
YOU... RAT!
GLARE
CRIK CRAK
I WOULD RATHER USE THE GRIND-CUTTER ON MY OWN BODY THAN GIVE IT UP TO A MONSTROUS CREATURE LIKE YOU!
EAT THIS!!
BOOM
BABOOM

Sign: Antechamber

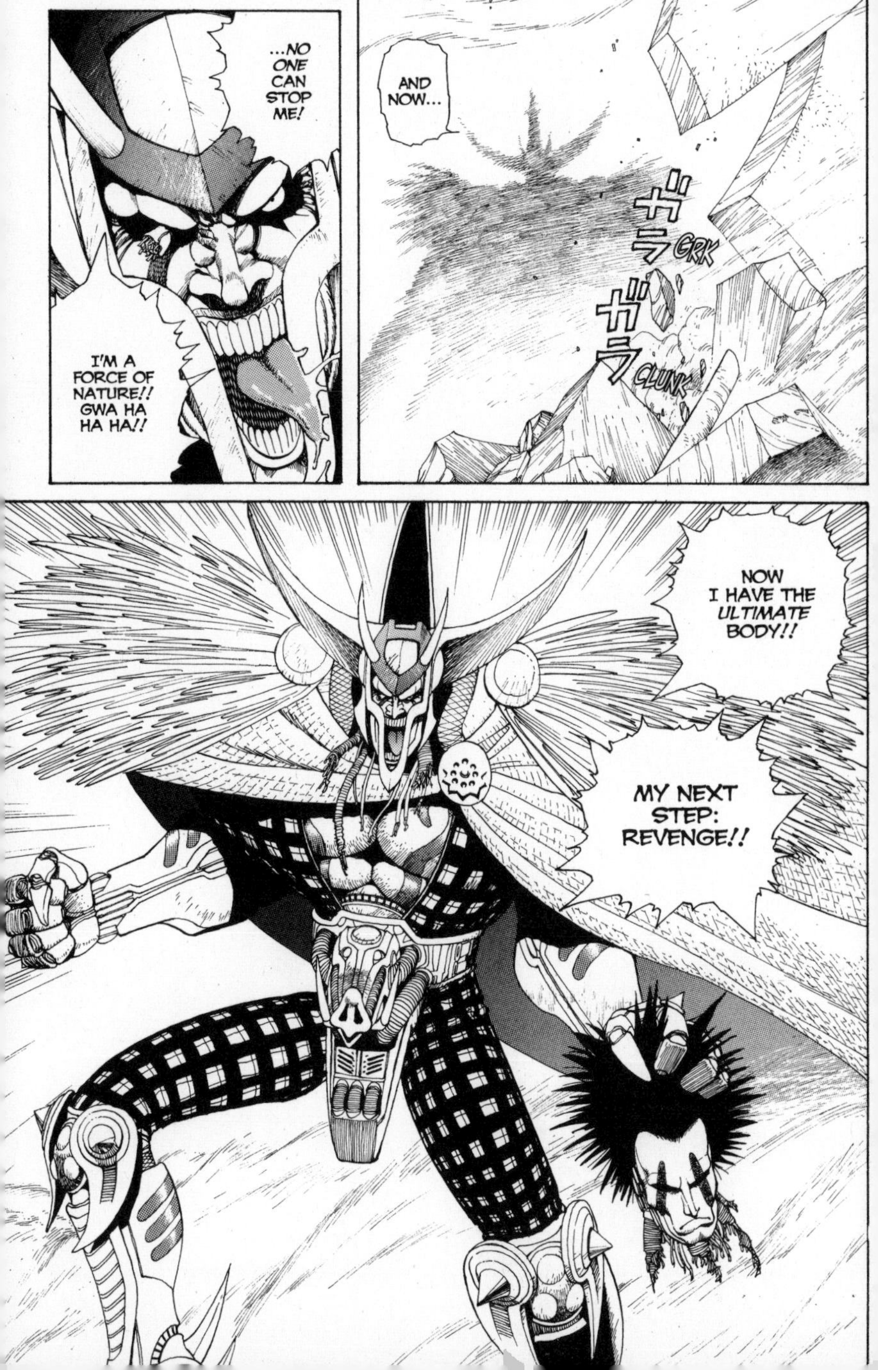
AND NOW...
ガラ GRK
ガラ CLUNK
...NO ONE CAN STOP ME!
I'M A FORCE OF NATURE!! GWA HA HA HA!!
NOW I HAVE THE *ULTIMATE* BODY!!
MY NEXT STEP: REVENGE!!

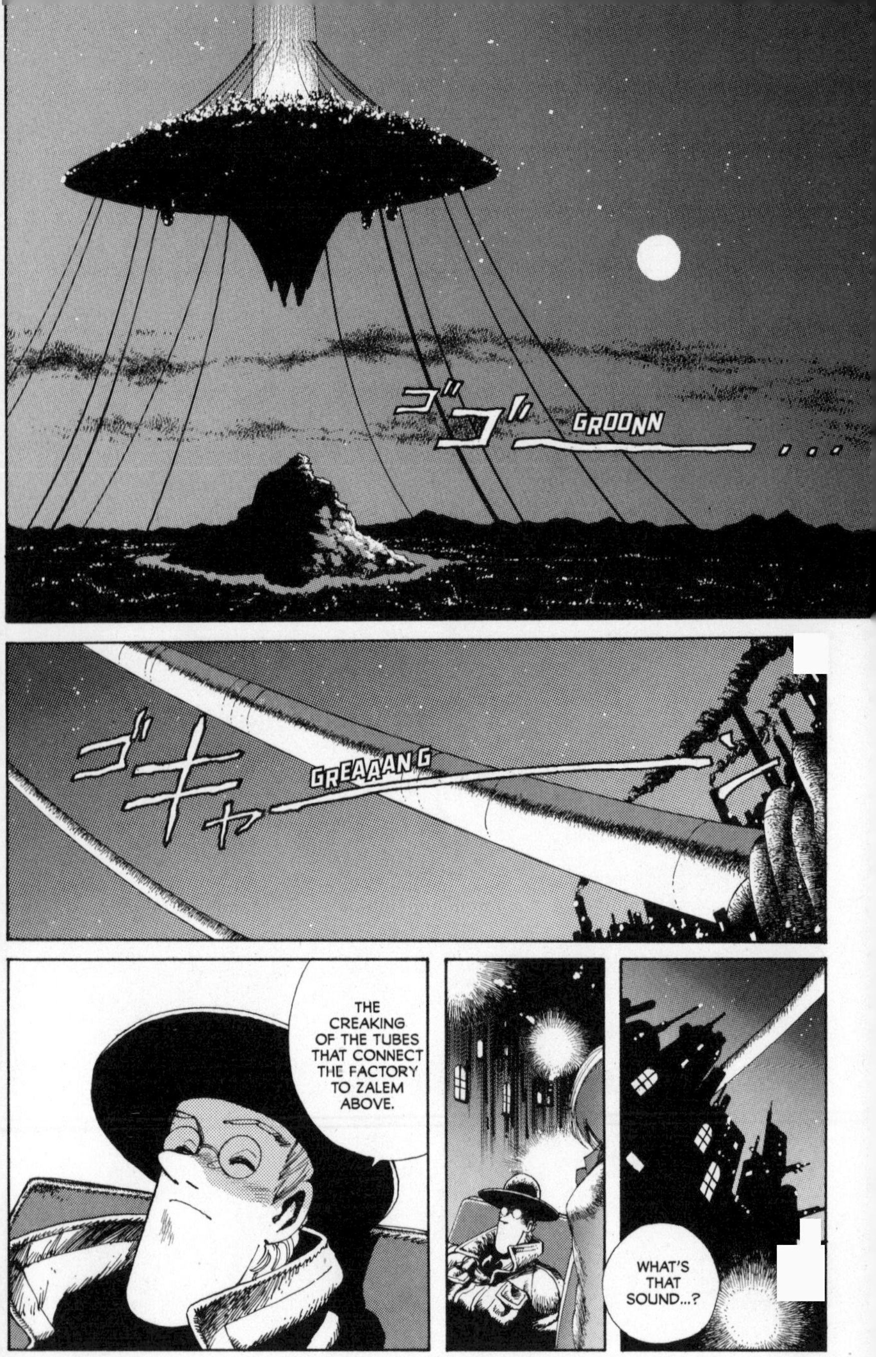
ゴゴー
GROONN
ゴギャー
GREAAANG
WHAT'S THAT SOUND...?
THE CREAKING OF THE TUBES THAT CONNECT THE FACTORY TO ZALEM ABOVE.

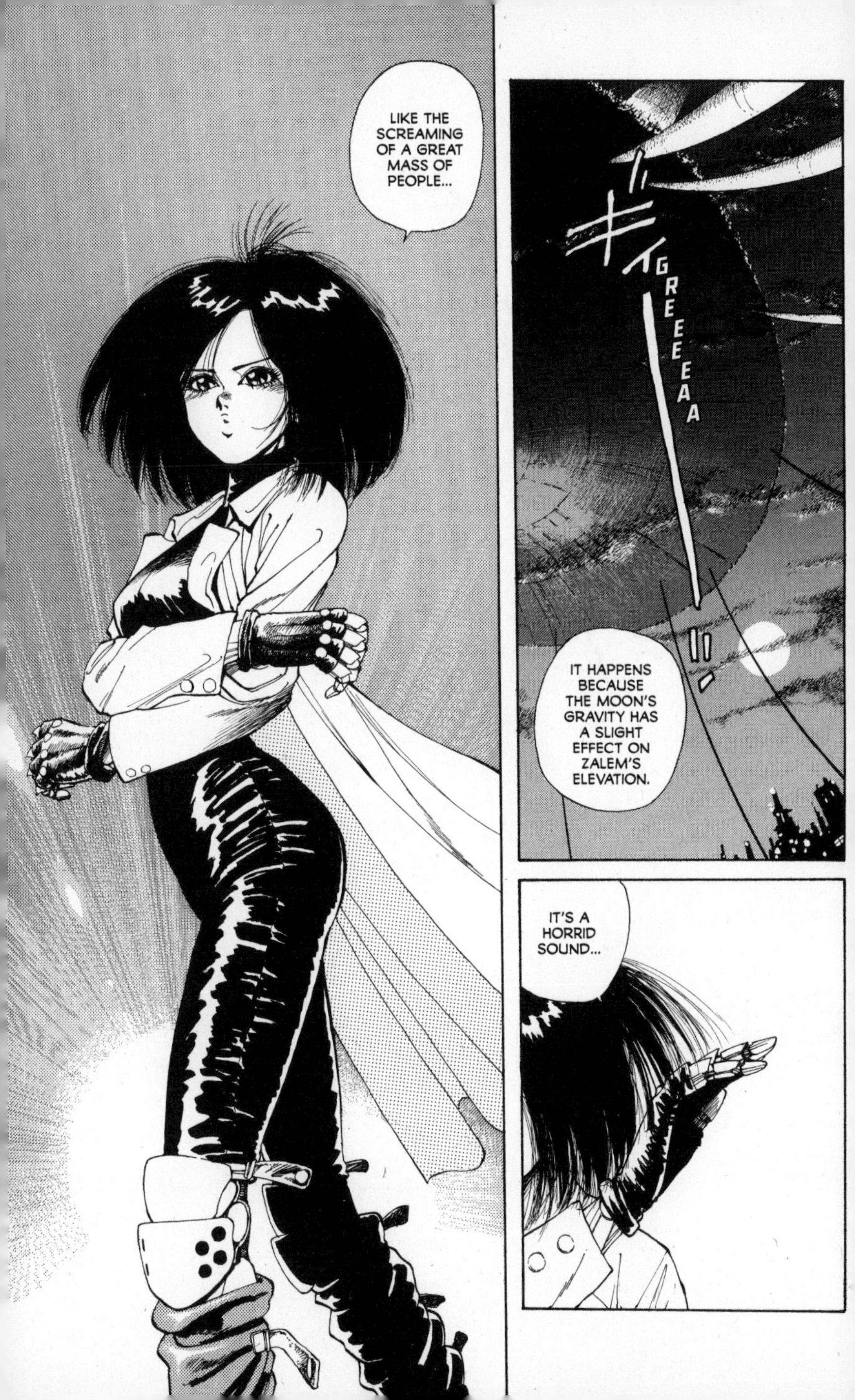
GREEEEAA!!
IT HAPPENS BECAUSE THE MOON'S GRAVITY HAS A SLIGHT EFFECT ON ZALEM'S ELEVATION.
IT'S A HORRID SOUND...
LIKE THE SCREAMING OF A GREAT MASS OF PEOPLE...

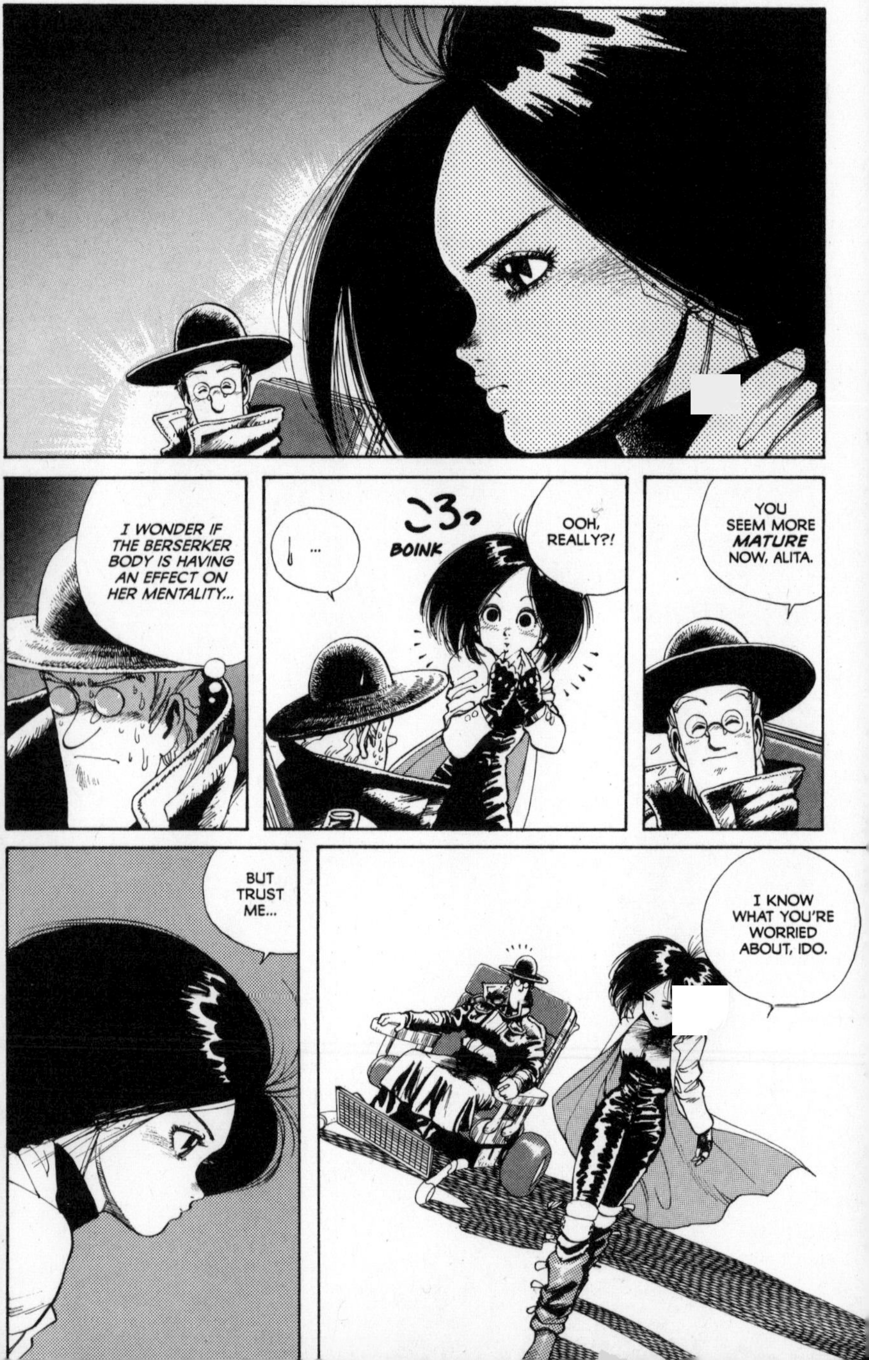
YOU SEEM MORE *MATURE* NOW, ALITA.
OOH, REALLY?!
こるっ
BOINK
...
I WONDER IF THE BERSERKER BODY IS HAVING AN EFFECT ON HER MENTALITY...
I KNOW WHAT YOU'RE WORRIED ABOUT, IDO.
BUT TRUST ME...

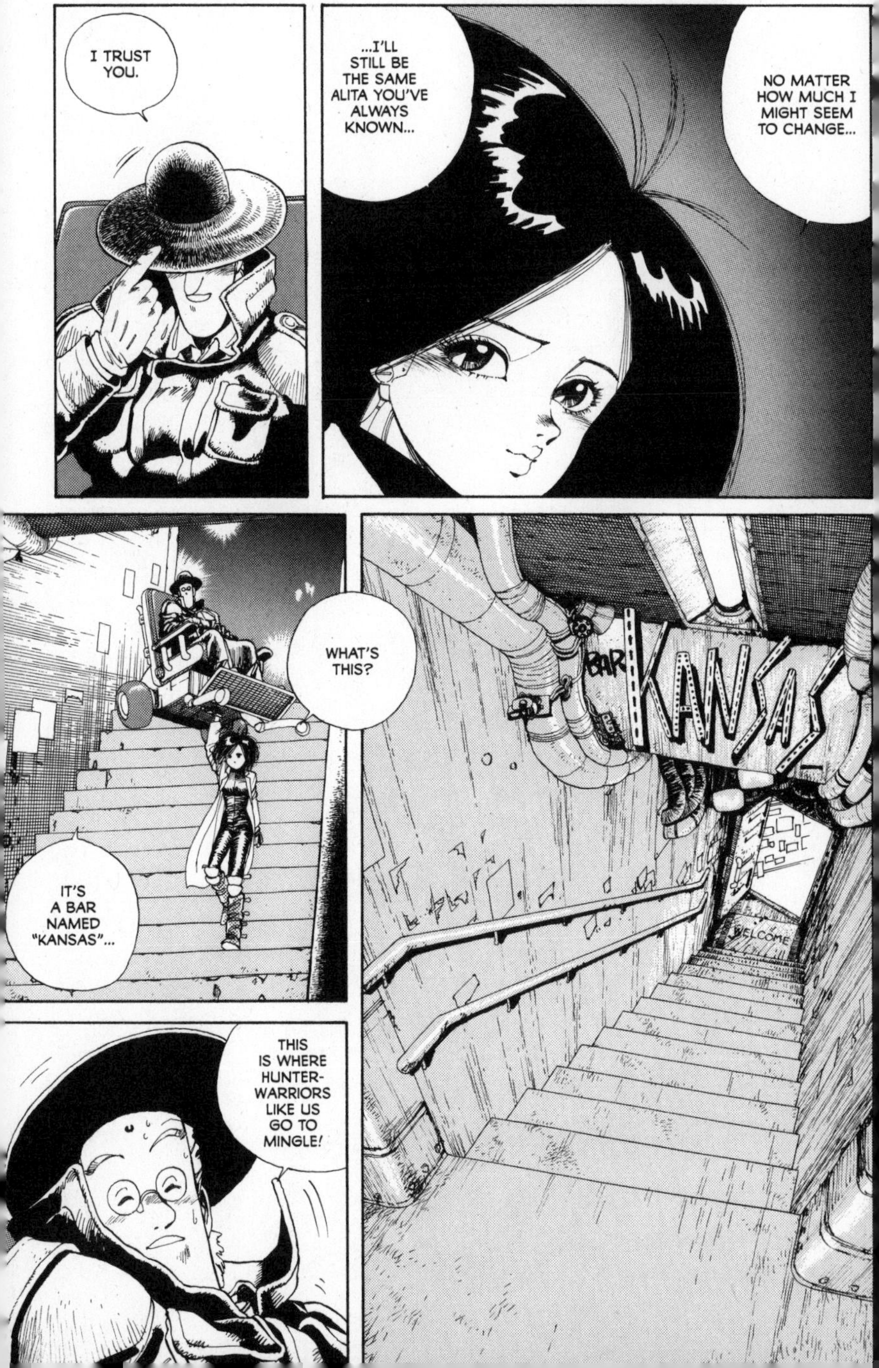
NO MATTER HOW MUCH I MIGHT SEEM TO CHANGE...
...I'LL STILL BE THE SAME ALITA YOU'VE ALWAYS KNOWN...
I TRUST YOU.
BAR
KANSAS
WELCOME
WHAT'S THIS?
IT'S A BAR NAMED "KANSAS"...
THIS IS WHERE HUNTER-WARRIORS LIKE US GO TO MINGLE!

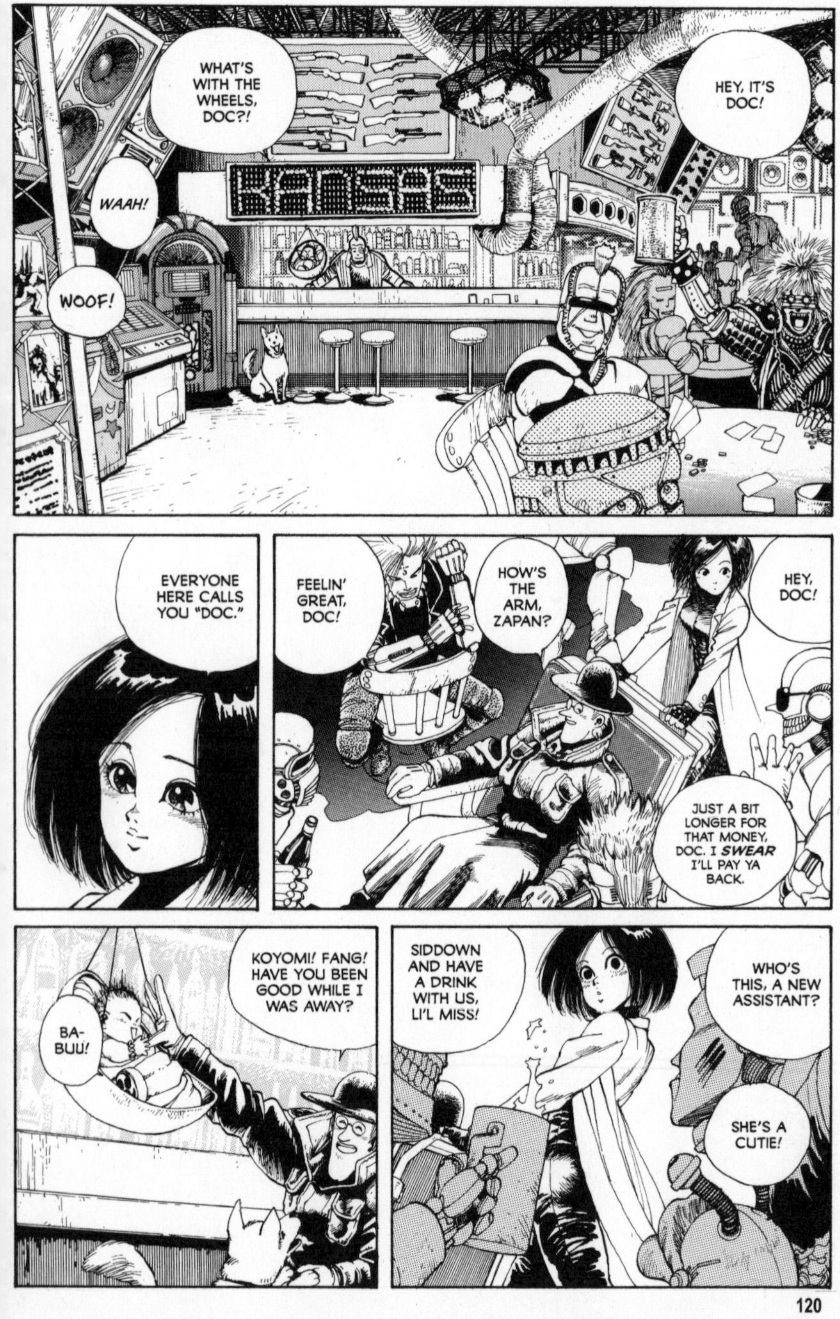
HEY, IT'S DOC!
WHAT'S WITH THE WHEELS, DOC?!
WAAH!
WOOF!
HEY, DOC!
HOW'S THE ARM, ZAPAN?
FEELIN' GREAT, DOC!
JUST A BIT LONGER FOR THAT MONEY, DOC. I *SWEAR* I'LL PAY YA BACK.
EVERYONE HERE CALLS YOU "DOC."
WHO'S THIS, A NEW ASSISTANT?
SIDDOWN AND HAVE A DRINK WITH US, LI'L MISS!
SHE'S A CUTIE!
KOYOMI! FANG! HAVE YOU BEEN GOOD WHILE I WAS AWAY?
BA-BUU!

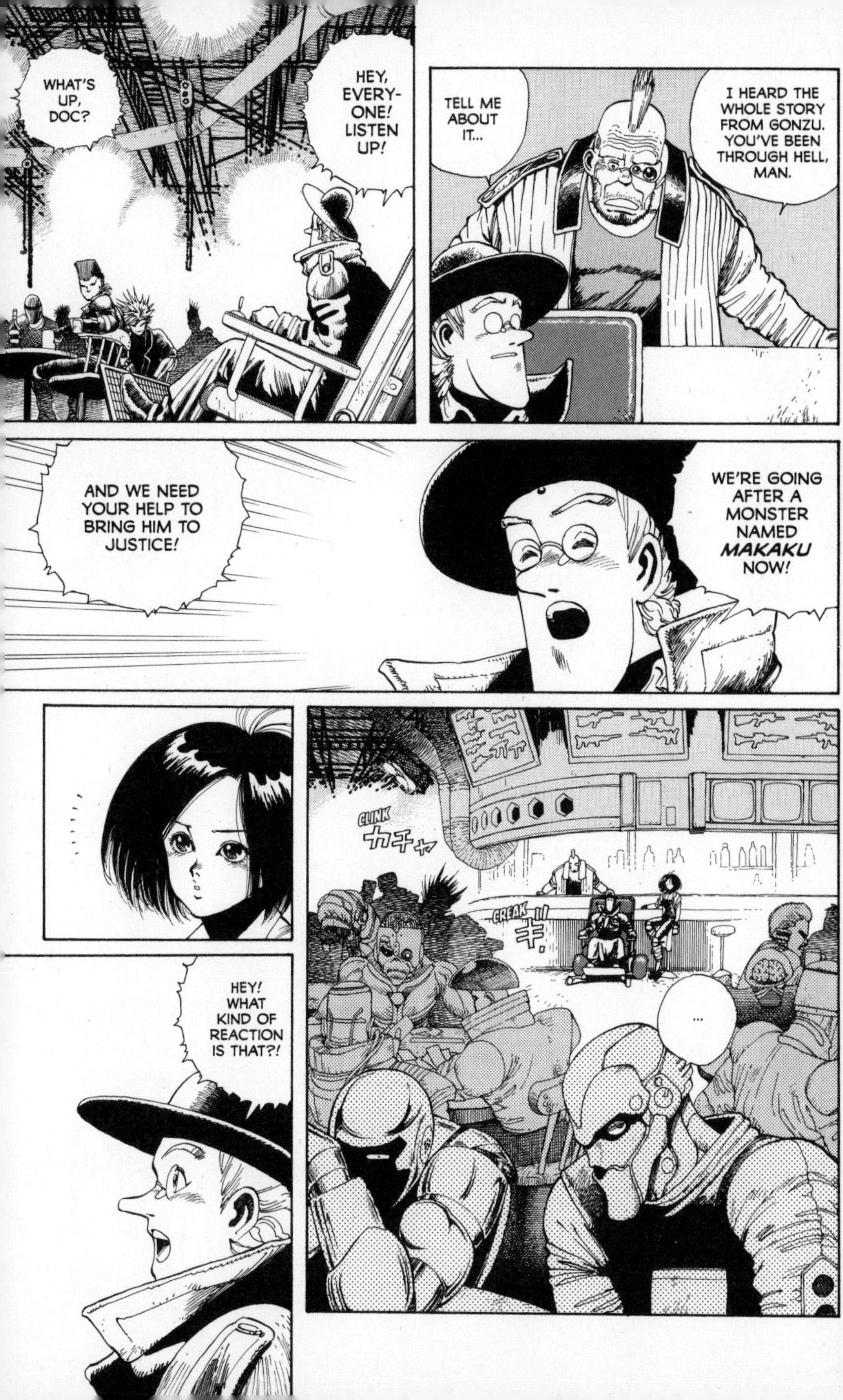
I HEARD THE WHOLE STORY FROM GONZU. YOU'VE BEEN THROUGH HELL, MAN.
TELL ME ABOUT IT...
HEY, EVERYONE! LISTEN UP!
WHAT'S UP, DOC?
WE'RE GOING AFTER A MONSTER NAMED *MAKAKU* NOW!
AND WE NEED YOUR HELP TO BRING HIM TO JUSTICE!
CLINK
カチャ
CREAK
ギ
...
HEY! WHAT KIND OF REACTION IS THAT?!

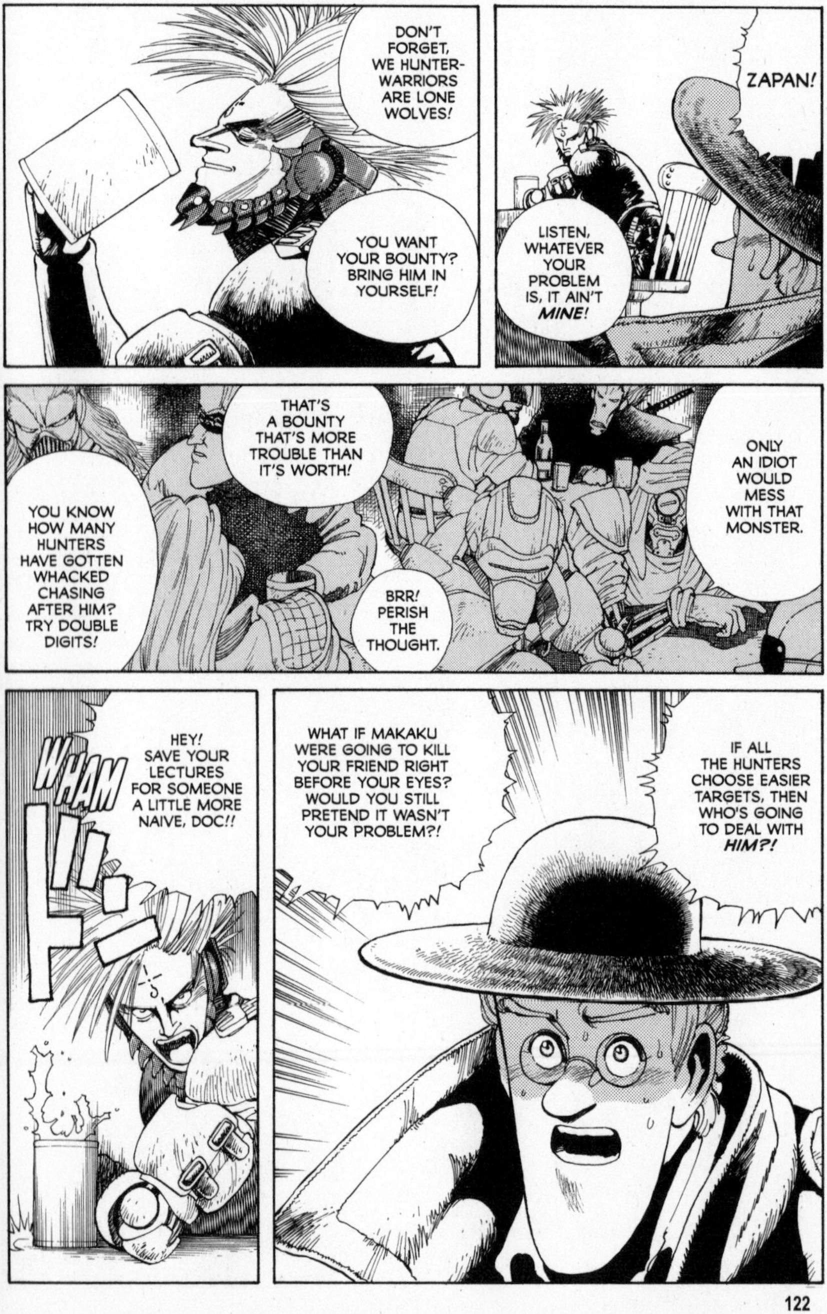
ZAPAN!
LISTEN, WHATEVER YOUR PROBLEM IS, IT AIN'T *MINE!*
DON'T FORGET, WE HUNTER-WARRIORS ARE LONE WOLVES!
YOU WANT YOUR BOUNTY? BRING HIM IN YOURSELF!
ONLY AN IDIOT WOULD MESS WITH THAT MONSTER.
THAT'S A BOUNTY THAT'S MORE TROUBLE THAN IT'S WORTH!
YOU KNOW HOW MANY HUNTERS HAVE GOTTEN WHACKED CHASING AFTER HIM? TRY DOUBLE DIGITS!
BRR! PERISH THE THOUGHT.
IF ALL THE HUNTERS CHOOSE EASIER TARGETS, THEN WHO'S GOING TO DEAL WITH *HIM?!*
WHAT IF MAKAKU WERE GOING TO KILL YOUR FRIEND RIGHT BEFORE YOUR EYES? WOULD YOU STILL PRETEND IT WASN'T YOUR PROBLEM?!
HEY! SAVE YOUR LECTURES FOR SOMEONE A LITTLE MORE NAIVE, DOC!!
WHAM

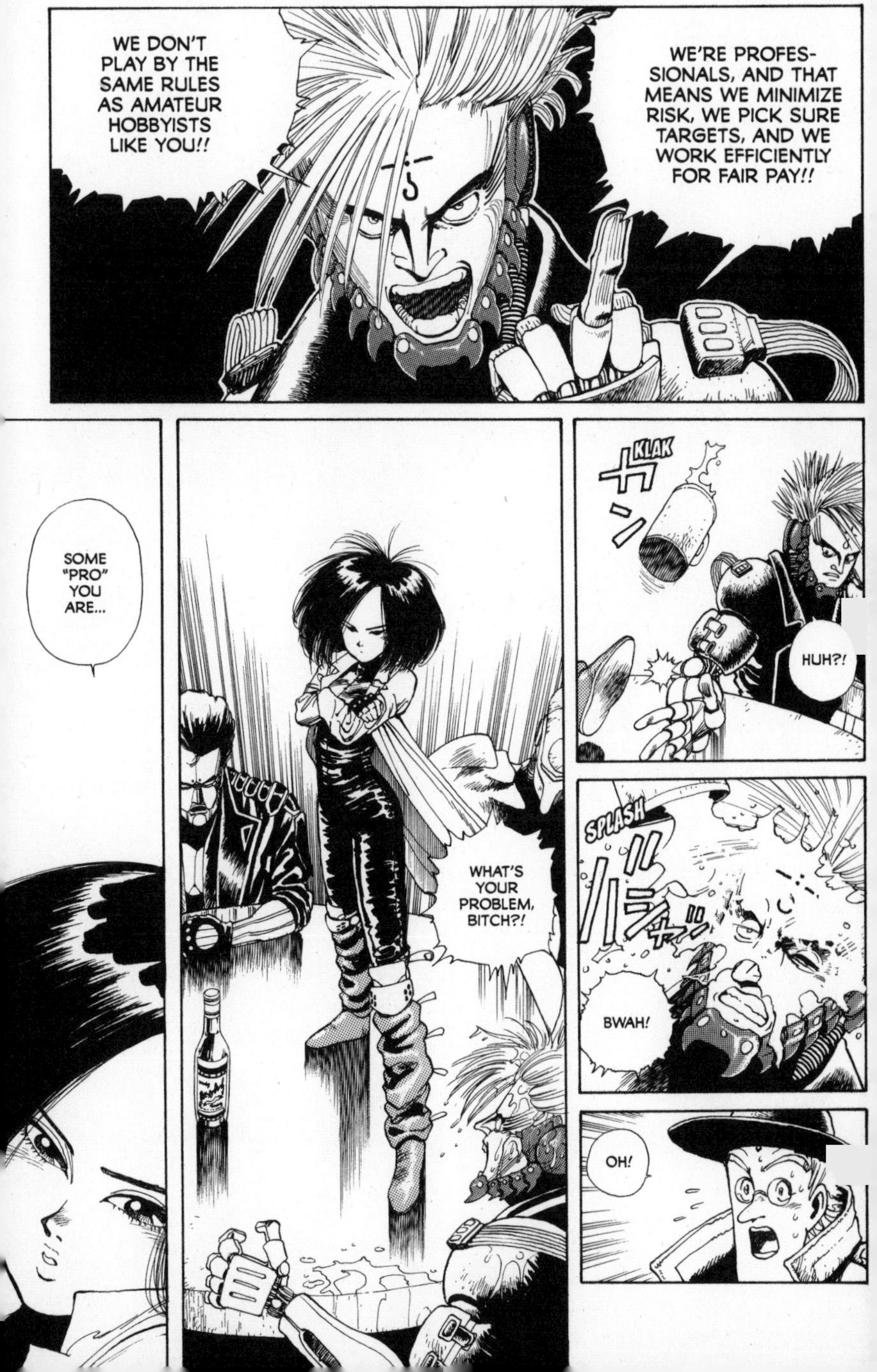
WE'RE PROFES-SIONALS, AND THAT MEANS WE MINIMIZE RISK, WE PICK SURE TARGETS, AND WE WORK EFFICIENTLY FOR FAIR PAY!!
WE DON'T PLAY BY THE SAME RULES AS AMATEUR HOBBYISTS LIKE YOU!!
KLAK
HUH?!
SPLASH
BWAH!
OH!
WHAT'S YOUR PROBLEM, BITCH?!
SOME "PRO" YOU ARE...

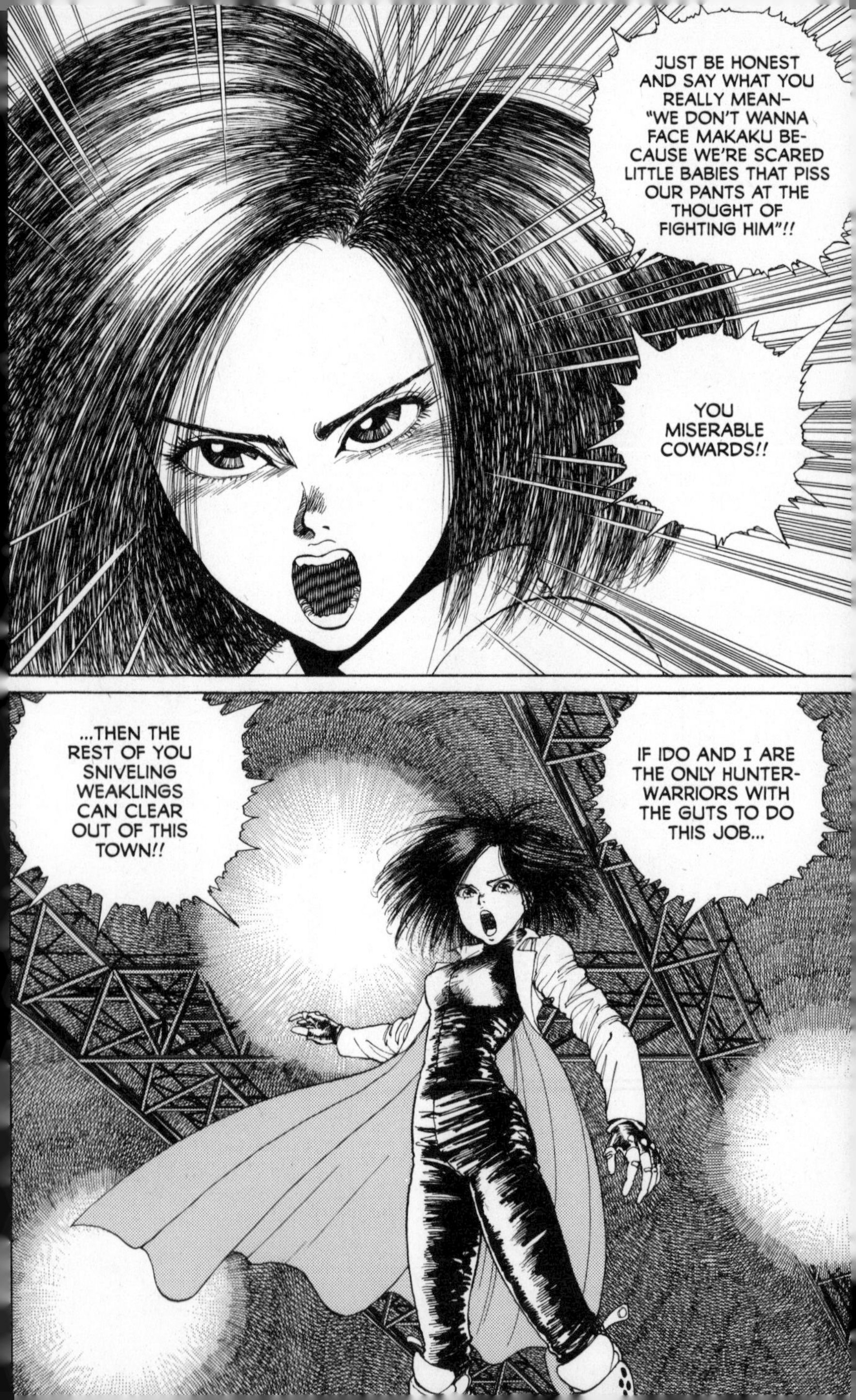
JUST BE HONEST AND SAY WHAT YOU REALLY MEAN– "WE DON'T WANNA FACE MAKAKU BE-CAUSE WE'RE SCARED LITTLE BABIES THAT PISS OUR PANTS AT THE THOUGHT OF FIGHTING HIM"!!
YOU MISERABLE COWARDS!!
IF IDO AND I ARE THE ONLY HUNTER-WARRIORS WITH THE GUTS TO DO THIS JOB...
...THEN THE REST OF YOU SNIVELING WEAKLINGS CAN CLEAR OUT OF THIS TOWN!!

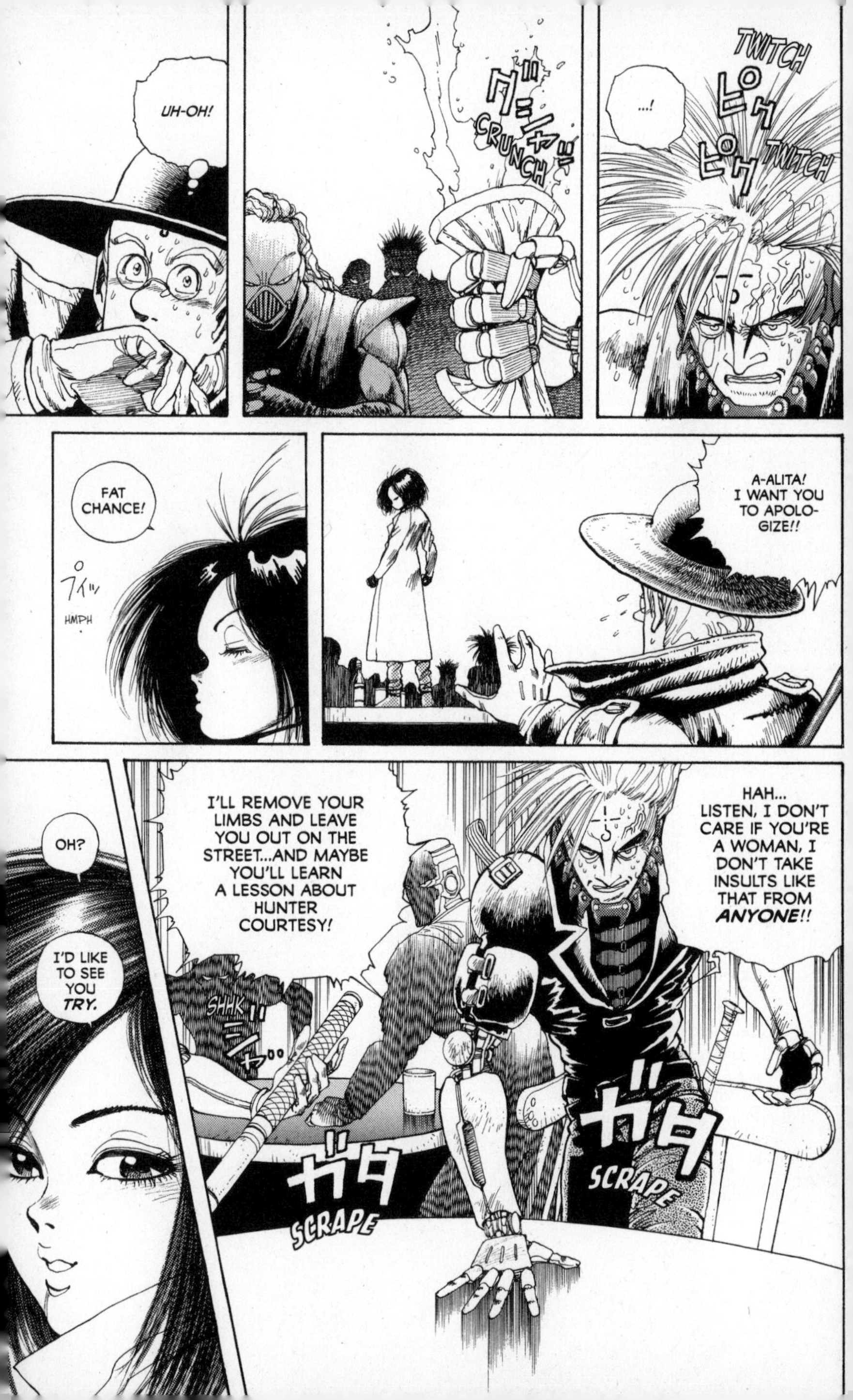

...!
TWITCH
TWITCH
CRUNCH
UH-OH!
A-ALITA! I WANT YOU TO APOLOGIZE!!
FAT CHANCE!
HMPH
HAH... LISTEN, I DON'T CARE IF YOU'RE A WOMAN, I DON'T TAKE INSULTS LIKE THAT FROM ANYONE!!
I'LL REMOVE YOUR LIMBS AND LEAVE YOU OUT ON THE STREET...AND MAYBE YOU'LL LEARN A LESSON ABOUT HUNTER COURTESY!
SHHK
ガタ
SCRAPE
ガタ
SCRAPE
OH?
I'D LIKE TO SEE YOU TRY.

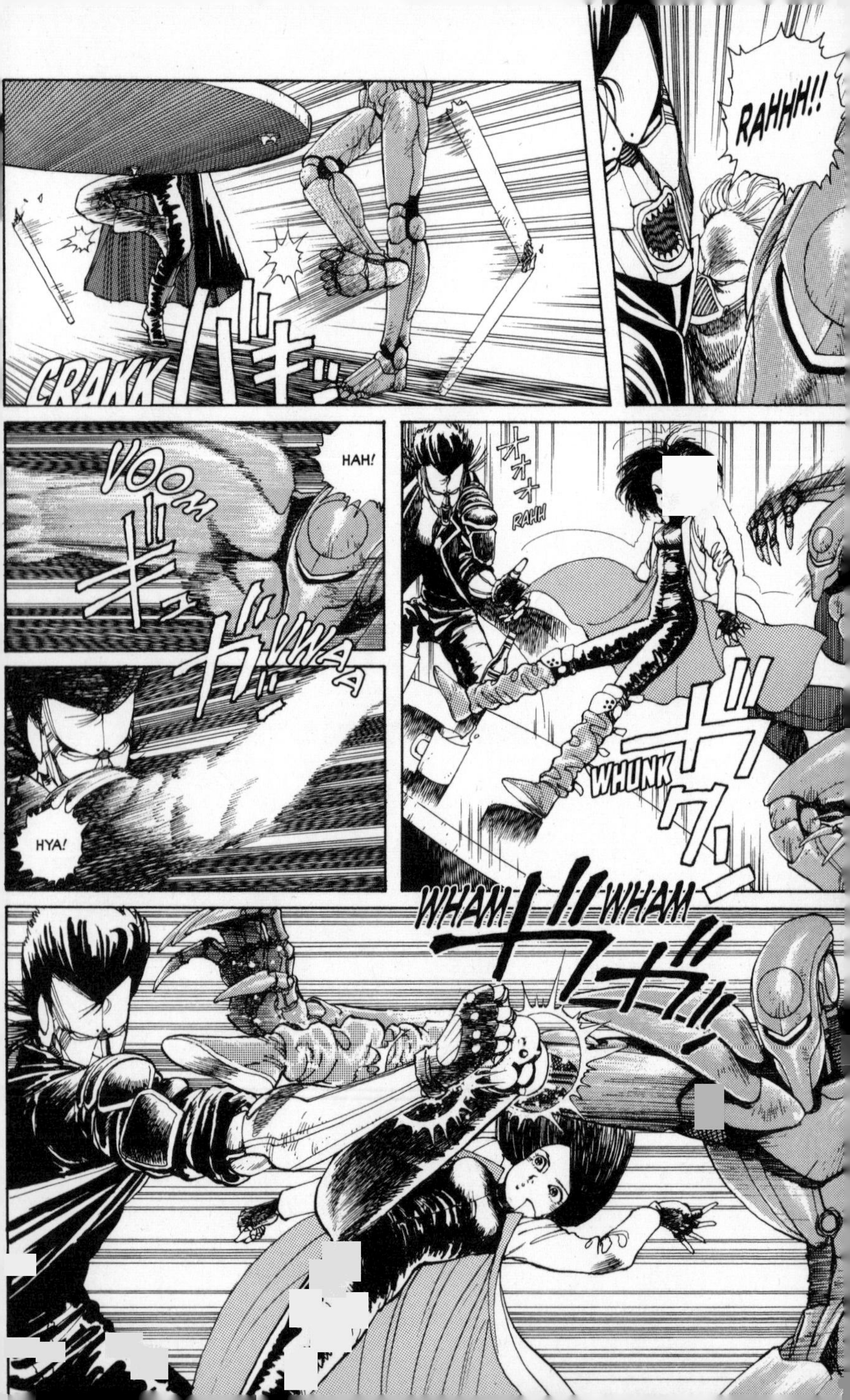
RAHHH!!
CRAKK
RAHH
WHUNK
HAH!
VOOM
VWAA
HYA!
WHAM
WHAM

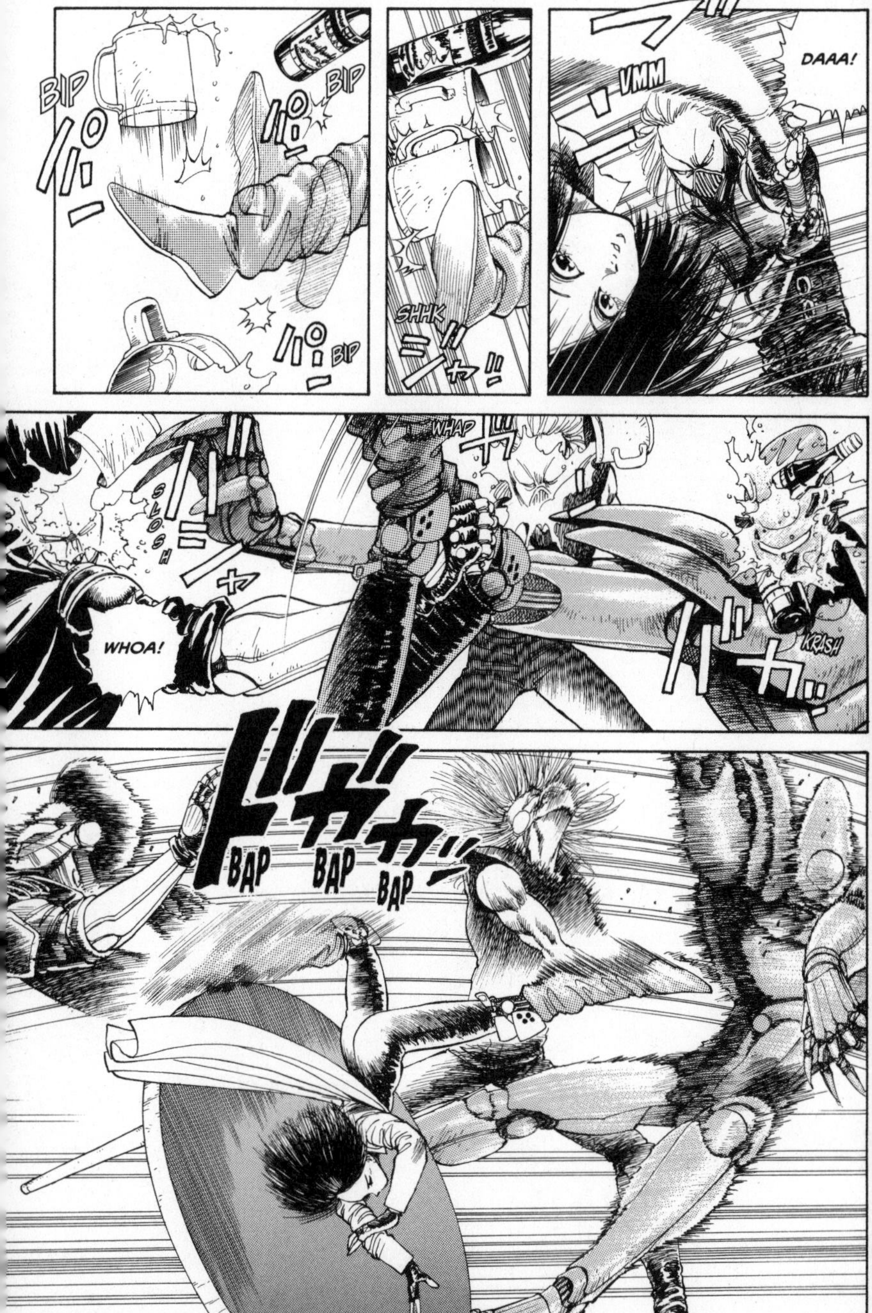
DAAA!
VMM
SHHK
BIP
BIP
BIP
WHAP
SLOSH
KRASH
WHOA!
BAP
BAP
BAP

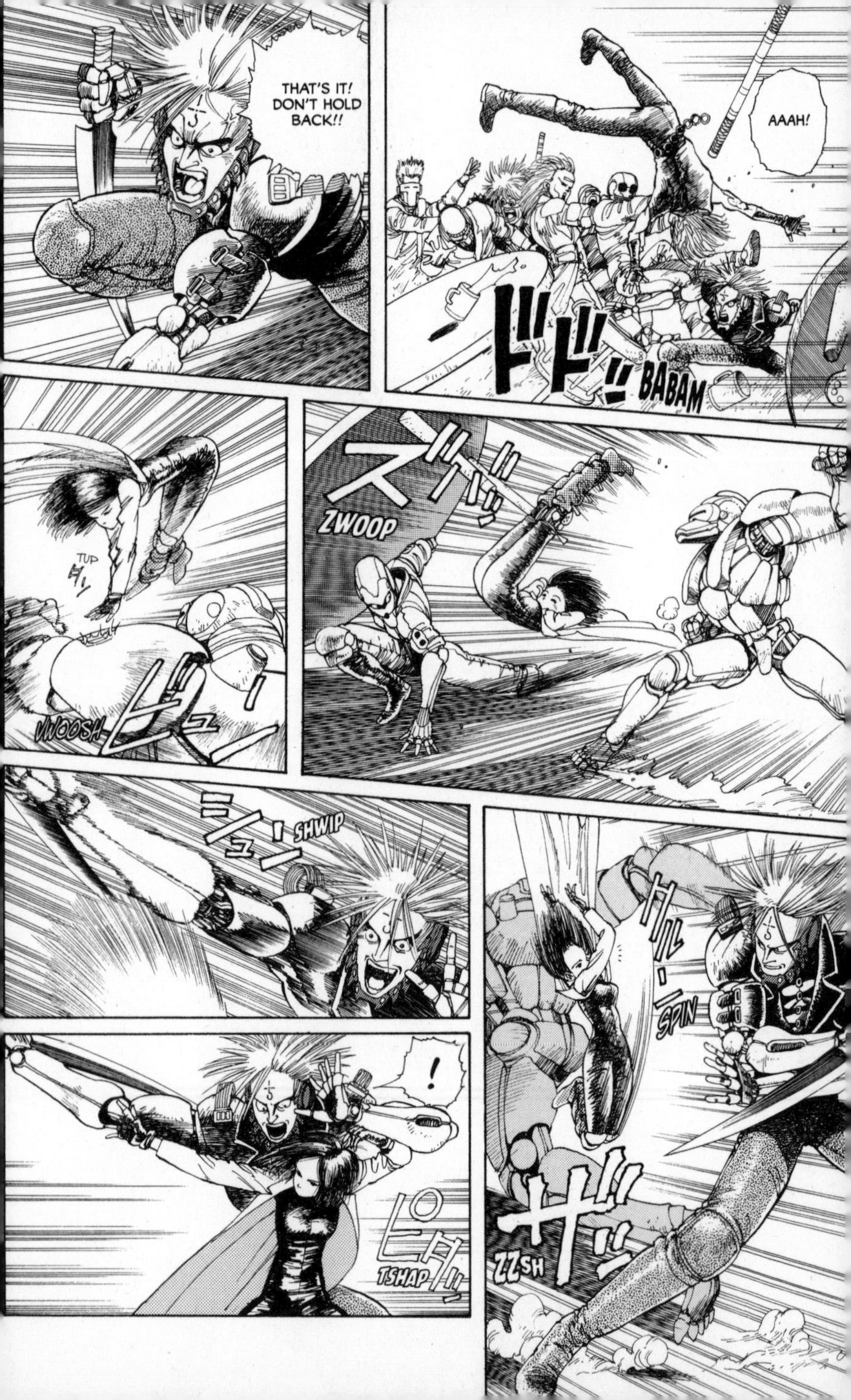
AAAH!
BABAM
THAT'S IT! DON'T HOLD BACK!!
ZWOOP
TUP
VWOOSH
SPIN
ZZSH
SHWIP
!
TSHAP

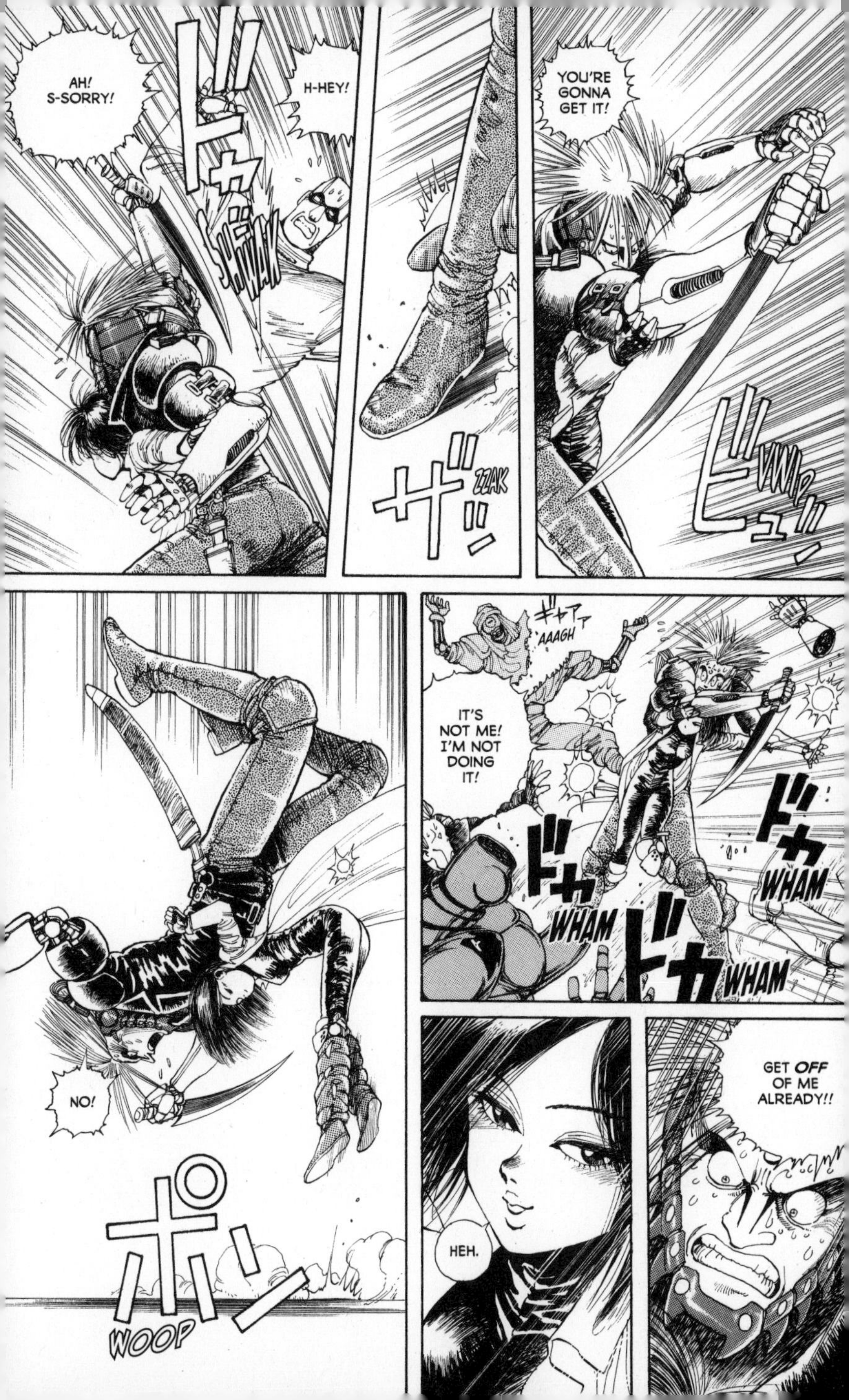
YOU'RE GONNA GET IT!
ZZAK
H-HEY!
AH! S-SORRY!
'AAAGH
IT'S NOT ME! I'M NOT DOING IT!
WHAM
WHAM
WHAM
GET OFF OF ME ALREADY!!
HEH.
NO!
WOOP

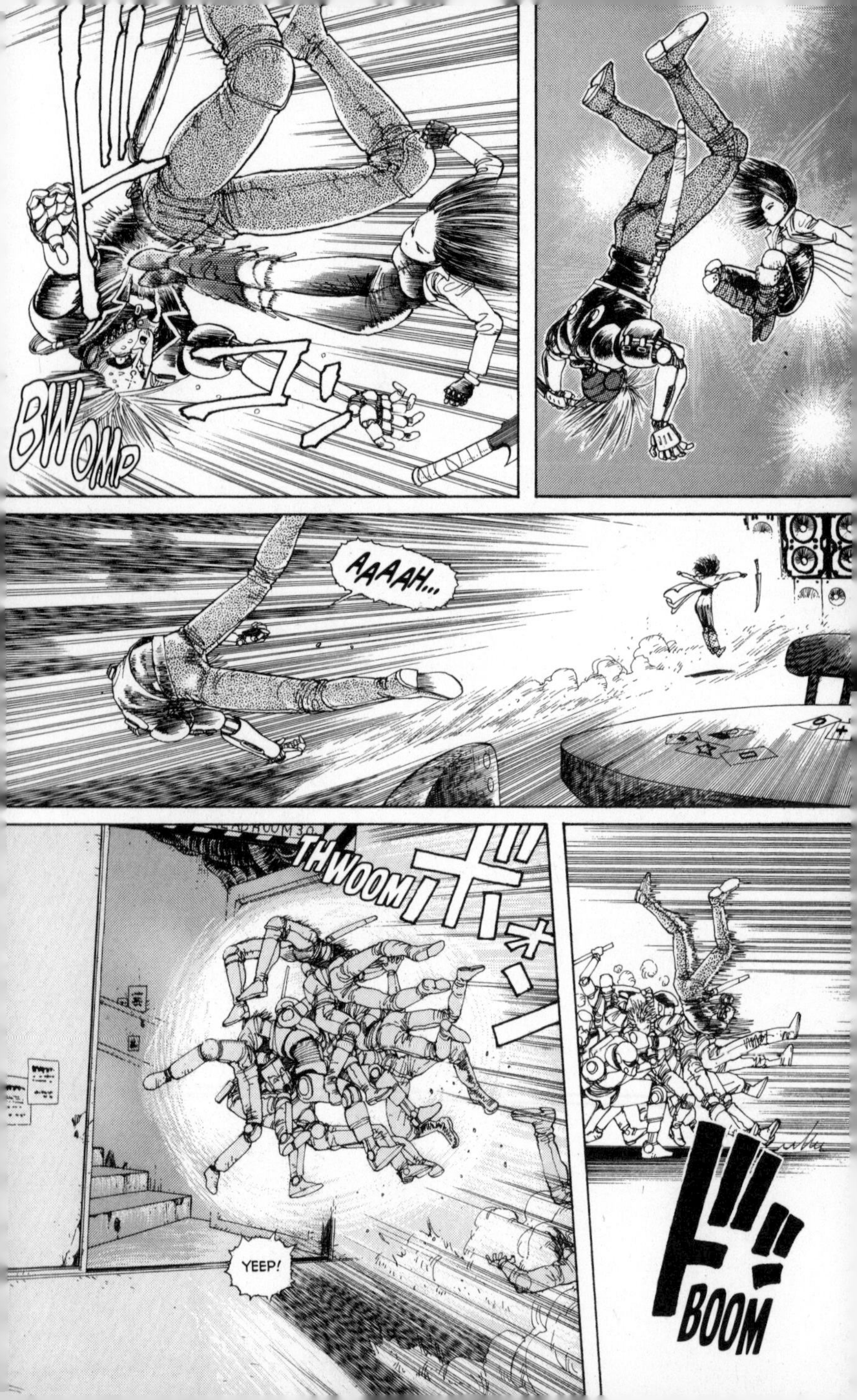
BWOMP
AAAAH...
BOOM
THWOOM
YEEP!

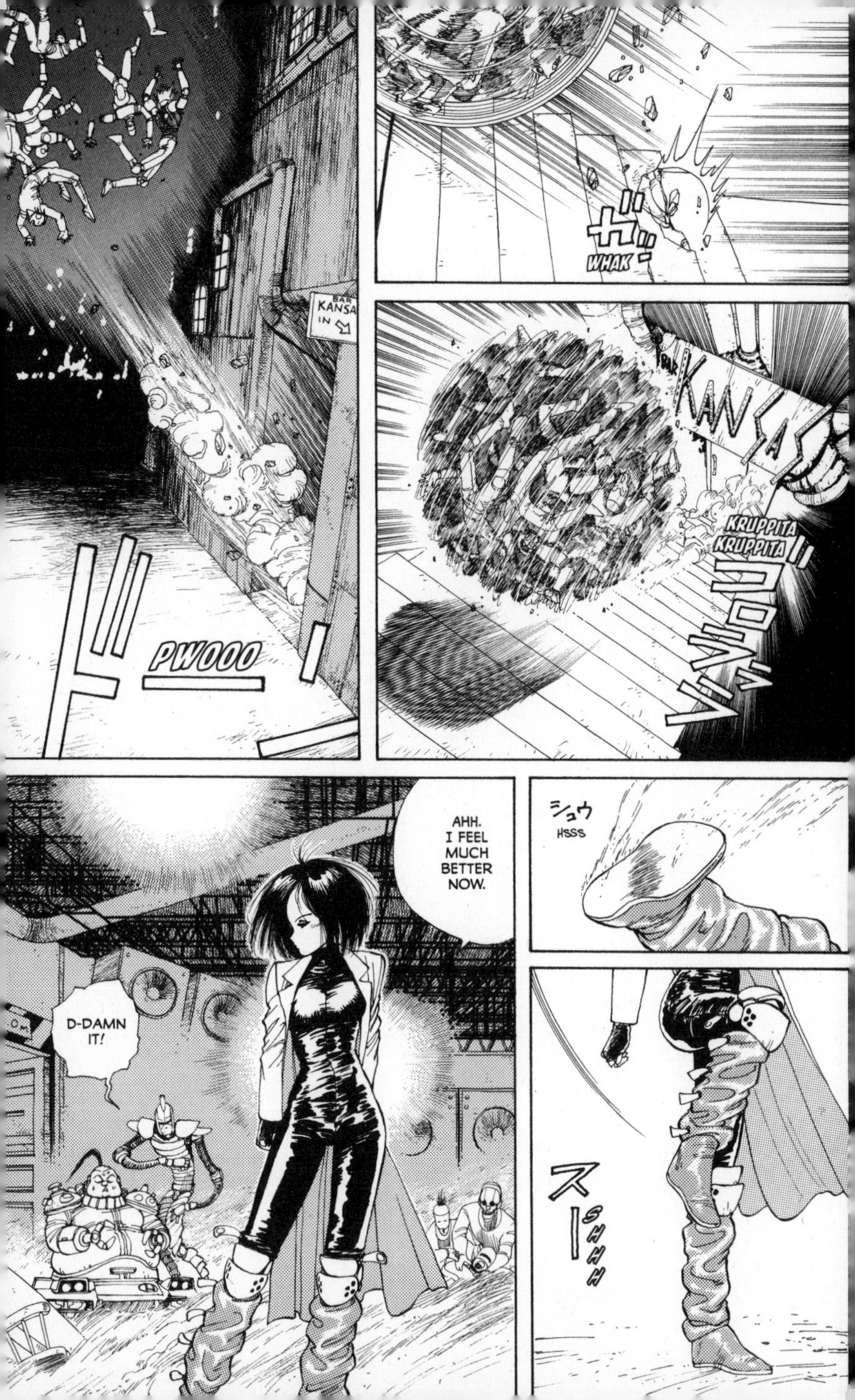
WHAK
KAN SA
KRUPPITA KRUPPITA
BAR
KANSA
IN
PWOOO
シュウ
HSSS
SHHH
AHH. I FEEL MUCH BETTER NOW.
D-DAMN IT!

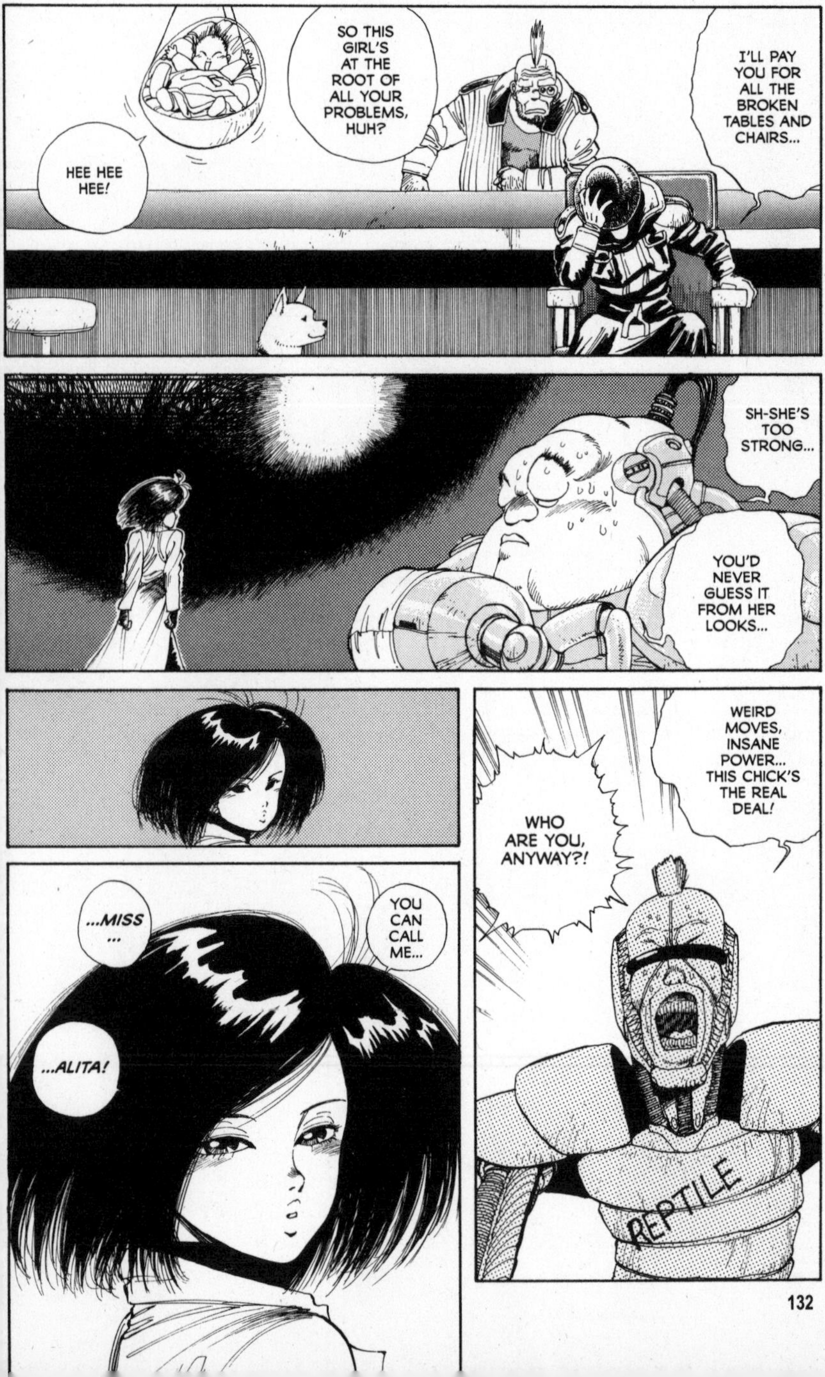
I'LL PAY YOU FOR ALL THE BROKEN TABLES AND CHAIRS...
SO THIS GIRL'S AT THE ROOT OF ALL YOUR PROBLEMS, HUH?
HEE HEE HEE!
SH-SHE'S TOO STRONG...
YOU'D NEVER GUESS IT FROM HER LOOKS...
WEIRD MOVES, INSANE POWER... THIS CHICK'S THE REAL DEAL!
WHO ARE YOU, ANYWAY?!
REPTILE
YOU CAN CALL ME...
...MISS ...
...ALITA!

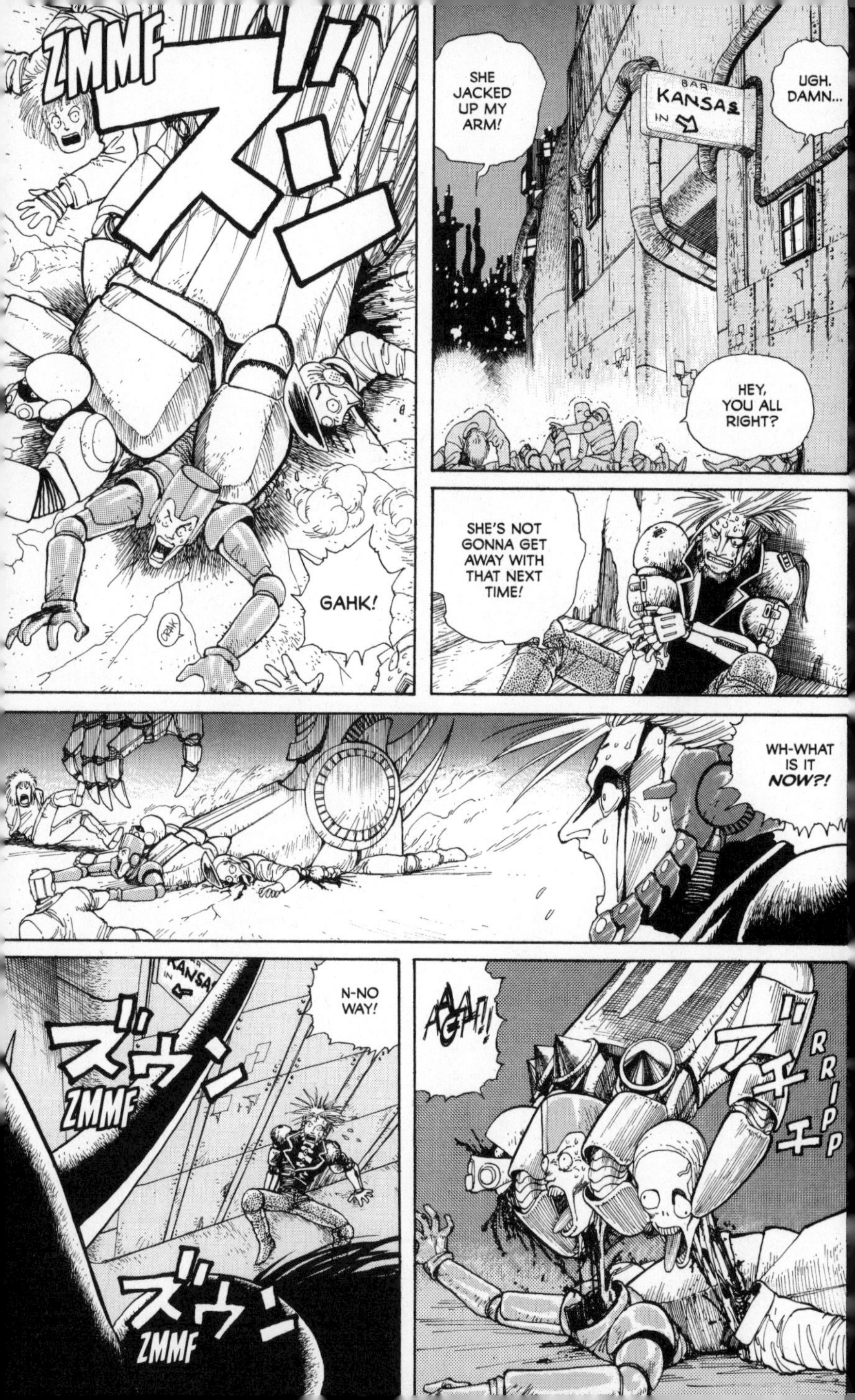
UGH. DAMN...
BAR
KANSAS
IN
SHE JACKED UP MY ARM!
HEY, YOU ALL RIGHT?
SHE'S NOT GONNA GET AWAY WITH THAT NEXT TIME!
ZMMF
ズン
GAHK!
CRAK
WH-WHAT IS IT *NOW?!*
RRIPP
ブチ
AAAGH!!
N-NO WAY!
KANSAS
IN
ズウン
ZMMF
ズウン
ZMMF

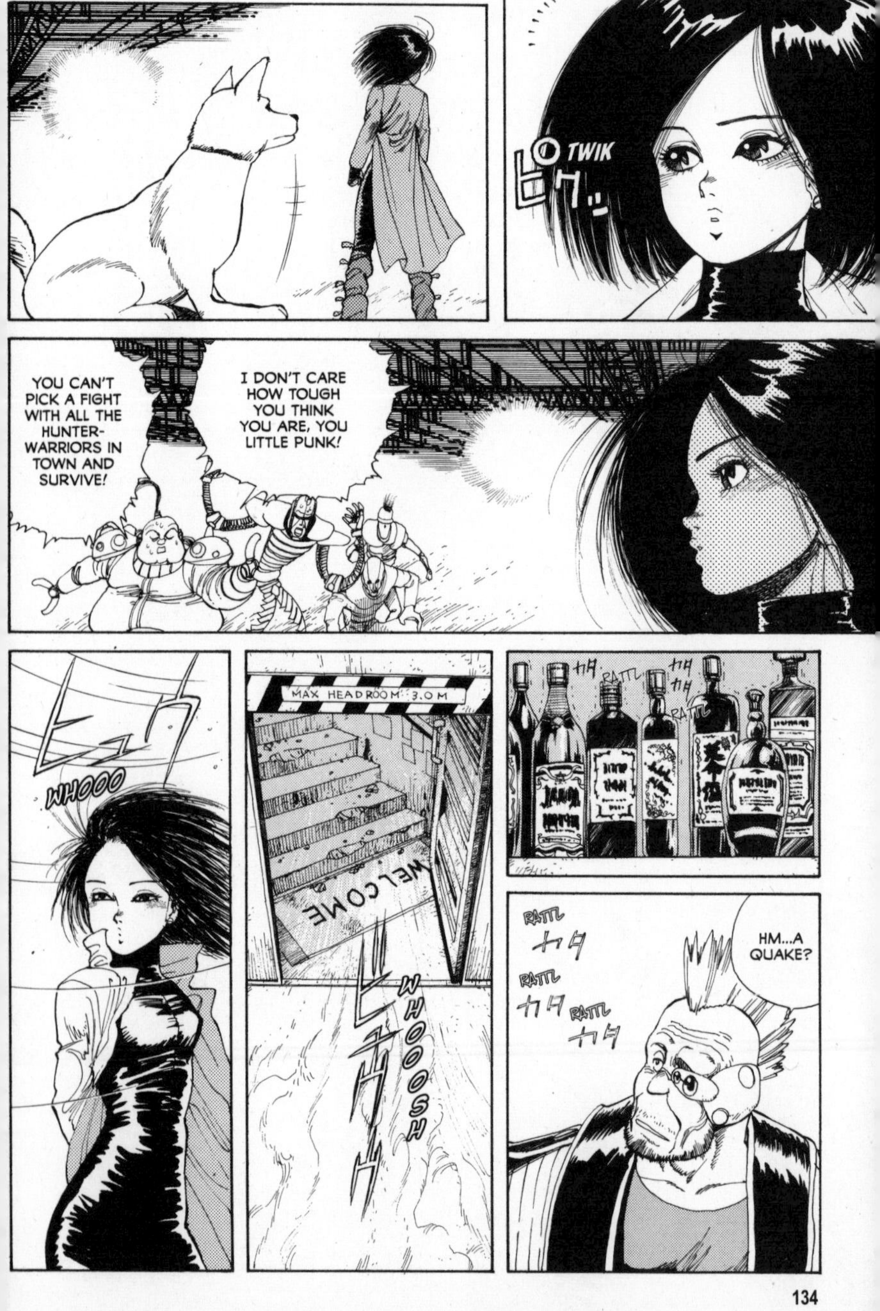
TWIK
I DON'T CARE HOW TOUGH YOU THINK YOU ARE, YOU LITTLE PUNK!
YOU CAN'T PICK A FIGHT WITH ALL THE HUNTER-WARRIORS IN TOWN AND SURVIVE!
RATTL
RATTL
RATTL
RATTL
カタ
RATTL
カタ
RATTL
カタ
HM...A QUAKE?
MAX HEADROOM 3.0 M
WELCOME
WHOOOSH
WHOOO

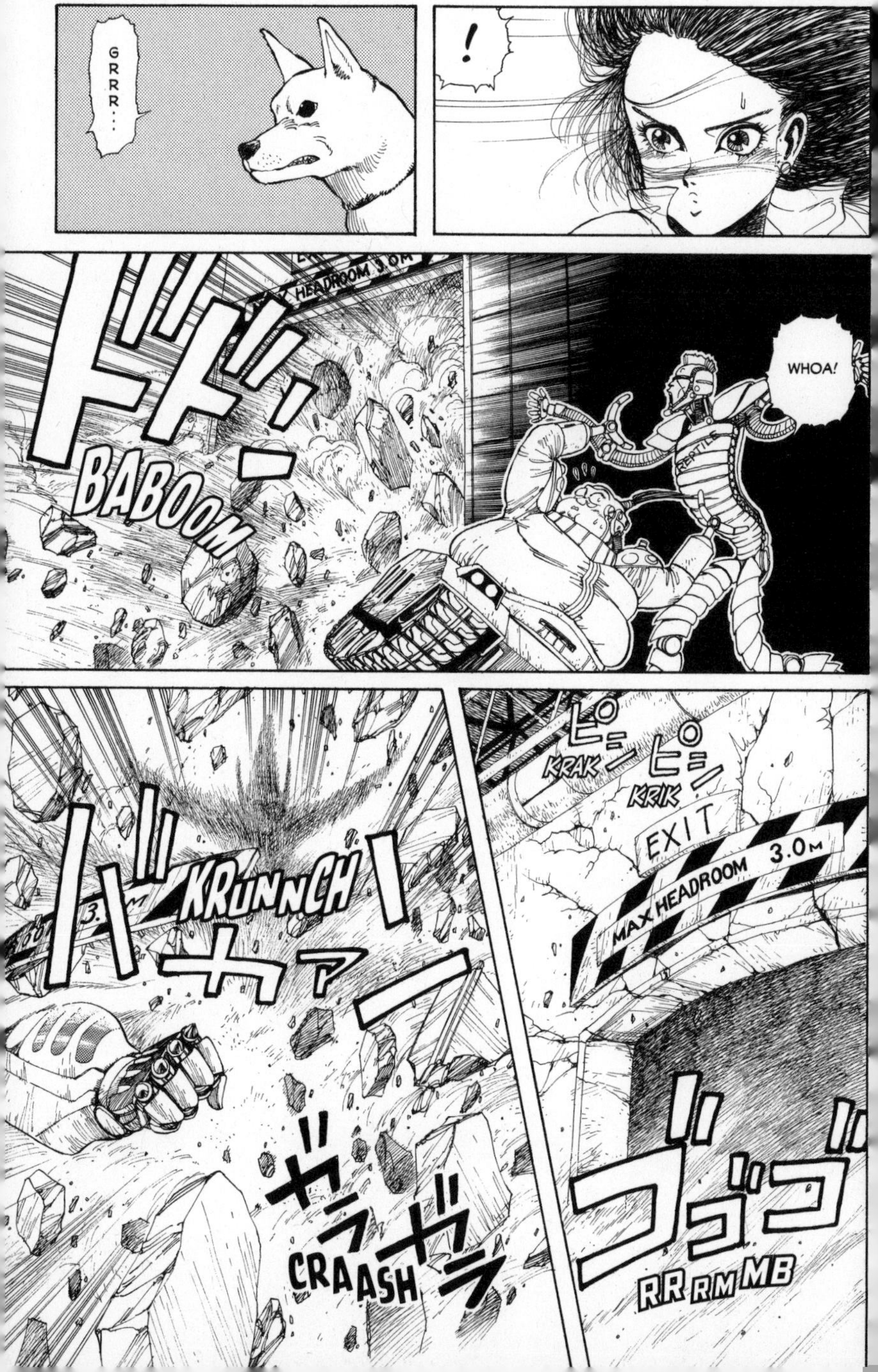
!
GRRR...
WHOA!
MAX HEADROOM 3.0M
REPTILE
BABOOM
KRAK
KRIK
EXIT
MAX HEADROOM 3.0M
RRRMMB
KRUNNCH
CRAASH

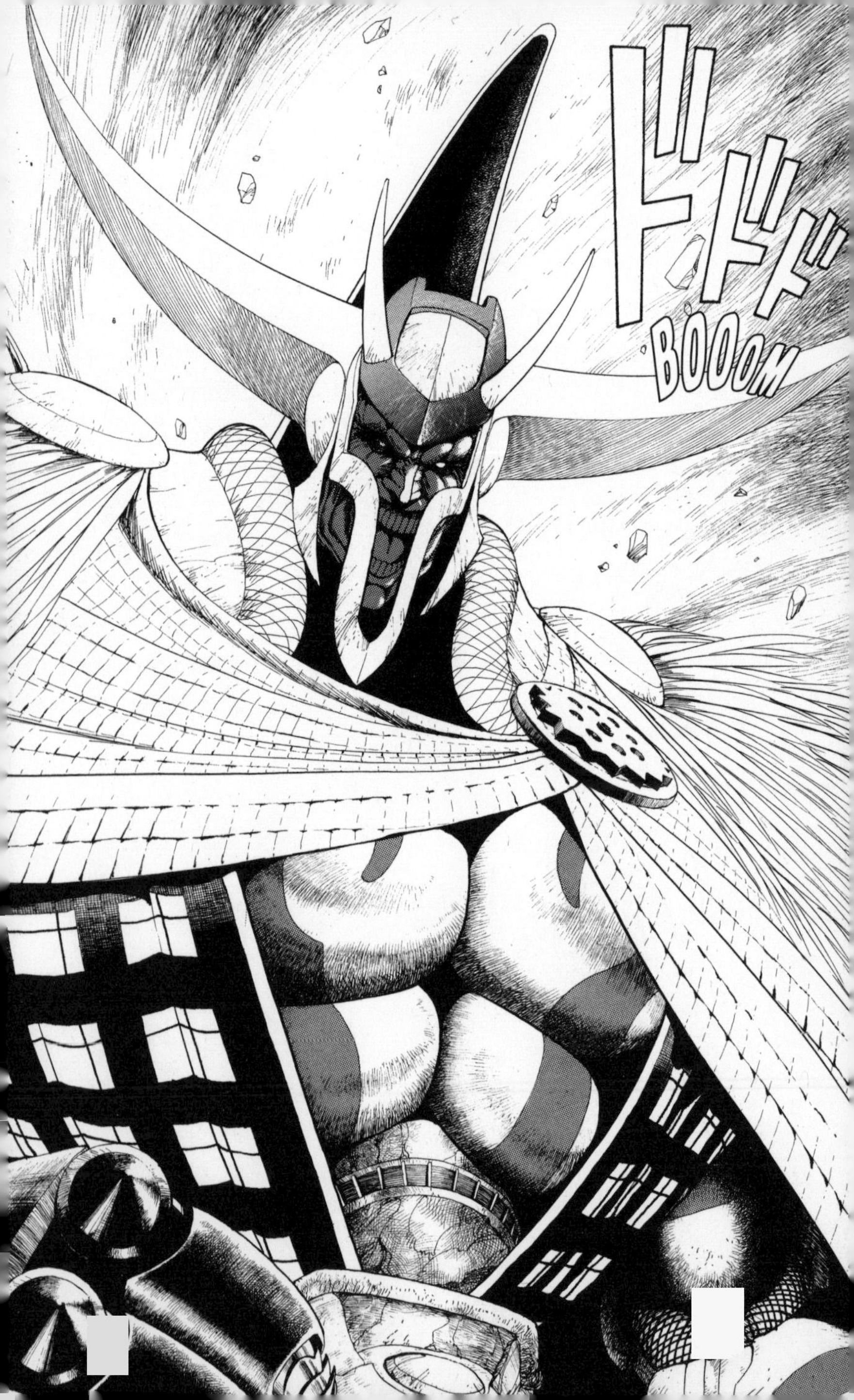
ドドドド
BOOOM

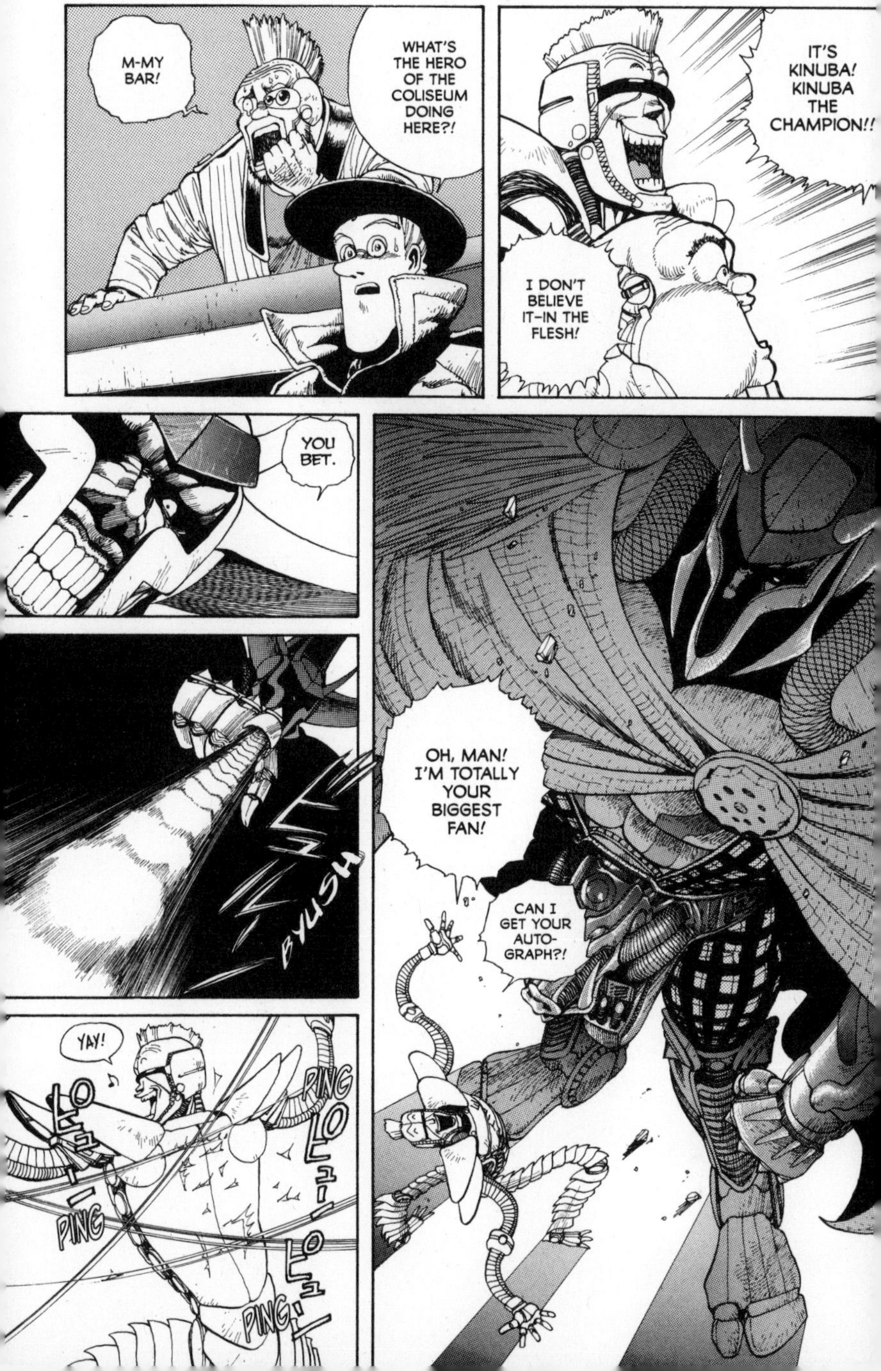
IT'S KINUBA! KINUBA THE CHAMPION!!
I DON'T BELIEVE IT–IN THE FLESH!
WHAT'S THE HERO OF THE COLISEUM DOING HERE?!
M-MY BAR!
OH, MAN! I'M TOTALLY YOUR BIGGEST FAN!
CAN I GET YOUR AUTO-GRAPH?!
YOU BET.
BYUSH
YAY!
PING
PING
PING!

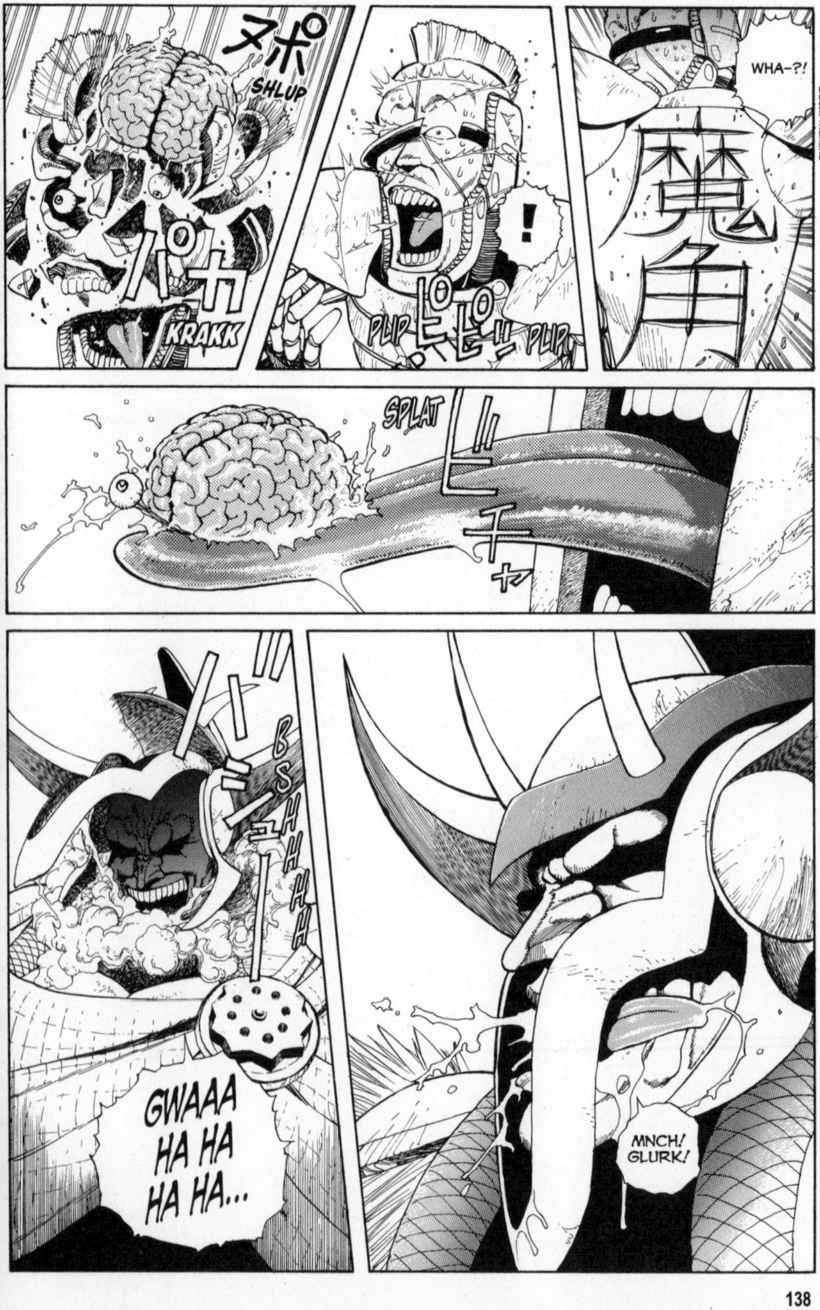
WHA-?!
魔角
!
PLIP ピピ!! PLIP
ヌポ
SHLUP
パカ
KRAKK
SPLAT
ビチャ
MNCH! GLURK!
BSHHHHHH
GWAAA HA HA HA HA...

Back: Makaku

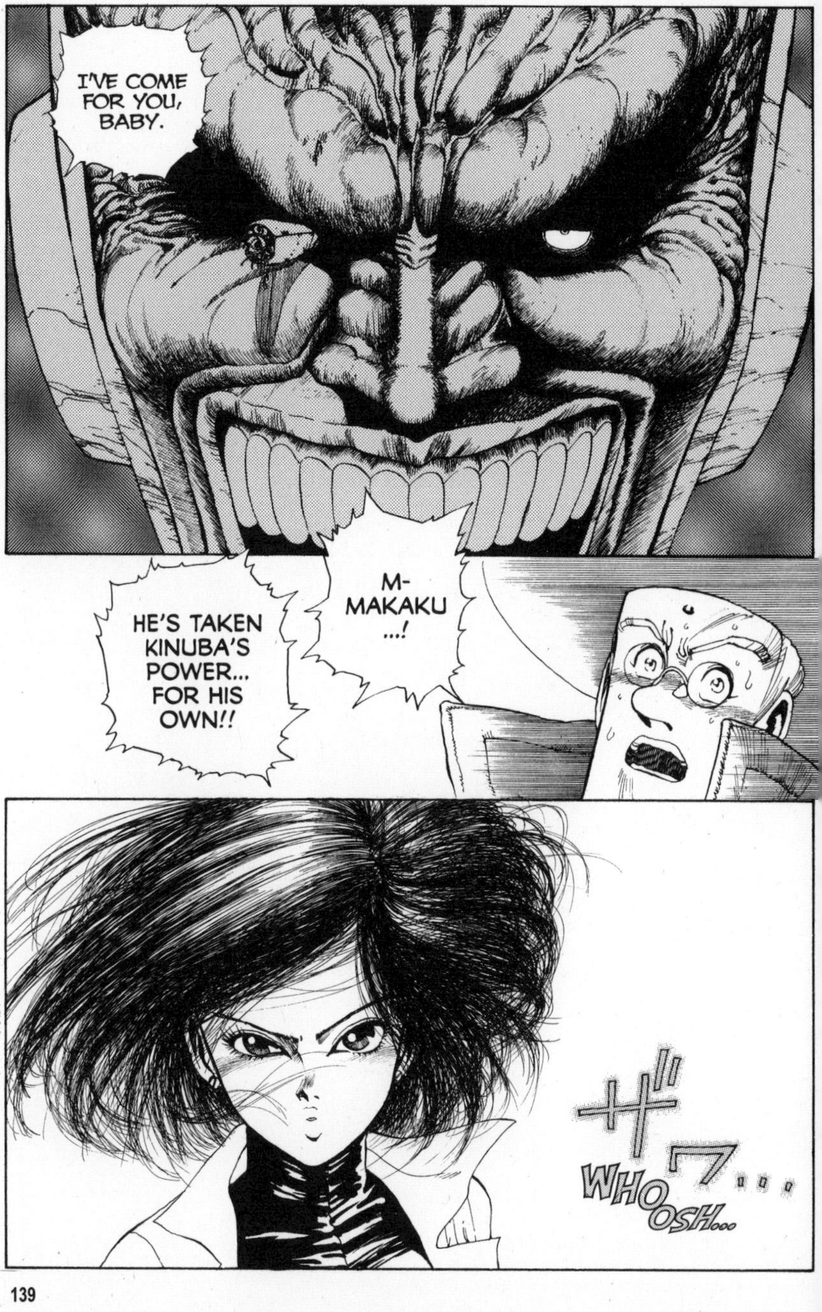

I'VE COME FOR YOU, BABY.
M-MAKAKU ...!
HE'S TAKEN KINUBA'S POWER... FOR HIS OWN!!
ザワ...
WHOOSH...

FIGHT_005 Trap at the Mouth of Hell

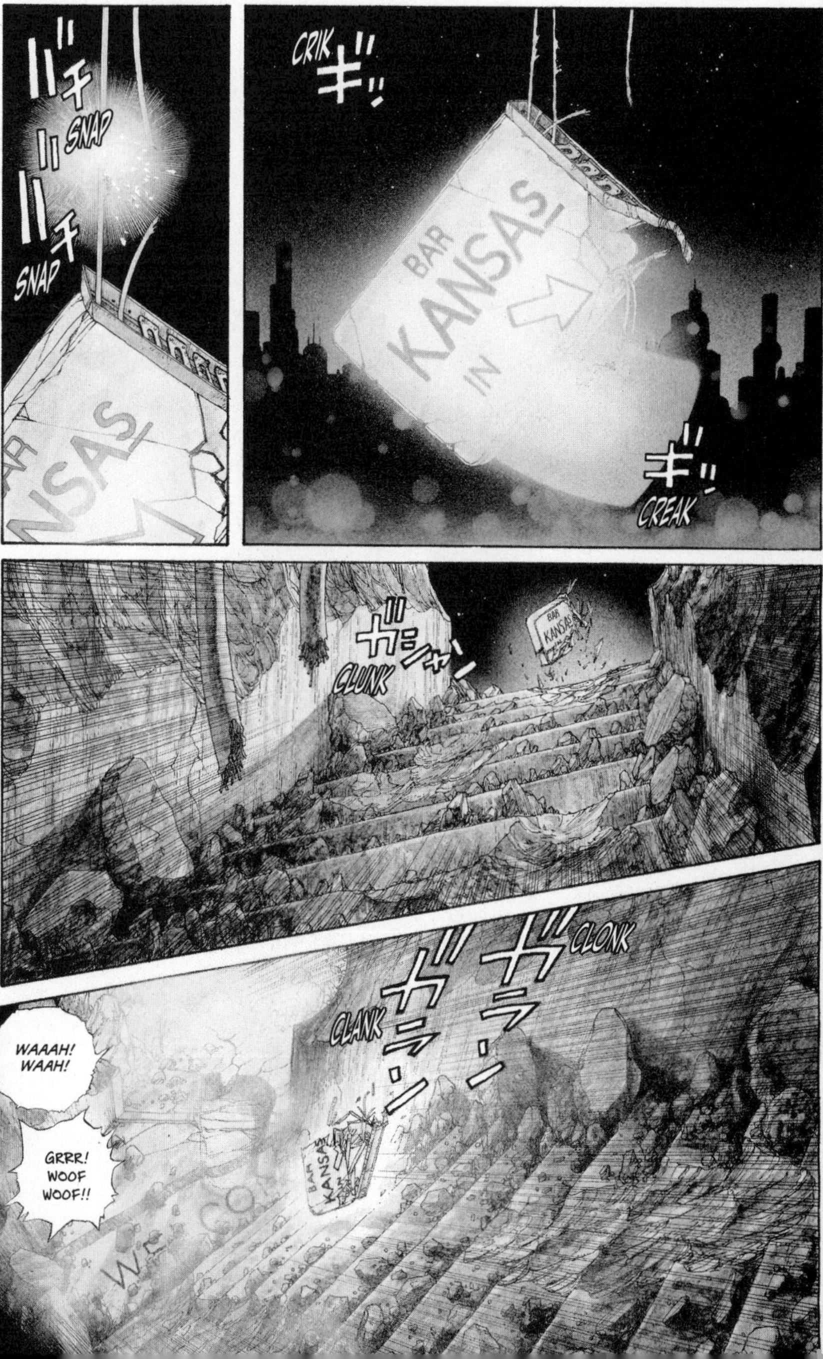
CRIK
BAR KANSAS IN
CREAK
SNAP
SNAP
CLUNK
BAR KANSAS
CLONK
CLANK
WAAAH! WAAH!
GRRR! WOOF WOOF!!
BAR KANSAS

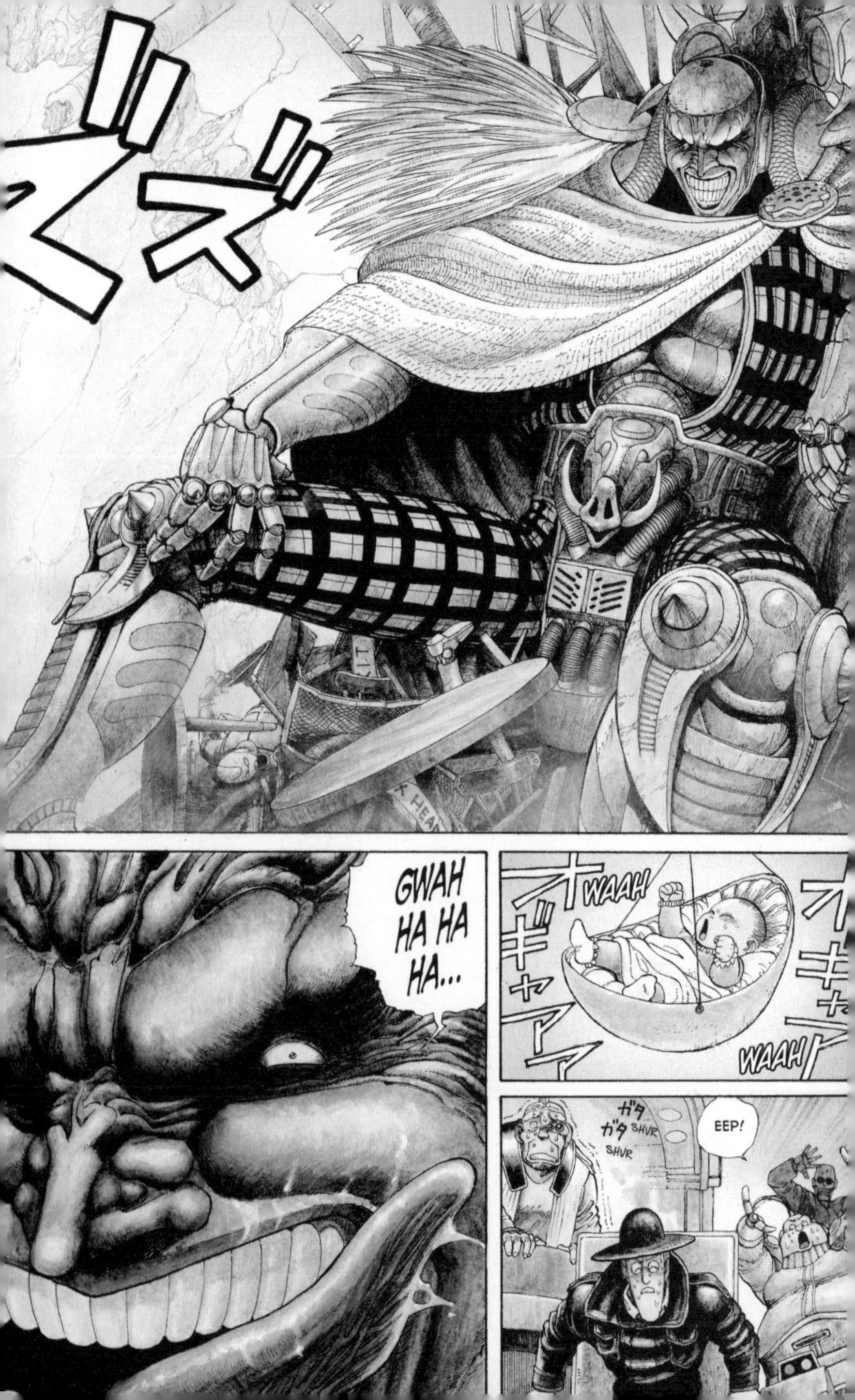

WAAH
WAAH
ガタ ガタ
SHUR SHUR
EEP!
GWAH HA HA HA...

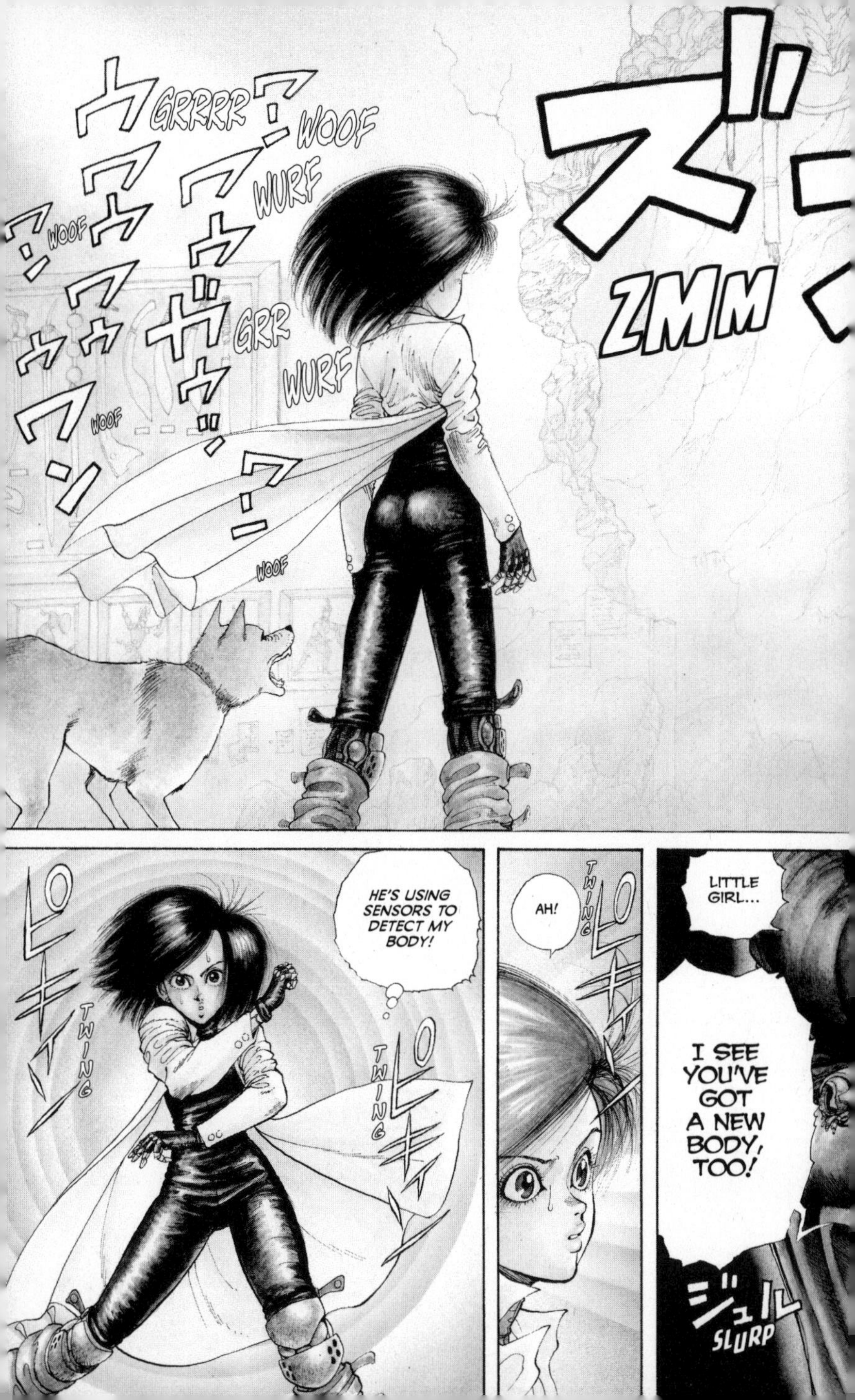
ZMM
GRRRR
WOOF
WURF
WOOF
GRR
WURF
WOOF
WOOF
LITTLE GIRL...
I SEE YOU'VE GOT A NEW BODY, TOO!
SLURP
AH!
TWING
HE'S USING SENSORS TO DETECT MY BODY!
TWING
TWING

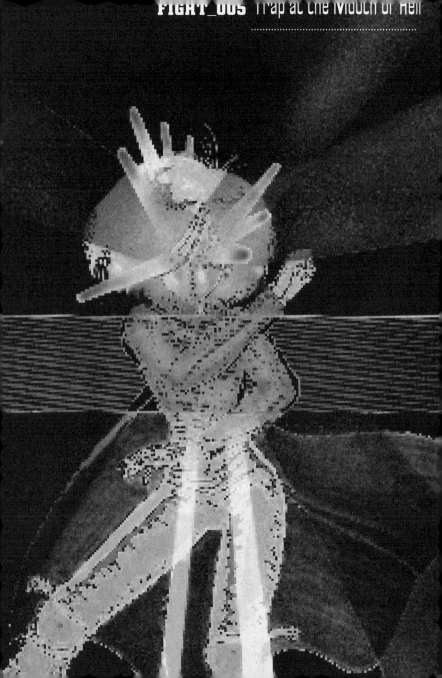

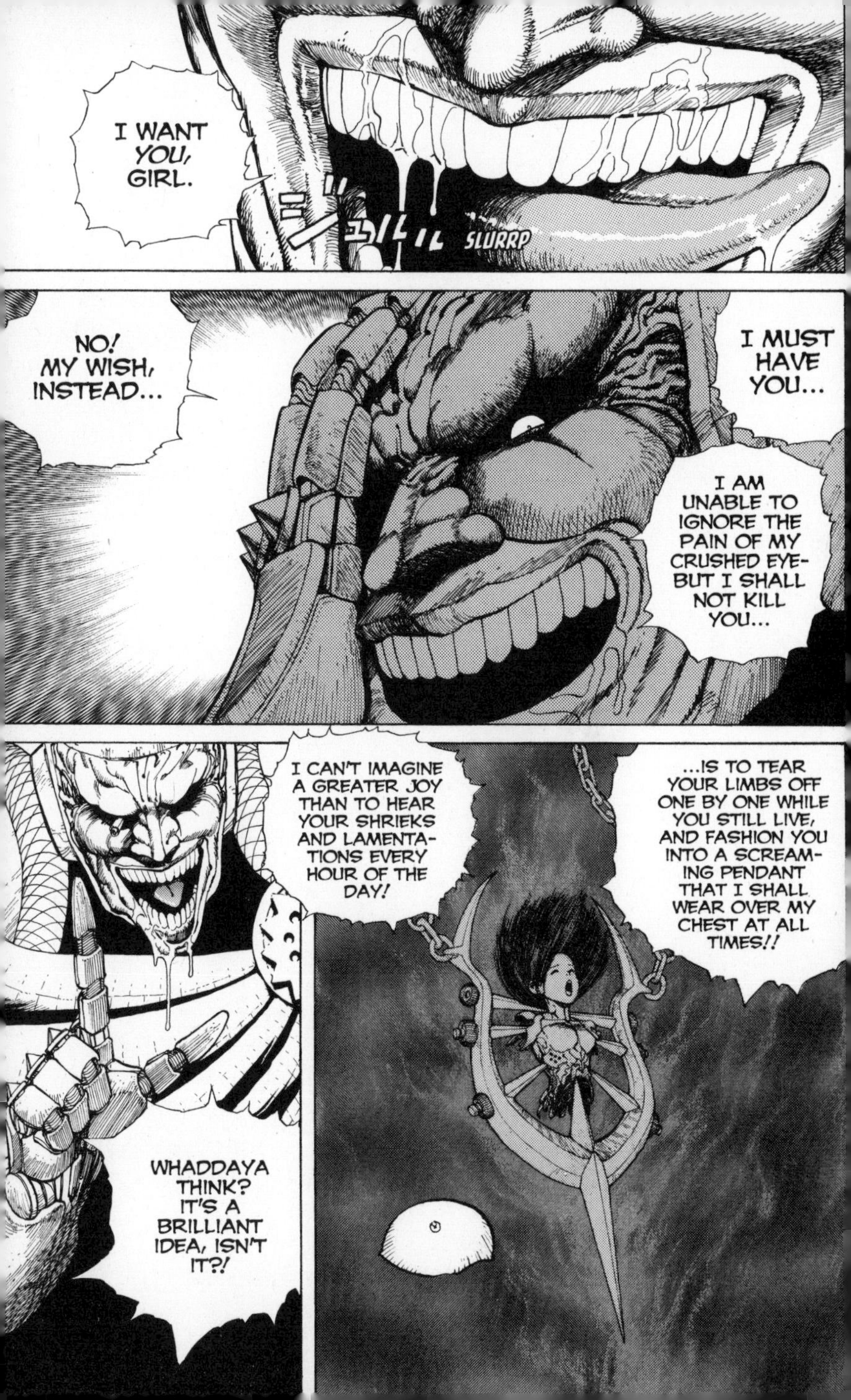
I WANT *YOU*, GIRL.
SLURRP
I MUST HAVE YOU...
I AM UNABLE TO IGNORE THE PAIN OF MY CRUSHED EYE- BUT I SHALL NOT KILL YOU...
NO! MY WISH, INSTEAD...
...IS TO TEAR YOUR LIMBS OFF ONE BY ONE WHILE YOU STILL LIVE, AND FASHION YOU INTO A SCREAMING PENDANT THAT I SHALL WEAR OVER MY CHEST AT ALL TIMES!!
I CAN'T IMAGINE A GREATER JOY THAN TO HEAR YOUR SHRIEKS AND LAMENTATIONS EVERY HOUR OF THE DAY!
WHADDAYA THINK? IT'S A BRILLIANT IDEA, ISN'T IT?!

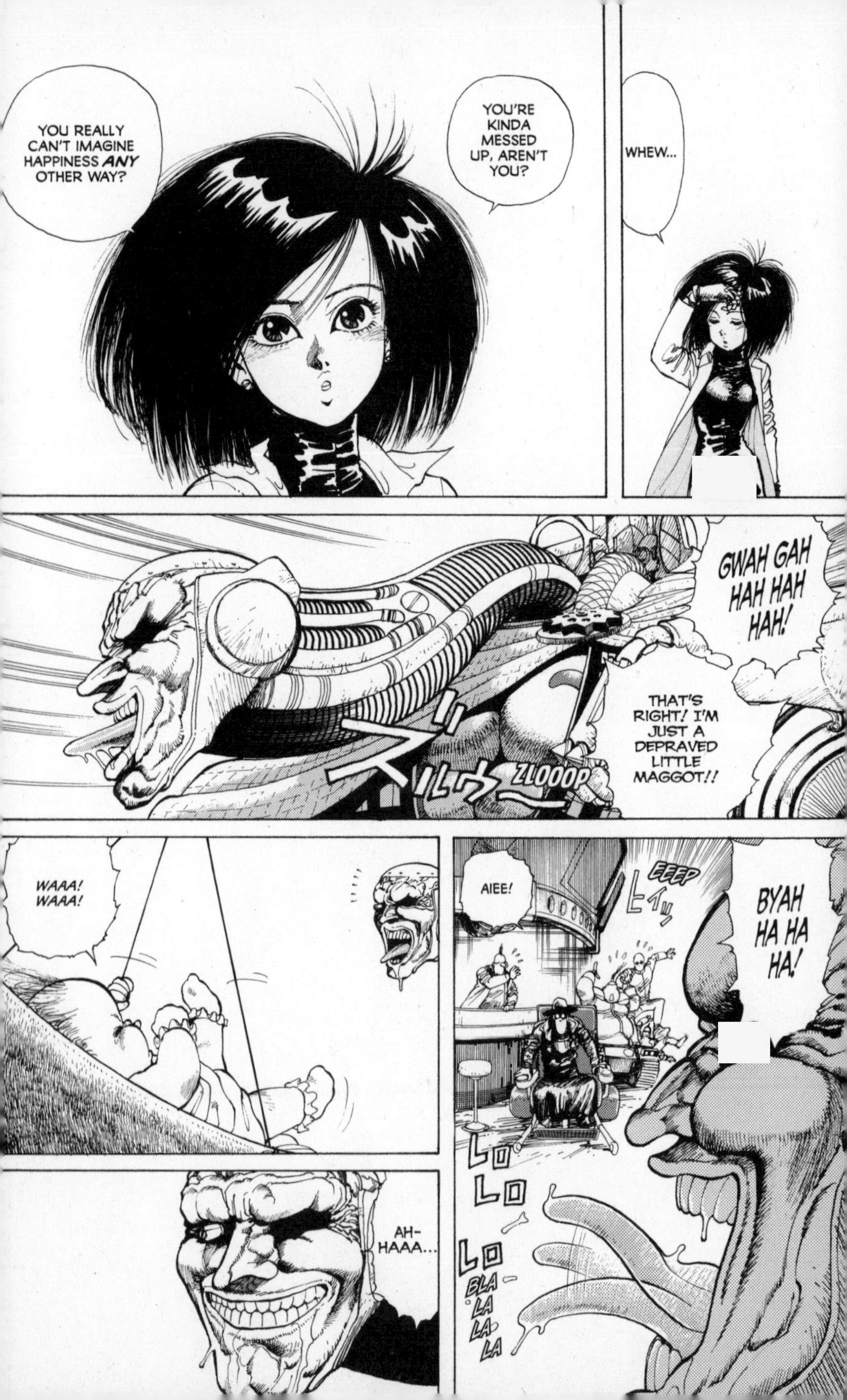
WHEW...
YOU'RE KINDA MESSED UP, AREN'T YOU?
YOU REALLY CAN'T IMAGINE HAPPINESS *ANY* OTHER WAY?
GWAH GAH HAH HAH HAH!
THAT'S RIGHT! I'M JUST A DEPRAVED LITTLE MAGGOT!!
ZLOOOP
BYAH HA HA HA!
EEEP
AIEE!
LO LO LO
BLA LA LA LA
WAAA! WAAA!
AH-HAAA...

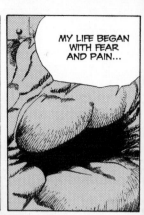

MY LIFE BEGAN WITH FEAR AND PAIN...
!
...
SOON, I UNDERSTOOD THE PRINCIPLE OF HOW TO CONQUER BOTH FEAR *AND* PAIN!
ブァーム
FRRRM
THESE TWO SENSATIONS FLOW FROM HIGH HILLS TO LOW VALLEYS LIKE WATER.
IN OTHER WORDS, I CAN PROTECT MYSELF FROM FEAR AND PAIN ONLY BY INFLICTING THEM ON OTHERS!
AND IN ORDER TO DO THAT, I REQUIRE *POWER!!*
ENOUGH POWER TO PLUNGE ALL OTHERS INTO TERROR AND ANGUISH-TO OBTAIN THAT IS MY LIFE'S AMBITION!!

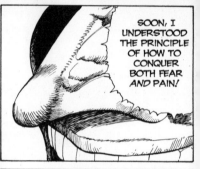

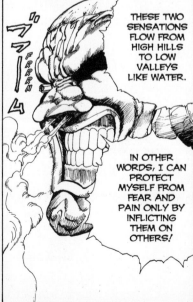

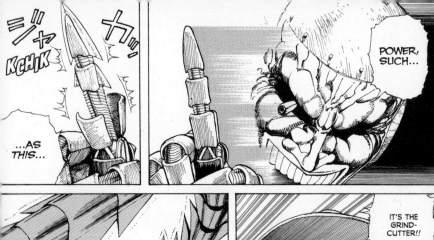

KCHIK

...AS THIS...

POWER, SUCH...

IT'S THE GRIND-CUTTER!!

GET AWAY FROM HIM, ALITA!!

VWOOOM

PAUSE

VMMM

ZRRRRING

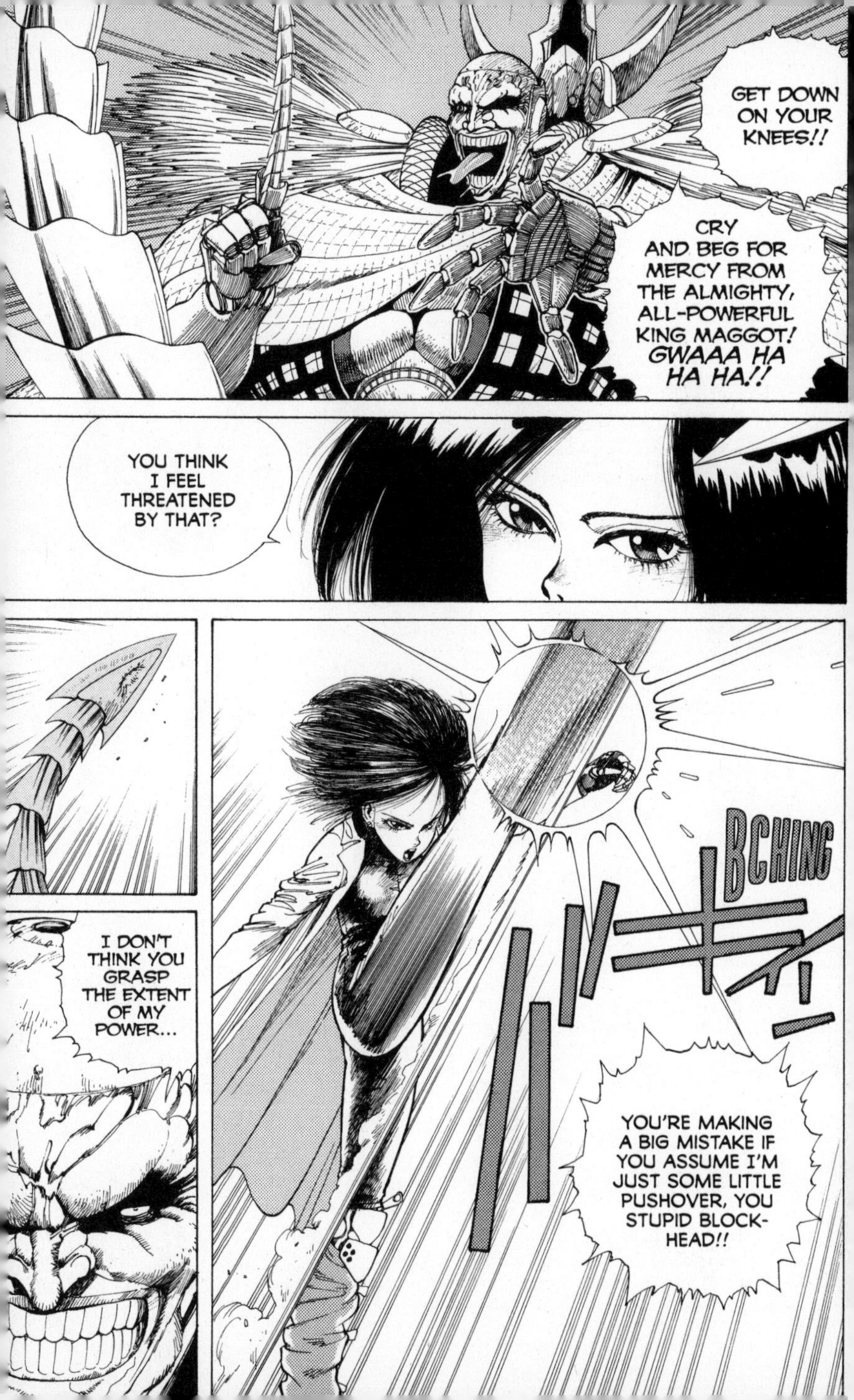

GET DOWN ON YOUR KNEES!!
CRY AND BEG FOR MERCY FROM THE ALMIGHTY, ALL-POWERFUL KING MAGGOT! *GWAAA HA HA HA!!*
YOU THINK I FEEL THREATENED BY THAT?
BCHING
YOU'RE MAKING A BIG MISTAKE IF YOU ASSUME I'M JUST SOME LITTLE PUSHOVER, YOU STUPID BLOCK-HEAD!!
I DON'T THINK YOU GRASP THE EXTENT OF MY POWER...

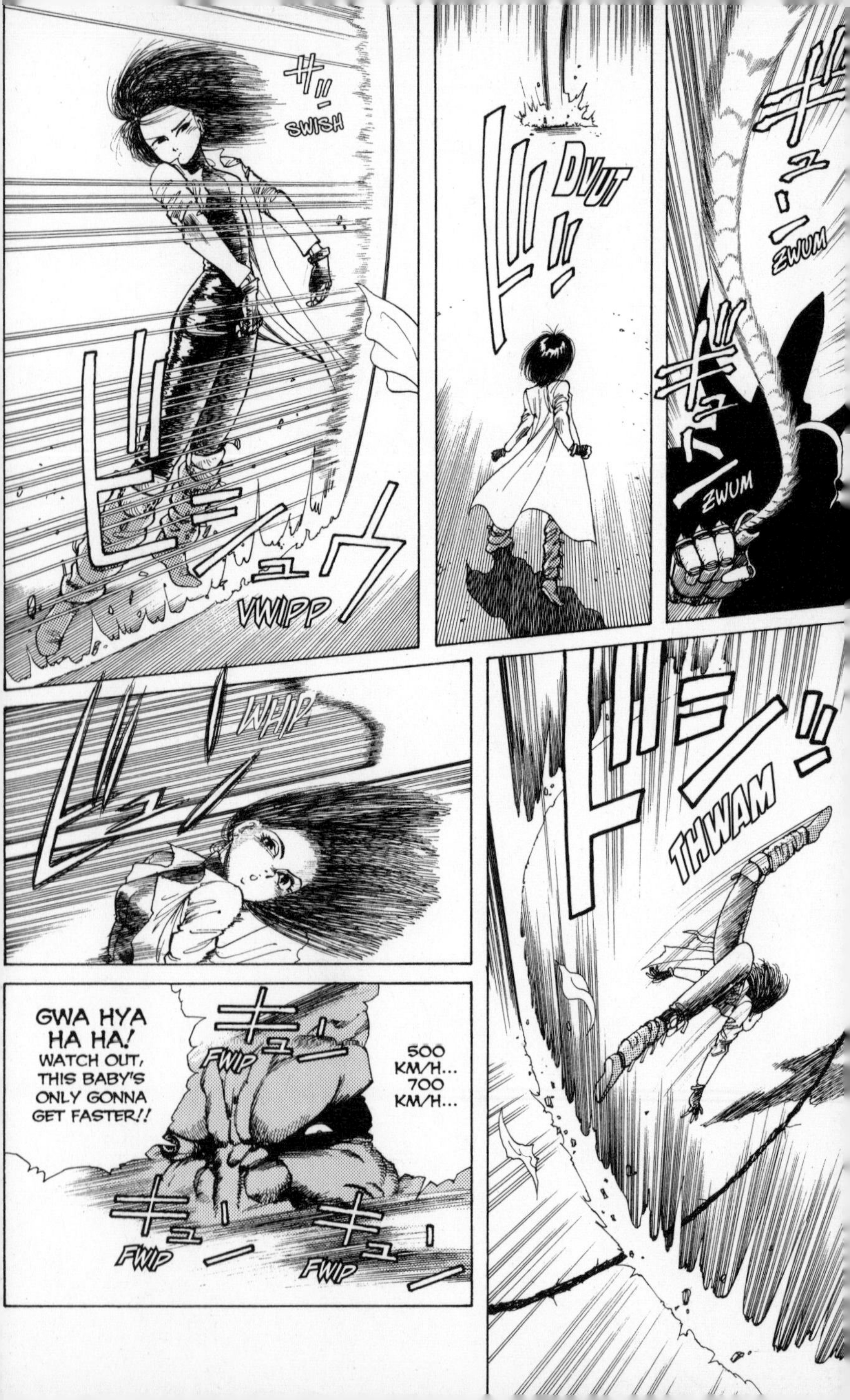

ZWUM
ZWUM
DVUT!!
SWISH
VWIPP
THWAM!!
WHIP
GWA HYA HA HA! WATCH OUT, THIS BABY'S ONLY GONNA GET FASTER!!
FWIP
500 KM/H... 700 KM/H...
FWIP
FWIP

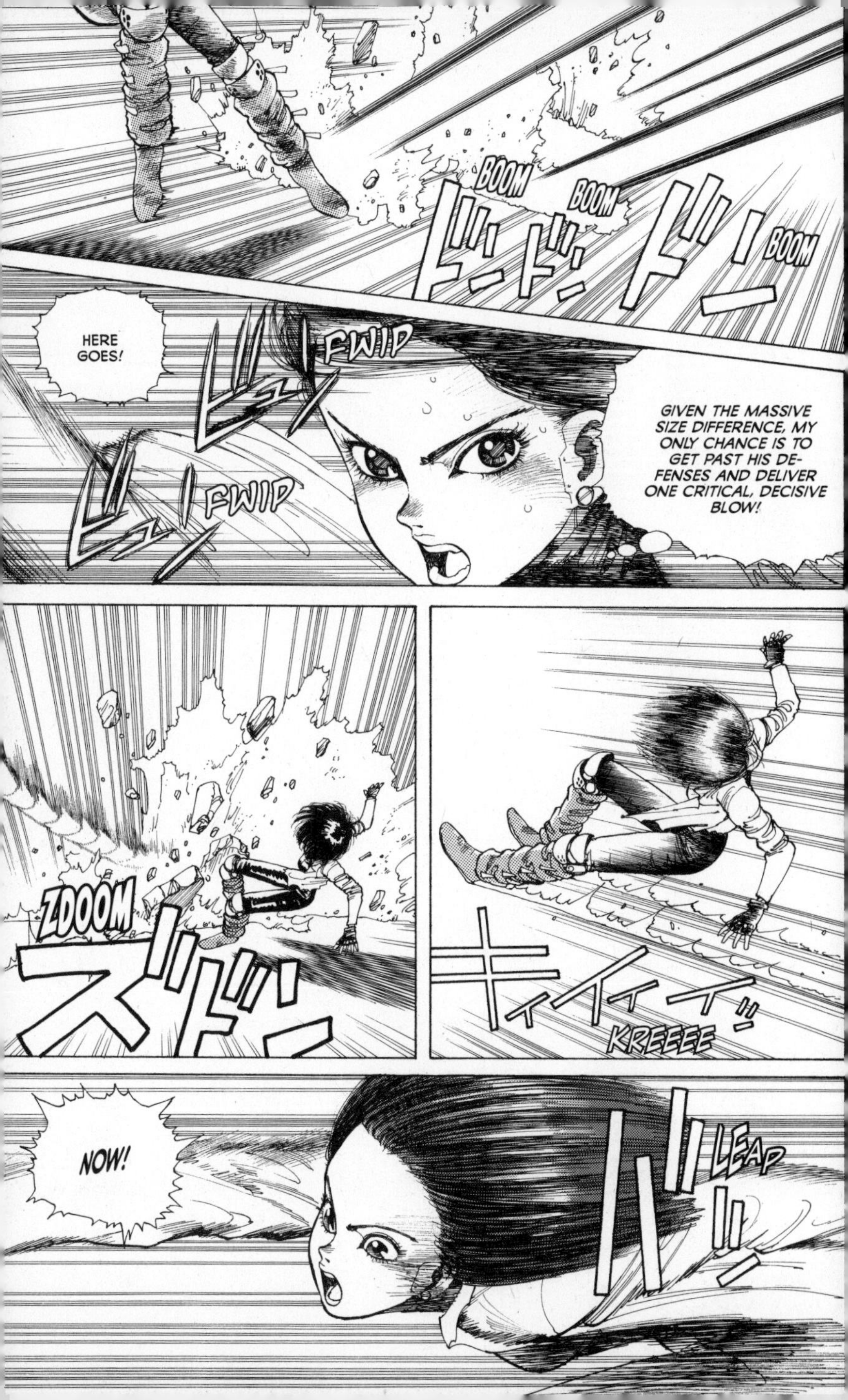

BOOM
BOOM
BOOM
GIVEN THE MASSIVE SIZE DIFFERENCE, MY ONLY CHANCE IS TO GET PAST HIS DEFENSES AND DELIVER ONE CRITICAL, DECISIVE BLOW!
FWIP
FWIP
HERE GOES!
KREEEE
ZDOOM
LEAP
NOW!

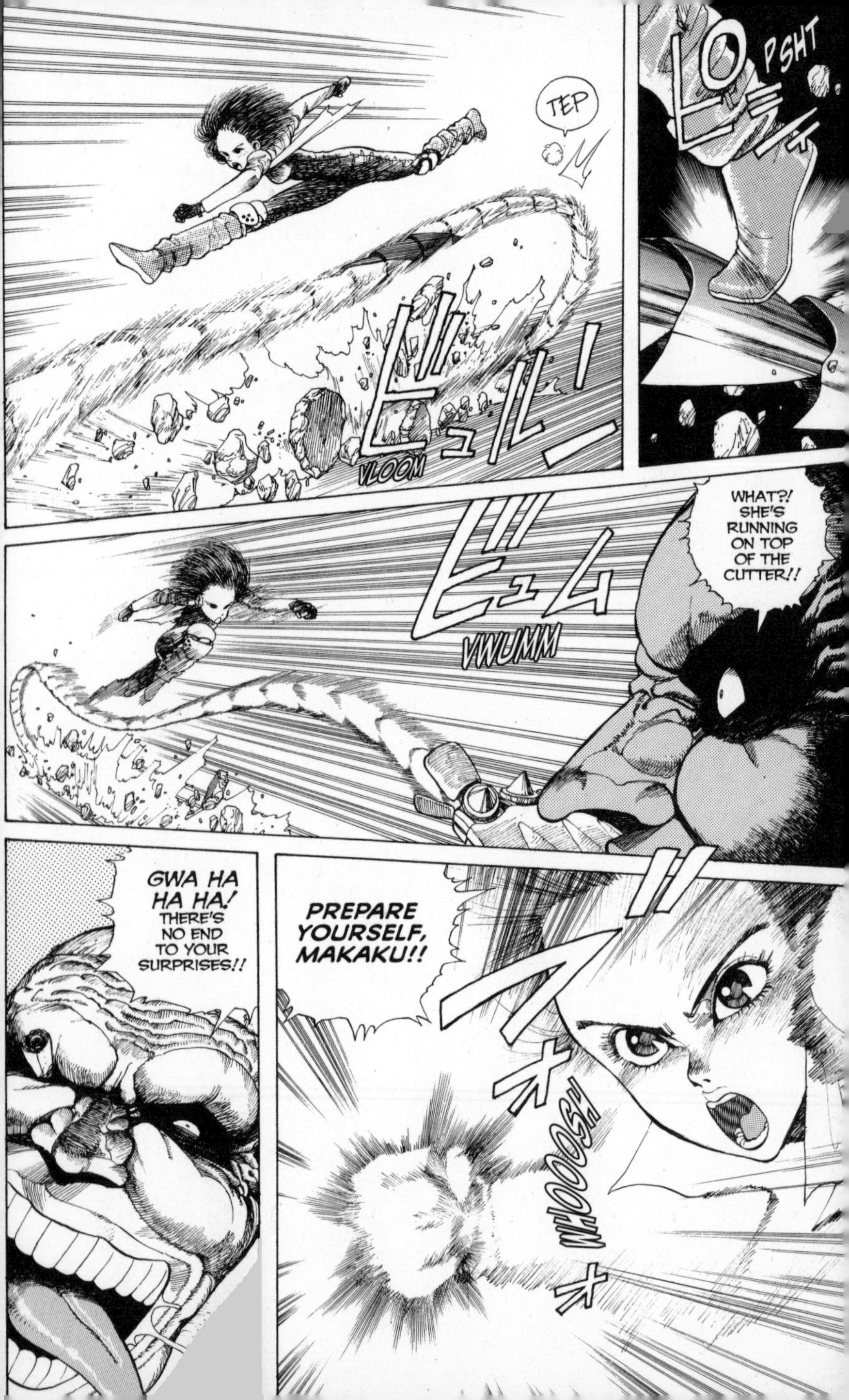
PSHT
TEP
VLOOM
WHAT?! SHE'S RUNNING ON TOP OF THE CUTTER!!
VWUMM
PREPARE YOURSELF, MAKAKU!!
WHOOOSH
GWA HA HA HA! THERE'S NO END TO YOUR SURPRISES!!

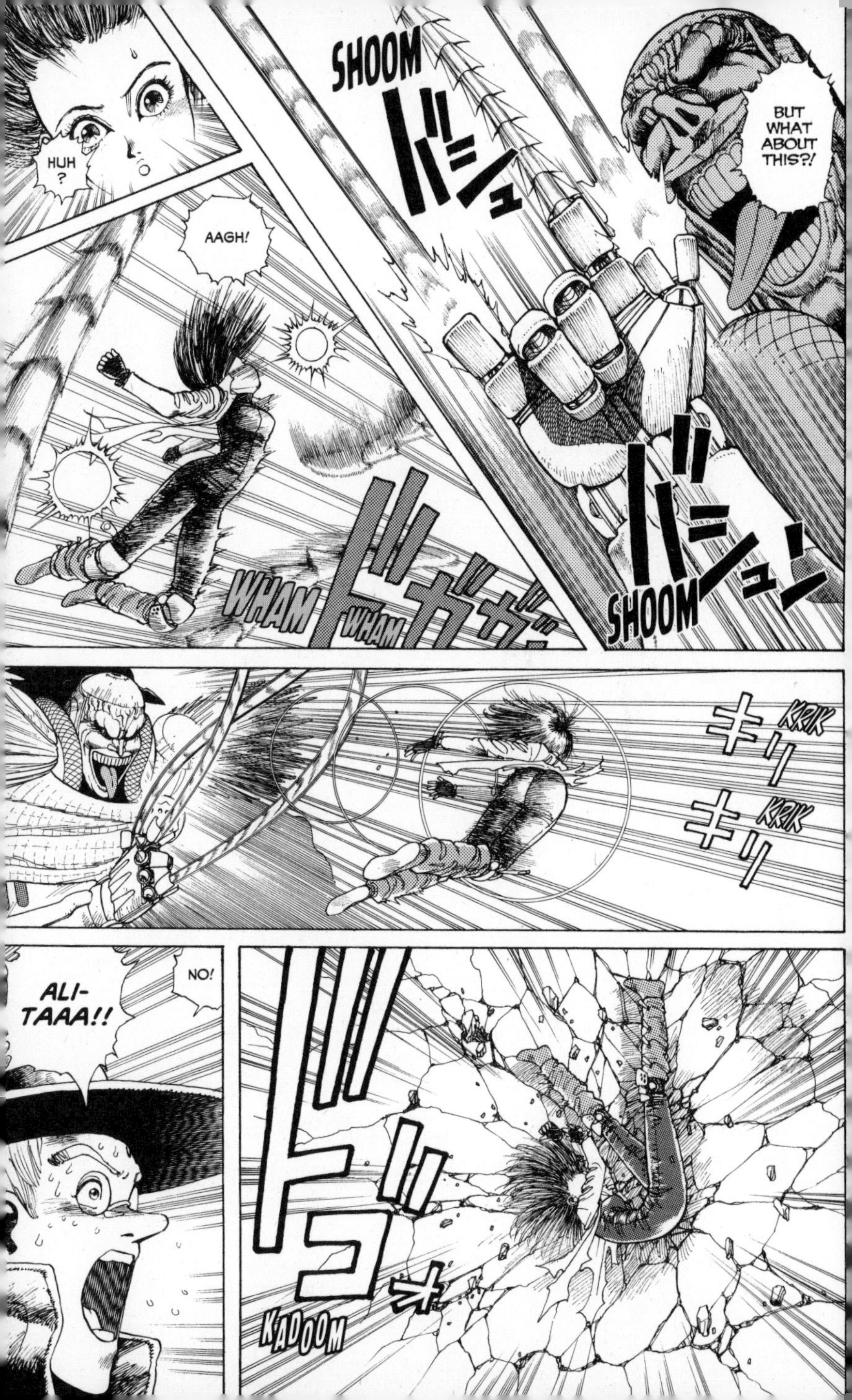
BUT WHAT ABOUT THIS?!
SHOOM
バシュ
SHOOM
バシュン
HUH?
AAGH!
WHAM
WHAM
ドガガ
KRIK
KRIK
キリキリ
KADOOM
ドゴォ
NO!
ALI-TAAA!!

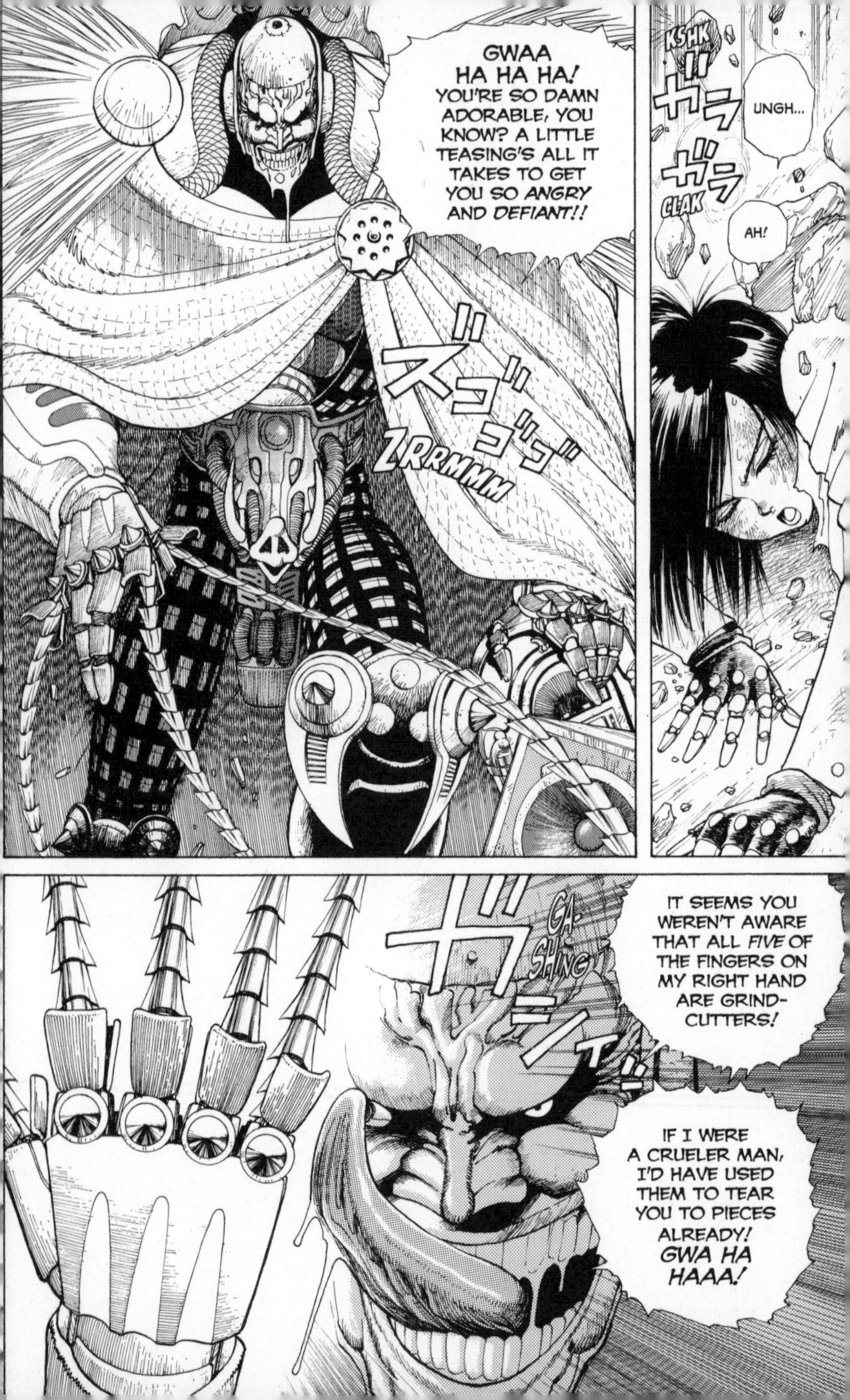
KSHK
ガラ
UNGH...
ガラ
CLAK
AH!
GWAA HA HA HA! YOU'RE SO DAMN ADORABLE, YOU KNOW? A LITTLE TEASING'S ALL IT TAKES TO GET YOU SO *ANGRY* AND *DEFIANT*!!
ZRRMMM
GA-SHING
IT SEEMS YOU WEREN'T AWARE THAT ALL *FIVE* OF THE FINGERS ON MY RIGHT HAND ARE GRIND-CUTTERS!
IF I WERE A CRUELER MAN, I'D HAVE USED THEM TO TEAR YOU TO PIECES ALREADY! *GWA HA HAAA!*

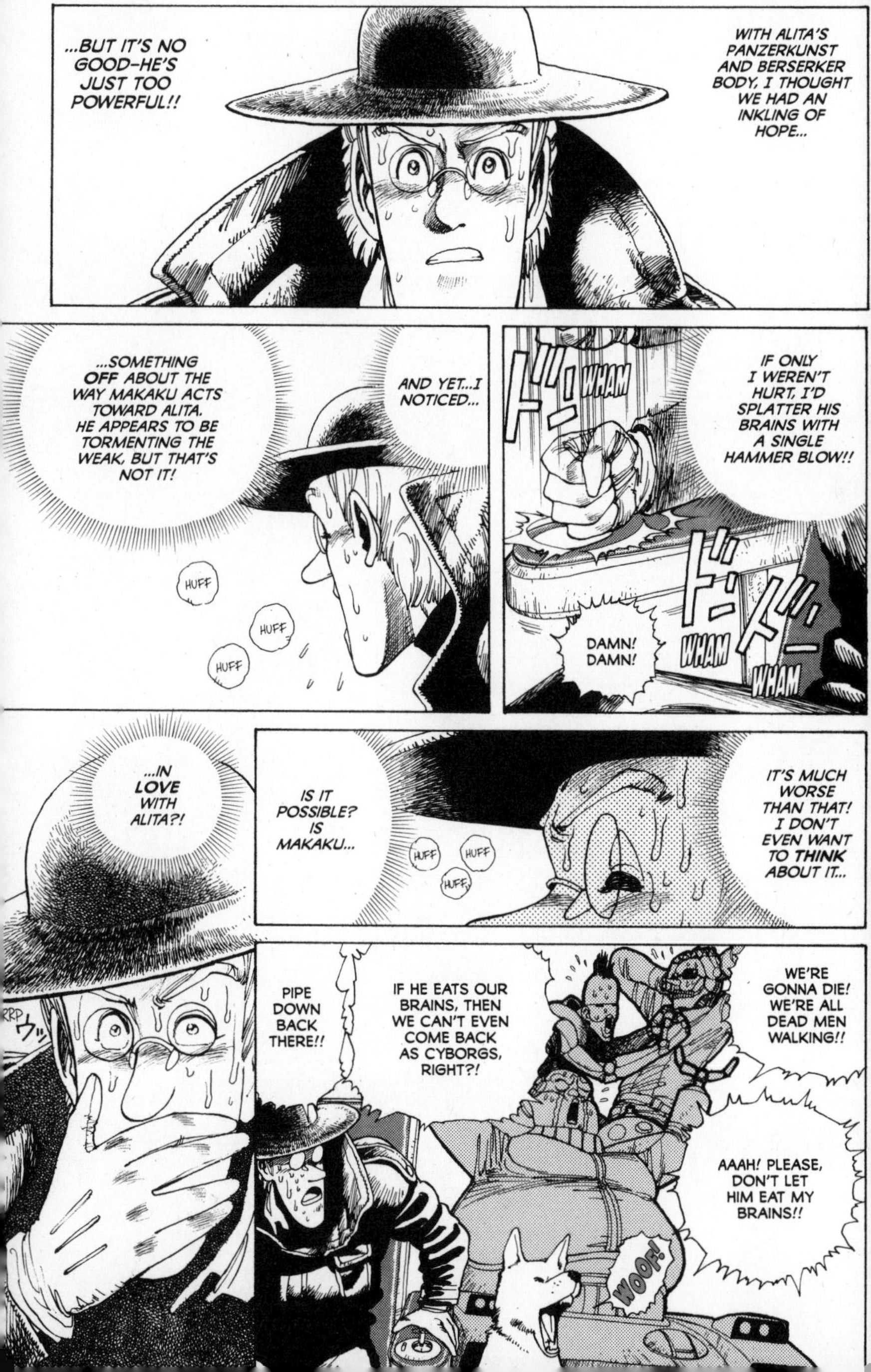
WITH ALITA'S PANZERKUNST AND BERSERKER BODY, I THOUGHT WE HAD AN INKLING OF HOPE...
...BUT IT'S NO GOOD–HE'S JUST TOO POWERFUL!!
IF ONLY I WEREN'T HURT, I'D SPLATTER HIS BRAINS WITH A SINGLE HAMMER BLOW!!
WHAM
DAMN! DAMN!
WHAM
WHAM
AND YET...I NOTICED...
...SOMETHING OFF ABOUT THE WAY MAKAKU ACTS TOWARD ALITA. HE APPEARS TO BE TORMENTING THE WEAK, BUT THAT'S NOT IT!
HUFF
HUFF
HUFF
IT'S MUCH WORSE THAN THAT! I DON'T EVEN WANT TO THINK ABOUT IT...
IS IT POSSIBLE? IS MAKAKU...
HUFF
HUFF
HUFF
WE'RE GONNA DIE! WE'RE ALL DEAD MEN WALKING!!
IF HE EATS OUR BRAINS, THEN WE CAN'T EVEN COME BACK AS CYBORGS, RIGHT?!
PIPE DOWN BACK THERE!!
AAAH! PLEASE, DON'T LET HIM EAT MY BRAINS!!
WOOF!
...IN LOVE WITH ALITA?!
RRP

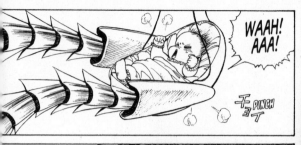

WAAH! AAA!

PINCH

WAAH WAAH

RIP!

K-KOYOMI!

VWIPP!!

OH!

GWAH HA HA HA!!

TREMBLE

P-PLEASE! NOT THE BABY! ANYTHING BUT THE BABY!!

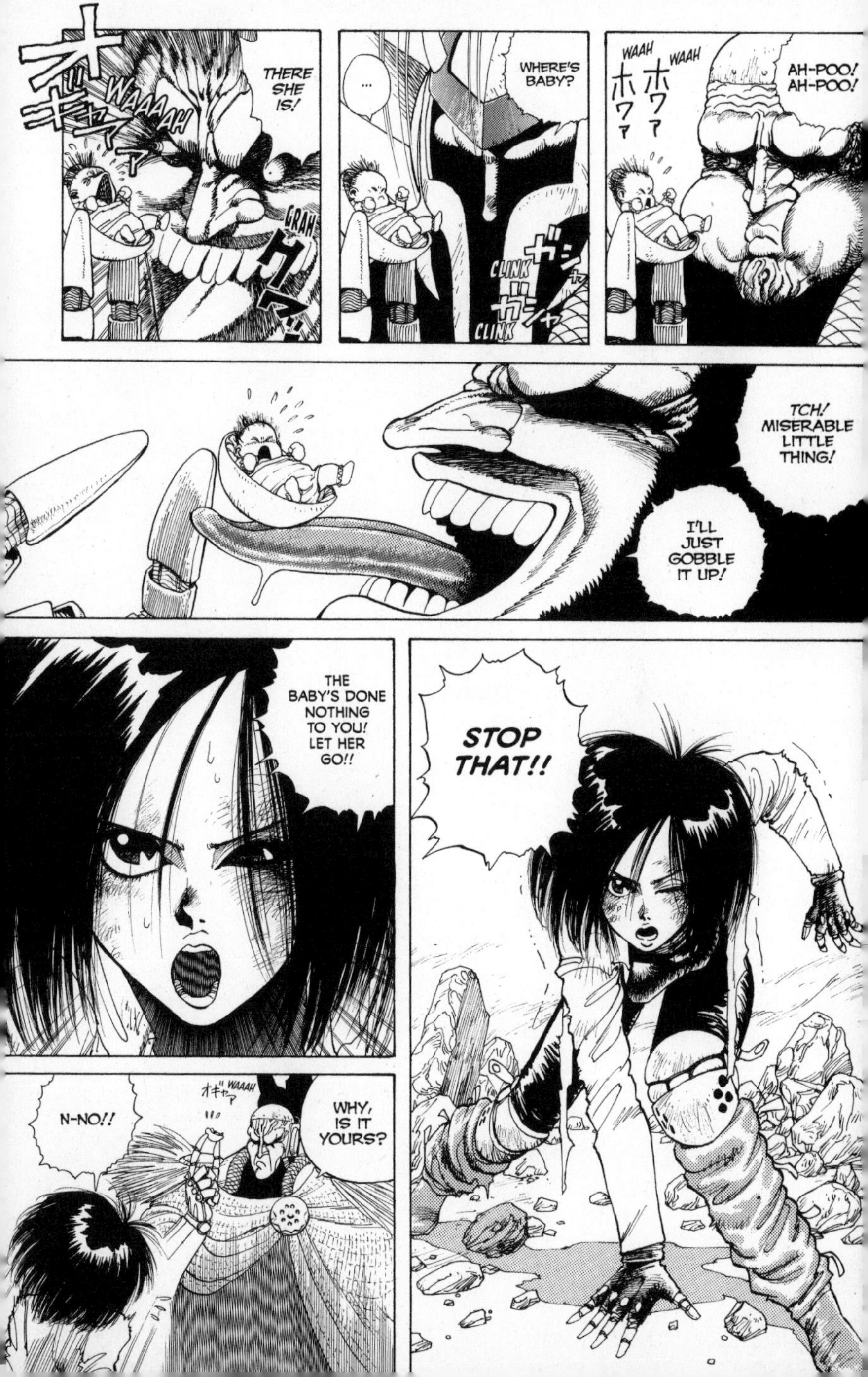
WAAH
ホワァ
WAAH
ホワァ
AH-POO! AH-POO!
WHERE'S BABY?
...
CLINK
ガシャ
CLINK
ガシャ
THERE SHE IS!
オギャア
WAAAAAH
GRAH
グワッ
TCH! MISERABLE LITTLE THING!
I'LL JUST GOBBLE IT UP!
STOP THAT!!
THE BABY'S DONE NOTHING TO YOU! LET HER GO!!
WHY, IS IT YOURS?
オギャア
WAAAH
N-NO!!

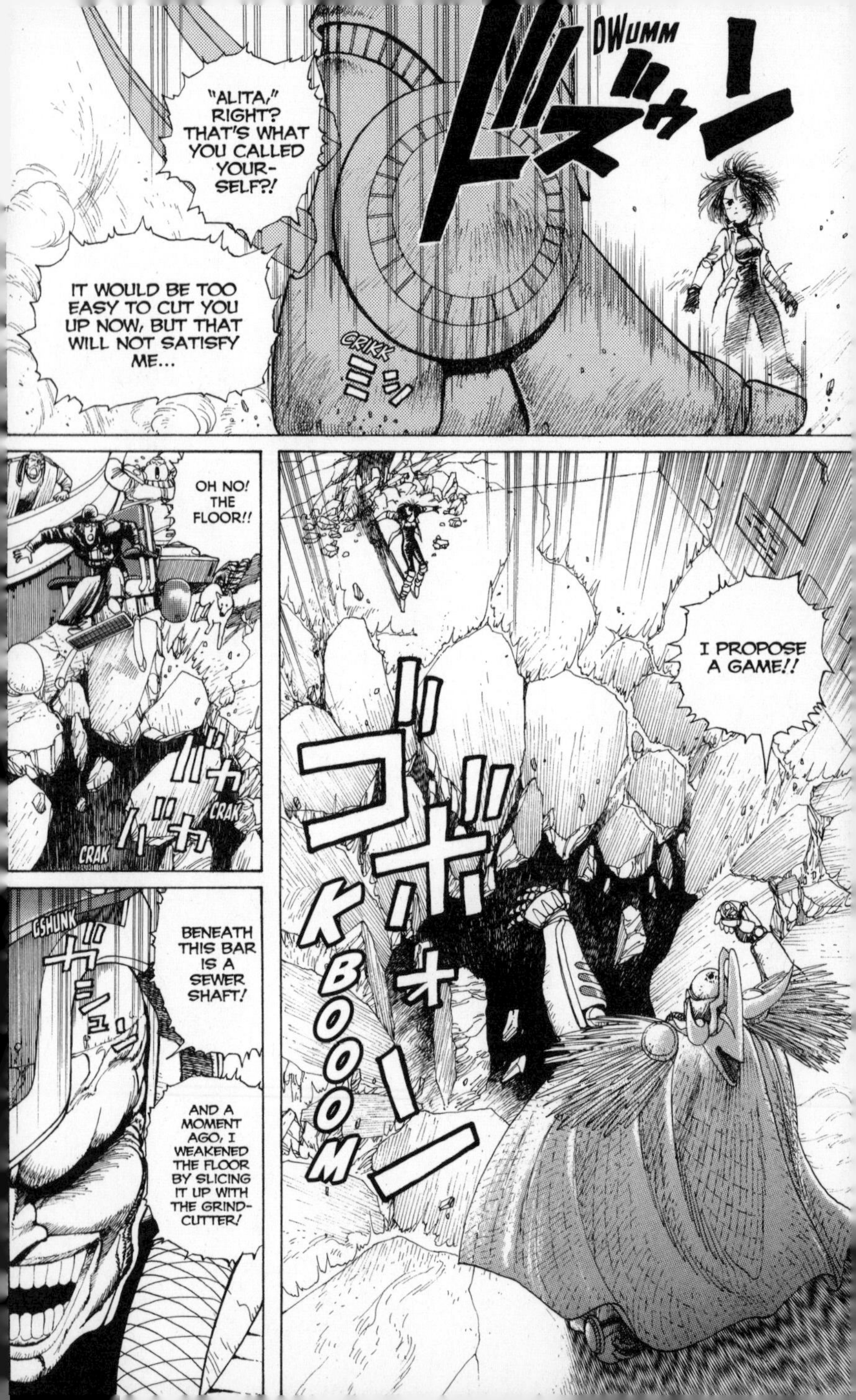
DWUMM
"ALITA," RIGHT? THAT'S WHAT YOU CALLED YOUR-SELF?!
IT WOULD BE TOO EASY TO CUT YOU UP NOW, BUT THAT WILL NOT SATISFY ME...
CRIKK
I PROPOSE A GAME!!
KBOOOOM
OH NO! THE FLOOR!!
CRAK
CRAK
GSHUNK
BENEATH THIS BAR IS A SEWER SHAFT!
AND A MOMENT AGO, I WEAKENED THE FLOOR BY SLICING IT UP WITH THE GRIND-CUTTER!

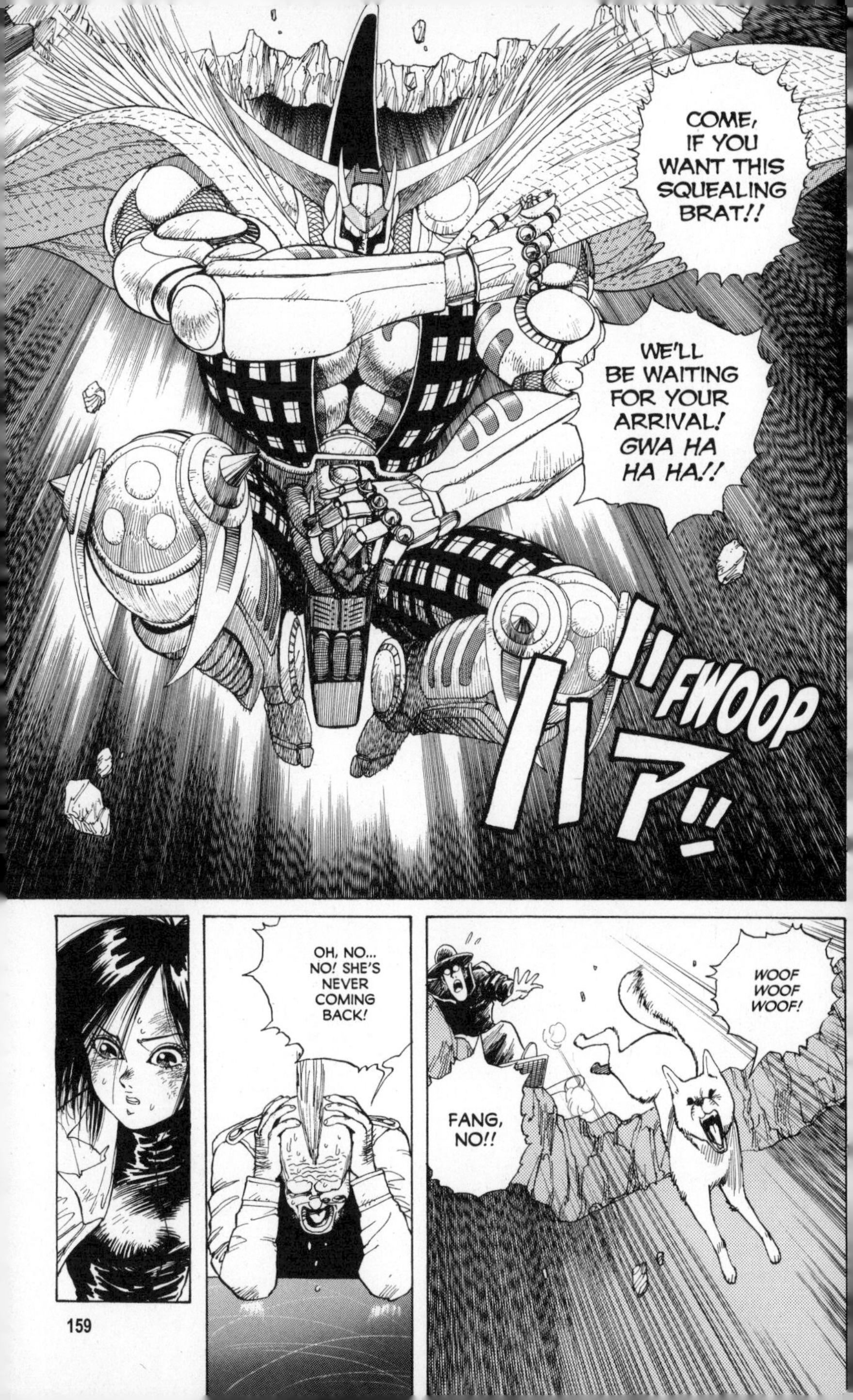
COME, IF YOU WANT THIS SQUEALING BRAT!!
WE'LL BE WAITING FOR YOUR ARRIVAL! GWA HA HA HA!!
FWOOP
WOOF WOOF WOOF!
FANG, NO!!
OH, NO... NO! SHE'S NEVER COMING BACK!

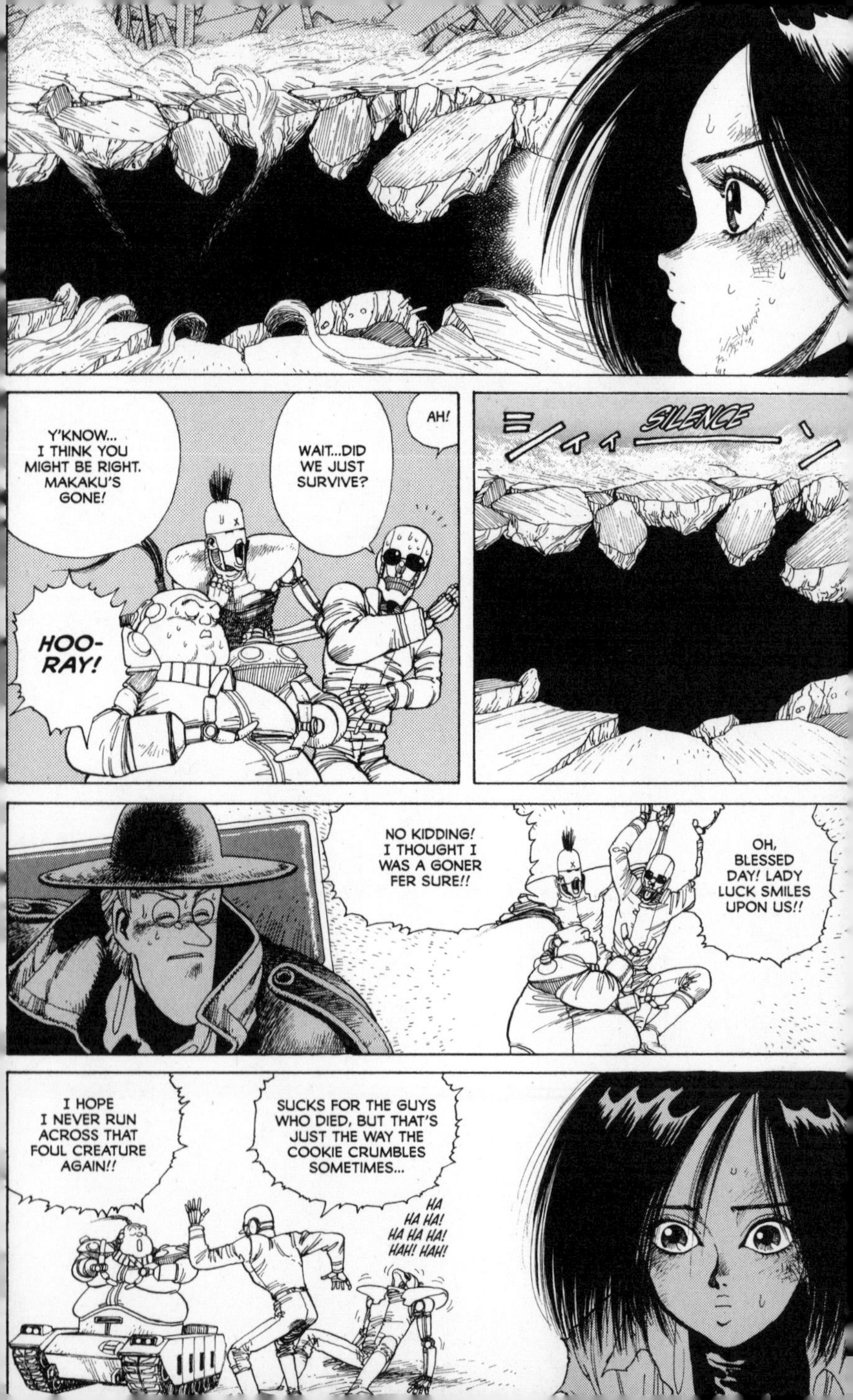
SILENCE
AH!
WAIT...DID WE JUST SURVIVE?
Y'KNOW... I THINK YOU MIGHT BE RIGHT. MAKAKU'S GONE!
HOO-RAY!
OH, BLESSED DAY! LADY LUCK SMILES UPON US!!
NO KIDDING! I THOUGHT I WAS A GONER FER SURE!!
SUCKS FOR THE GUYS WHO DIED, BUT THAT'S JUST THE WAY THE COOKIE CRUMBLES SOMETIMES...
I HOPE I NEVER RUN ACROSS THAT FOUL CREATURE AGAIN!!
HA HA HA! HA HA HA! HAH! HAH!

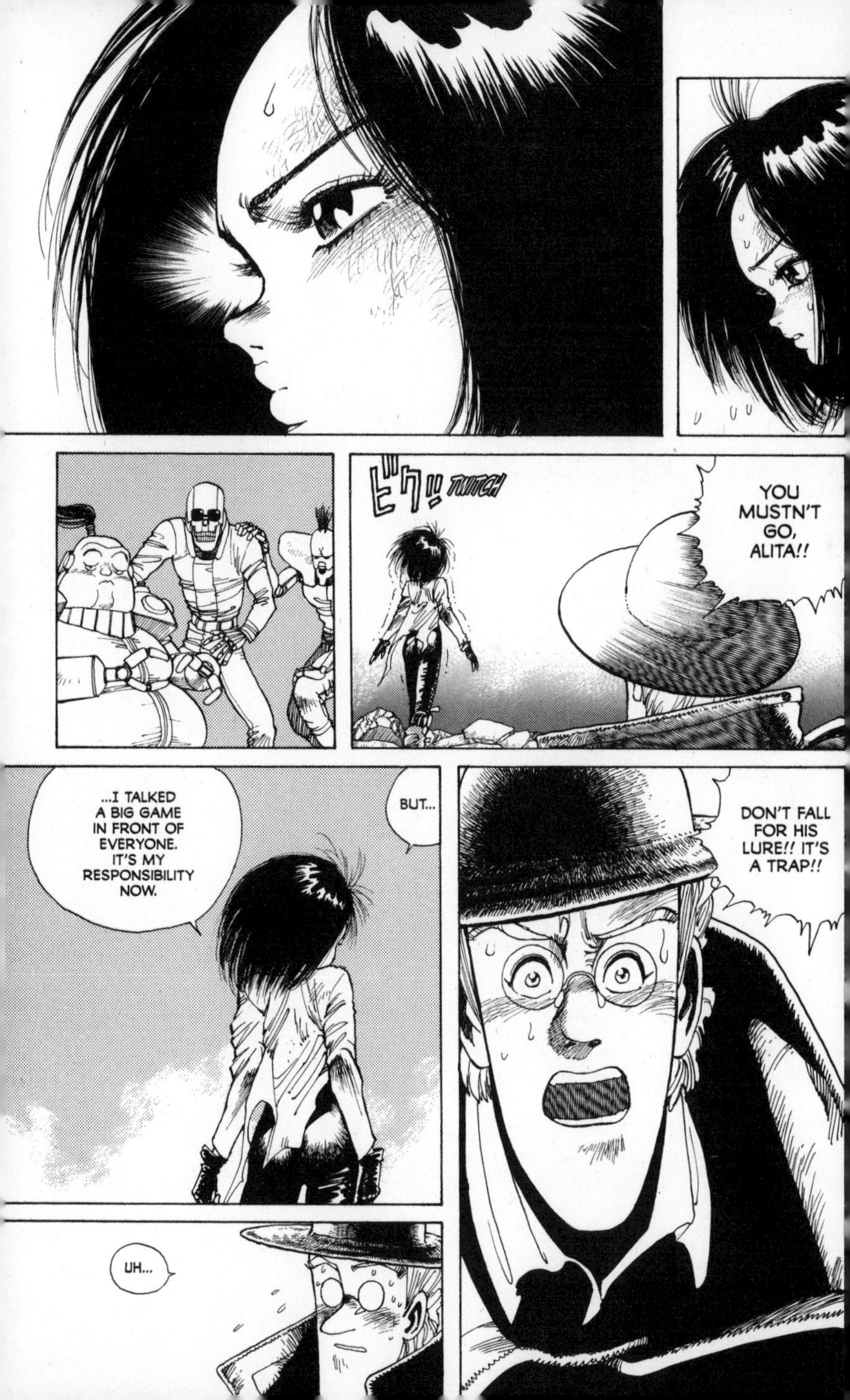
ビク!! TWITCH
YOU MUSTN'T GO, ALITA!!
DON'T FALL FOR HIS LURE!! IT'S A TRAP!!
BUT...
...I TALKED A BIG GAME IN FRONT OF EVERYONE. IT'S MY RESPONSIBILITY NOW.
UH...

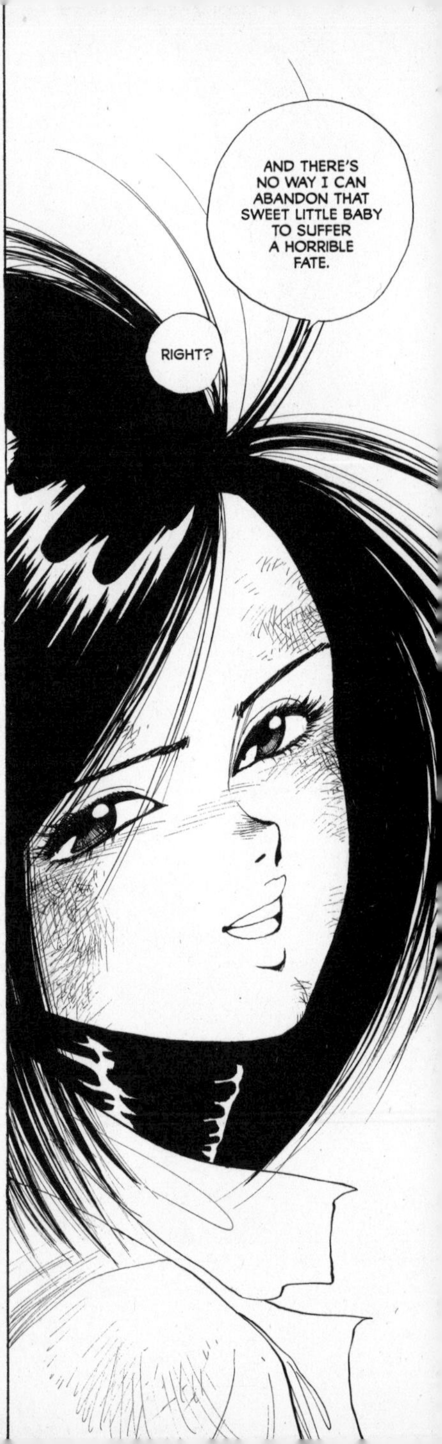
AND THERE'S NO WAY I CAN ABANDON THAT SWEET LITTLE BABY TO SUFFER A HORRIBLE FATE.
RIGHT?

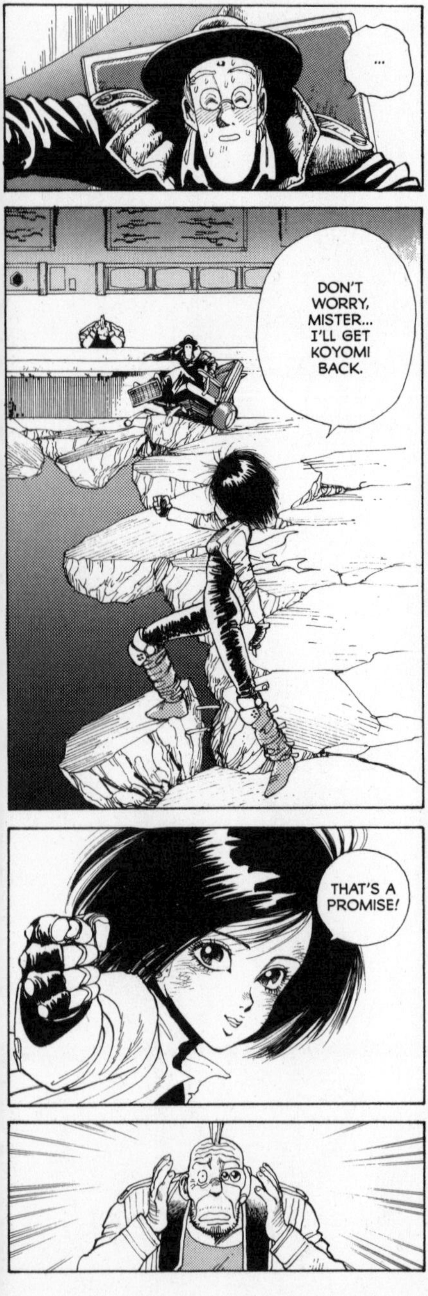
...
DON'T WORRY, MISTER... I'LL GET KOYOMI BACK.
THAT'S A PROMISE!

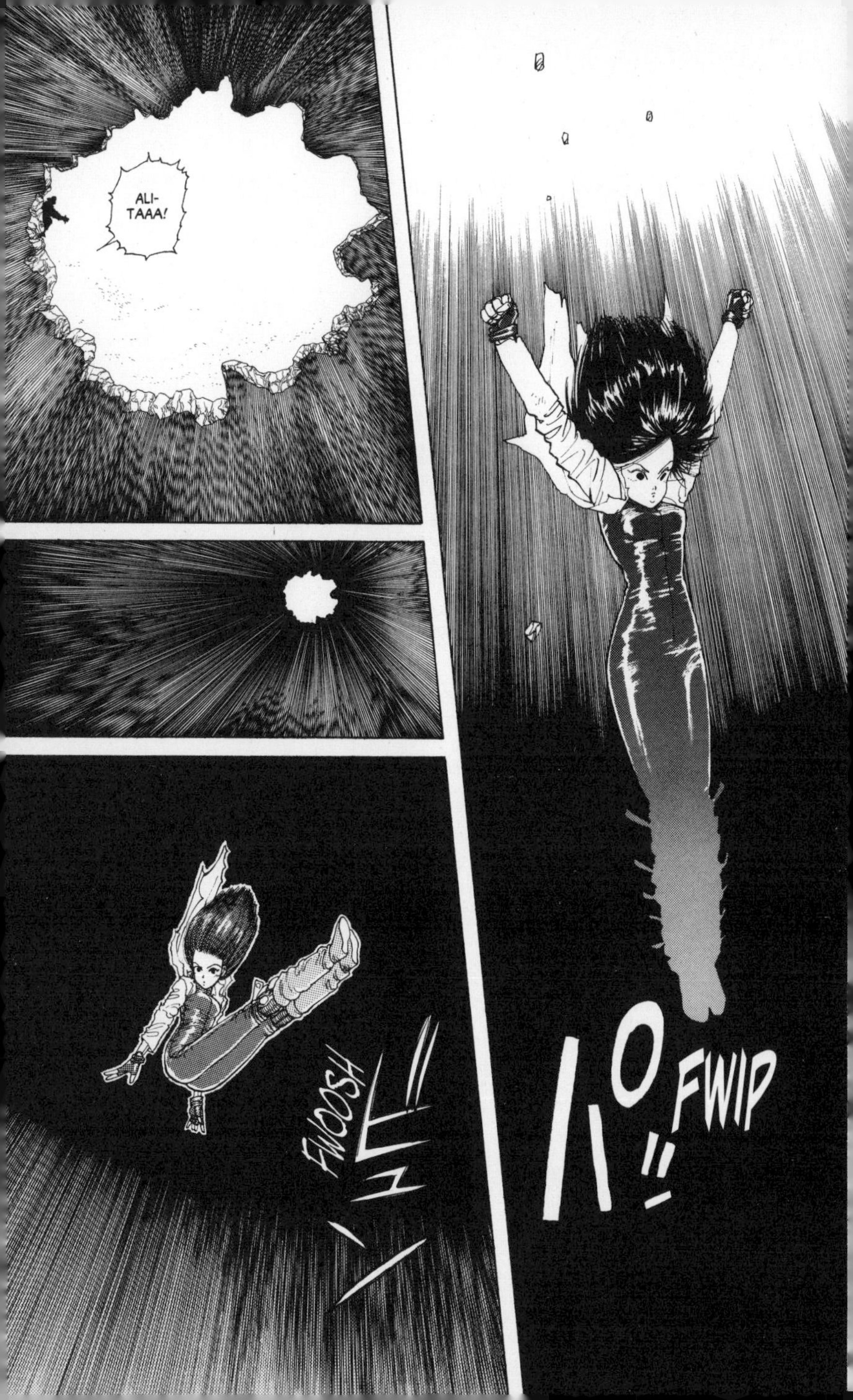
FWIP
ALI-TAAA!
FWOOSH

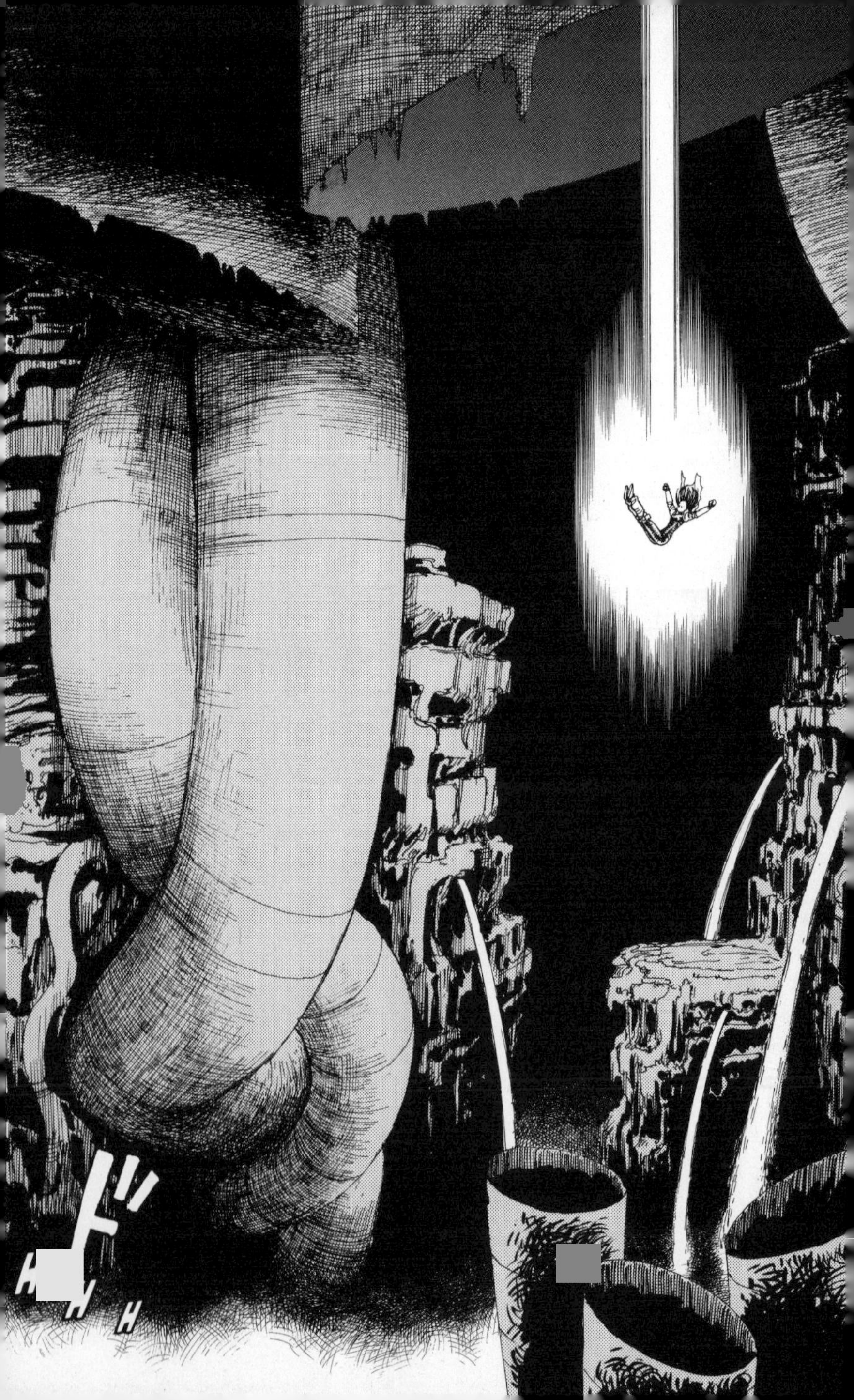
ド

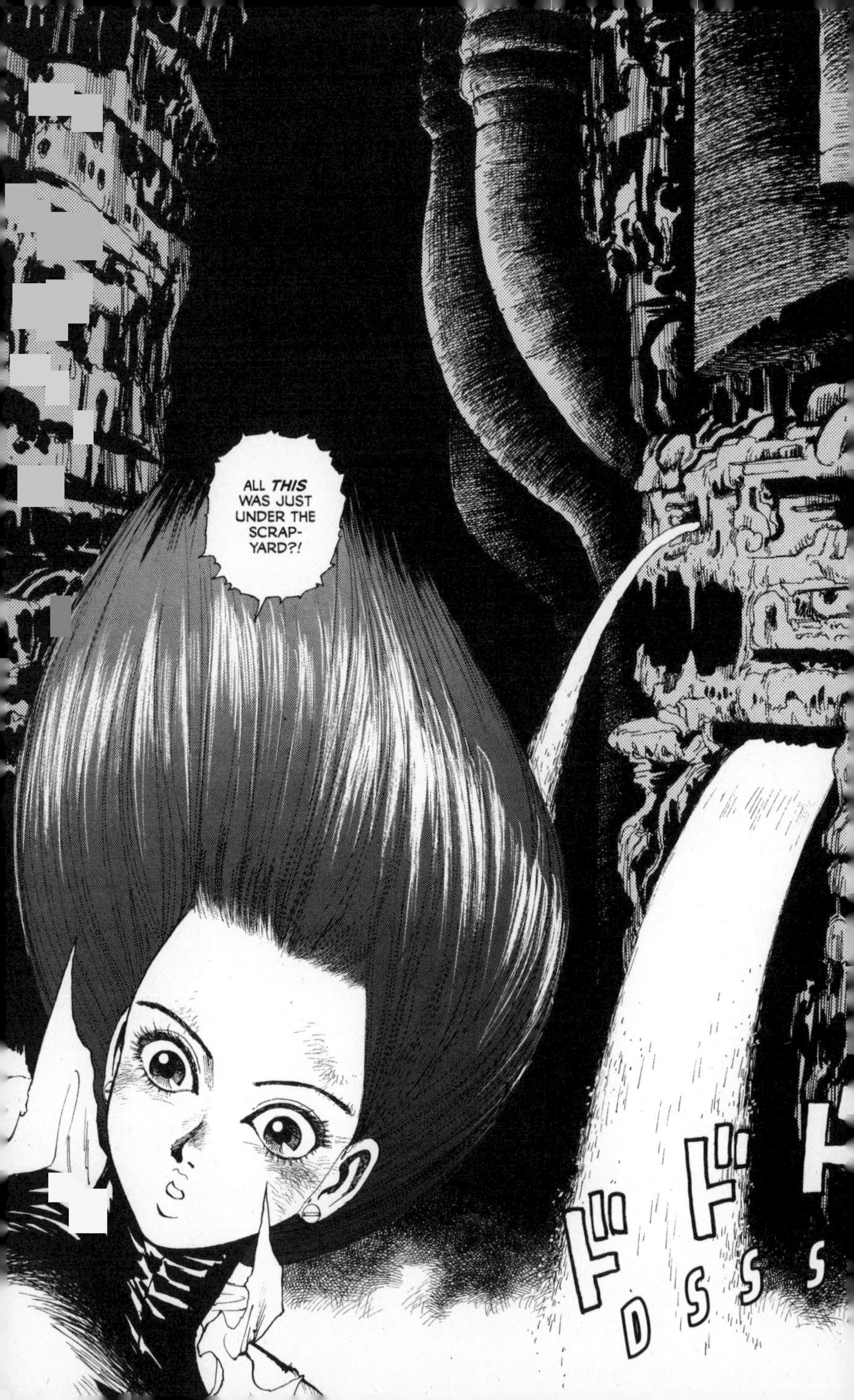
ALL THIS WAS JUST UNDER THE SCRAP-YARD?!
DSSS

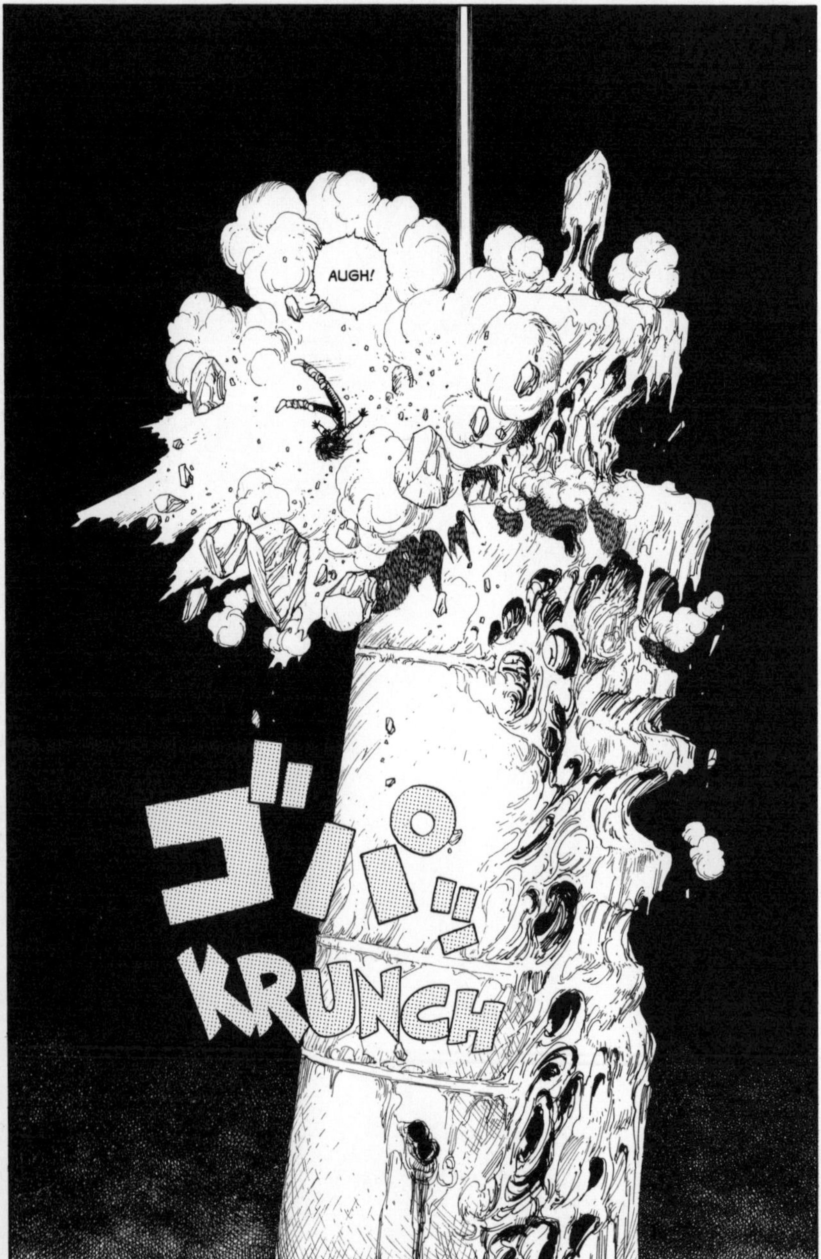
AUGH!
ゴバッ
KRUNCH

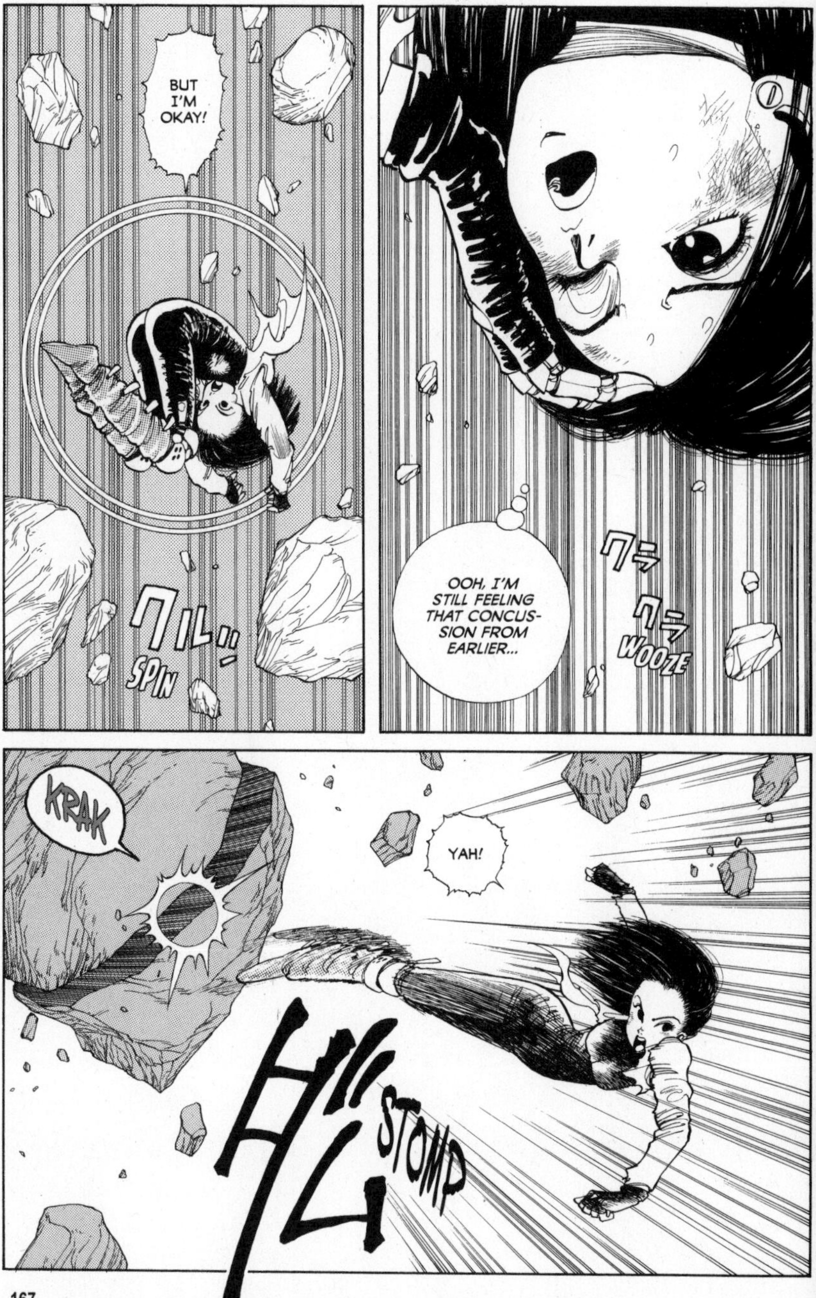
OOH, I'M STILL FEELING THAT CONCUSSION FROM EARLIER...
クラ クラ
WOOZE
BUT I'M OKAY!
クルッ
SPIN
YAH!
KRAK
ドム
STOMP

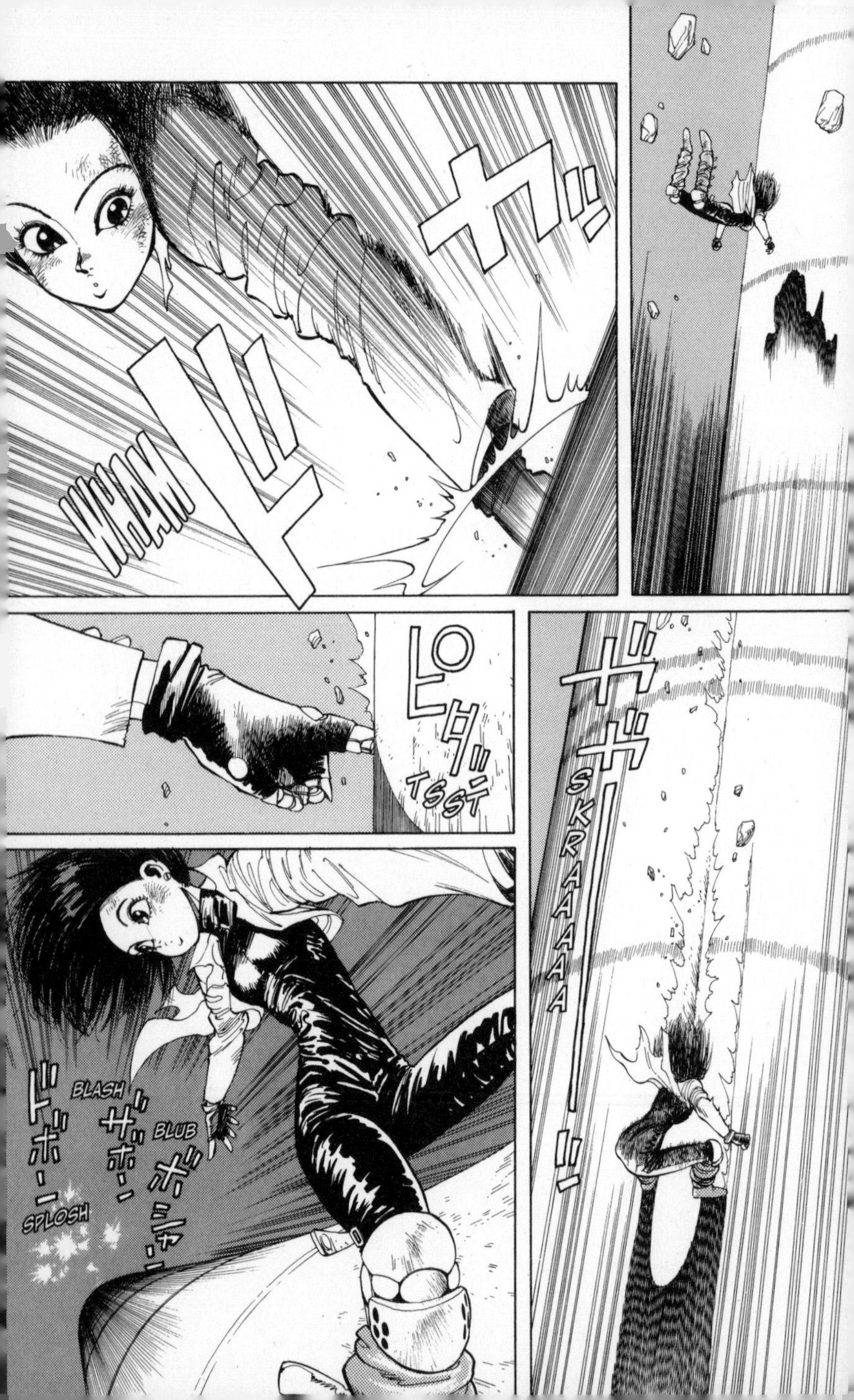
WHAM
SKRAAAAAAA
TSST
BLASH
BLUB
SPLOSH

CLUNK

MAKA-KU.

WHERE ARE YOU?

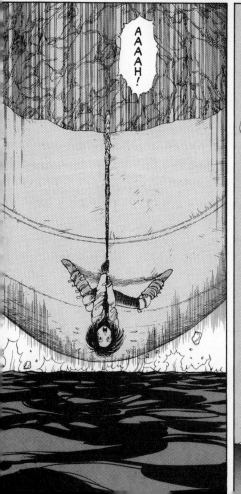

AAAAH!

HUH?

GRRGK

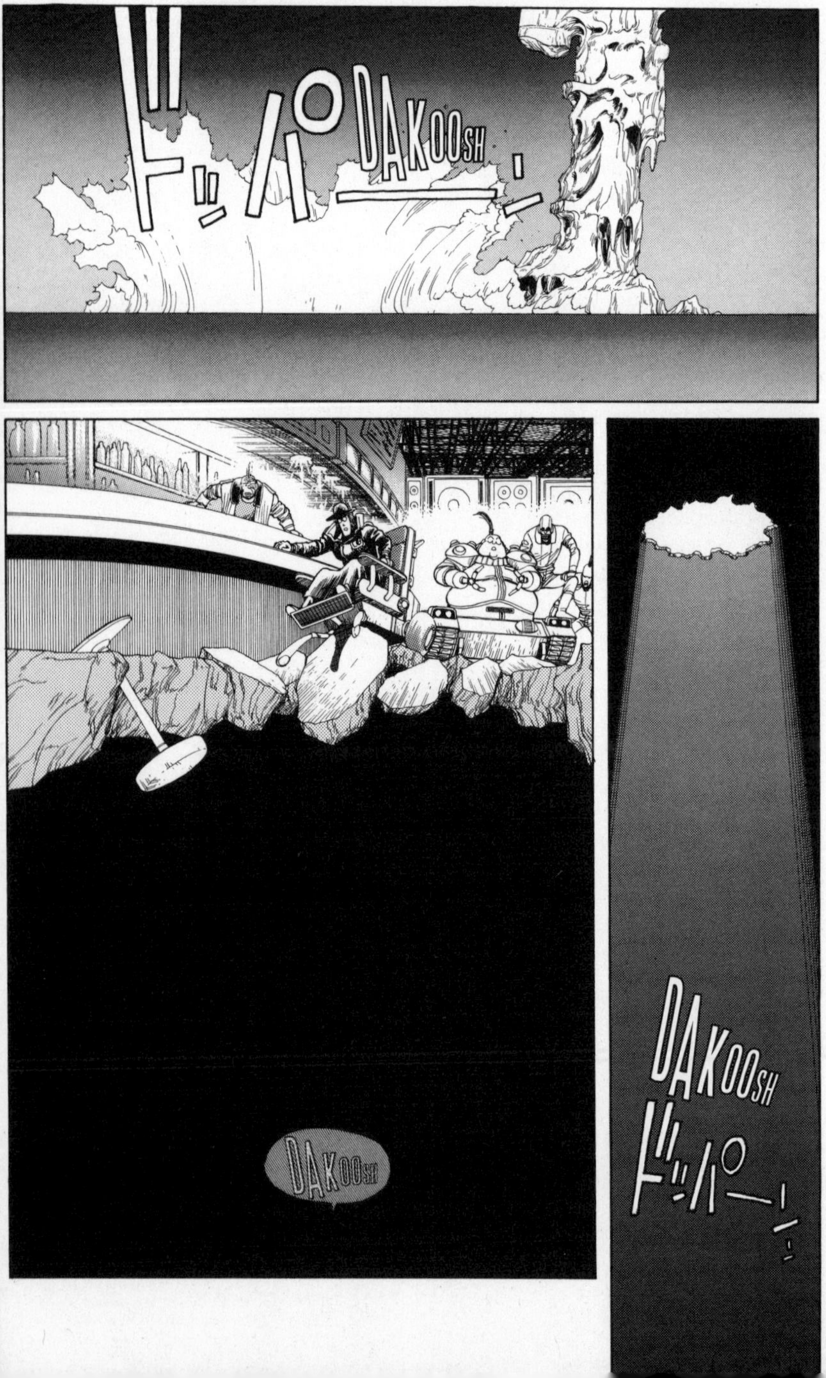
ドッパーー
DAKOOSH
DAKOOSH
ドッパーー
DAKOOSH

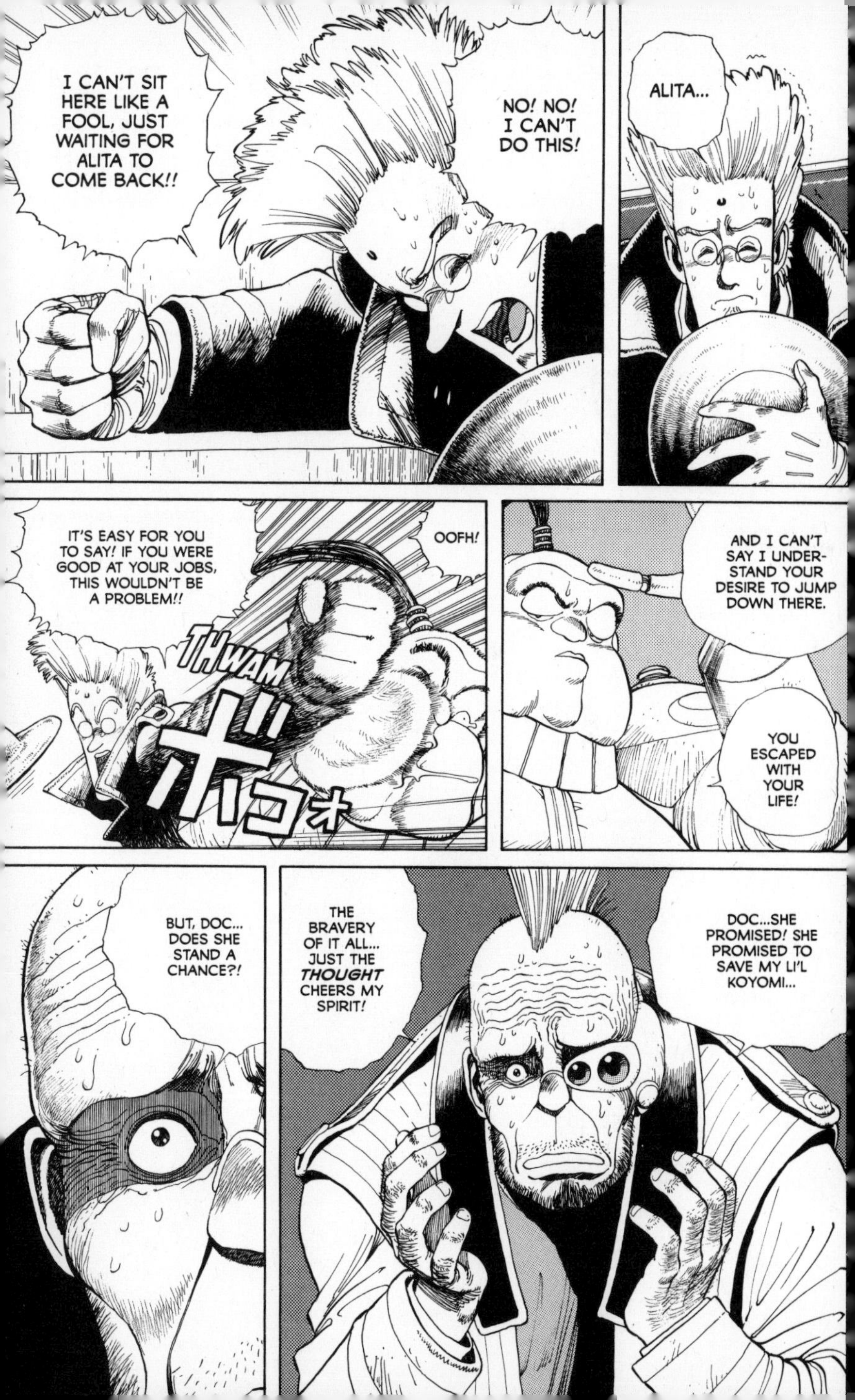
ALITA...
NO! NO! I CAN'T DO THIS!
I CAN'T SIT HERE LIKE A FOOL, JUST WAITING FOR ALITA TO COME BACK!!
AND I CAN'T SAY I UNDER-STAND YOUR DESIRE TO JUMP DOWN THERE.
YOU ESCAPED WITH YOUR LIFE!
OOFH!
IT'S EASY FOR YOU TO SAY! IF YOU WERE GOOD AT YOUR JOBS, THIS WOULDN'T BE A PROBLEM!!
THWAM
ボコォ
DOC...SHE PROMISED! SHE PROMISED TO SAVE MY LI'L KOYOMI...
THE BRAVERY OF IT ALL... JUST THE *THOUGHT* CHEERS MY SPIRIT!
BUT, DOC... DOES SHE STAND A CHANCE?!

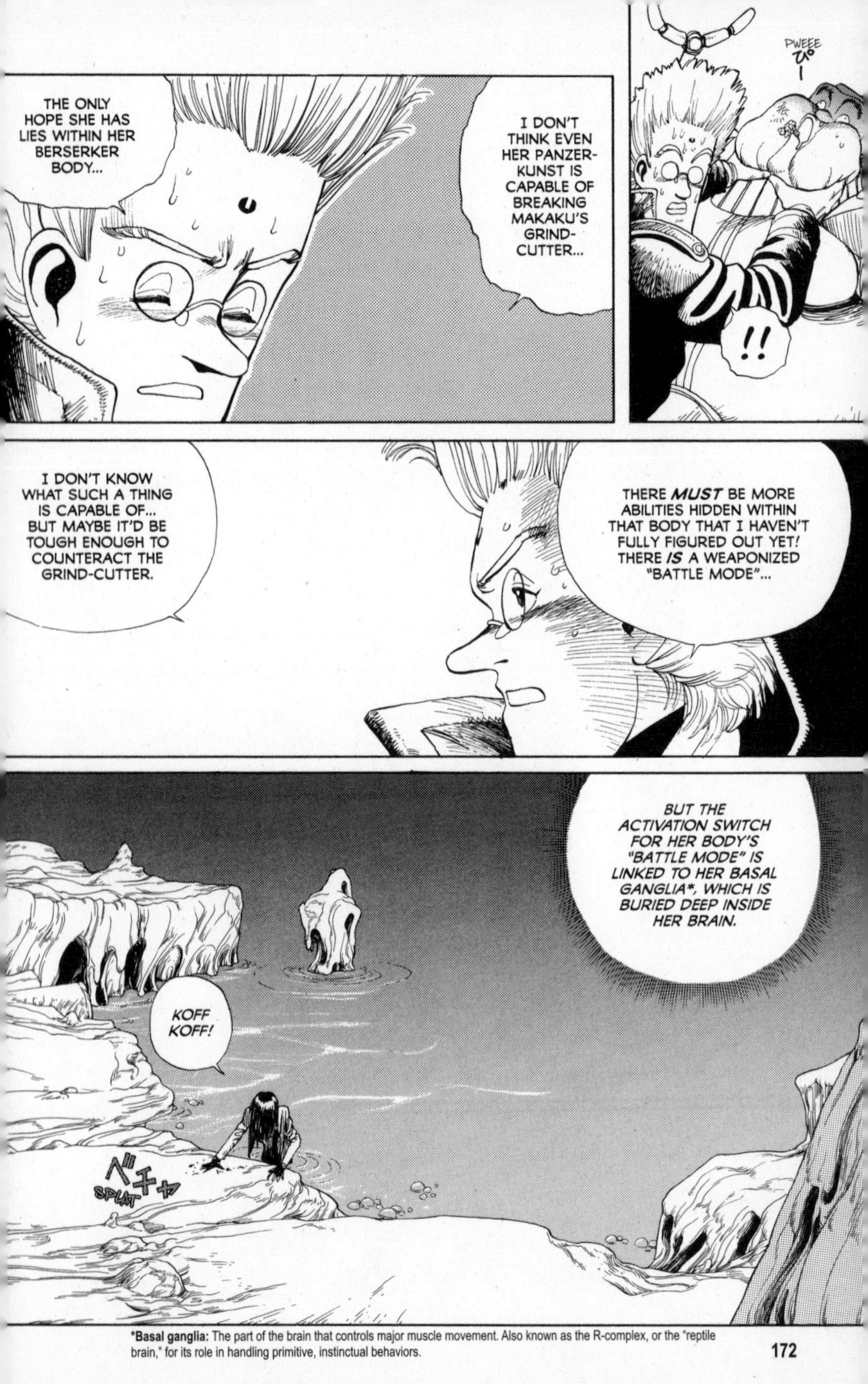
PWEEE
!!
I DON'T THINK EVEN HER PANZER-KUNST IS CAPABLE OF BREAKING MAKAKU'S GRIND-CUTTER...
THE ONLY HOPE SHE HAS LIES WITHIN HER BERSERKER BODY...
THERE *MUST* BE MORE ABILITIES HIDDEN WITHIN THAT BODY THAT I HAVEN'T FULLY FIGURED OUT YET! THERE *IS* A WEAPONIZED "BATTLE MODE"...
I DON'T KNOW WHAT SUCH A THING IS CAPABLE OF... BUT MAYBE IT'D BE TOUGH ENOUGH TO COUNTERACT THE GRIND-CUTTER.
BUT THE ACTIVATION SWITCH FOR HER BODY'S "BATTLE MODE" IS LINKED TO HER BASAL GANGLIA, WHICH IS BURIED DEEP INSIDE HER BRAIN.*
KOFF KOFF!
SPLAT

***Basal ganglia:** The part of the brain that controls major muscle movement. Also known as the R-complex, or the "reptile brain," for its role in handling primitive, instinctual behaviors.

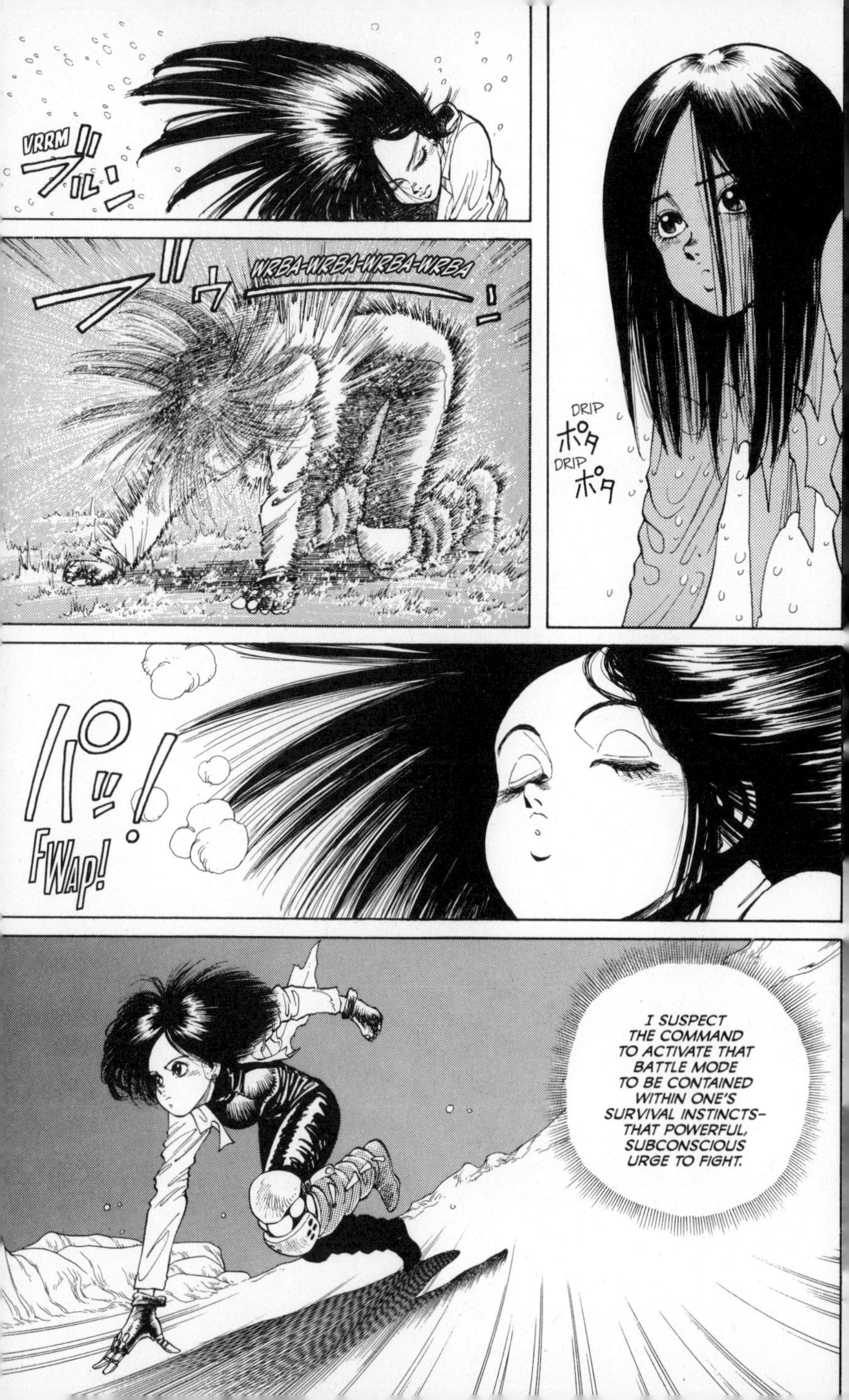
DRIP
ポタ
DRIP
ポタ
VRRM
WRBA-WRBA-WRBA-WRBA
FWAP!
I SUSPECT THE COMMAND TO ACTIVATE THAT BATTLE MODE TO BE CONTAINED WITHIN ONE'S SURVIVAL INSTINCTS– THAT POWERFUL, SUBCONSCIOUS URGE TO FIGHT.

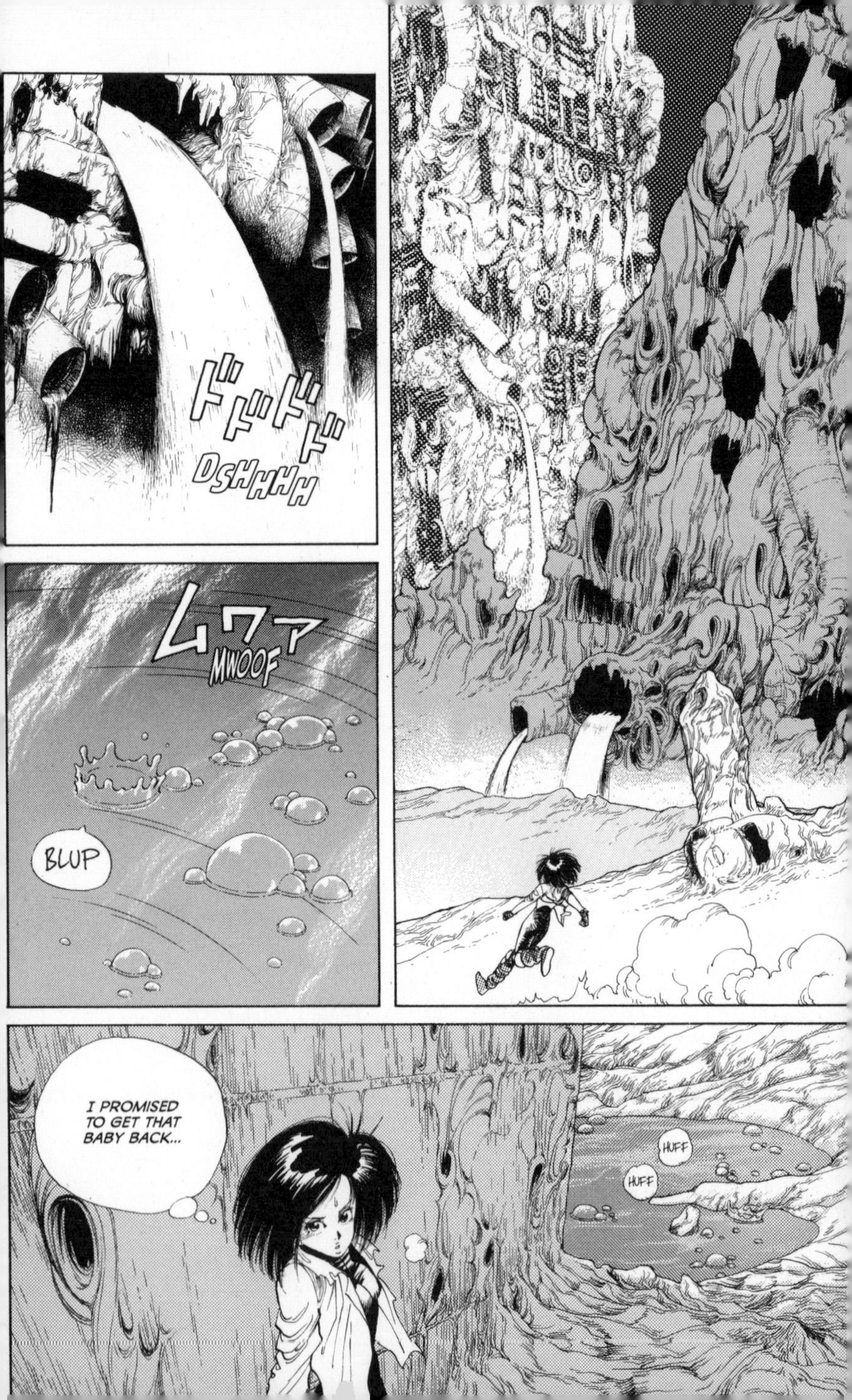
ドドドド
DSHHHH
ムワア
MWOOF
BLUP
I PROMISED TO GET THAT BABY BACK...
HUFF
HUFF

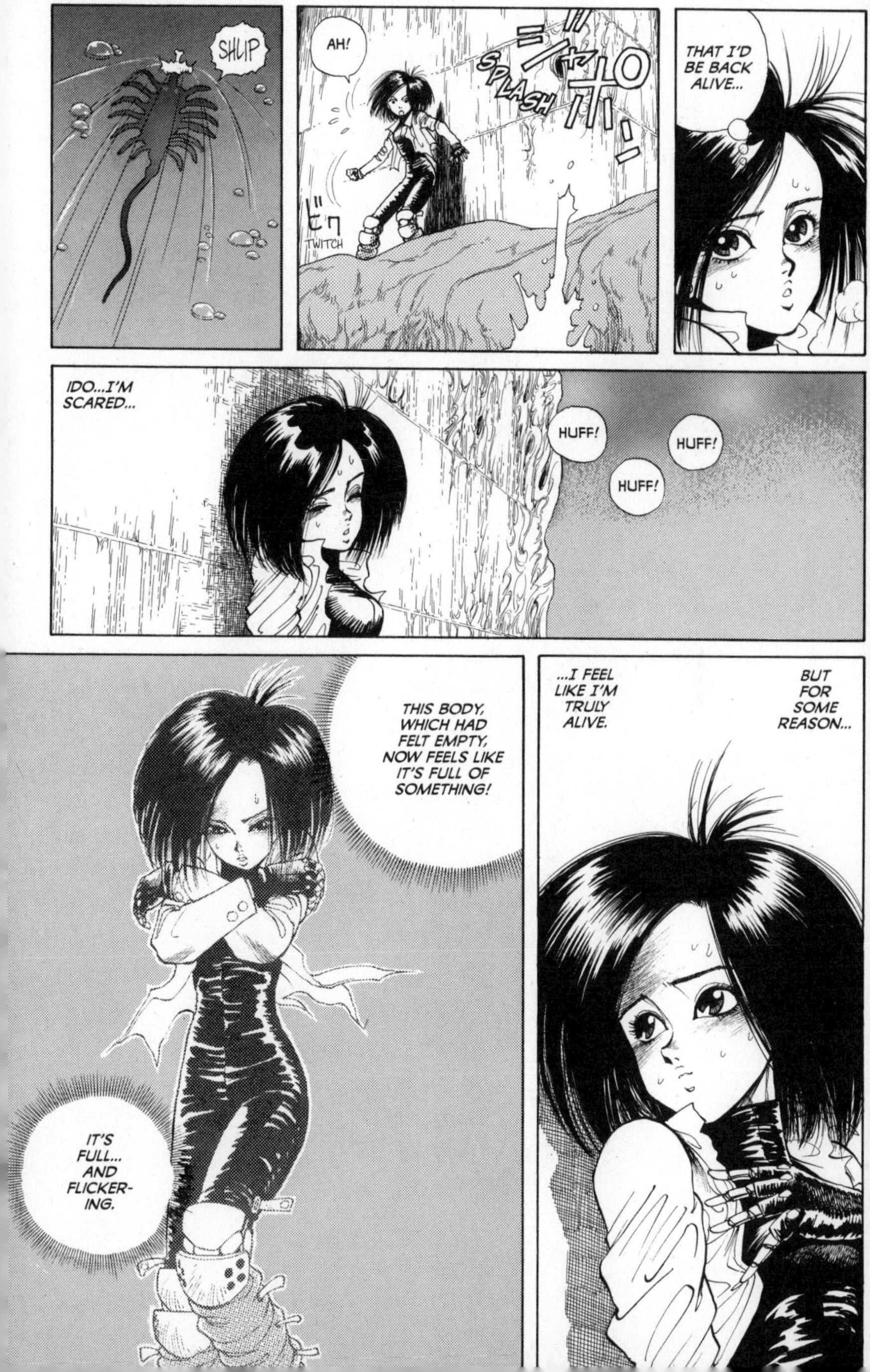
THAT I'D BE BACK ALIVE...
AH!
SPLASH
TWITCH
SHLIP
IDO...I'M SCARED...
HUFF!
HUFF!
HUFF!
BUT FOR SOME REASON...
...I FEEL LIKE I'M TRULY ALIVE.
THIS BODY, WHICH HAD FELT EMPTY, NOW FEELS LIKE IT'S FULL OF SOMETHING!
IT'S FULL... AND FLICKER-ING.

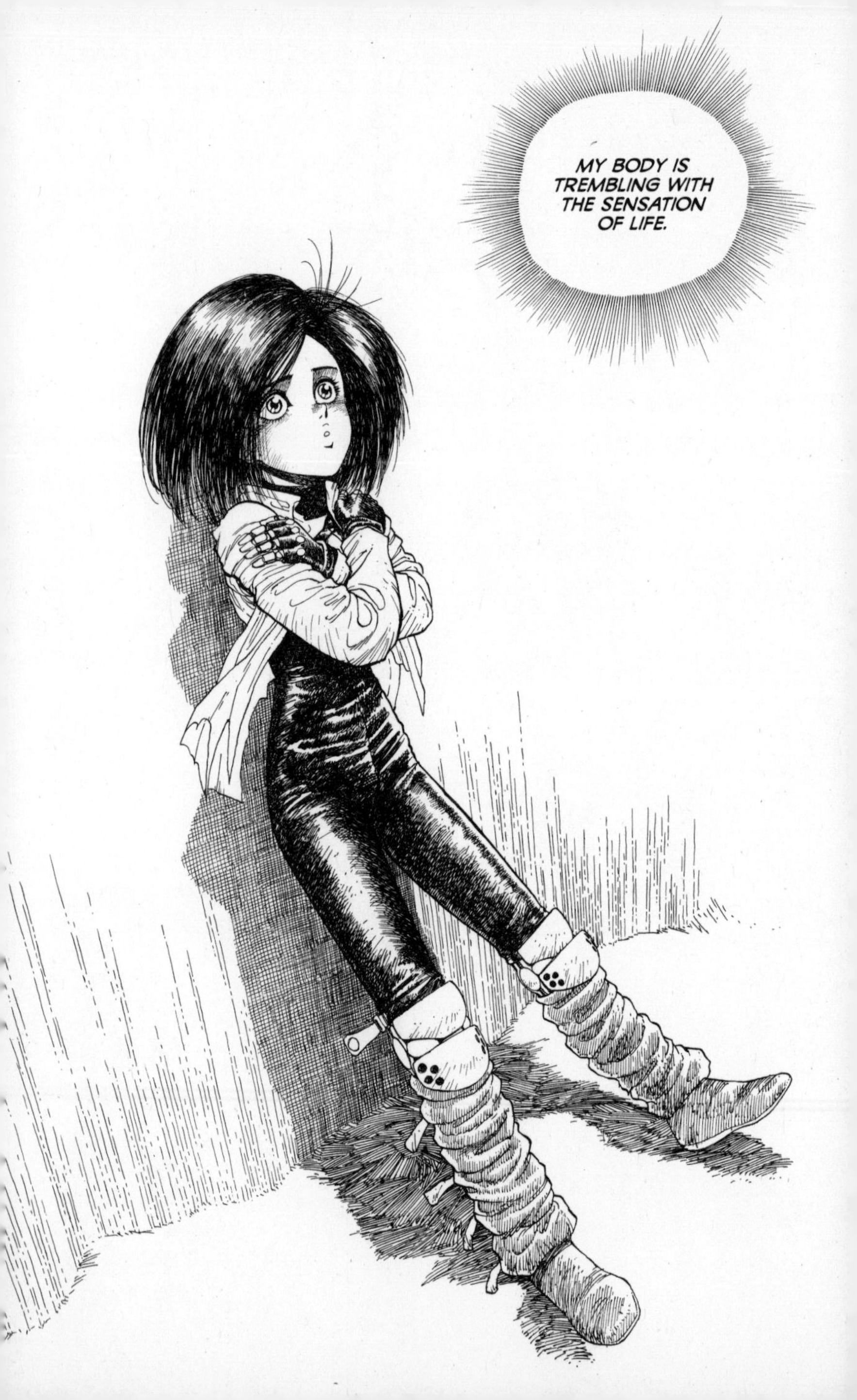
MY BODY IS TREMBLING WITH THE SENSATION OF LIFE.

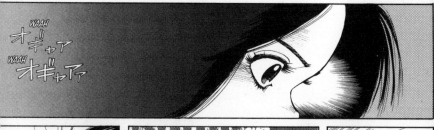

WAAH
オギャア

WAAH
オギャァァ

HUP

WAAH
オギャア

WAAH
オギャァ

THAT'S KOYOMI!

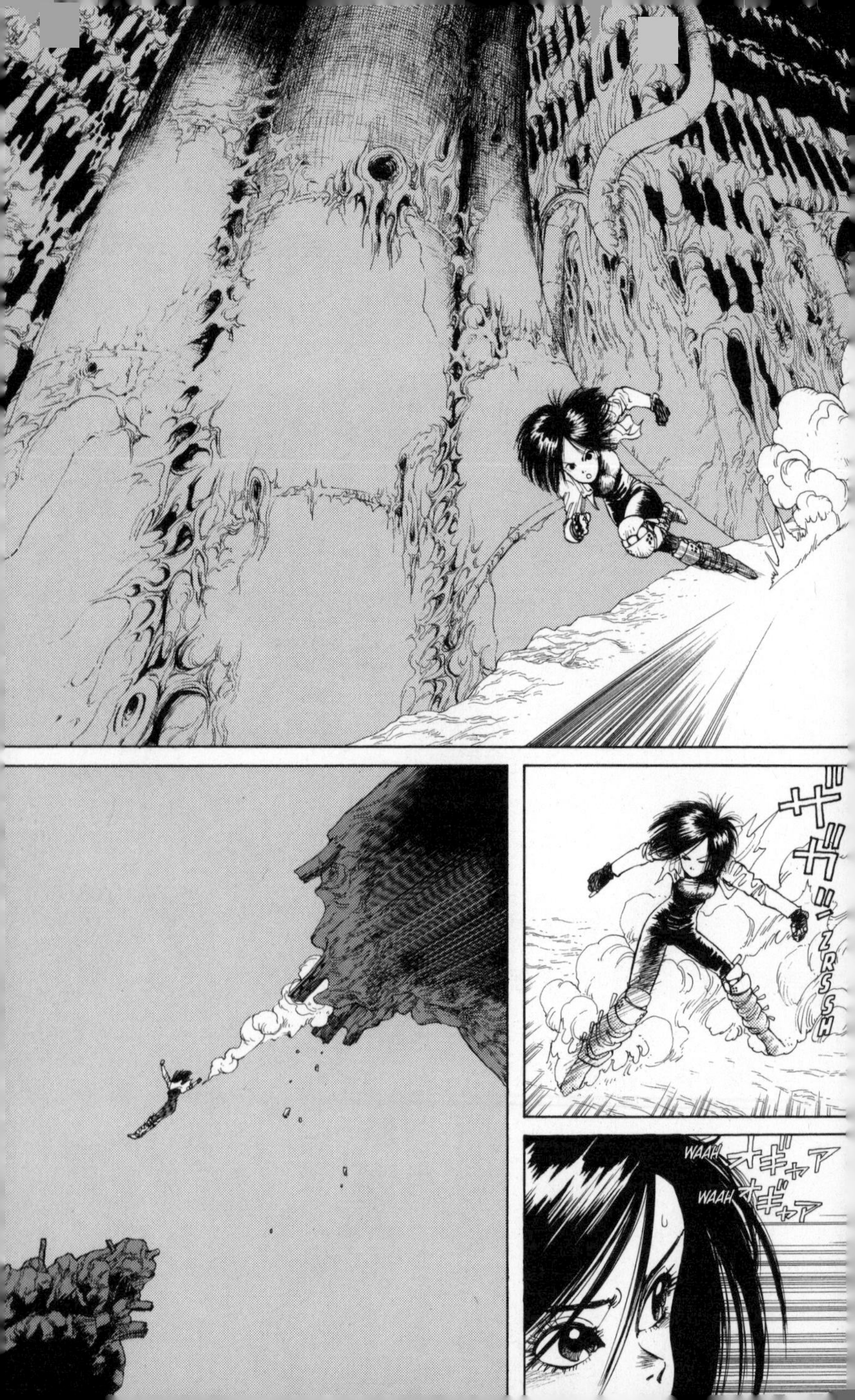
ザガ
ZRSSH
WAAH オギャア
WAAH オギャア

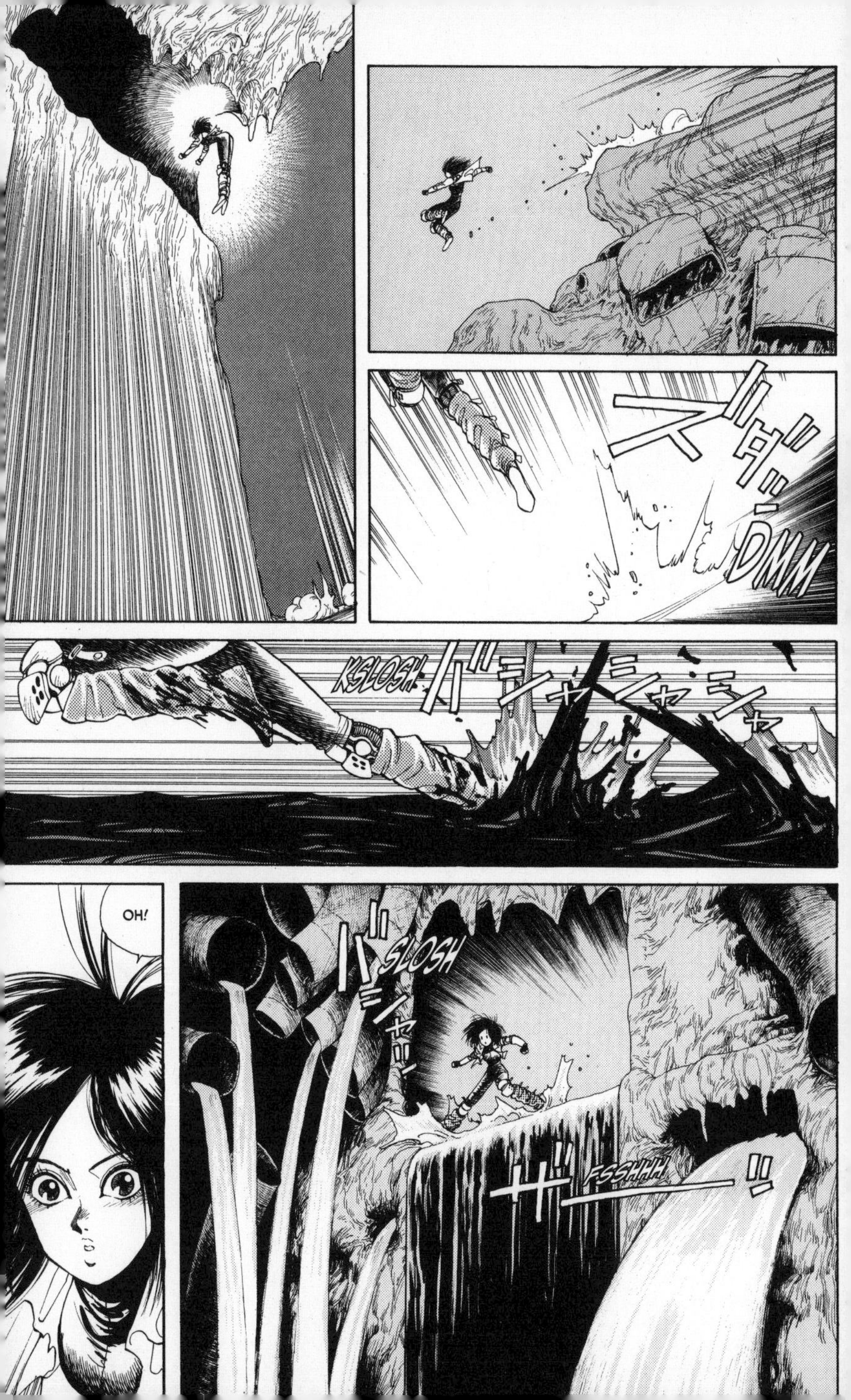
DMM
KSLOSH
SLOSH
FSSHHH
OH!

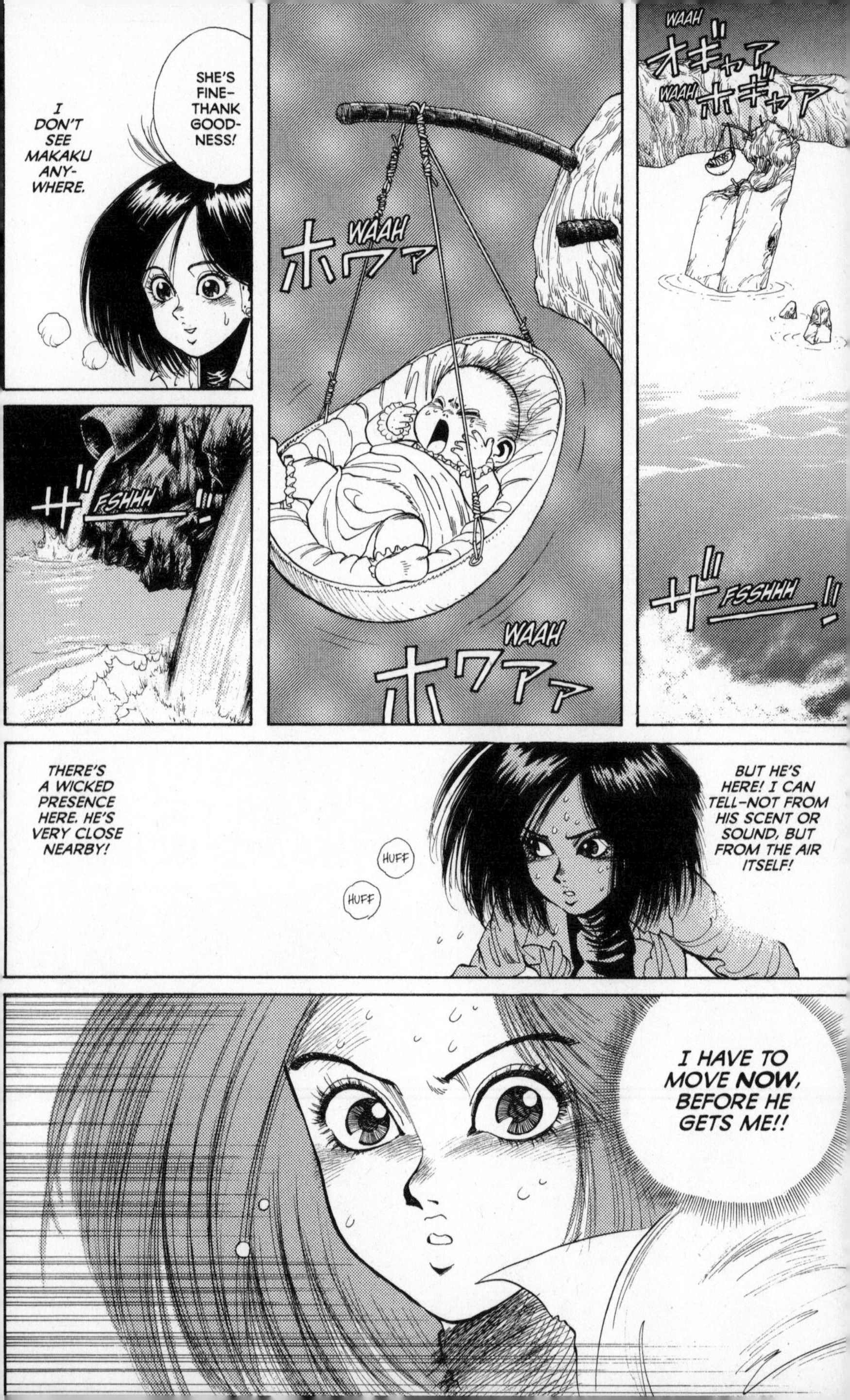
WAAH
WAAH
FSSHHH!!
WAAH
WAAH
SHE'S FINE—THANK GOODNESS!
I DON'T SEE MAKAKU ANYWHERE.
FSHHH
BUT HE'S HERE! I CAN TELL—NOT FROM HIS SCENT OR SOUND, BUT FROM THE AIR ITSELF!
HUFF
HUFF
THERE'S A WICKED PRESENCE HERE. HE'S VERY CLOSE NEARBY!
I HAVE TO MOVE **NOW**, BEFORE HE GETS ME!!

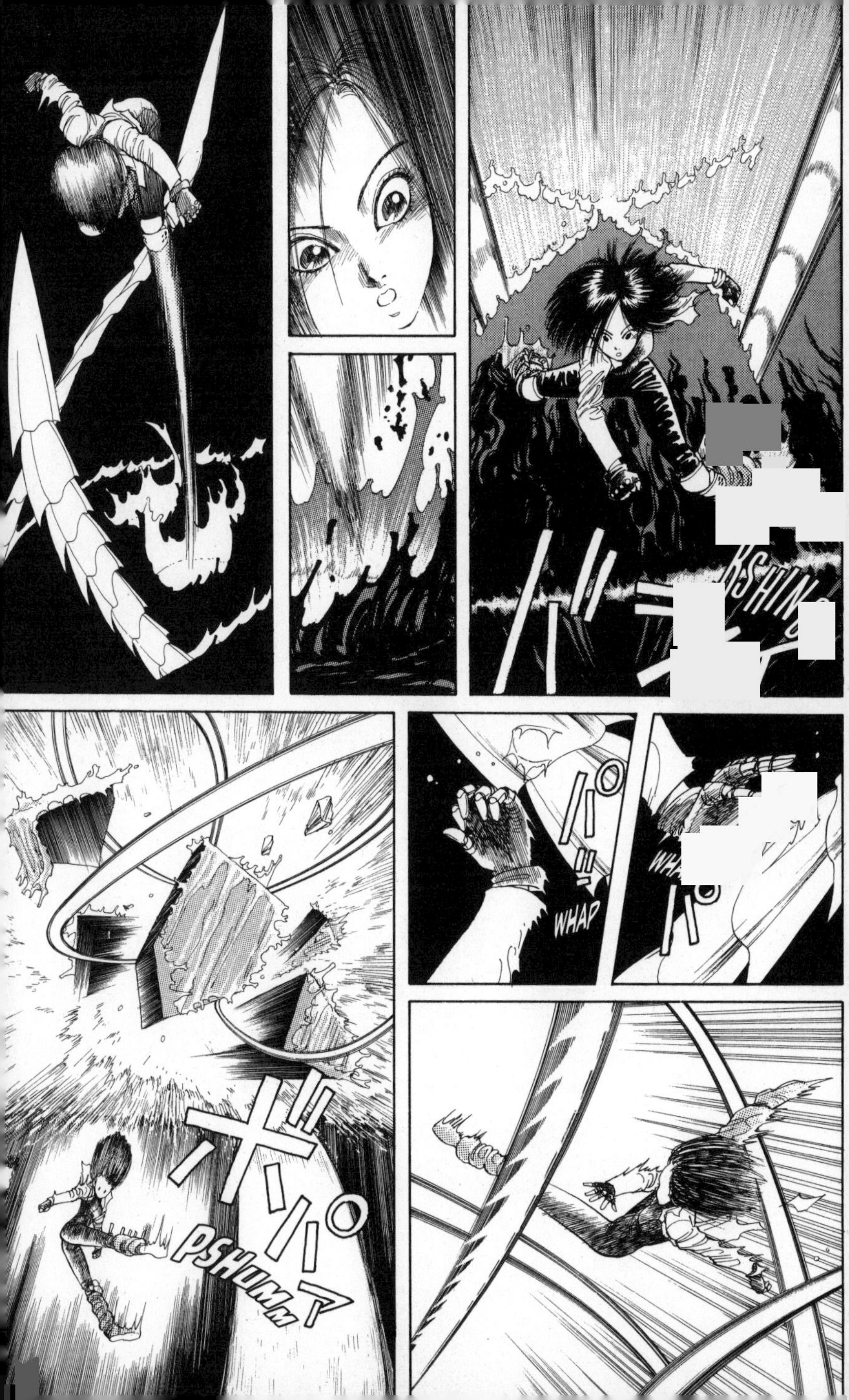
WHAP
PSHUMM

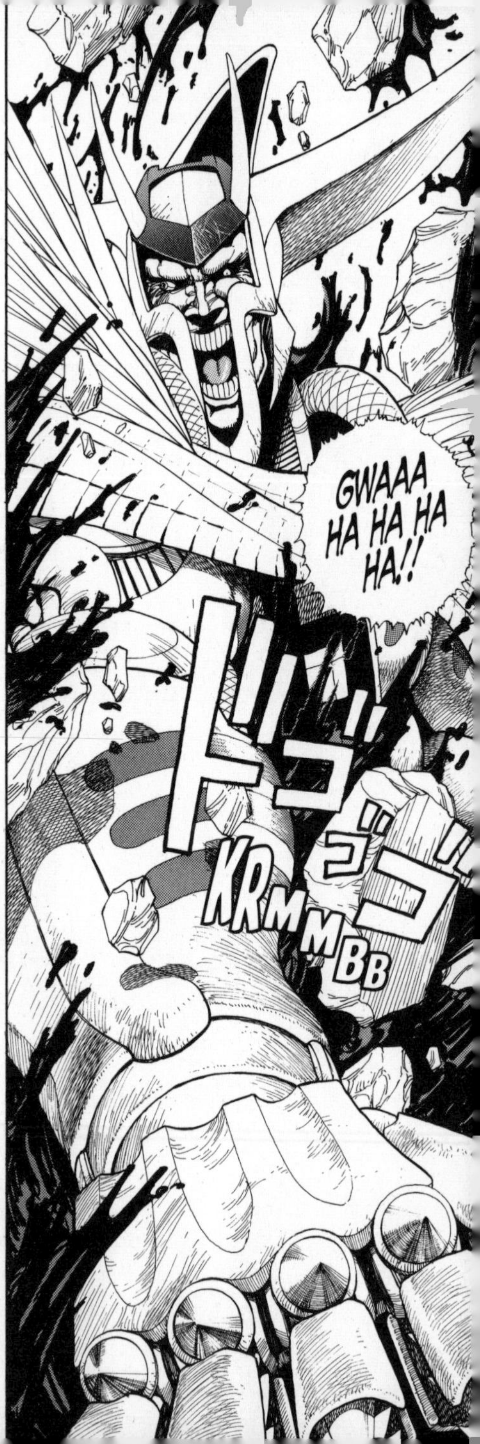
GWAAA HA HA HA HA!!
KRMMMBB

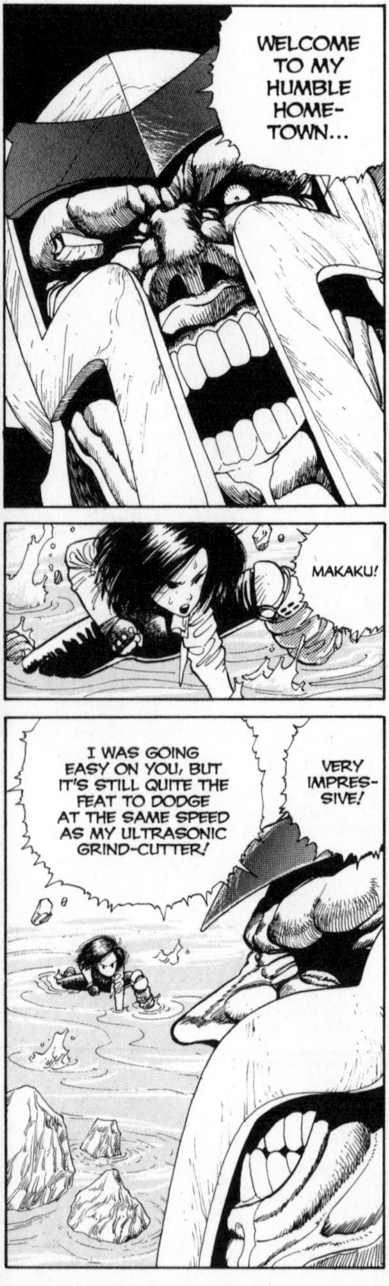
WELCOME TO MY HUMBLE HOME-TOWN...
MAKAKU!
VERY IMPRES-SIVE!
I WAS GOING EASY ON YOU, BUT IT'S STILL QUITE THE FEAT TO DODGE AT THE SAME SPEED AS MY ULTRASONIC GRIND-CUTTER!

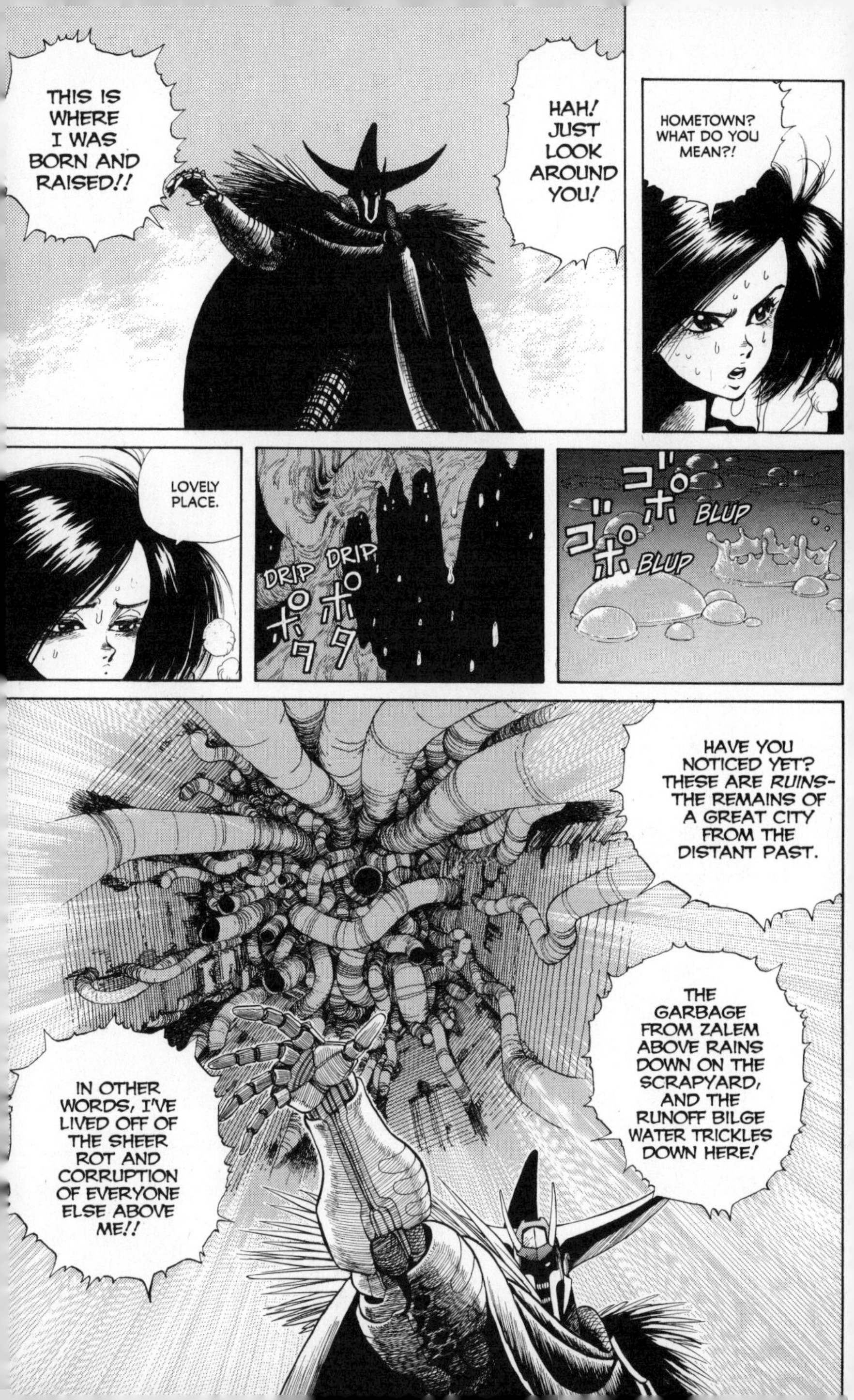
HOMETOWN? WHAT DO YOU MEAN?!
HAH! JUST LOOK AROUND YOU!
THIS IS WHERE I WAS BORN AND RAISED!!
ゴポ BLUP
ゴポ BLUP
DRIP DRIP
ポタ ポタ
LOVELY PLACE.
HAVE YOU NOTICED YET? THESE ARE *RUINS*- THE REMAINS OF A GREAT CITY FROM THE DISTANT PAST.
THE GARBAGE FROM ZALEM ABOVE RAINS DOWN ON THE SCRAPYARD, AND THE RUNOFF BILGE WATER TRICKLES DOWN HERE!
IN OTHER WORDS, I'VE LIVED OFF OF THE SHEER ROT AND CORRUPTION OF EVERYONE ELSE ABOVE ME!!

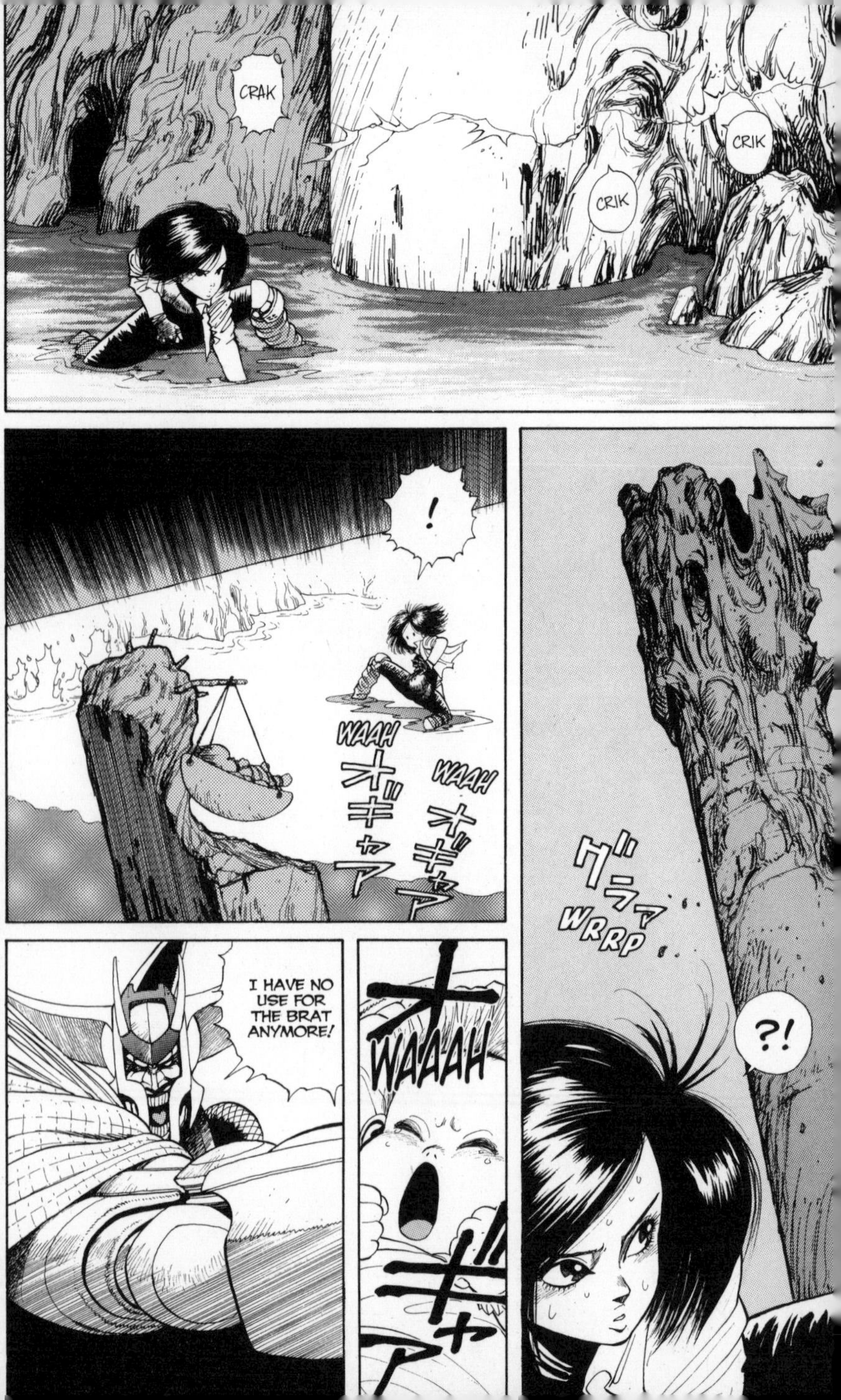
CRIK
CRIK
CRAK
グラァ
WRRP
?!
!
WAAH
オギャア
WAAH
オギャア
オギャア
WAAAH
I HAVE NO USE FOR THE BRAT ANYMORE!

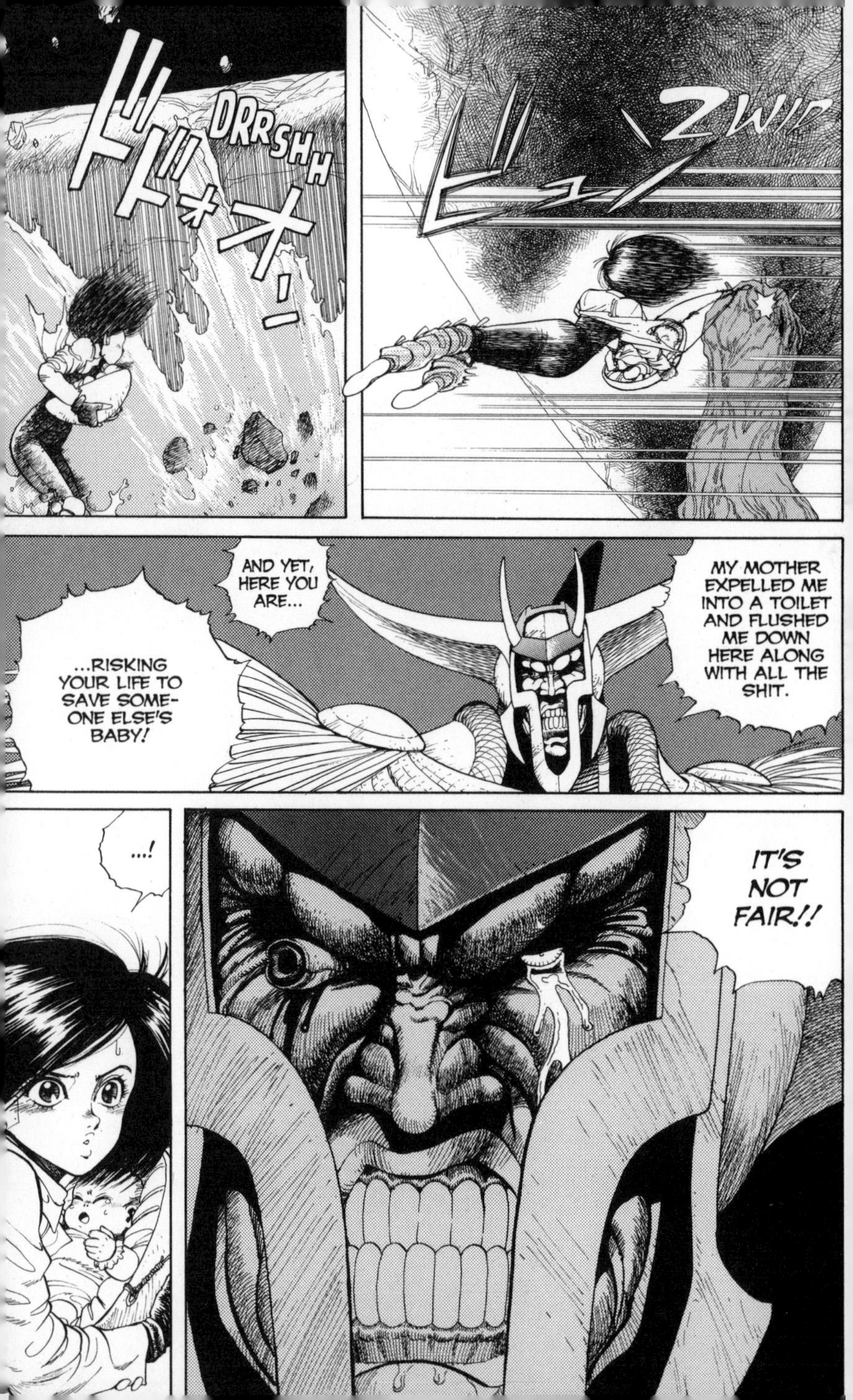
ビュン
ZWIP
ドドォオー
DRRSHH
MY MOTHER EXPELLED ME INTO A TOILET AND FLUSHED ME DOWN HERE ALONG WITH ALL THE SHIT.
AND YET, HERE YOU ARE...
...RISKING YOUR LIFE TO SAVE SOME-ONE ELSE'S BABY!
IT'S NOT FAIR!!
...!

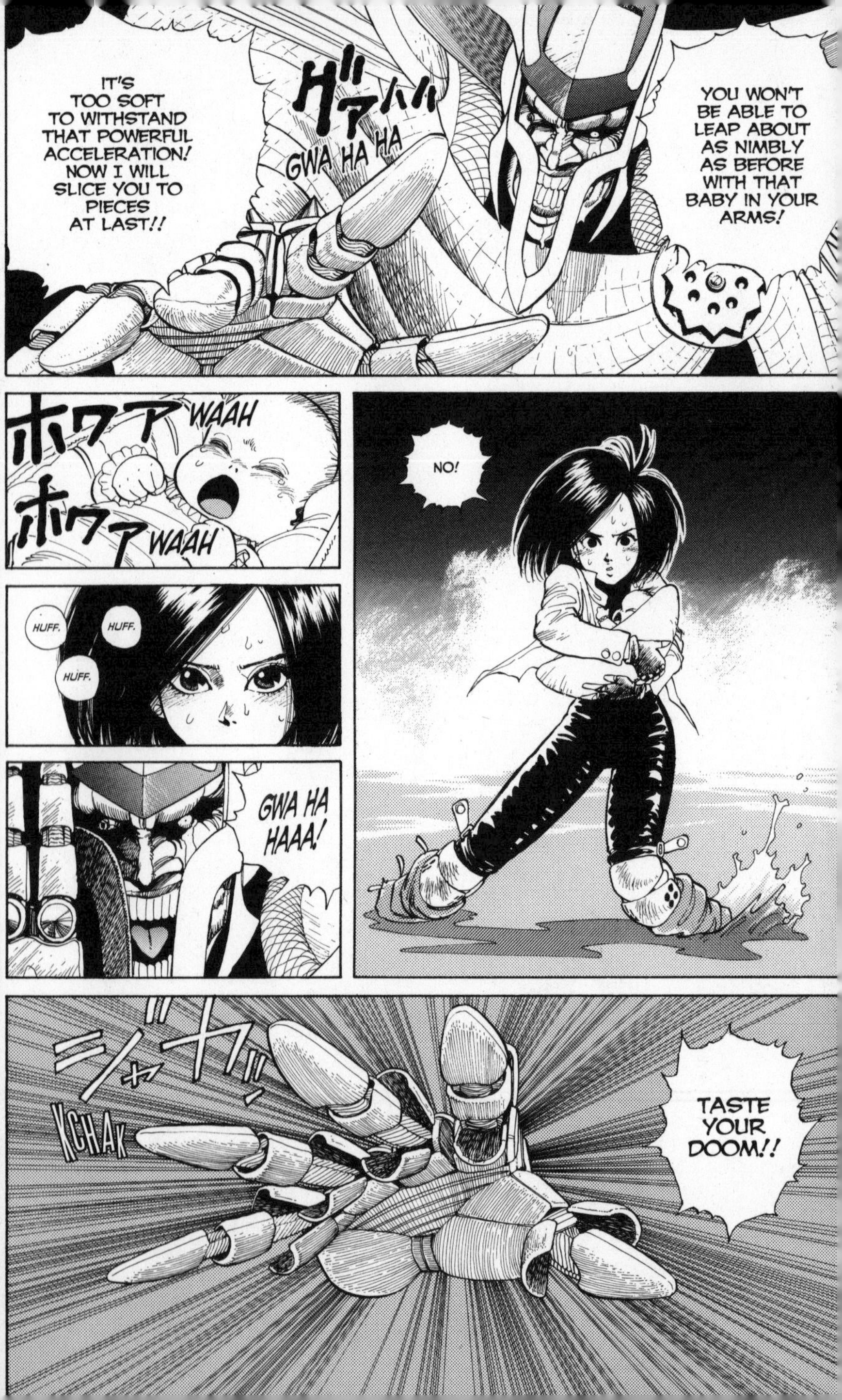
YOU WON'T BE ABLE TO LEAP ABOUT AS NIMBLY AS BEFORE WITH THAT BABY IN YOUR ARMS!
GWA HA HA
IT'S TOO SOFT TO WITHSTAND THAT POWERFUL ACCELERATION! NOW I WILL SLICE YOU TO PIECES AT LAST!!
NO!
ホワア WAAH
ホワア WAAH
HUFF.
HUFF.
HUFF.
GWA HA HAAA!
TASTE YOUR DOOM!!
KCHAK

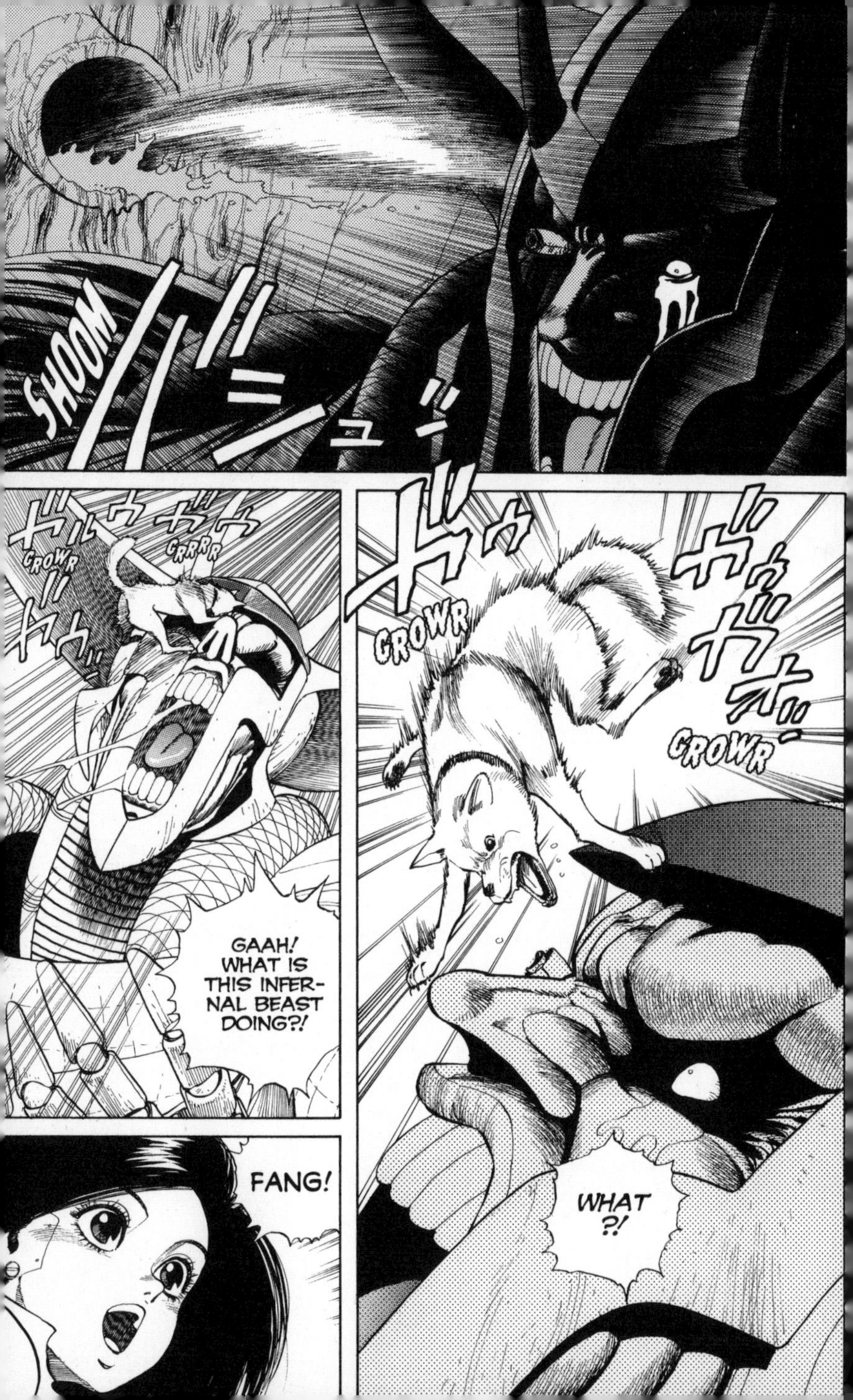
SHOOM
GROWR
GROWR
WHAT ?!
GRRRR
GROWR
GAAH! WHAT IS THIS INFER-NAL BEAST DOING?!
FANG!

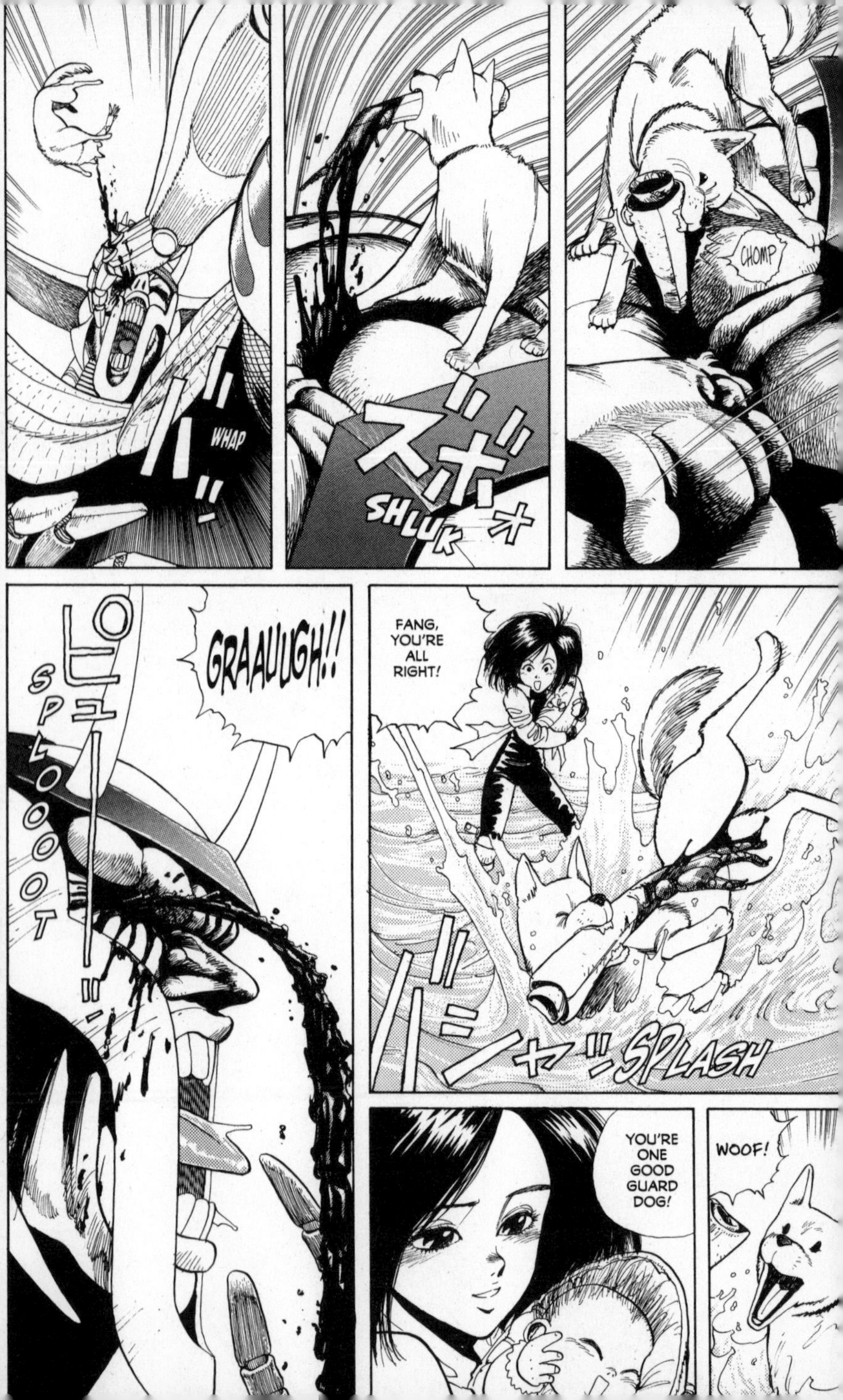
CHOMP
ズボォ
SHLUK
WHAP
FANG, YOU'RE ALL RIGHT!
SPLASH
WOOF!
YOU'RE ONE GOOD GUARD DOG!
GRAAUUGH!!
ピュー
SPLOOOOOT

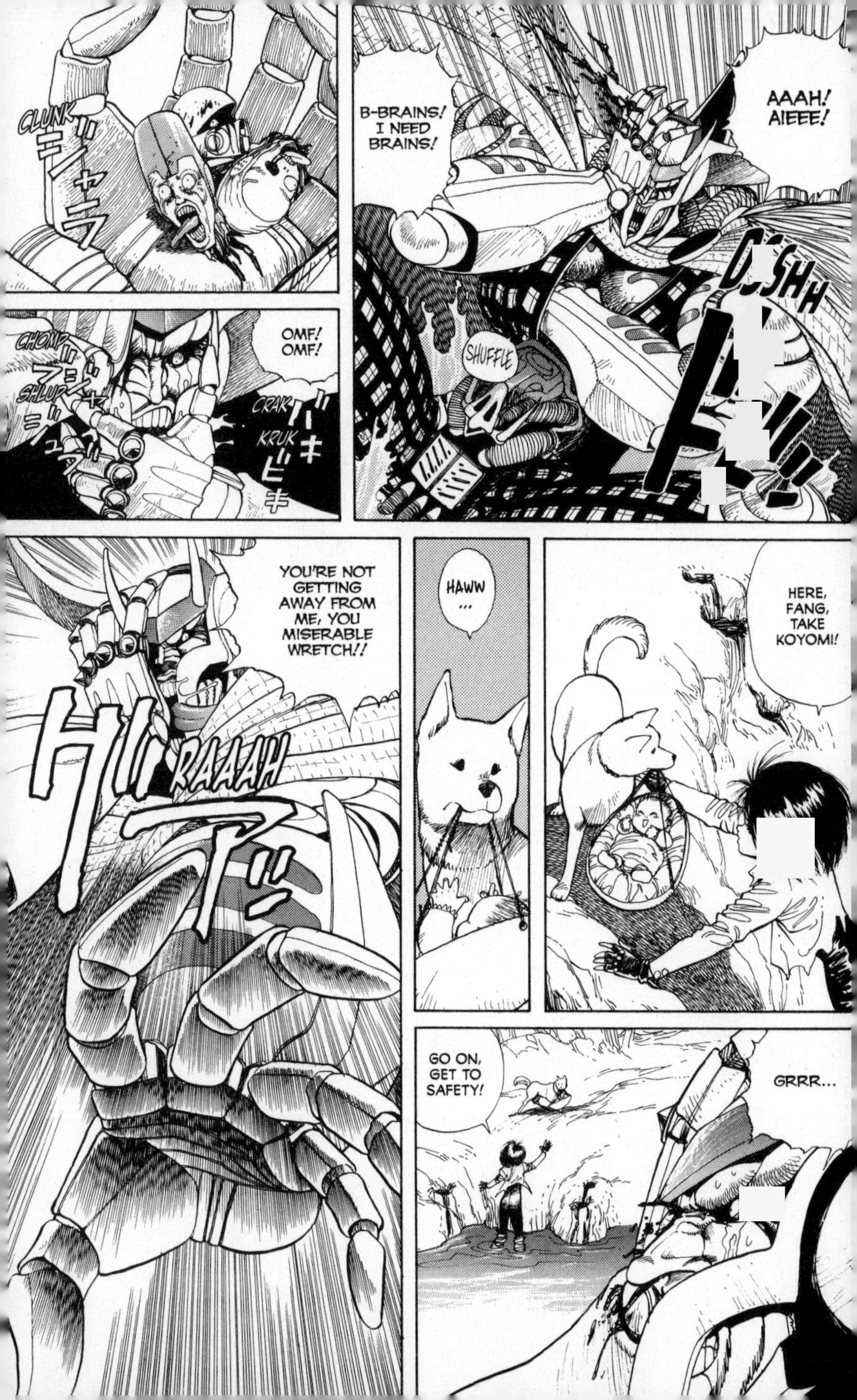
AAAH! AIEEE!
B-BRAINS! I NEED BRAINS!
DSHH
SHUFFLE
CLUNK
OMF! OMF!
CHOMP
SHLUP
CRAK
KRUK
HERE, FANG, TAKE KOYOMI!
HAWW ...
GRRR...
GO ON, GET TO SAFETY!
YOU'RE NOT GETTING AWAY FROM ME, YOU MISERABLE WRETCH!!
RAAAH

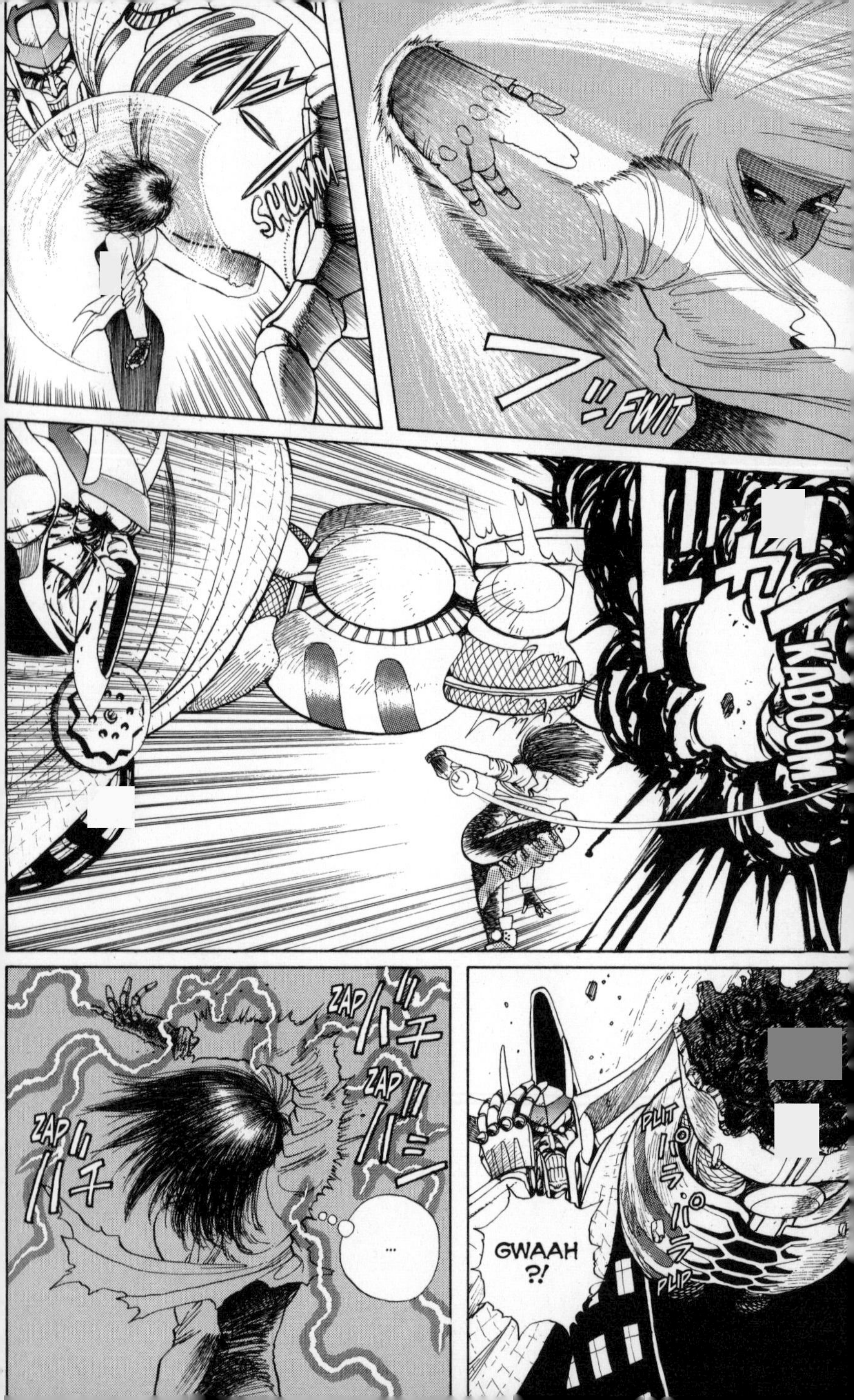
FWIT
SHUMM
KABOOM
PLIT
PLIP
GWAAH ?!
ZAP
ZAP
ZAP
...

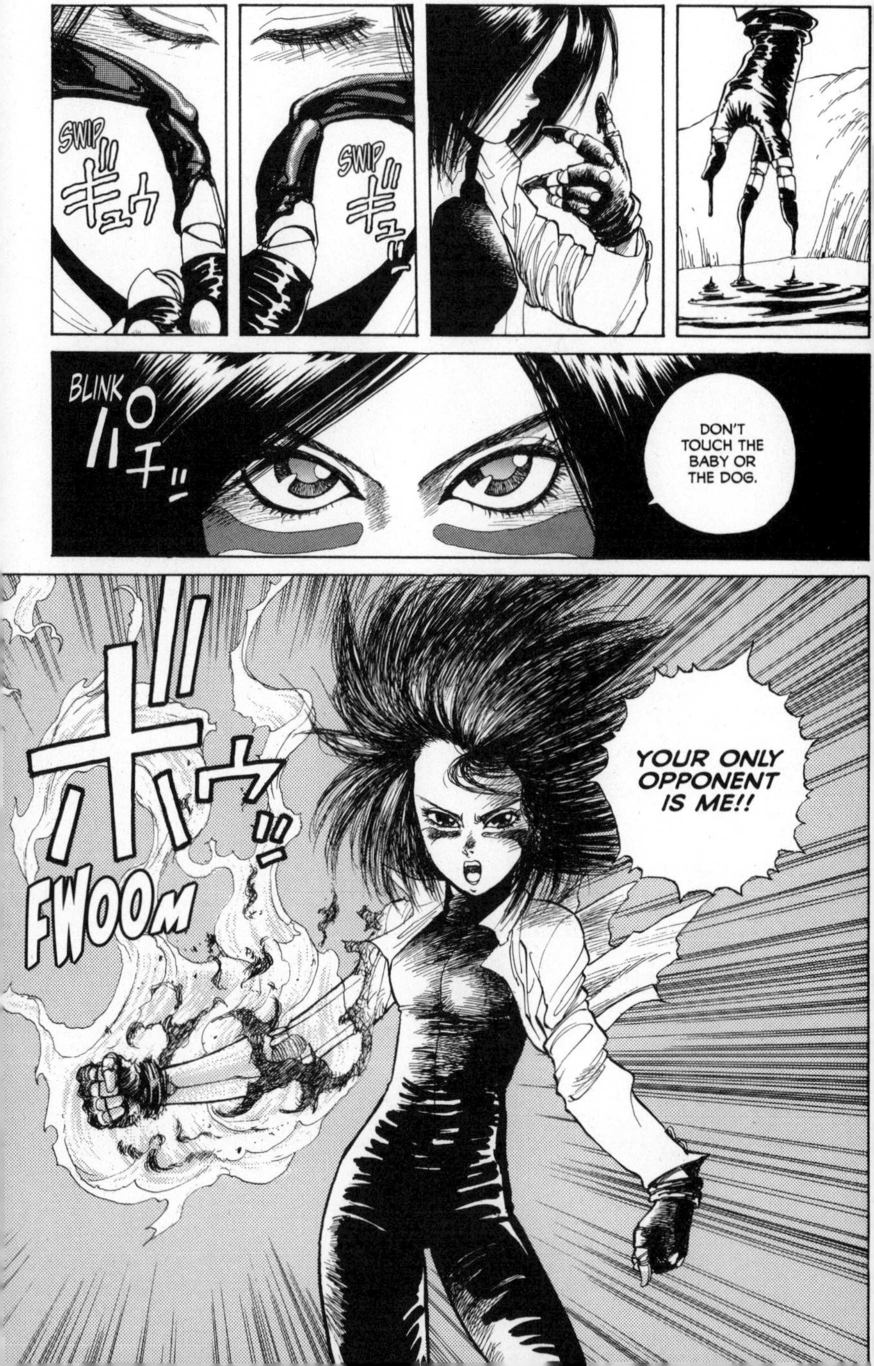
SWIP
ギュッ
SWIP
ギュウ
DON'T TOUCH THE BABY OR THE DOG.
BLINK
パチッ
YOUR ONLY OPPONENT IS ME!!
ボウッ
FWOOM

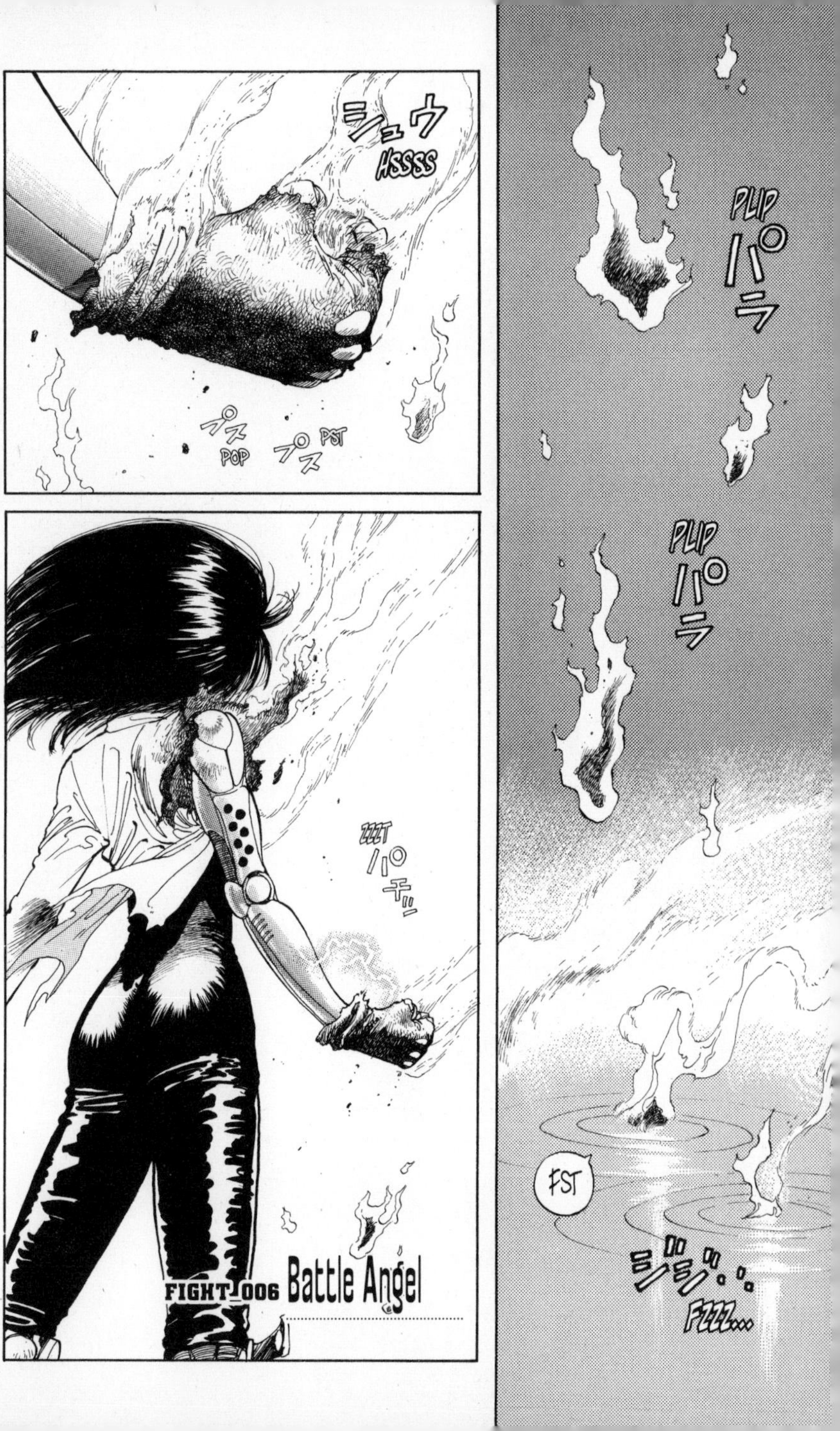
PLIP
パラ
PLIP
パラ
FST
ジジ…
FZZZ...
シュウ
HSSSS
プス
POP
プス
PST
ZZZT
パチッ

FIGHT_006 Battle Angel

FIGHT_006 Battle Angel

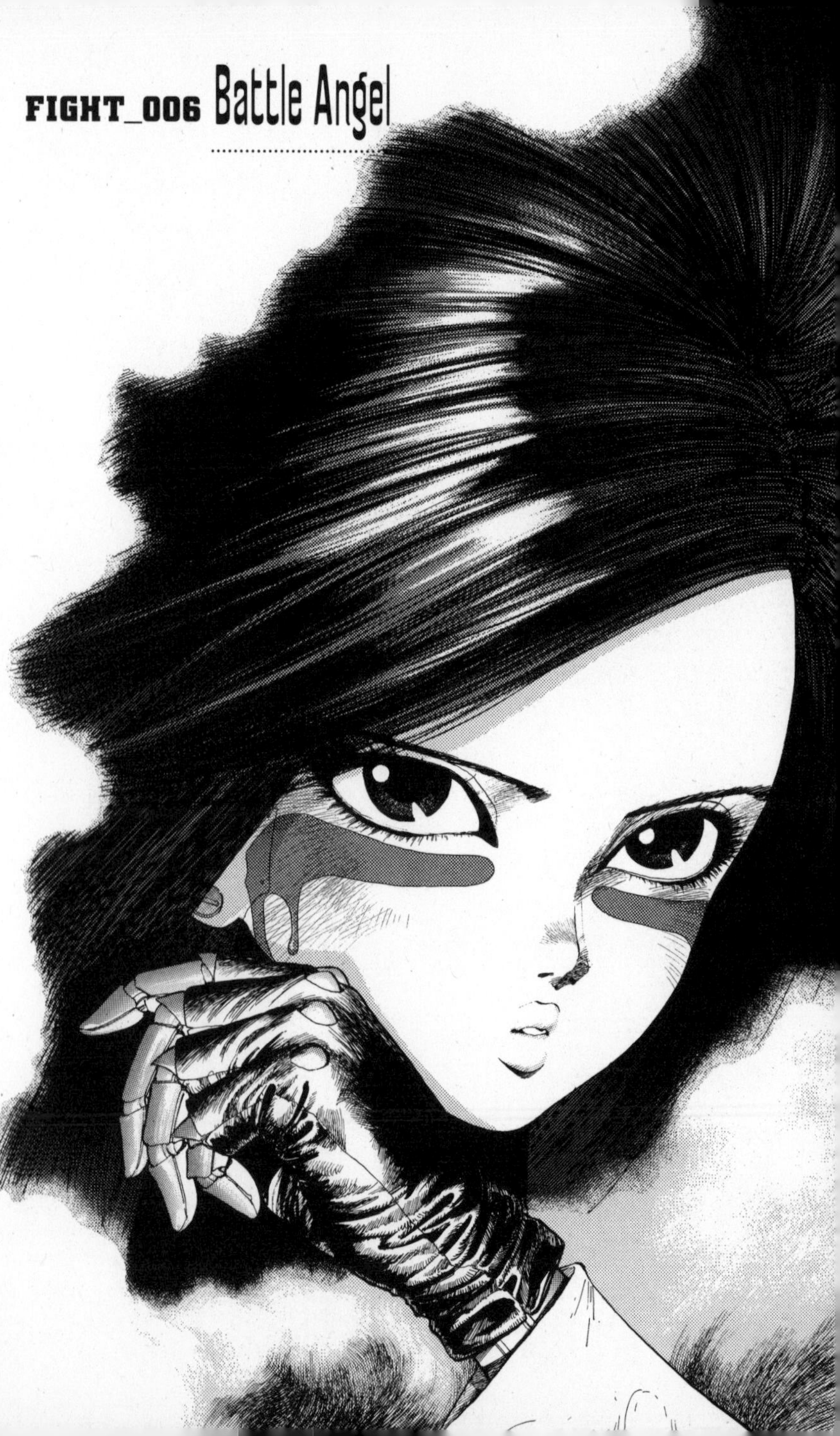

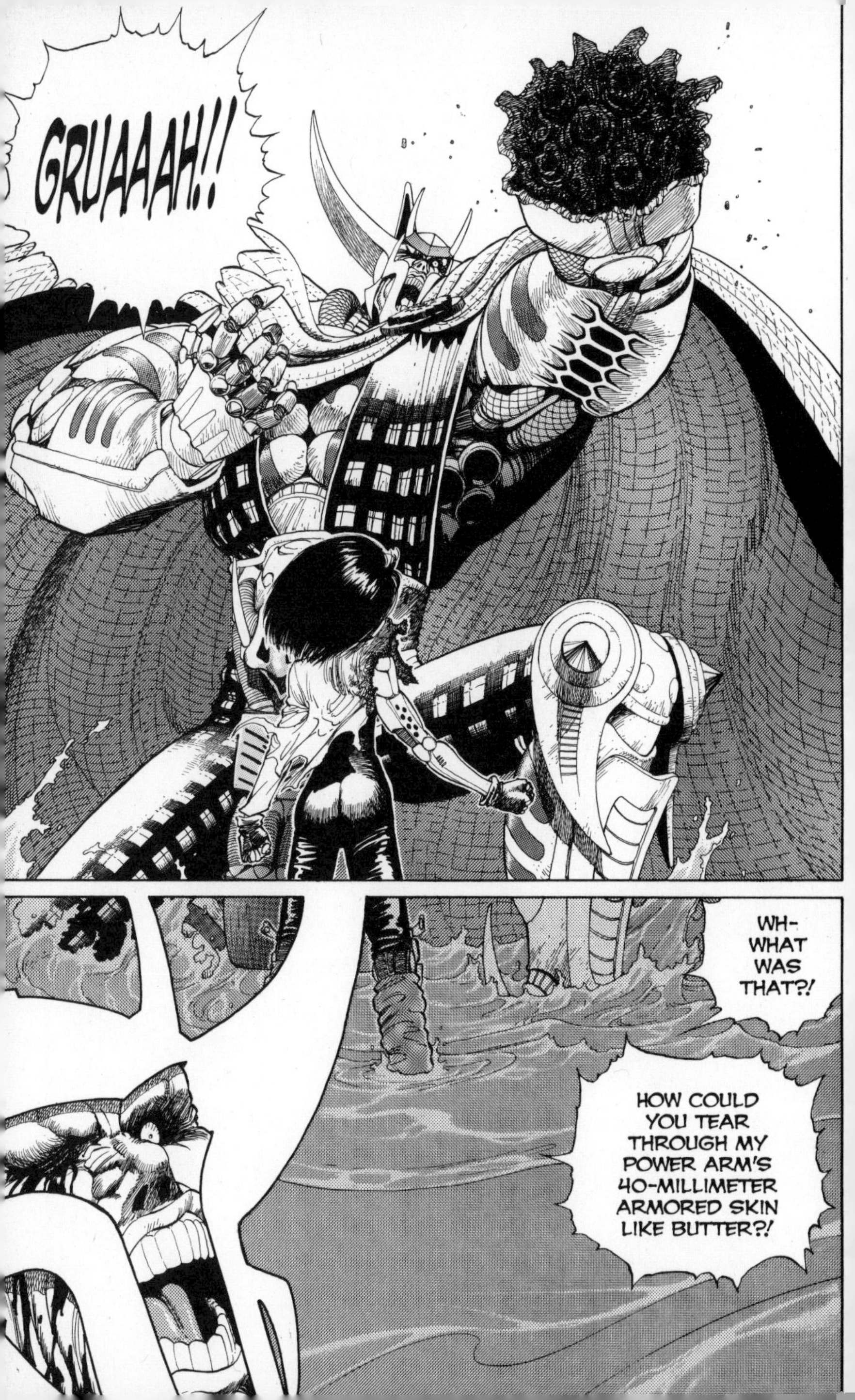
GRUAAAH!!
WH- WHAT WAS THAT?!
HOW COULD YOU TEAR THROUGH MY POWER ARM'S 40-MILLIMETER ARMORED SKIN LIKE BUTTER?!

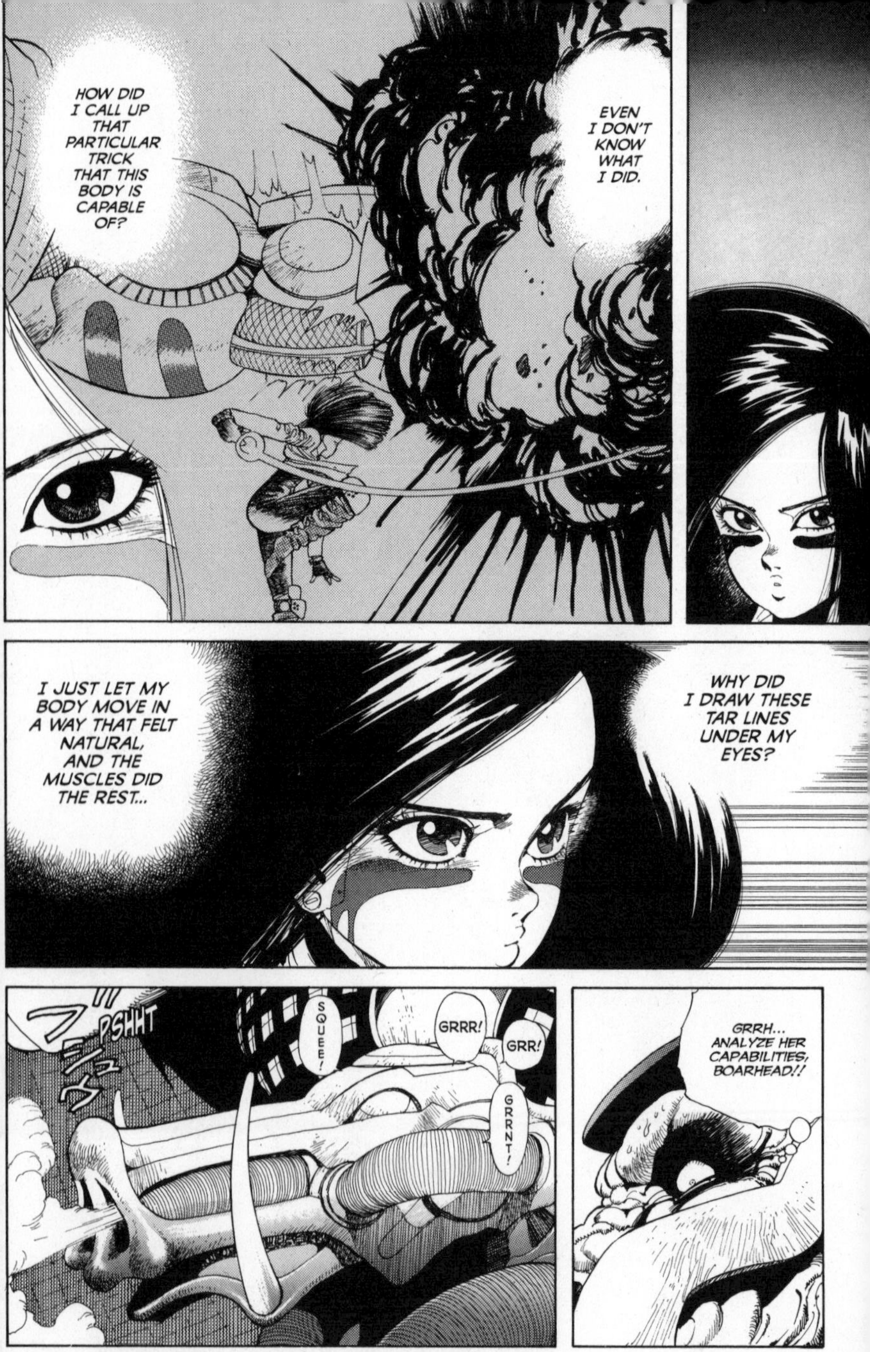
EVEN I DON'T KNOW WHAT I DID.
HOW DID I CALL UP THAT PARTICULAR TRICK THAT THIS BODY IS CAPABLE OF?
WHY DID I DRAW THESE TAR LINES UNDER MY EYES?
I JUST LET MY BODY MOVE IN A WAY THAT FELT NATURAL, AND THE MUSCLES DID THE REST...
GRRH... ANALYZE HER CAPABILITIES, BOARHEAD!!
GRR!
GRRR!
SQUEE!
GRRNT!
PSHHT

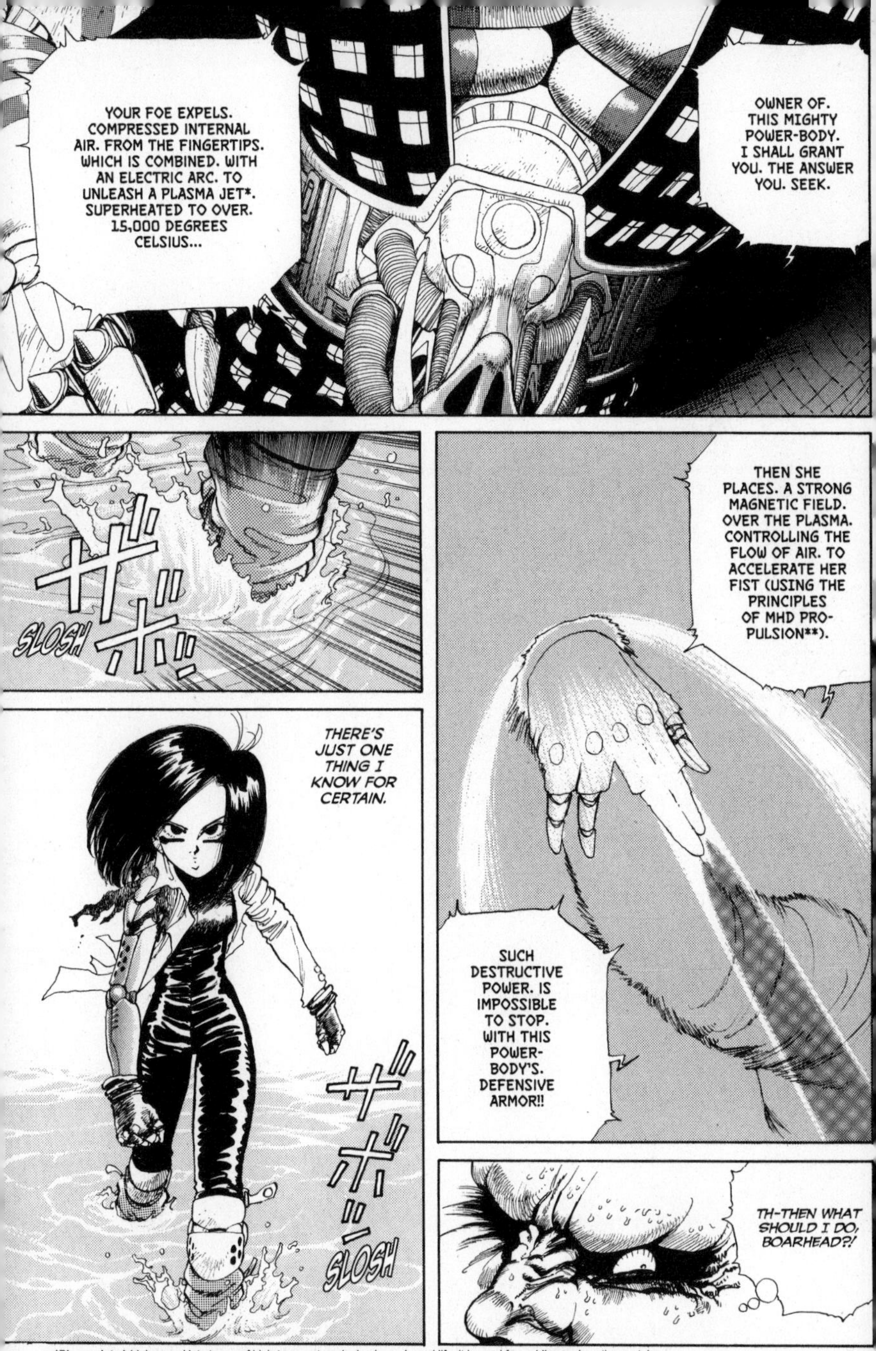
OWNER OF. THIS MIGHTY POWER-BODY. I SHALL GRANT YOU. THE ANSWER YOU. SEEK.
YOUR FOE EXPELS. COMPRESSED INTERNAL AIR. FROM THE FINGERTIPS. WHICH IS COMBINED. WITH AN ELECTRIC ARC. TO UNLEASH A PLASMA JET*. SUPERHEATED TO OVER. 15,000 DEGREES CELSIUS...
THEN SHE PLACES. A STRONG MAGNETIC FIELD. OVER THE PLASMA. CONTROLLING THE FLOW OF AIR. TO ACCELERATE HER FIST (USING THE PRINCIPLES OF MHD PROPULSION**).
SUCH DESTRUCTIVE POWER. IS IMPOSSIBLE TO STOP. WITH THIS POWER-BODY'S. DEFENSIVE ARMOR!!
TH-THEN WHAT SHOULD I DO, BOARHEAD?!
SLOSH
THERE'S JUST ONE THING I KNOW FOR CERTAIN.
SLOSH

***Plasma jet:** A high-speed jet stream of high-temperature, ionized gas. In real life, it is used for welding and casting metal.

****MHD (Magnetohydrodynamics) propulsion:** The application of magnetohydrodynamics to conductive plasma to produce a propulsive force. The "caterpillar drive" for the new nuclear submarine in the movie *The Hunt for Red October* uses the same concept.

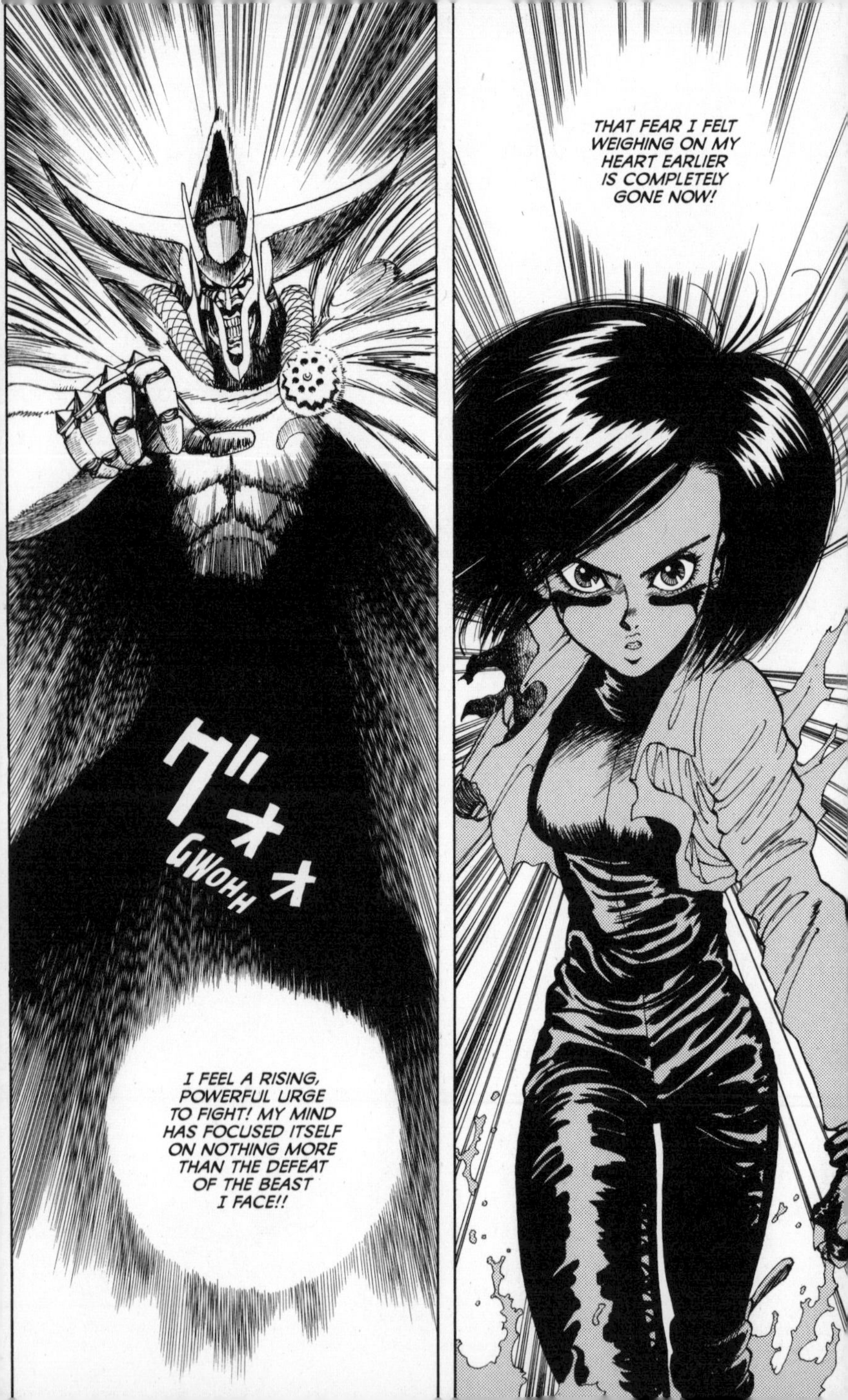
THAT FEAR I FELT WEIGHING ON MY HEART EARLIER IS COMPLETELY GONE NOW!
グオオ
GWOHH
I FEEL A RISING, POWERFUL URGE TO FIGHT! MY MIND HAS FOCUSED ITSELF ON NOTHING MORE THAN THE DEFEAT OF THE BEAST I FACE!!

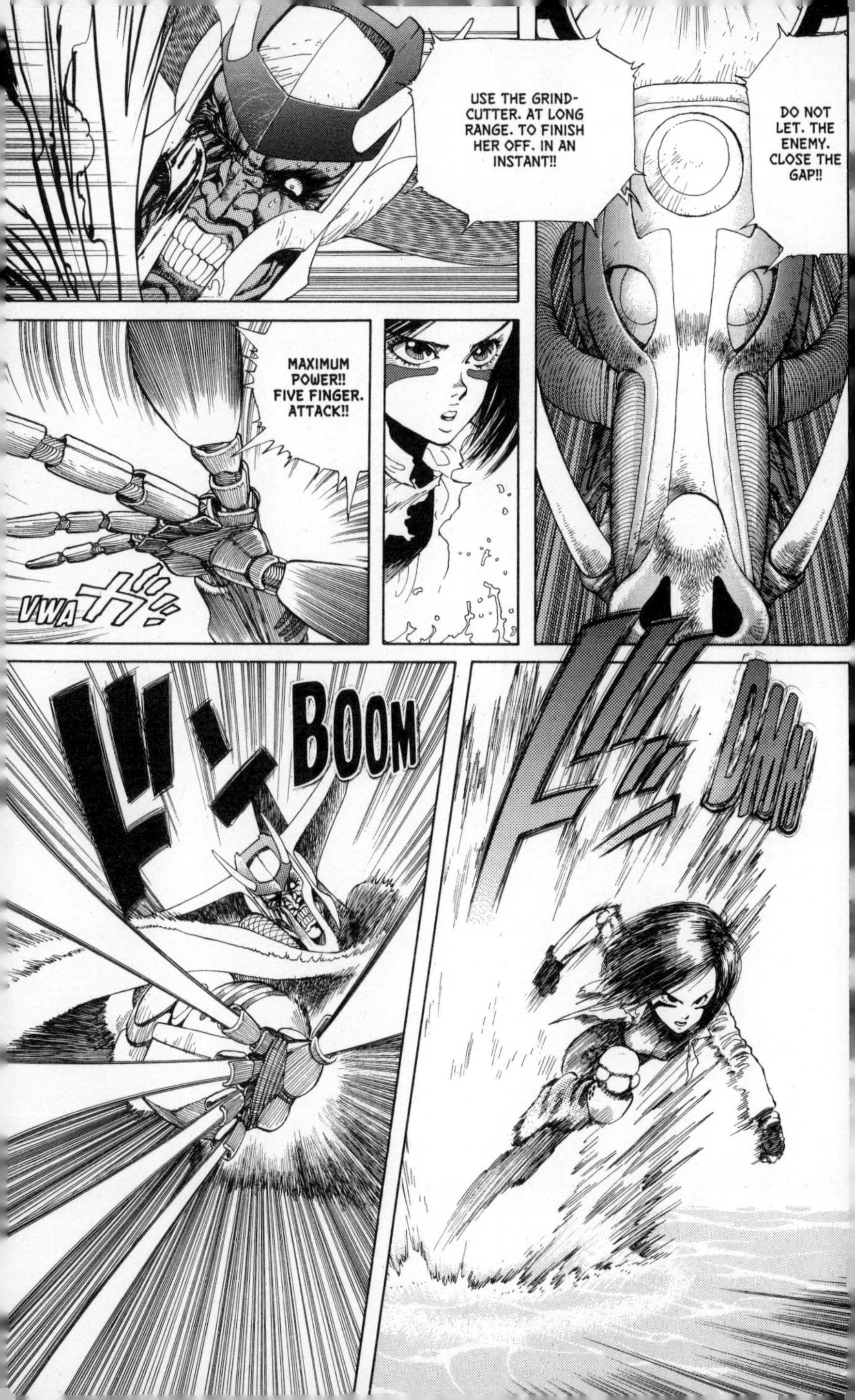
DO NOT LET. THE ENEMY. CLOSE THE GAP!!
USE THE GRIND-CUTTER. AT LONG RANGE. TO FINISH HER OFF. IN AN INSTANT!!
MAXIMUM POWER!! FIVE FINGER. ATTACK!!
VWA
DMM
BOOM

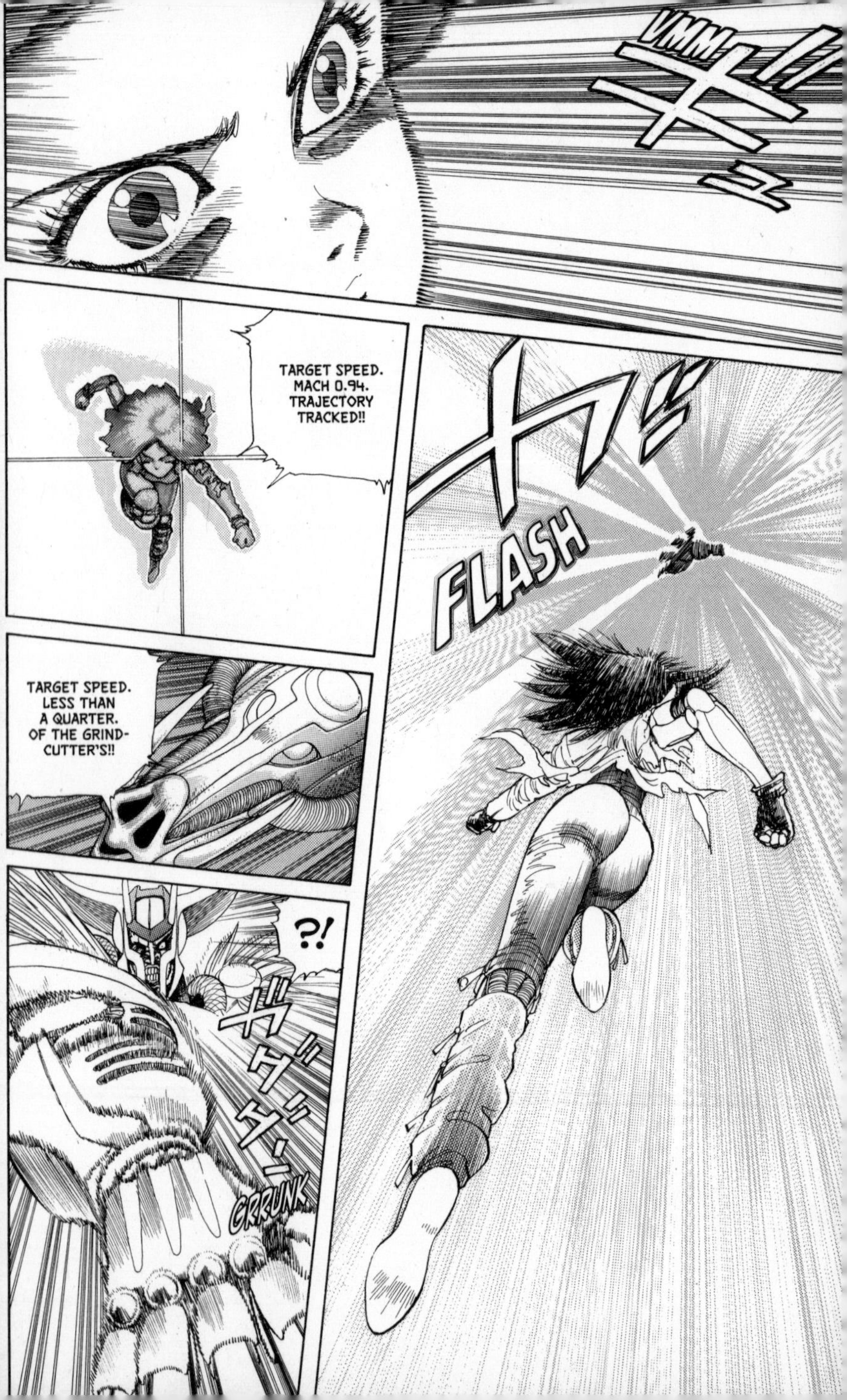
VMMM!!
FLASH
TARGET SPEED. MACH 0.94. TRAJECTORY TRACKED!!
TARGET SPEED. LESS THAN A QUARTER. OF THE GRIND-CUTTER'S!!
?!
CRRUNK

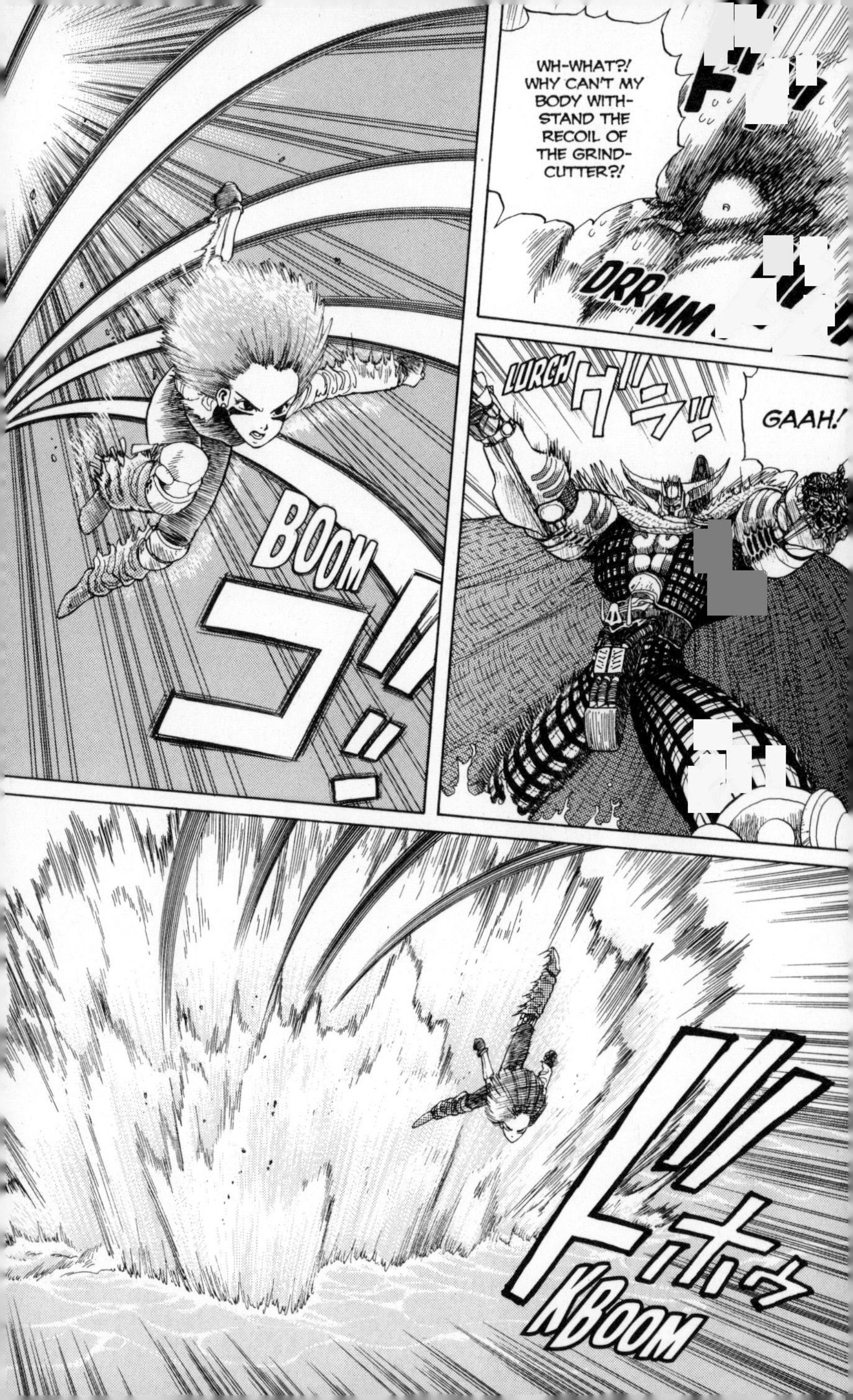
WH-WHAT?! WHY CAN'T MY BODY WITH-STAND THE RECOIL OF THE GRIND-CUTTER?!
DRRMM
LURCH
GAAH!
BOOM
KBOOM

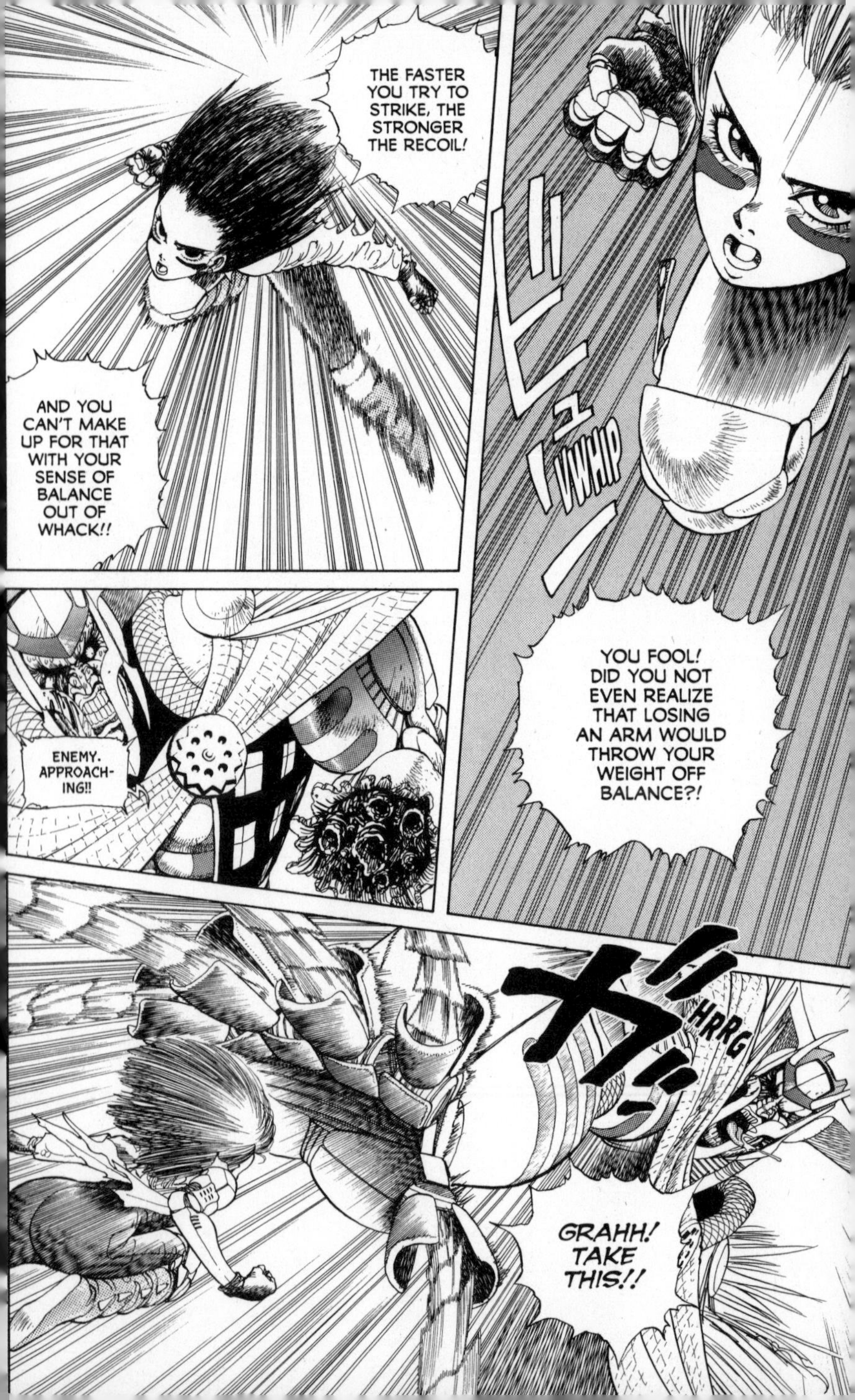
VWHIP
YOU FOOL! DID YOU NOT EVEN REALIZE THAT LOSING AN ARM WOULD THROW YOUR WEIGHT OFF BALANCE?!
THE FASTER YOU TRY TO STRIKE, THE STRONGER THE RECOIL!
AND YOU CAN'T MAKE UP FOR THAT WITH YOUR SENSE OF BALANCE OUT OF WHACK!!
ENEMY. APPROACHING!!
HRRG
GRAHH! TAKE THIS!!

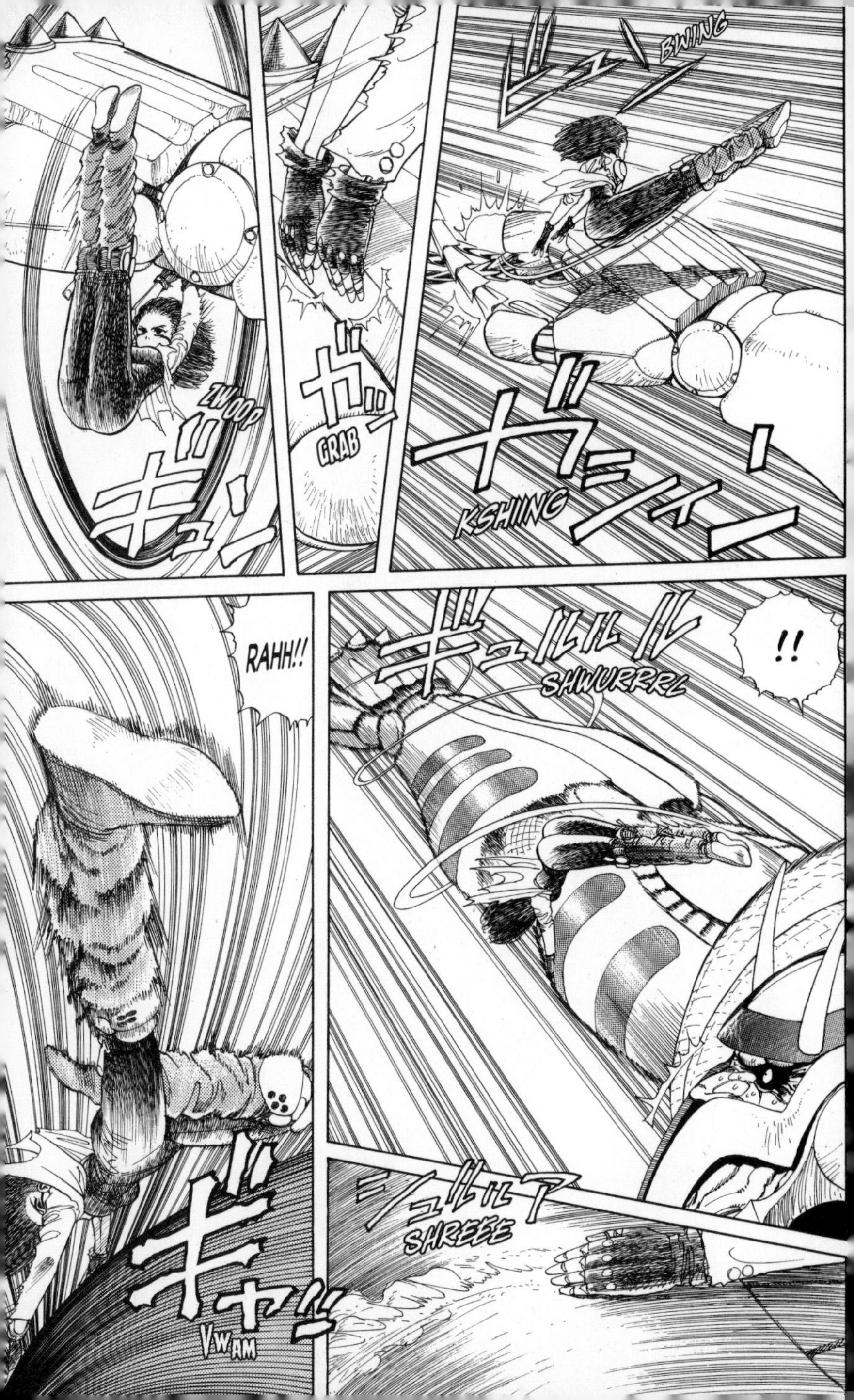
BWING
KSHIING
GRAB
ZWOOP
!!
SHWURRRL
SHREEE
RAHH!!
VWAM

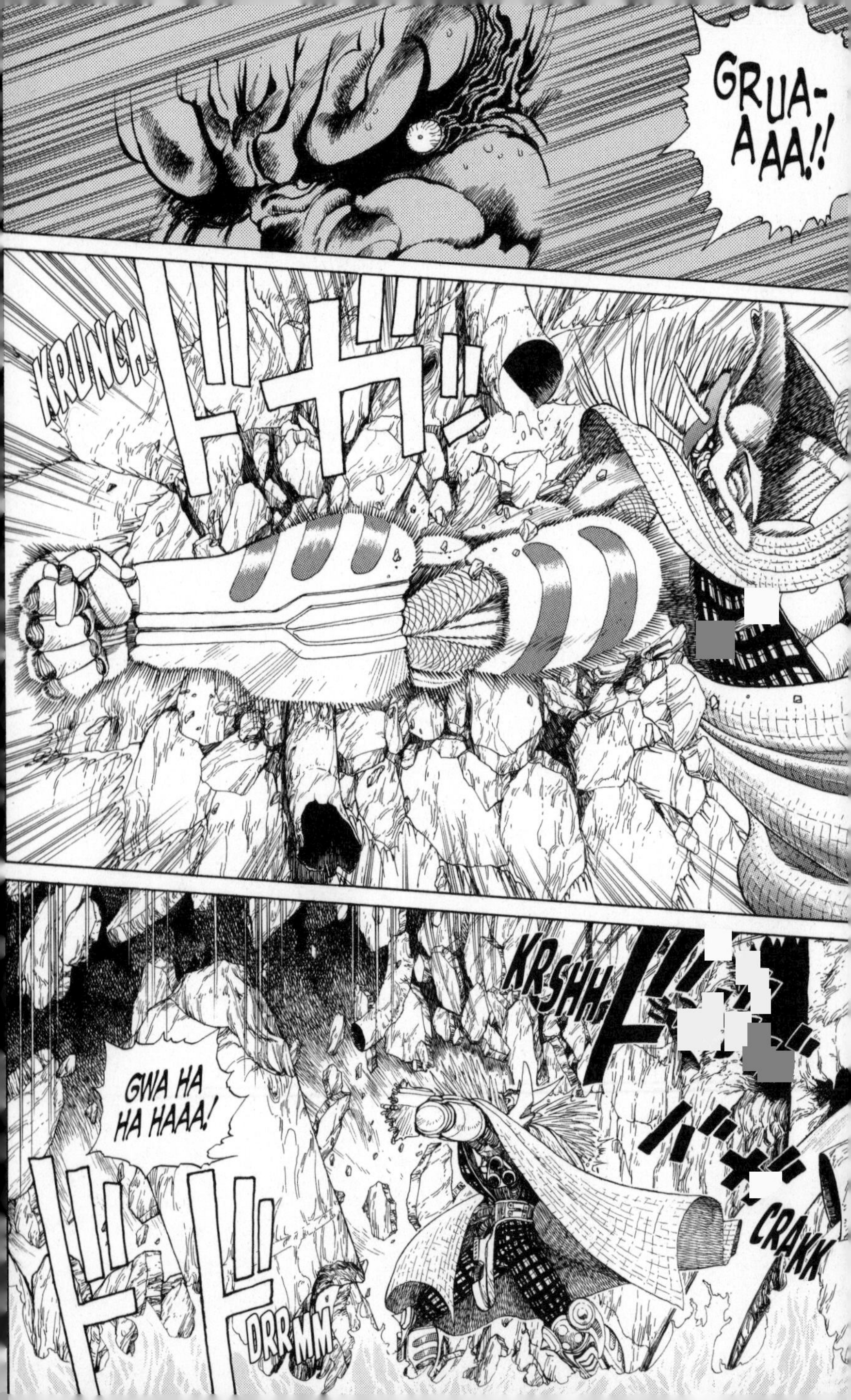
GRUA-AAA!!
KRUNCH
KRSHH
CRAKK
GWA HA HA HAAA!
DRRMM

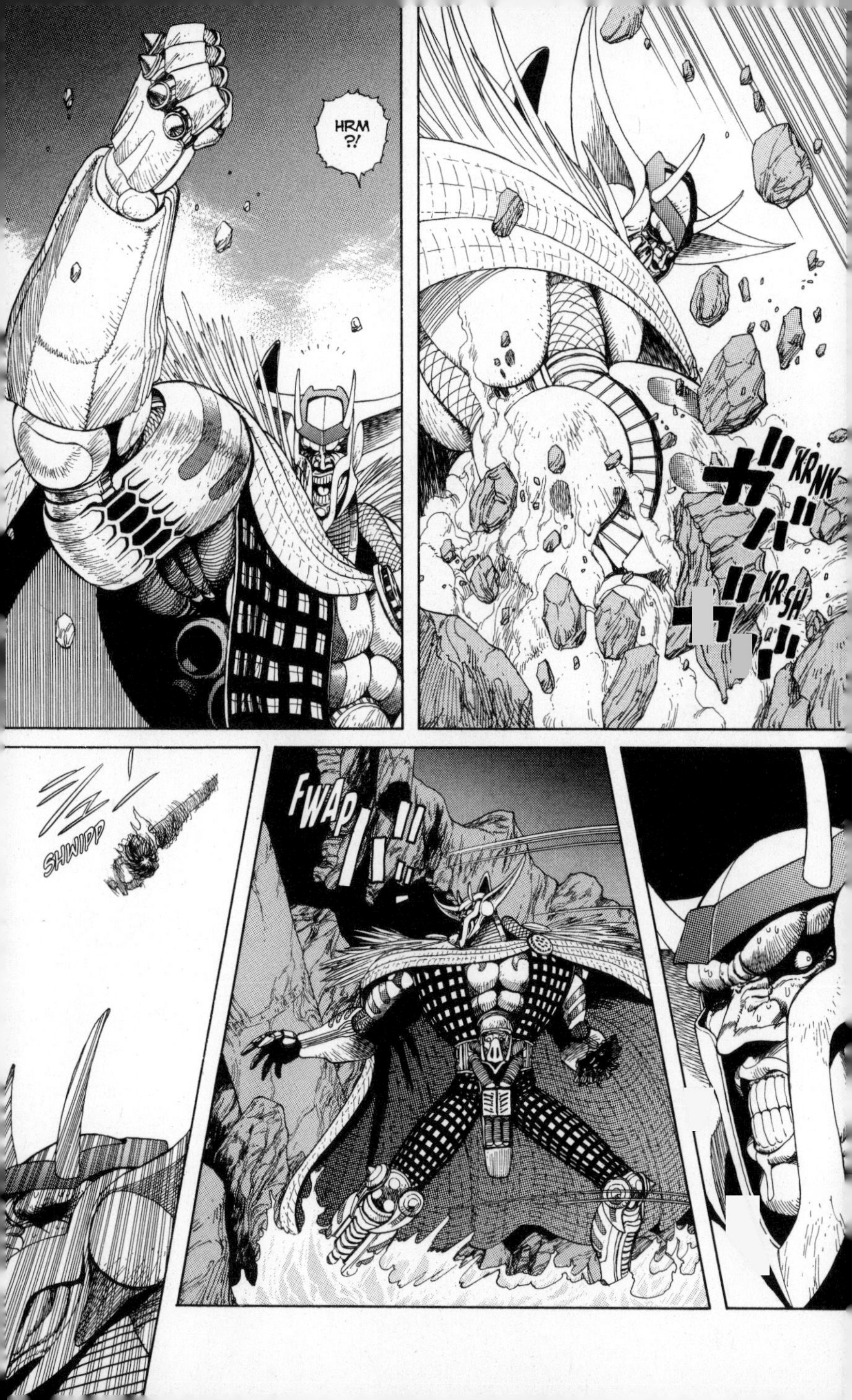
KRNK
KRSH
HRM ?!
FWAP
SHWIPP

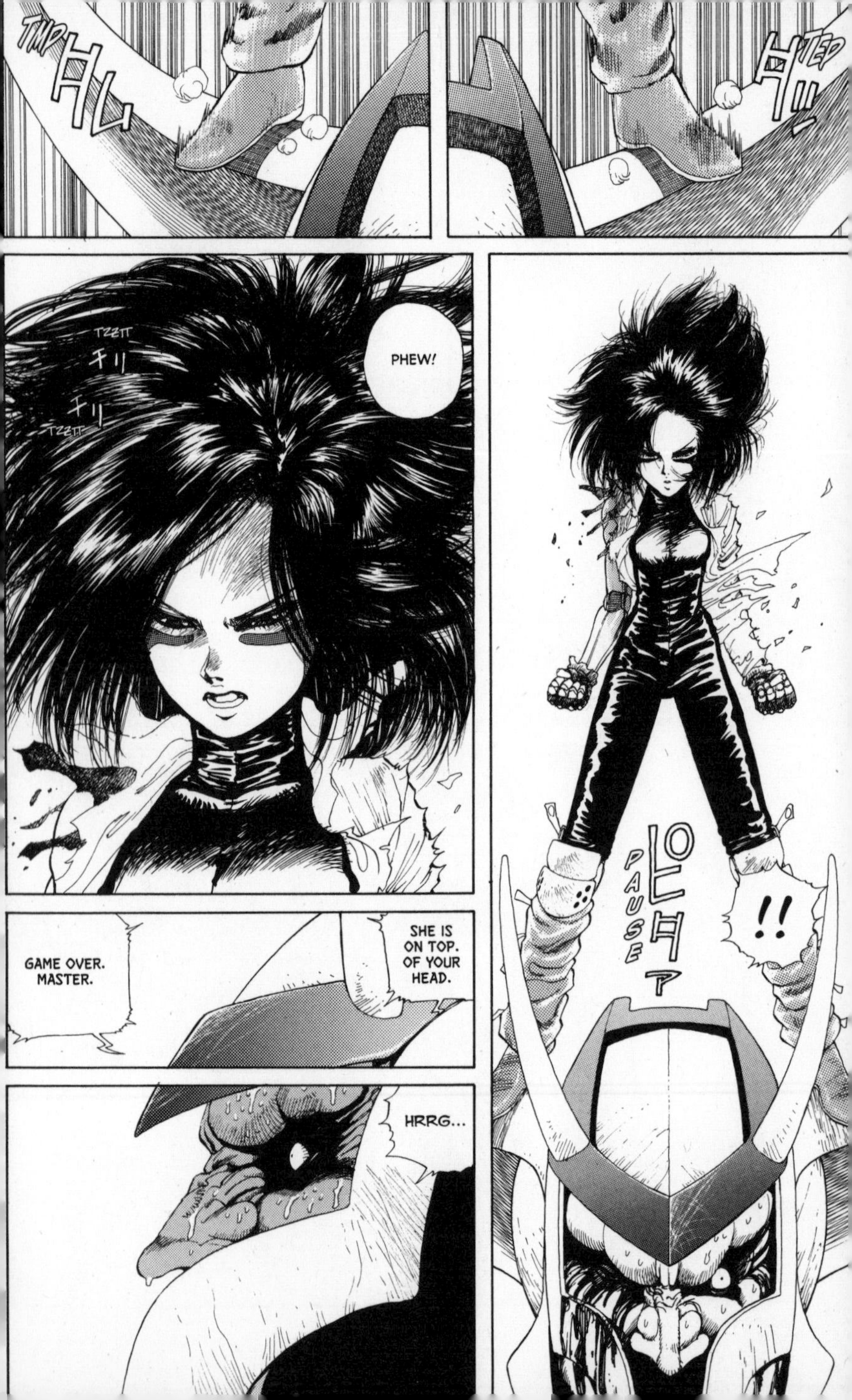
TED
TMD
!!
PAUSE
PHEW!
TZZTT
TZZTT
SHE IS ON TOP. OF YOUR HEAD.
GAME OVER. MASTER.
HRRG...

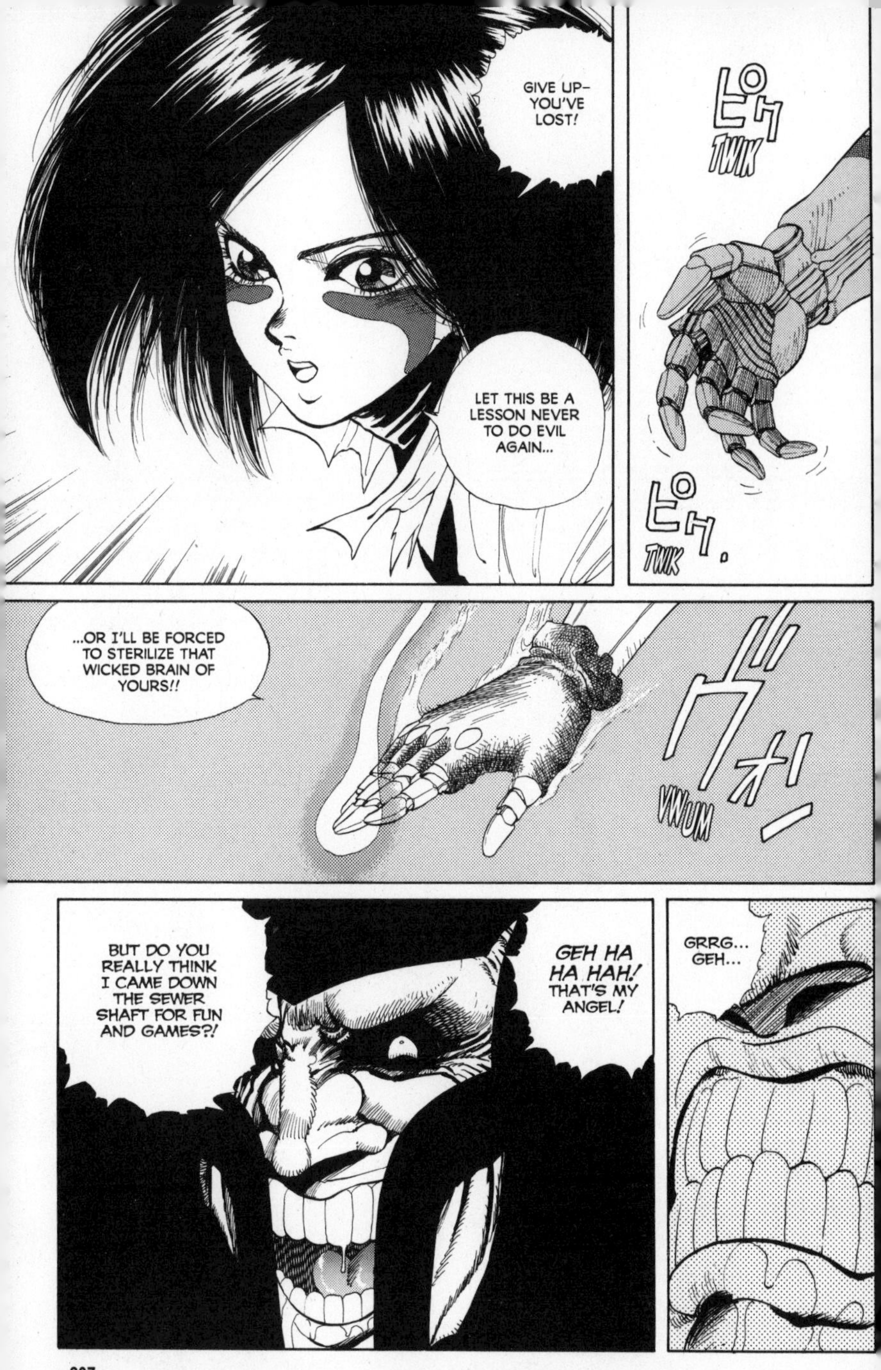
ピク
TWIK
ピク。
TWIK
GIVE UP— YOU'VE LOST!
LET THIS BE A LESSON NEVER TO DO EVIL AGAIN...
VNUM
...OR I'LL BE FORCED TO STERILIZE THAT WICKED BRAIN OF YOURS!!
GRRG... GEH...
GEH HA HA HAH! THAT'S MY ANGEL!
BUT DO YOU REALLY THINK I CAME DOWN THE SEWER SHAFT FOR FUN AND GAMES?!

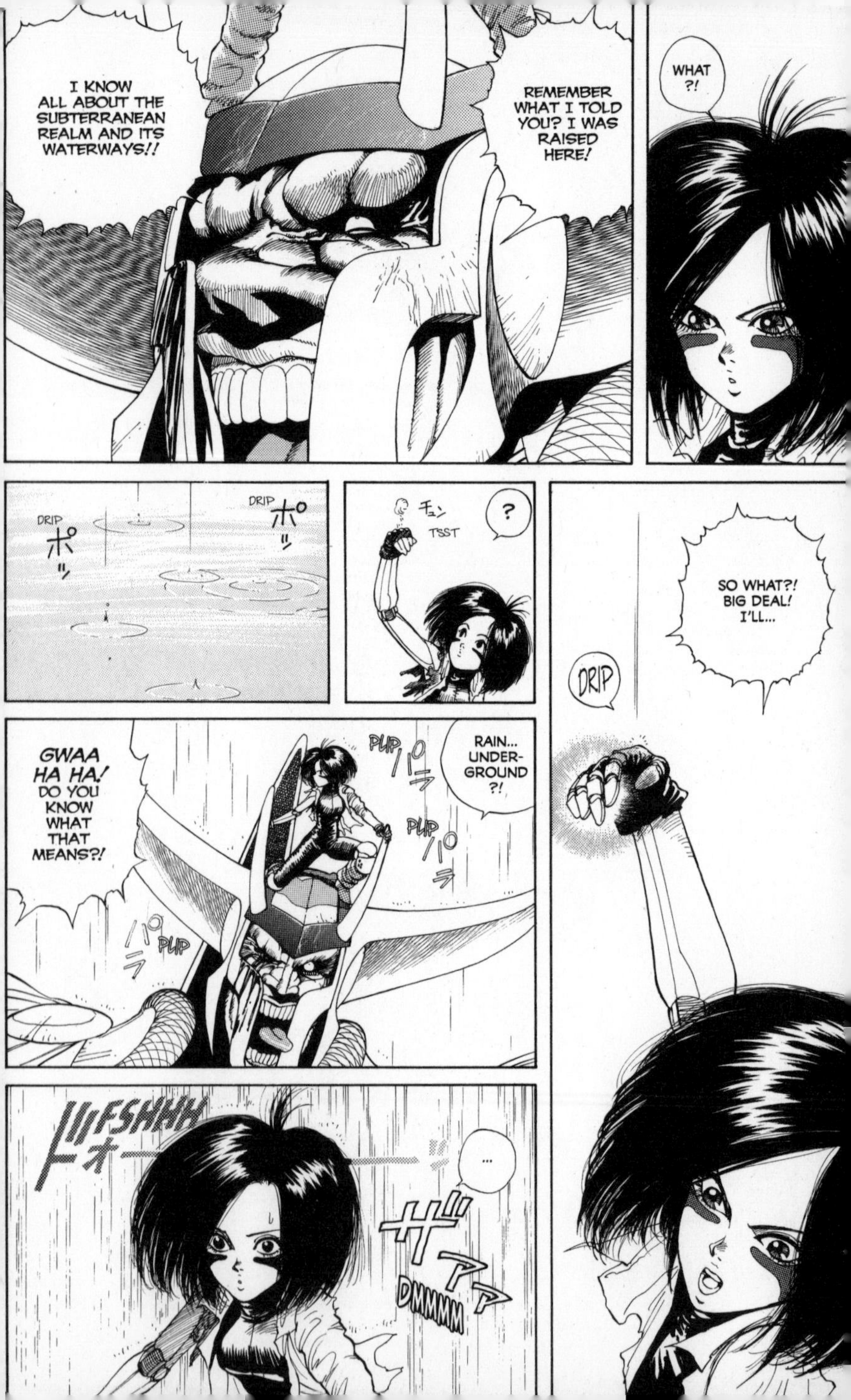
WHAT ?!
REMEMBER WHAT I TOLD YOU? I WAS RAISED HERE!
I KNOW ALL ABOUT THE SUBTERRANEAN REALM AND ITS WATERWAYS!!
SO WHAT?! BIG DEAL! I'LL...
DRIP
?
TSST
DRIP
DRIP
RAIN... UNDERGROUND ?!
PLIP
PLIP
GWAA HA HA! DO YOU KNOW WHAT THAT MEANS?!
PLIP
...
DMMMM
FSHHH

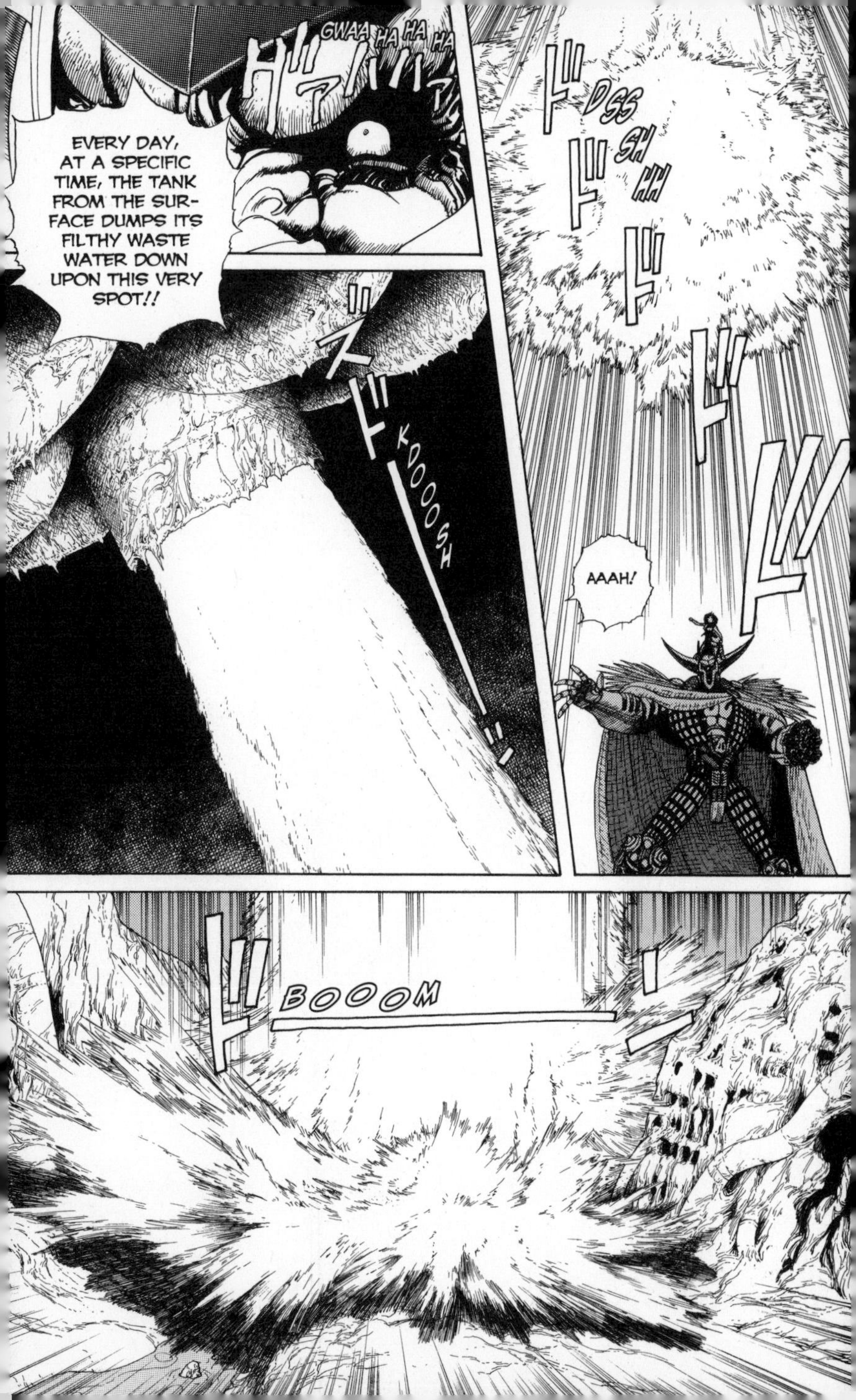
DSSSHHH
AAAH!
GWAA HA HA HA
EVERY DAY, AT A SPECIFIC TIME, THE TANK FROM THE SUR-FACE DUMPS ITS FILTHY WASTE WATER DOWN UPON THIS VERY SPOT!!
KDOOOSH
BOOOM

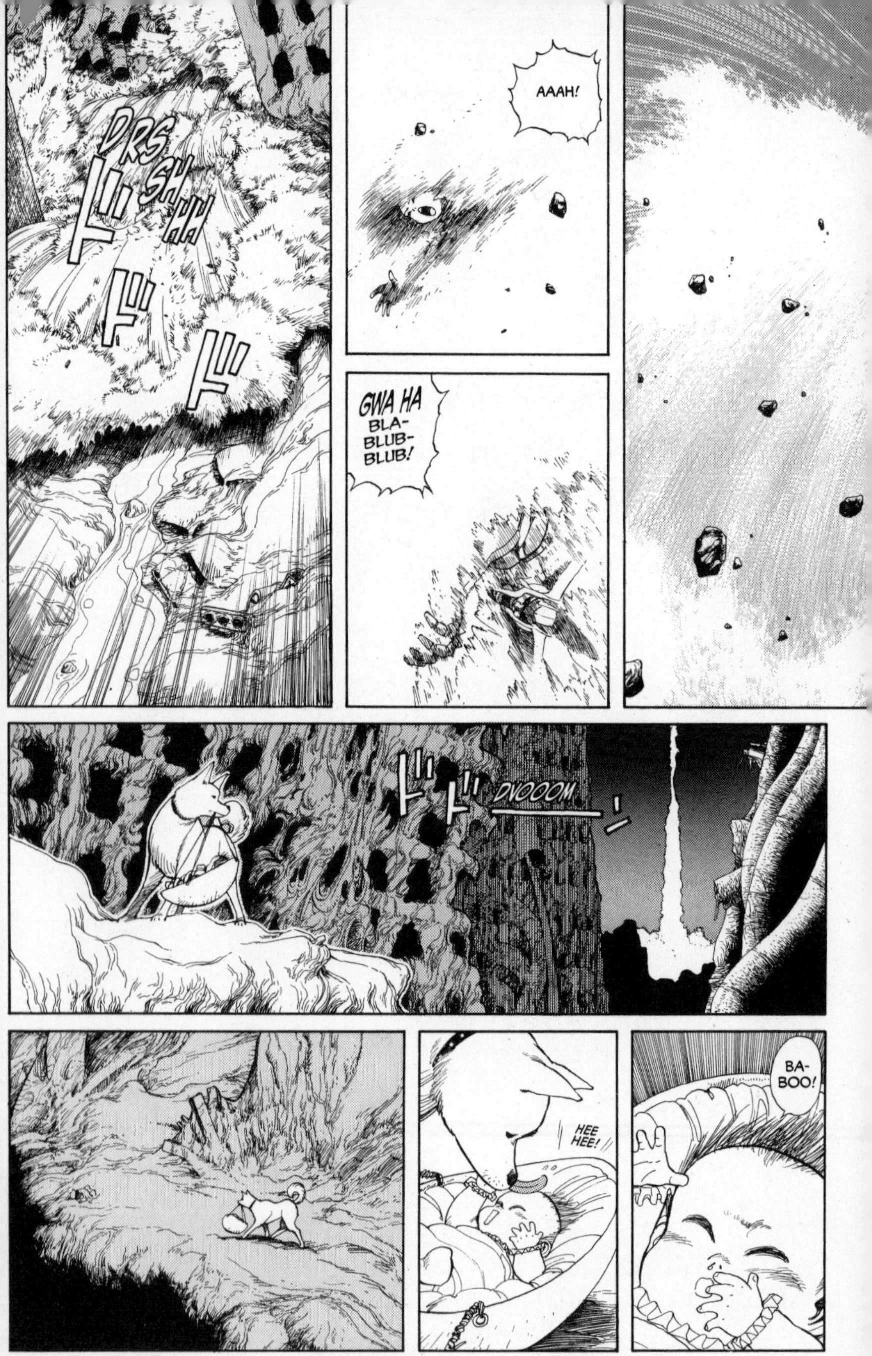
AAAH!
GWA HA BLA-BLUB-BLUB!
DRSSHHH
ドドド
ドド DVOOOM
BA-BOO!
HEE HEE!

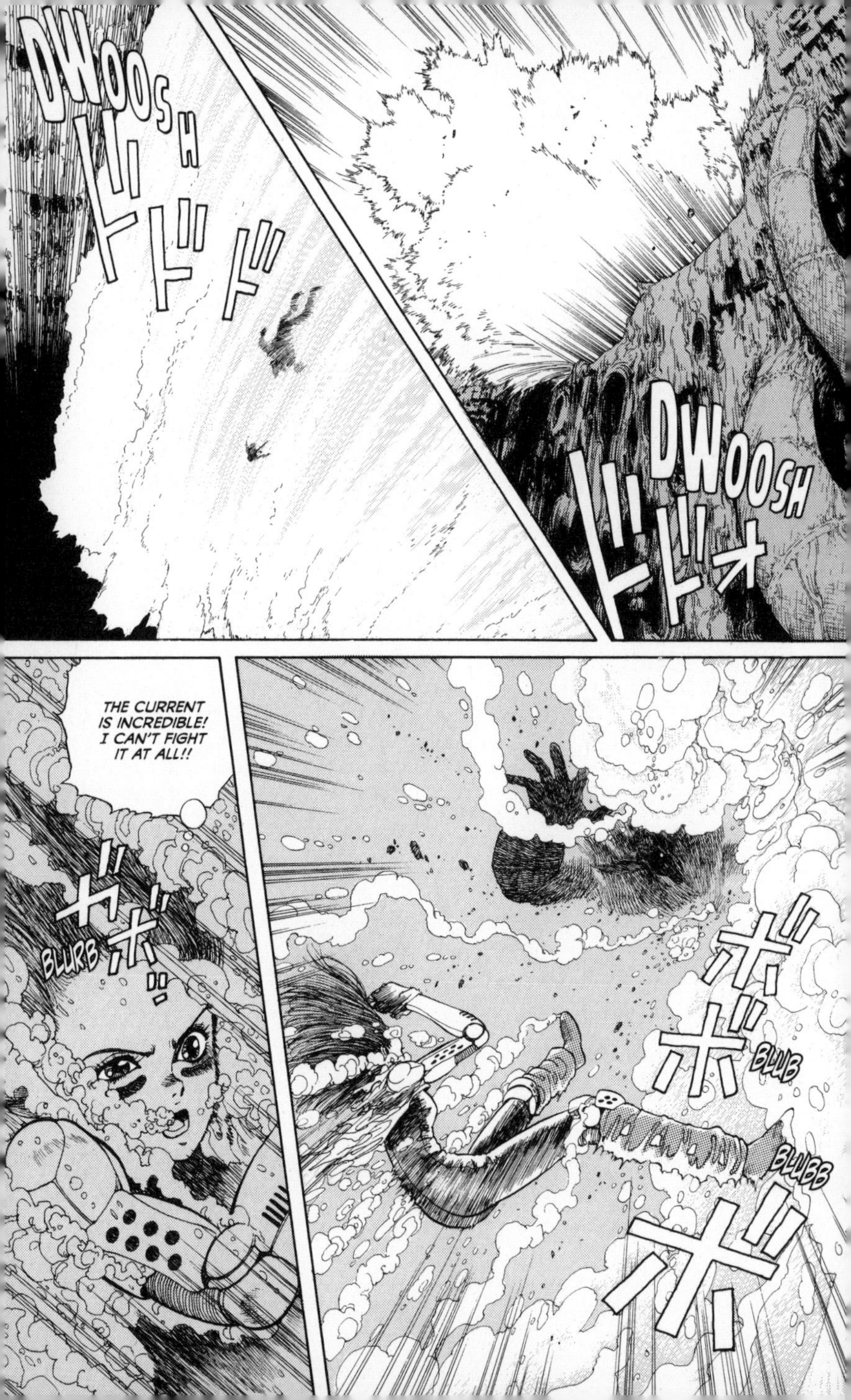
DWOOSH
DWOOSH
BLUB
BLUBB
THE CURRENT IS INCREDIBLE! I CAN'T FIGHT IT AT ALL!!
BLURB

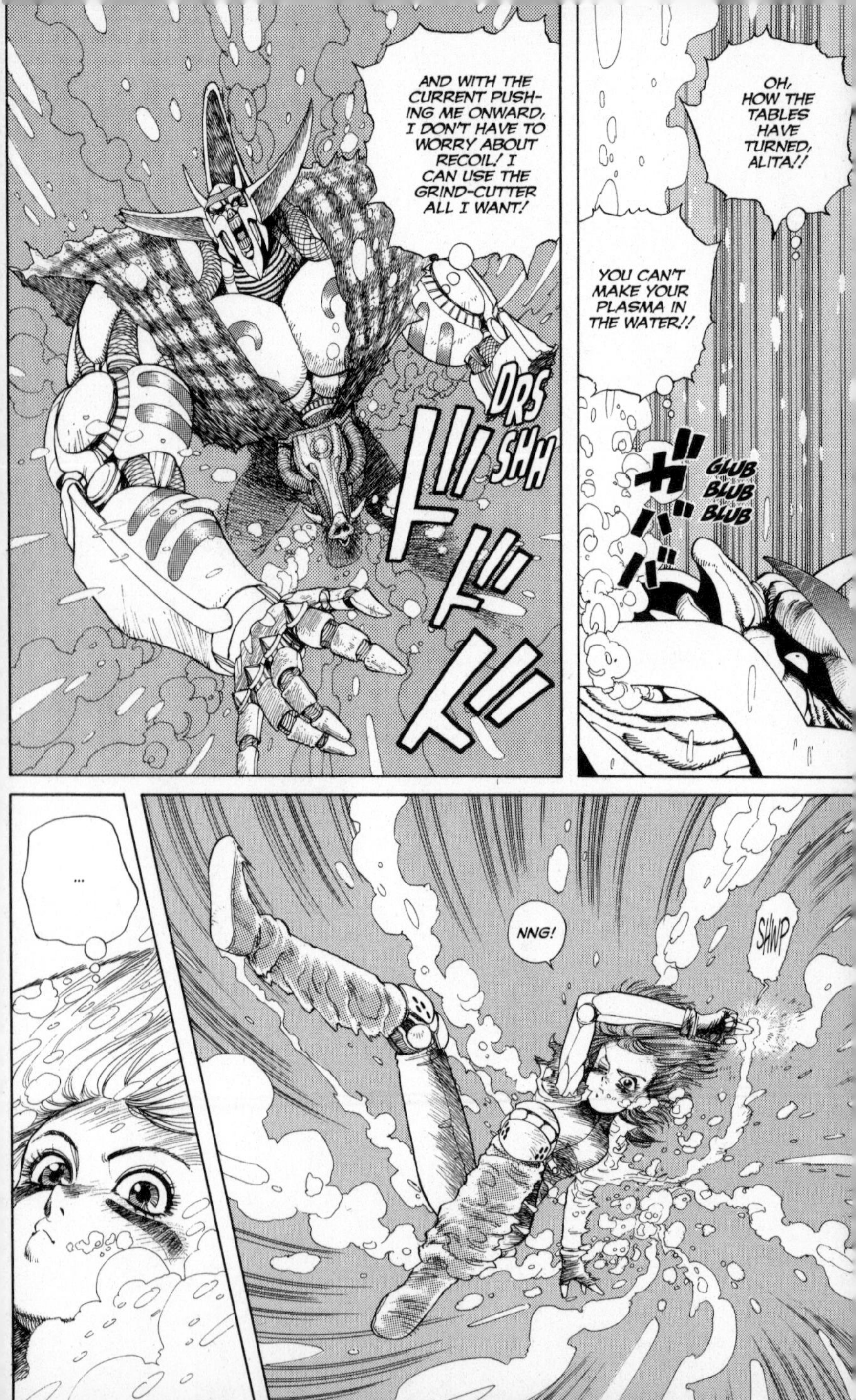
OH, HOW THE TABLES HAVE TURNED, ALITA!!
YOU CAN'T MAKE YOUR PLASMA IN THE WATER!!
GLUB BLUB BLUB
AND WITH THE CURRENT PUSHING ME ONWARD, I DON'T HAVE TO WORRY ABOUT RECOIL! I CAN USE THE GRIND-CUTTER ALL I WANT!
DRS SHH
NNG!
SHWP
...

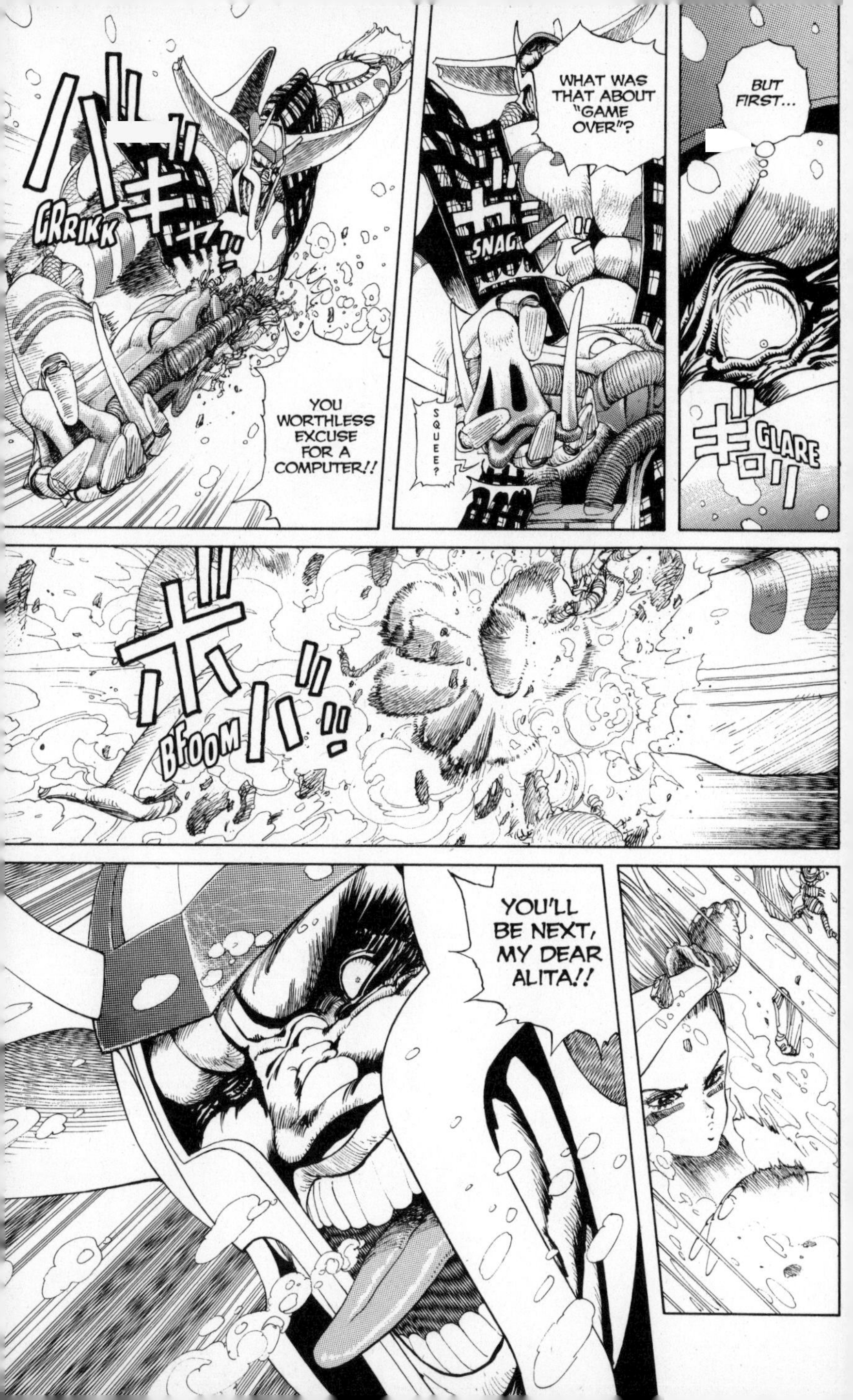
BUT FIRST...
GLARE
WHAT WAS THAT ABOUT "GAME OVER"?
SNAG
SQUEE?
GRRIKK
YOU WORTHLESS EXCUSE FOR A COMPUTER!!
BFOOM
YOU'LL BE NEXT, MY DEAR ALITA!!

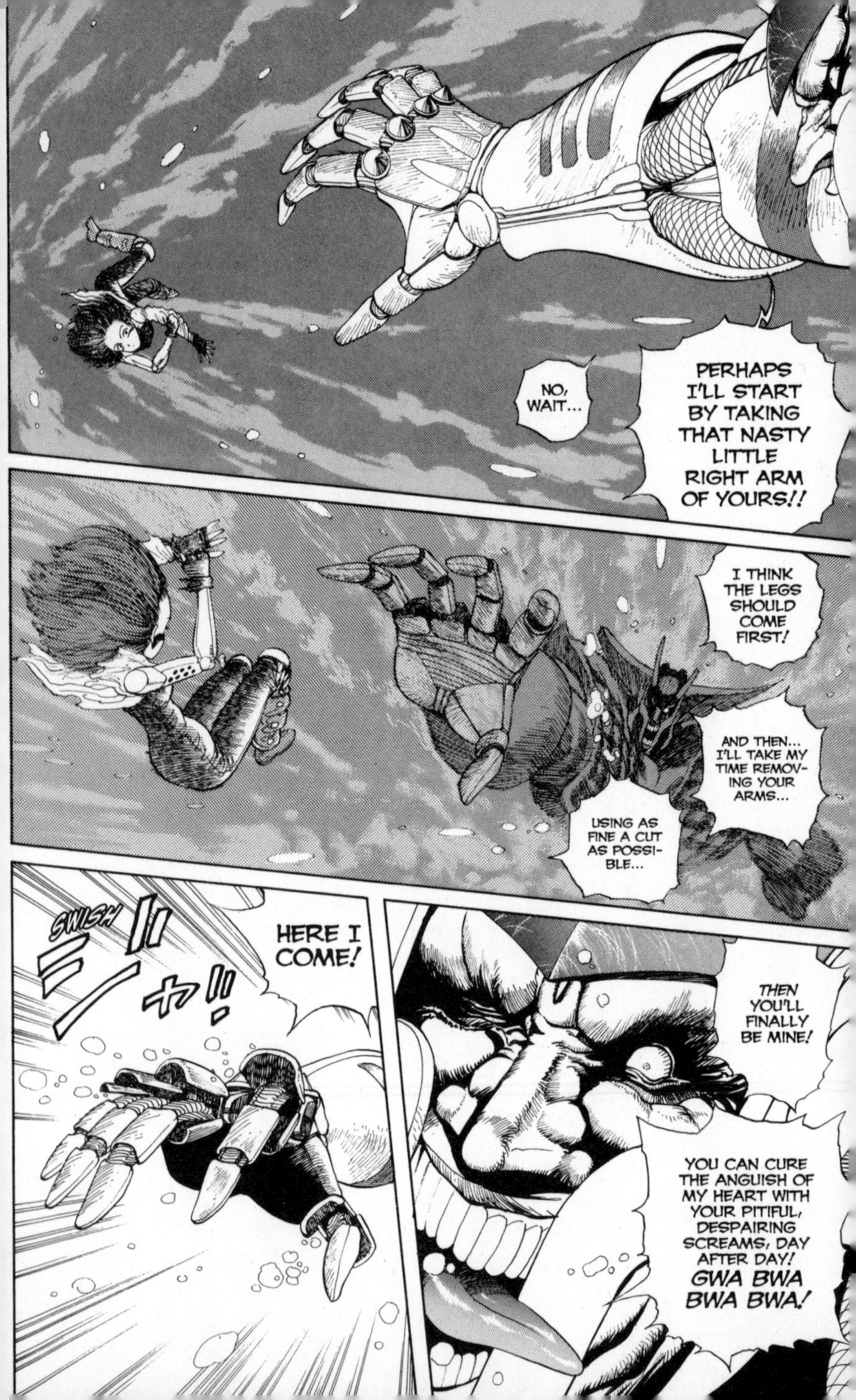
PERHAPS I'LL START BY TAKING THAT NASTY LITTLE RIGHT ARM OF YOURS!!
NO, WAIT...
I THINK THE LEGS SHOULD COME FIRST!
AND THEN... I'LL TAKE MY TIME REMOVING YOUR ARMS...
USING AS FINE A CUT AS POSSIBLE...
THEN YOU'LL FINALLY BE MINE!
YOU CAN CURE THE ANGUISH OF MY HEART WITH YOUR PITIFUL, DESPAIRING SCREAMS, DAY AFTER DAY! GWA BWA BWA BWA!
SWISH
HERE I COME!

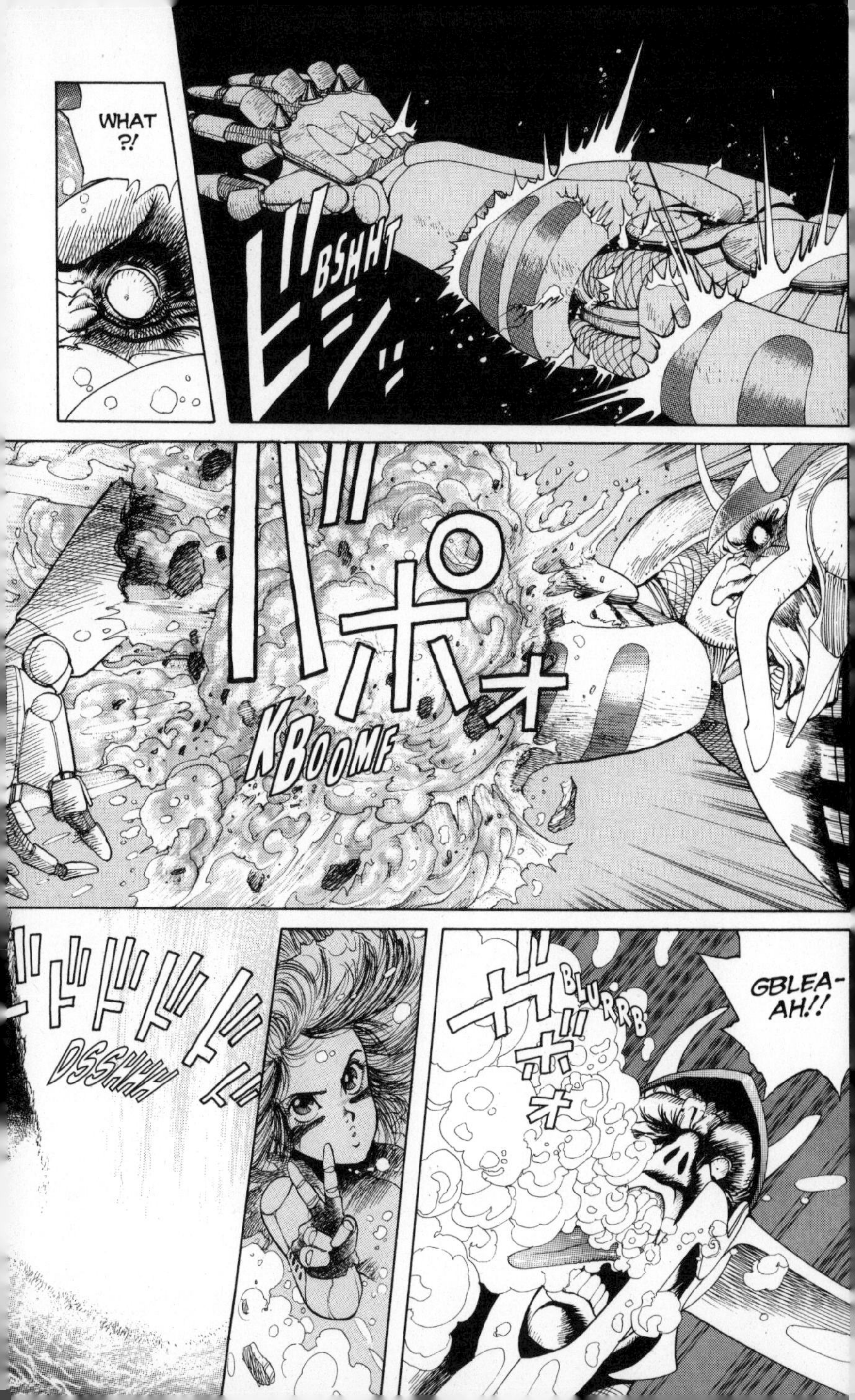
BSHHT
WHAT ?!
KBOOMF
BLURRRB
GBLEA-AH!!
DSSHHH

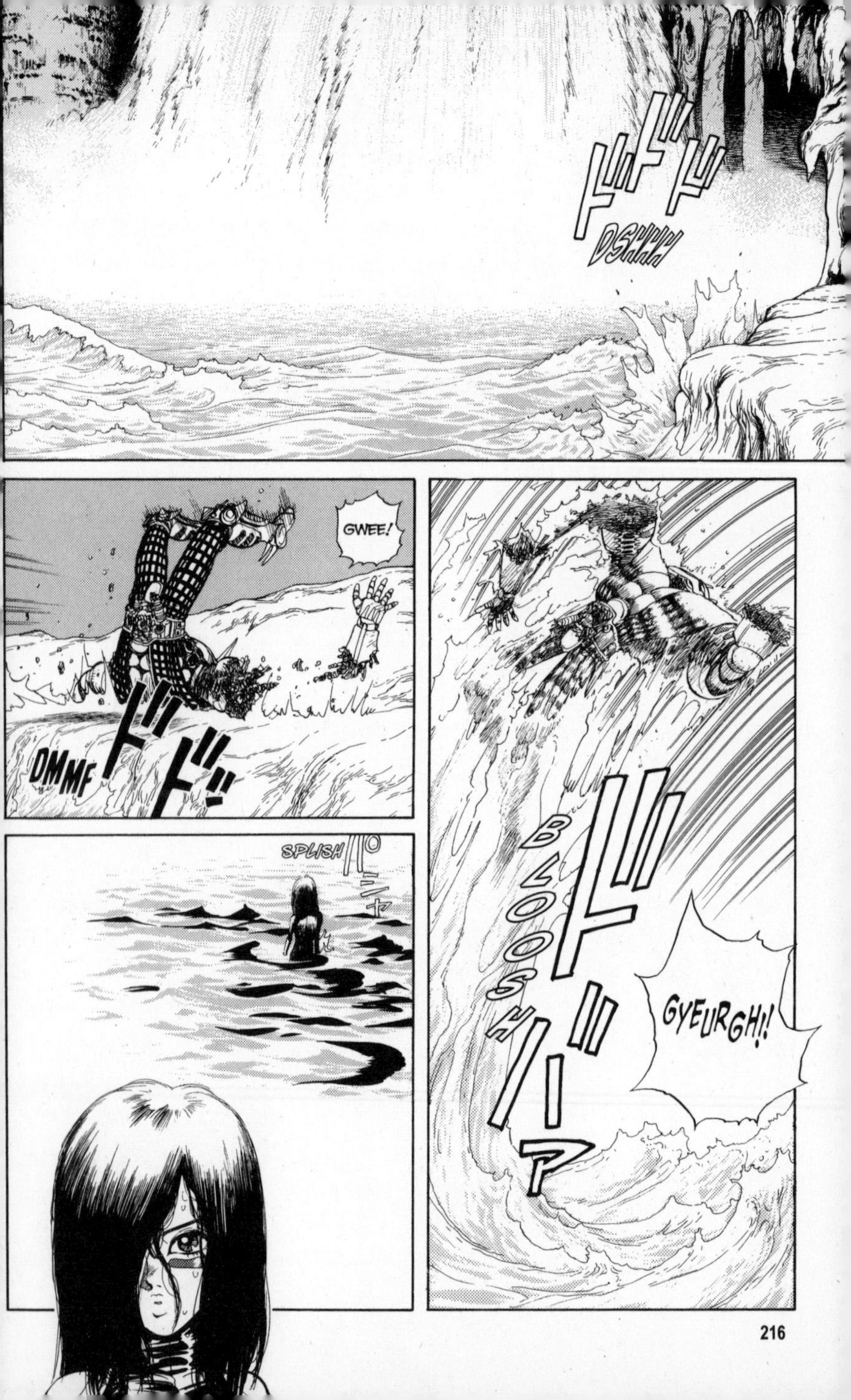
DSHHH
BLOOSH
GYEURGH!!
GWEE!
DMMF
SPLISH

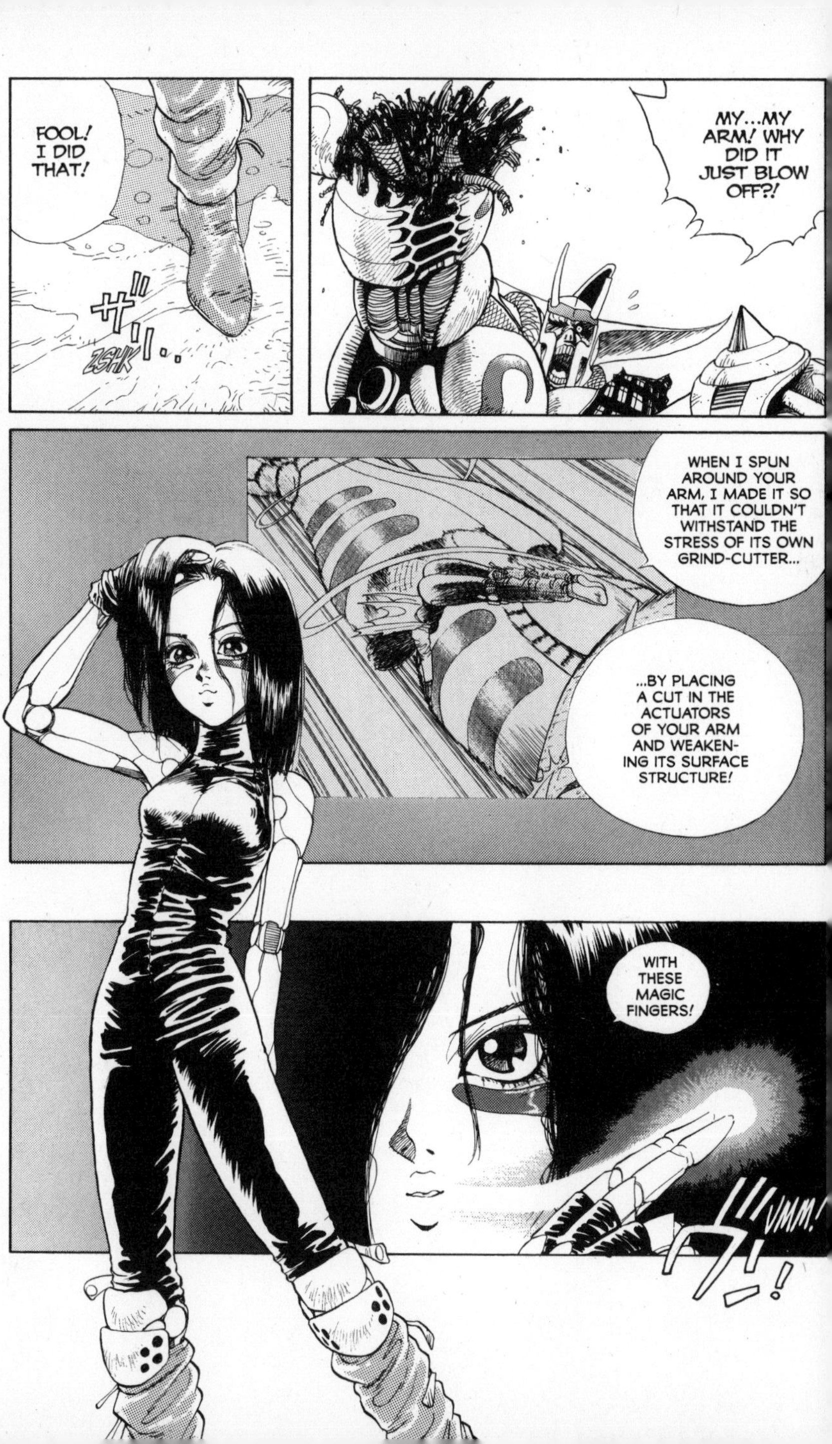
MY...MY ARM! WHY DID IT JUST BLOW OFF?!
FOOL! I DID THAT!
ZSHK
WHEN I SPUN AROUND YOUR ARM, I MADE IT SO THAT IT COULDN'T WITHSTAND THE STRESS OF ITS OWN GRIND-CUTTER...
...BY PLACING A CUT IN THE ACTUATORS OF YOUR ARM AND WEAKEN-ING ITS SURFACE STRUCTURE!
WITH THESE MAGIC FINGERS!
VMM!

The Factories and the Deckmen

EXPLAINED!

THE WORD "FACTORY" NORMALLY MAKES ONE THINK OF A MANUFACTURING PLACE, BUT IN THE SCRAPYARD, IT'S MORE SYNONYMOUS WITH "GOVERNMENT OFFICE."

THE FACTORIES ARE THE MANAGEMENT CENTERS FOR THE VARIOUS INDUSTRIAL COMPLEXES OF THE SCRAPYARD, AND WORK FOR THE BENEFIT OF ZALEM.

VIRTUALLY ALL THE FOOD AND INDUSTRIAL GOODS MANUFACTURED IN THE SCRAPYARD ARE SENT UP TO ZALEM THROUGH THE FACTORIES.

THERE ARE ELEVEN DIFFERENT MANAGEMENT CENTERS IN THE SCRAPYARD, FROM FACTORY II TO FACTORY IIII.

THERE ARE NO HUMANS IN THE CENTERS. ALL HUMAN INTERFACING IS DONE THROUGH SPECIAL CYBORG PROCESSORS CALLED "DECKMEN."

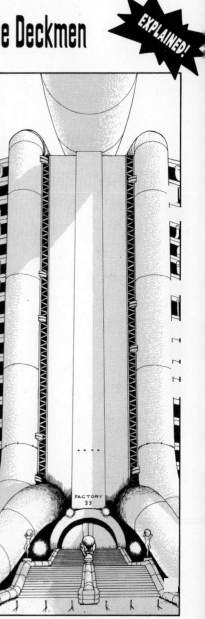

FACTORY
33
FRONT ENTRANCE OF A FACTORY

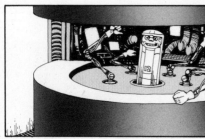

12
DECKMAN IN OPERATION CYLINDER

8
17
3
21
35
11
VARIOUS DECKMEN

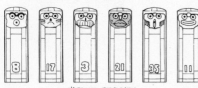

THE BIRTH OF DECKMAN #10!

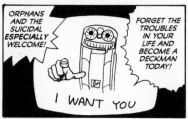

FORGET THE TROUBLES IN YOUR LIFE AND BECOME A DECKMAN TODAY!
ORPHANS AND THE SUICIDAL ESPECIALLY WELCOME!
15
I WANT YOU
I AHWAYS WANTED TA BE A DECK-MAN, EVAH SINCE I WAS A KID.
MY DAYS AS A HUMAN END TODAY!
DON'T MOVE, WE'RE MAKING A LIIITTLE INCISION TO REMOVE YOUR FACIAL FLESH AND LANGUAGE CENTERS.
15
YAY!
BEGIN OPERA-TION!
BLURCH
SPLUT
SPAK
15
WHY'D YA WANNA BE A DECKMAN, BABY?
FOH MY OWN WEASONS ...
MWAH!
15
10

The End.

DECKMEN DO FEATURE BIOLOGICAL BRAINS IN PLACE OF COMPUTER CHIPS, BUT THEY ARE ESSENTIALLY ZALEMITE SLAVES (ROBOTS) WITH NO HUMAN DESIRES OR FREE WILL.

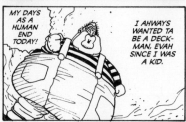

THE DECKMAN'S BODY MOVES THROUGHOUT A LINEAR TUBE SYSTEM THAT CONNECTS IT TO OTHER SYSTEM FUNCTIONS THAT ACT LIKE ITS LIMBS.

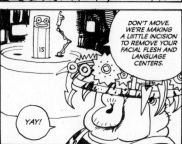

10

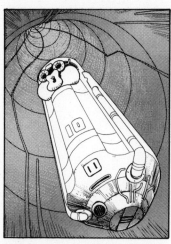

DECKMAN TRAVELING THROUGH LINEAR TUBE

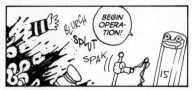

THERE ARE STILL MANY MYSTERIES REMAINING ABOUT THE FACTORIES AND ZALEM, BUT THESE WILL SLOWLY BUT SURELY BE REVEALED AS THE STORY MOVES ONWARD.

YUKITO.
1991. 8. 9.

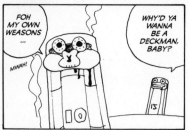

Translation Notes

Battle Angel Alita, Alita

The original title of the *Battle Angel Alita* series in Japan is *Ganmu* (which the author styles *Gunnm*), a portmanteau of the kanji characters for "gun" and "dream." Likewise, the protagonist's name is not Alita, but "Gally" (Garii).

At the time of its original translation to English in the mid-1990s, the title of the series (and its namesake) were changed to make it more appealing to an English-speaking audience, especially given the niche audience for manga at the time. As the demand for stories from Japan has grown over the years, such changes to the core presentation of these creative works are now largely seen as unnecessary or distracting. However, in recognition of the familiarity among Western readers with *Battle Angel Alita* over the many years of its publication (continuing through the sequel series *Battle Angel Alita: Last Order* and the live-action film), these changes will remain in place for this edition, with any alterations noted here.

Makaku, page 138

Although the name "Makaku" is normally written in the phonetic katakana alphabet, his "autograph," as seen tattooed onto this hapless hunter's back, is written in kanji characters that tell us his name is meant to sound like "demon horns."

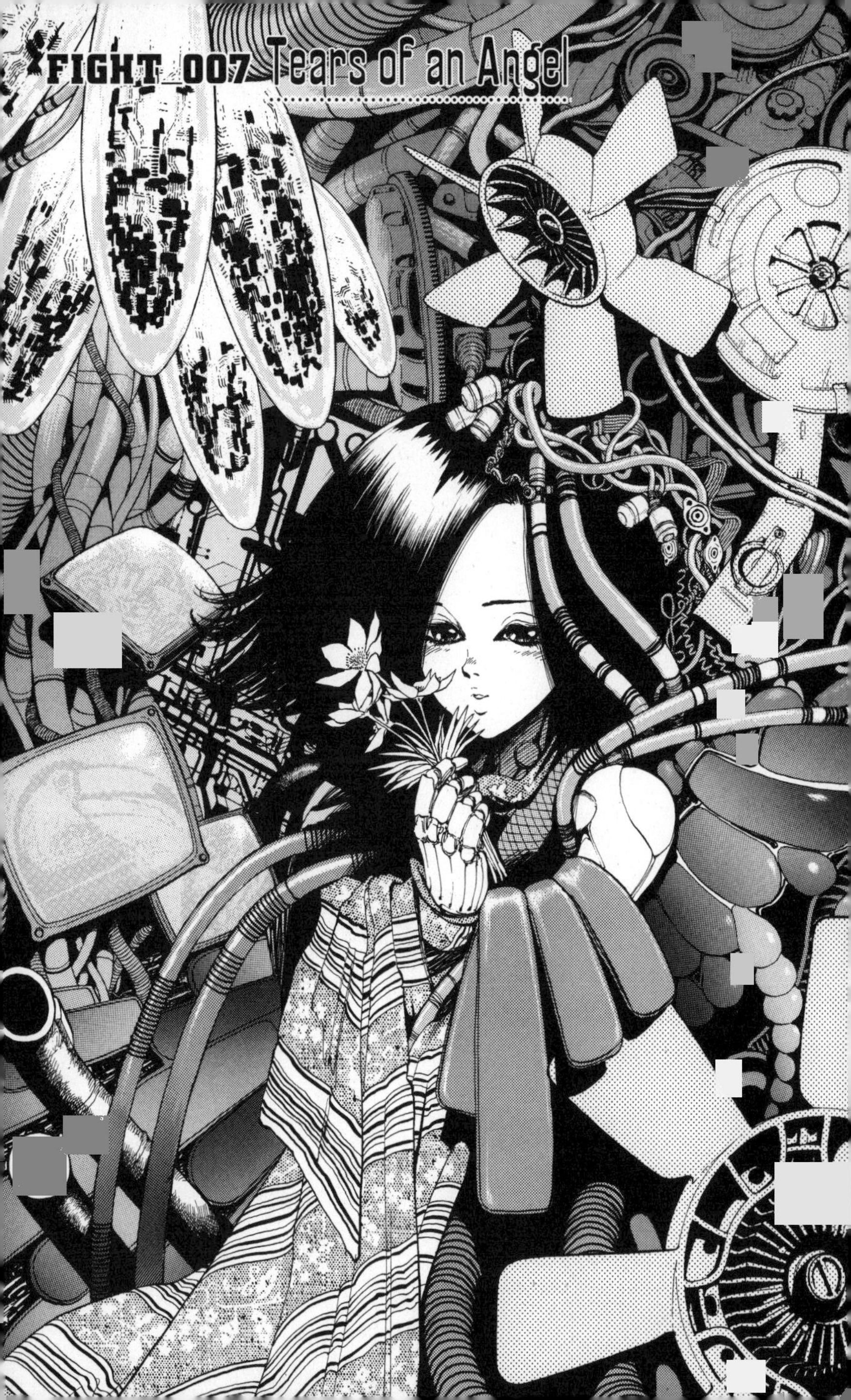
FIGHT_007 Tears of an Angel

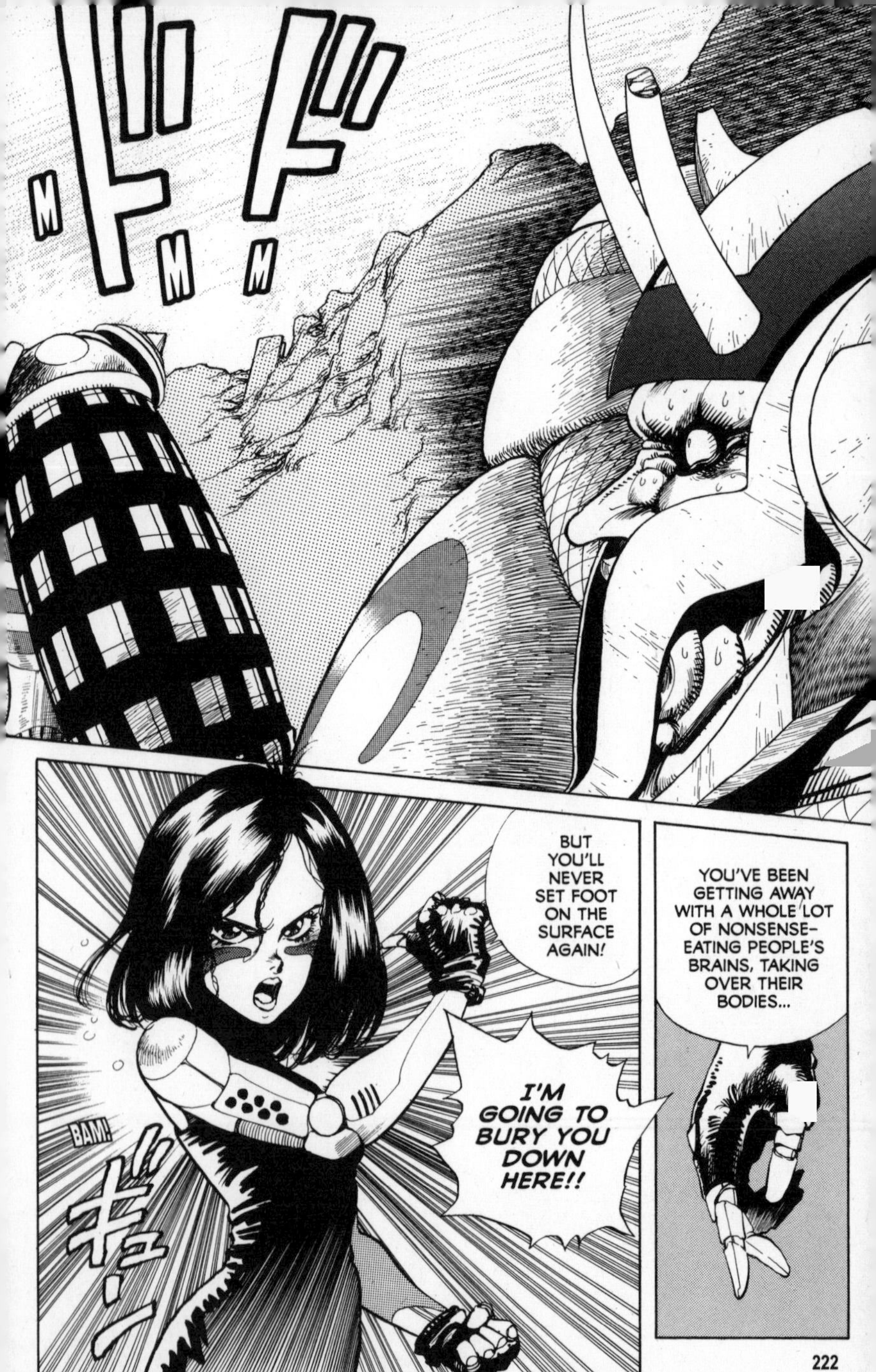
MドMドM
YOU'VE BEEN GETTING AWAY WITH A WHOLE LOT OF NONSENSE– EATING PEOPLE'S BRAINS, TAKING OVER THEIR BODIES...
BUT YOU'LL NEVER SET FOOT ON THE SURFACE AGAIN!
I'M GOING TO BURY YOU DOWN HERE!!
BAM!
ギュー

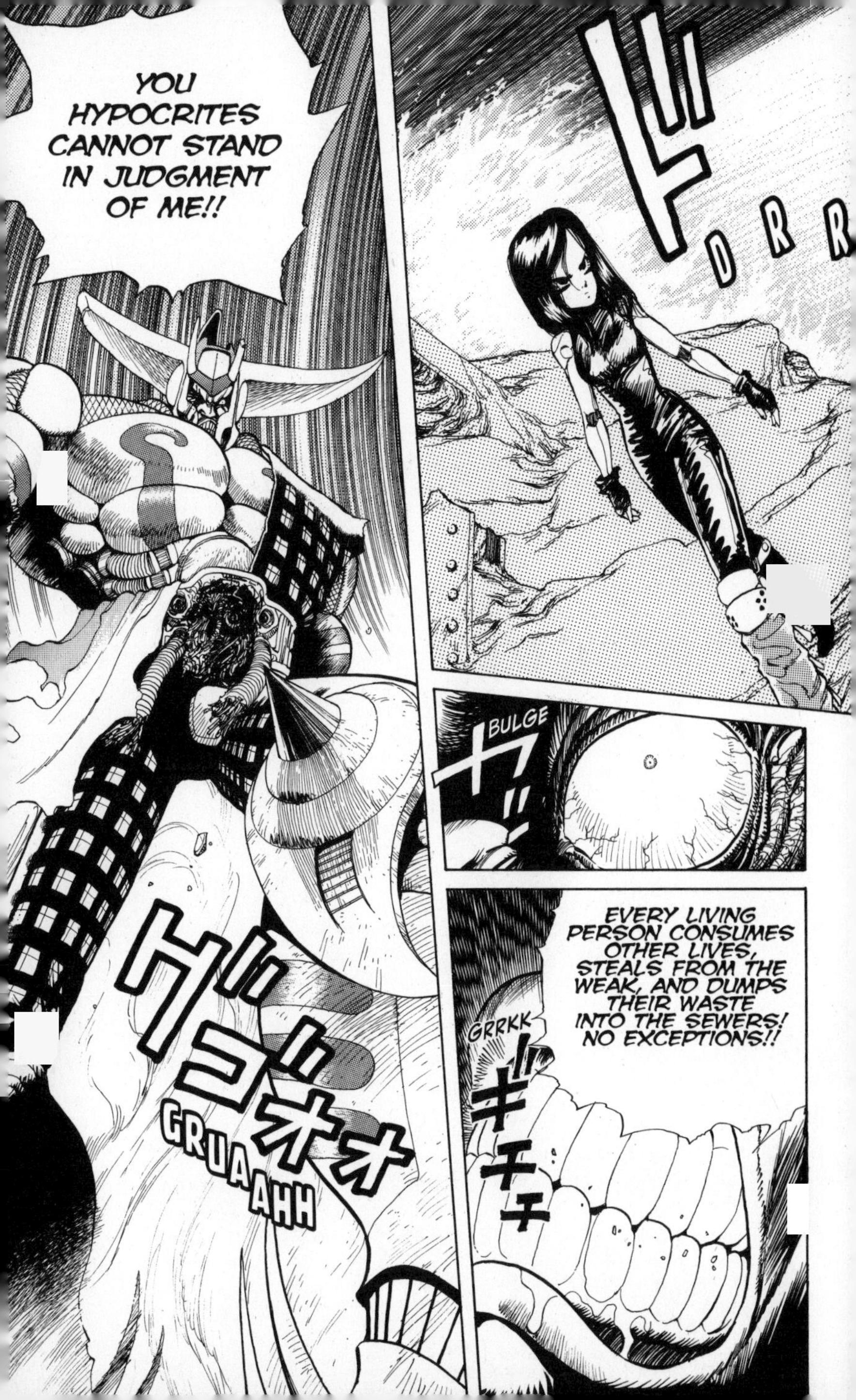
DRRR
BULGE
EVERY LIVING PERSON CONSUMES OTHER LIVES, STEALS FROM THE WEAK, AND DUMPS THEIR WASTE INTO THE SEWERS! NO EXCEPTIONS!!
GRRKK
YOU HYPOCRITES CANNOT STAND IN JUDGMENT OF ME!!
GRUAAHH

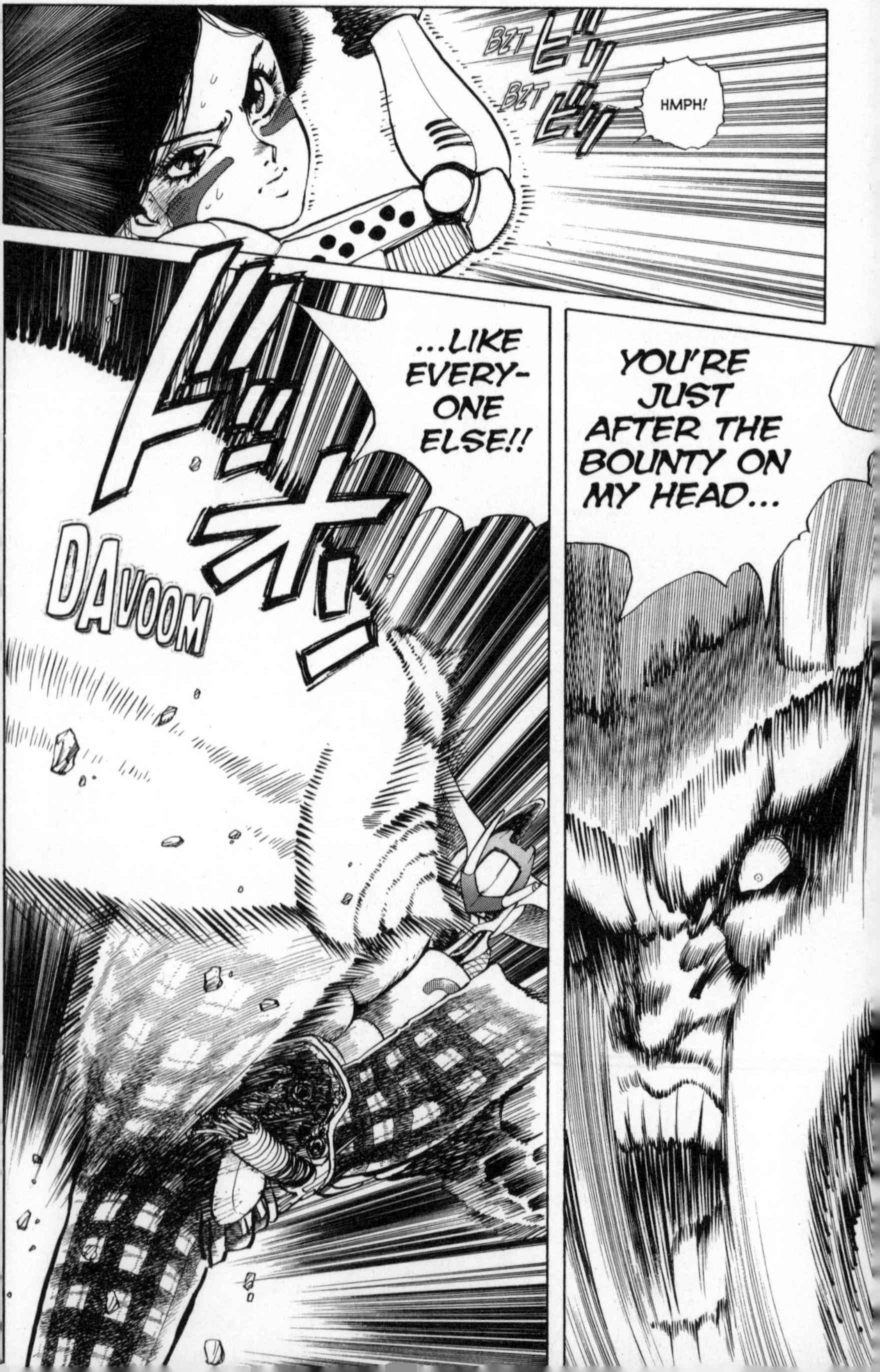
BZT
BZT
HMPH!
YOU'RE JUST AFTER THE BOUNTY ON MY HEAD...
...LIKE EVERY-ONE ELSE!!
DAVOOM

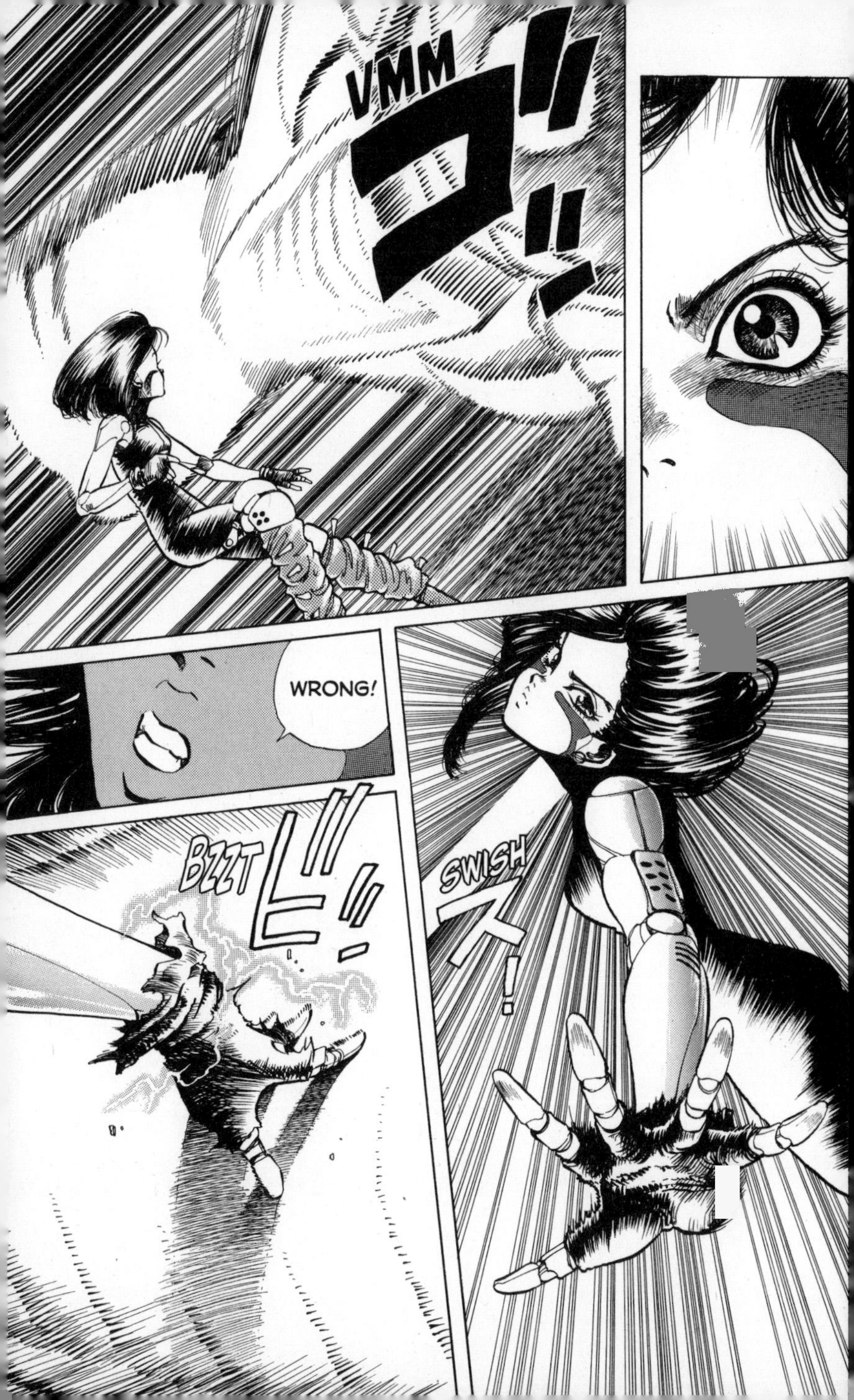
VMM
SWISH
WRONG!
BZZT

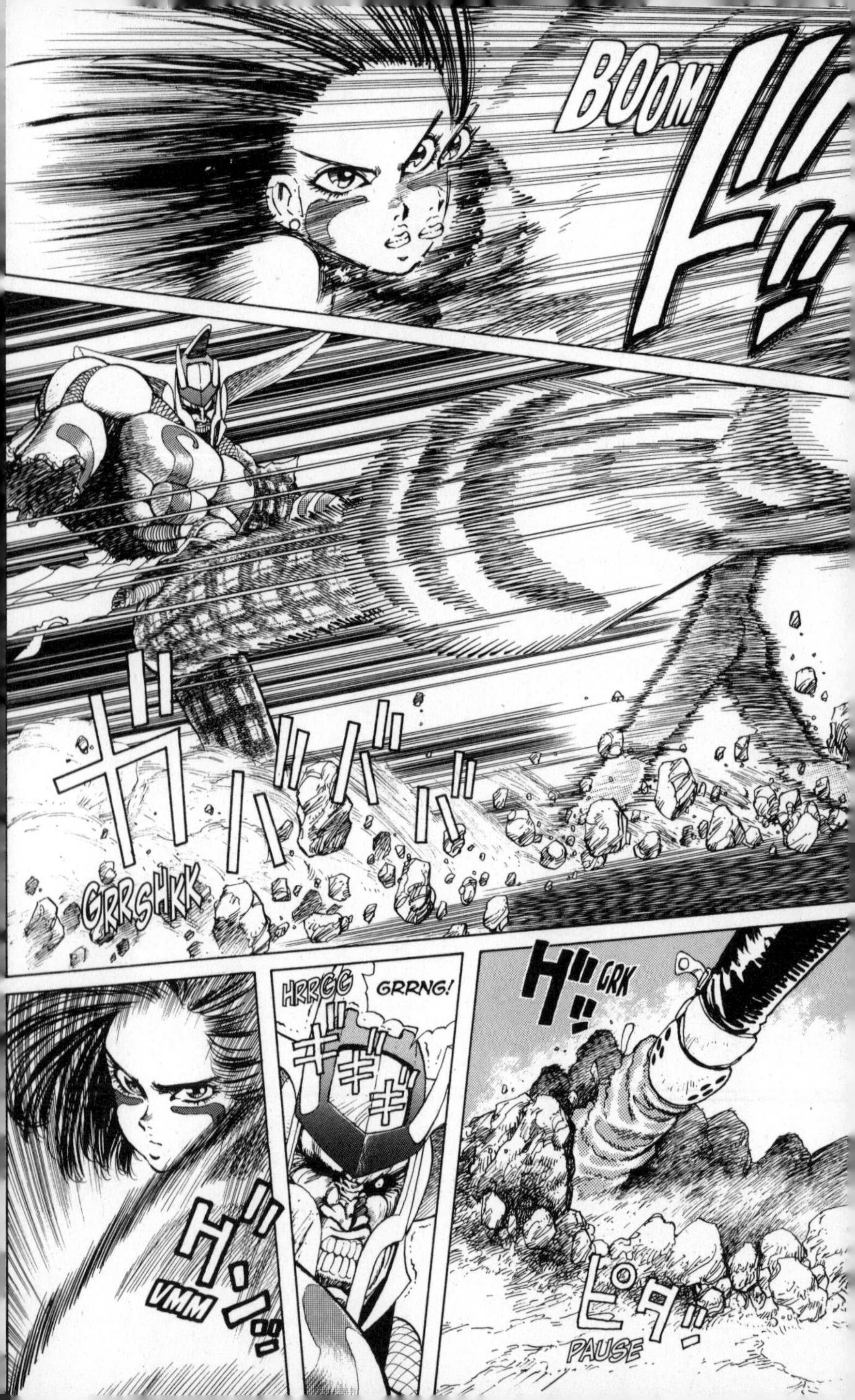

BOOM
GRRSHKK
GRK
PAUSE
HRRGG
GRRNG!
VMM

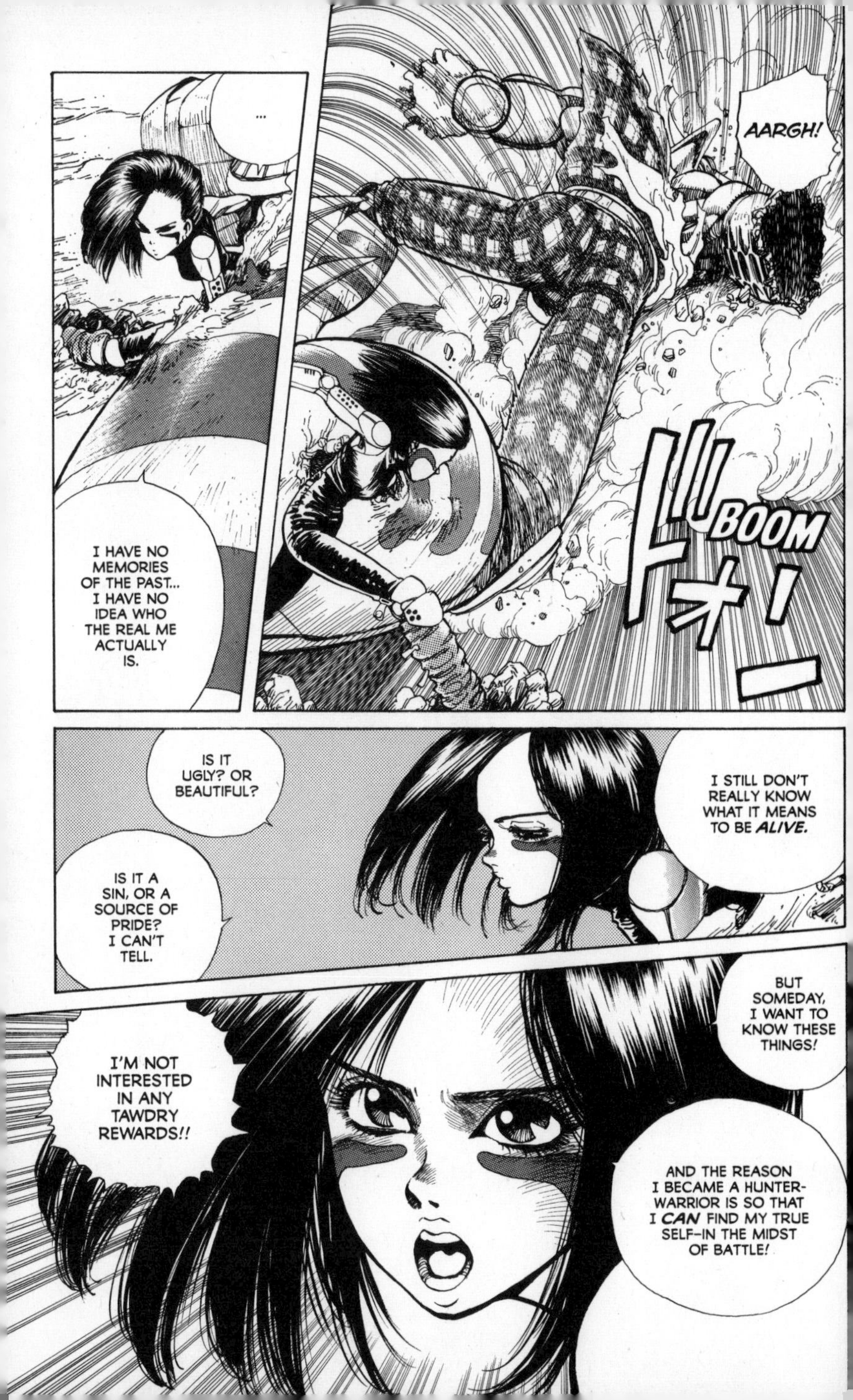
AARGH!
BOOM
...
I HAVE NO MEMORIES OF THE PAST... I HAVE NO IDEA WHO THE REAL ME ACTUALLY IS.
I STILL DON'T REALLY KNOW WHAT IT MEANS TO BE *ALIVE.*
IS IT UGLY? OR BEAUTIFUL?
IS IT A SIN, OR A SOURCE OF PRIDE? I CAN'T TELL.
BUT SOMEDAY, I WANT TO KNOW THESE THINGS!
I'M NOT INTERESTED IN ANY TAWDRY REWARDS!!
AND THE REASON I BECAME A HUNTER-WARRIOR IS SO THAT I *CAN* FIND MY TRUE SELF—IN THE MIDST OF BATTLE!

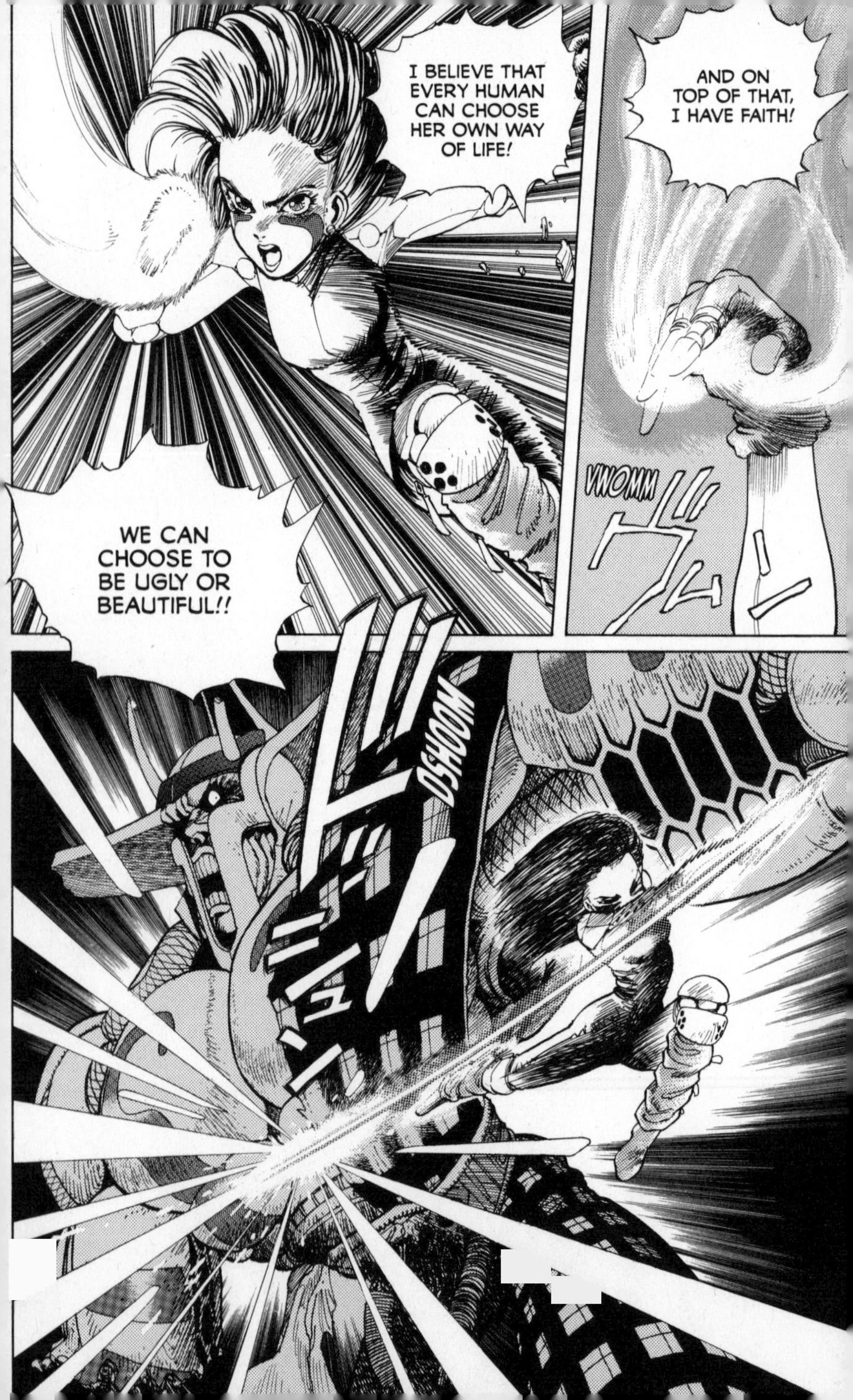
AND ON TOP OF THAT, I HAVE FAITH!
VWOMM
I BELIEVE THAT EVERY HUMAN CAN CHOOSE HER OWN WAY OF LIFE!
WE CAN CHOOSE TO BE UGLY OR BEAUTIFUL!!
DSHOOM

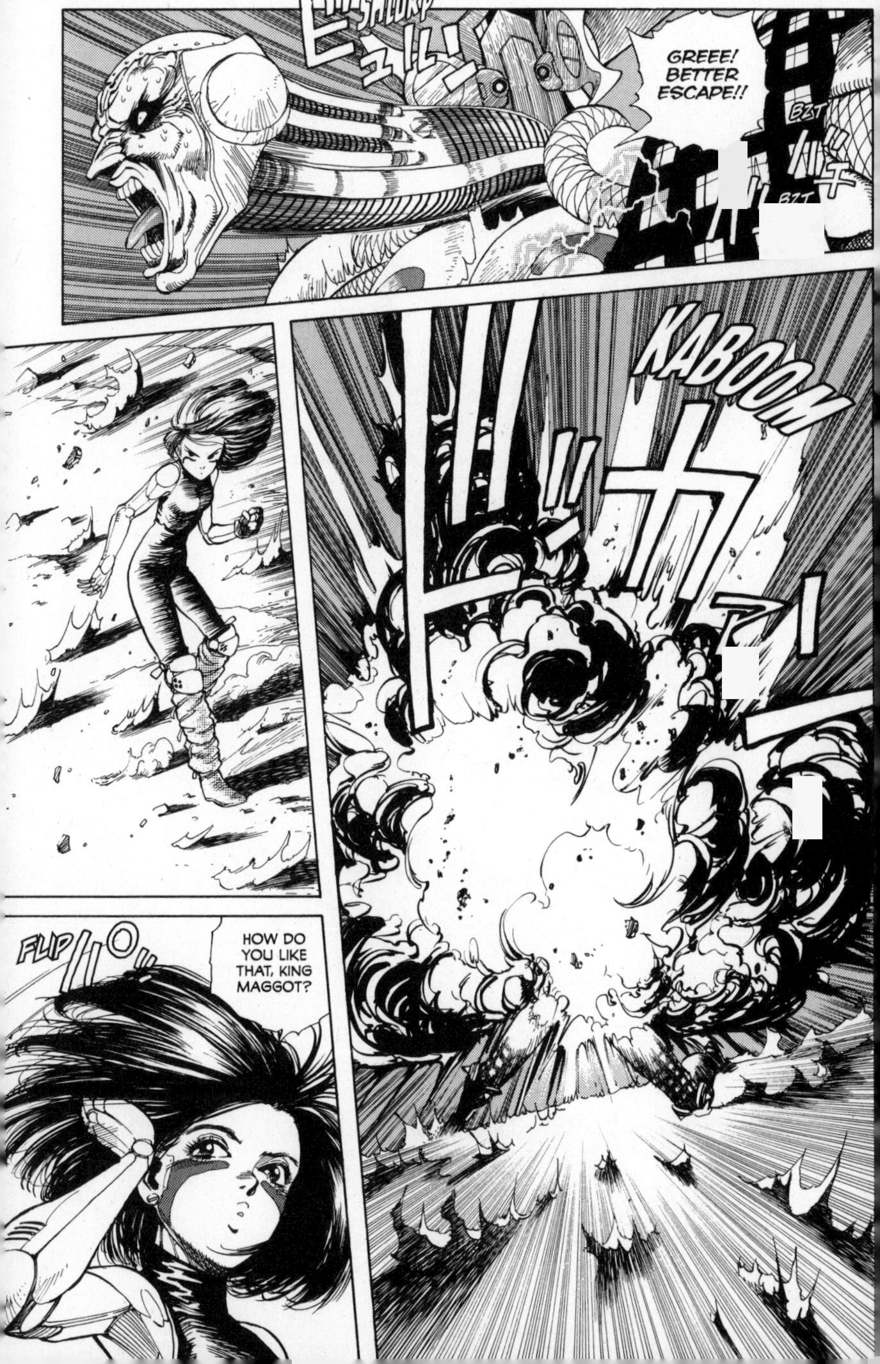

GREEE! BETTER ESCAPE!!
BZT
BZT
SHLURP
KABOOM
FLIP
HOW DO YOU LIKE THAT, KING MAGGOT?

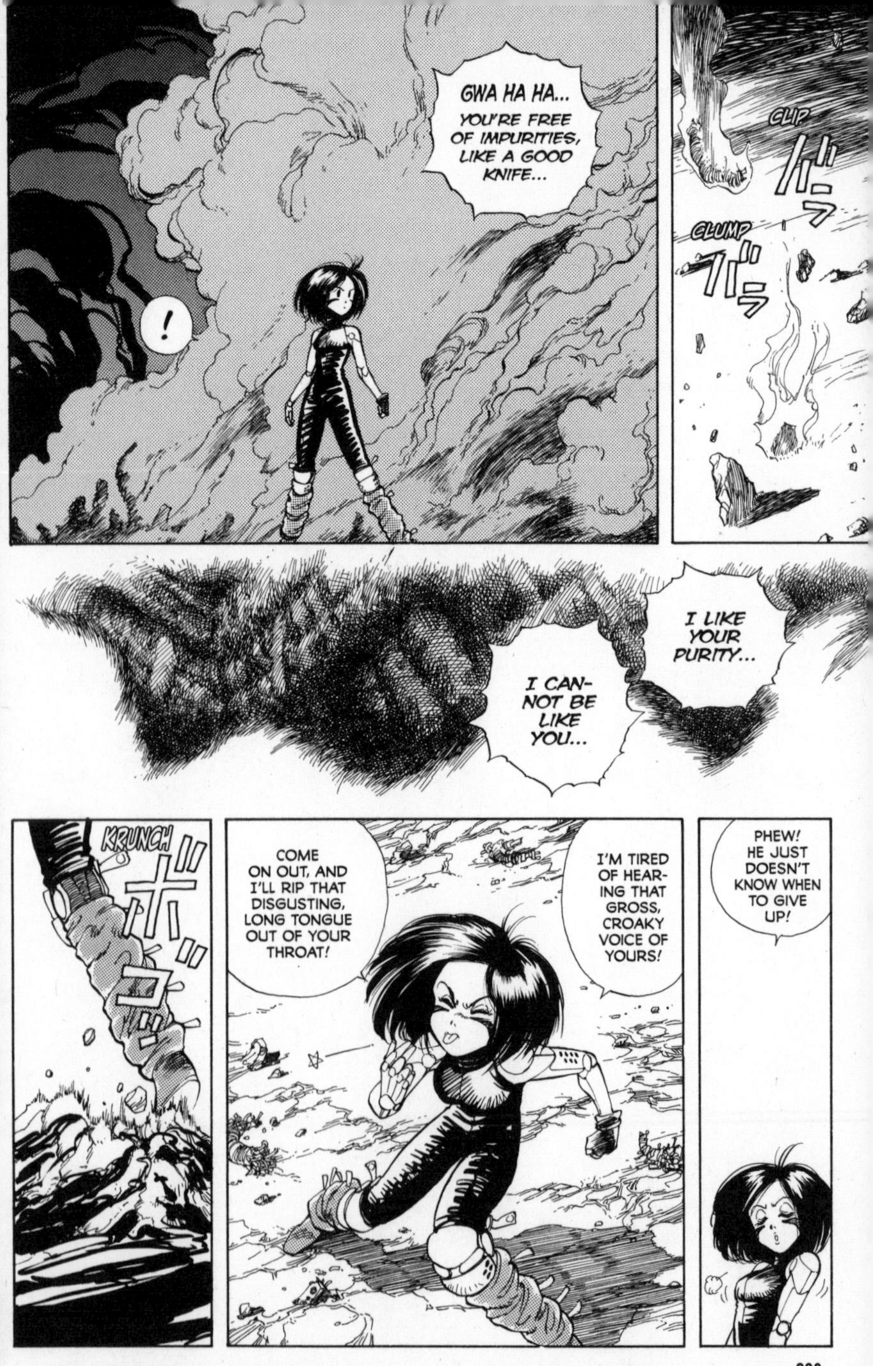

CLIP
CLUMP
GWA HA HA... YOU'RE FREE OF IMPURITIES, LIKE A GOOD KNIFE...
!
I LIKE YOUR PURITY...
I CAN-NOT BE LIKE YOU...
PHEW! HE JUST DOESN'T KNOW WHEN TO GIVE UP!
I'M TIRED OF HEAR-ING THAT GROSS, CROAKY VOICE OF YOURS!
COME ON OUT, AND I'LL RIP THAT DISGUSTING, LONG TONGUE OUT OF YOUR THROAT!
KRUNCH

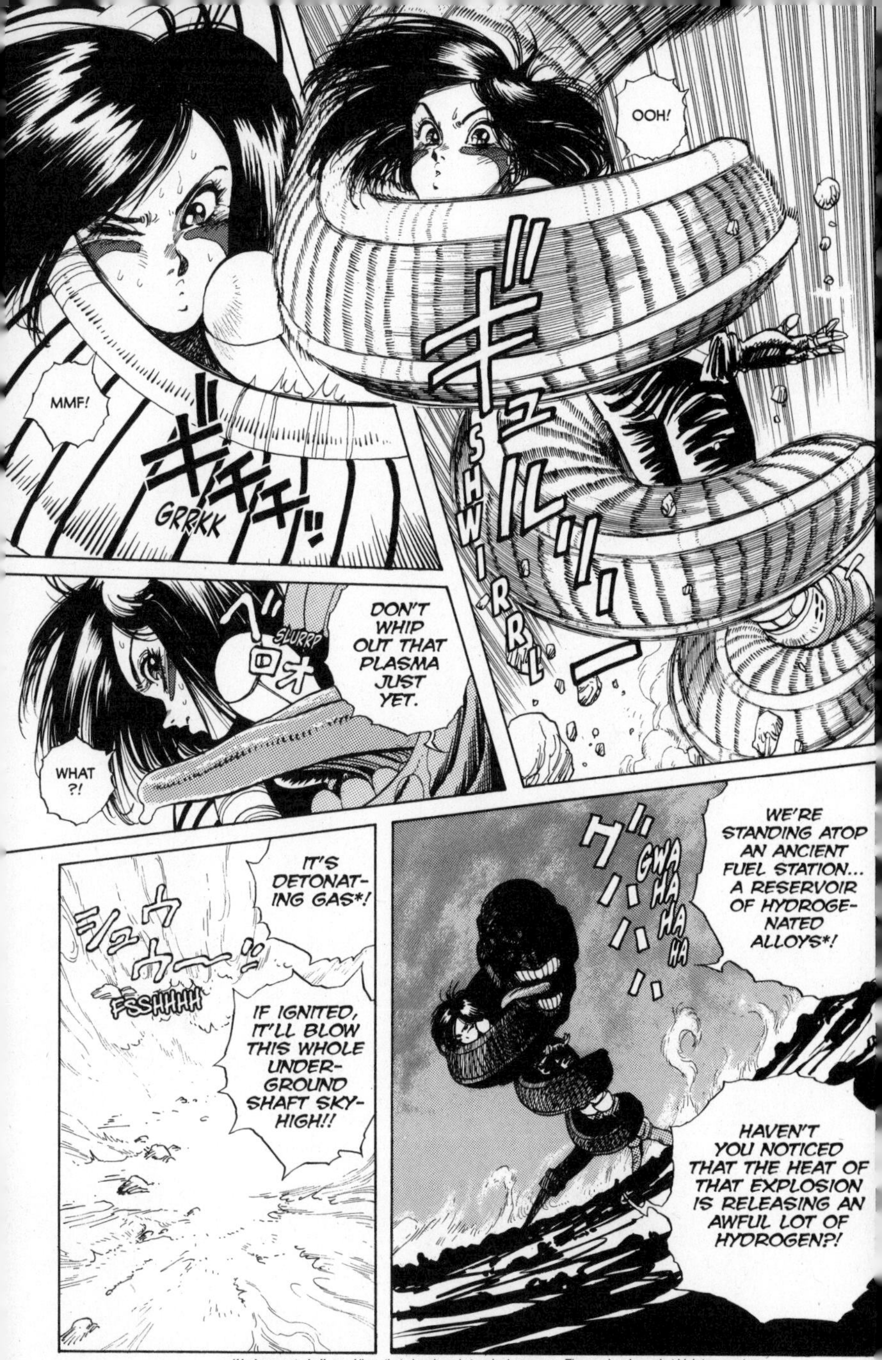

OOH!
SHWIRRRL
MMF!
GRRKK
DON'T WHIP OUT THAT PLASMA JUST YET.
SLURRP
WHAT?!
WE'RE STANDING ATOP AN ANCIENT FUEL STATION... A RESERVOIR OF HYDROGENATED ALLOYS*!
GWA HA HA HA HA
HAVEN'T YOU NOTICED THAT THE HEAT OF THAT EXPLOSION IS RELEASING AN AWFUL LOT OF HYDROGEN?!
IT'S DETONATING GAS*!
FSSHHHH
IF IGNITED, IT'LL BLOW THIS WHOLE UNDERGROUND SHAFT SKY-HIGH!!

***Hydrogenated alloys:** Alloys that absorb and store hydrogen gas. The gas is released at high temperatures.

***Detonating gas:** A 2:1 mixture of hydrogen and oxygen gases. It explodes when ignited, producing water as a result.

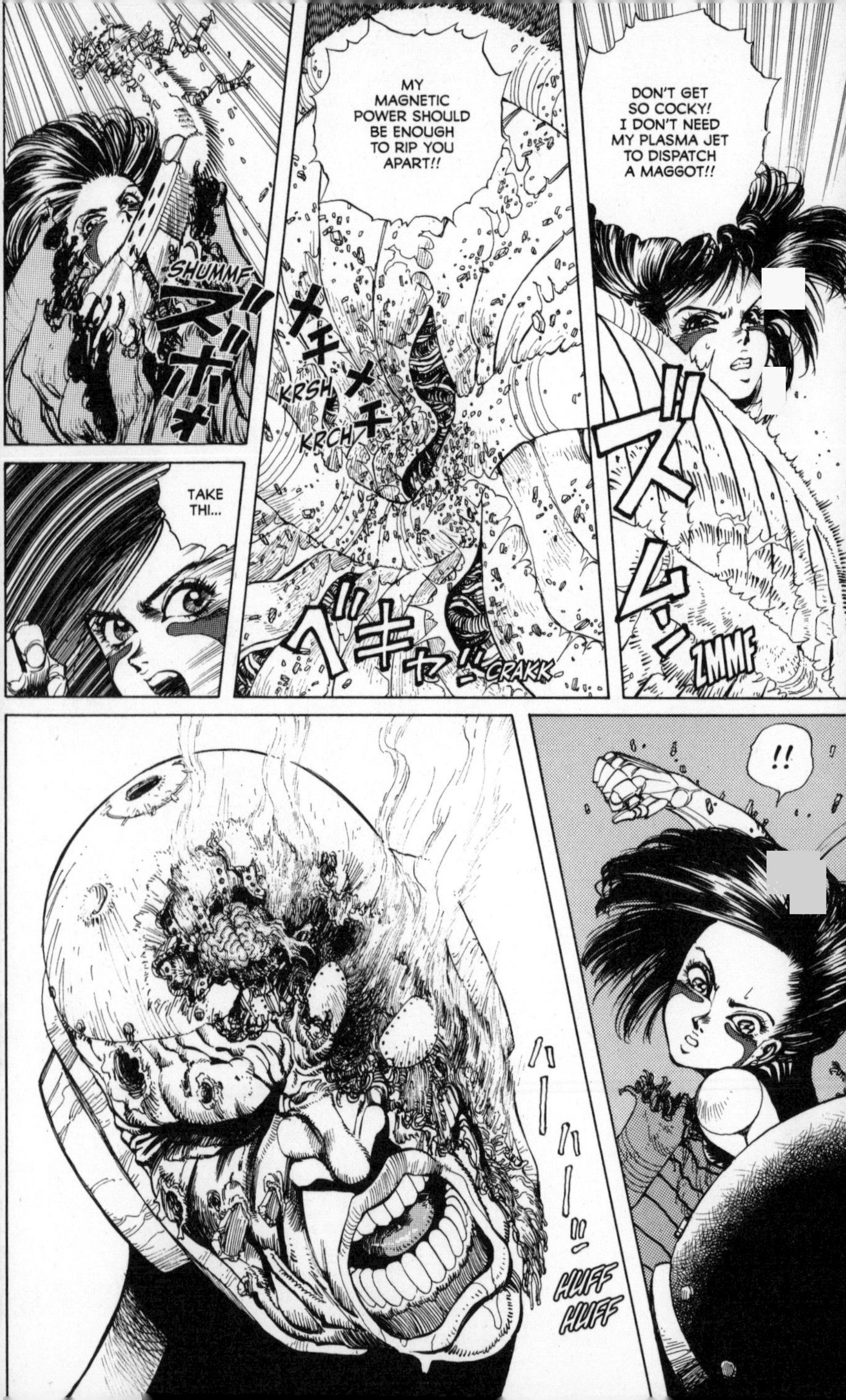
DON'T GET SO COCKY! I DON'T NEED MY PLASMA JET TO DISPATCH A MAGGOT!!
ZMMF
MY MAGNETIC POWER SHOULD BE ENOUGH TO RIP YOU APART!!
KRSH
KRCH
CRAKK
SHUMMF
TAKE THI...
!!
HUFF HUFF

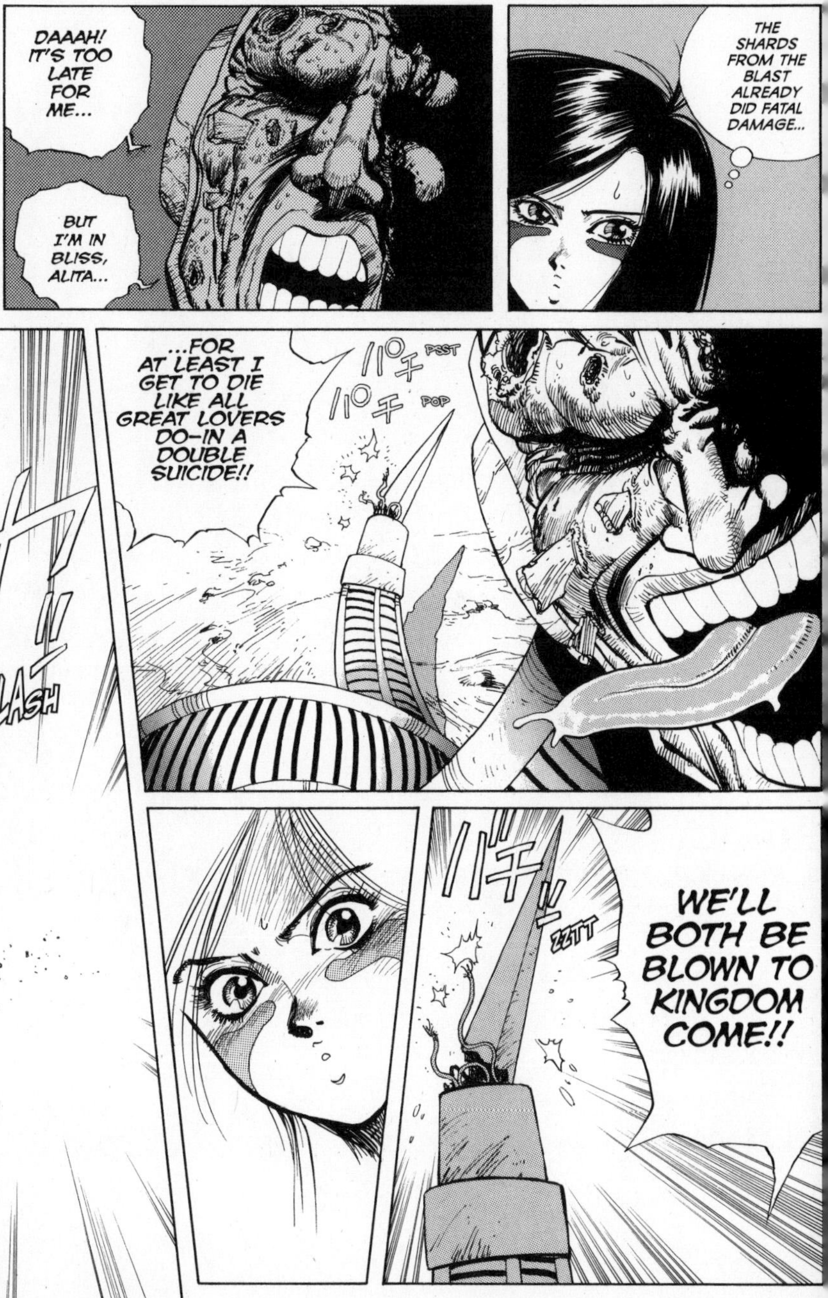
THE SHARDS FROM THE BLAST ALREADY DID FATAL DAMAGE...
DAAAH! IT'S TOO LATE FOR ME...
BUT I'M IN BLISS, ALITA...
...FOR AT LEAST I GET TO DIE LIKE ALL GREAT LOVERS DO—IN A DOUBLE SUICIDE!!
PSST
POP
WE'LL BOTH BE BLOWN TO KINGDOM COME!!
ZZTT
FLASH

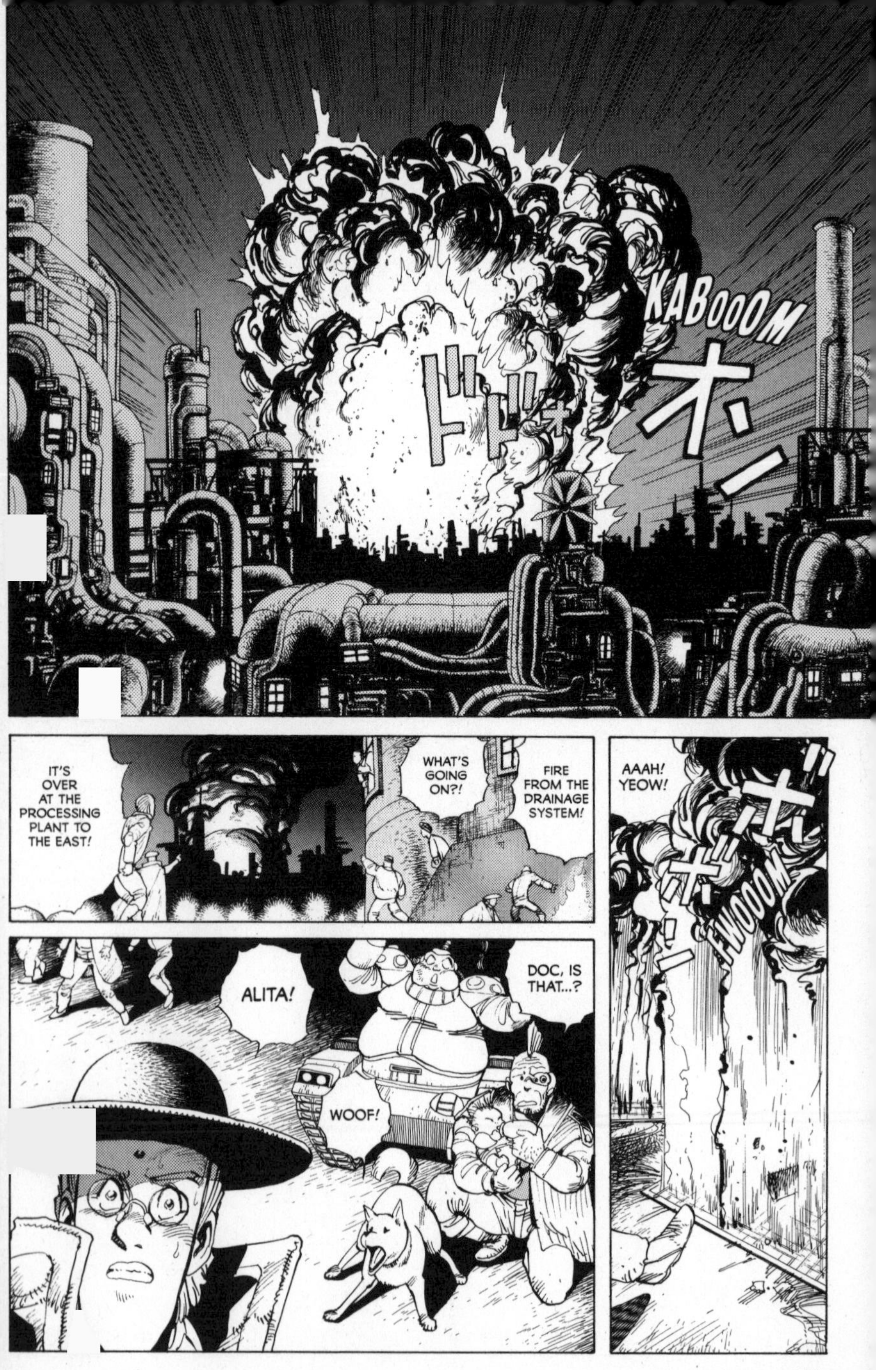
KABOOOM
AAAH! YEOW!
FWOOOM
FIRE FROM THE DRAINAGE SYSTEM!
WHAT'S GOING ON?!
IT'S OVER AT THE PROCESSING PLANT TO THE EAST!
DOC, IS THAT...?
ALITA!
WOOF!

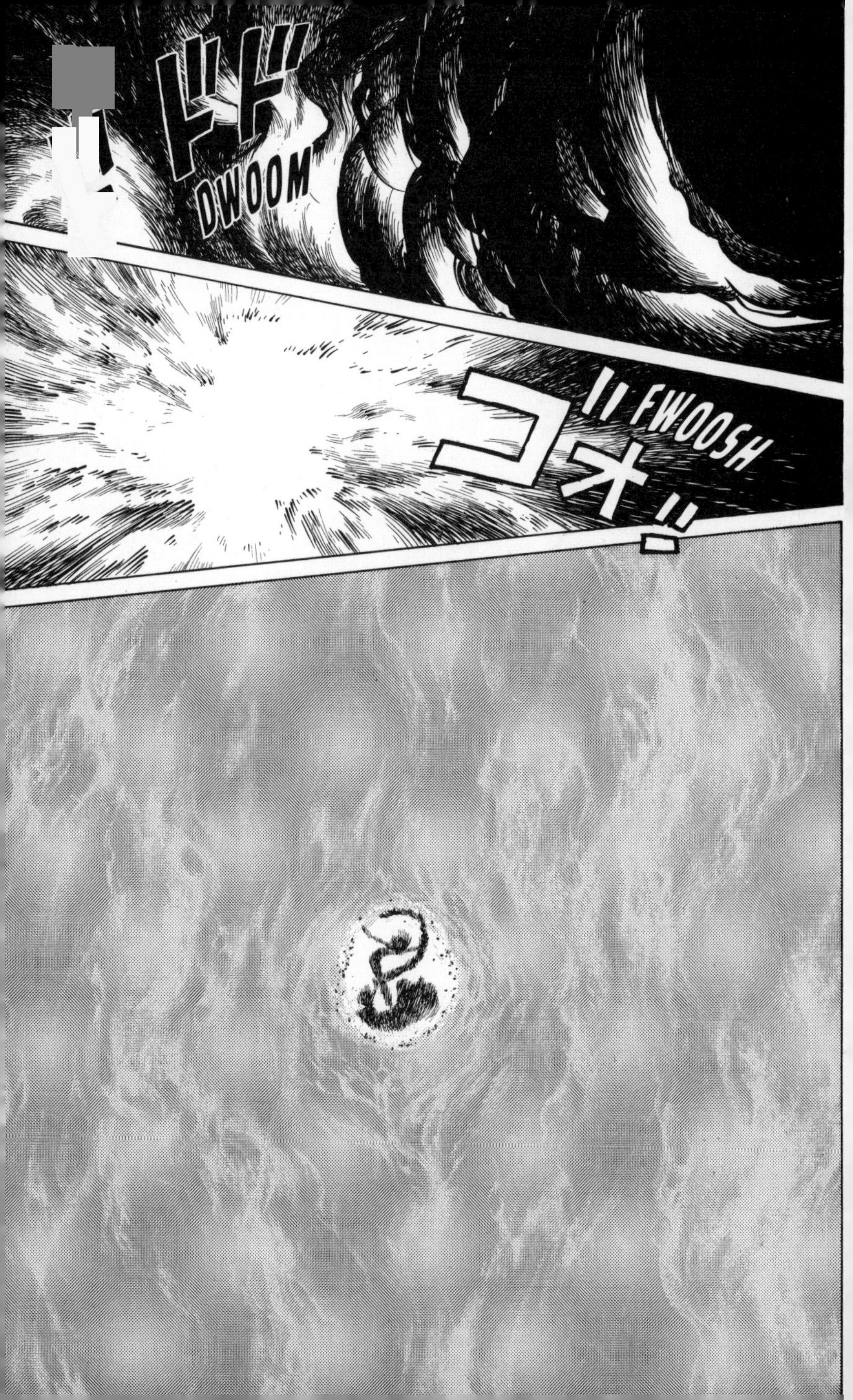
DWOOM
FWOOSH

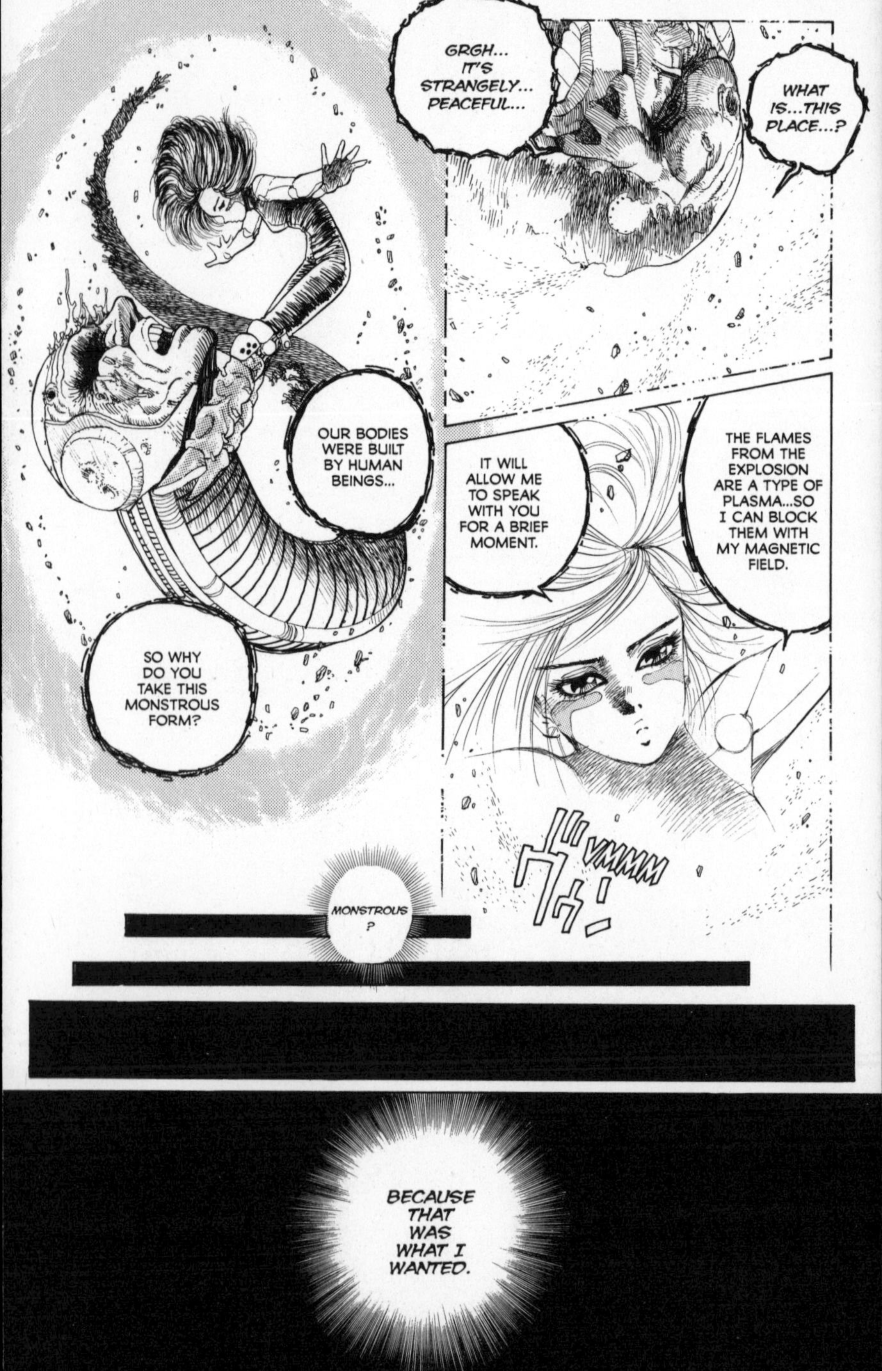
GRGH... IT'S STRANGELY... PEACEFUL...
WHAT IS...THIS PLACE...?
THE FLAMES FROM THE EXPLOSION ARE A TYPE OF PLASMA...SO I CAN BLOCK THEM WITH MY MAGNETIC FIELD.
IT WILL ALLOW ME TO SPEAK WITH YOU FOR A BRIEF MOMENT.
VMMMM
OUR BODIES WERE BUILT BY HUMAN BEINGS...
SO WHY DO YOU TAKE THIS MONSTROUS FORM?
MONSTROUS ?
BECAUSE THAT WAS WHAT I WANTED.

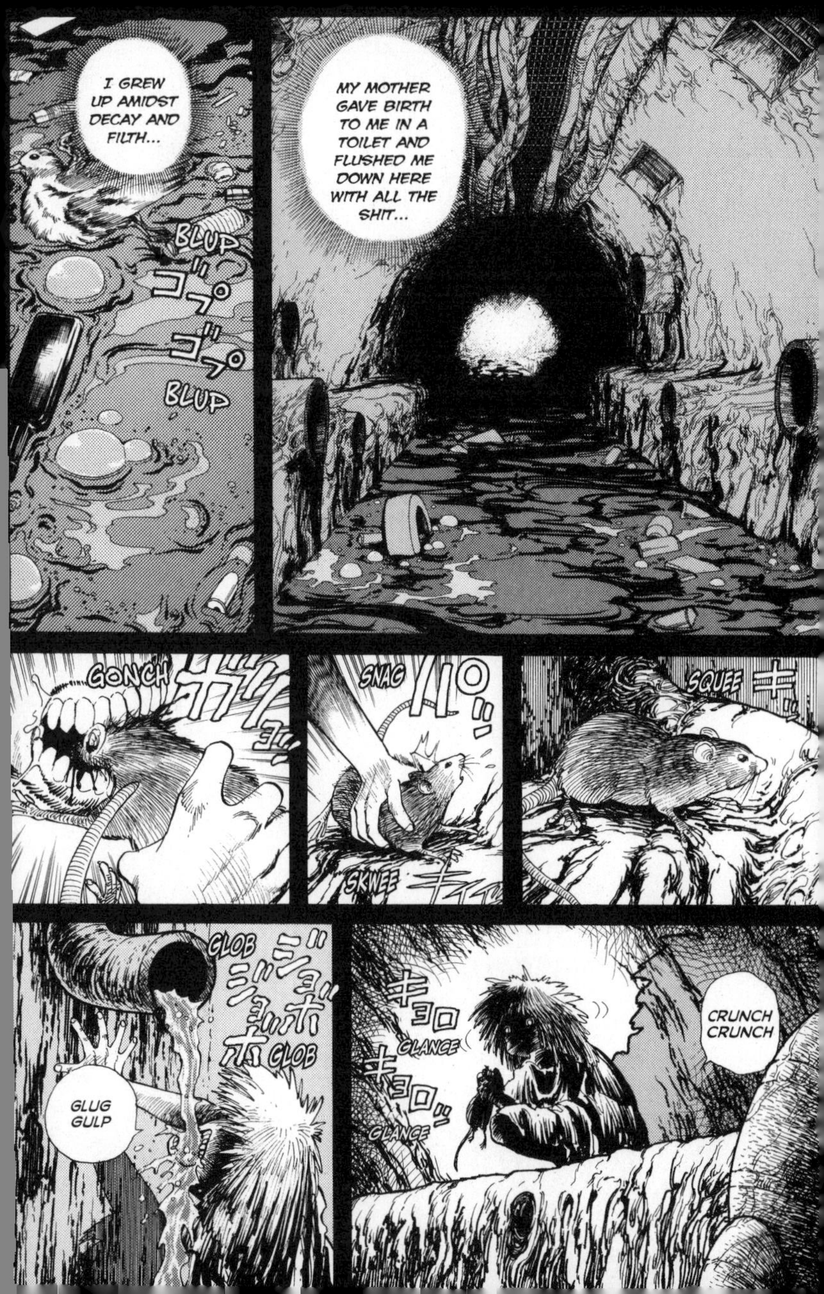
MY MOTHER GAVE BIRTH TO ME IN A TOILET AND FLUSHED ME DOWN HERE WITH ALL THE SHIT...
I GREW UP AMIDST DECAY AND FILTH...
BLUP
BLUP
SQUEE
SNAG
SKWEE
GONCH
GLANCE
GLANCE
CRUNCH CRUNCH
GLOB
GLOB
GLUG GULP

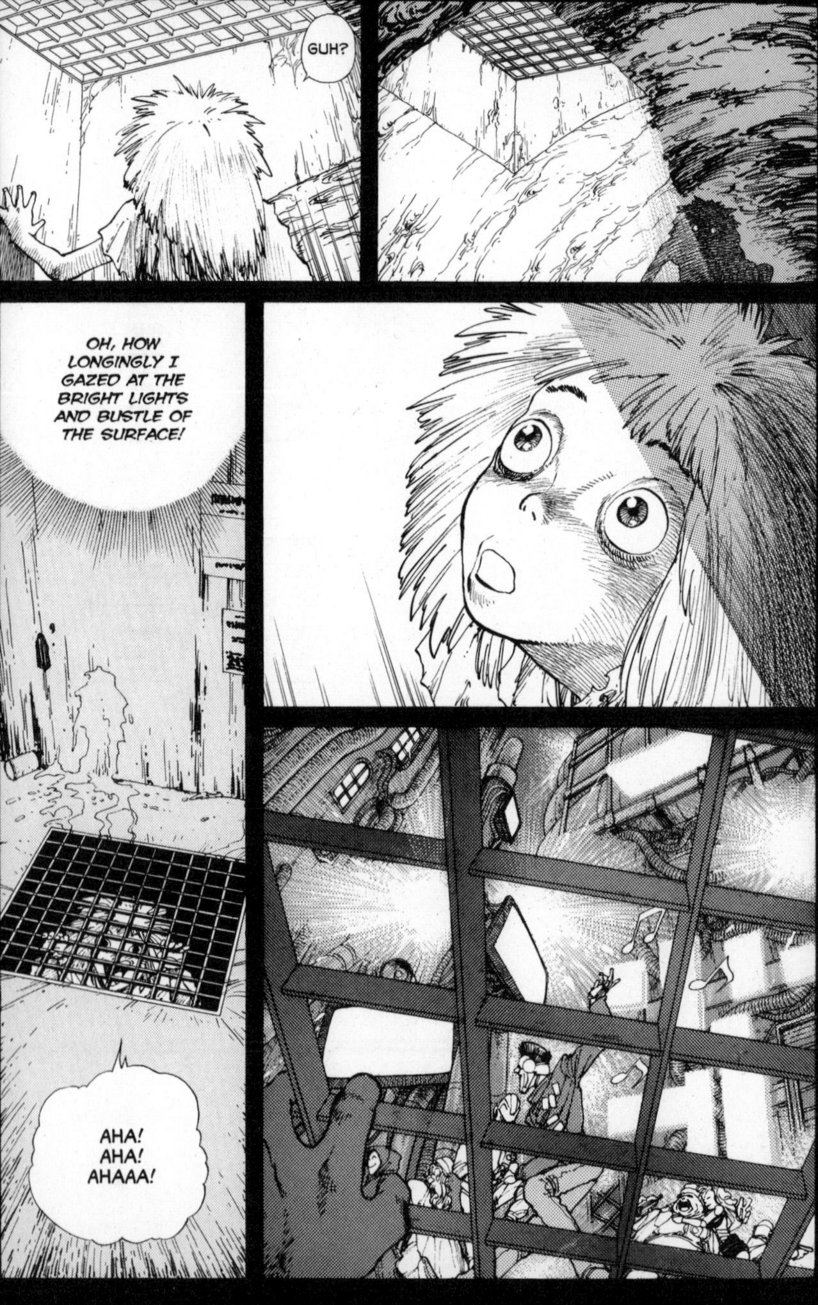
GUH?
OH, HOW LONGINGLY I GAZED AT THE BRIGHT LIGHTS AND BUSTLE OF THE SURFACE!
AHA! AHA! AHAAA!

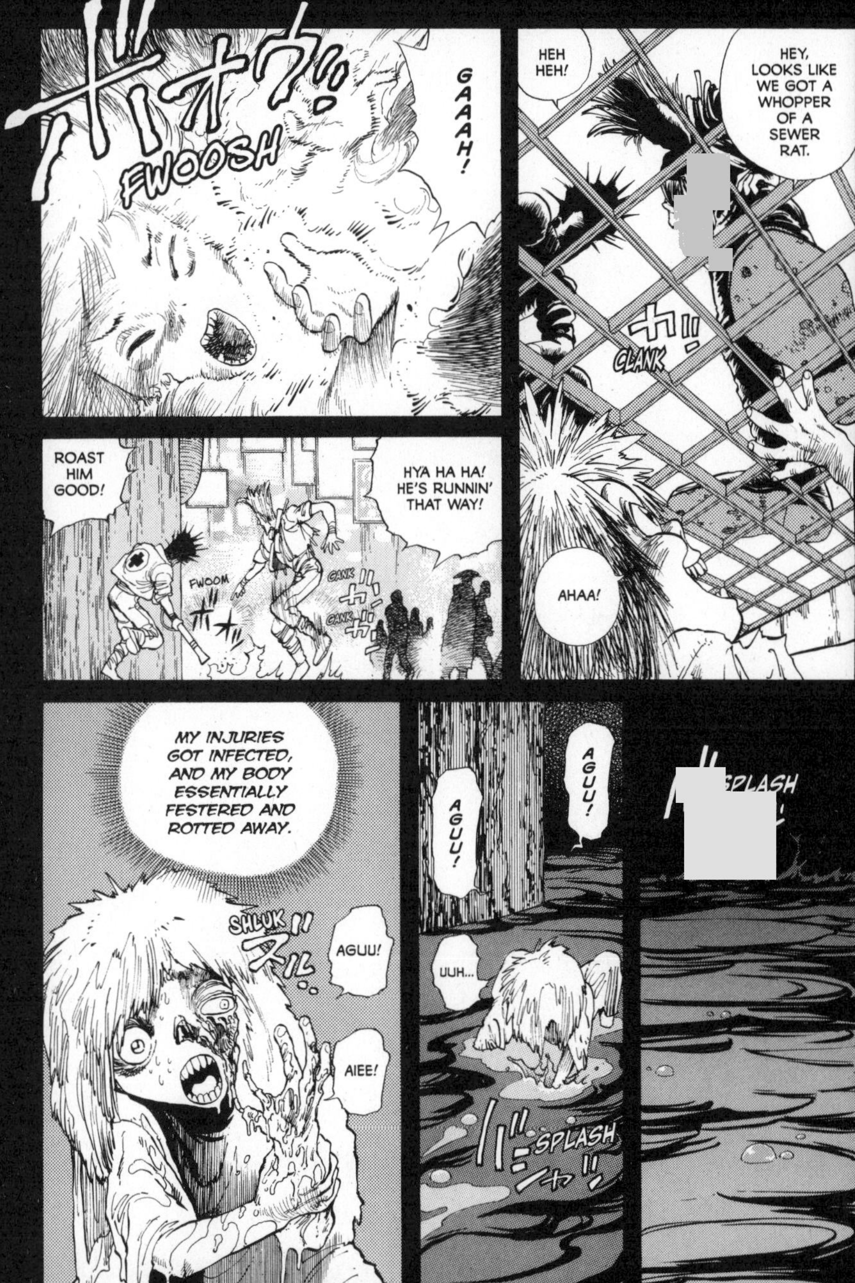
HEY, LOOKS LIKE WE GOT A WHOPPER OF A SEWER RAT.
HEH HEH!
CLANK
AHAA!
FWOOSH
GAAAAH!
HYA HA HA! HE'S RUNNIN' THAT WAY!
ROAST HIM GOOD!
FWOOM
CANK
CANK
SPLASH
AGUU!
AGUU!
UUH...
SPLASH
MY INJURIES GOT INFECTED, AND MY BODY ESSENTIALLY FESTERED AND ROTTED AWAY.
SHLUK
AGUU!
AIEE!

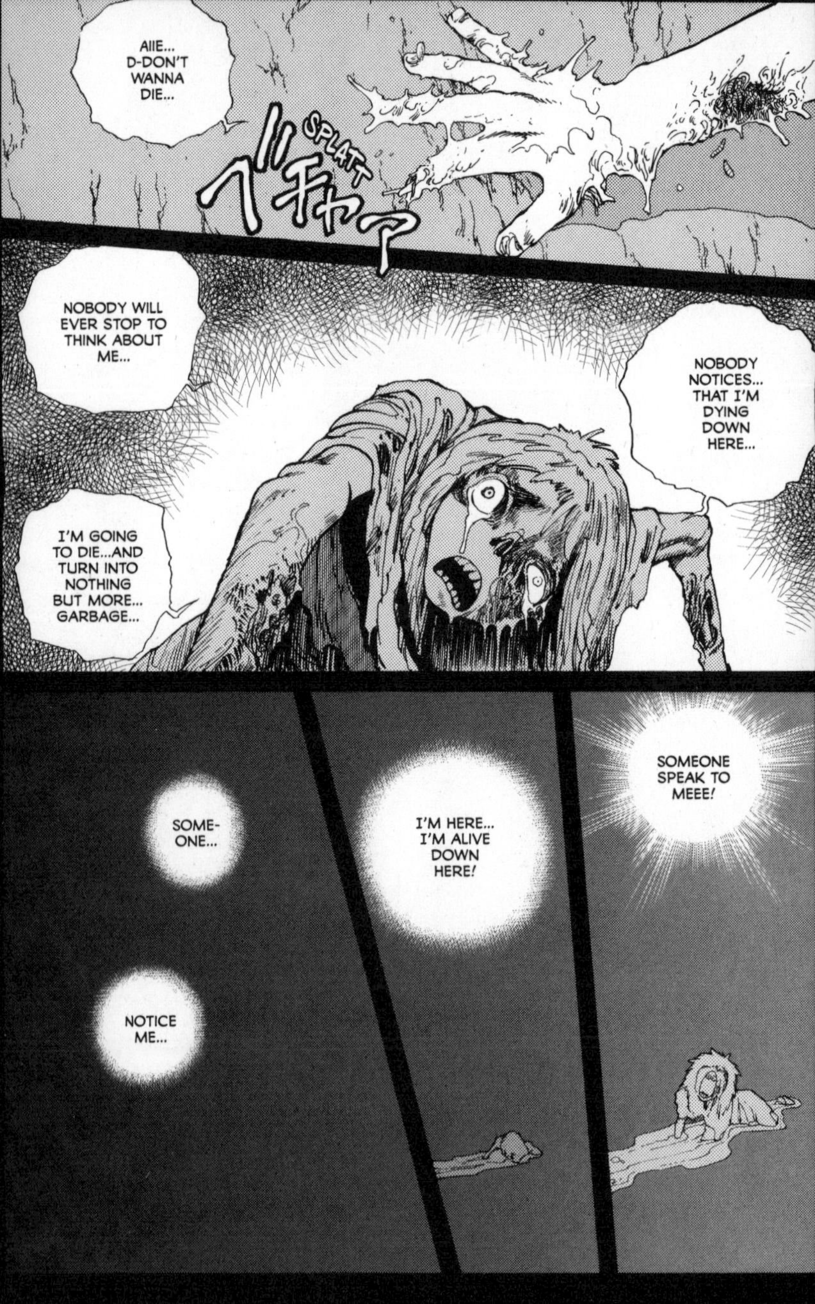
AIIE... D-DON'T WANNA DIE...
SPLATT
ベチャア
NOBODY NOTICES... THAT I'M DYING DOWN HERE...
NOBODY WILL EVER STOP TO THINK ABOUT ME...
I'M GOING TO DIE...AND TURN INTO NOTHING BUT MORE... GARBAGE...
SOMEONE SPEAK TO MEEE!
I'M HERE... I'M ALIVE DOWN HERE!
SOME-ONE...
NOTICE ME...

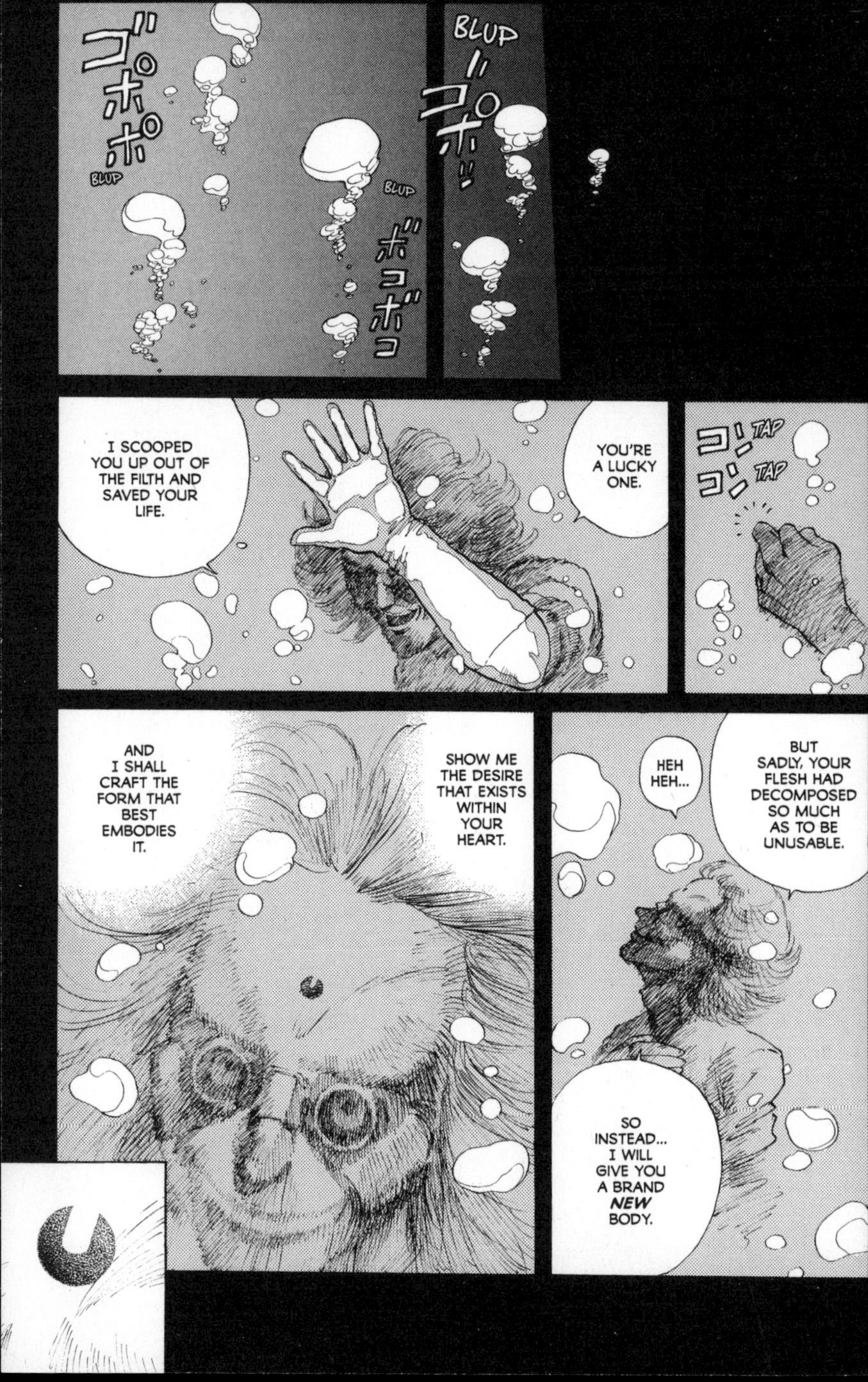
BLUP
ゴポ!!
ゴポポ
BLUP
BLUP
ボコボコ
コン TAP
コン TAP
YOU'RE A LUCKY ONE.
I SCOOPED YOU UP OUT OF THE FILTH AND SAVED YOUR LIFE.
BUT SADLY, YOUR FLESH HAD DECOMPOSED SO MUCH AS TO BE UNUSABLE.
HEH HEH...
SO INSTEAD... I WILL GIVE YOU A BRAND NEW BODY.
SHOW ME THE DESIRE THAT EXISTS WITHIN YOUR HEART.
AND I SHALL CRAFT THE FORM THAT BEST EMBODIES IT.

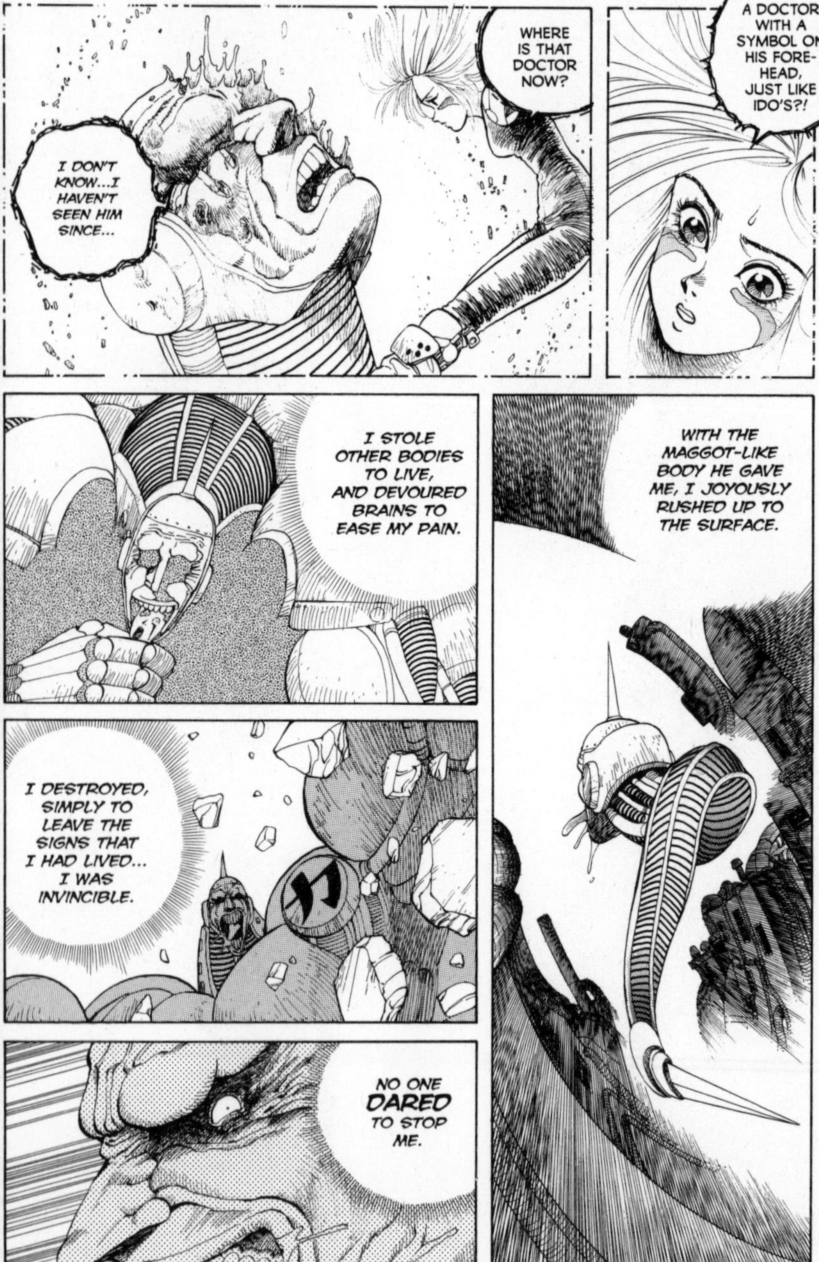
A DOCTOR WITH A SYMBOL ON HIS FORE-HEAD, JUST LIKE IDO'S?!
WHERE IS THAT DOCTOR NOW?
I DON'T KNOW...I HAVEN'T SEEN HIM SINCE...
WITH THE MAGGOT-LIKE BODY HE GAVE ME, I JOYOUSLY RUSHED UP TO THE SURFACE.
I STOLE OTHER BODIES TO LIVE, AND DEVOURED BRAINS TO EASE MY PAIN.
I DESTROYED, SIMPLY TO LEAVE THE SIGNS THAT I HAD LIVED... I WAS INVINCIBLE.
NO ONE DARED TO STOP ME.

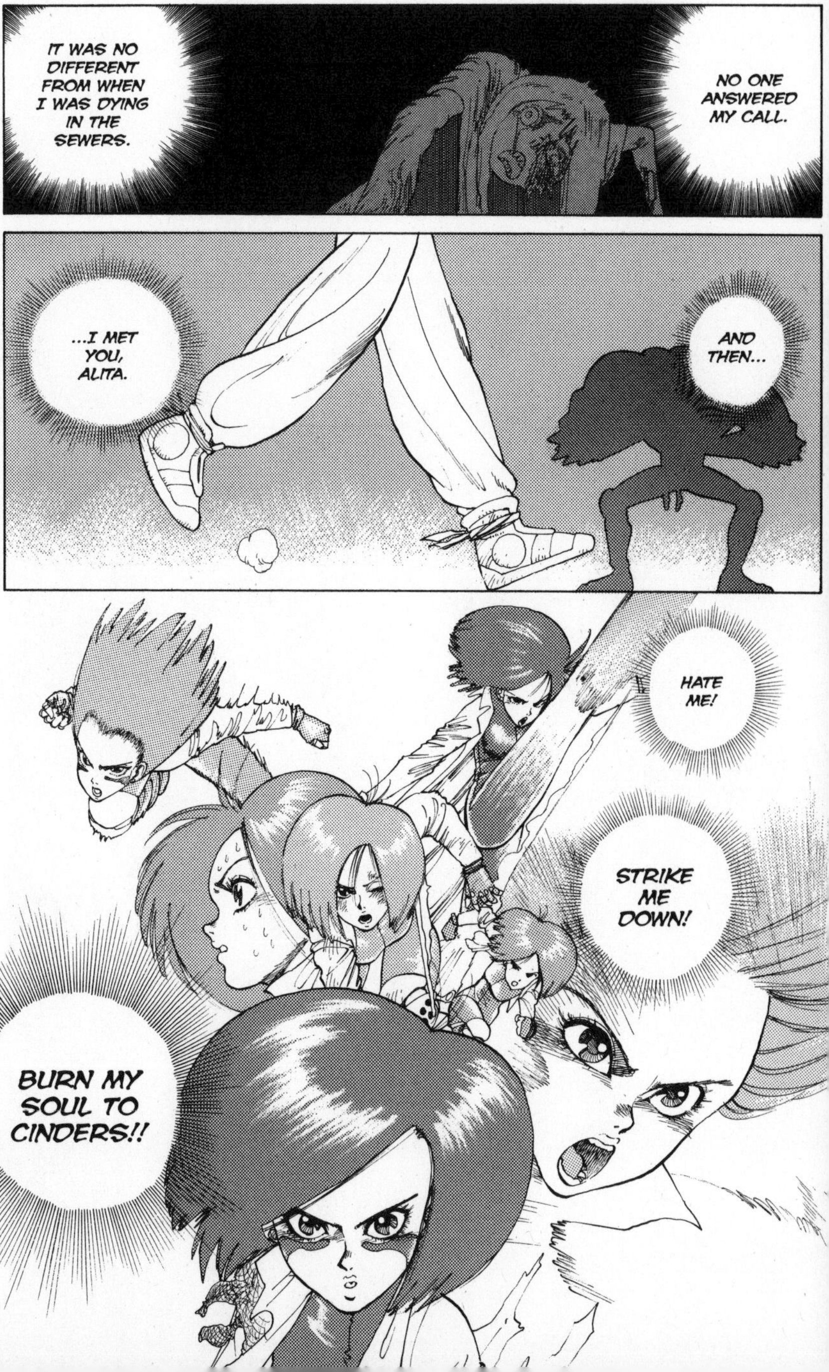
NO ONE ANSWERED MY CALL.
IT WAS NO DIFFERENT FROM WHEN I WAS DYING IN THE SEWERS.
AND THEN...
...I MET YOU, ALITA.
HATE ME!
STRIKE ME DOWN!
BURN MY SOUL TO CINDERS!!

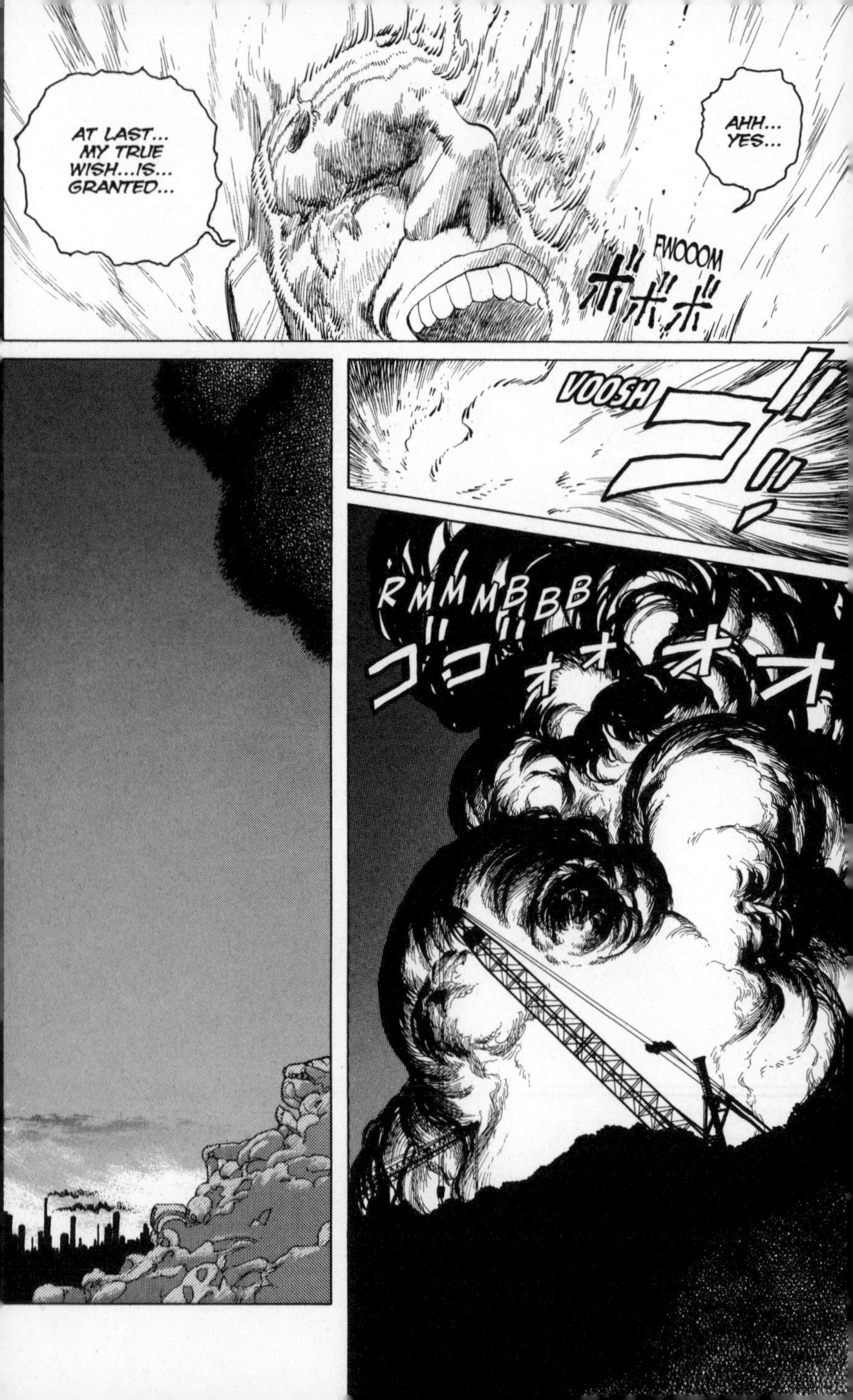
AHH... YES...
AT LAST... MY TRUE WISH...IS... GRANTED...
FWOOOM
ボボボ
VOOSH
ゴッ
RMMMBBB
ゴゴオオオ

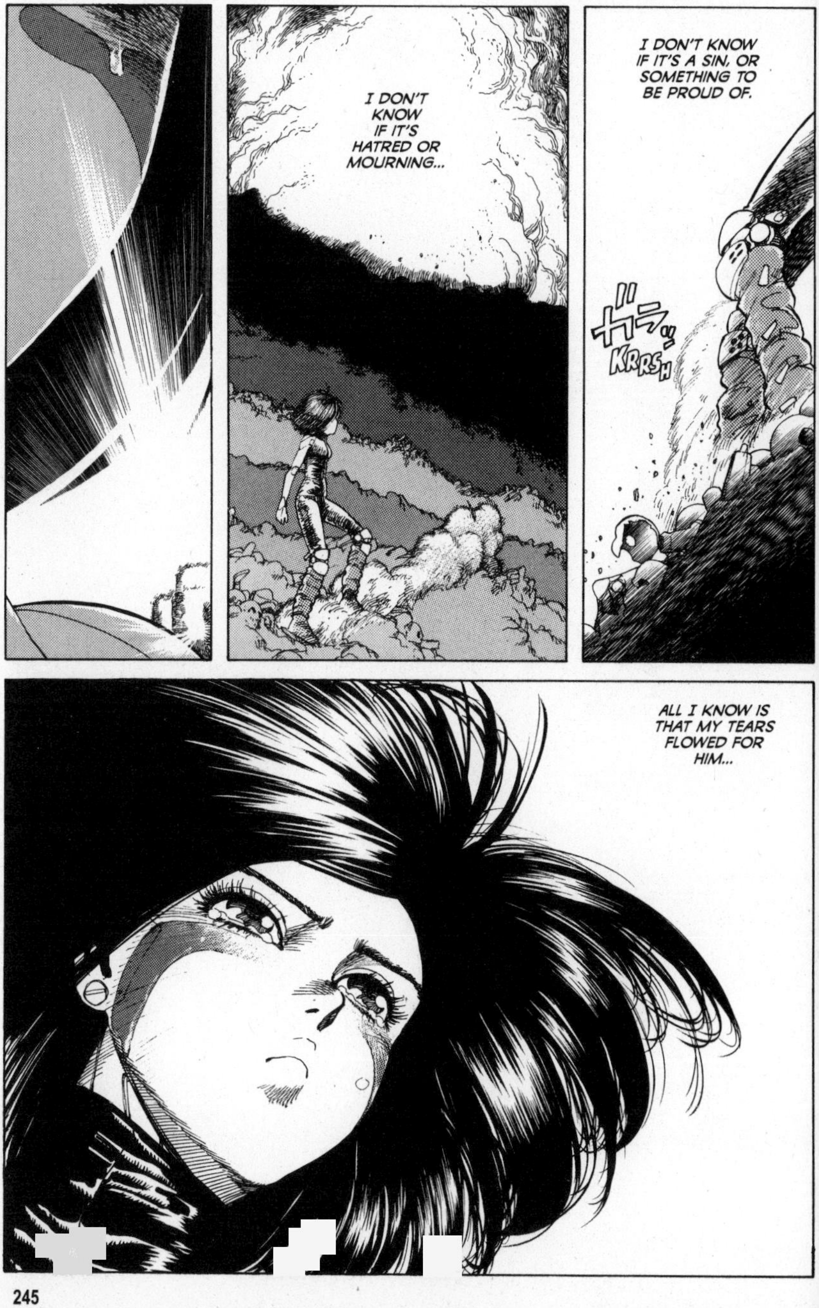
I DON'T KNOW IF IT'S A SIN, OR SOMETHING TO BE PROUD OF.
ガラッ
KRRSH
I DON'T KNOW IF IT'S HATRED OR MOURNING...
ALL I KNOW IS THAT MY TEARS FLOWED FOR HIM...

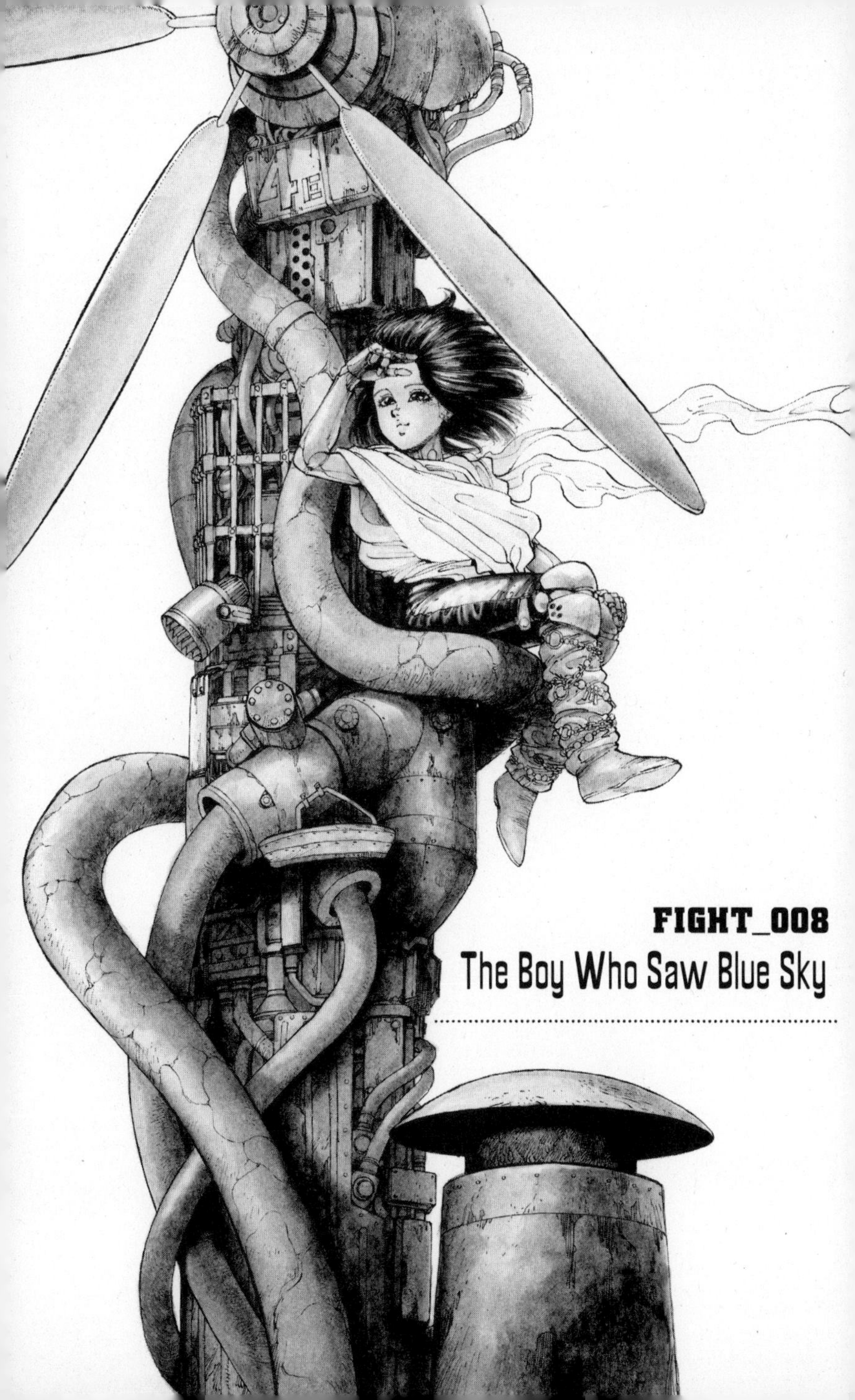

FIGHT_008

The Boy Who Saw Blue Sky

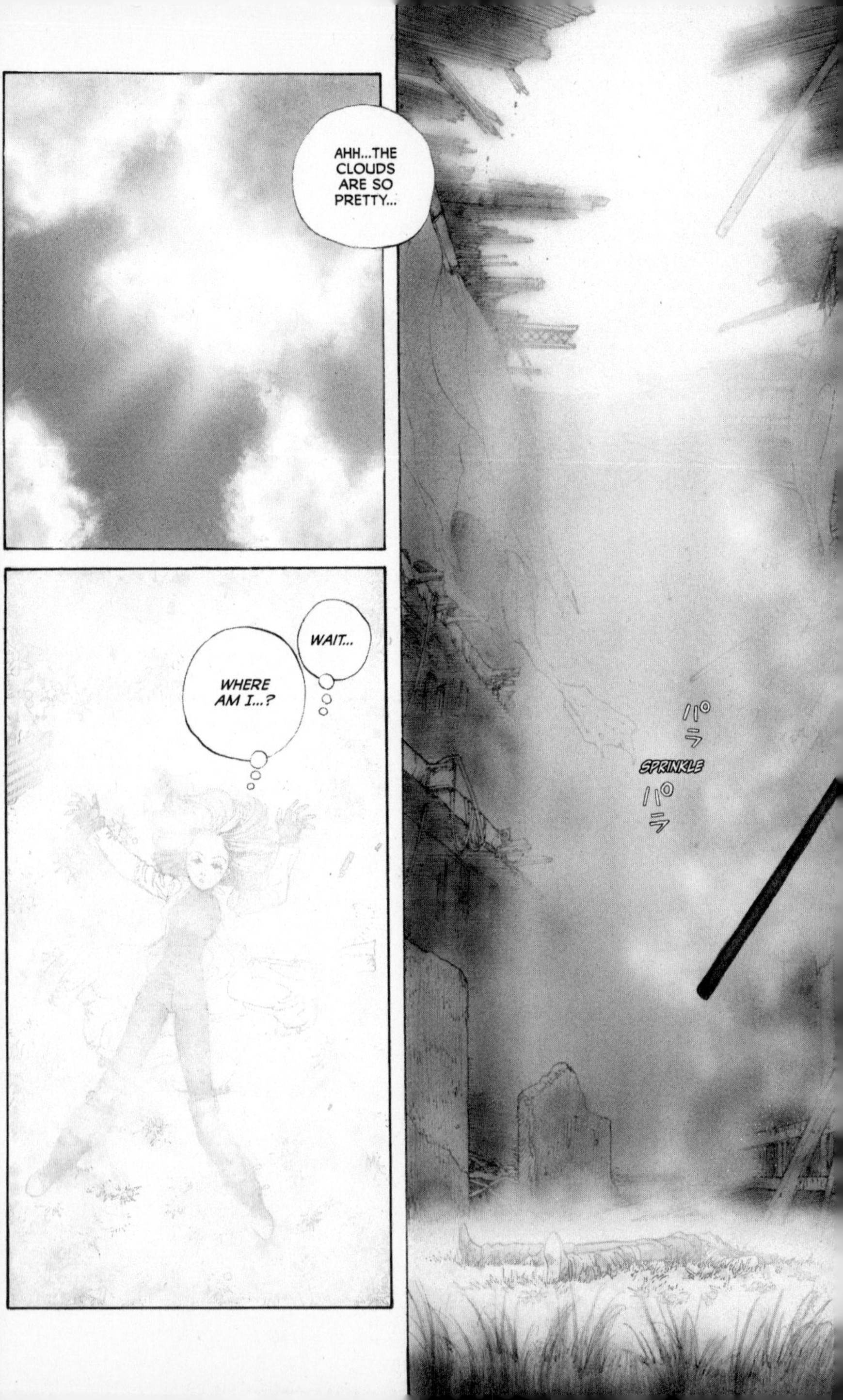
パラ
SPRINKLE
パラ
AHH...THE CLOUDS ARE SO PRETTY...
WAIT...
WHERE AM I...?

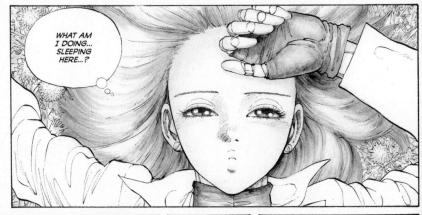

WHAT AM I DOING... SLEEPING HERE...?

?

あはははははは
HA HA HA HA HA HA HA

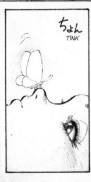

ちょん
TINK

FLUTTER
ひら
FLUTTER
ひら
FLUTTER
ひら

WHAT'CHA DOIN' DOWN THERE?

WHO...?

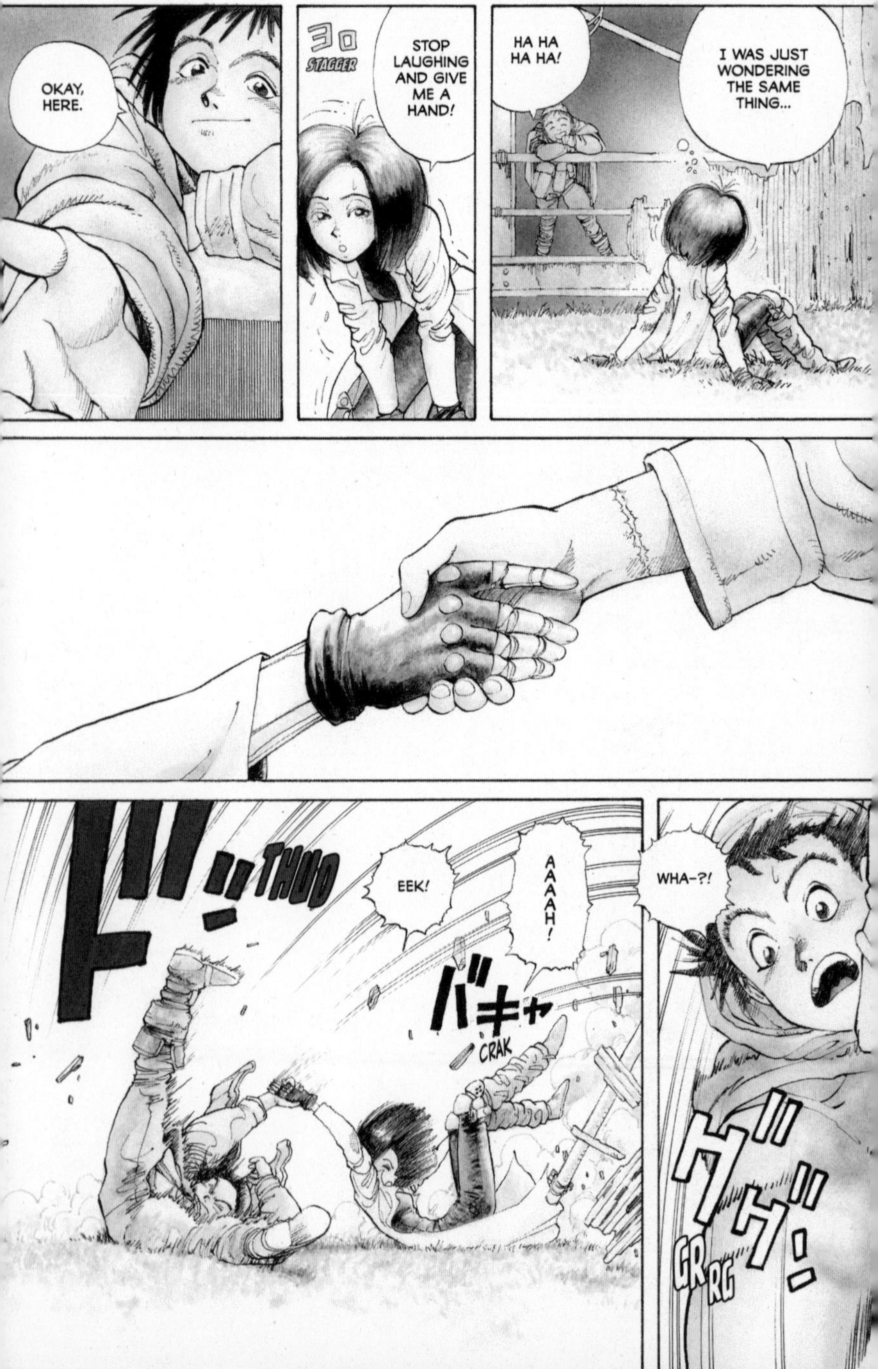
I WAS JUST WONDERING THE SAME THING...
HA HA HA HA!
STOP LAUGHING AND GIVE ME A HAND!
ヨロ
STAGGER
OKAY, HERE.
WHA-?!
GRRG
AAAAH!
EEK!
THUD
バキャ
CRAK

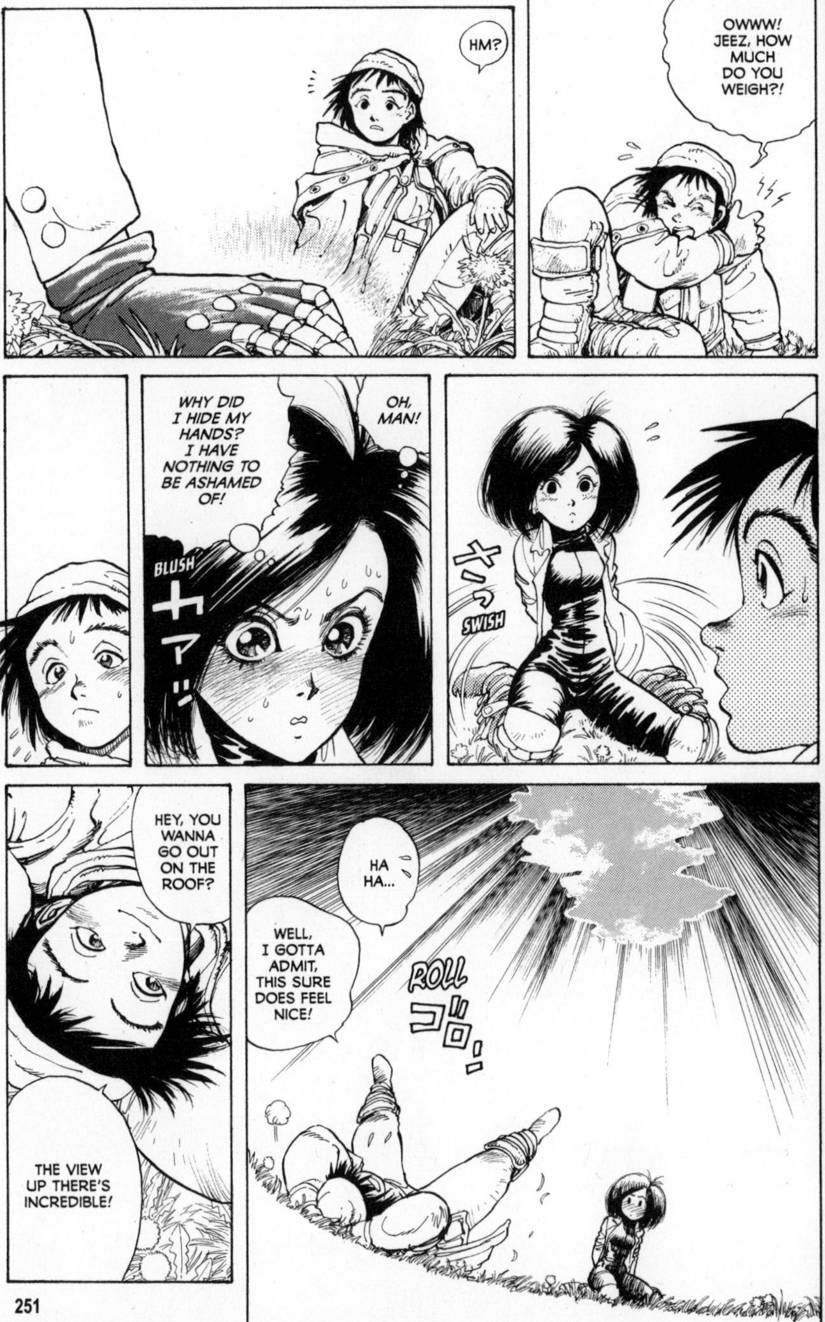
OWWW! JEEZ, HOW MUCH DO YOU WEIGH?!
HM?
SWISH
OH, MAN!
WHY DID I HIDE MY HANDS? I HAVE NOTHING TO BE ASHAMED OF!
BLUSH
HA HA...
WELL, I GOTTA ADMIT, THIS SURE DOES FEEL NICE!
ROLL
HEY, YOU WANNA GO OUT ON THE ROOF?
THE VIEW UP THERE'S INCREDIBLE!

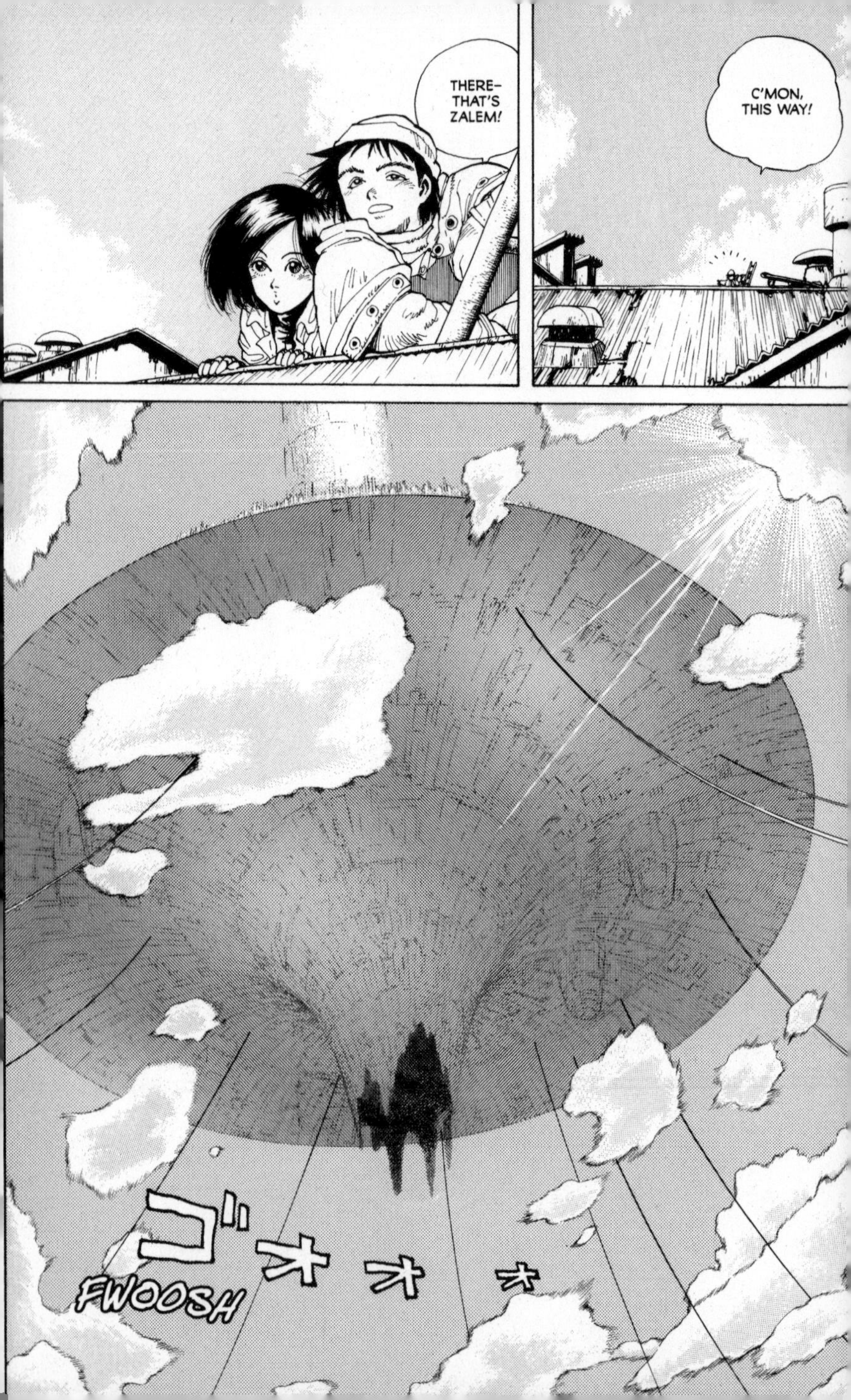
C'MON, THIS WAY!
THERE— THAT'S ZALEM!
ゴオオォ
FWOOSH

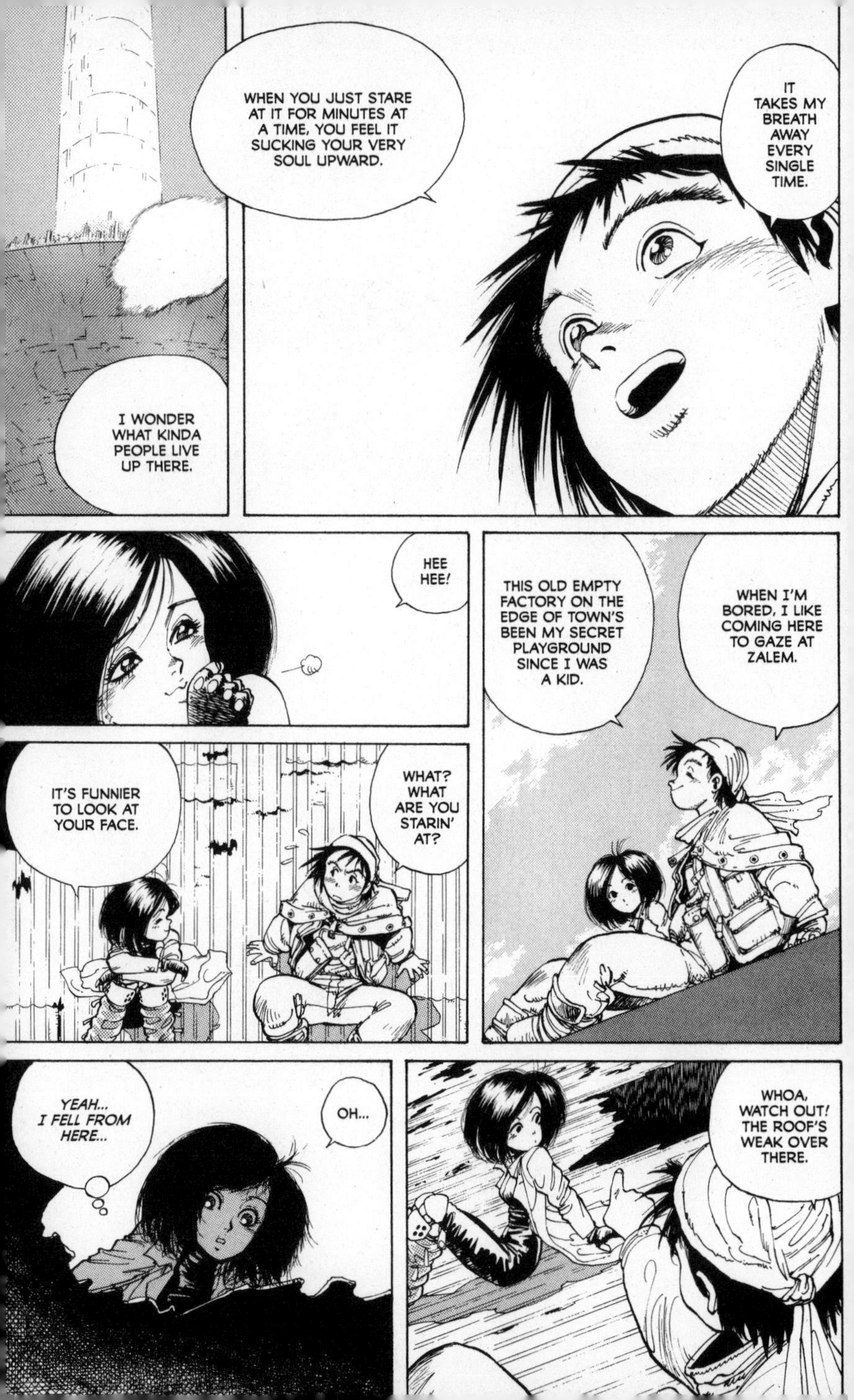
IT TAKES MY BREATH AWAY EVERY SINGLE TIME.
WHEN YOU JUST STARE AT IT FOR MINUTES AT A TIME, YOU FEEL IT SUCKING YOUR VERY SOUL UPWARD.
I WONDER WHAT KINDA PEOPLE LIVE UP THERE.
WHEN I'M BORED, I LIKE COMING HERE TO GAZE AT ZALEM.
THIS OLD EMPTY FACTORY ON THE EDGE OF TOWN'S BEEN MY SECRET PLAYGROUND SINCE I WAS A KID.
HEE HEE!
WHAT? WHAT ARE YOU STARIN' AT?
IT'S FUNNIER TO LOOK AT YOUR FACE.
WHOA, WATCH OUT! THE ROOF'S WEAK OVER THERE.
OH...
YEAH... I FELL FROM HERE...

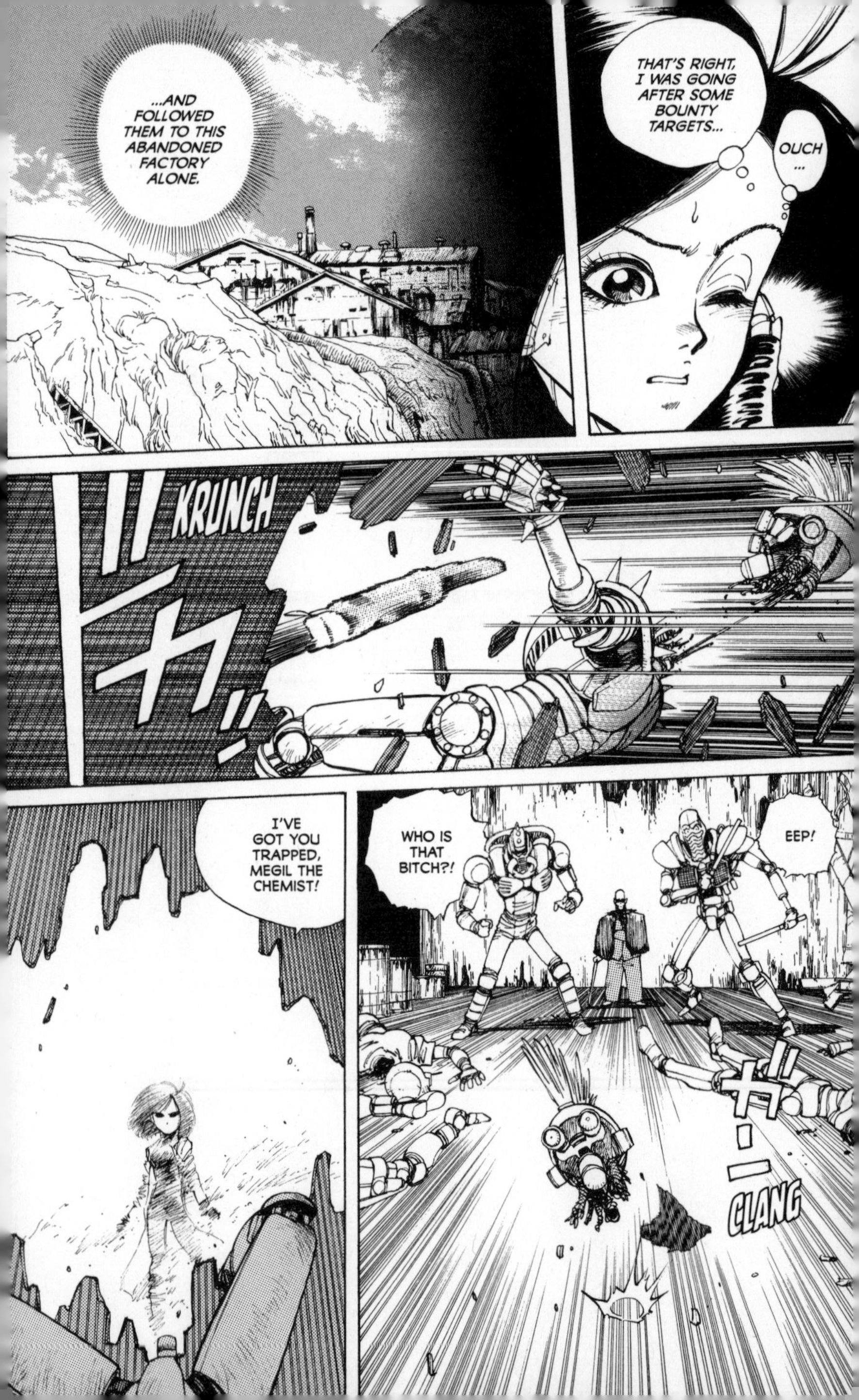
THAT'S RIGHT, I WAS GOING AFTER SOME BOUNTY TARGETS...
OUCH ...
...AND FOLLOWED THEM TO THIS ABANDONED FACTORY ALONE.
KRUNCH
EEP!
WHO IS THAT BITCH?!
CLANG
I'VE GOT YOU TRAPPED, MEGIL THE CHEMIST!

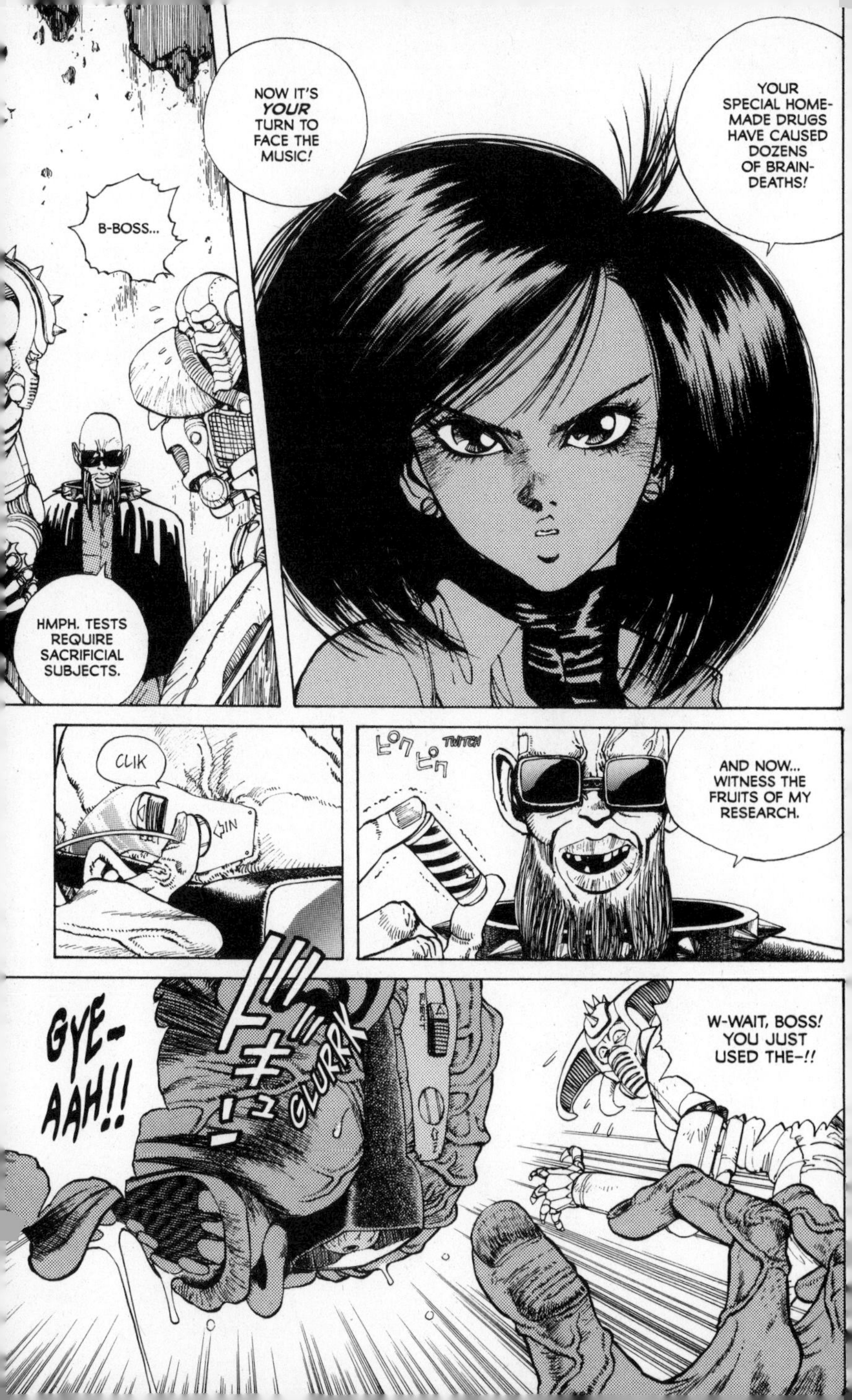
YOUR SPECIAL HOME-MADE DRUGS HAVE CAUSED DOZENS OF BRAIN-DEATHS!
NOW IT'S *YOUR* TURN TO FACE THE MUSIC!
B-BOSS...
HMPH. TESTS REQUIRE SACRIFICIAL SUBJECTS.
ピク ピク
TWITCH
AND NOW... WITNESS THE FRUITS OF MY RESEARCH.
CLIK
W-WAIT, BOSS! YOU JUST USED THE–!!
GLURRK
GYE-AAH!!

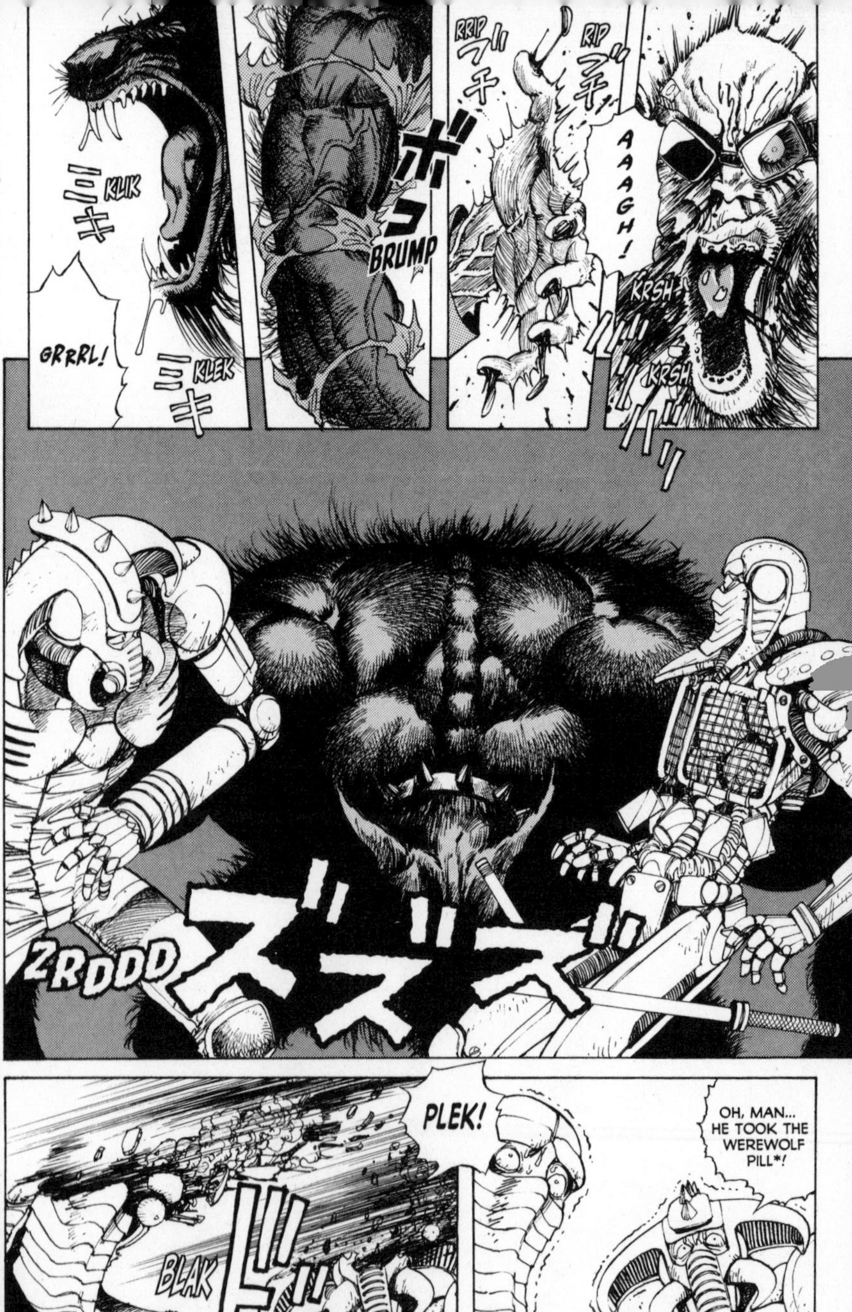
AAAAGH!
KRSH
KRSH
RIP
RRIP
BRUMP
KLIK
GRRRL!
KLEK
ZRDDD
OH, MAN... HE TOOK THE WEREWOLF PILL*!
PLEK!
BLAK

***Werewolf pill:** A drug that reduces conscious thought and elevates bestial attack instincts. This self-suggestion forces the user to believe that he is a beast, and is so potent that it can alter the body and raise subliminal power to the maximum extent possible.

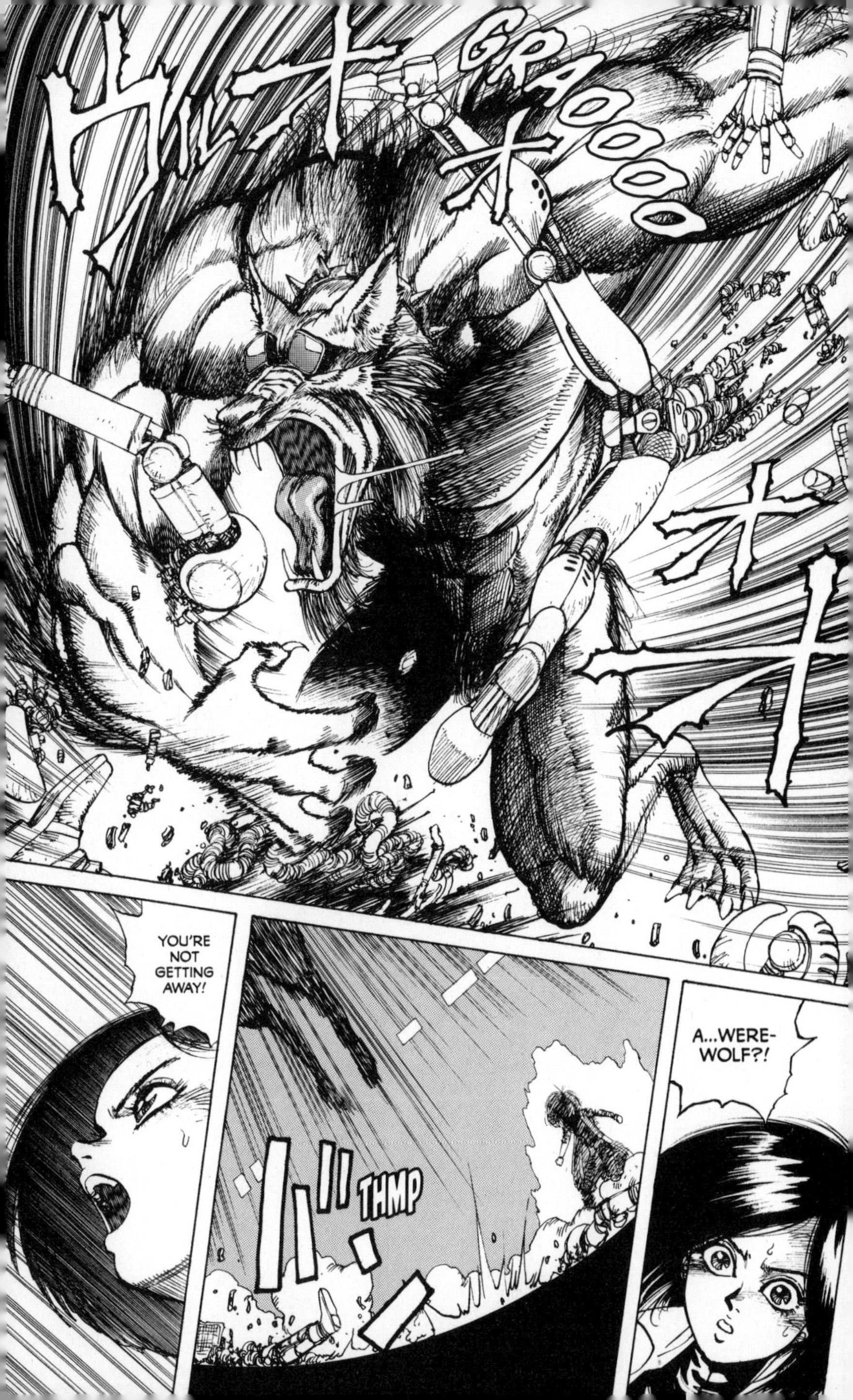
GRAOOOOO
A...WERE-WOLF?!
THMP
YOU'RE NOT GETTING AWAY!

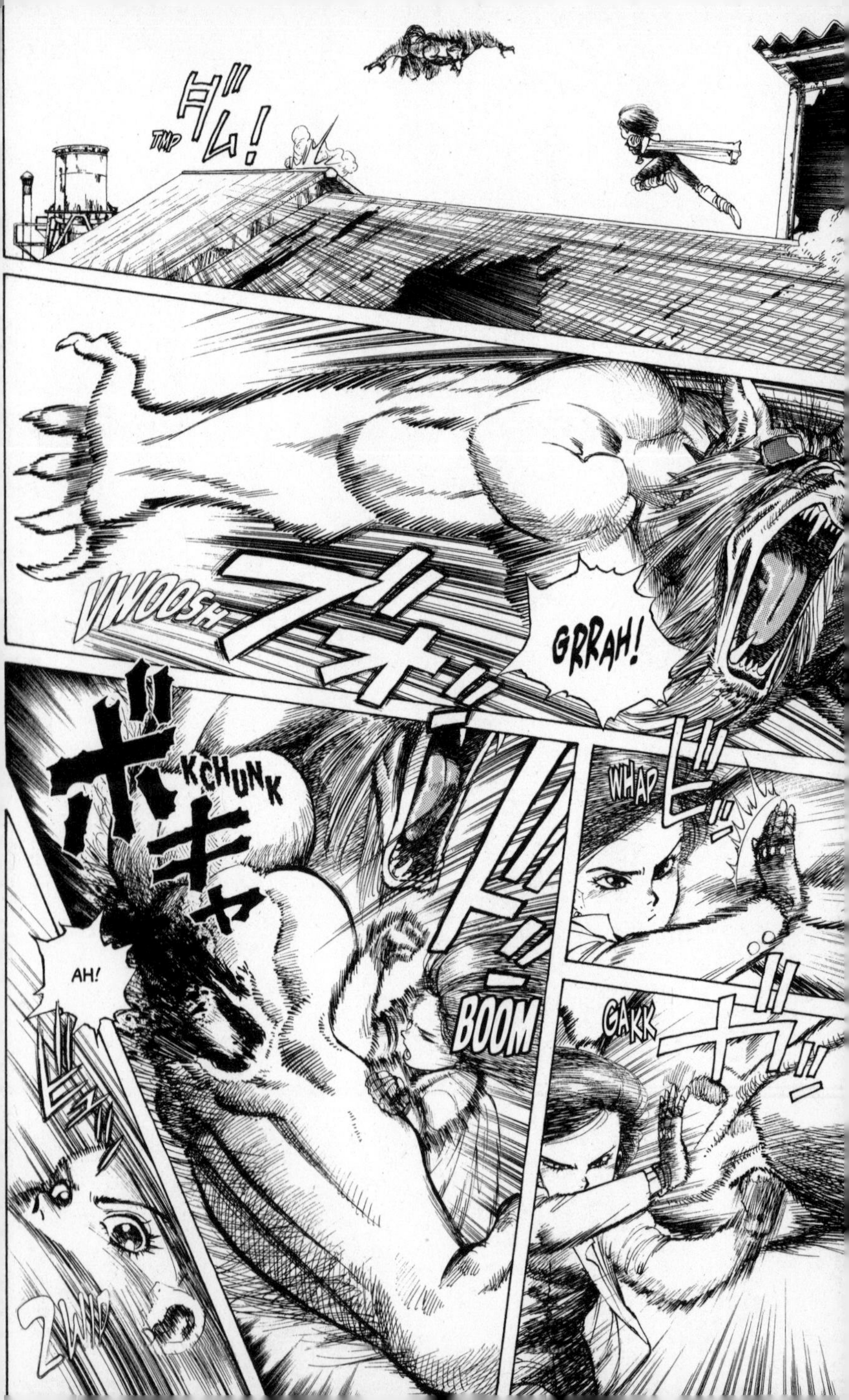
TMP
ダム!
GRRAH!
VWOOSH
フォッ
WHAP
GAKK
KCHUNK
ボキャ
BOOM
AH!
ZWIP

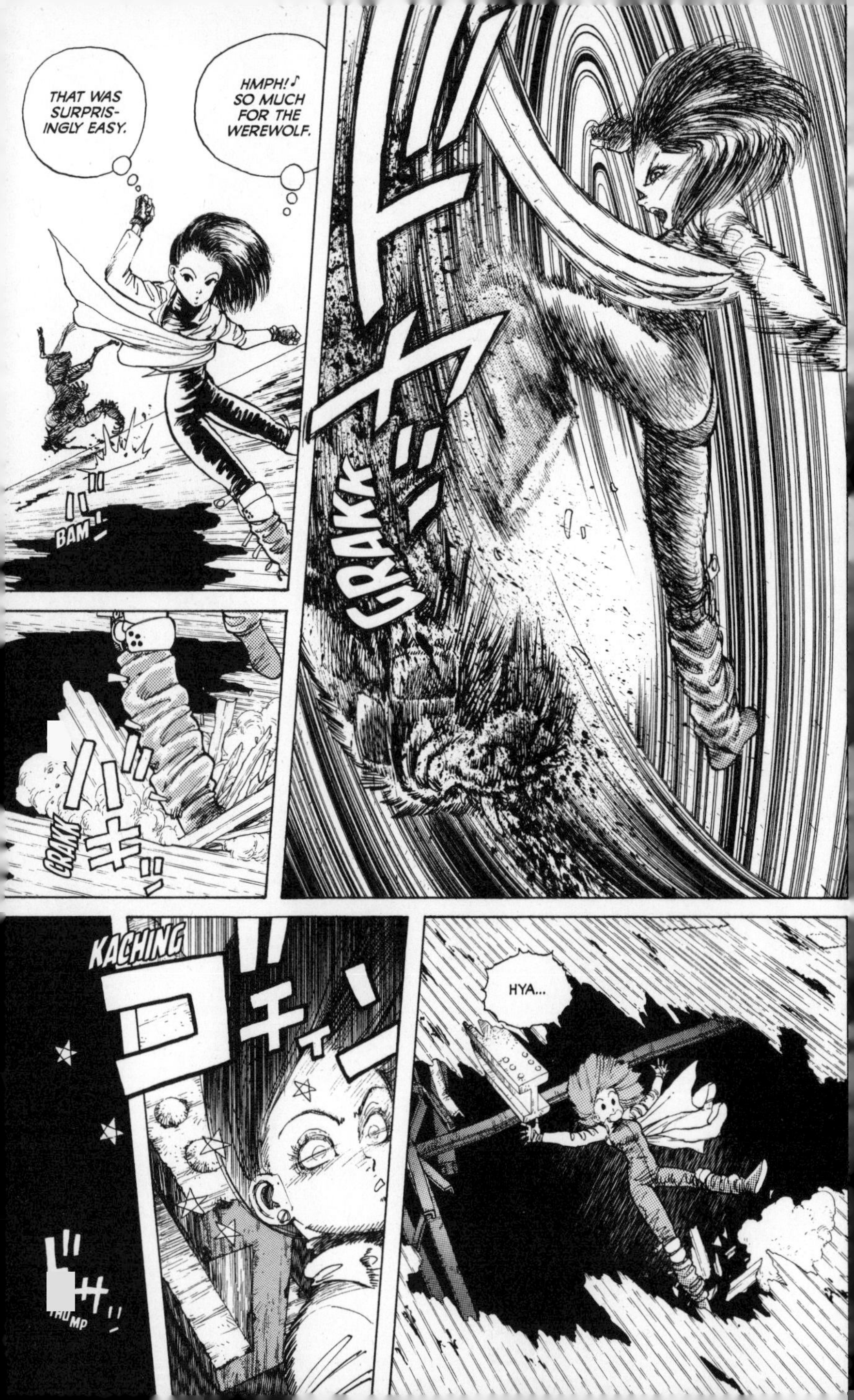
GRAKK
HMPH! ♪ SO MUCH FOR THE WEREWOLF.
THAT WAS SURPRISINGLY EASY.
BAM
GRAKK
HYA...
KACHING
THUMP

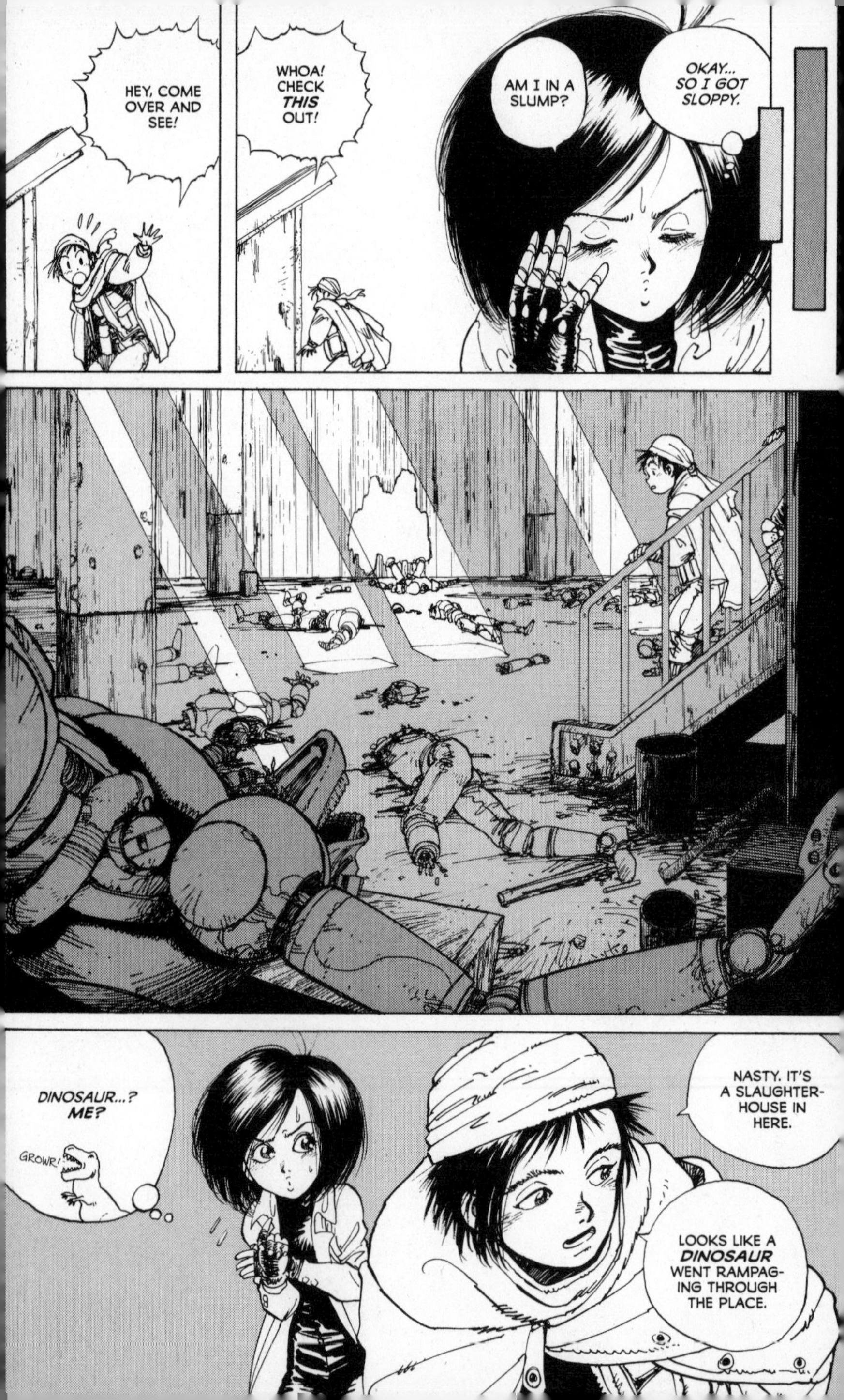
OKAY... SO I GOT SLOPPY.
AM I IN A SLUMP?
WHOA! CHECK *THIS* OUT!
HEY, COME OVER AND SEE!
NASTY. IT'S A SLAUGHTER-HOUSE IN HERE.
LOOKS LIKE A ***DINOSAUR*** WENT RAMPAGING THROUGH THE PLACE.
*DINOSAUR...? **ME?***
GROWR!

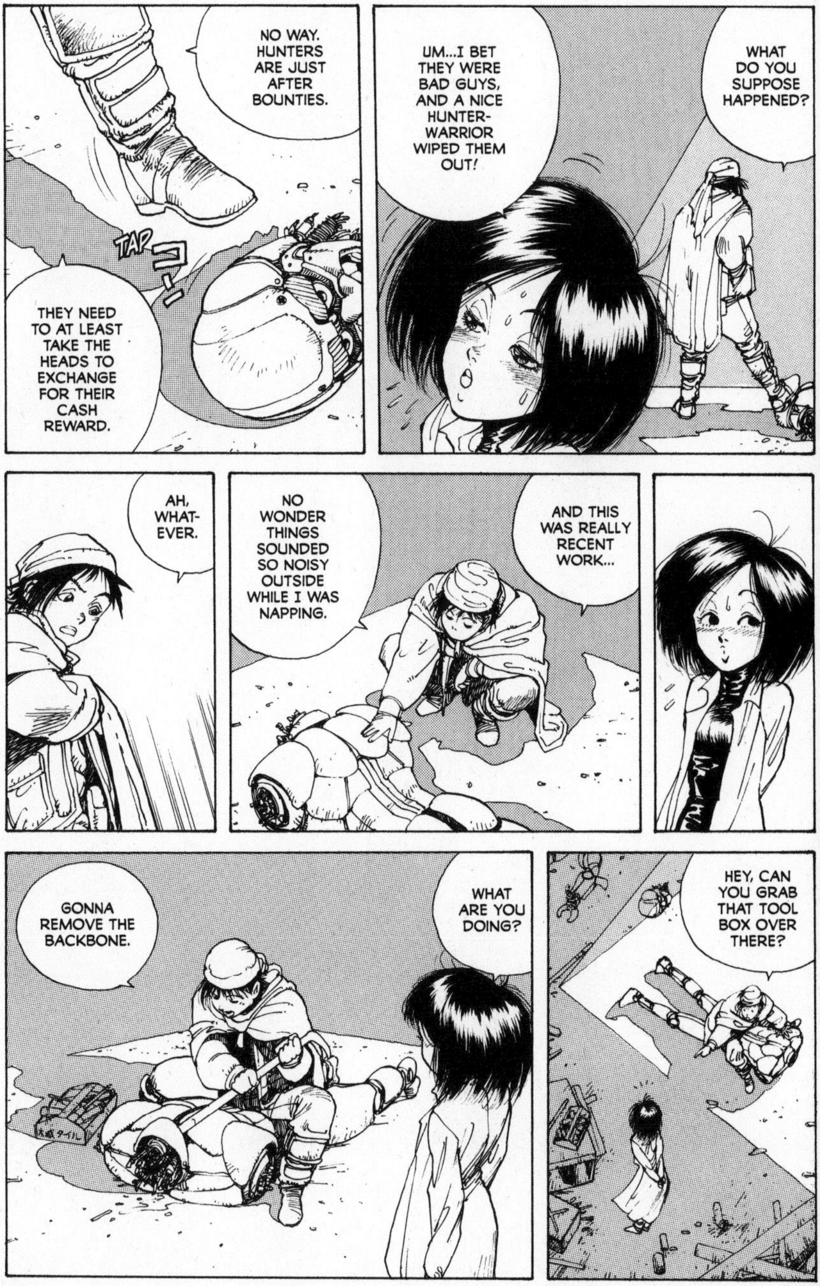
WHAT DO YOU SUPPOSE HAPPENED?
UM...I BET THEY WERE BAD GUYS, AND A NICE HUNTER-WARRIOR WIPED THEM OUT!
NO WAY. HUNTERS ARE JUST AFTER BOUNTIES.
TAP
THEY NEED TO AT LEAST TAKE THE HEADS TO EXCHANGE FOR THEIR CASH REWARD.
AND THIS WAS REALLY RECENT WORK...
NO WONDER THINGS SOUNDED SO NOISY OUTSIDE WHILE I WAS NAPPING.
AH, WHATEVER.
HEY, CAN YOU GRAB THAT TOOL BOX OVER THERE?
WHAT ARE YOU DOING?
GONNA REMOVE THE BACKBONE.

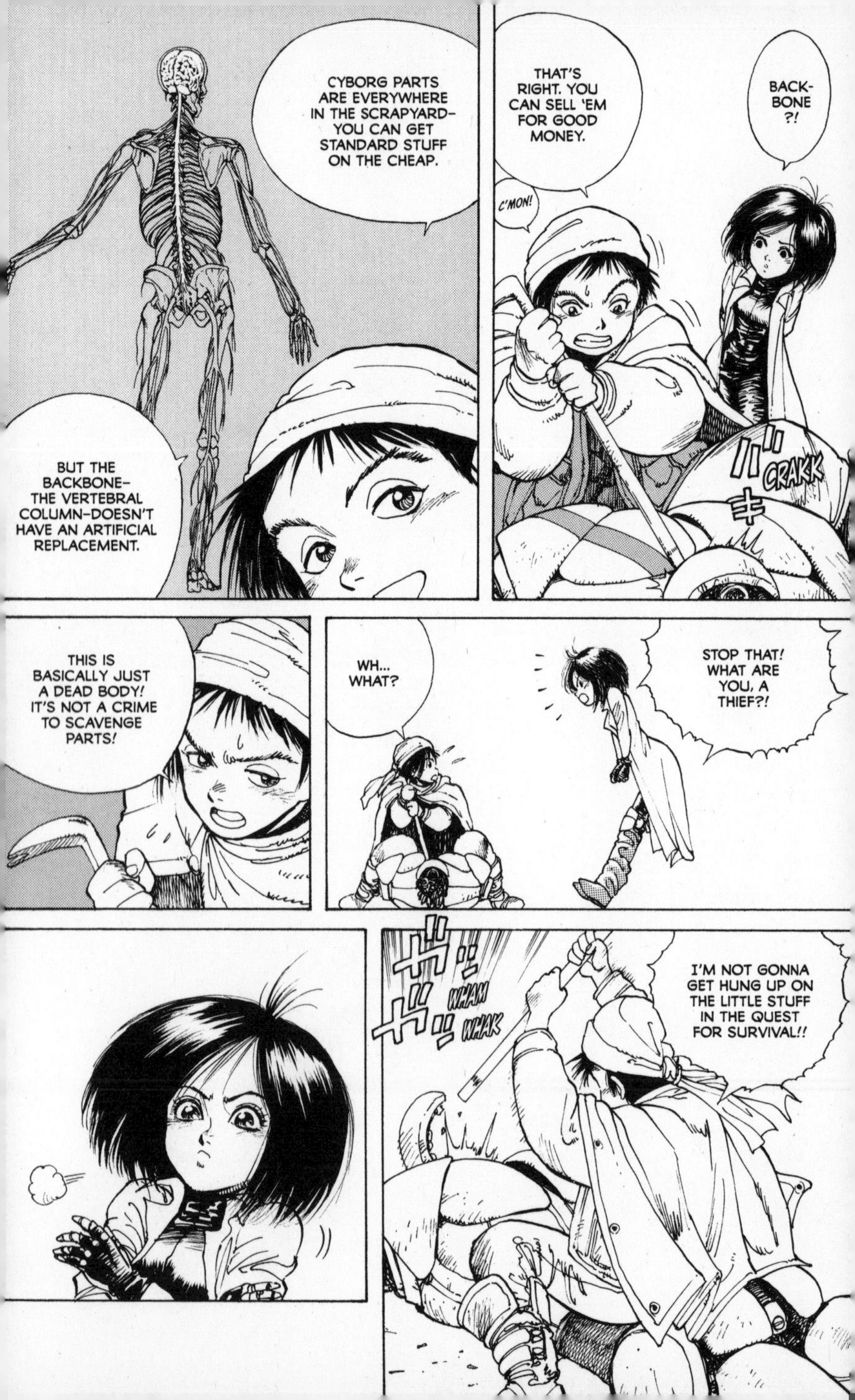
BACK-BONE ?!
THAT'S RIGHT. YOU CAN SELL 'EM FOR GOOD MONEY.
C'MON!
CRAKK
CYBORG PARTS ARE EVERYWHERE IN THE SCRAPYARD–YOU CAN GET STANDARD STUFF ON THE CHEAP.
BUT THE BACKBONE–THE VERTEBRAL COLUMN–DOESN'T HAVE AN ARTIFICIAL REPLACEMENT.
STOP THAT! WHAT ARE YOU, A THIEF?!
WH... WHAT?
THIS IS BASICALLY JUST A DEAD BODY! IT'S NOT A CRIME TO SCAVENGE PARTS!
I'M NOT GONNA GET HUNG UP ON THE LITTLE STUFF IN THE QUEST FOR SURVIVAL!!
WHAM
WHAK

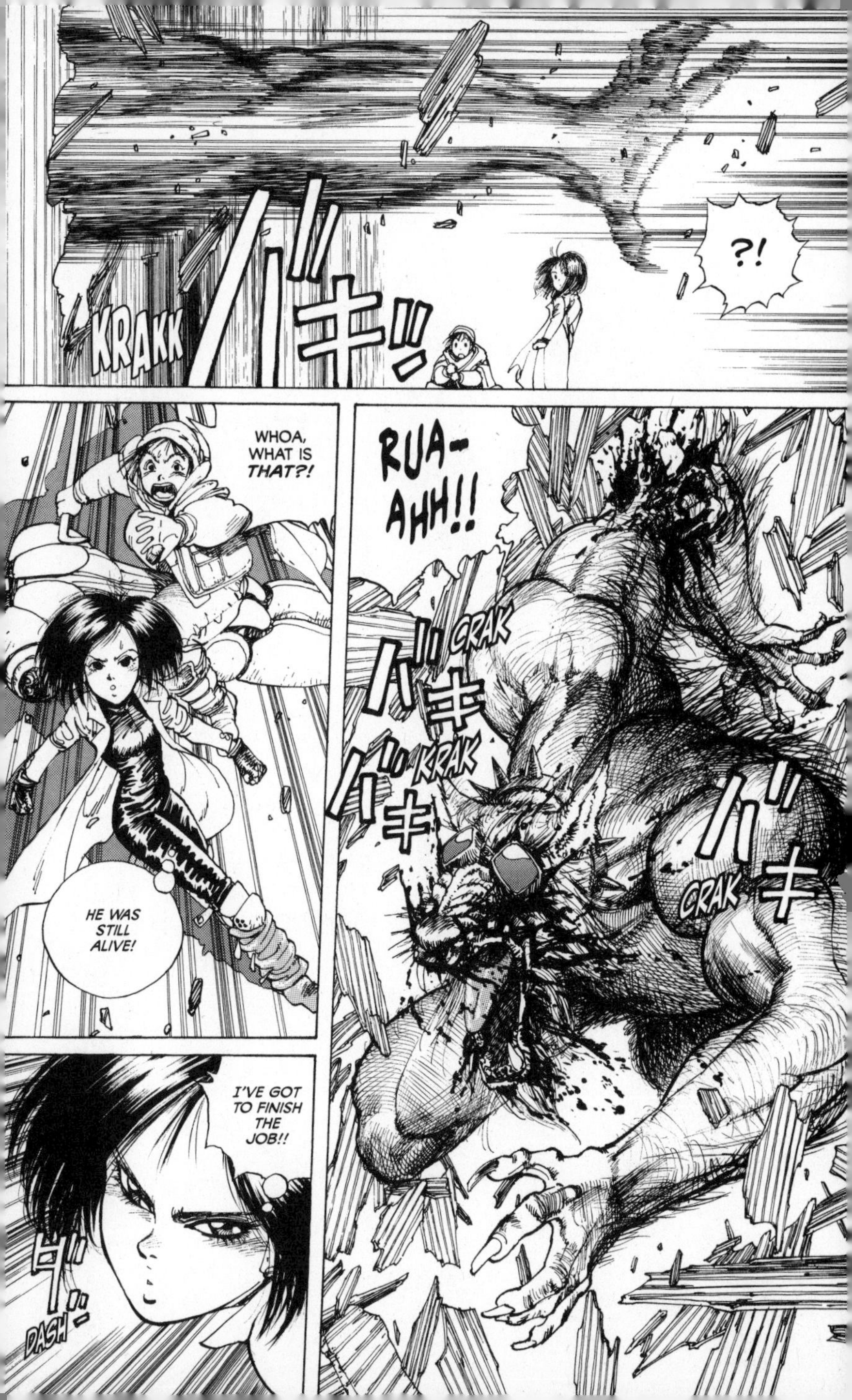
?!
バキッ
KRAKK
RUA-AHH!!
バキ CRAK
バキ KRAK
バキ CRAK
WHOA, WHAT IS THAT?!
HE WAS STILL ALIVE!
I'VE GOT TO FINISH THE JOB!!
ダッ DASH

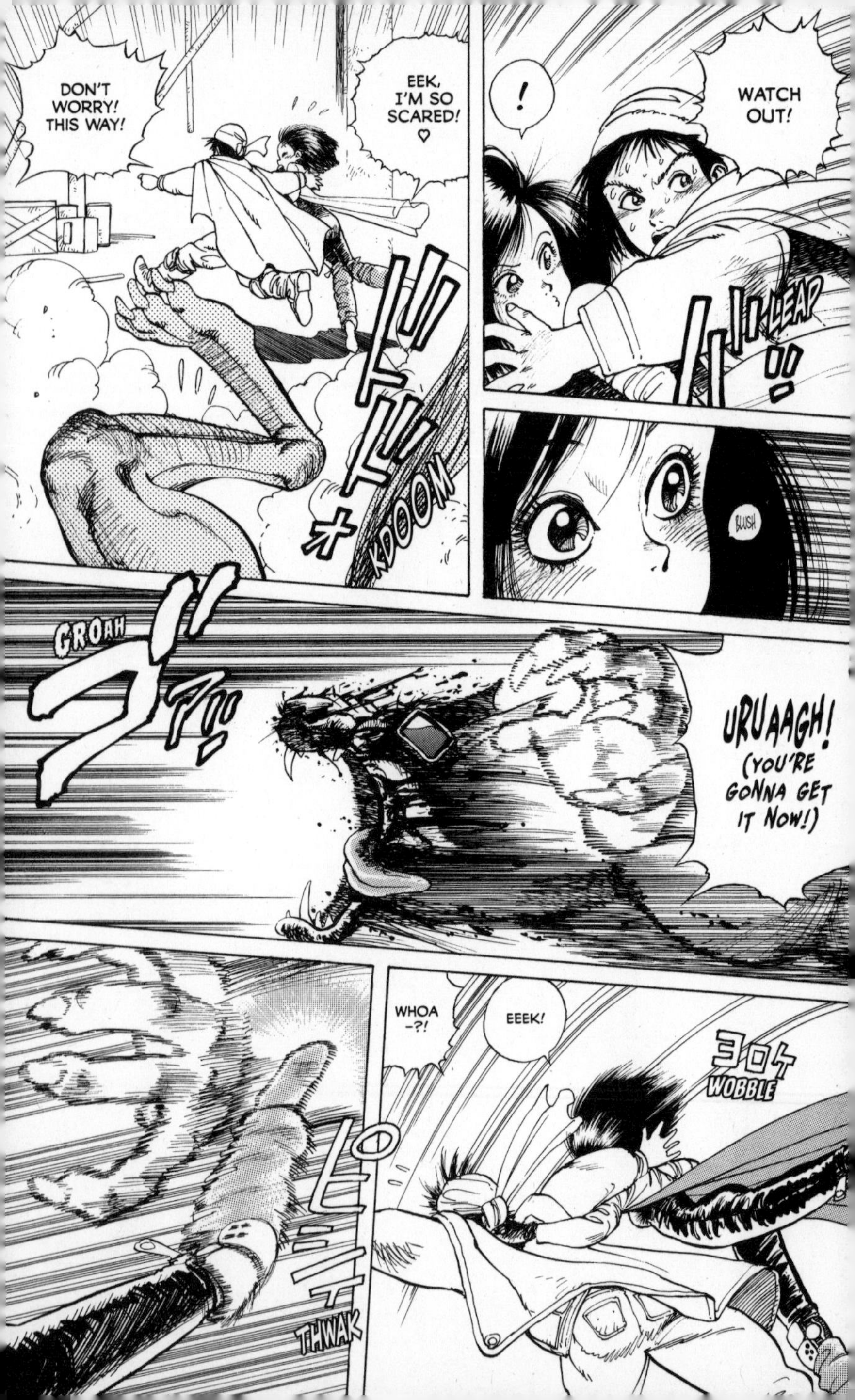
WATCH OUT!
!
LEAP
BLUSH
EEK, I'M SO SCARED! ♡
DON'T WORRY! THIS WAY!
KDOOM
URUAAGH! (YOU'RE GONNA GET IT NOW!)
GROAH
WOBBLE
EEEK!
WHOA -?!
THWAK

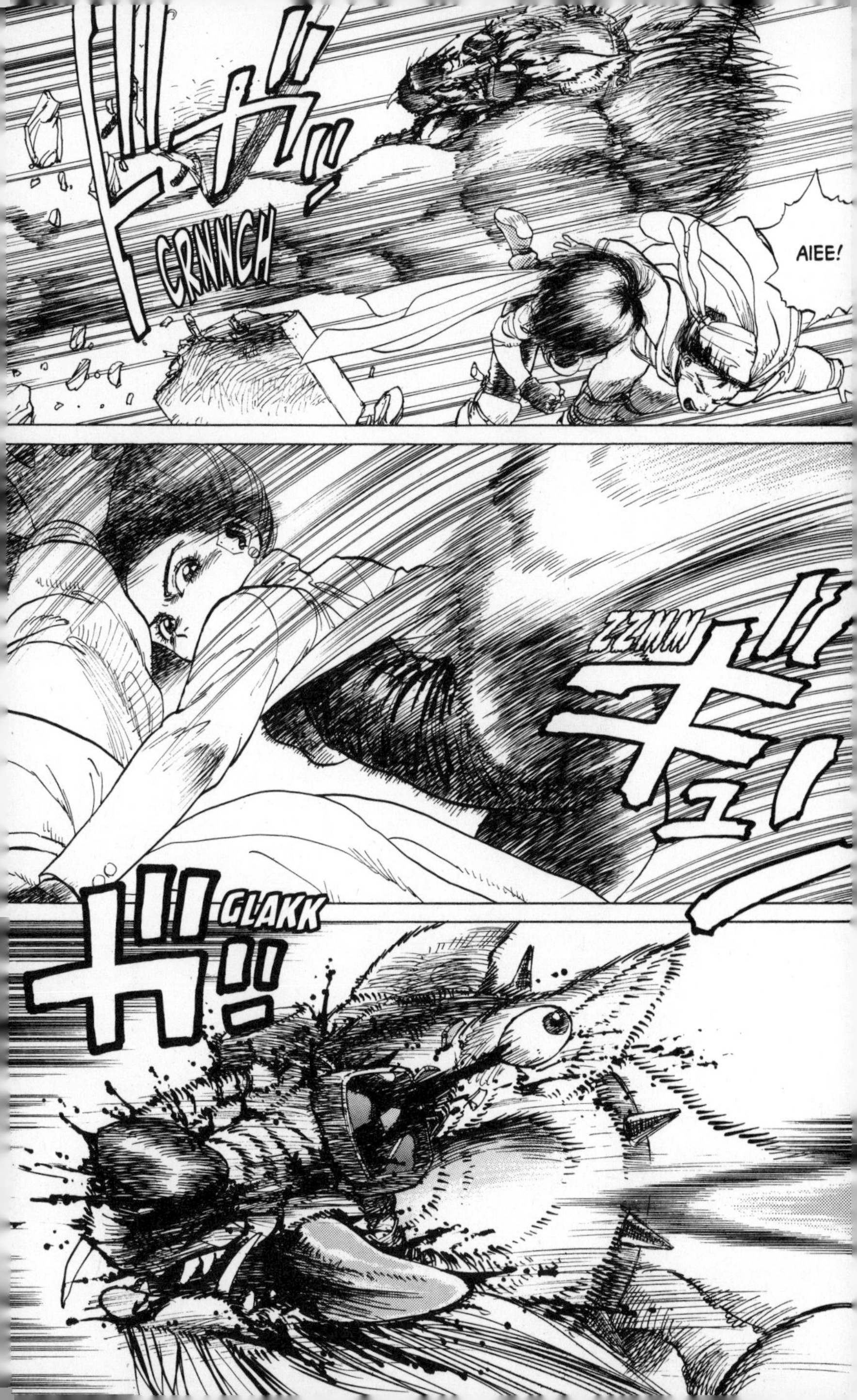
AIEE!
CRNNCH
ZZMN
GLAKK

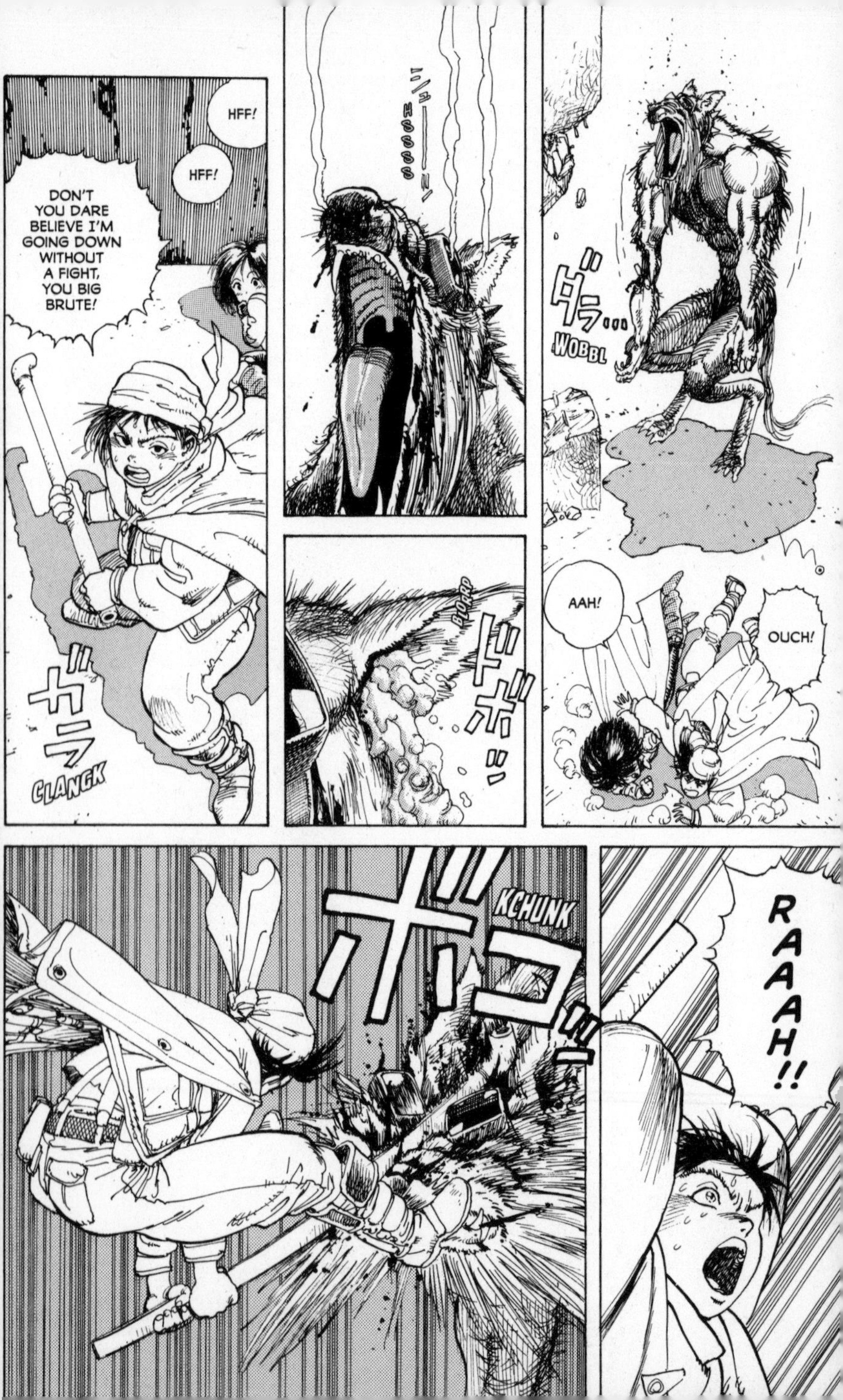
WOBBL
OUCH!
AAH!
HSSSS
BORRP
HFF!
HFF!
DON'T YOU DARE BELIEVE I'M GOING DOWN WITHOUT A FIGHT, YOU BIG BRUTE!
CLANGK
RAAAH!!
KCHUNK

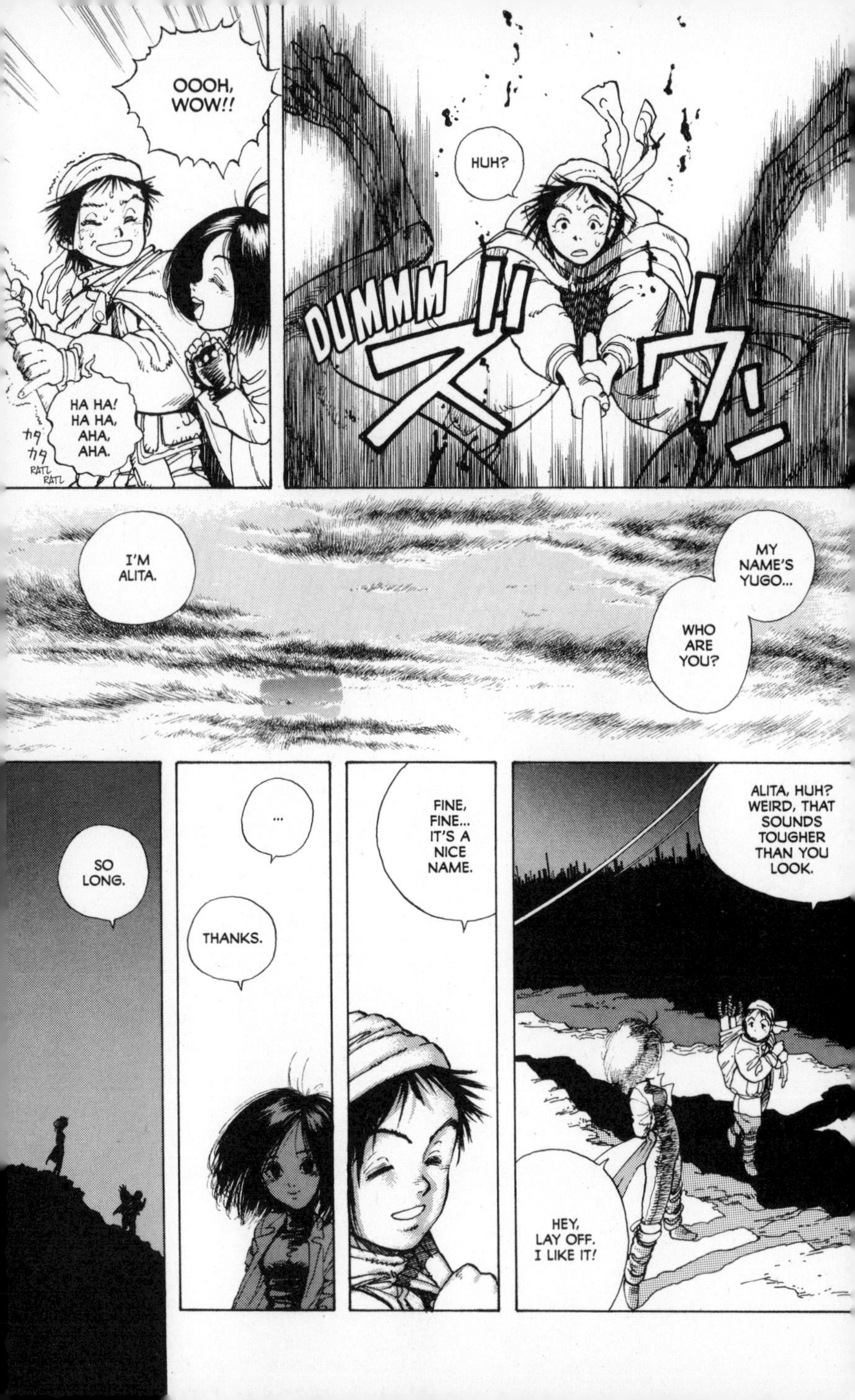
HUH?
DUMMM
ズウー
OOOH, WOW!!
HA HA! HA HA, AHA, AHA.
カタ カタ
RATL RATL
MY NAME'S YUGO...
WHO ARE YOU?
I'M ALITA.
ALITA, HUH? WEIRD, THAT SOUNDS TOUGHER THAN YOU LOOK.
HEY, LAY OFF. I LIKE IT!
FINE, FINE... IT'S A NICE NAME.
...
THANKS.
SO LONG.

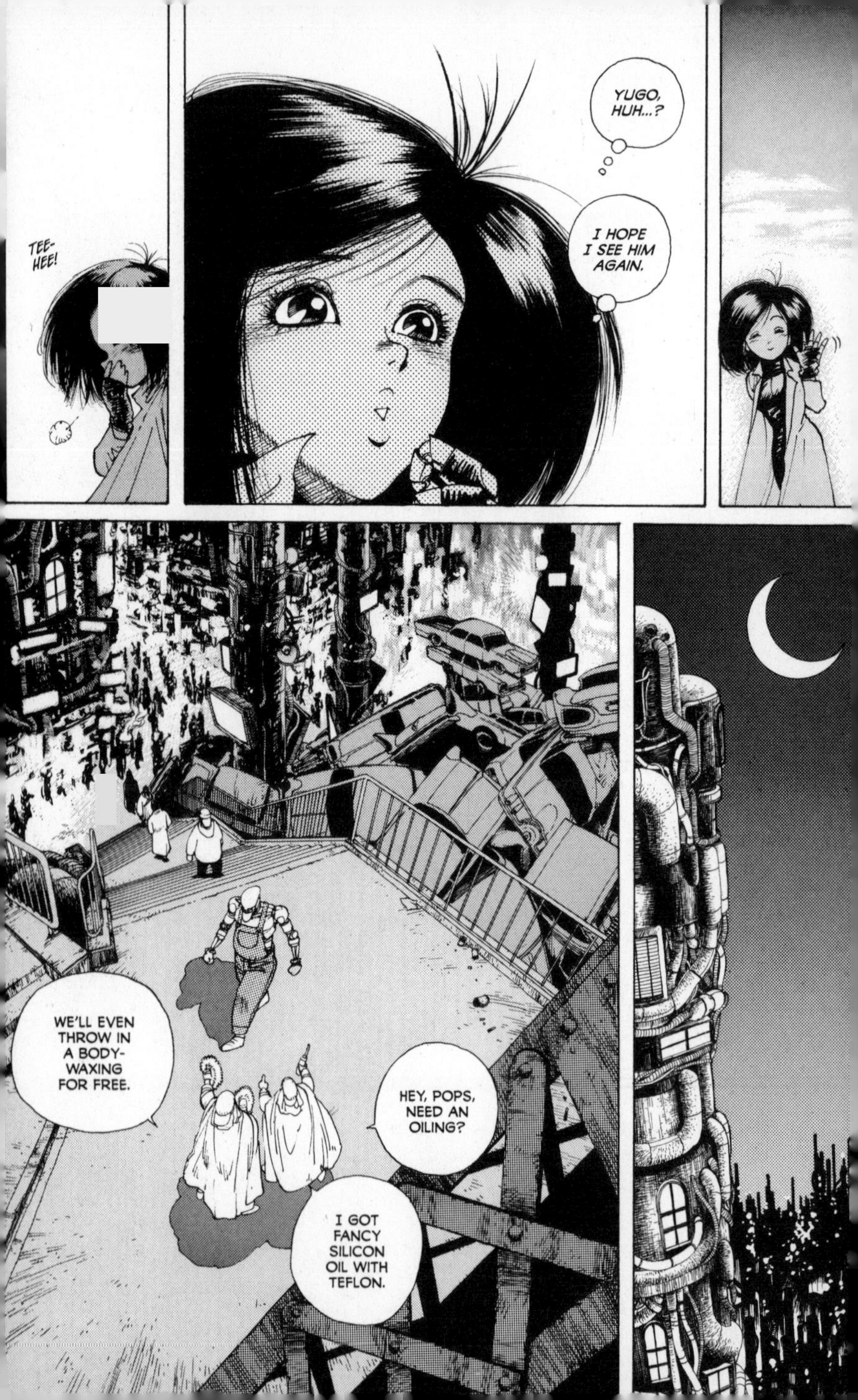
YUGO, HUH...?
I HOPE I SEE HIM AGAIN.
TEE-HEE!
HEY, POPS, NEED AN OILING?
I GOT FANCY SILICON OIL WITH TEFLON.
WE'LL EVEN THROW IN A BODY-WAXING FOR FREE.

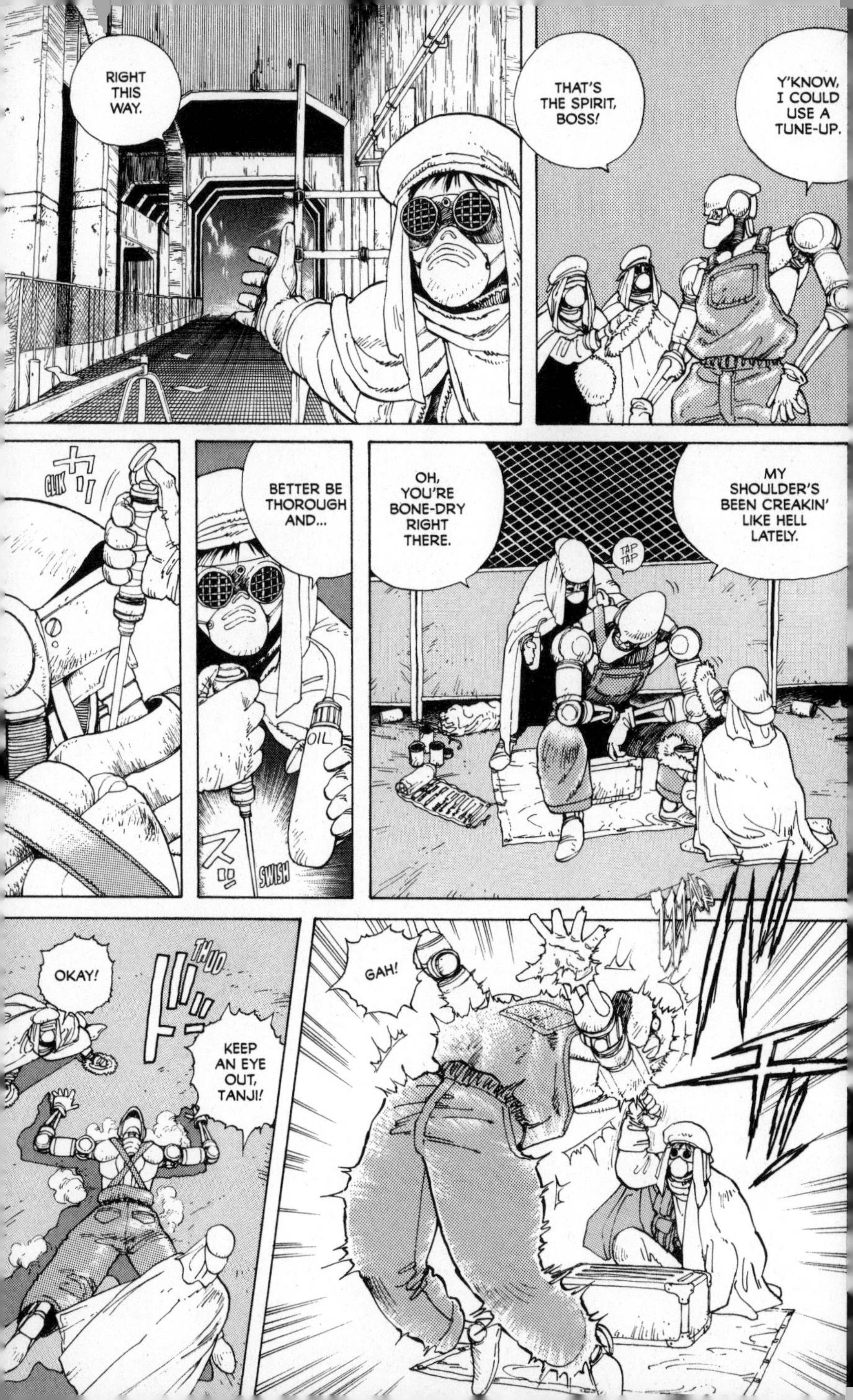
Y'KNOW, I COULD USE A TUNE-UP.
THAT'S THE SPIRIT, BOSS!
RIGHT THIS WAY.
MY SHOULDER'S BEEN CREAKIN' LIKE HELL LATELY.
TAP TAP
OH, YOU'RE BONE-DRY RIGHT THERE.
BETTER BE THOROUGH AND...
OIL
SWISH
CLIK
GAH!
THUD
OKAY!
KEEP AN EYE OUT, TANJI!

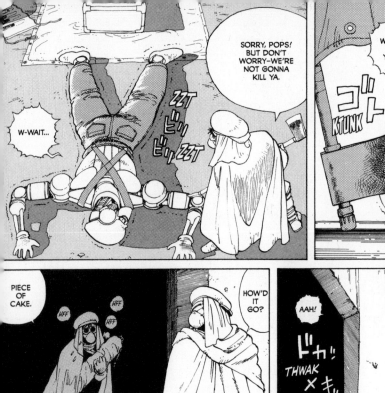

WH-WHAT ARE YOU...?!
ゴト
KTUNK
SORRY, POPS! BUT DON'T WORRY–WE'RE NOT GONNA KILL YA.
ZZT
ビッ
ビッ
ZZT
W-WAIT...
AAH!
ドカッ
THWAK
メキッ
RRIP
HOW'D IT GO?
PIECE OF CAKE.
HFF
HFF
HFF
THIS'LL BAG US AT LEAST FIFTY GRAND.
TH-THIEF! GIVE BACK MY SPINE...!
ピク
TIK
ピク
TIK

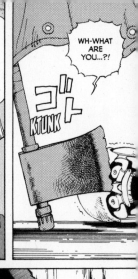

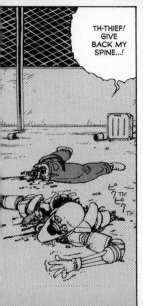

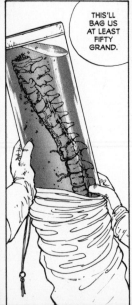

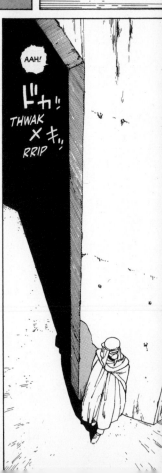

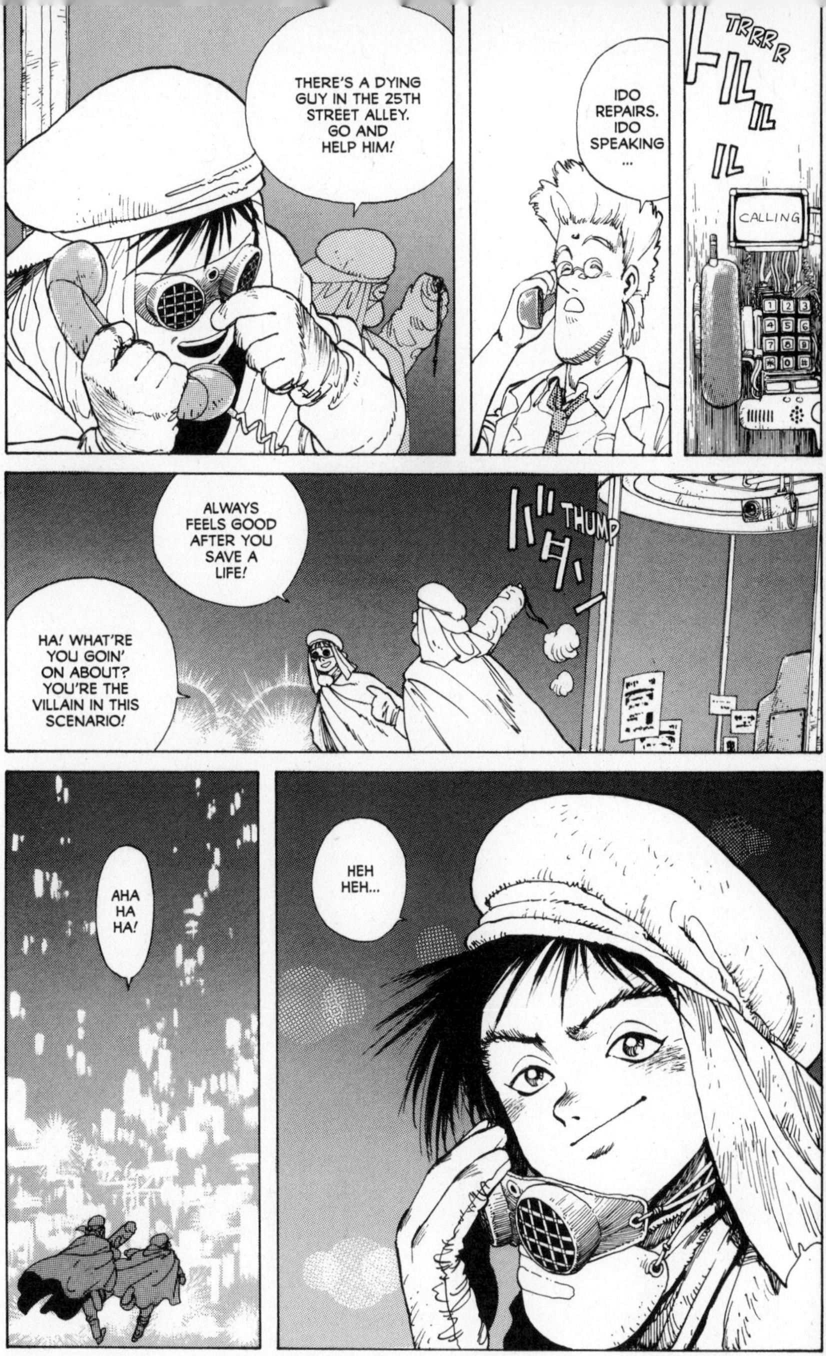
TRRRR
CALLING
IDO REPAIRS. IDO SPEAKING ...
THERE'S A DYING GUY IN THE 25TH STREET ALLEY. GO AND HELP HIM!
THUMP
ALWAYS FEELS GOOD AFTER YOU SAVE A LIFE!
HA! WHAT'RE YOU GOIN' ON ABOUT? YOU'RE THE VILLAIN IN THIS SCENARIO!
HEH HEH...
AHA HA HA!

FIGHT_009 Iron Maiden

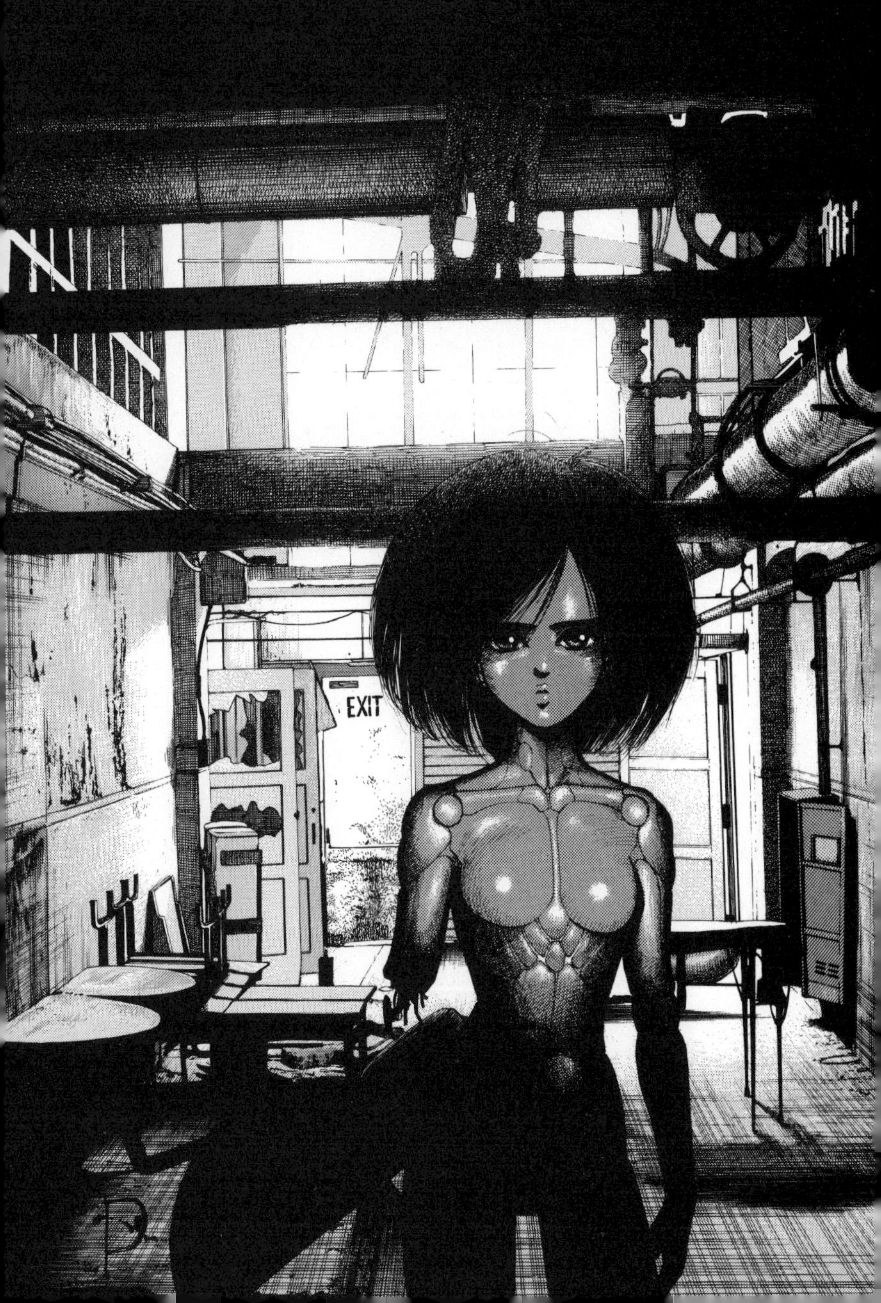
EXIT

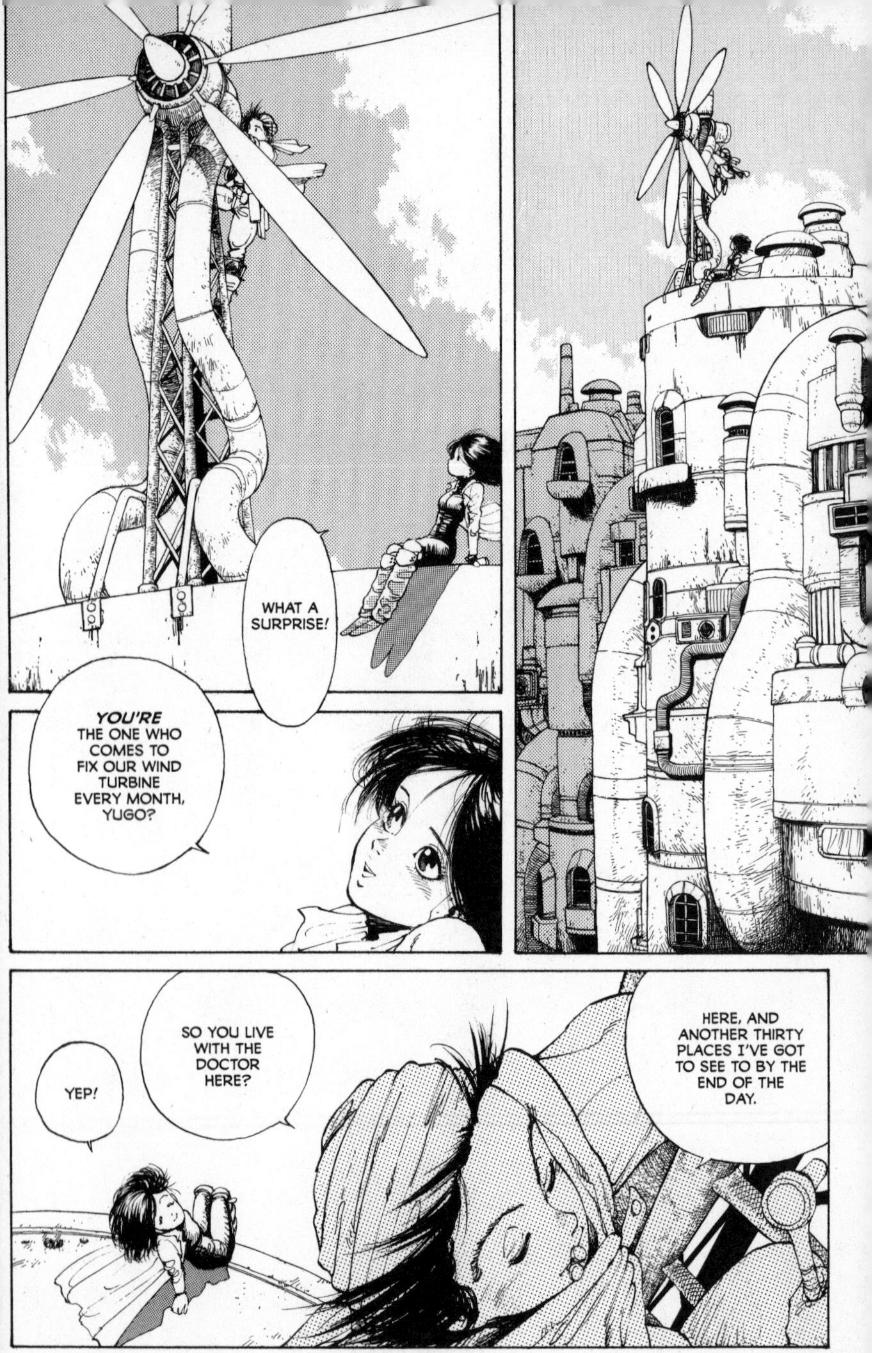
WHAT A SURPRISE!
YOU'RE THE ONE WHO COMES TO FIX OUR WIND TURBINE EVERY MONTH, YUGO?
HERE, AND ANOTHER THIRTY PLACES I'VE GOT TO SEE TO BY THE END OF THE DAY.
SO YOU LIVE WITH THE DOCTOR HERE?
YEP!

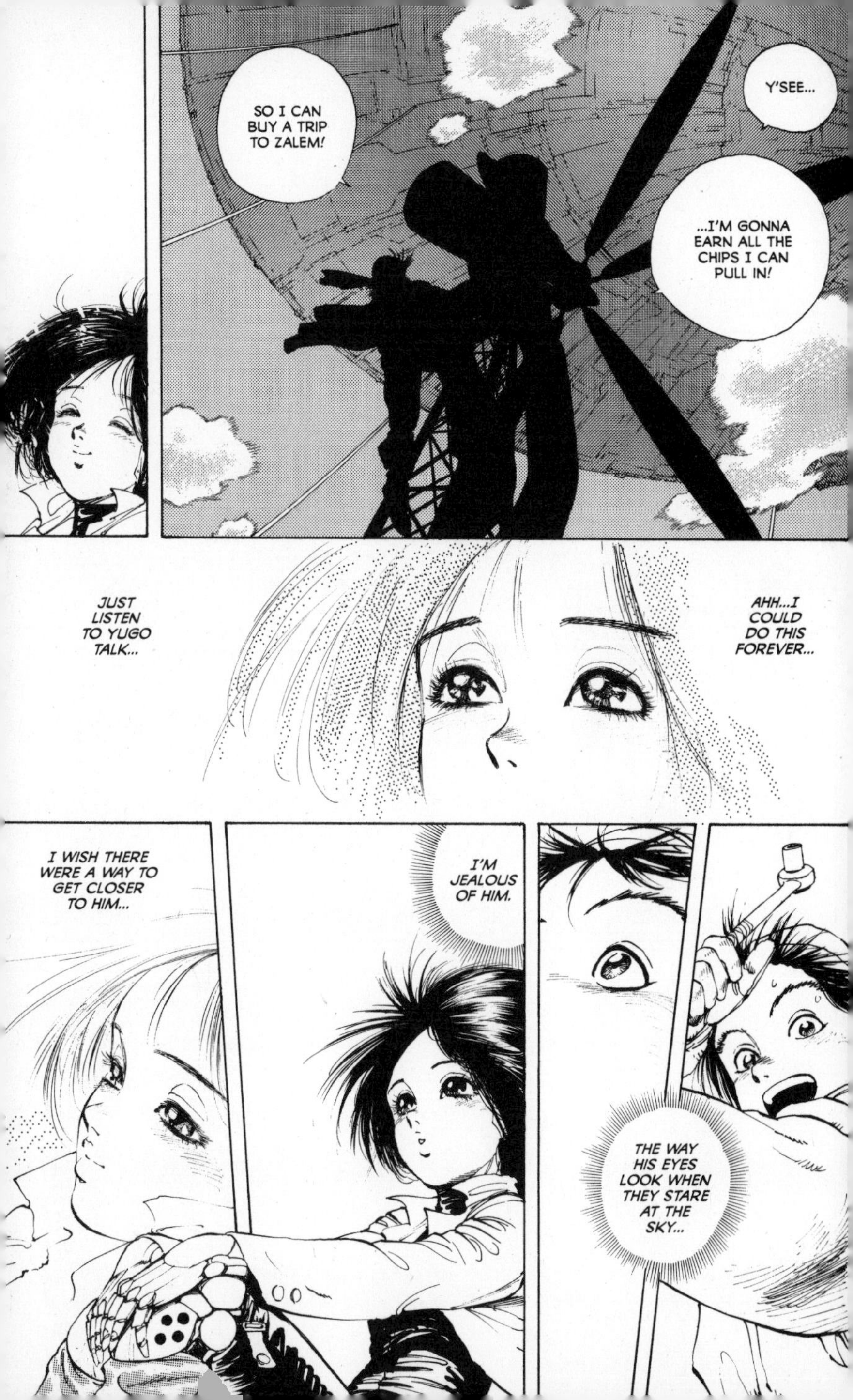
Y'SEE...
...I'M GONNA EARN ALL THE CHIPS I CAN PULL IN!
SO I CAN BUY A TRIP TO ZALEM!
AHH...I COULD DO THIS FOREVER...
JUST LISTEN TO YUGO TALK...
THE WAY HIS EYES LOOK WHEN THEY STARE AT THE SKY...
I'M JEALOUS OF HIM.
I WISH THERE WERE A WAY TO GET CLOSER TO HIM...

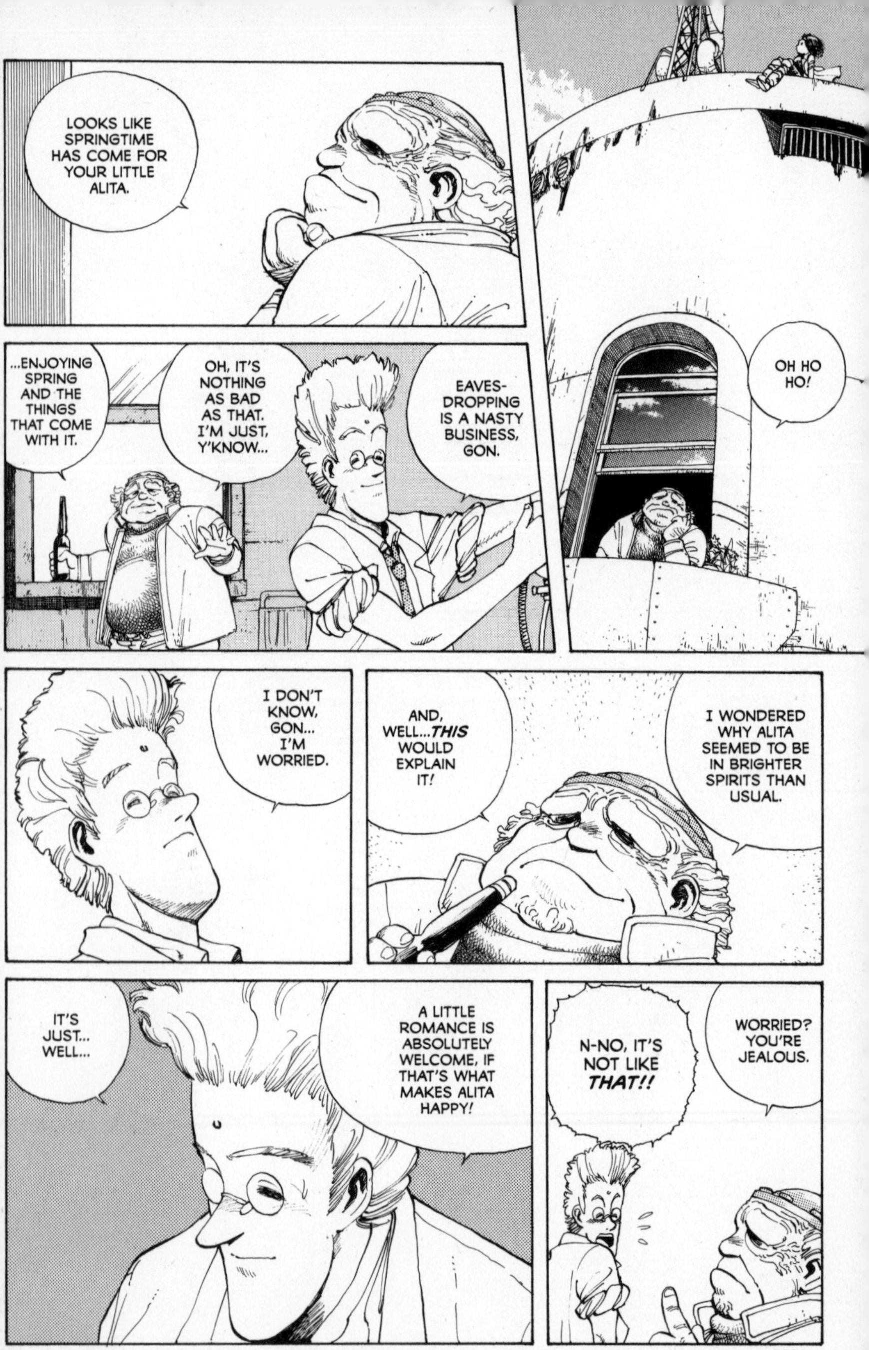
OH HO HO!
LOOKS LIKE SPRINGTIME HAS COME FOR YOUR LITTLE ALITA.
EAVES-DROPPING IS A NASTY BUSINESS, GON.
OH, IT'S NOTHING AS BAD AS THAT. I'M JUST, Y'KNOW...
...ENJOYING SPRING AND THE THINGS THAT COME WITH IT.
I WONDERED WHY ALITA SEEMED TO BE IN BRIGHTER SPIRITS THAN USUAL.
AND, WELL...*THIS* WOULD EXPLAIN IT!
I DON'T KNOW, GON... I'M WORRIED.
WORRIED? YOU'RE JEALOUS.
N-NO, IT'S NOT LIKE *THAT!!*
A LITTLE ROMANCE IS ABSOLUTELY WELCOME, IF THAT'S WHAT MAKES ALITA HAPPY!
IT'S JUST... WELL...

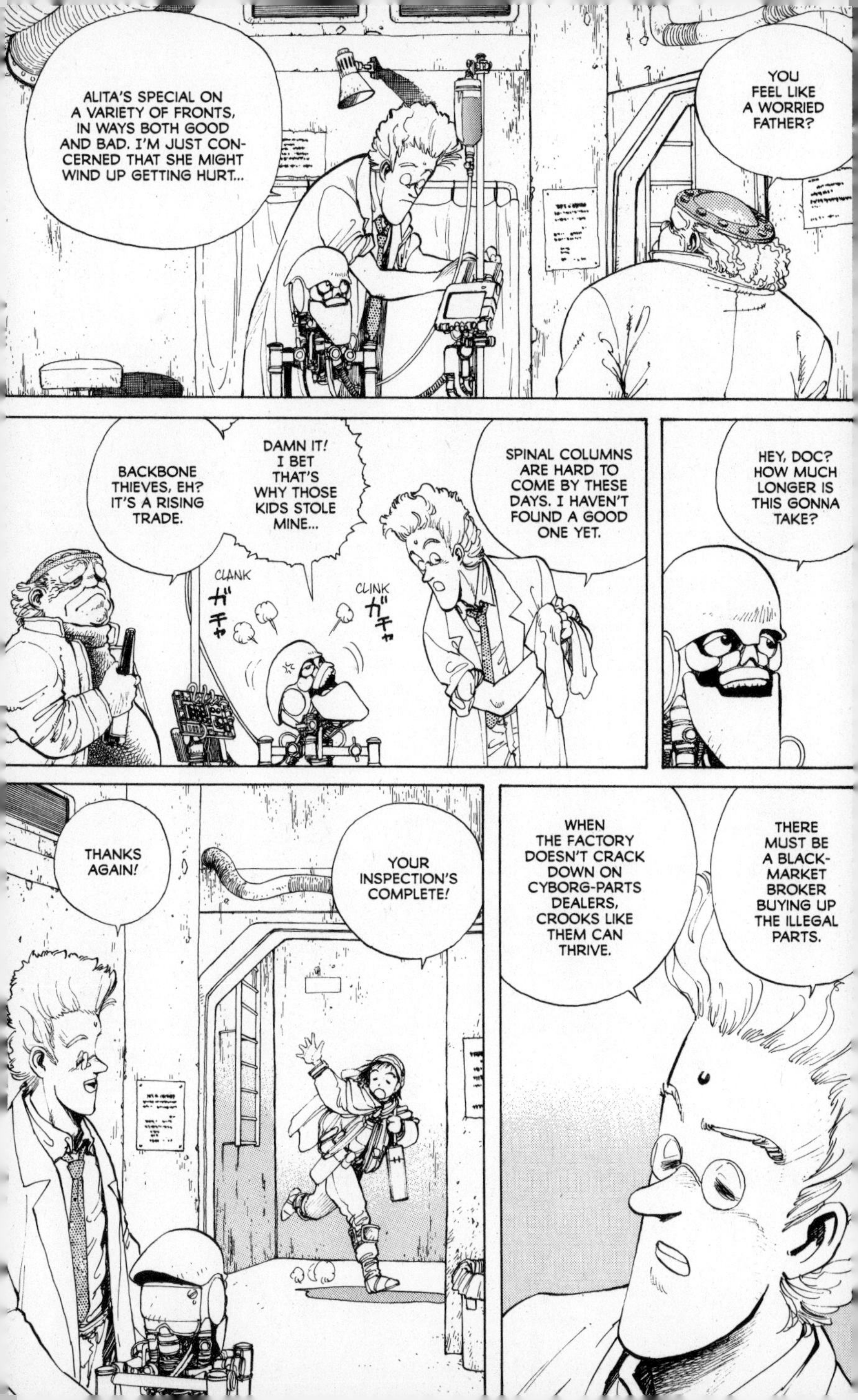
YOU FEEL LIKE A WORRIED FATHER?
ALITA'S SPECIAL ON A VARIETY OF FRONTS, IN WAYS BOTH GOOD AND BAD. I'M JUST CONCERNED THAT SHE MIGHT WIND UP GETTING HURT...
HEY, DOC? HOW MUCH LONGER IS THIS GONNA TAKE?
SPINAL COLUMNS ARE HARD TO COME BY THESE DAYS. I HAVEN'T FOUND A GOOD ONE YET.
DAMN IT! I BET THAT'S WHY THOSE KIDS STOLE MINE...
BACKBONE THIEVES, EH? IT'S A RISING TRADE.
CLINK ガチャ
CLANK ガチャ
THERE MUST BE A BLACK-MARKET BROKER BUYING UP THE ILLEGAL PARTS.
WHEN THE FACTORY DOESN'T CRACK DOWN ON CYBORG-PARTS DEALERS, CROOKS LIKE THEM CAN THRIVE.
YOUR INSPECTION'S COMPLETE!
THANKS AGAIN!

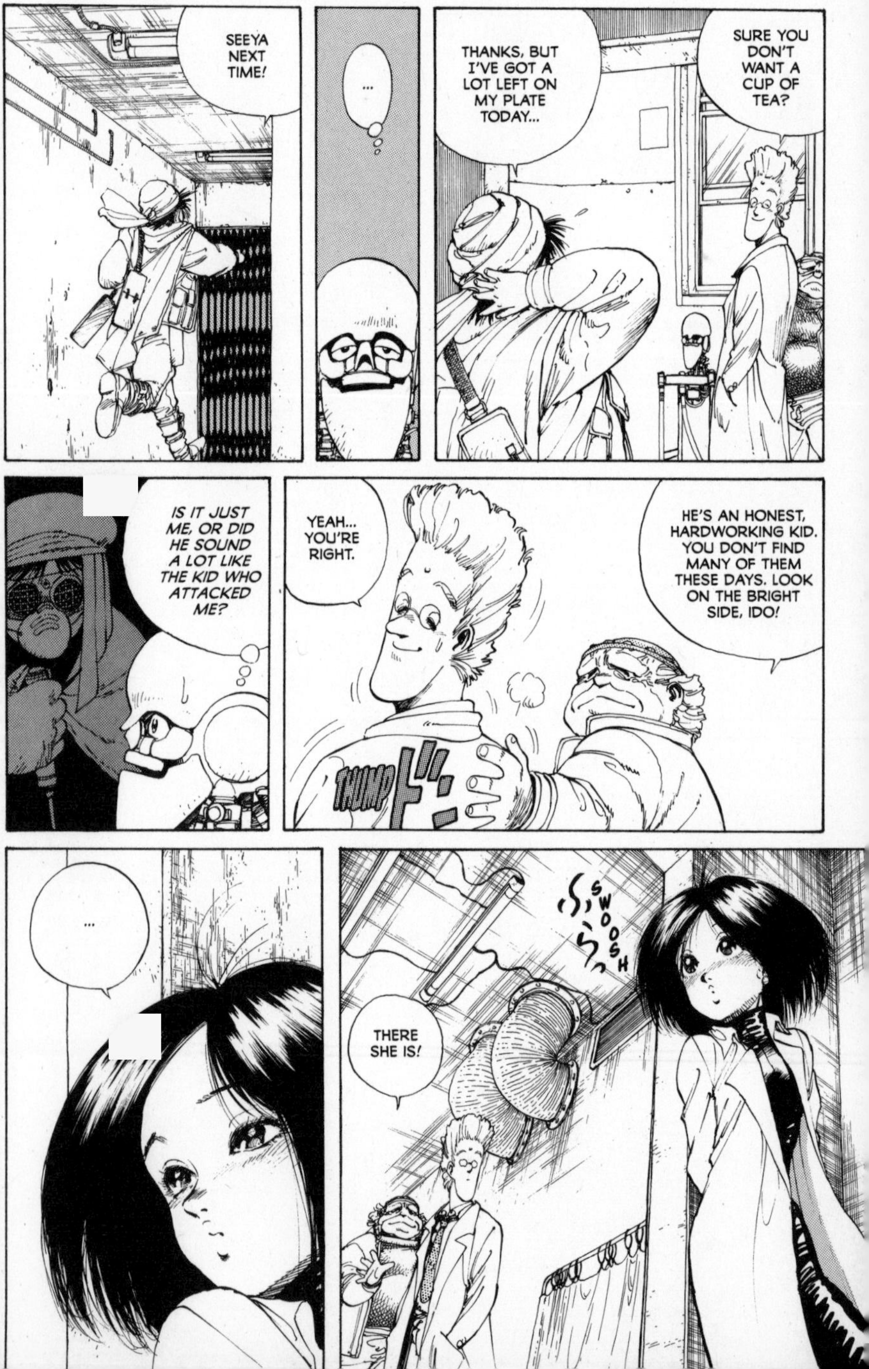
SURE YOU DON'T WANT A CUP OF TEA?
THANKS, BUT I'VE GOT A LOT LEFT ON MY PLATE TODAY...
...
SEEYA NEXT TIME!
HE'S AN HONEST, HARDWORKING KID. YOU DON'T FIND MANY OF THEM THESE DAYS. LOOK ON THE BRIGHT SIDE, IDO!
YEAH... YOU'RE RIGHT.
THUMP
IS IT JUST ME, OR DID HE SOUND A LOT LIKE THE KID WHO ATTACKED ME?
SWOOSH
THERE SHE IS!
...

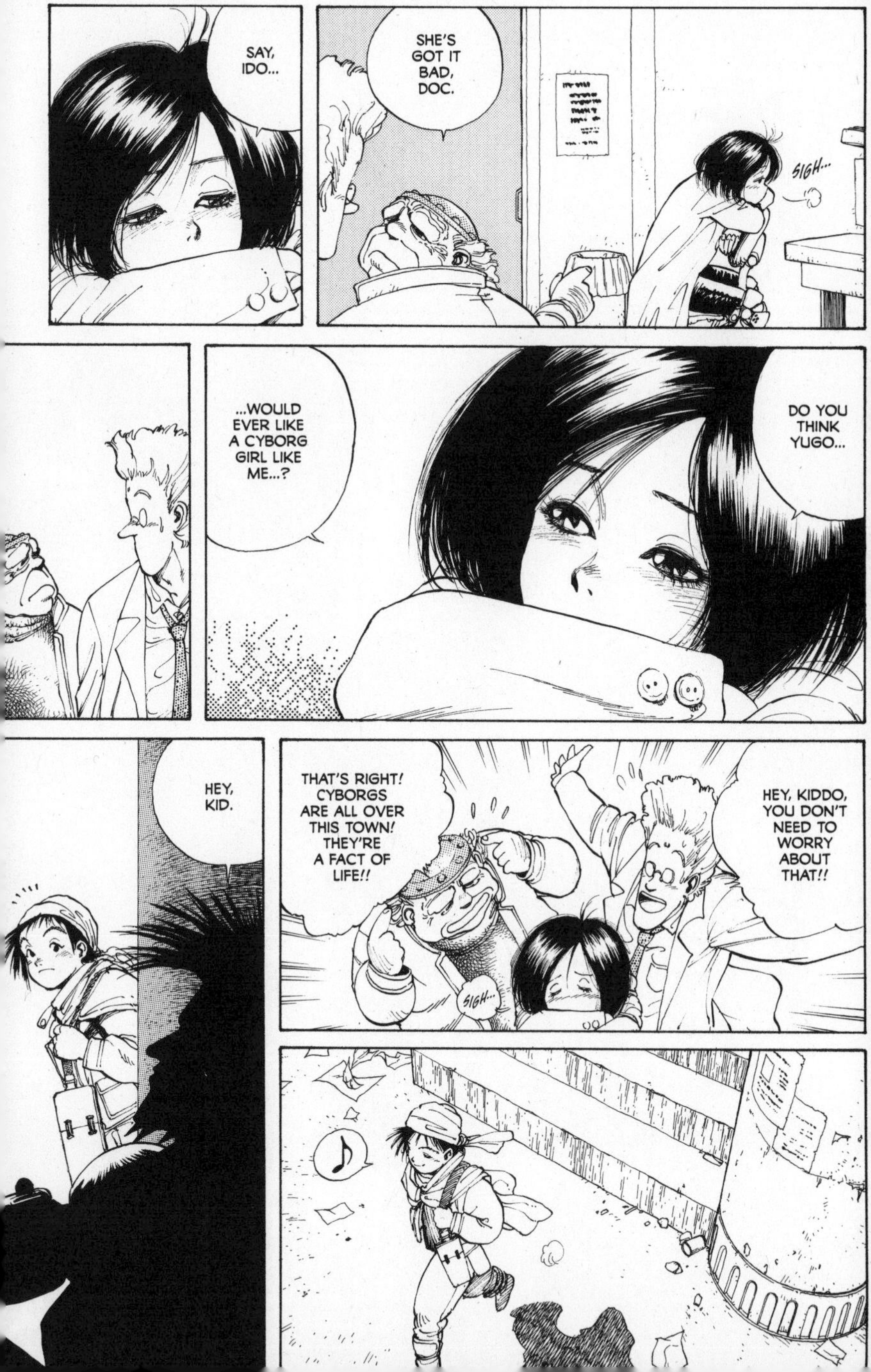
SIGH...
SHE'S GOT IT BAD, DOC.
SAY, IDO...
DO YOU THINK YUGO...
...WOULD EVER LIKE A CYBORG GIRL LIKE ME...?
HEY, KIDDO, YOU DON'T NEED TO WORRY ABOUT THAT!!
THAT'S RIGHT! CYBORGS ARE ALL OVER THIS TOWN! THEY'RE A FACT OF LIFE!!
SIGH...
♪
HEY, KID.

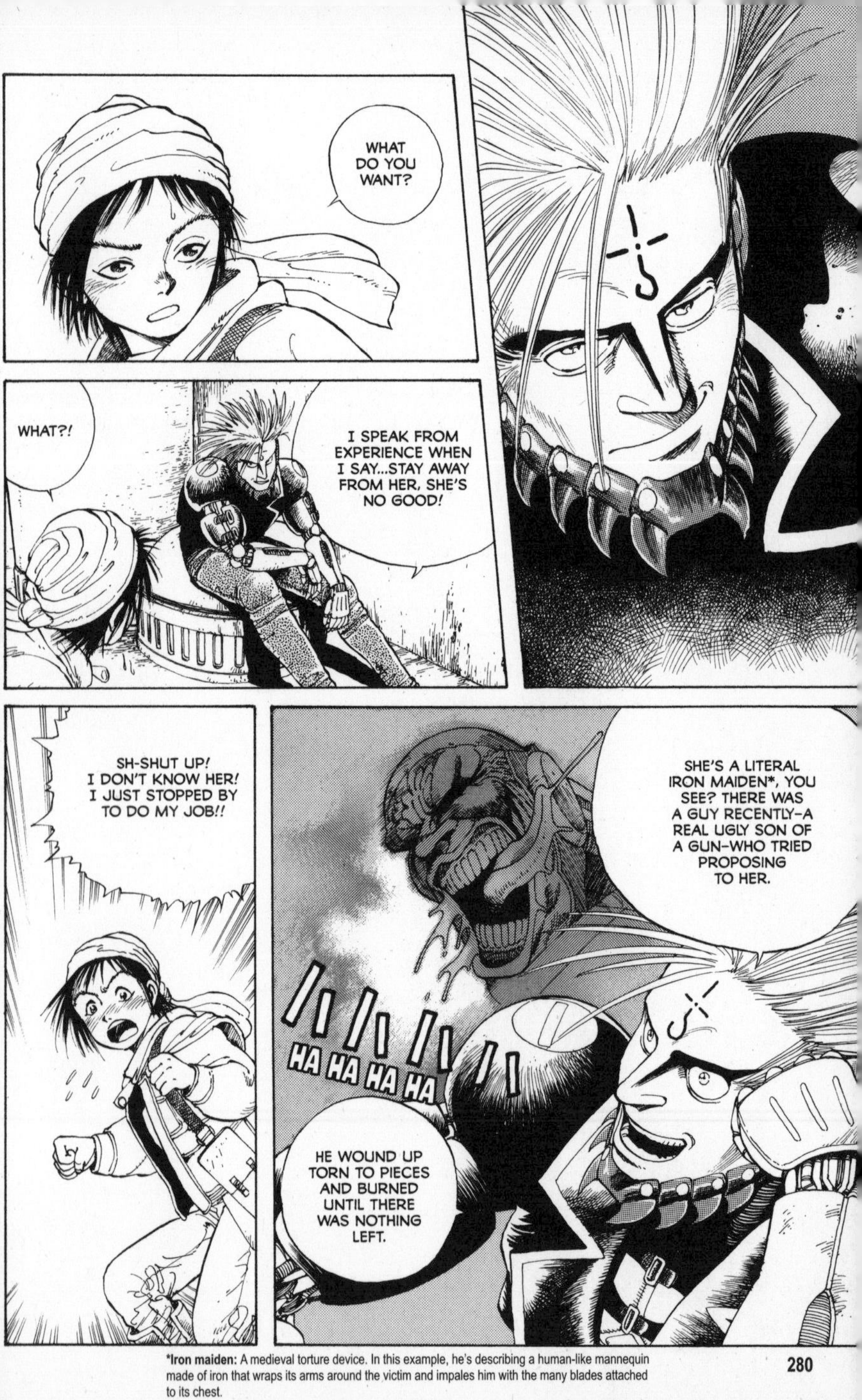
WHAT DO YOU WANT?
I SPEAK FROM EXPERIENCE WHEN I SAY...STAY AWAY FROM HER, SHE'S NO GOOD!
WHAT?!
SHE'S A LITERAL IRON MAIDEN*, YOU SEE? THERE WAS A GUY RECENTLY–A REAL UGLY SON OF A GUN–WHO TRIED PROPOSING TO HER.
HA HA HA HA
HE WOUND UP TORN TO PIECES AND BURNED UNTIL THERE WAS NOTHING LEFT.
SH-SHUT UP! I DON'T KNOW HER! I JUST STOPPED BY TO DO MY JOB!!

***Iron maiden:** A medieval torture device. In this example, he's describing a human-like mannequin made of iron that wraps its arms around the victim and impales him with the many blades attached to its chest.

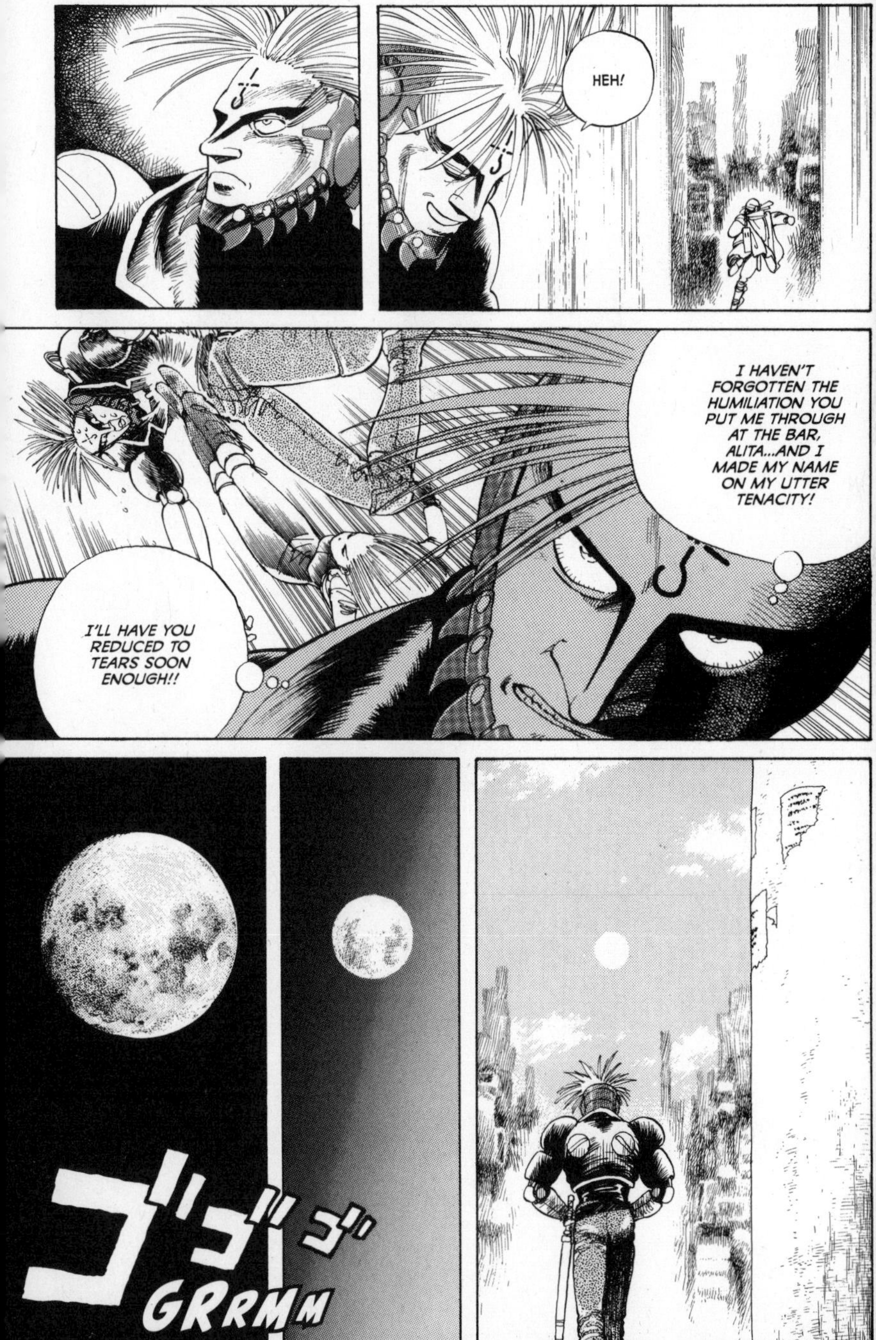
HEH!
I HAVEN'T FORGOTTEN THE HUMILIATION YOU PUT ME THROUGH AT THE BAR, ALITA...AND I MADE MY NAME ON MY UTTER TENACITY!
I'LL HAVE YOU REDUCED TO TEARS SOON ENOUGH!!
ゴゴゴ
GRRMM

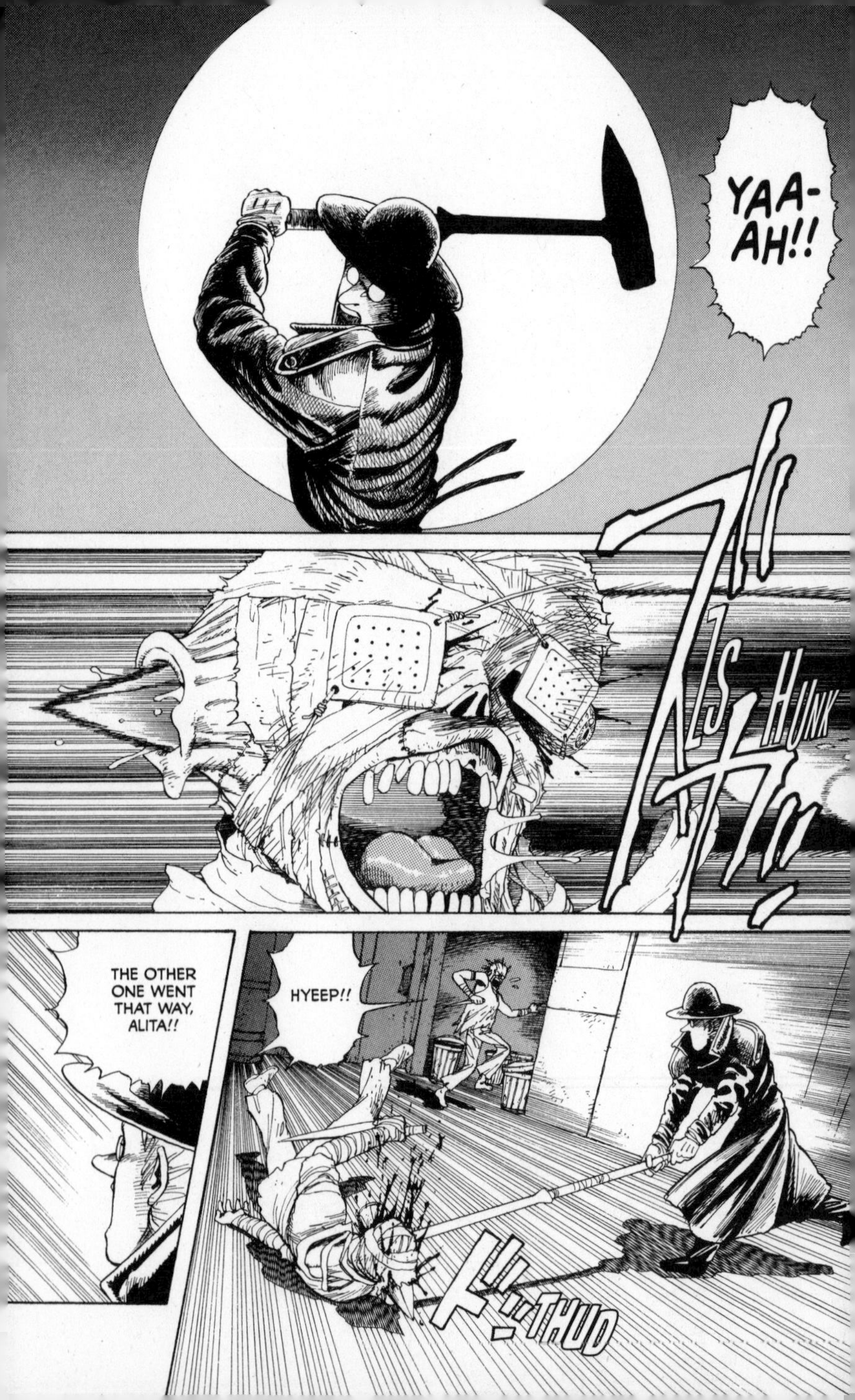
YAA-
AH!!
SHUNK
HYEEP!!
THUD
THE OTHER ONE WENT THAT WAY, ALITA!!

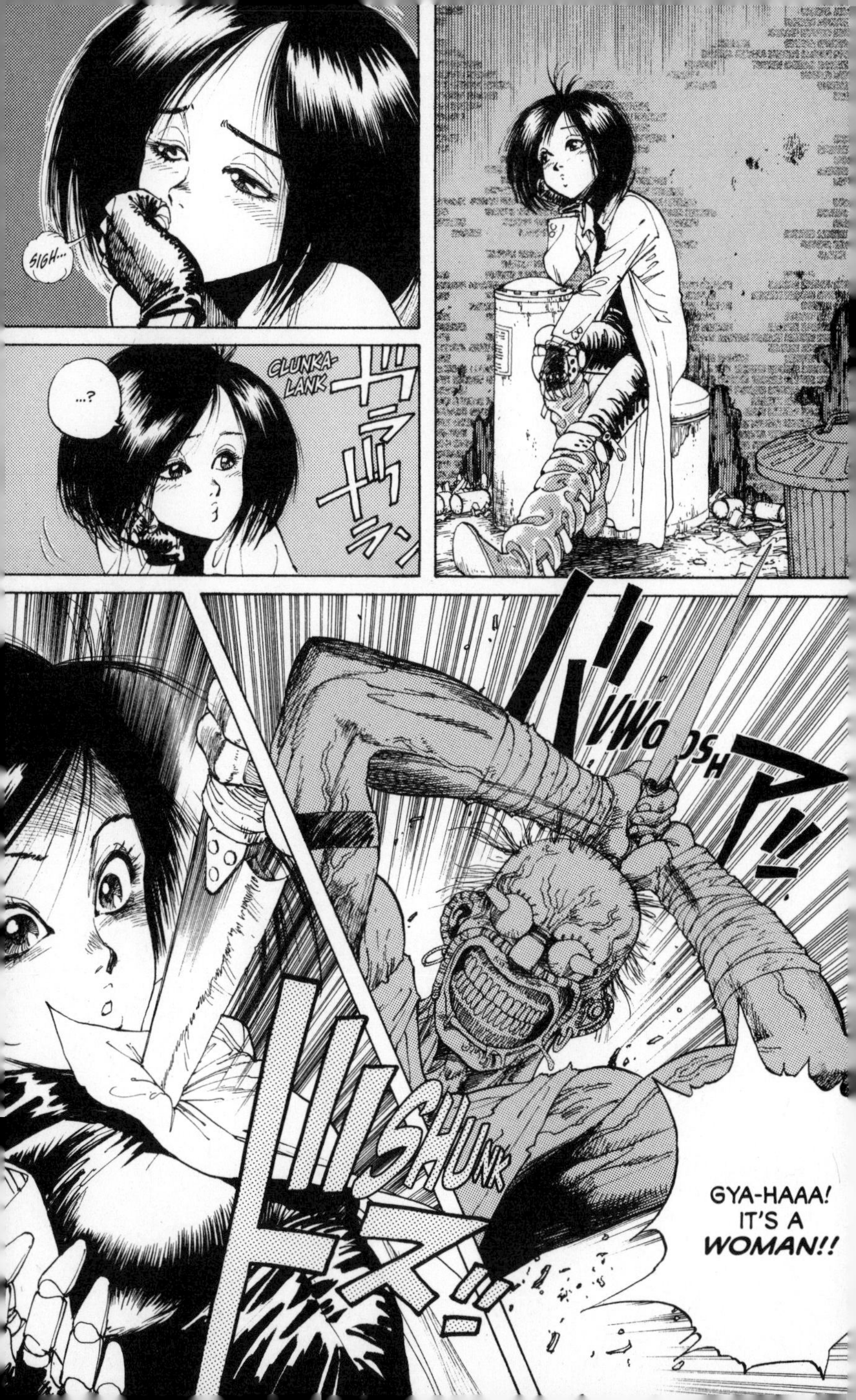
SIGH...
...?
CLUNKA-LANK
VWOOSH
GYA-HAAA! IT'S A WOMAN!!
SHUNK

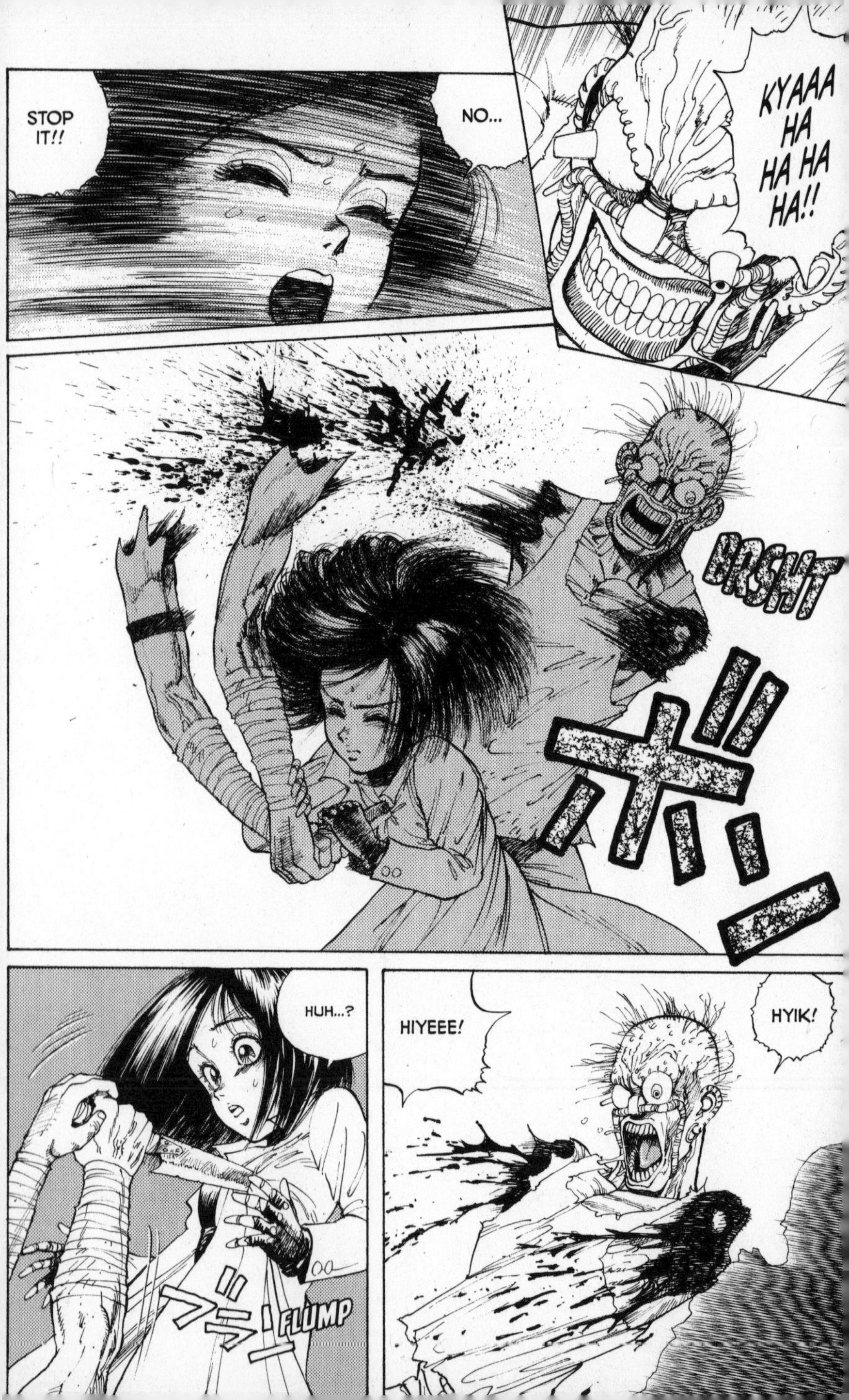
KYAAA HA HA HA HA!!
NO...
STOP IT!!
HYIK!
HIYEEE!
HUH...?
FLUMP

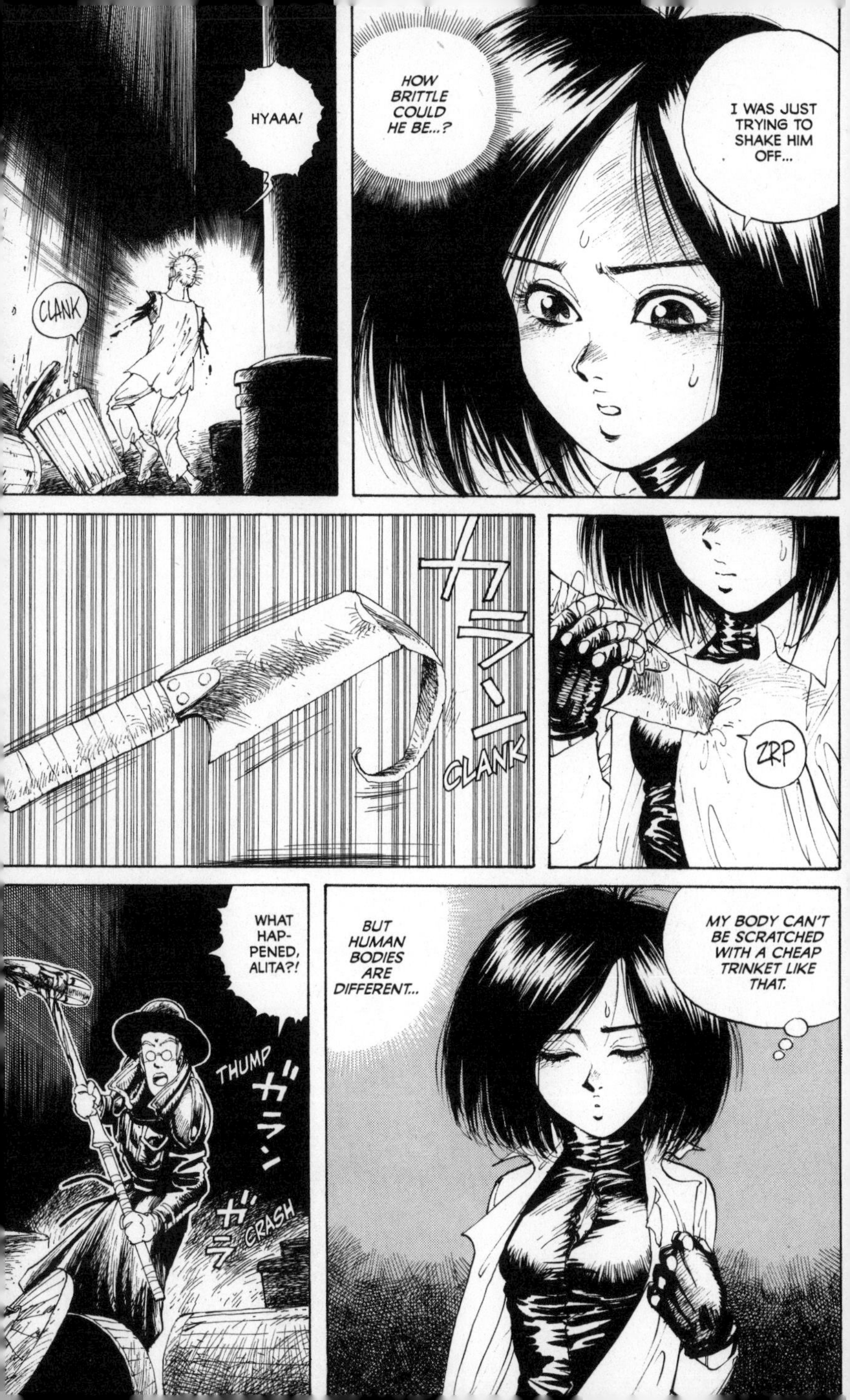
I WAS JUST TRYING TO SHAKE HIM OFF...
HOW BRITTLE COULD HE BE...?
HYAAA!
CLANK
ZRP
カラン
CLANK
MY BODY CAN'T BE SCRATCHED WITH A CHEAP TRINKET LIKE THAT.
BUT HUMAN BODIES ARE DIFFERENT...
WHAT HAP-PENED, ALITA?!
THUMP
ガラン
ガラ
CRASH

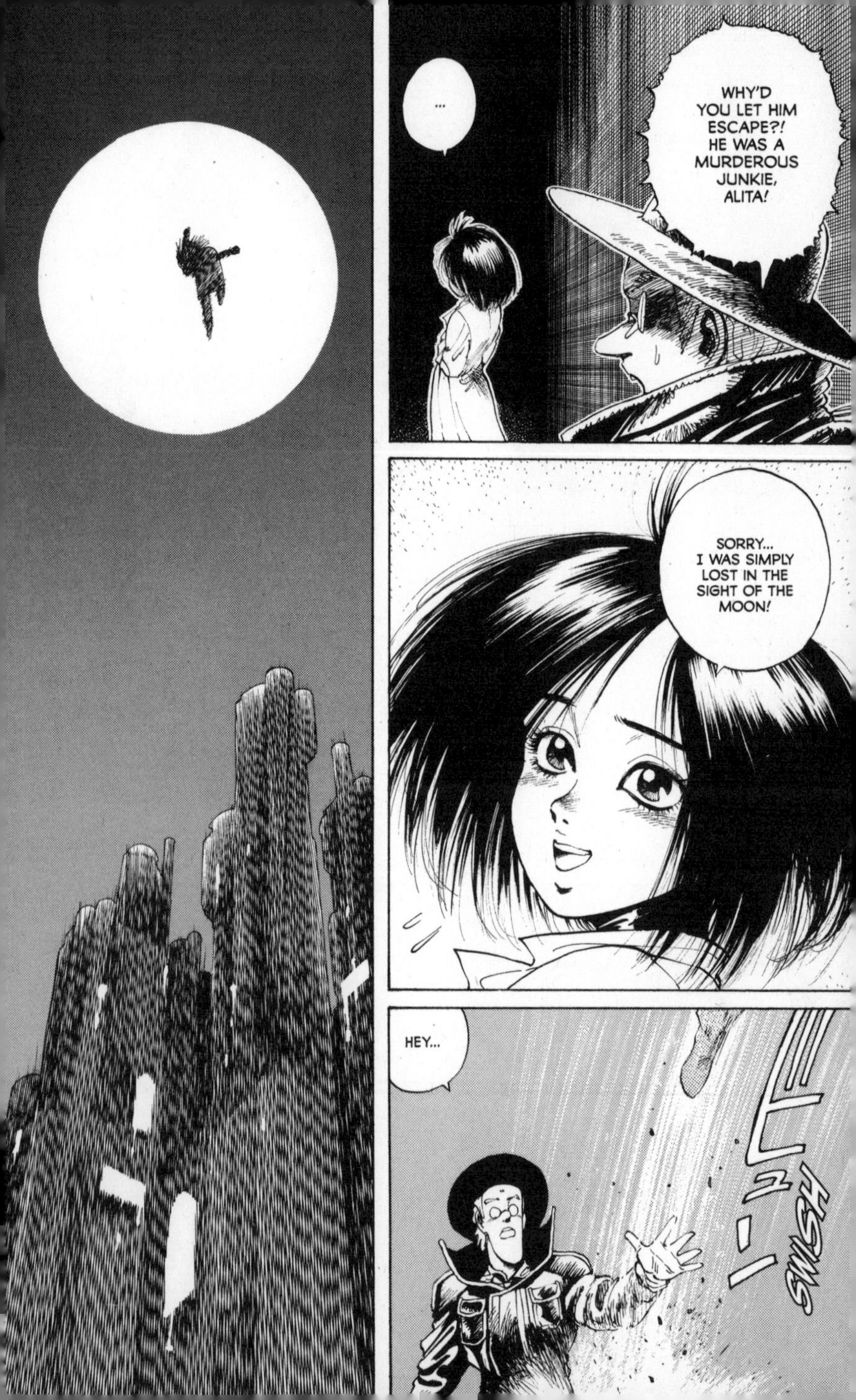
WHY'D YOU LET HIM ESCAPE?! HE WAS A MURDEROUS JUNKIE, ALITA!
...
SORRY... I WAS SIMPLY LOST IN THE SIGHT OF THE MOON!
HEY...
SWISH

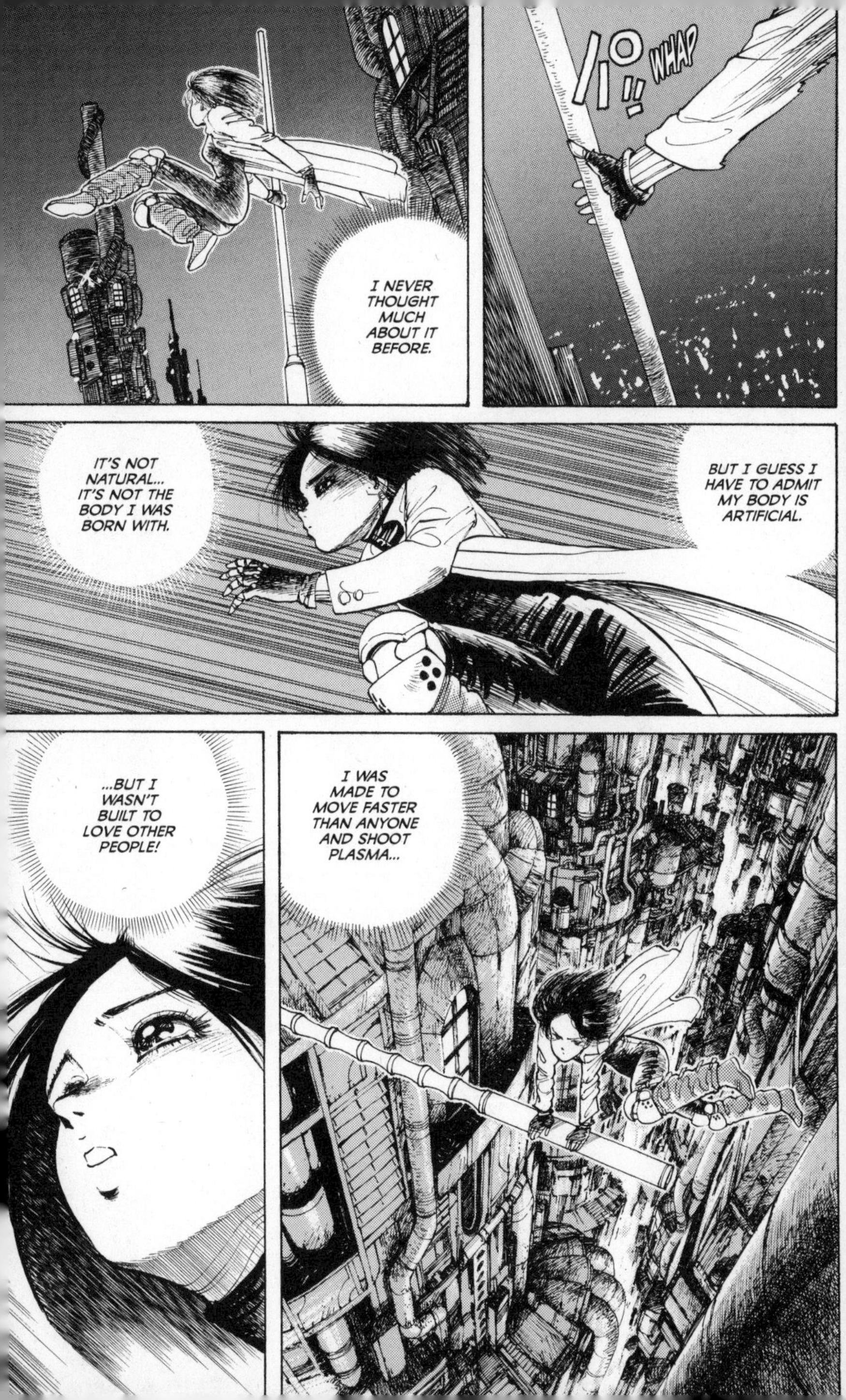
WHAP
I NEVER THOUGHT MUCH ABOUT IT BEFORE.
BUT I GUESS I HAVE TO ADMIT MY BODY IS ARTIFICIAL.
IT'S NOT NATURAL... IT'S NOT THE BODY I WAS BORN WITH.
I WAS MADE TO MOVE FASTER THAN ANYONE AND SHOOT PLASMA...
...BUT I WASN'T BUILT TO LOVE OTHER PEOPLE!

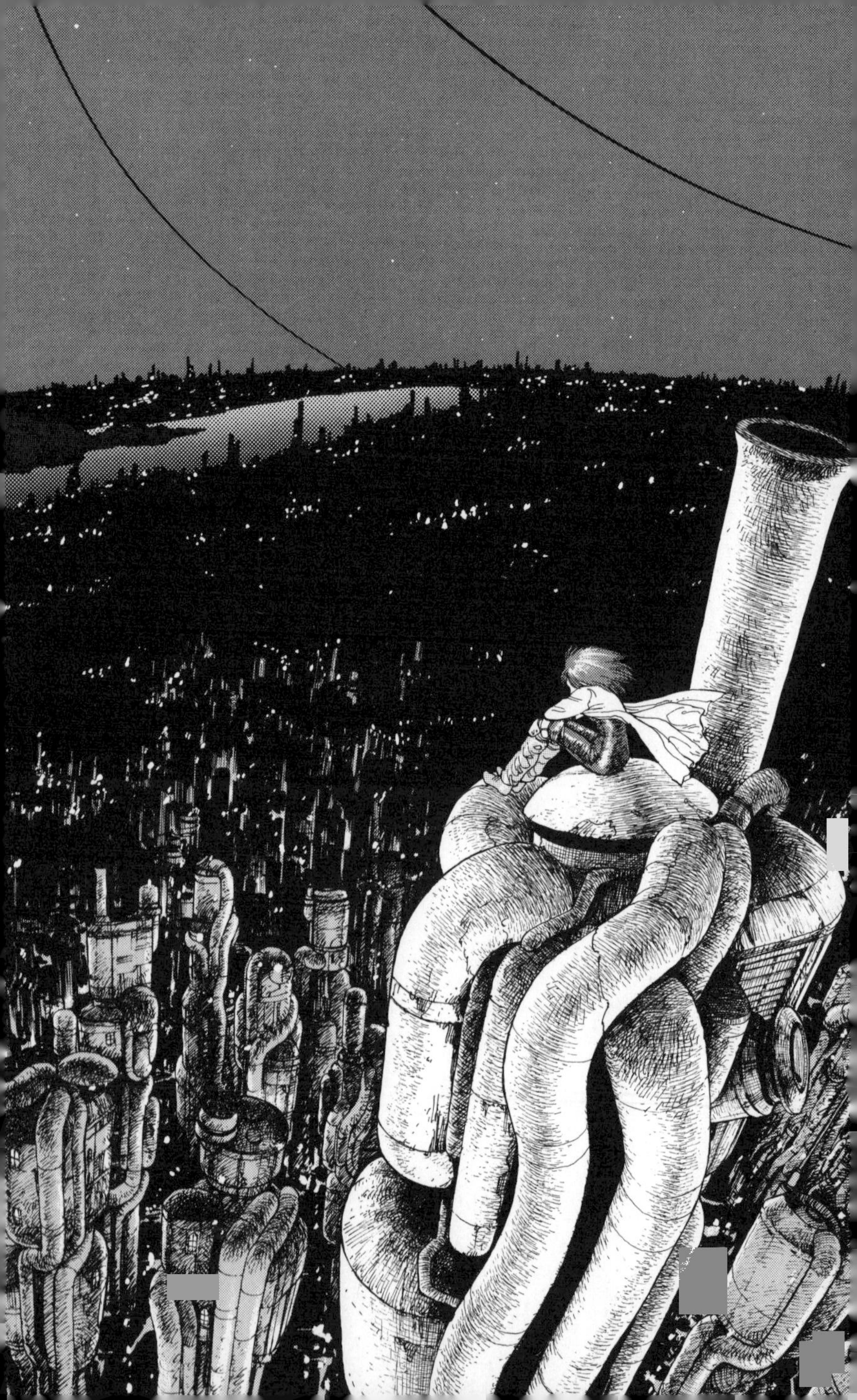

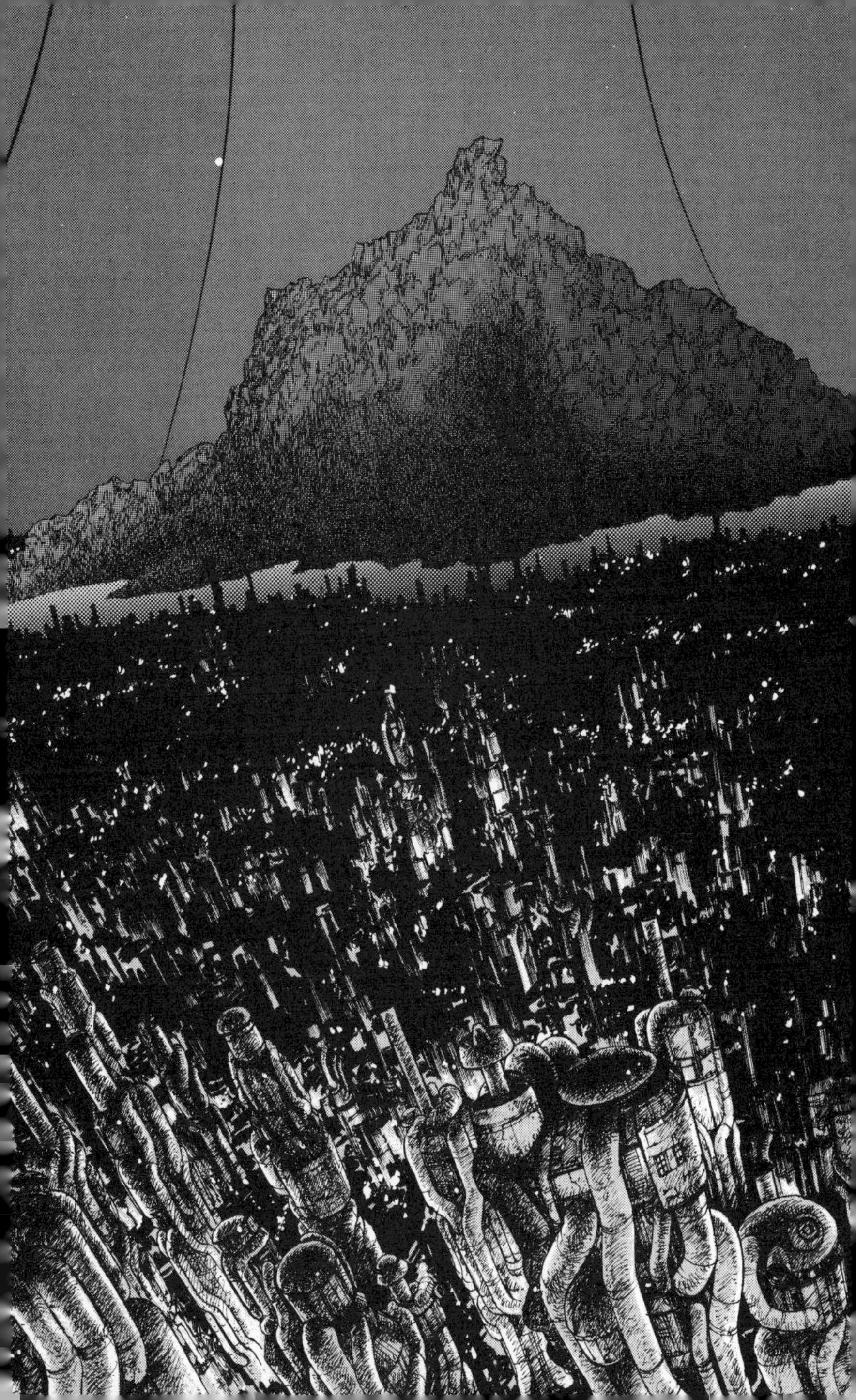

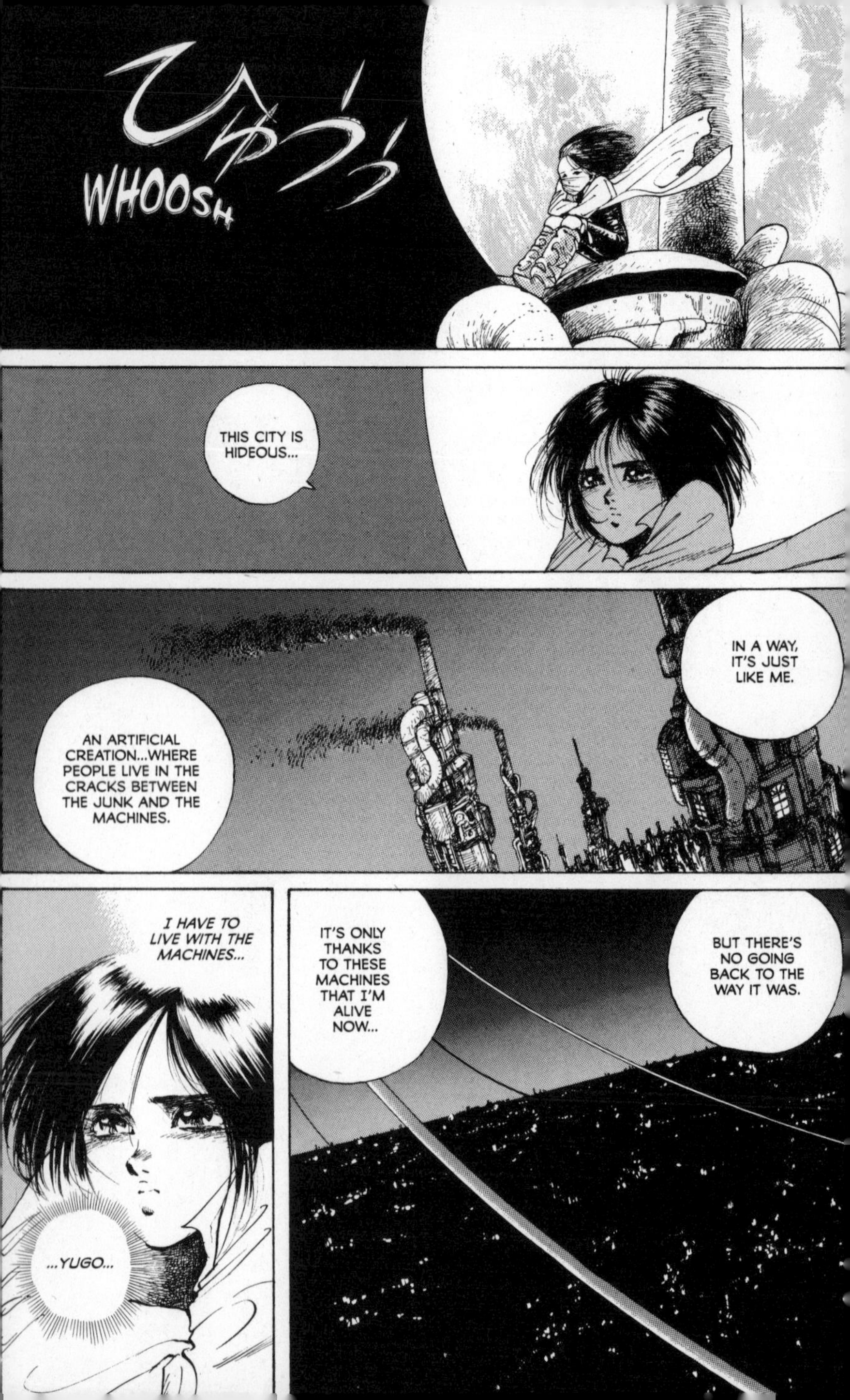

WHOOSH
THIS CITY IS HIDEOUS...
IN A WAY, IT'S JUST LIKE ME.
AN ARTIFICIAL CREATION...WHERE PEOPLE LIVE IN THE CRACKS BETWEEN THE JUNK AND THE MACHINES.
BUT THERE'S NO GOING BACK TO THE WAY IT WAS.
IT'S ONLY THANKS TO THESE MACHINES THAT I'M ALIVE NOW...
I HAVE TO LIVE WITH THE MACHINES...
...YUGO...

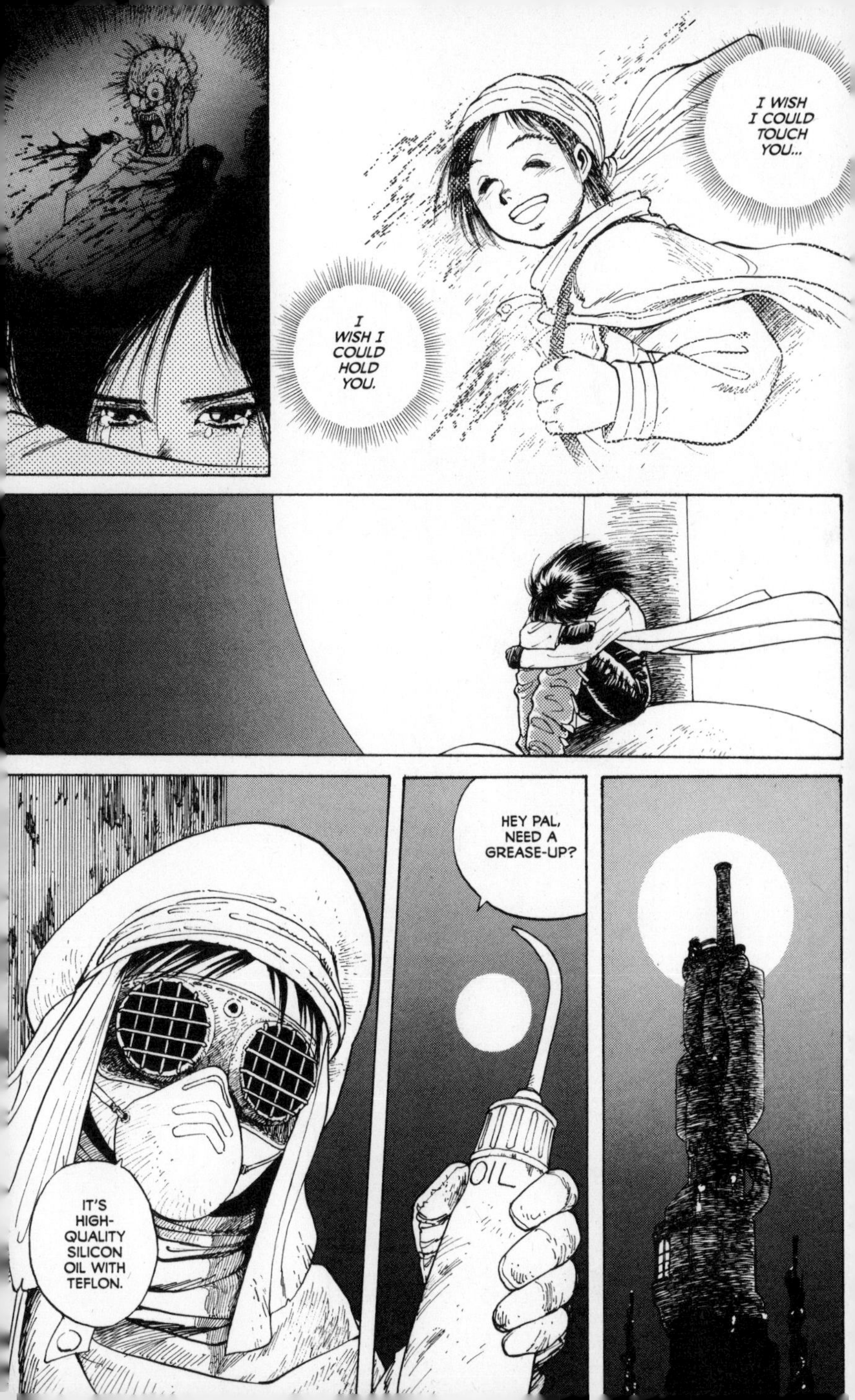
I WISH I COULD TOUCH YOU...
I WISH I COULD HOLD YOU.
HEY PAL, NEED A GREASE-UP?
OIL
IT'S HIGH-QUALITY SILICON OIL WITH TEFLON.

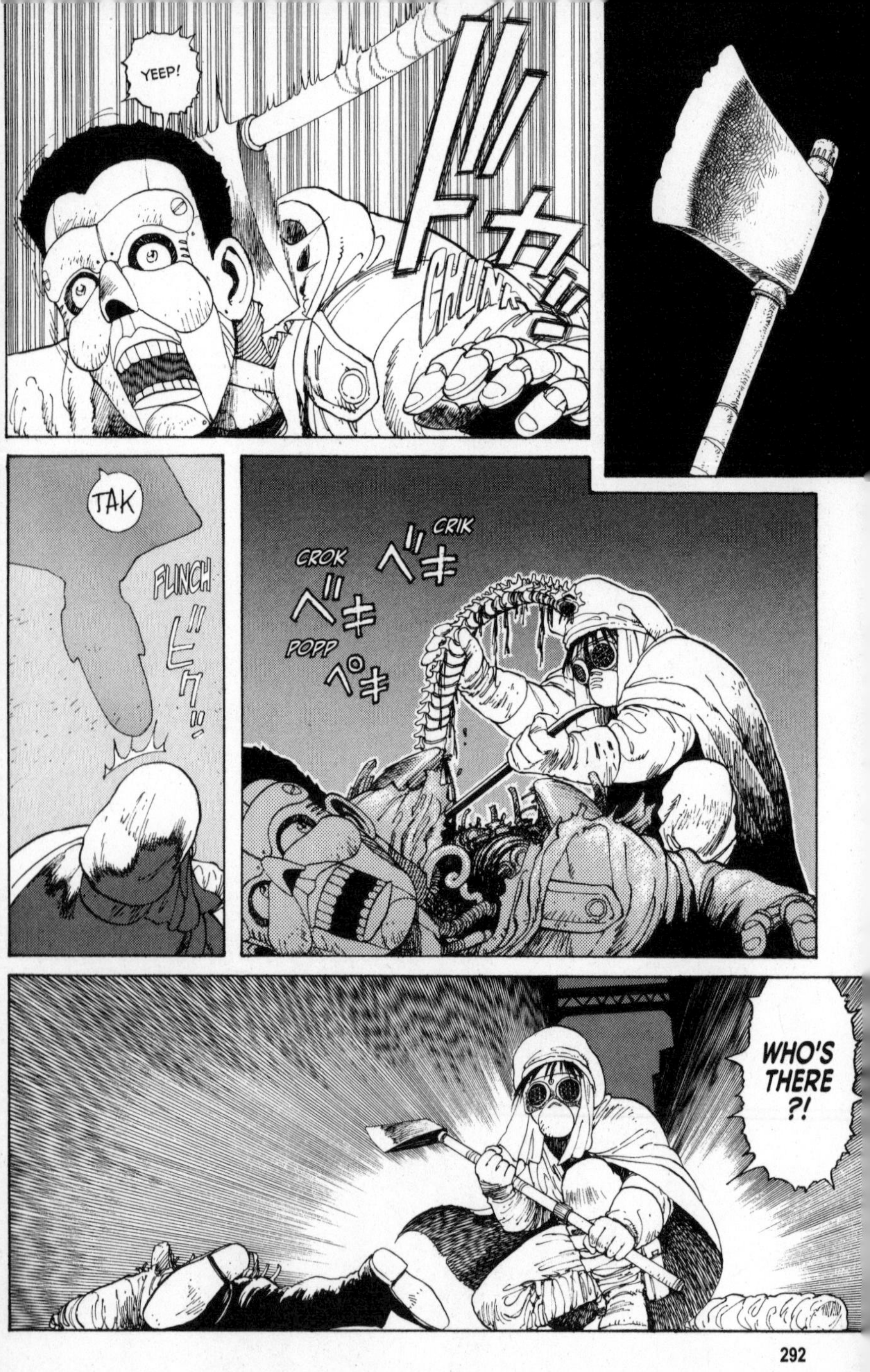
ドカッ
YEEP!
CHUNK
CRIK
ベキ
CROK
ベキ
POPP
ペキ
TAK
FLINCH
ビクッ
WHO'S THERE ?!

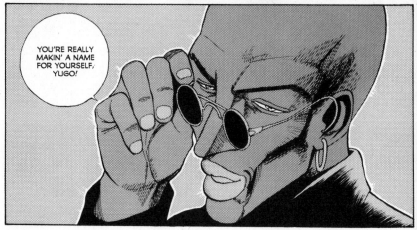

YOU'RE REALLY MAKIN' A NAME FOR YOURSELF, YUGO!

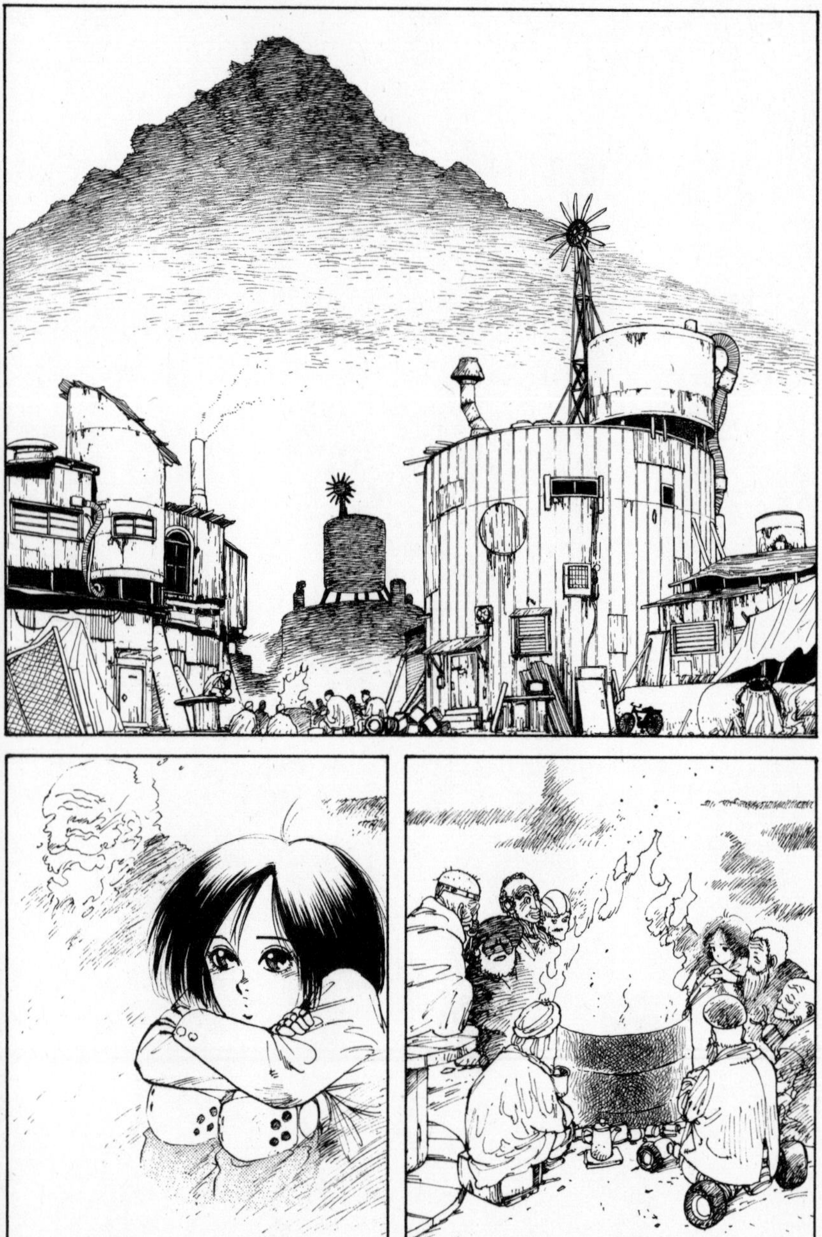

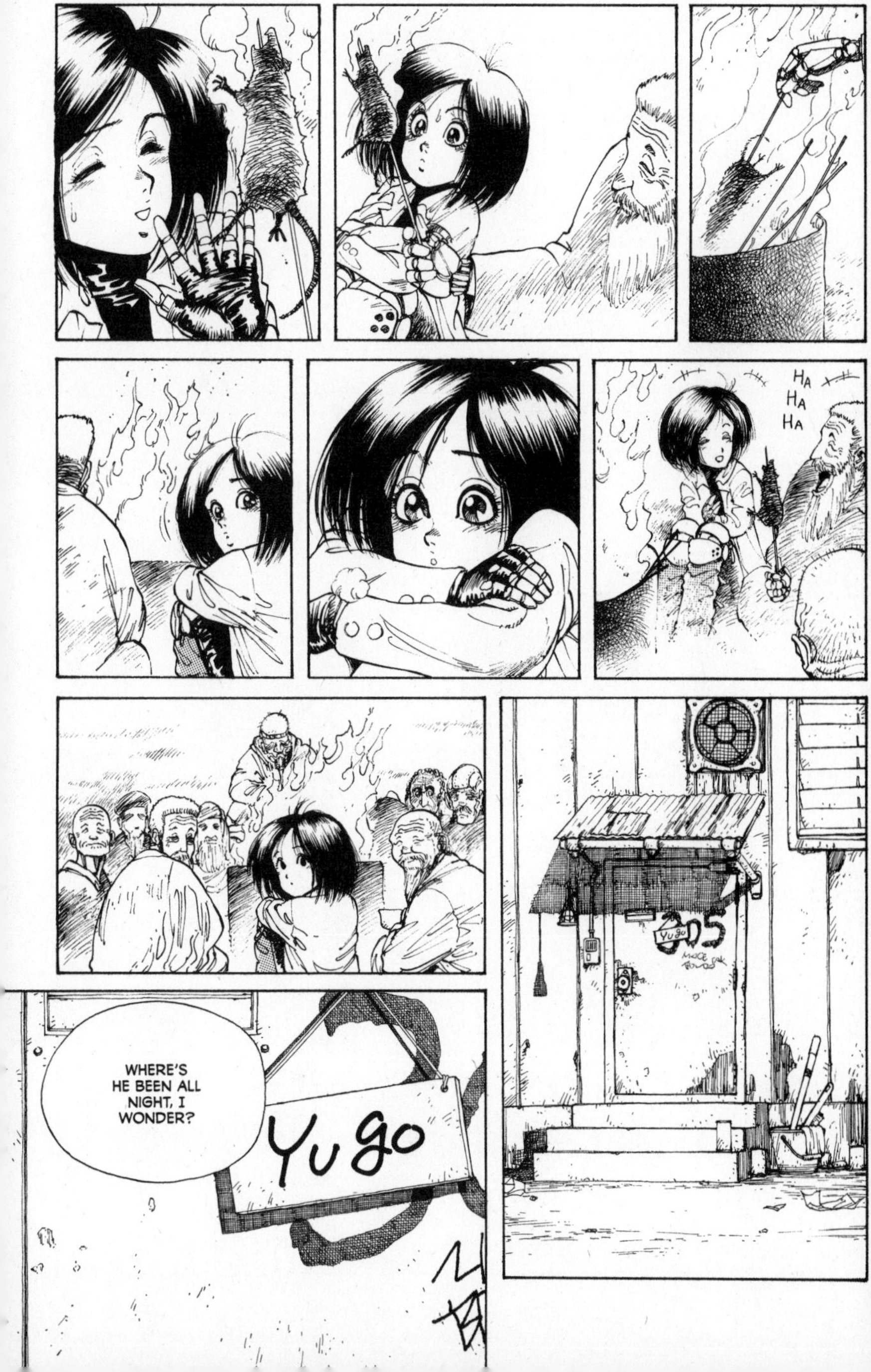
HA
HA
HA
Yugo
WHERE'S HE BEEN ALL NIGHT, I WONDER?
Yugo

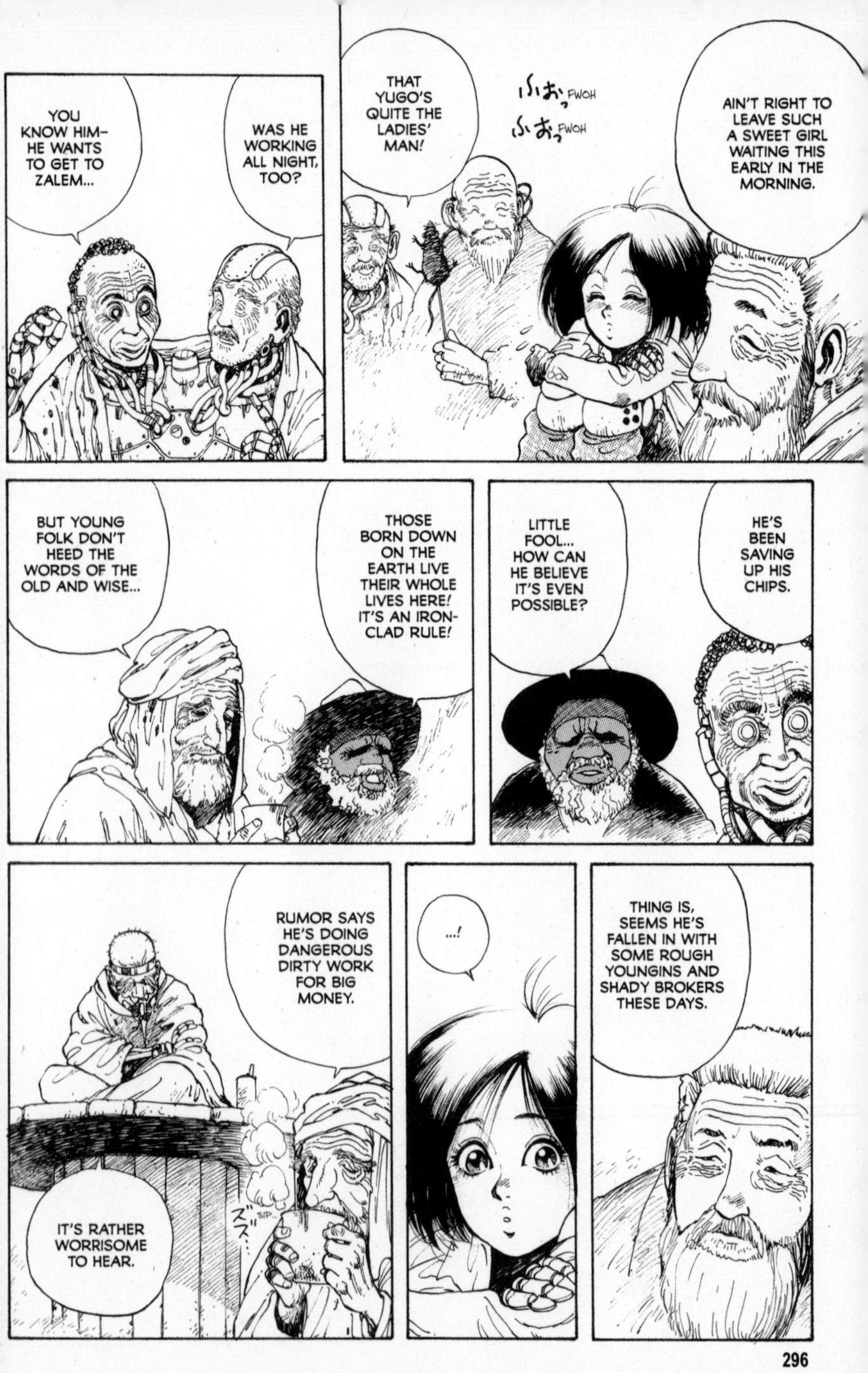
AIN'T RIGHT TO LEAVE SUCH A SWEET GIRL WAITING THIS EARLY IN THE MORNING.
ふおっ FWOH
ふおっ FWOH
THAT YUGO'S QUITE THE LADIES' MAN!
WAS HE WORKING ALL NIGHT, TOO?
YOU KNOW HIM– HE WANTS TO GET TO ZALEM...
HE'S BEEN SAVING UP HIS CHIPS.
LITTLE FOOL... HOW CAN HE BELIEVE IT'S EVEN POSSIBLE?
THOSE BORN DOWN ON THE EARTH LIVE THEIR WHOLE LIVES HERE! IT'S AN IRON-CLAD RULE!
BUT YOUNG FOLK DON'T HEED THE WORDS OF THE OLD AND WISE...
THING IS, SEEMS HE'S FALLEN IN WITH SOME ROUGH YOUNGINS AND SHADY BROKERS THESE DAYS.
...!
RUMOR SAYS HE'S DOING DANGEROUS DIRTY WORK FOR BIG MONEY.
ズズ... SIP...
IT'S RATHER WORRISOME TO HEAR.

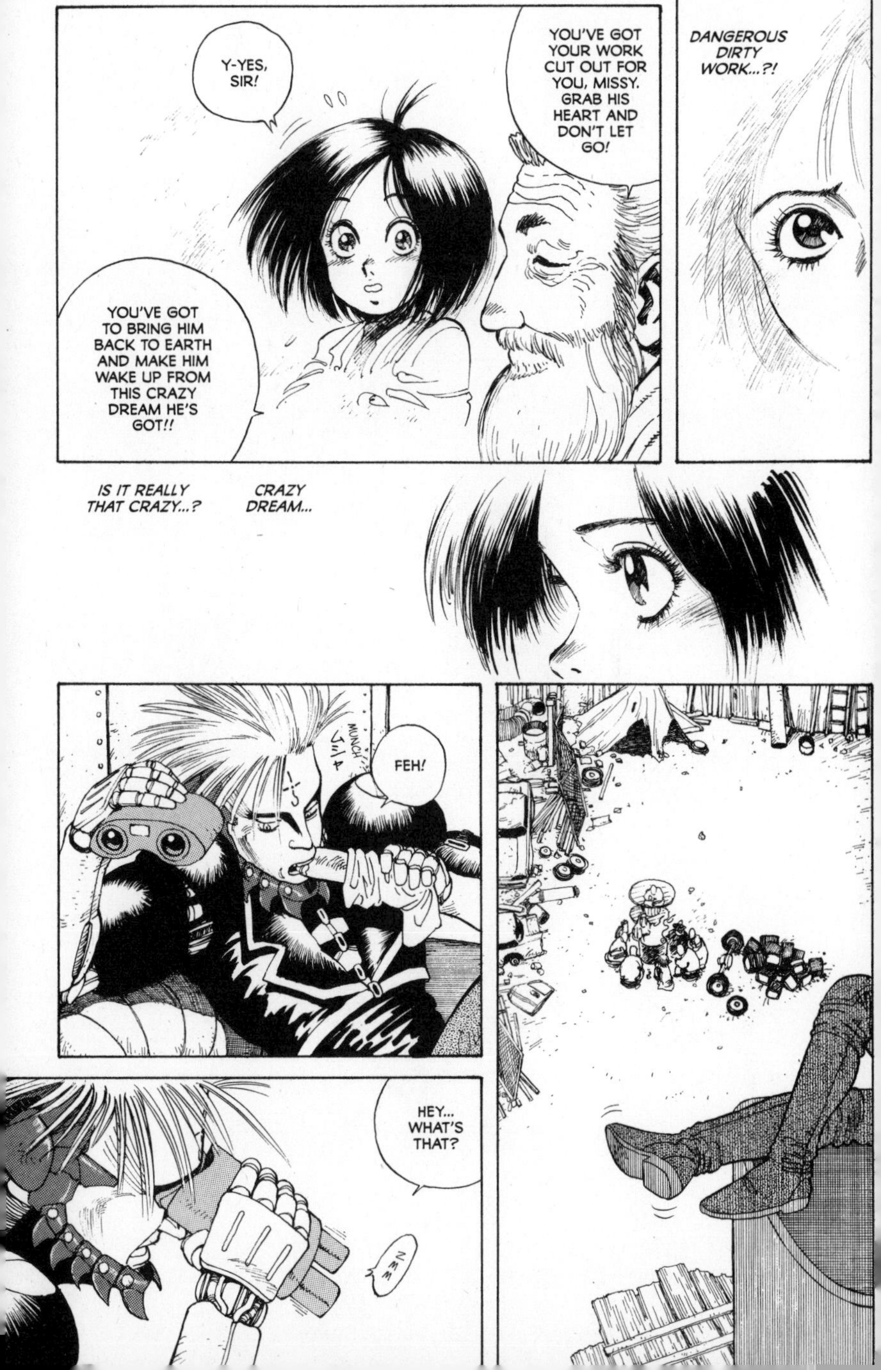
DANGEROUS DIRTY WORK...?!
YOU'VE GOT YOUR WORK CUT OUT FOR YOU, MISSY. GRAB HIS HEART AND DON'T LET GO!
Y-YES, SIR!
YOU'VE GOT TO BRING HIM BACK TO EARTH AND MAKE HIM WAKE UP FROM THIS CRAZY DREAM HE'S GOT!!
CRAZY DREAM...
IS IT REALLY THAT CRAZY...?
MUNCH
FEH!
HEY... WHAT'S THAT?

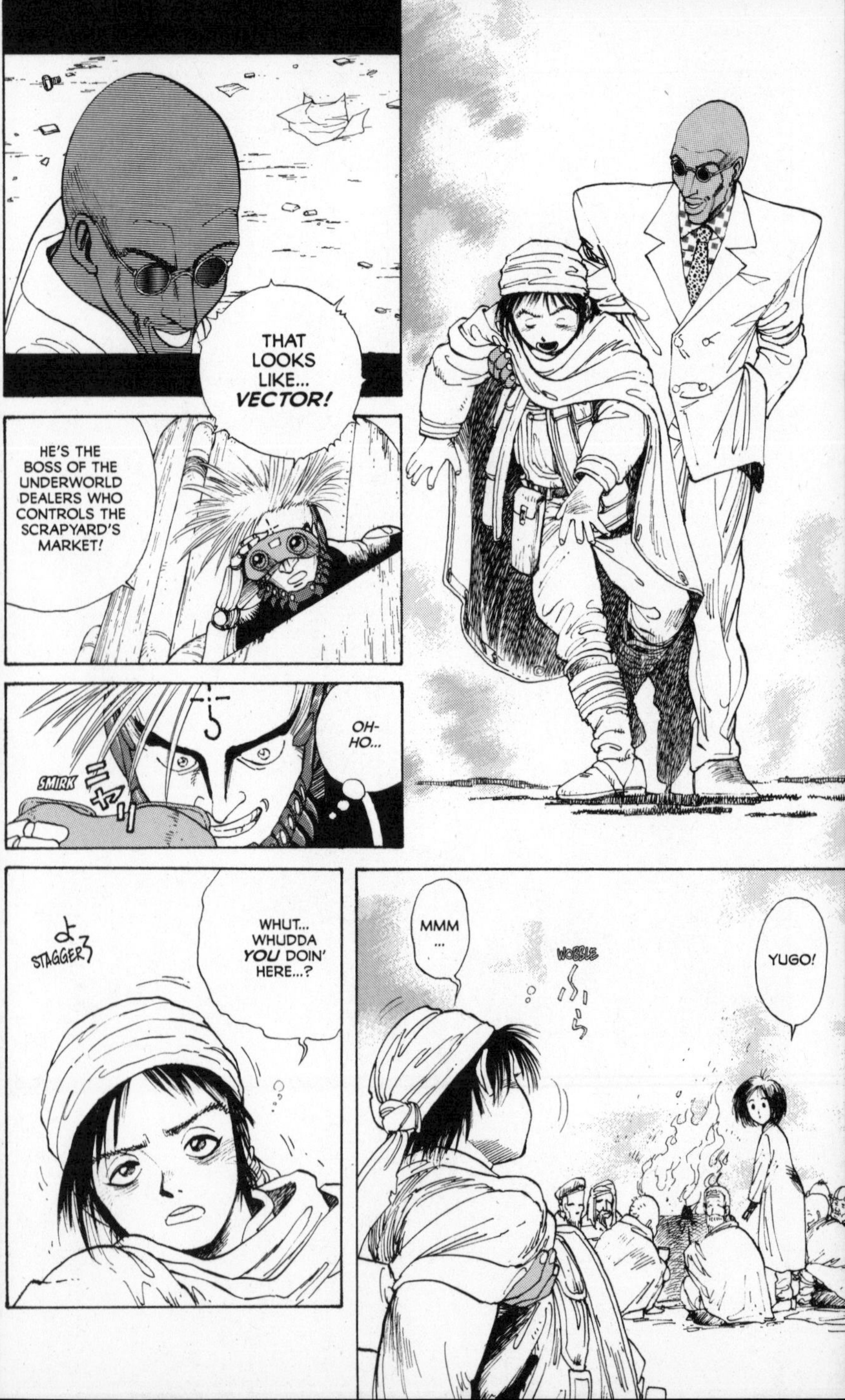

THAT LOOKS LIKE... VECTOR!
HE'S THE BOSS OF THE UNDERWORLD DEALERS WHO CONTROLS THE SCRAPYARD'S MARKET!
OH-HO...
SMIRK
YUGO!
WOBBLE
MMM ...
WHUT... WHUDDA YOU DOIN' HERE...?
STAGGER

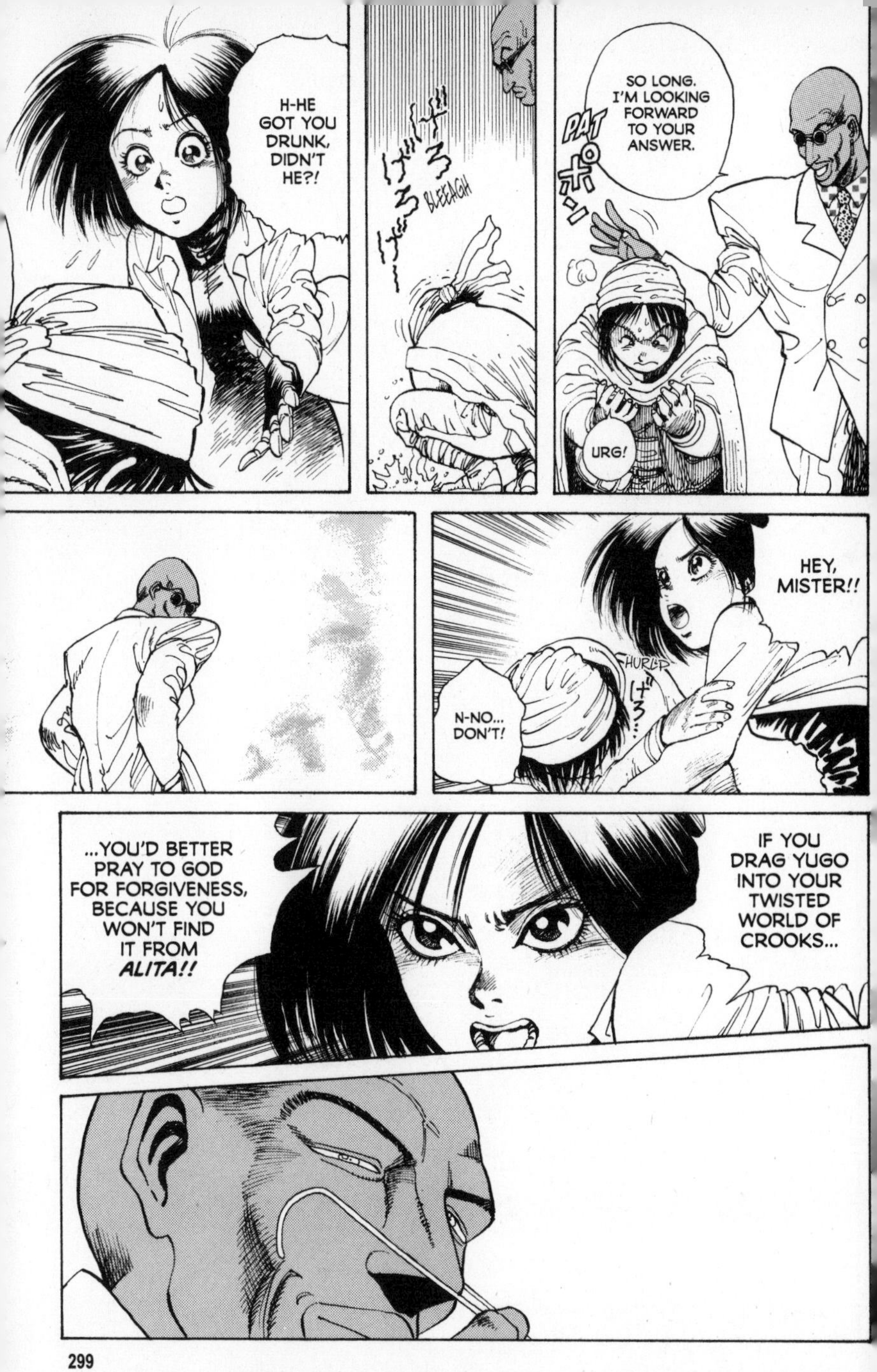
SO LONG. I'M LOOKING FORWARD TO YOUR ANSWER.
PAT
URG!
BLEEAGH
H-HE GOT YOU DRUNK, DIDN'T HE?!
HEY, MISTER!!
HURLP
N-NO... DON'T!
IF YOU DRAG YUGO INTO YOUR TWISTED WORLD OF CROOKS...
...YOU'D BETTER PRAY TO GOD FOR FORGIVENESS, BECAUSE YOU WON'T FIND IT FROM *ALITA!!*

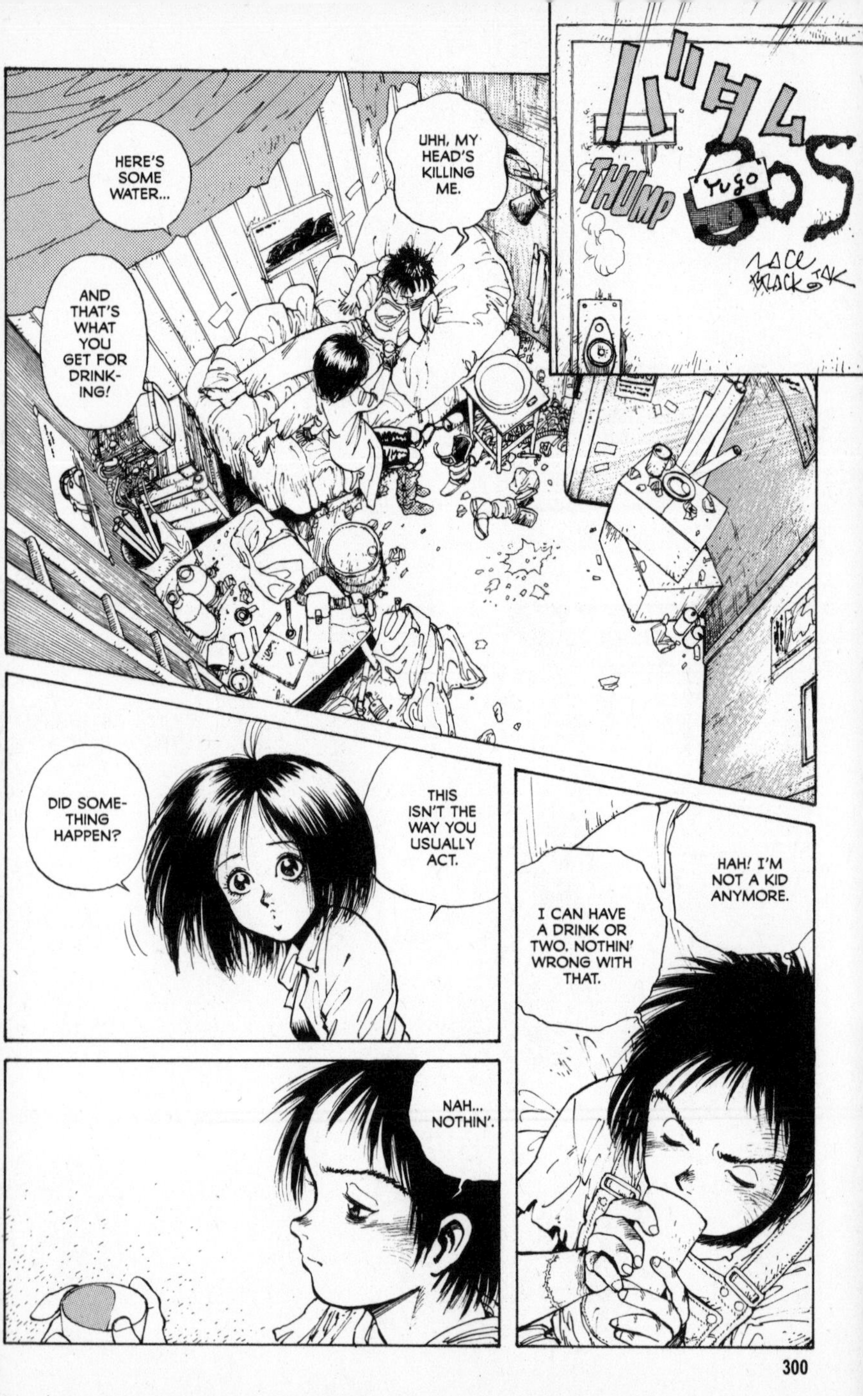
THUMP
YUGO
UHH, MY HEAD'S KILLING ME.
HERE'S SOME WATER...
AND THAT'S WHAT YOU GET FOR DRINK-ING!
HAH! I'M NOT A KID ANYMORE.
I CAN HAVE A DRINK OR TWO. NOTHIN' WRONG WITH THAT.
THIS ISN'T THE WAY YOU USUALLY ACT.
DID SOME-THING HAPPEN?
NAH... NOTHIN'.

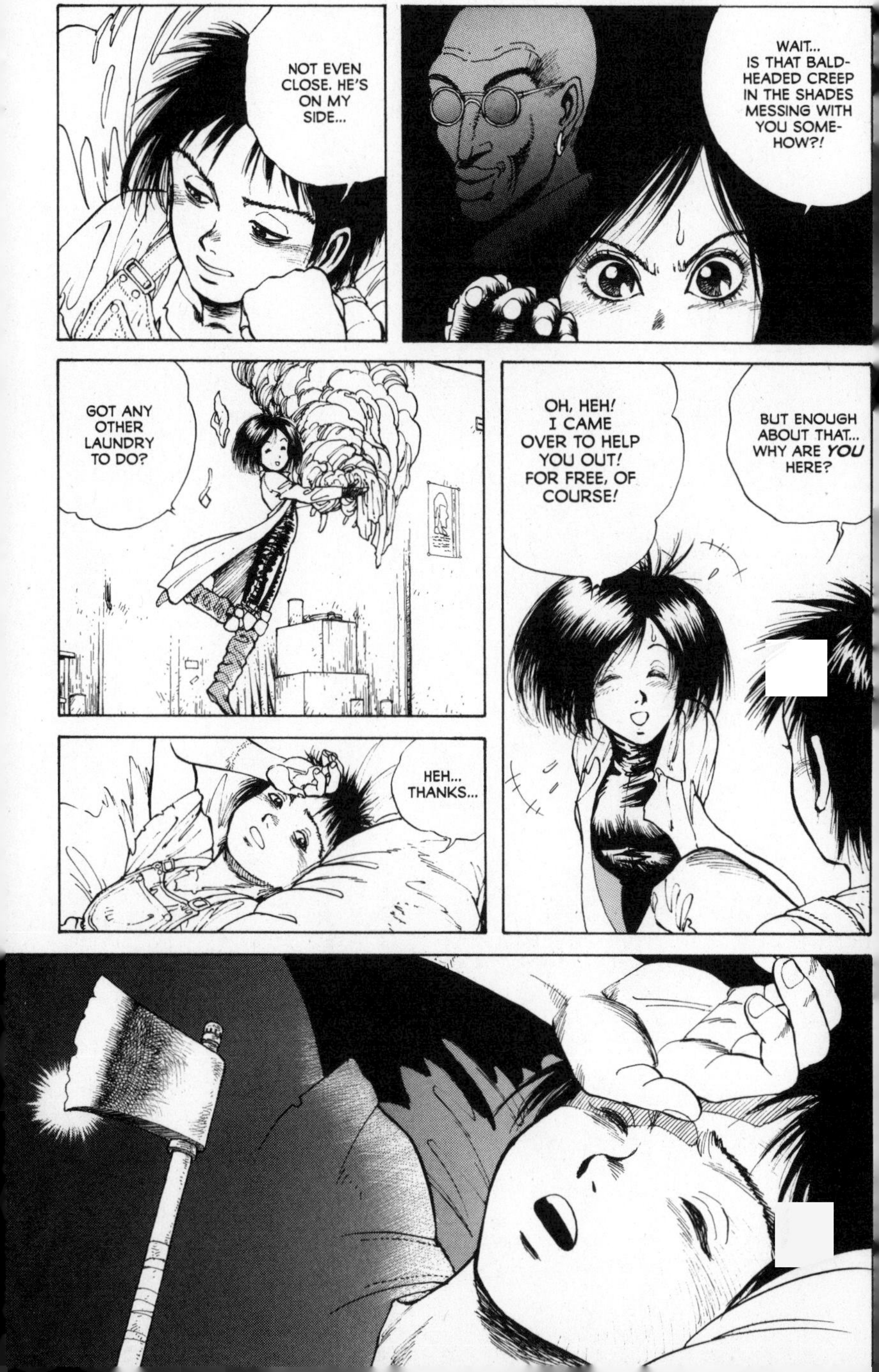
WAIT... IS THAT BALD-HEADED CREEP IN THE SHADES MESSING WITH YOU SOME-HOW?!
NOT EVEN CLOSE. HE'S ON MY SIDE...
BUT ENOUGH ABOUT THAT... WHY ARE *YOU* HERE?
OH, HEH! I CAME OVER TO HELP YOU OUT! FOR FREE, OF COURSE!
GOT ANY OTHER LAUNDRY TO DO?
HEH... THANKS...

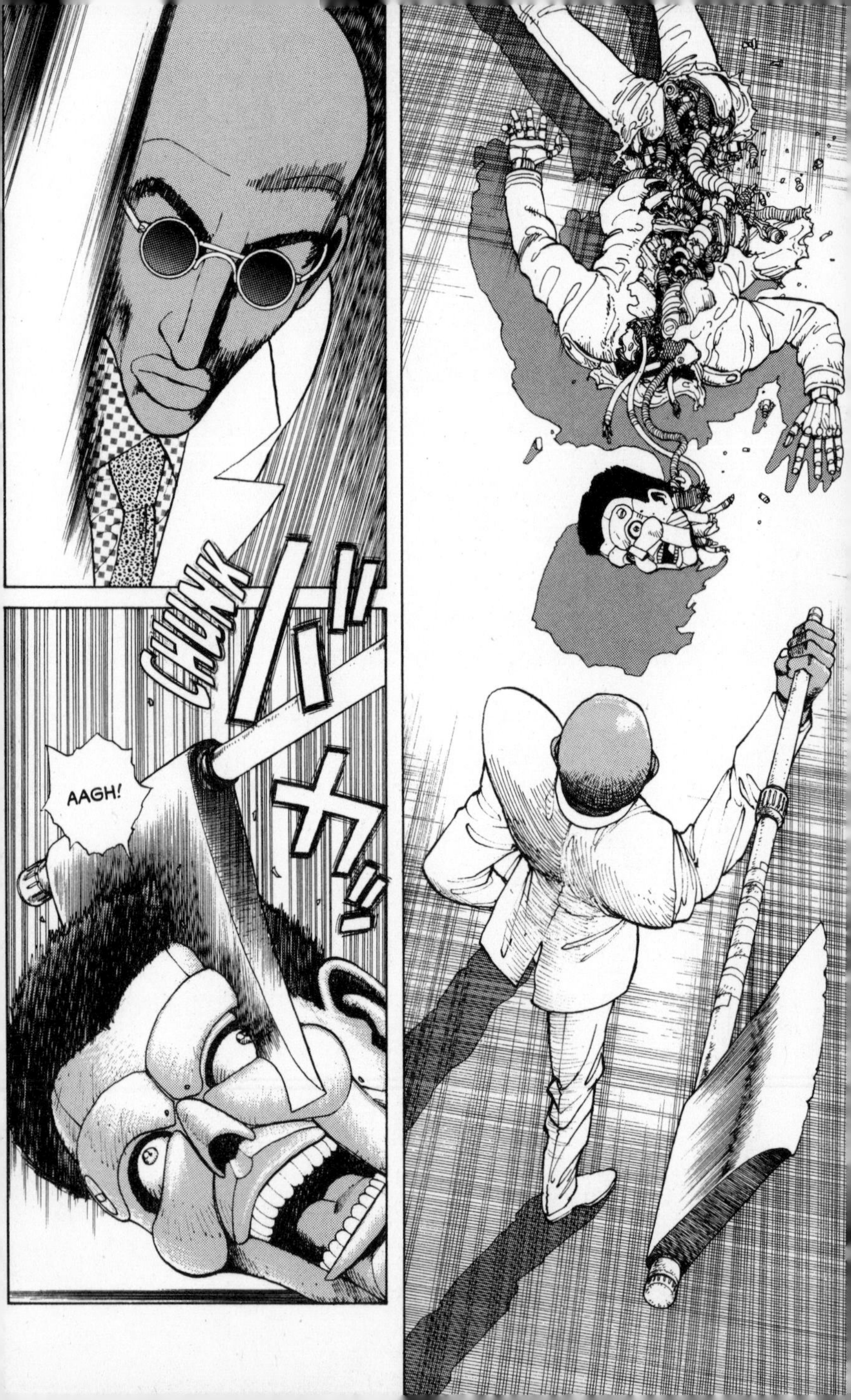
CHUNK
AAGH!

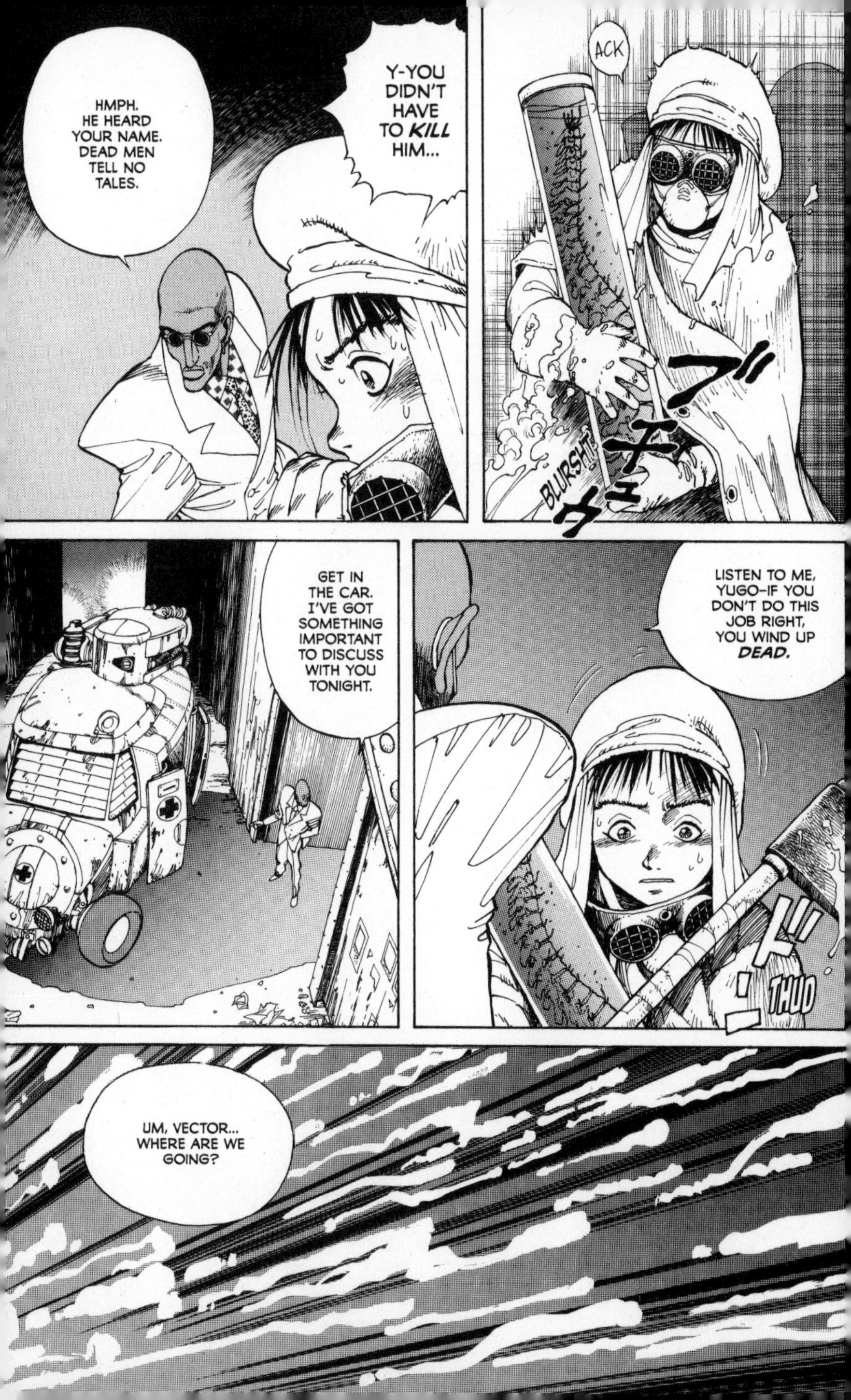
ACK
BLURSH!
Y-YOU DIDN'T HAVE TO *KILL* HIM...
HMPH. HE HEARD YOUR NAME. DEAD MEN TELL NO TALES.
LISTEN TO ME, YUGO–IF YOU DON'T DO THIS JOB RIGHT, YOU WIND UP *DEAD.*
THUD
GET IN THE CAR. I'VE GOT SOMETHING IMPORTANT TO DISCUSS WITH YOU TONIGHT.
UM, VECTOR... WHERE ARE WE GOING?

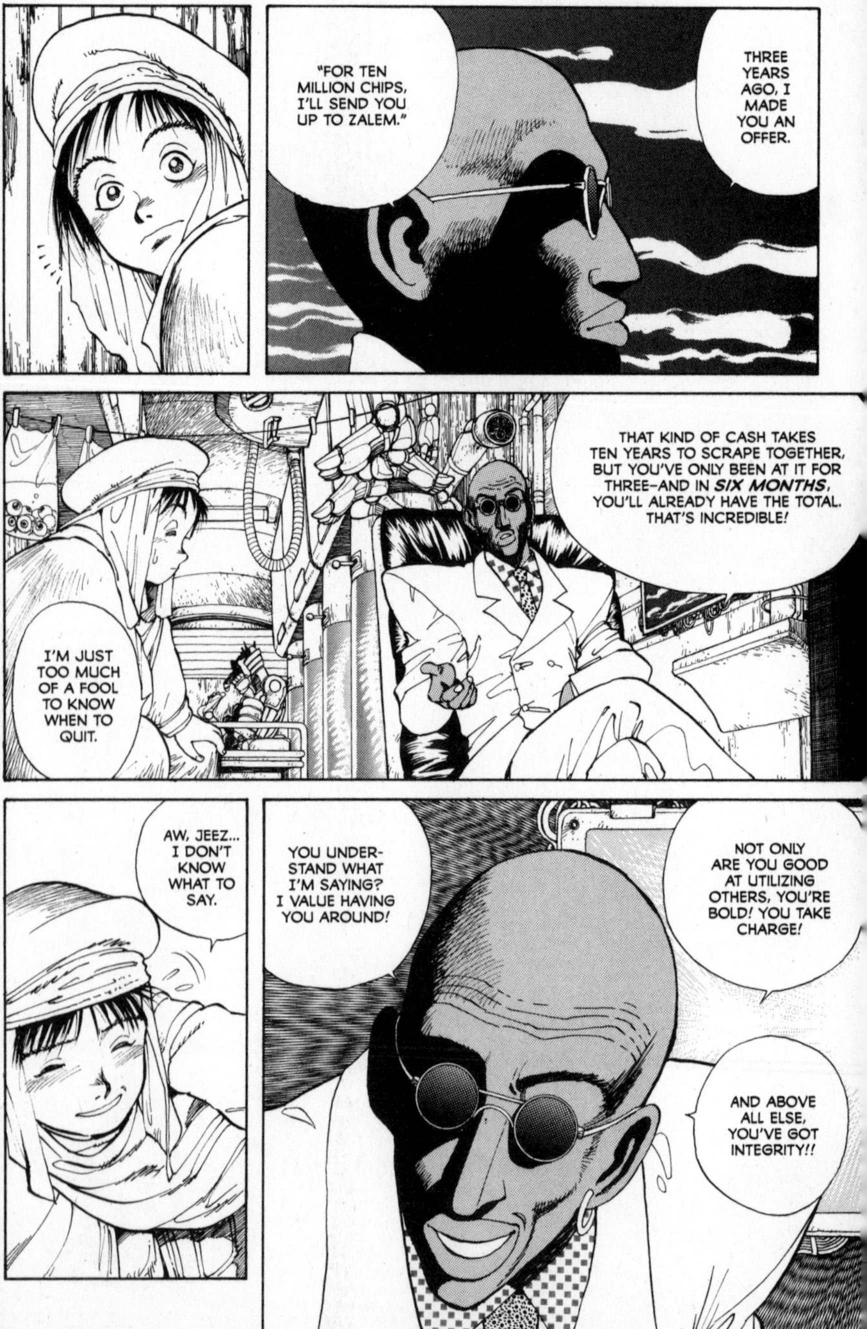
THREE YEARS AGO, I MADE YOU AN OFFER.
"FOR TEN MILLION CHIPS, I'LL SEND YOU UP TO ZALEM."
THAT KIND OF CASH TAKES TEN YEARS TO SCRAPE TOGETHER, BUT YOU'VE ONLY BEEN AT IT FOR THREE—AND IN *SIX MONTHS*, YOU'LL ALREADY HAVE THE TOTAL. THAT'S INCREDIBLE!
I'M JUST TOO MUCH OF A FOOL TO KNOW WHEN TO QUIT.
NOT ONLY ARE YOU GOOD AT UTILIZING OTHERS, YOU'RE BOLD! YOU TAKE CHARGE!
YOU UNDER-STAND WHAT I'M SAYING? I VALUE HAVING YOU AROUND!
AND ABOVE ALL ELSE, YOU'VE GOT INTEGRITY!!
AW, JEEZ... I DON'T KNOW WHAT TO SAY.

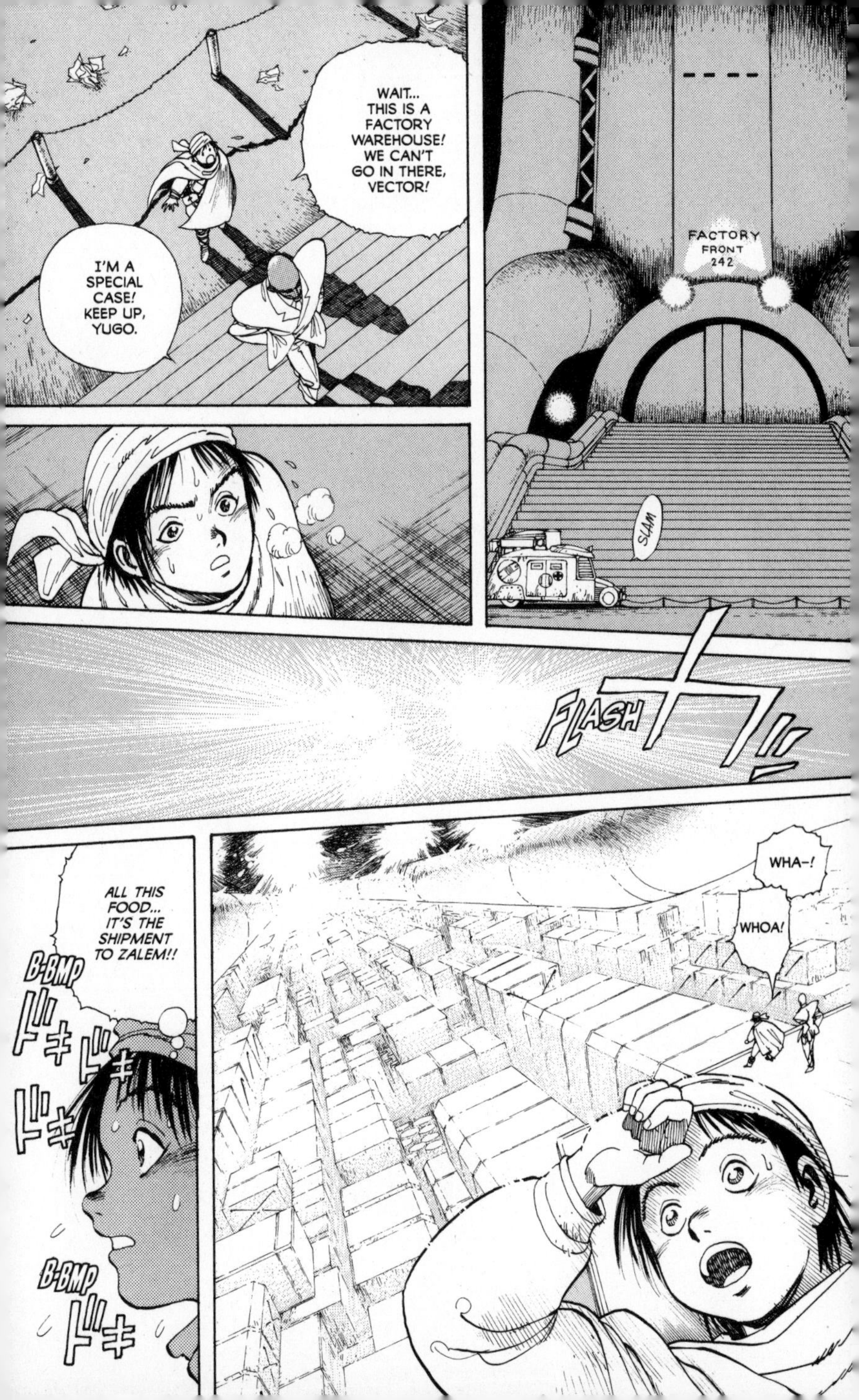
FACTORY FRONT 242
SLAM
WAIT... THIS IS A FACTORY WAREHOUSE! WE CAN'T GO IN THERE, VECTOR!
I'M A SPECIAL CASE! KEEP UP, YUGO.
FLASH
WHA-!
WHOA!
ALL THIS FOOD... IT'S THE SHIPMENT TO ZALEM!!
B-BMP
ドキドキ
ドキ
B-BMP
ドキ

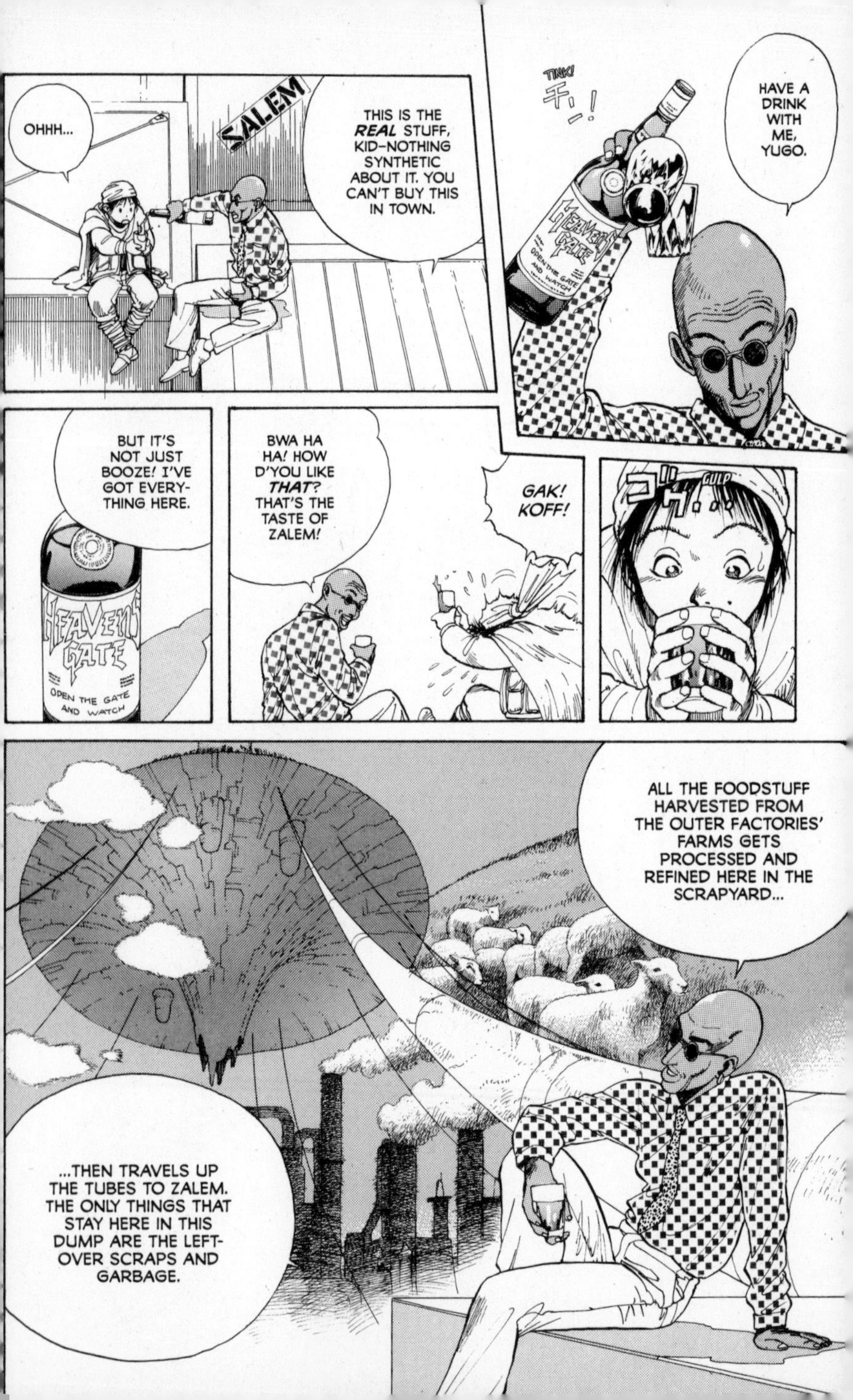
TINK!
HAVE A DRINK WITH ME, YUGO.
HEAVEN'S GATE
OPEN THE GATE AND WATCH
SALEM
THIS IS THE *REAL* STUFF, KID—NOTHING SYNTHETIC ABOUT IT. YOU CAN'T BUY THIS IN TOWN.
OHHH...
GULP
GAK! KOFF!
BWA HA HA! HOW D'YOU LIKE *THAT*? THAT'S THE TASTE OF ZALEM!
BUT IT'S NOT JUST BOOZE! I'VE GOT EVERYTHING HERE.
HEAVEN'S GATE
OPEN THE GATE AND WATCH
ALL THE FOODSTUFF HARVESTED FROM THE OUTER FACTORIES' FARMS GETS PROCESSED AND REFINED HERE IN THE SCRAPYARD...
...THEN TRAVELS UP THE TUBES TO ZALEM. THE ONLY THINGS THAT STAY HERE IN THIS DUMP ARE THE LEFTOVER SCRAPS AND GARBAGE.

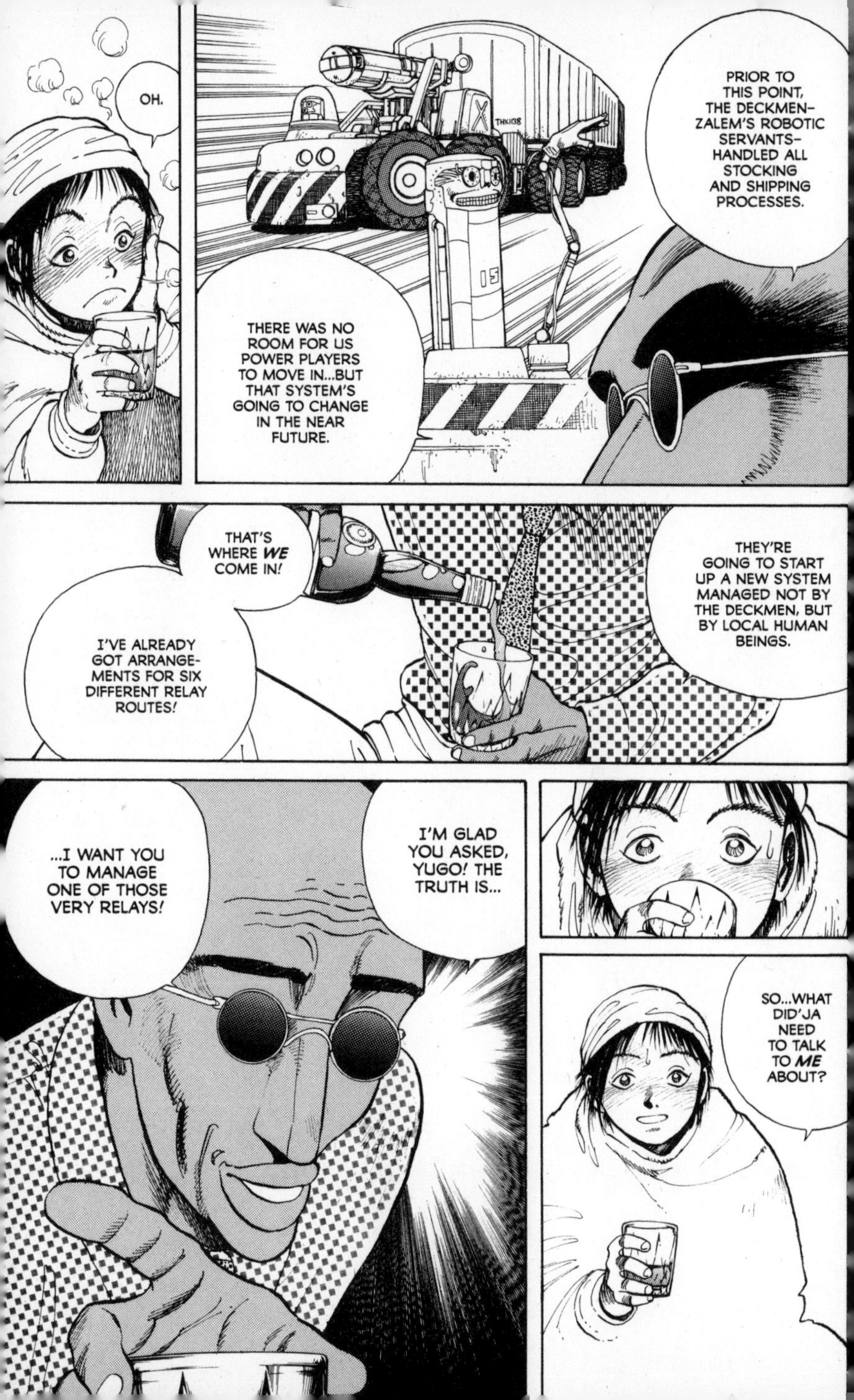
PRIOR TO THIS POINT, THE DECKMEN–ZALEM'S ROBOTIC SERVANTS–HANDLED ALL STOCKING AND SHIPPING PROCESSES.
THERE WAS NO ROOM FOR US POWER PLAYERS TO MOVE IN...BUT THAT SYSTEM'S GOING TO CHANGE IN THE NEAR FUTURE.
OH.
THEY'RE GOING TO START UP A NEW SYSTEM MANAGED NOT BY THE DECKMEN, BUT BY LOCAL HUMAN BEINGS.
THAT'S WHERE *WE* COME IN!
I'VE ALREADY GOT ARRANGE-MENTS FOR SIX DIFFERENT RELAY ROUTES!
SO...WHAT DID'JA NEED TO TALK TO *ME* ABOUT?
I'M GLAD YOU ASKED, YUGO! THE TRUTH IS...
...I WANT YOU TO MANAGE ONE OF THOSE VERY RELAYS!

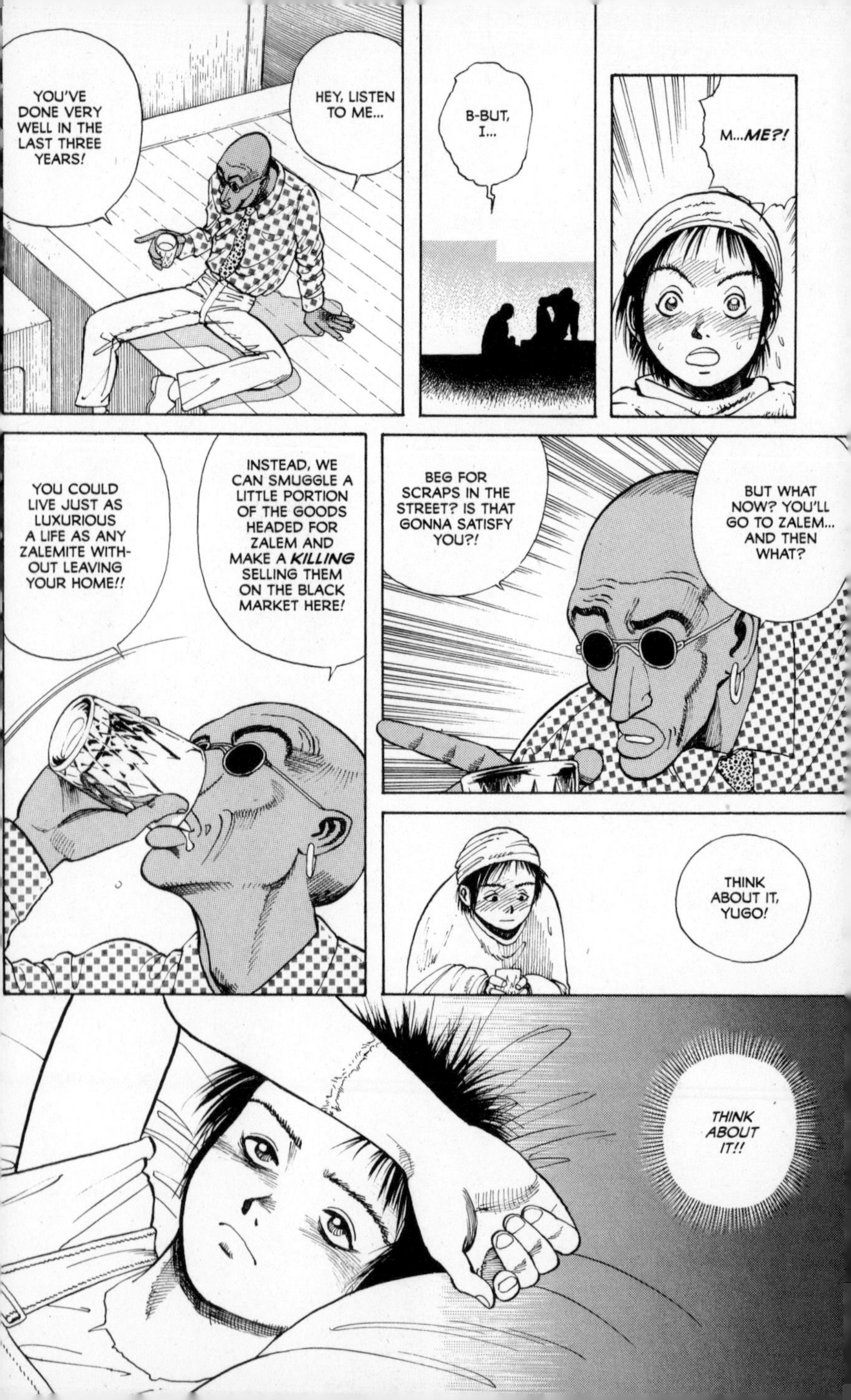
M...*ME?!*
B-BUT, I...
HEY, LISTEN TO ME...
YOU'VE DONE VERY WELL IN THE LAST THREE YEARS!
BUT WHAT NOW? YOU'LL GO TO ZALEM... AND THEN WHAT?
BEG FOR SCRAPS IN THE STREET? IS THAT GONNA SATISFY YOU?!
THINK ABOUT IT, YUGO!
INSTEAD, WE CAN SMUGGLE A LITTLE PORTION OF THE GOODS HEADED FOR ZALEM AND MAKE A *KILLING* SELLING THEM ON THE BLACK MARKET HERE!
YOU COULD LIVE JUST AS LUXURIOUS A LIFE AS ANY ZALEMITE WITHOUT LEAVING YOUR HOME!!
THINK ABOUT IT!!

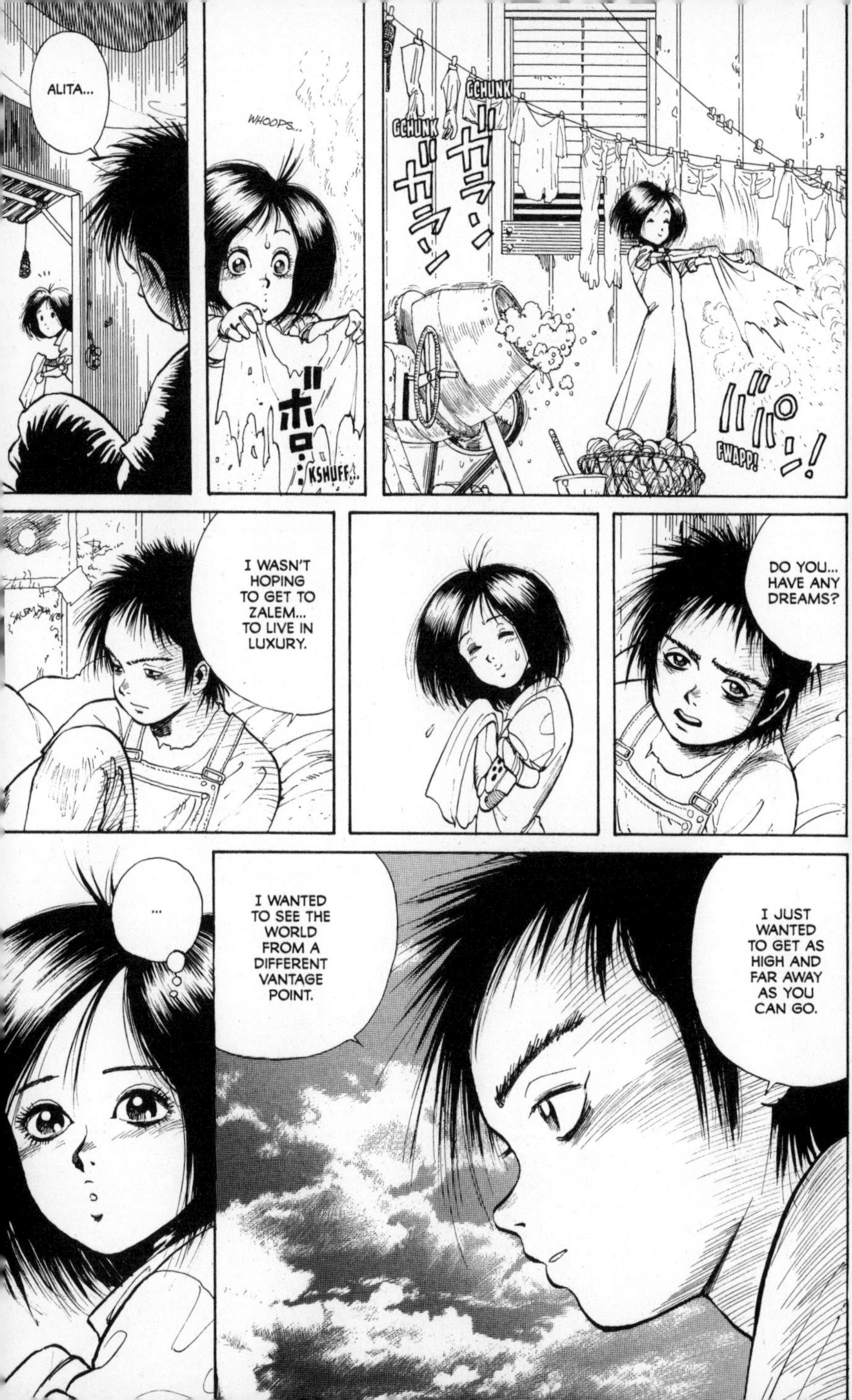

GCHUNK
GCHUNK
FWAPP!
WHOOPS...
KSHUFF...
ALITA...
DO YOU... HAVE ANY DREAMS?
I WASN'T HOPING TO GET TO ZALEM... TO LIVE IN LUXURY.
I JUST WANTED TO GET AS HIGH AND FAR AWAY AS YOU CAN GO.
I WANTED TO SEE THE WORLD FROM A DIFFERENT VANTAGE POINT.
...

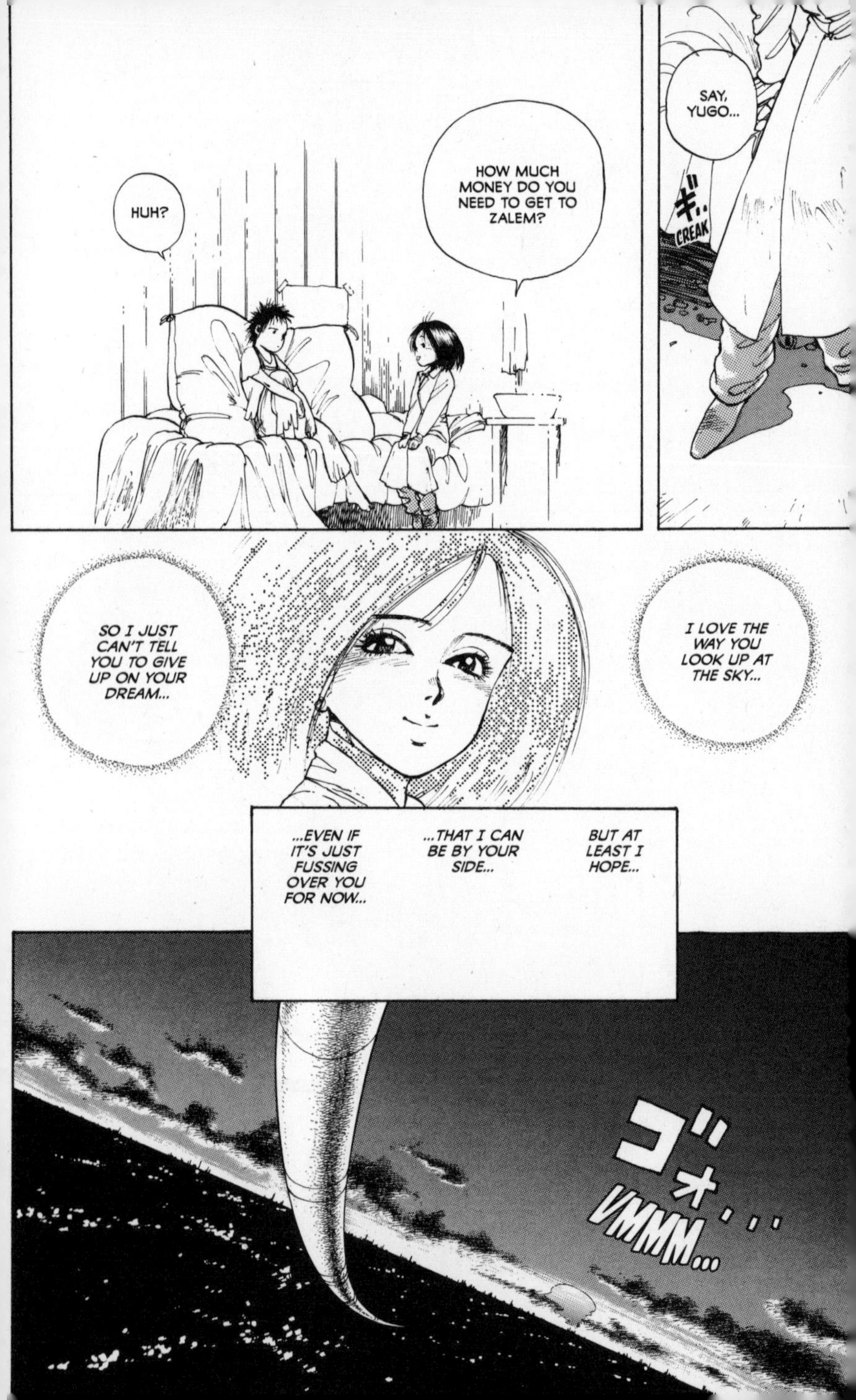

SAY, YUGO...
ギ
CREAK
HOW MUCH MONEY DO YOU NEED TO GET TO ZALEM?
HUH?
I LOVE THE WAY YOU LOOK UP AT THE SKY...
SO I JUST CAN'T TELL YOU TO GIVE UP ON YOUR DREAM...
BUT AT LEAST I HOPE...
...THAT I CAN BE BY YOUR SIDE...
...EVEN IF IT'S JUST FUSSING OVER YOU FOR NOW...
VMMM...

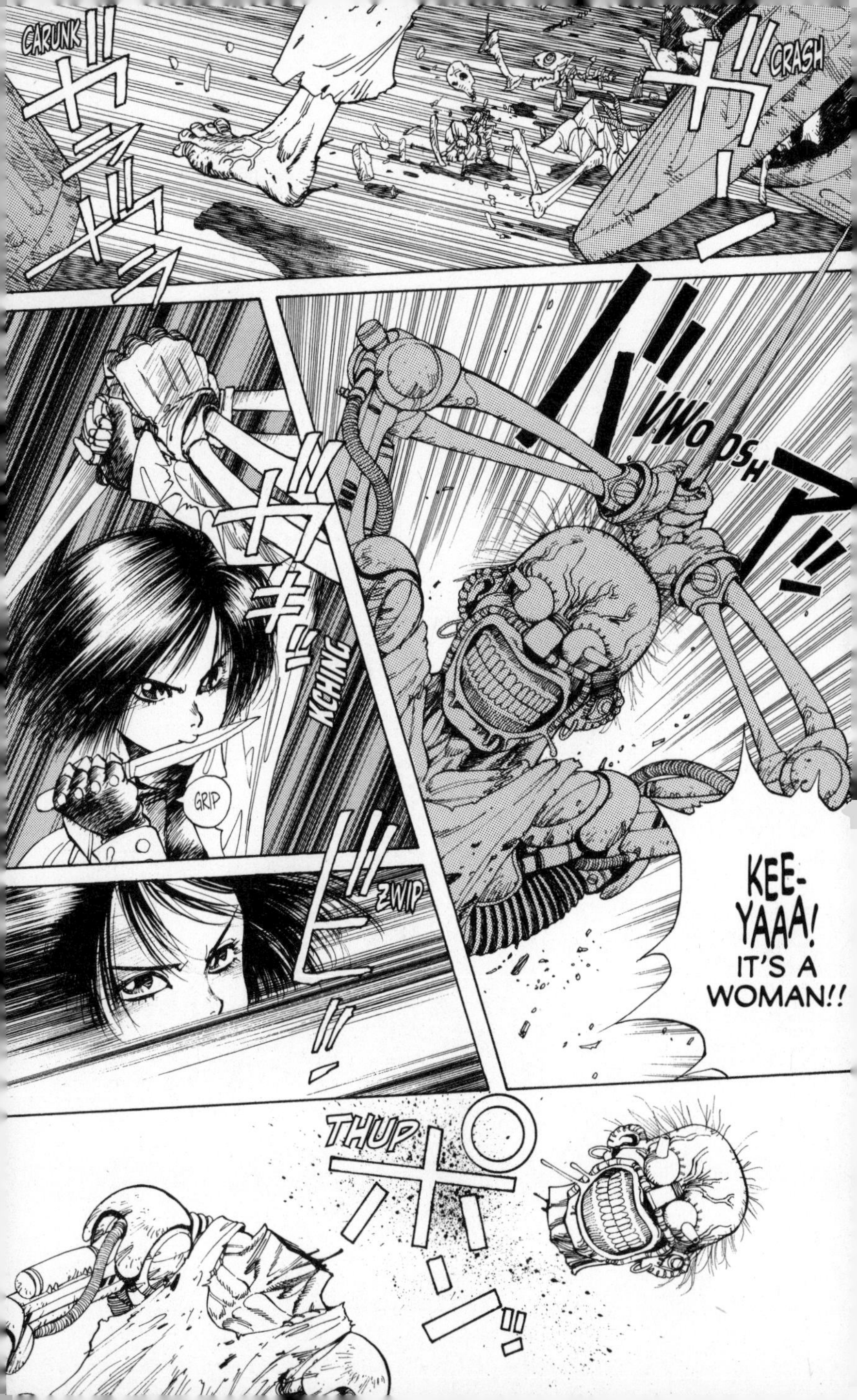
CRASH
CARUNK
VWOOSH
KEE-YAAA! IT'S A WOMAN!!
KCHING
GRIP
ZWIP
THUP

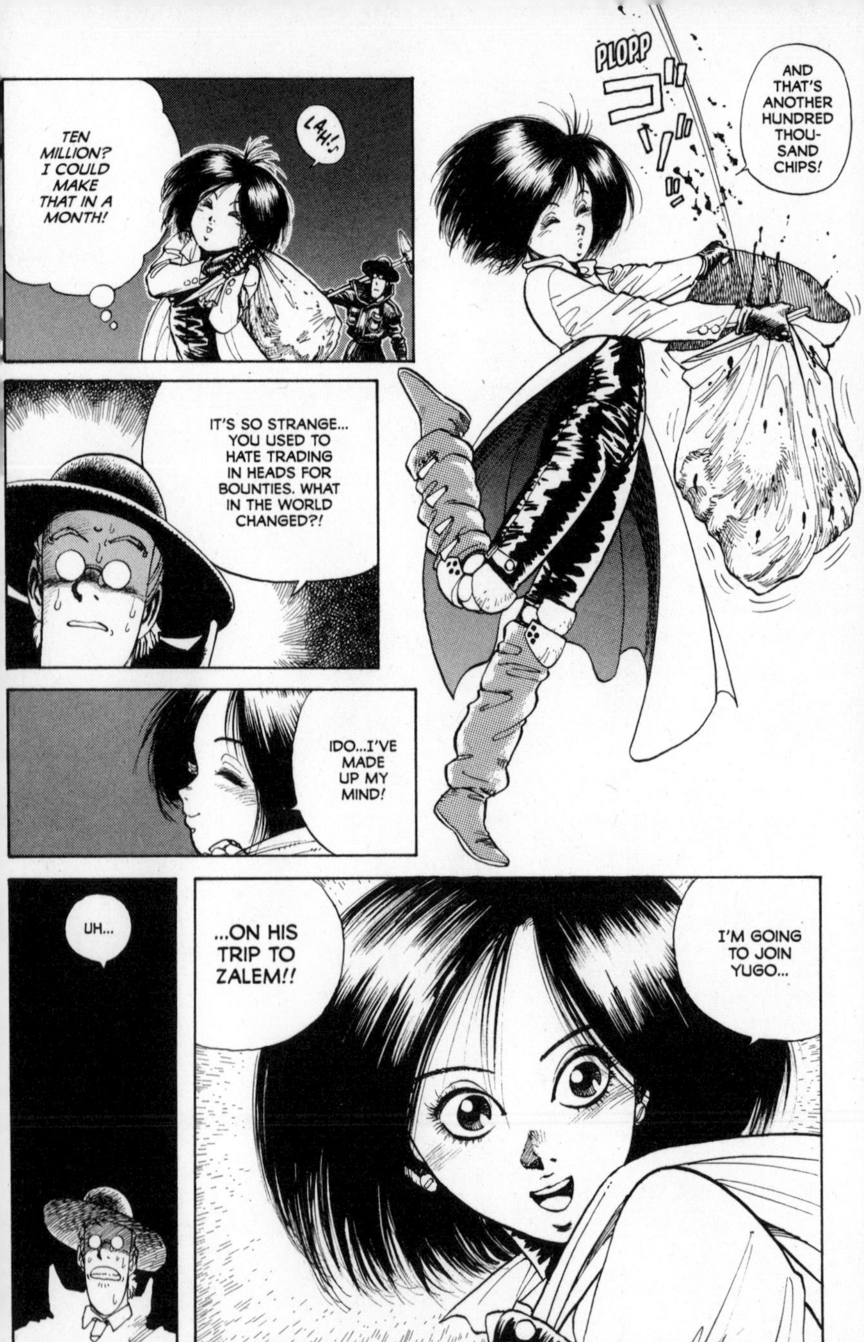
PLOPP
AND THAT'S ANOTHER HUNDRED THOU-SAND CHIPS!
LAH!
TEN MILLION? I COULD MAKE THAT IN A MONTH!
IT'S SO STRANGE... YOU USED TO HATE TRADING IN HEADS FOR BOUNTIES. WHAT IN THE WORLD CHANGED?!
IDO...I'VE MADE UP MY MIND!
I'M GOING TO JOIN YUGO...
...ON HIS TRIP TO ZALEM!!
UH...

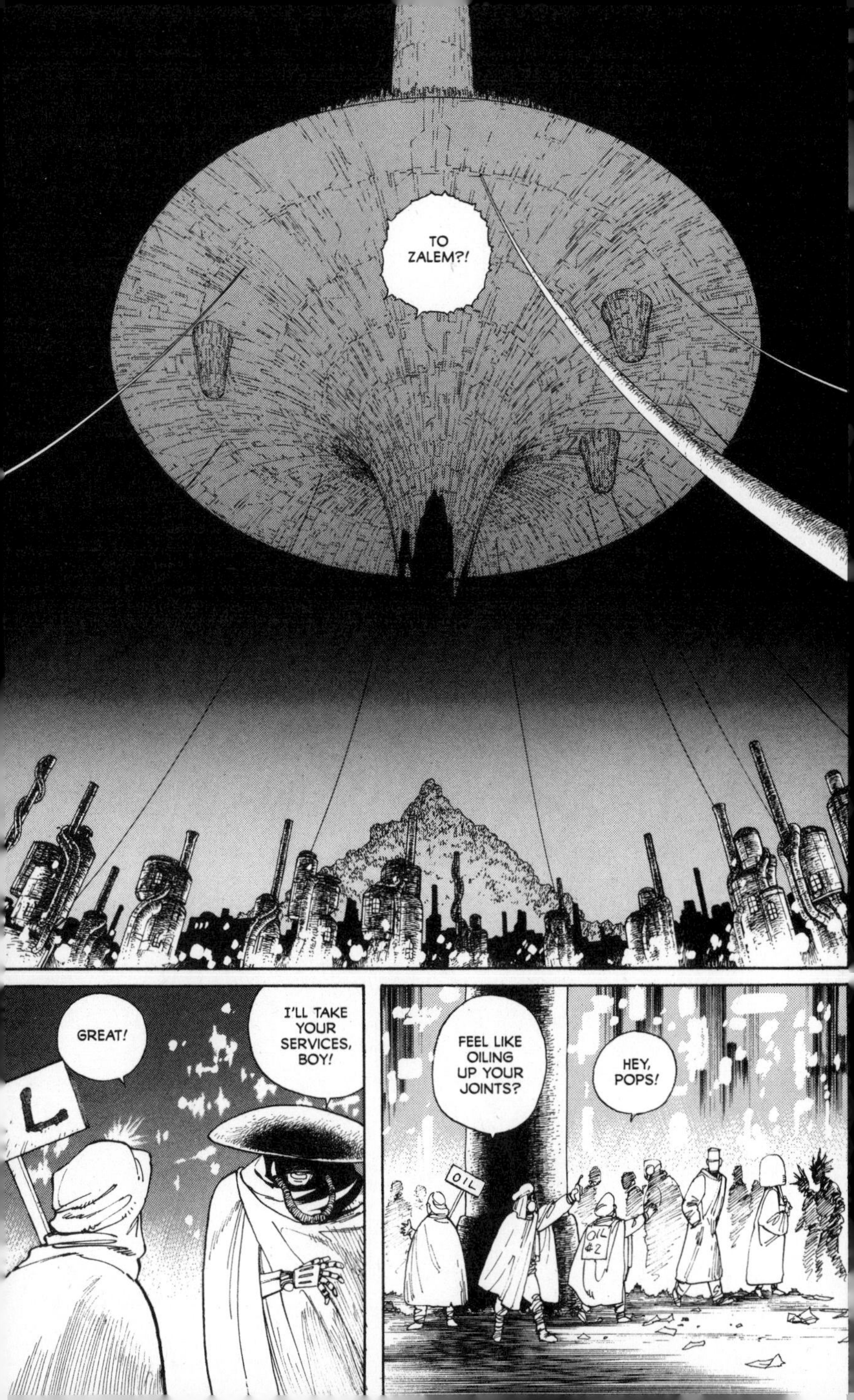
TO ZALEM?!
HEY, POPS!
FEEL LIKE OILING UP YOUR JOINTS?
OIL
OIL #2
I'LL TAKE YOUR SERVICES, BOY!
GREAT!
L

HEE HEE!

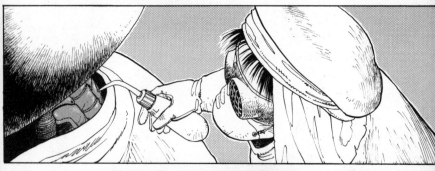

HEH... SO *THIS* IS HOW YOU'VE BEEN DOING IT!

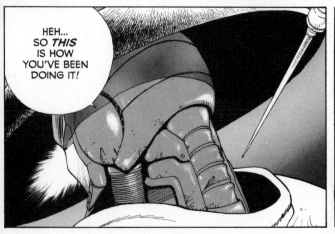

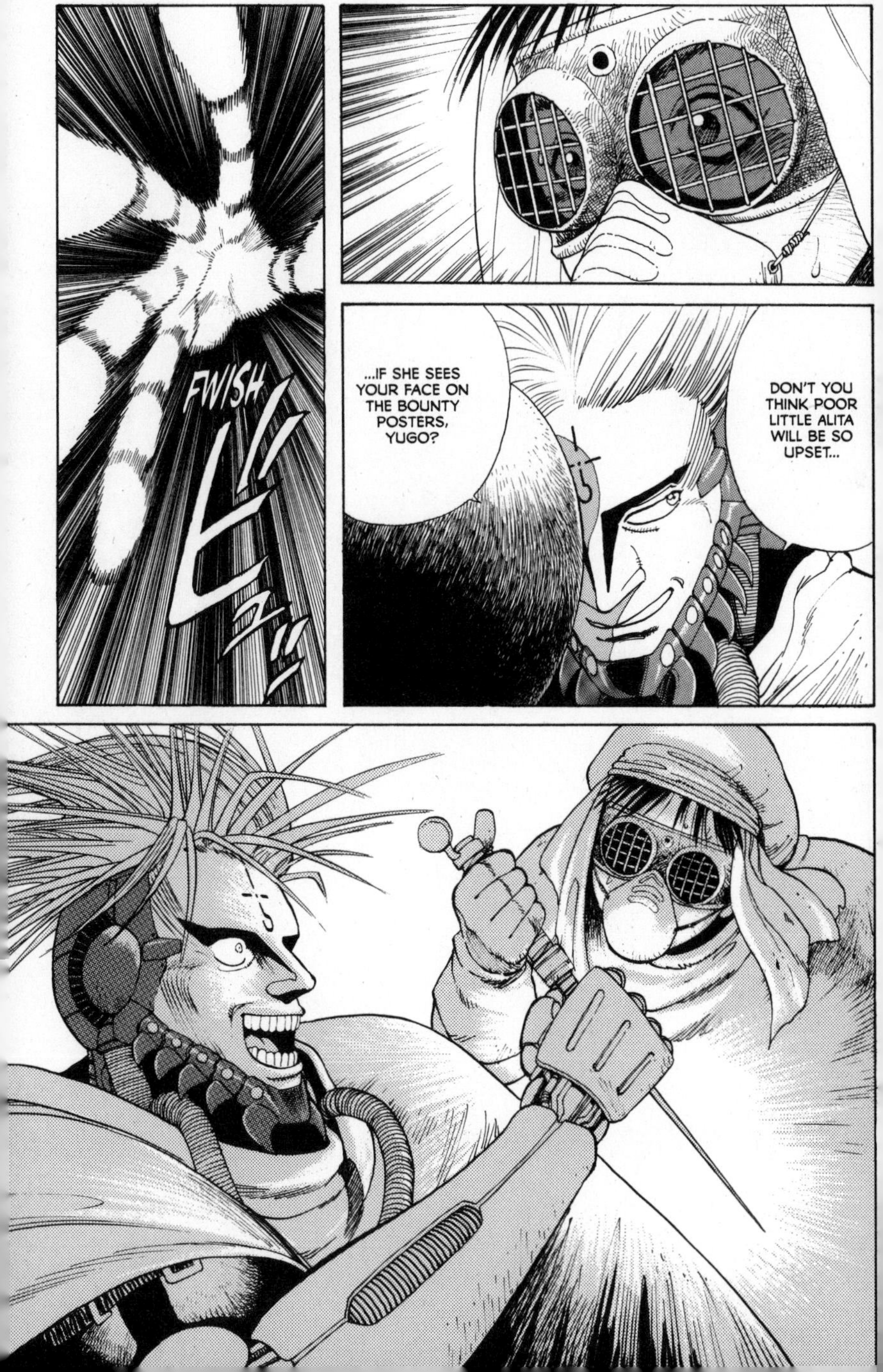
DON'T YOU THINK POOR LITTLE ALITA WILL BE SO UPSET...
...IF SHE SEES YOUR FACE ON THE BOUNTY POSTERS, YUGO?
FWISH

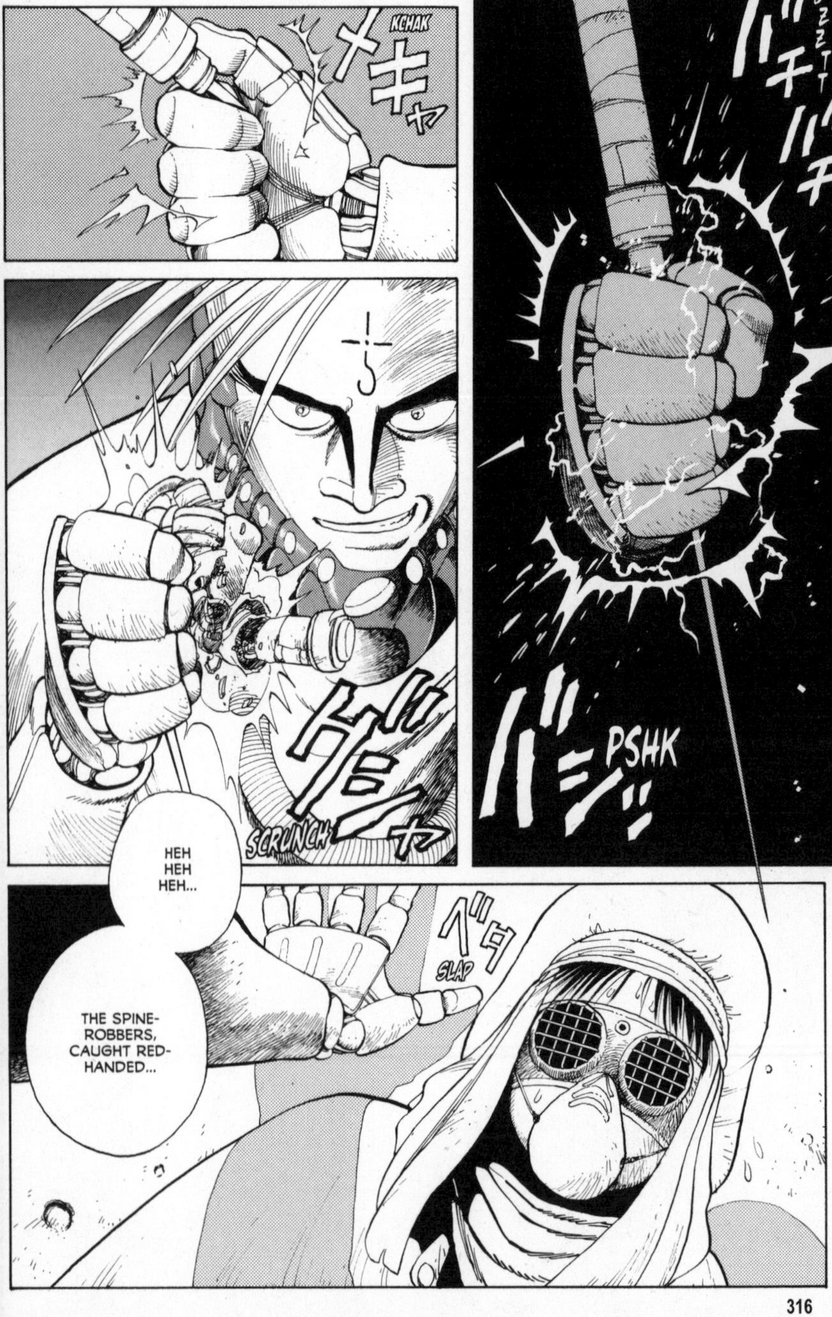
バチバチ
BZZTTT
バシッ
PSHK
メキャ
KCHAK
グシャ
SCRUNCH
ベタ
SLAP
HEH HEH HEH...
THE SPINE-ROBBERS, CAUGHT RED-HANDED...

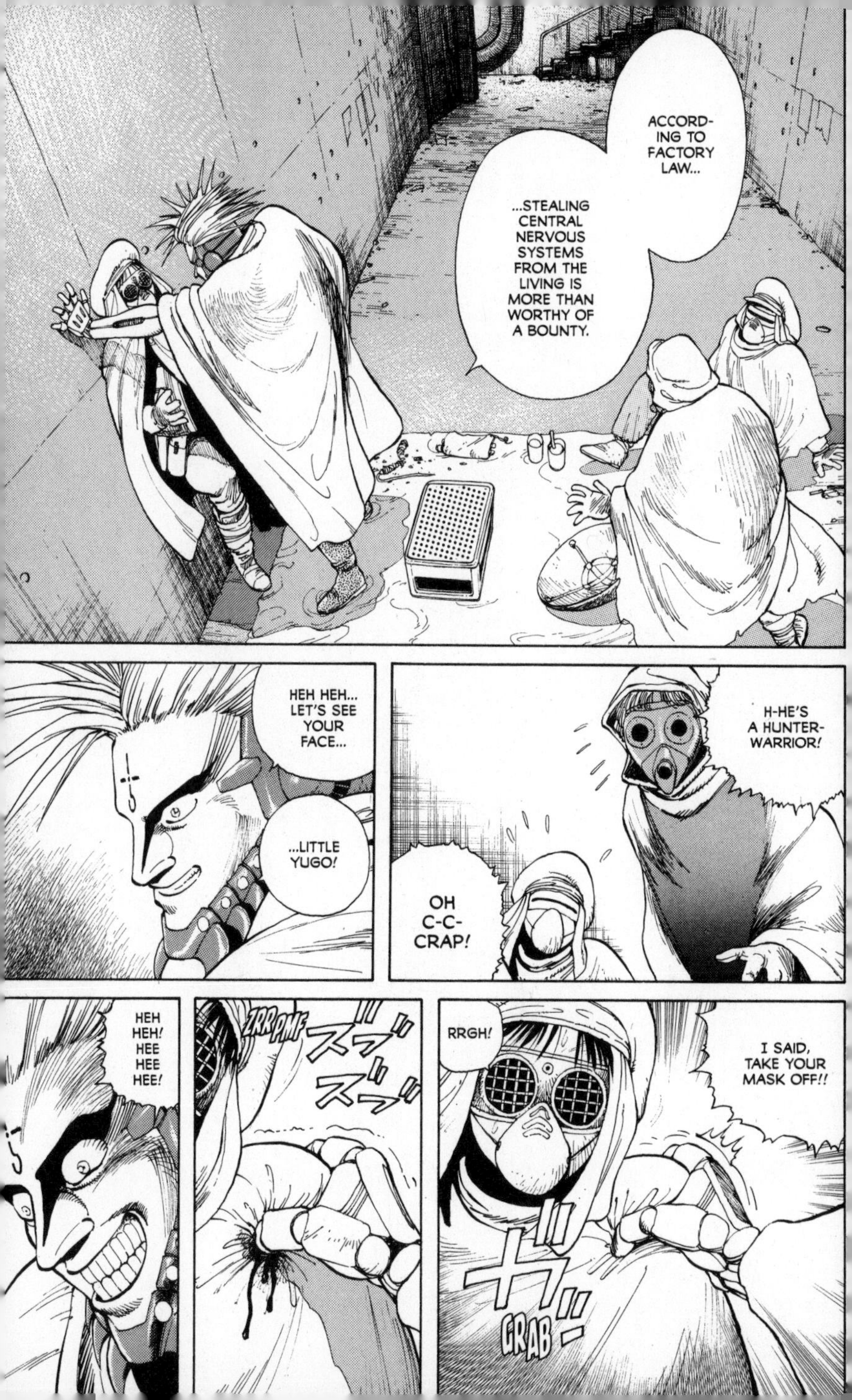
ACCORD-
ING TO
FACTORY
LAW...
...STEALING
CENTRAL
NERVOUS
SYSTEMS
FROM THE
LIVING IS
MORE THAN
WORTHY OF
A BOUNTY.
H-HE'S
A HUNTER-
WARRIOR!
OH
C-C-
CRAP!
HEH HEH...
LET'S SEE
YOUR
FACE...
...LITTLE
YUGO!
I SAID,
TAKE YOUR
MASK OFF!!
RRGH!
ガッ
GRAB
ZRR PMF
ズブッ
ズブッ
HEH
HEH!
HEE
HEE
HEE!

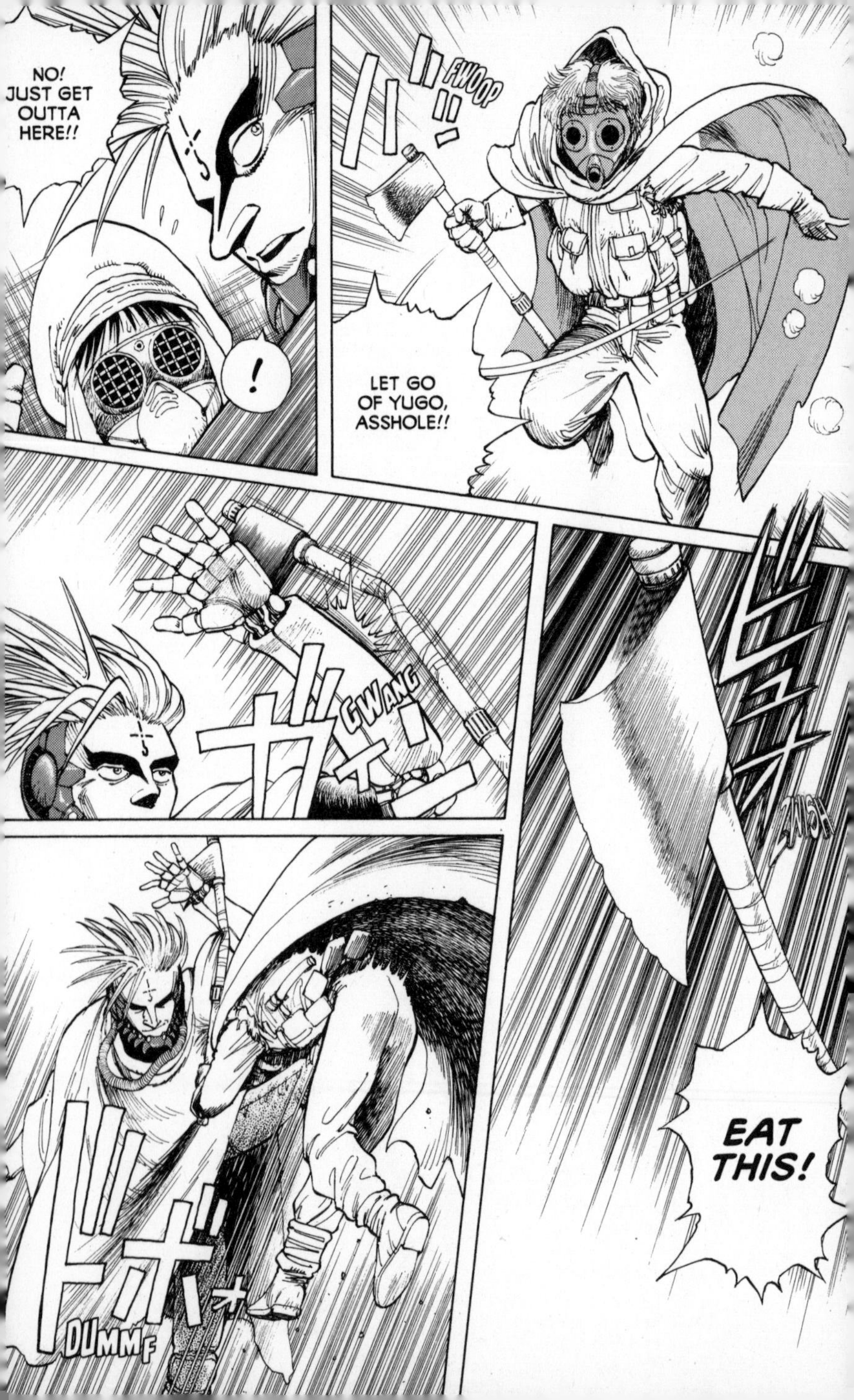
FWOOP
LET GO OF YUGO, ASSHOLE!!
NO! JUST GET OUTTA HERE!!
!
ZWISH
EAT THIS!
GWANG
DUMMF

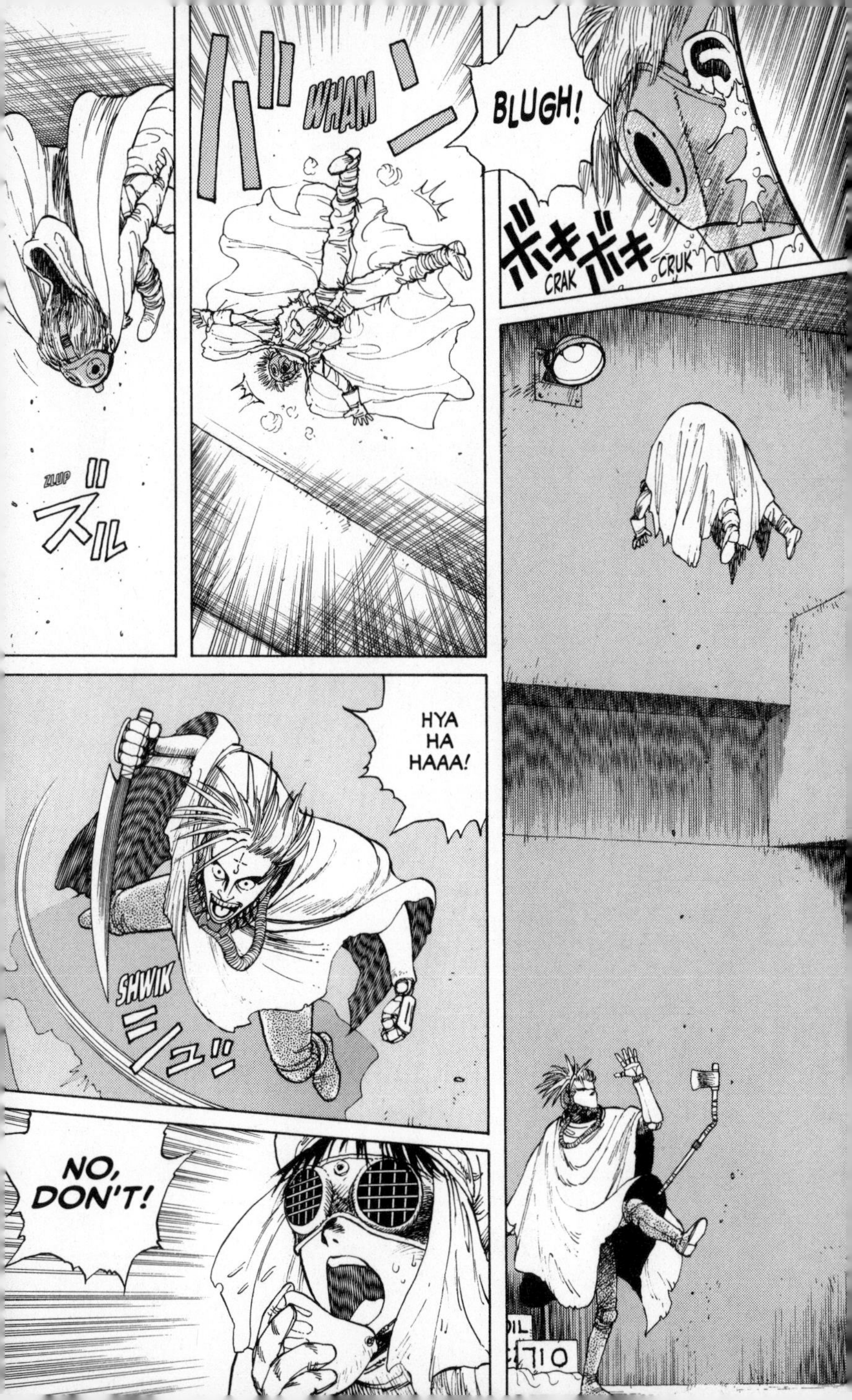
BLUGH!
ボキ CRAK
ボキ CRUK
バーン
WHAM
ズル
ZLUP
OIL
710
HYA HA HAAA!
SHWIK
ミシュッ
NO, DON'T!

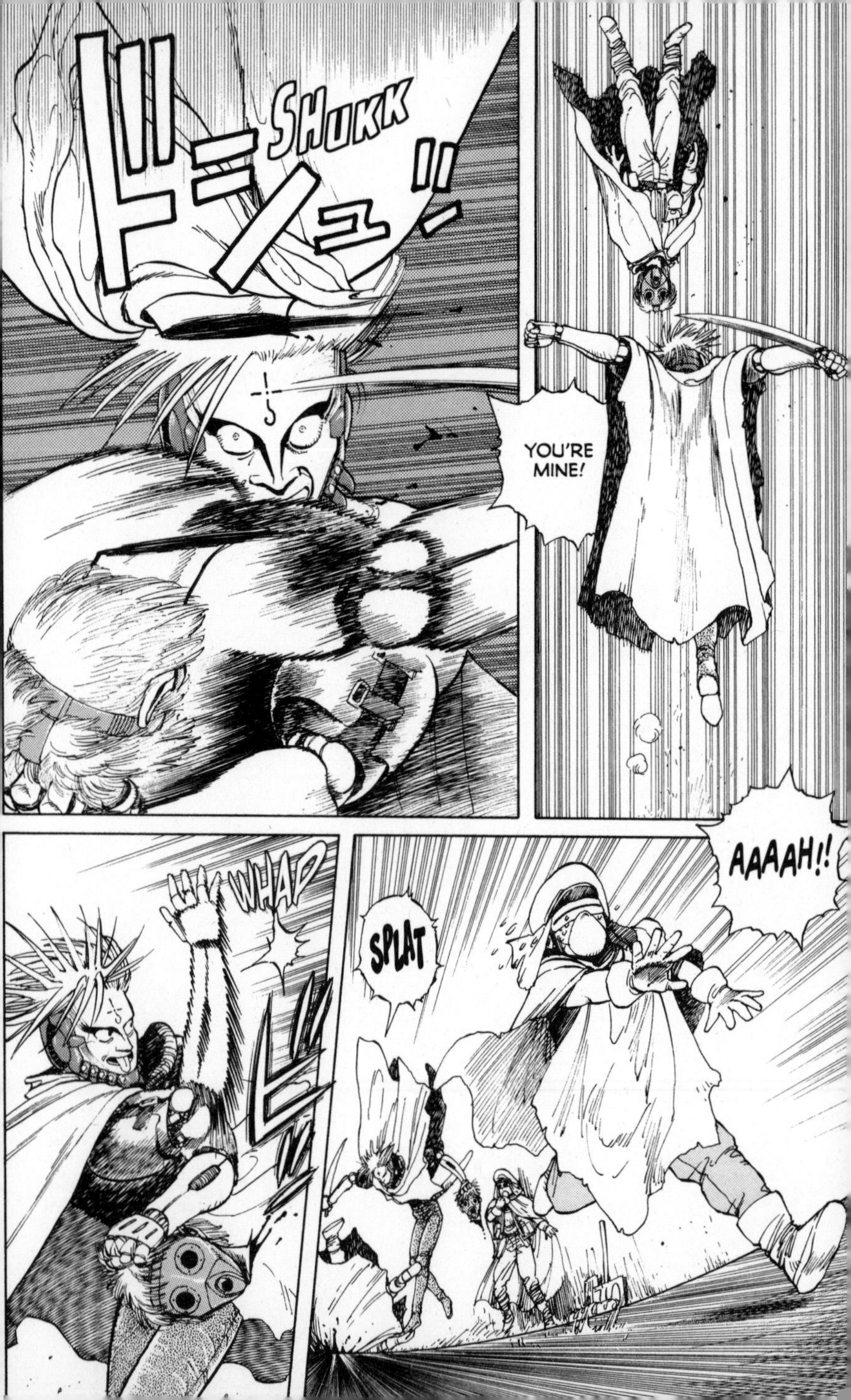

YOU'RE MINE!
ドシュー
SHUKK
AAAAH!!
SPLAT
WHAP

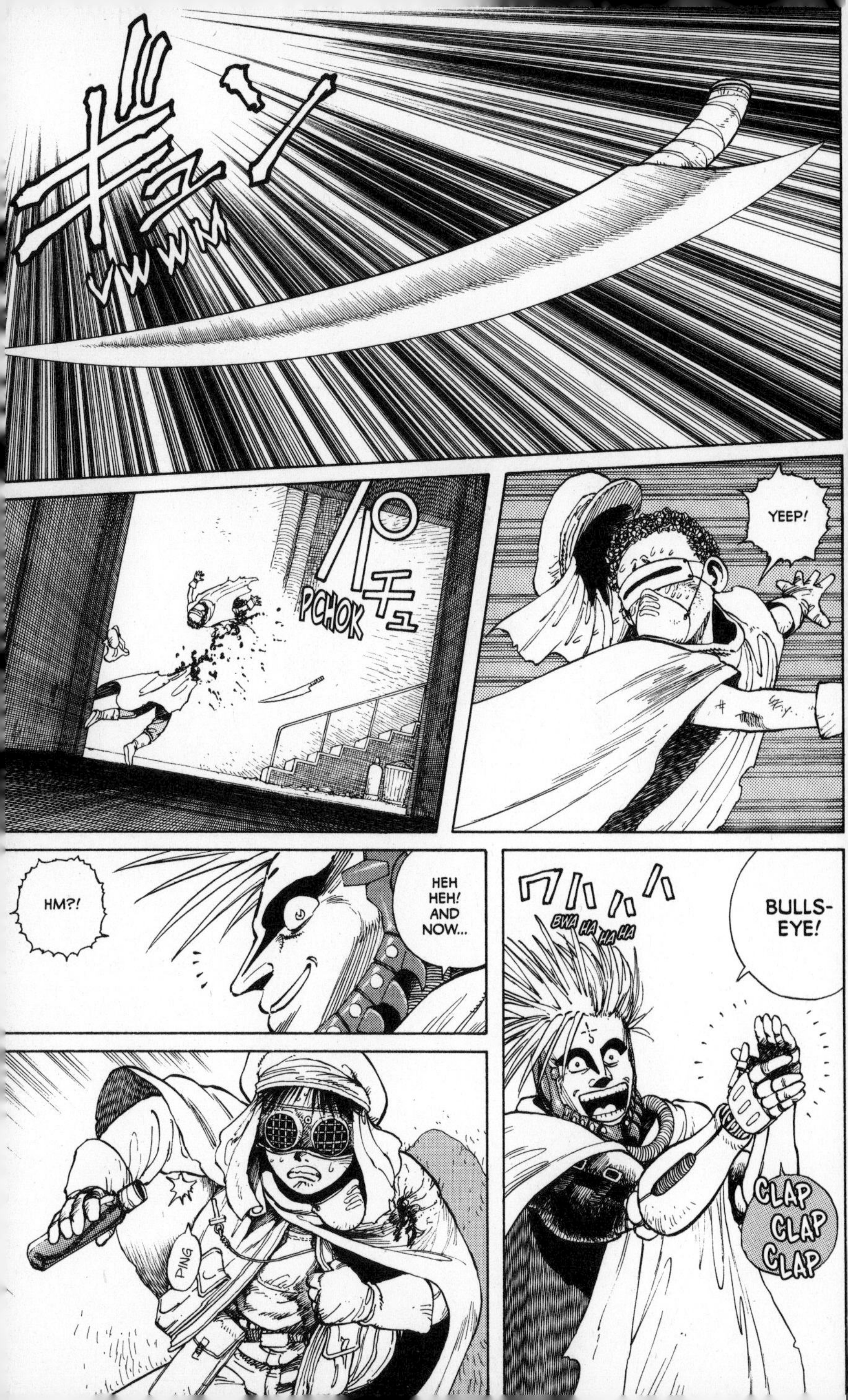
VWWM
YEEP!
パチュ
PCHOK
ワハハハ
BWA HA HA HA
BULLS-EYE!
CLAP CLAP CLAP
HEH HEH! AND NOW...
HM?!
PING

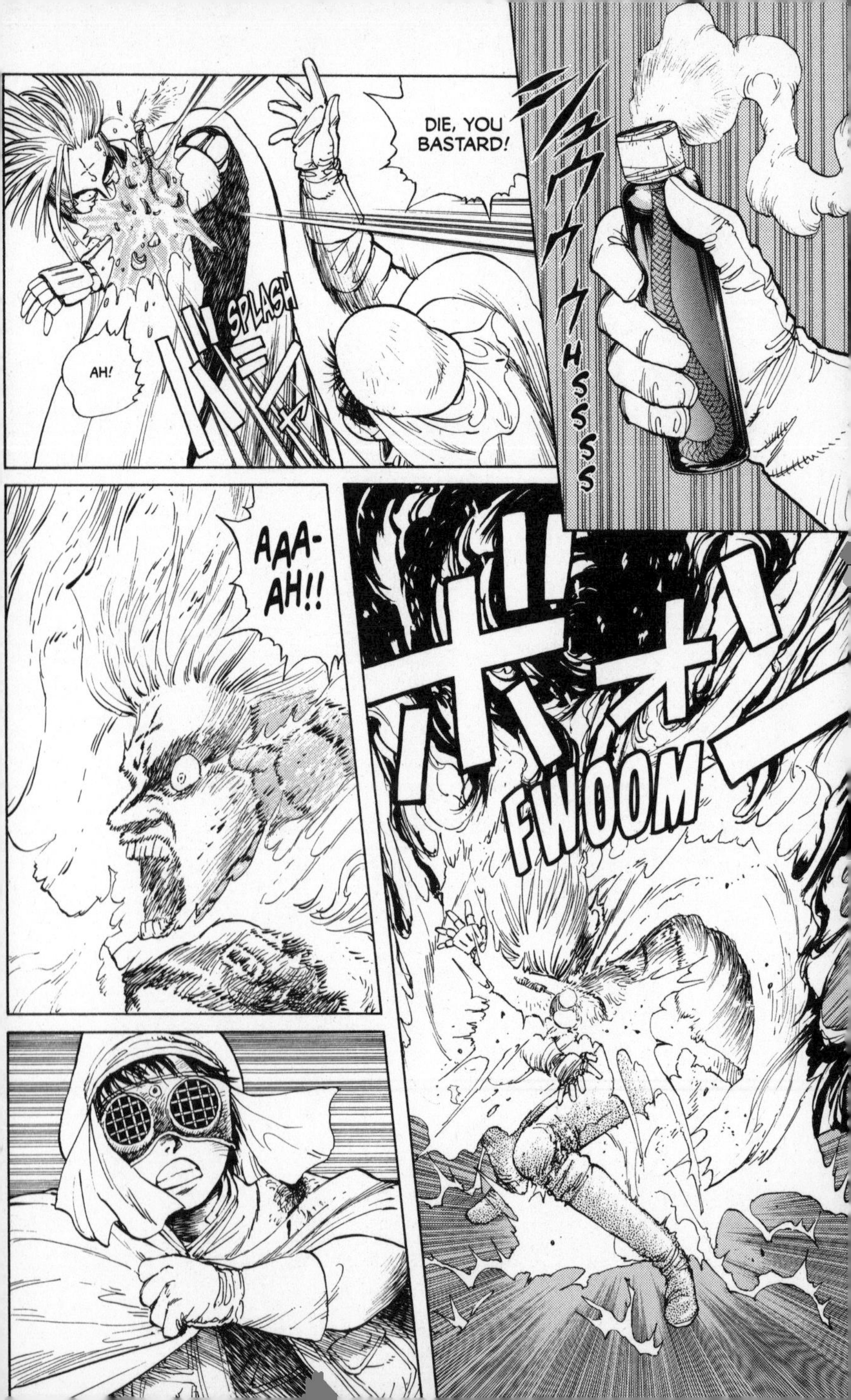
HSSSSS
DIE, YOU BASTARD!
SPLASH
AH!
FWOOM
AAA-AH!!

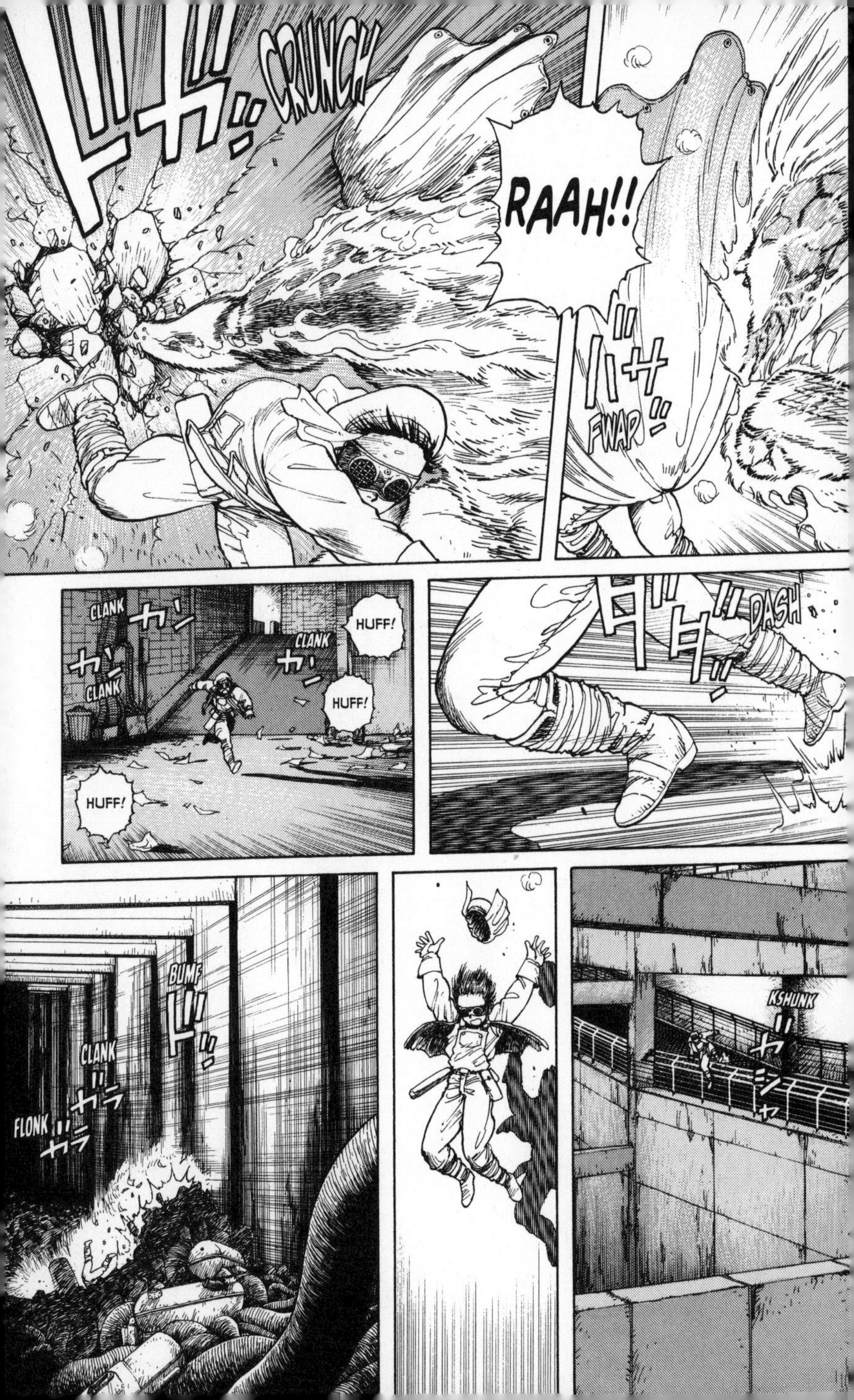
RAAH!!
FWAP!!
CRUNCH
DASH
CLANK
HUFF!
CLANK
HUFF!
CLANK
HUFF!
KSHUNK
BUMF
CLANK
FLONK

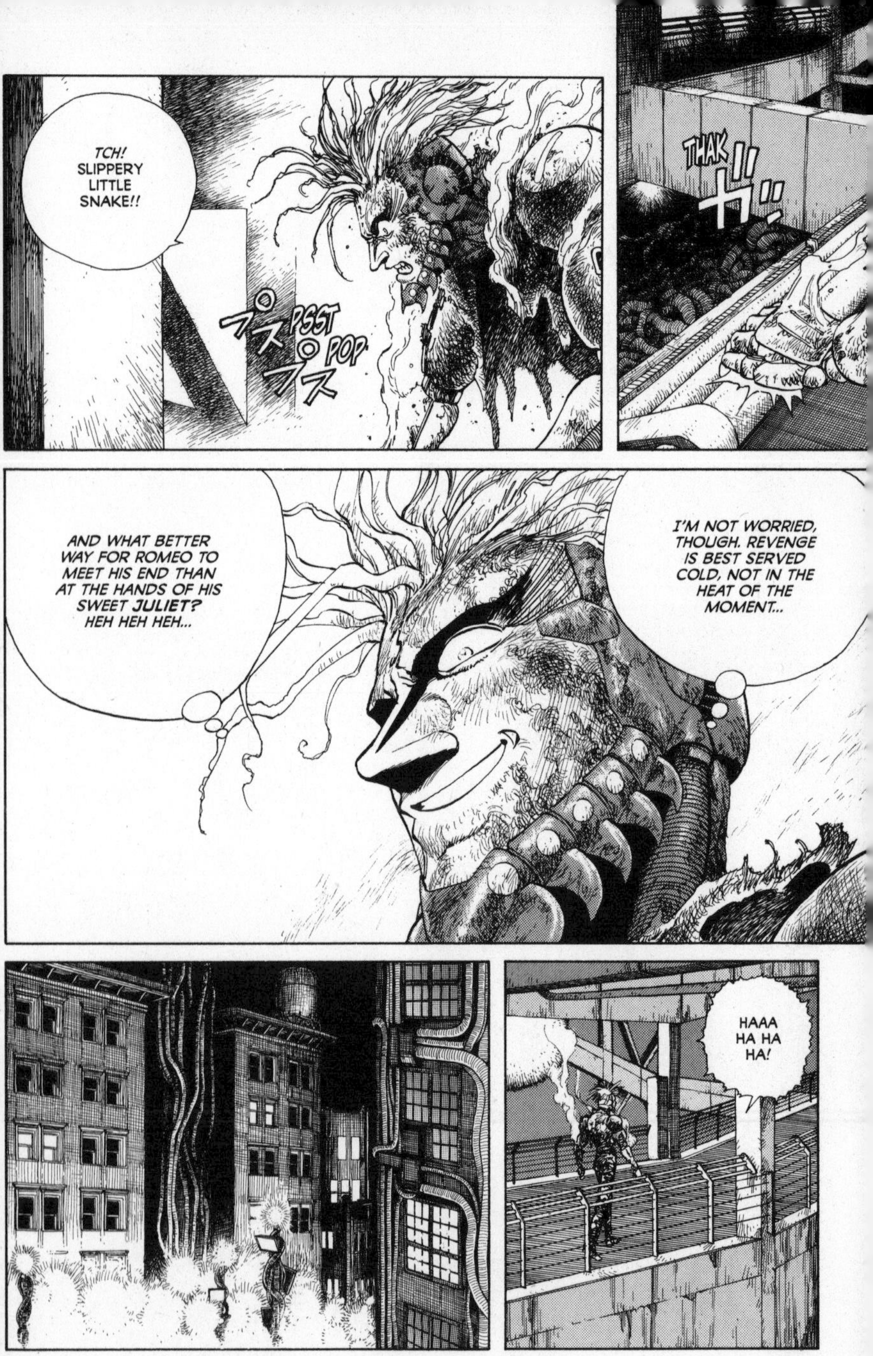

THAK
ガッ
TCH! SLIPPERY LITTLE SNAKE!!
PSST
POP
I'M NOT WORRIED, THOUGH. REVENGE IS BEST SERVED COLD, NOT IN THE HEAT OF THE MOMENT...
AND WHAT BETTER WAY FOR ROMEO TO MEET HIS END THAN AT THE HANDS OF HIS SWEET **JULIET?** HEH HEH HEH...
HAAA HA HA HA!

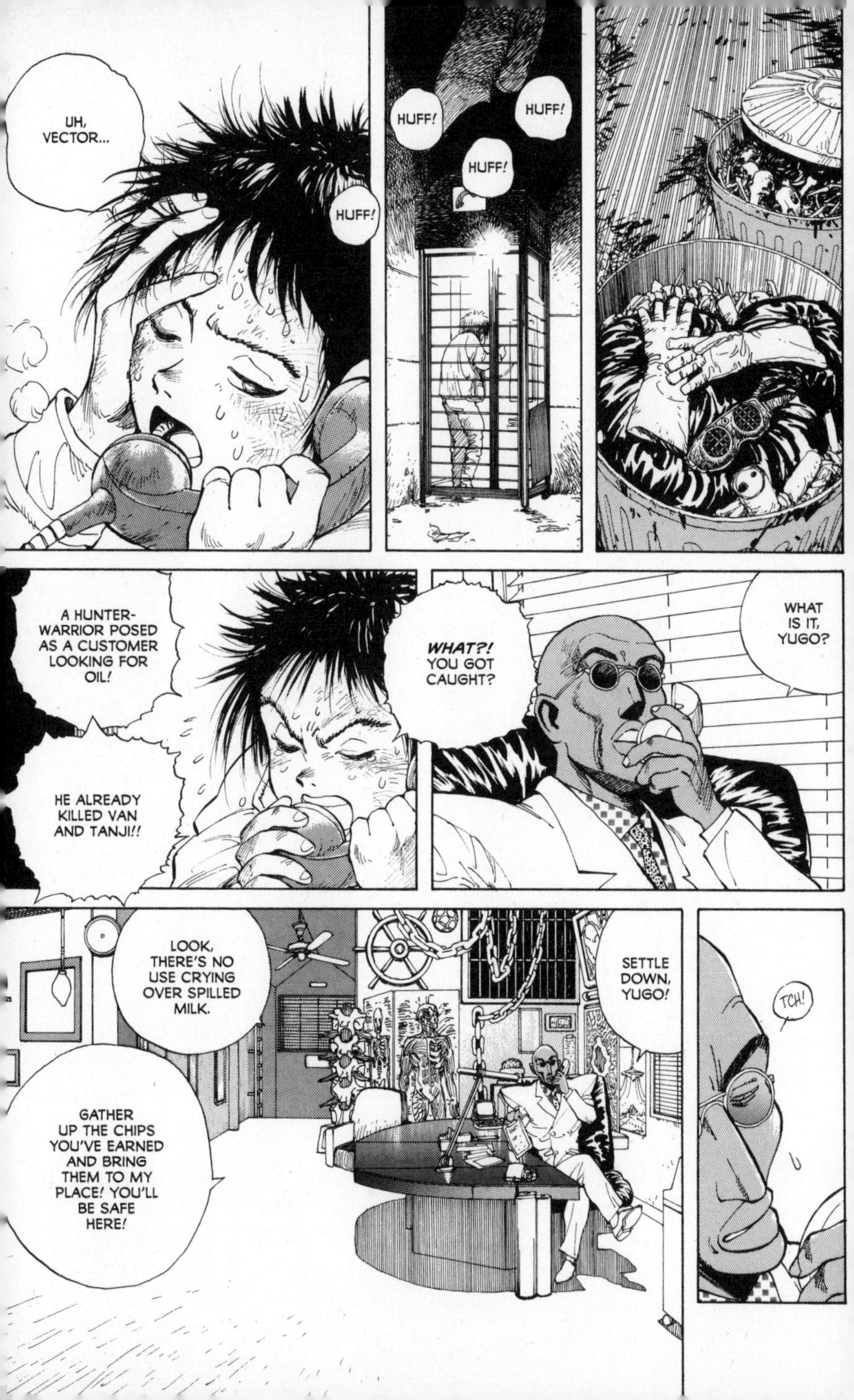
HUFF!
HUFF!
HUFF!
HUFF!
UH, VECTOR...
WHAT IS IT, YUGO?
WHAT?! YOU GOT CAUGHT?
A HUNTER-WARRIOR POSED AS A CUSTOMER LOOKING FOR OIL!
HE ALREADY KILLED VAN AND TANJI!!
TCH!
SETTLE DOWN, YUGO!
LOOK, THERE'S NO USE CRYING OVER SPILLED MILK.
GATHER UP THE CHIPS YOU'VE EARNED AND BRING THEM TO MY PLACE! YOU'LL BE SAFE HERE!

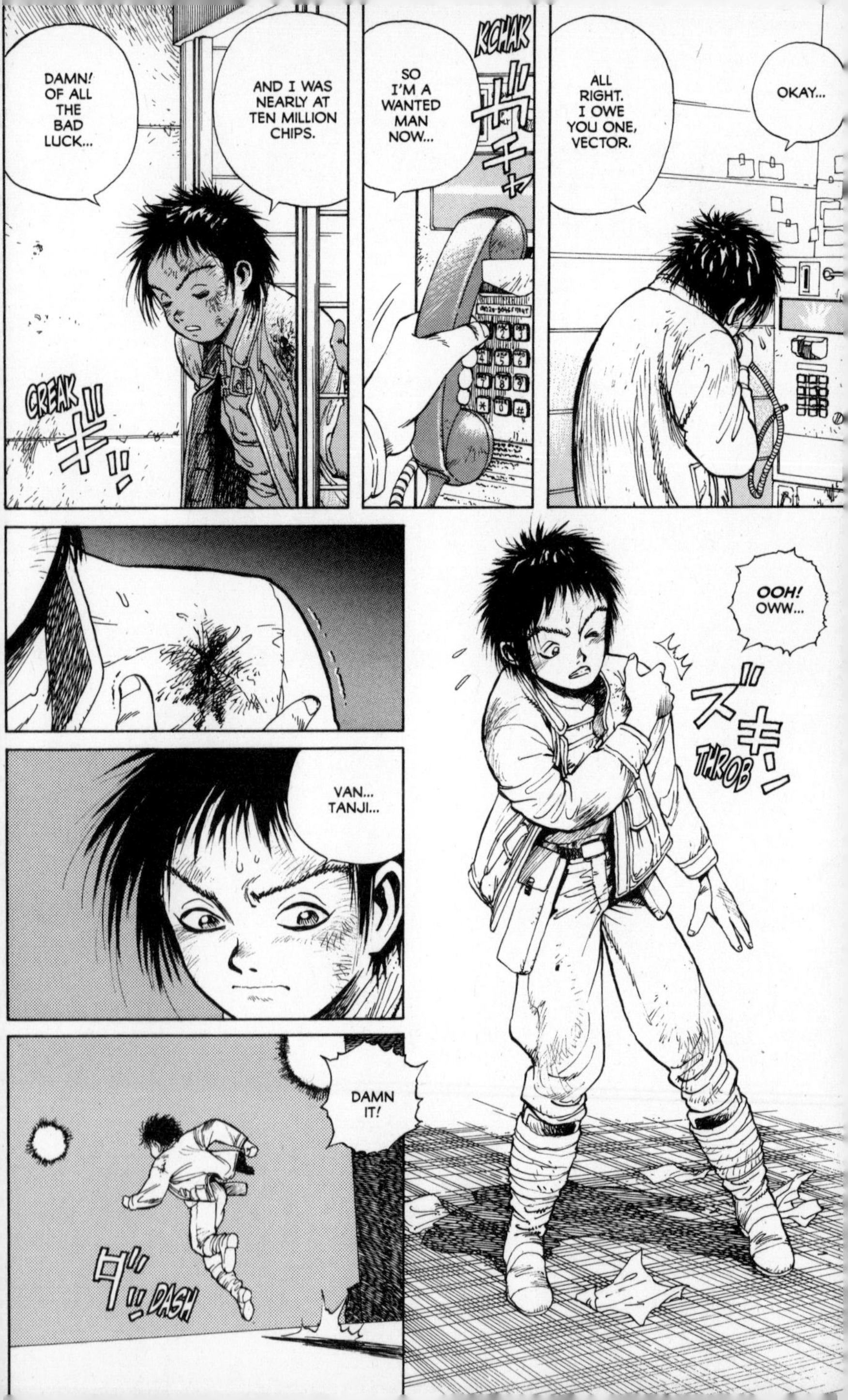

OKAY...
ALL RIGHT. I OWE YOU ONE, VECTOR.
KCHAK
SO I'M A WANTED MAN NOW...
AND I WAS NEARLY AT TEN MILLION CHIPS.
DAMN! OF ALL THE BAD LUCK...
CREAK
OOH! OWW...
THROB
VAN... TANJI...
DAMN IT!
DASH

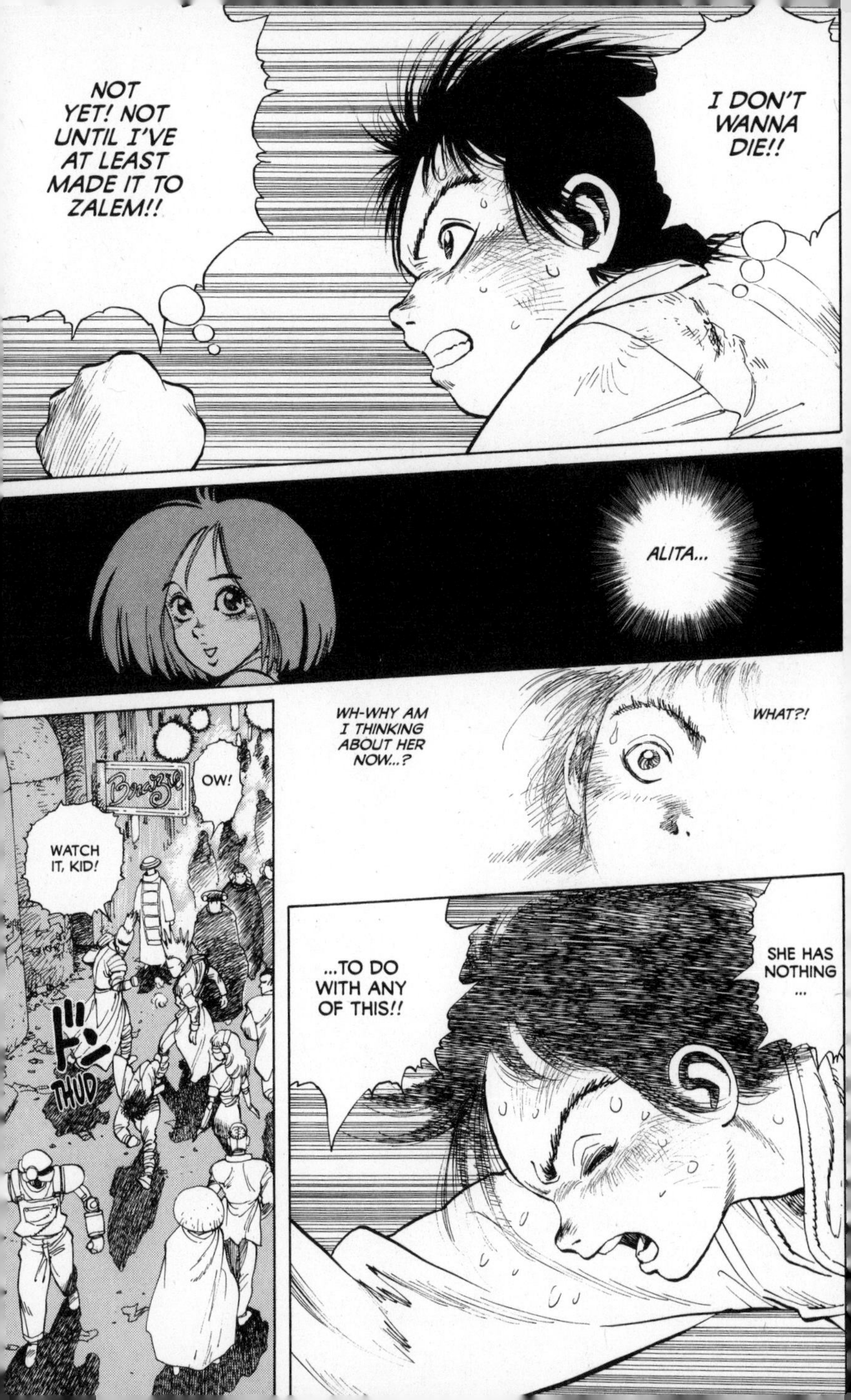
I DON'T WANNA DIE!!
NOT YET! NOT UNTIL I'VE AT LEAST MADE IT TO ZALEM!!
ALITA...
WHAT?!
WH-WHY AM I THINKING ABOUT HER NOW...?
SHE HAS NOTHING ...
...TO DO WITH ANY OF THIS!!
OW!
WATCH IT, KID!
ドン
THUD

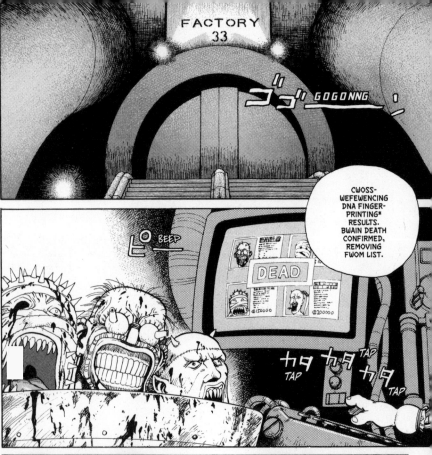

FACTORY 33

ゴゴ GOGONNG

BEEP

DEAD

$150,000 $200,000

CWOSS-WEFEWENCING DNA FINGER-PRINTING* RESULTS. BWAIN DEATH CONFIRMED, REMOVING FWOM LIST.

タ タ タ タ TAP
TAP   TAP

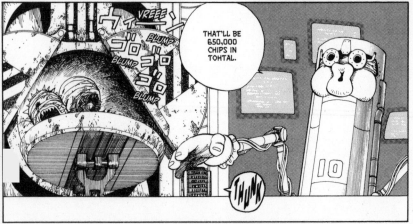

VREEEEE
ウィーーン
ゴロ
BLUMP
ゴロ
BLUMP
ゴロ
BLUMP

THAT'LL BE 650,000 CHIPS IN TOHTAL.

THUNK

10

*DNA Fingerprinting: An analysis of DNA (deoxyribonucleic acid), the building block of genetics, to determine a subject's identity.

328

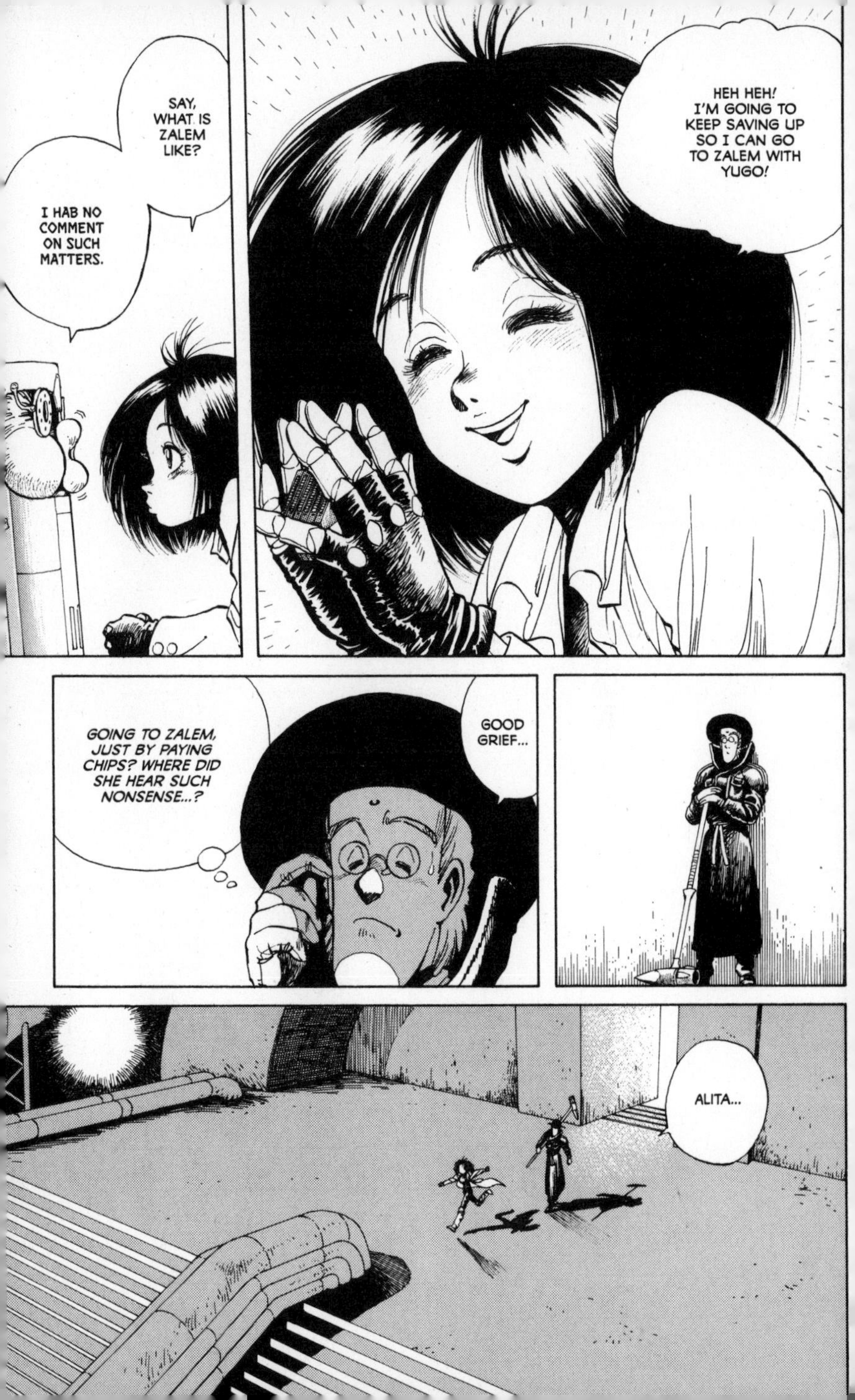
HEH HEH! I'M GOING TO KEEP SAVING UP SO I CAN GO TO ZALEM WITH YUGO!
SAY, WHAT IS ZALEM LIKE?
I HAB NO COMMENT ON SUCH MATTERS.
GOOD GRIEF...
GOING TO ZALEM, JUST BY PAYING CHIPS? WHERE DID SHE HEAR SUCH NONSENSE...?
ALITA...

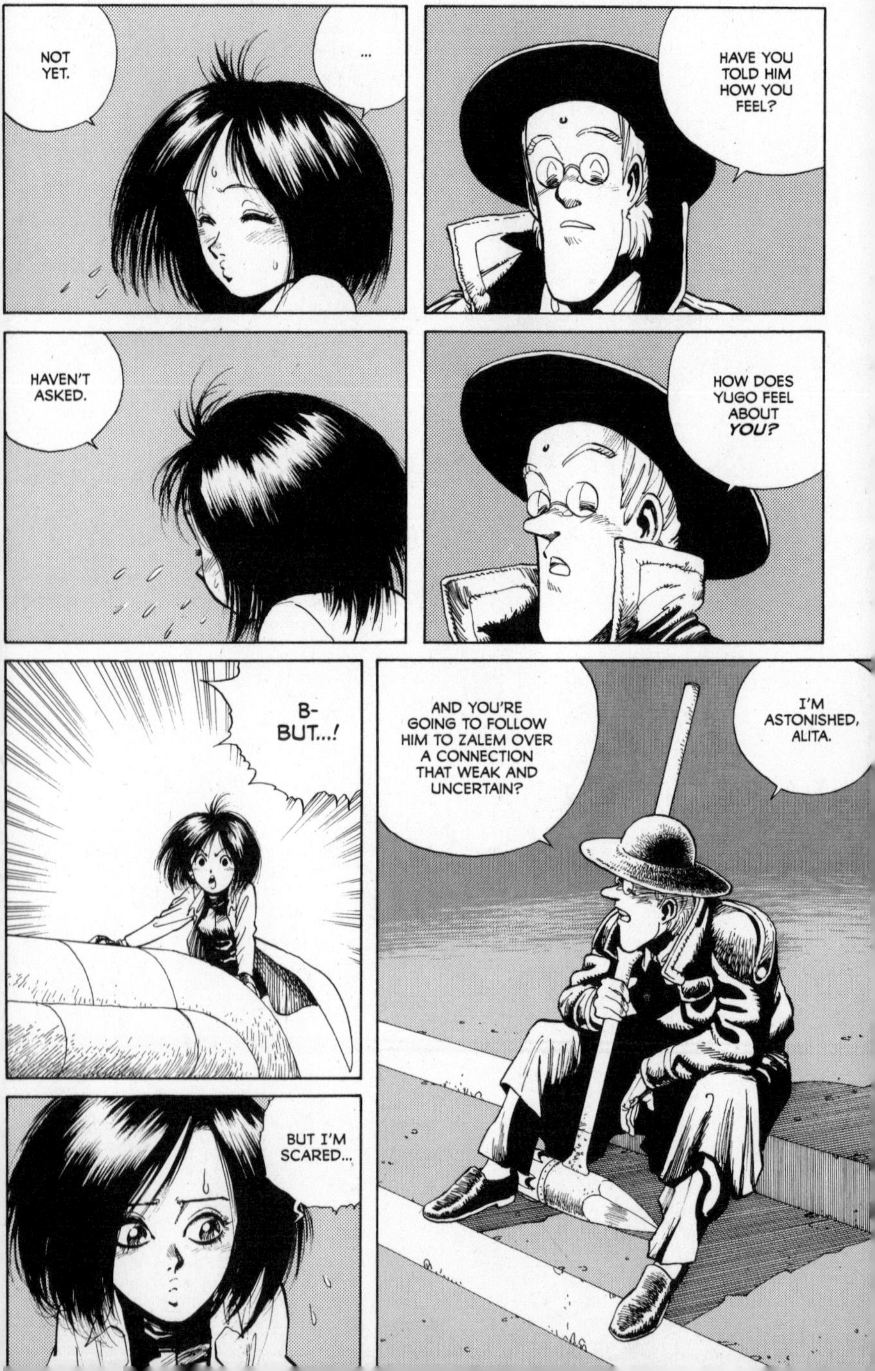
HAVE YOU TOLD HIM HOW YOU FEEL?
...
NOT YET.
HOW DOES YUGO FEEL ABOUT *YOU?*
HAVEN'T ASKED.
I'M ASTONISHED, ALITA.
AND YOU'RE GOING TO FOLLOW HIM TO ZALEM OVER A CONNECTION THAT WEAK AND UNCERTAIN?
B-BUT...!
BUT I'M SCARED...

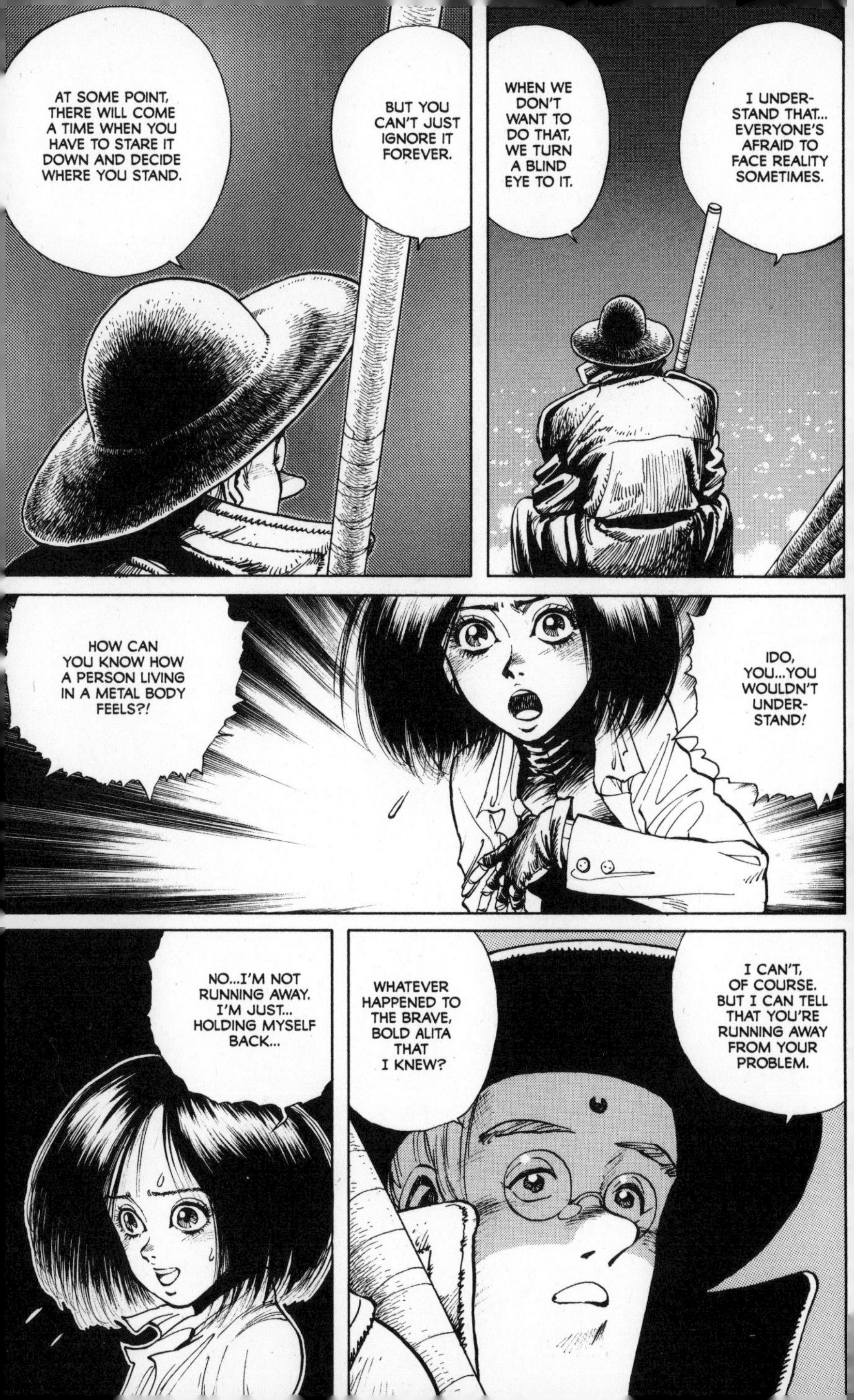
I UNDERSTAND THAT... EVERYONE'S AFRAID TO FACE REALITY SOMETIMES.
WHEN WE DON'T WANT TO DO THAT, WE TURN A BLIND EYE TO IT.
BUT YOU CAN'T JUST IGNORE IT FOREVER.
AT SOME POINT, THERE WILL COME A TIME WHEN YOU HAVE TO STARE IT DOWN AND DECIDE WHERE YOU STAND.
IDO, YOU...YOU WOULDN'T UNDERSTAND!
HOW CAN YOU KNOW HOW A PERSON LIVING IN A METAL BODY FEELS?!
I CAN'T, OF COURSE. BUT I CAN TELL THAT YOU'RE RUNNING AWAY FROM YOUR PROBLEM.
WHATEVER HAPPENED TO THE BRAVE, BOLD ALITA THAT I KNEW?
NO...I'M NOT RUNNING AWAY. I'M JUST... HOLDING MYSELF BACK...

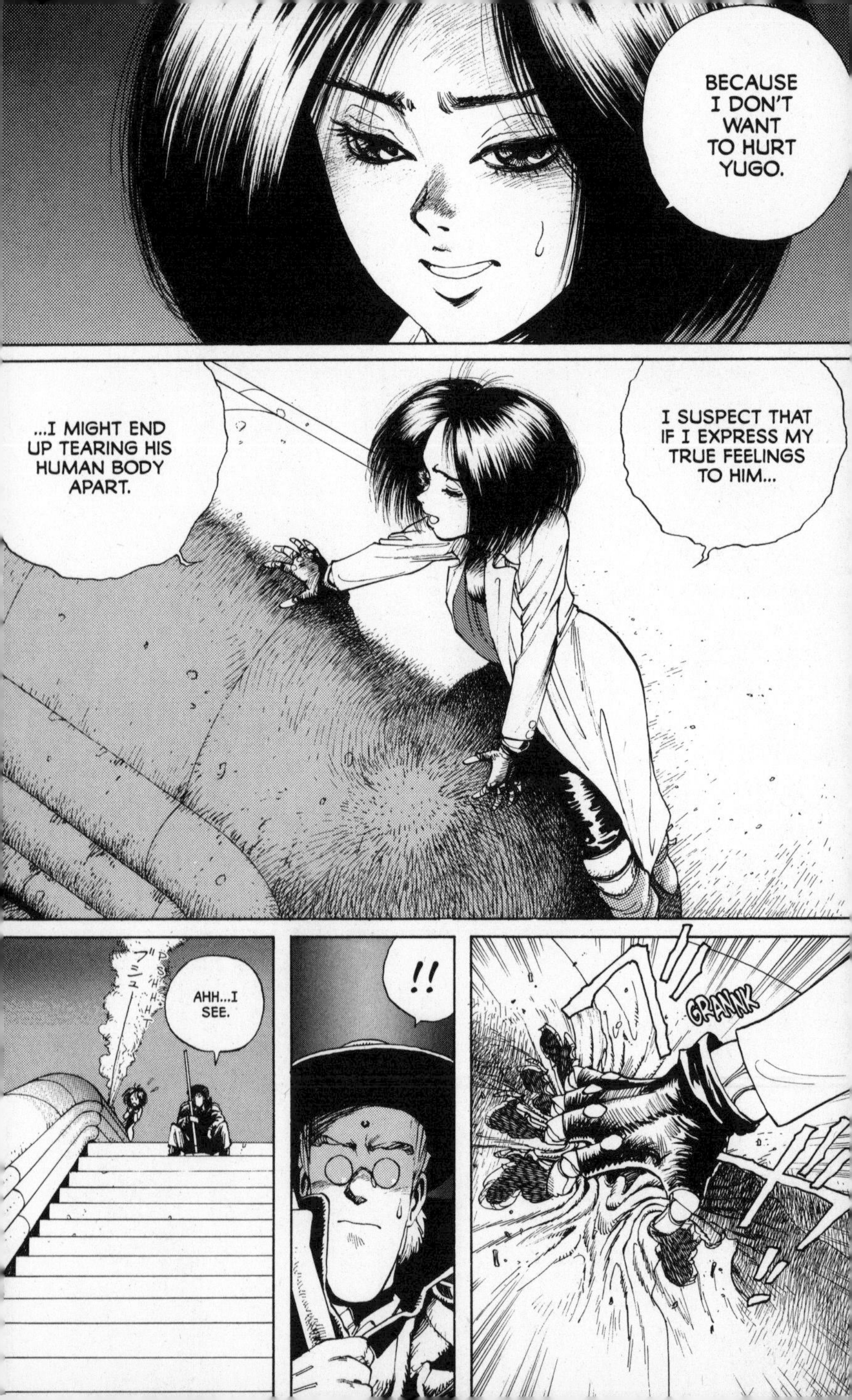
BECAUSE I DON'T WANT TO HURT YUGO.
I SUSPECT THAT IF I EXPRESS MY TRUE FEELINGS TO HIM...
...I MIGHT END UP TEARING HIS HUMAN BODY APART.
GRANNK
!!
AHH...I SEE.
ブシュ
PSHHHT

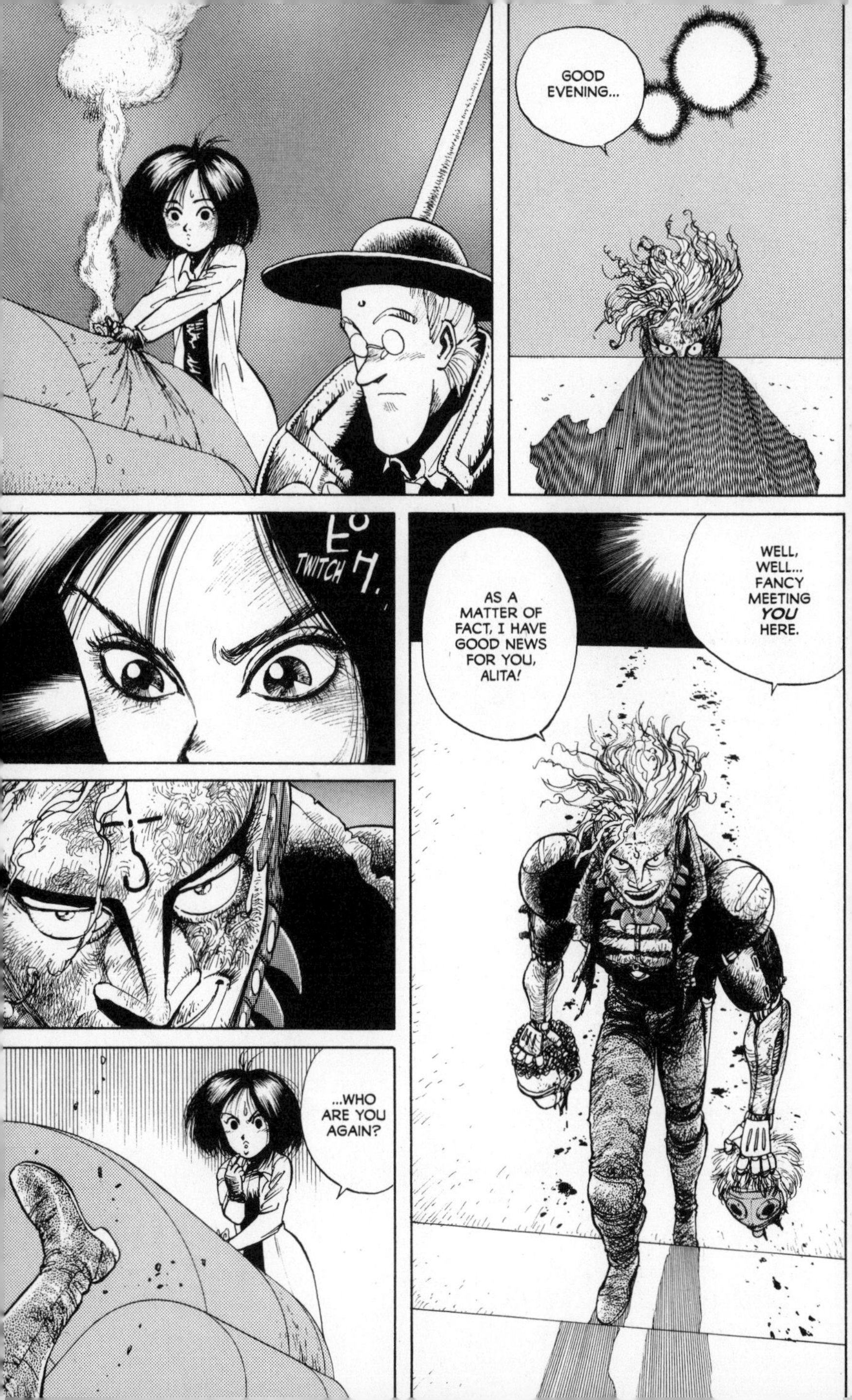
GOOD EVENING...
WELL, WELL... FANCY MEETING *YOU* HERE.
AS A MATTER OF FACT, I HAVE GOOD NEWS FOR YOU, ALITA!
TWITCH
...WHO ARE YOU AGAIN?

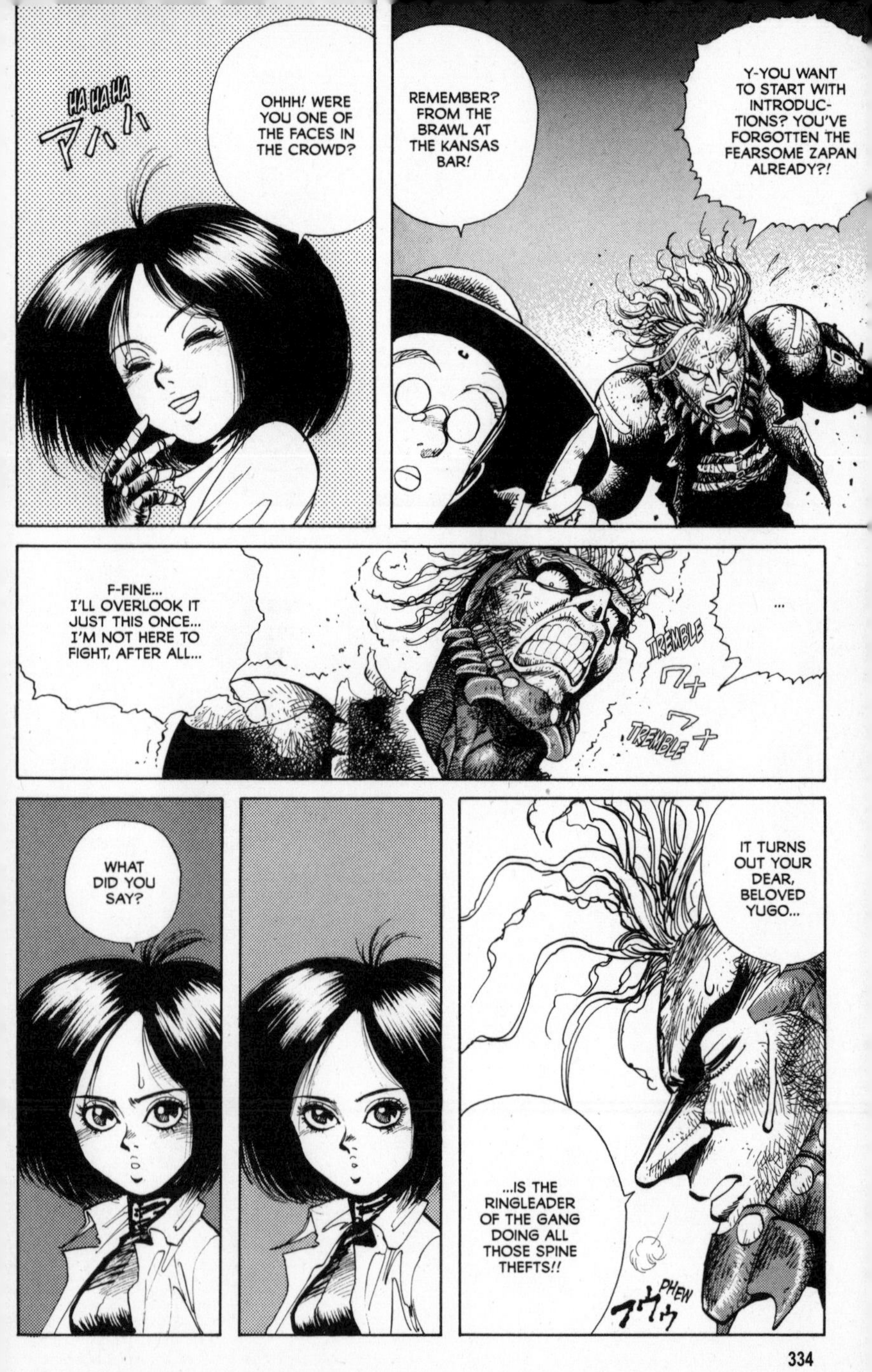
Y-YOU WANT TO START WITH INTRODUCTIONS? YOU'VE FORGOTTEN THE FEARSOME ZAPAN ALREADY?!
REMEMBER? FROM THE BRAWL AT THE KANSAS BAR!
OHHH! WERE YOU ONE OF THE FACES IN THE CROWD?
HA HA HA
アハハ
...
TREMBLE
ワナ
ワナ
TREMBLE
F-FINE... I'LL OVERLOOK IT JUST THIS ONCE... I'M NOT HERE TO FIGHT, AFTER ALL...
IT TURNS OUT YOUR DEAR, BELOVED YUGO...
...IS THE RINGLEADER OF THE GANG DOING ALL THOSE SPINE THEFTS!!
PHEW
フウゥ
WHAT DID YOU SAY?

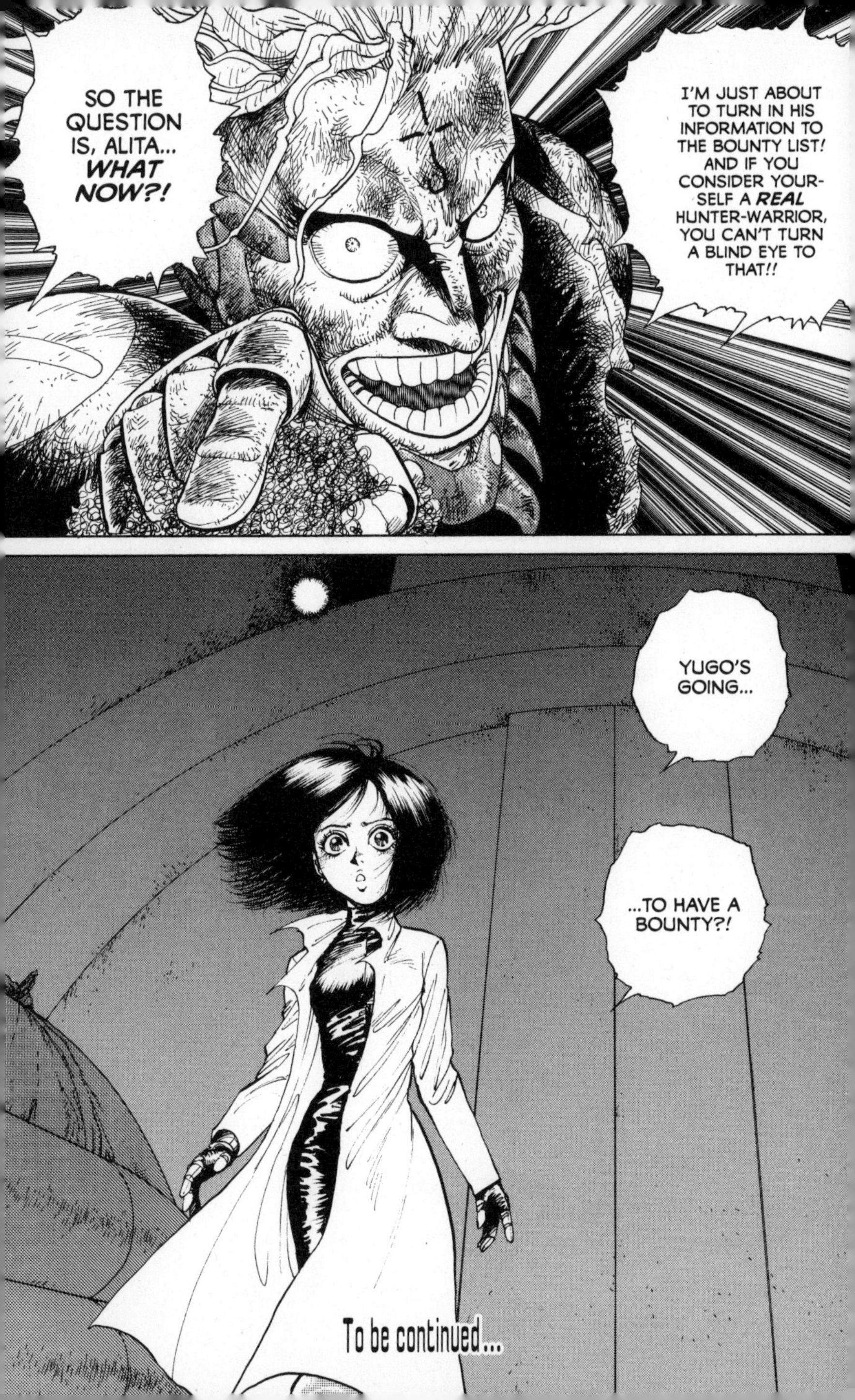
I'M JUST ABOUT TO TURN IN HIS INFORMATION TO THE BOUNTY LIST! AND IF YOU CONSIDER YOUR-SELF A REAL HUNTER-WARRIOR, YOU CAN'T TURN A BLIND EYE TO THAT!!
SO THE QUESTION IS, ALITA... WHAT NOW?!
YUGO'S GOING...
...TO HAVE A BOUNTY?!
To be continued...

Battle Angel Alita Paperback volume 1 is a work of fiction. Names, characters, places, and incidents are the products of the author's imagination or are used fictitiously. Any resemblance to actual events, locales, or persons, living or dead, is entirely coincidental.

Published in the United States by Kodansha Comics, an imprint of Kodansha USA Publishing, LLC, New York.

Publication rights for this English edition arranged through Kodansha Ltd., Tokyo.

Firs … okyo,

Printed … essneck.

www.kodansha.us

9 8 7 6 5 4
Translation: Stephen Paul
Lettering: Scott O. Brown, Evan Hayden
Editing: Ajani Oloye, Alejandro Arbona
Kodansha Comics edition cover design by Phil Balsman

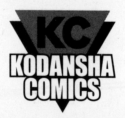

Publisher: Kiichiro Sugawara

Director of publishing services: Ben Applegate
Associate director of operations: Stephen Pakula
Publishing services associate managing editor: Madison Salters
Production managers: Emi Lotto, Angela Zurlo